CLARK

PROPAGANDA AND
PROMOTIONAL ACTIVITIES

———————

AN ANNOTATED BIBLIOGRAPHY

Propaganda and Promotional Activities

AN ANNOTATED BIBLIOGRAPHY

PREPARED UNDER THE DIRECTION OF THE ADVISORY
COMMITTEE ON PRESSURE GROUPS AND PROPAGANDA,
THE SOCIAL SCIENCE RESEARCH COUNCIL

Edited by

HAROLD D. LASSWELL

RALPH D. CASEY

BRUCE LANNES SMITH

With a New Introduction by Harold D. Lasswell

THE UNIVERSITY OF CHICAGO PRESS
CHICAGO AND LONDON

Library of Congress Catalog Card Number: 75–77979

THE UNIVERSITY OF CHICAGO PRESS, CHICAGO, 60637
THE UNIVERSITY OF CHICAGO PRESS, LTD., LONDON W.C.1

© 1935 by The University of Minnesota
© renewed 1962 by Harold D. Lasswell
1969 Introduction © 1969 by Harold D. Lasswell
All rights reserved
Originally published 1935. This edition reissued 1969
Printed in the United States of America

CONTENTS

v

PART III. PROPAGANDA CLASSIFIED BY THE RESPONSE TO BE ELICITED

PART IV. THE SYMBOLS AND PRACTICES OF WHICH PROPAGANDA MAKES USE OR TO WHICH IT ADAPTS ITSELF

CONTENTS

PART V. THE CHANNELS OF PROPAGANDA

PART VI. THE MEASUREMENT OF THE EFFECTS OF PROPAGANDA

PREFACE

The practice of scientific propaganda has permeated the Great Society until scientists and laymen view it today with curiosity and even with alarm. The stream of writing on the subject has been fed by public relations counselors, advertisers, sociologists, social psychologists, political scientists, economists, journalists, and lawyers. From the efforts of these specialists a common fund of fact and interpretation is gradually emerging, on the basis of which there may be developed a consensus upon sound principles of public policy concerning the functions of propaganda and its social control. At present, however, the specialists tend to work in isolation, and without the stimulation of professional contact or of a common scientific tradition. Propagandists are without a professional organization or publication devoted to their calling.

The difficulties that impede the sharing of experience among those who seek to understand or control propaganda are accentuated by the meagerness of dependable guides to the whole body of accumulated literature. Scientific treatises and journals, sensational periodicals, and popular books, are all sources of some value; yet so serious are the limitations of specialized theory and professional pride that valuable citations are neglected by scholar and practitioner alike. The ephemeral nature of many of the media in which propaganda is described often shares the fugitive character of propaganda material itself.

In view of the importance of stimulating the scientific analysis of the function of propaganda in contemporary civilization, the Social Science Research Council in 1931 appointed a Committee on Pressure Groups and Propaganda to investigate the existing state of research in the field and to survey the subject itself in greater detail. In a series of conferences with specialists in propaganda analysis and active propaganda management, this committee learned of the existence of hitherto unexplored documents and received numerous suggestions for fruitful research. Handicapped by the fragmentary character of the pioneer bibliographies now available, the Council's committee found itself impelled by its own need for a view of the entire field to engage in the preparation of a bibliographic aid to research.

That such a bibliography could be more than a simple list of references was clear to the committee. It was therefore decided that informative annotations should be added, and the whole work developed to serve as a research tool for the use of specialists in the social sciences, as well as for a more general public. In an effort to break down the barriers of language, foreign-language books and articles were canvassed as exhaustively as possible, although the sheer bulk of the literature made it necessary to reject all but very representative citations.

Plan of Classification

Since compilation of the bibliography afforded an unusual opportunity to outline the entire field of propaganda study, the committee adopted the present classification only after the consideration of several alternative plans. It is self-evident why the plan it has finally employed includes Part I, on " Propaganda Strategy and Technique," and Parts II, III, V, and VI, entitled " Propaganda Classified by the Name of the Promoting Group," " Propaganda Classified by the Response to be Elicited," " The Channels of Propaganda," and " The Measurement of the Effects of Propaganda." Part IV, " The Symbols and Practices of Which Propaganda Makes Use or to Which It Adapts Itself," and Part VII, " Propaganda and Censorship in Modern Society," may require a word of explanation. They represent an effort to meet the problem of placing contemporary promotional effort in relation to the total setting in which it operates.

Since this purpose requires lengthy analysis of modern culture in its historical development, it was felt to be a task far beyond the scope of the present undertaking. Yet so fundamental for the study and management of propaganda is the body of available symbols and practices of the community that it was considered imperative to choose some means of exhibiting these interrelationships. Anyone who strives to elicit responses from others by means of propaganda is circumscribed and abetted by the vocabularies, organized prejudices, and habitual preoccupations of the community, and his skill consists in maneuvering successfully within these limits. Since any detail of the total configuration may be adapted to or adopted by the propagandist, the editorial task was to select publications that showed the relevance of several aspects of the total situation, without covering the whole field of the social sciences. Thus the section on " The Symbols and Practices of Which Propaganda Makes Use or to Which It Adapts Itself " presents representative studies of the genesis of collective attitudes toward typical groups, persons, policies, doctrines, institutions, and practices. Some of these titles examine the distribution of habitual practices, or the whole social and political symbolism of a definite historical situation. All the references listed here analyze the currents of " public opinion " without generalizing principles of propaganda, or seeking to evaluate with special care the effect of propaganda on social change. By giving emphasis in this section to the social panorama within which propaganda takes place, the compilers have hoped to indicate the partial and uncoordinated condition of existing research in the propaganda field, and tacitly to illustrate the potentialities of cooperation among the social sciences for the development of greater conceptual soundness and methodological skill.

The scientific analysis of propaganda often casts light upon the judgments of social and political philosophers who desire to conserve various social values in the name of ethical codes and political formulas. For the attainment of these ends it has often been proposed to censor promotional activities or to control them in some other way. Therefore Part VII, the final section of the bibliography, is devoted to " Propaganda and Censorship in Modern Society," and references have been included that describe and criticize the history, technique, and results of various means of preventive and punitive control. Propaganda both expresses and intensifies conflicting interests and sentiments in modern society, and efforts at reintegration have varied from " proportional representation " and " economic advisory councils " to " corporative " and " soviet " states. Titles suggesting the nature of these readjustments have been listed in Part VII, Section A, Subdivision 3. Since the principal emphasis of the volume is on propaganda methods, this entire section has been curtailed severely, to include only titles of a representative character.

Scope

So voluminous is the material which has been employed in the effort to sway " public opinion " that this bibliography is limited, in principle, to studies, rather than illustrations, of propaganda. Some important collections of propaganda in private or public libraries are noted, since the usual guides to scholarly material do not mention pamphlets, leaflets, posters, stickers, films, photographs, and similar matter. Research institutions and certain researches now in preparation are also cited in order to add to the working value of this publication.

Throughout the volume every effort has been made to include titles from all fields in which conscious promotion is prominent. Because of the impracticability of presenting a complete list of all publications of interest to the student of propaganda technique and its consequences, it has been found desirable to represent many such fields by quoting only their most characteristic documentation. The goal, in a word, has been inclusive scope and adequate sampling.

Sources

The sources used include card files of the New York Public Library and of the Library of Congress; the International Index to Periodicals and the Reader's Guide; the Index to Legal Periodicals; the List of Published Theses; book review sections of leading journals in the social sciences; materials collected privately by the compilers in various parts of the world; materials collected privately by members of the Committee on Pressure Groups and Propaganda of the Social Science Research Council, and others, and placed at the disposal of the compilers; materials cited in standard treatises on propaganda, journalism, social psychology, advertising, etc.; articles in the available volumes of the *Encyclopedia of the Social Sciences;* and certain previous bibliographies of propaganda or closely related topics, which are listed in the Appendix. It is hoped that later editions of this work will make use of foreign-language sources whose development on this occasion was precluded by limited time and resources.

Nature of the Annotations

The annotations, which are necessarily terse, descriptive, and analytic, are confined for the most part to titles characteristic of the section in which they are found, or to the work of prominent authorities. Where the convenience of the reader made exceptions advisable, however, this rule has been set aside.

Cross-Referencing

Obviously, the overlapping of subjects complicates the problem of arranging titles according to a logic useful to all readers. To offset this, recourse may be had to the subject index, the detailed table of contents, and the cross references. The latter have been arranged with the idea of indicating as many alternative sections of possible relevance as could be indicated without adding to the reader's confusion.

Collaboration Invited

Naturally, this bibliography will never be complete. This is due partly to the lack of a literature on a number of the topics involved; partly to the inaccessibility or confidential nature of some of the literature in existence; partly to limited time and resources on the part of the bibliographers; and partly to the fact that diminutive groups now among us may be the sprouting seeds, though unrecognized, of the significant propaganda groups of our times.

To offset these difficulties, and to correct any errors that may have crept in despite the care with which the entries were prepared, the freest criticism by readers is invited. Reissue of the bibliography from time to time is contemplated, when required by the development of research.

ACKNOWLEDGMENTS

In preparing this bibliography the editors have relied for assistance, particularly in matters of verification and annotation, upon the following members of the Social Science Research Council Committee on Pressure Groups and Propaganda: Professor Merle Curti, Smith College; Professor Harold F. Gosnell, University of Chicago; Professor E. Pendleton Herring, Jr., Harvard University; Professor Peter Odegard, Ohio State University; Professor Schuyler Wallace, Columbia University; and Professor Kimball Young, University of Wisconsin. This counsel was supplemented in many cases by the critical assistance of other experts. Among those from whom special aid has been sought and received should be named Professor Harwood L. Childs, Princeton University; Professor Ralph Haswell Lutz, Stanford University; Professor Roland S. Vaile, University of Minnesota; and Professor W. F. G. Thacher, University of Oregon.

A very heavy burden of editorial responsibility has been put upon the staff of the University of Minnesota Press, and it is desired to acknowledge here the care and discrimination they have exercised.

The author of the introductory essay on " The Study and Practice of Propaganda " wishes to express his indebtedness to his co-editors for thoughtful suggestions, many of which were adopted.

H. D. L.
R. D. C.
B. L. S.

INTRODUCTION (1969): WHAT NEXT?

Harold D. Lasswell

I

During the decades since the Committee on Pressure Groups and Propaganda concluded its work and the annotated bibliography was released in 1935, many of the objectives of the original undertaking have been bountifully fulfilled. A truly spectacular convergence of interest has brought the study of communication into the center of intellectual concern.

The members of the original committee were bound together by a unifying interest in comprehending the strategy of managed communication and in providing a firmer scholarly basis for interpreting the significance of the phenomenon itself. It was evident that a multitude of specialists in the social sciences and related disciplines were approaching the subject from many directions but that they had a very foggy view of the field as a whole. Hence the immediate aim of the Committee was to provide an accessible map of communication studies, giving emphasis to the manipulative dimension and to researches having high empirical content. The members of the Committee were grateful for the rich classical and post-classical inheritance of speculative analysis and impressionistic comment. They were hopeful of passing beyond this, however, by subjecting "plausible guesses" to disciplined empirical investigation. It would not be far wrong to say that although Marxism had greatly influenced the study and practice of propaganda, the subject was dominated by "remarksists." One of the seven parts of the annotated bibliography was devoted to the "measurement of the effects of propaganda"; however, an attempt was made in each of the parts to give preference to researches which employed analytic or quantitative technique. Where possible, theoretical books and articles were chosen if the categories used had promise of being made operational, and if the authors showed familiarity with empirical work.

It has not escaped the eye of commentators that the original committee set up by the Social Science Research Council was a packed court. It was stacked with political scientists (Casey, Gosnell, Herring, Odegard, Wallace, and myself), and the historian and the social psychologist members (Curti and Young) were in tune with their colleagues. Another influential committee, initiated a few years later by the Humanities Division of the Rockefeller Foundation (David Stevens and John Marshall), was broader in disciplinary affiliation; but its members, too, could scarcely be called political innocents (e.g., Lyman Bryson, educator, Hans Speier, sociologist, Paul Lazarsfeld and Hadley Cantril, social psychologists).

The political scientists, in particular, were policy oriented, not in the limited sense of being wholly preoccupied with current affairs, or with the fortunes of a single candidate, party, or issue, but in the larger sense of concern with long-range goals and strategic options. They wanted to contribute to scientific knowledge and skill; at the same time, they hoped that the cultivation of communication research would give a differential benefit to popular government. It was a common view that despotisms, autocracies, and oligarchies were the beneficiaries of ignorance among the friends of popular rule about how to mobilize the latent assets of the system.

It would be a mistake to suppose that these champions of shared power were under the impression that scientific advances could be made forthwith. They were not unaware of the generations that separated the revival of learning in the West from the impressive position occupied by the natural and biological sciences in today's society. The prime initiators of active research programs, Charles E. Merriam and his colleagues, took it for granted that they were supporting a social movement that could not come into its own for generations. They did not, however, assume that no significant contributions of a scientific or policy character could be expected in the meantime. On the contrary, they believed that public and official opinion would benefit from an ever-rising level of dependable information about historical and current trends and of valid explanations of the initiation, diffusion, and restriction of these changes.

As William James, John Dewey, and their colleagues had made relatively clear, the components of a problem-solving orientation can be conveniently summarized in terms of five intellectual tasks: the clarification of goal, the description of trend, the analysis of conditions, the projection of developments, and the invention, evaluation, and selection of alternatives. The alternatives vary from short-range, narrowly circumscribed objectives and strategies to middle- and long-range programs. The clarification of goals provides the contextual map in terms of which these alternatives can be developed. For instance, those who commit themselves to human dignity, not indignity, are concerned with operating in the present in ways that increase the probability that coming events will conform to their preference profile. Even those who concede that "preferences" and "descriptions" cannot be sharply distinguished recognize that a scientific enterprise may legitimately begin with a postulated and operationally specified preference and proceed to discover the factors that explain the conditions of occurrence of the events in question. If a large degree of freedom of communication is postulated as a long-run goal (as a partial realization of human dignity), scientific work can proceed by searching for the "myths" and "techniques" that work for or against freedom. All the available tools of theory formation, and of data gathering and processing, can be mobilized to accomplish the task.

That the members of the Committee were concerned with problems of democratic policy is indicated in many ways. The concluding section, for instance, was focused on "Propaganda and Censorship in Modern Society," which dealt with a major preoccupation of all who concern themselves with freedom.

2

I indicated in the first paragraph that "many" of the objectives of the original committee have been substantially realized. For instance, the scientific study of communication has ramified throughout the academic community. It must, of course, be acknowledged that the social scientists who initiated the investigation of propaganda were unmistakable amateurs in linguistics. Not a single member of the committee was a qualified expert in the study of language. But the semantic component of linguistics has been subsequently affected by the stress laid on the importance of vocabulary and by the quantitative improvisations adapted to describing the content of public media or to surveying public opinion. These latter improvisations were themselves adapted from studies in literature and cryptography, and were stimulated from the beginning by the preoccupation of social psychologists with measurement. The terms "cybernetics," "information theory," and "computer programming" are sufficient to call to mind some of the most impressive advances in theory and procedure in recent times. There is the rapidly emerging field of "zoosemiotics" (Seboek) concerned with the evolution and the use of signs in all living forms, a line of inquiry that has been accelerated by renewed interest in the role of gesture and of other body features in communication. Other developments in the study and management of communication are suggested by the television debates between political candidates, the use of satellites, the furor over "hidden persuaders" in commercial advertising, the reliance on drugs and hypnosis in the psychiatric treatment of mental disorders, the tactics of "brainwashing," the innovation of teaching machines, detailed research on socialization in advanced as well as traditional societies, the concern with the dynamics of racial bias, and the emphasis on communication and ecumenicalism.

3

Nevertheless, one must comment on the persistent failure of modern societies to devise institutions equipped to harness the instruments of communication to the clarification of the policy options of public officials and private persons. I refer, in particular, to the neglect of the *appraisal* function applied to the performance of the media themselves. It has often been proposed that a deliberate attempt should be made to survey and report on the adequacy of the news and commentary available to the citizens who live in the various parts of the country and in cities and towns of different sizes. *The Report of the Commission on Freedom of the Press* (the Hutchins Commission, 1947) recommended "the establishment of a new and independent agency to appraise and report annually upon the performance of the press."

The obstacles in the path are not intellectual. Theoretical models of the flow of communication have been adumbrated in great profusion since the publication of the simple formula *Who says what in what channel to whom with what effect?*

The point has been repeatedly made that a continuing appraisal is possible at any level of coverage desired. For instance, it is not necessary to include every broadcast of radio or television or every edition of every newspaper or magazine. Sampling techniques are available to economize the choice of representative media. The advantages of combining *qualitative exhibits* with *quantitative summaries* of information have been underlined. When variations in headlines or in the front page of newspapers are reproduced, they dramatize differences in relative prominence and slant. Excerpts from broadcasts arouse immediate interest. Hence reports need not be dull even when they are soundly disciplined by quantitative procedures.

The criteria to be used in reporting on the contents of the media are not obscure. The requirements made articulate in the Commission's report have won general approval. In brief they include: a truthful, comprehensive, and intelligent account of the day's events in a context which gives them meaning; a forum for the exchange of comment and criticism; the projection of a representative picture of the constituent groups in the society; the presentation and clarification of the goals and values of the society; full access to the day's intelligence.

An important point in implementing the proposal is to recognize the differences to be expected between the *interpreters* of research and the researchers themselves. Interpreters and researchers can agree that the conception of a free forum implies the balanced presentation of divergent statements of fact and opinion. Hence the appraising agency must be able to report on the universe of factual and opinion statements and to summarize the degree to which the coverage in a particular channel or group of channels reflects the universe. The interpreters and the researchers may not agree whether a given pattern of content is "balanced" or not; and it is important to emphasize these differences of interpretation, since they mobilize interest in the act of appraisal. A structural means of keeping the distinction clear between interpretative and research statements is to operate through a two-pronged organization, one branch specializing in asking questions of researchers and interpreting the answers, the other composed of researchers. The former can be recruited from citizens who are acknowledged leaders of a wide sample of the interlaced constituencies in the body politic. Clearly, the way to win public confidence in the integrity of an operation is to make it a model of candor and competence.

It is generally agreed that the appraising body must *look* independent and competent as well as *be* what it looks. Hence the personnel must possess the pluralistic connections appropriate to a pluralized society, and the sources of financial support must be diversified. The originators of the Hutchins Commission leaned over backward to disassociate themselves from the communications industry. Of course they publicized that the initial funds came from Henry R. Luce. Partly because Luce was not altogether pleased by what he heard of the direction taken by the Commission, other sources were turned to when the original grant proved insufficient. William B. Benton stepped into the breach. Note that the Commission did not imply that a structure specializing in appraisal must never include influential figures from the media or accept gifts from commercial sources. The principle of impartiality does not require the exclusion of members of the media industries if they measure up to the levels of statesmanship that are often exemplified in American business. It is well known that some leaders win the confidence of their fellows beyond the boundaries of an occupation without losing their reputations for integrity. Such exponents of the common interest, whether businessmen or not, are indispensable to civic and public order.

Why, if the intellectual difficulties are not formidable, has the proposal failed to be realized? I shall not dwell on the timidity of possible sources of funds, whether private foundations or business corporations. Rather, I shall comment on those who specialize in the study of communication. The recently risen field of communications research has been so absorbed in improving the technical procedures required that practitioners have given modest attention to their social responsibilities. The older professions, notably law and medicine, are *relatively* responsive to the demands of the community that they help to assess and improve the *aggregate* realization of justice or health in society. True professions are expected to go beyond private skills to public enlightenment concerning the aggregate realization of value outcomes. A communications profession with a firm grasp of its responsibilities would long since have taken the initiative to organize continuing agencies to observe and report on the functioning of communication institutions. As it is, timidity and technicalization go hand in hand on the shady side of the street.

4

I commented favorably on the scientific advances of recent decades. Impressive as the record is, at least two remarkable gaps remain. First, no comprehensive theory of communication in biological and cultural processes has been generally accepted. Second, the study of the role of communication in culture is held back by the absence of thorough research on basic trends of attention and perspective among those who participate in the policy processes of government, business, churches, or other national and transnational groups. There is, as yet, no great chain of research centers specializing in the improvement and application of the techniques required to establish such time series, and in the discovery of their interdependence with more commonly available series that refer to population, production, prices, wars, rebellions (and the like). Consequently our knowledge of the interconnections between changes in perspectives, operations, and resources remains unnecessarily fragmentary. What the Natural Bureau for Economic Research (and parallel agencies) has been able to do for some features of economic change has not yet been done for the variables of group attention, value demand, indentification, and expectation.

Such an institution is not to be confused with the policy-oriented agencies referred to in report of the Commission on Freedom of the Press. These institutions would serve different though complementary purposes. Policy institutions could benefit from the depth perspective possible to *Centers of Historical and Comparative Research on Communication;* and policy institutions would continually pose new problems whose historic roots and connections need to be exposed.

5

Whatever qualifications may be made, the many-sided study of symbols and signs in the life of man and of all living forms is bound to illuminate new dimensions of insight and understanding as it moves toward universality in time and space. Whatever the "ultimate" theory of communication may be, it will no doubt continue to underline the creative role of "central process" ("brain," "mind") in guiding man's impact on his cultural and biological evolution. To interpose in the sequence of perception of current events a contextual map of past, present, and future aims and strategies is to open new paths of expression. In a word: to communicate is to liberate.

THE STUDY AND PRACTICE OF PROPAGANDA
By HAROLD D. LASSWELL

THE STUDY AND PRACTICE OF PROPAGANDA

By HAROLD D. LASSWELL

Not bombs nor bread, but words, pictures, songs, parades, and many similar devices are the typical means of making propaganda. Not the purpose but the method distinguishes propaganda from the management of men by violence, boycott, bribery, and similar means of social control. Propaganda relies on symbols to attain its end: the manipulation of collective attitudes.

In the sixteenth century, when the Roman Catholic church used the word to refer to its own missionary activity, propaganda was a descriptive and non-controversial term. But the expression fell on evil days during the World War of 1914-18, when inconvenient news and opinion was stigmatized as " enemy propaganda." Hence it is common for modern promoters of attitudes to borrow the prestige of words like *education, information, public relations,* and *publicity.* For analytical purposes, however, it is permissible to give the word an objective meaning, and to say that anybody who uses " representations " to influence collective responses is a propagandist.

It is important, when using this word objectively, to delimit its scope in relation to terms like *pedagogy* and *education.* Pedagogy is the transmission of a skill, like reading, writing, and arithmetic; propaganda strives to organize attitudes of love and hate, divorced from the transmission of skill.

Thus far propaganda has been defined as *method;* it can also be defined as *process.* In this sense propaganda is the transmission of attitudes that are recognized as *controversial* within a given community. Education is a process of transmitting skills and *accepted* attitudes. Thus the inculcation of respect for Martin Luther in a devout Prussian village is a process of education in terms of the village, but a process of propaganda in terms of the whole of Germany or of the world.

It is often serviceable to have a separate name for symbols that spread more or less rapidly with a minimum of conscious promotional effort. Many of the dancing manias and crazes that have swept portions of the world have seemed to rise from nowhere in particular and to rage like epidemics throughout a population. Under the influence of medical usage such cases are often treated as examples of *contagion* or *psychic infection,* permitting the term propaganda to be reserved for instances of the dissemination of symbols or practices in which there is a large element of premeditation.

Another word that is marginal to propaganda is *news.* If we are justified in calling news any representation of events that reaches the attention of large numbers of a community and arouses expressions of interest on their part, it is evident that some news may be propaganda, but that all propaganda is not news. The term *publicity* might even be limited to news instigated by someone who expects to extract a tangible advantage from the attitudes molded by it. *Advertising* thus becomes " paid publicity."

All these closely connected terms — propaganda, pedagogy, education, contagion, news, publicity, and advertising — are used in intercrossing senses in the common speech of different periods and in the technical jargon of different specialists. As usual in such matters, it is less important to impose a homogeneous vocabulary than to induce a common critical attitude toward the usage in particular contexts.

The Extent of Propaganda

Propaganda in the United States is notable for its quantity and for the high degree of specialization that has arisen in connection with it. Some propagandists serve several clients at the same time, advising them on the whole field of their relations with the public. Such propagandists may call themselves "publicity men" or "public relations counsels." Other propagandists are connected with a single interest, possibly serving behind the scenes, as when a "vice-president" or "advisor to the president" is in fact the responsible head of public relations. Advertising agencies specialize in handling media of communication for a number of clients.

In the boom days E. Pendleton Herring was able to account for over five hundred national organizations with headquarters in Washington, D. C. Consciousness of propaganda was vastly stimulated during the war, when the Committee on Public Information was active and "enemy propaganda" was a means of stigmatizing inconvenient ideas. The prestige of propaganda was greatly heightened, and after the war many former agents of the government remained in Washington and New York hoping to take advantage of their skill and "contacts." There were said to be no fewer than five thousand press agents in New York. Large expenditures on advertising were favored by many as a form of "goodwill" investment that would prove more lucrative than the payment of taxes. In the boom year of 1928 the advertising bill of the United States was between one and a half and two billion dollars; of this sum the newspapers alone got $765,000,000. In the presidential campaign of the same year $16,500,000 was spent by the national and state committees of the Republican and Democratic parties, exclusive of the sums spent by individuals and local agencies. In the same year three-fifths of the $50,000,000 expended by the Protestant missionary societies of the world was raised in North America. The total propaganda bill of the country cannot be exactly given; but no doubt the sums spent by the foregoing agencies and in the interests of the causes named constitute the bulk of it, unless we decide to include in the computation a large fraction of the cost of our school system. Propaganda consciousness continued to be stimulated by the fear of Communist propaganda, and by praise of the showmanship of Mussolini and Hitler. The Federal Trade Commission conducted the widely heralded investigation of the propaganda activities of the public utility companies (the National Electric Light Association, renamed the Edison Institute) and legislative investigating committees connected the name of one of the best-known publicity men in the United States with the German dye trust and indirectly with the German government. Academic interest became constantly more lively, as can be readily seen in the literature cited in the present volume.

Although accompanied by much less public awareness, the pre-war use of propaganda in the United States was extensive and in some measure effective. The war with Spain has come to be understood in part in the light of the circulation war between Joseph Pulitzer and William Randolph Hearst. Several colorful incidents attended the propaganda of the northern states in foreign countries during the Civil War; and the astuteness of Benjamin Franklin in winning the sympathy of influential circles in France for the cause of the seceding Americans has come to be greatly admired. Controversies over the adoption of the Constitution, the limitation of slavery, and the control of the currency were landmarks in the growth of political propaganda in this country.

Concurrently the resort to propaganda by public and private agencies abroad has attained impressive dimensions. From 1866 until 1893 the German government had available for propaganda purposes the confiscated property of the Hanoverian dynasty; after the World War the unpopularity of " secret diplomacy " led to the inclusion of various secret funds in regular government budgets. The high-water mark of these avowed sums came in 1926–27, when the amount was in excess of twelve million marks, of which an unknown proportion went to propaganda as distinct from espionage. Secret funds connected with the struggle over the Ruhr have been estimated to be nearly twice as high.

The long history of the Catholic church is inextricably bound up with propaganda agencies and methods. The College of Propaganda, organized in 1622 to spread the faith, is believed to have spent about four billion dollars in the nineteenth century. In 1927 the number of foreign missionaries of the Roman church was given as twenty-five thousand; the corresponding figure for world Protestantism was twenty-nine thousand. Strenuous efforts to convert the peoples who were pressing upon the later Roman Empire were in no small degree responsible for the potent historical rôle the bishops of Rome came gradually to play. The Papacy and not the imperial authority became the most vivid symbol of unity in the West.

The investiture controversy beginning in the eleventh century has been characterized by James Westfall Thompson as " the first event in medieval Europe before the Crusades which attracted the attention of each and every class in society." The Cluny reform had already given rise to a large polemical literature, which grew rapidly when the issue between Henry IV and Gregory VII took shape. Sixty-five tracts are still in existence from the years 1085 to 1112 (Mirbt).

In the struggle between Emperor Frederick II and the Papacy, as Otto Vehse has shown, a secular agency for the first time stood fully equipped to do battle with the church on terms of equal, if not superior, technical competence. Frederick II, who learned his methods from Pope Innocent III, improved upon his master, and for a time the secular power scored advances on the ecclesiastical. Pope Innocent IV, however, reborrowed from the emperor and by the middle of the thirteenth century the two antagonists were again on equal footing.

The use of propaganda in the Crusades, in the Reformation and Counter-Reformation, in the Puritan Revolution, the French Revolution, and the Russian Revolution is better known. In the earlier Roman world there is evidence that organized propaganda had its share in the spread of the Egyptian Isis and the Persian Mithras worships until they were the dominant religions in the first two centuries of the Empire (W. L. Westermann). Julius Caesar seems to have relied upon Aulus Hirtius to assist in keeping his military exploits before the public. Alexander the Great certainly influenced the historical work of Kallisthenes which fostered his propaganda of divinity. (See Wilhelm Bauer's discussion of the evidence.) The verses of Solon of

Athens (594 B. C.) have also been cited as an early example of the use of literature for political propaganda or public instruction.

The beginning of the imperial era of Chinese history is said by Marcel Granet to be distinguished by a regrouping of classes which had long been foreshadowed, and by a reform of manners and morals for which both the propaganda of certain teachers of morals and the action of the government had a share of responsibility. The spread of Buddhism throughout India, China, Korea, and Japan was fostered by the celibate monks; indeed, the propaganda on behalf of Buddhism is to be ranked alongside the propagandas of Christianity and Islam in the list of major promotional achievements of all time.

The Technique of Propaganda

These reminders of the scope of propaganda in the contemporary and historical affairs of man no doubt enliven the search to understand the methods that have proved effective in propaganda work. The technique of successful propaganda can be discussed most vividly by concentrating some attention upon a definite campaign.

The recent senatorial investigation of the efforts of the American Steamship Owners' Association to influence ship subsidies may be deemed timely and representative.* This association was organized in 1906, and a number of its members profit by federal contracts for ocean mail, obtaining a subsidy which they, and others, justify as essential to an American merchant marine. Stimulated by criticisms directed against subsidies, the members of this association who benefited from mail contracts contributed one-fifth of one per cent of their mail receipts to a propaganda fund in 1932. Their propaganda was handled by a director appointed by the association's Committee on Shipping Information.

One of his first acts was to " contact " three clipping bureaus, which were instructed to collect everything favorable and everything adverse to the American merchant marine. Thus the active centers of support and attack were spotted. If the undesired material printed by a particular paper or association was syndicated, the editors were told that their columns were being used for propaganda. The Washington lobbyist who had been representing shipping interests at the capital for thirty-five years supplied the information that made it possible to classify the members of Congress into friendly, hostile, and indifferent. An early

* An Investigation of Air Mail and Ocean Mail Contracts (hearings before a Special Committee on Investigation of Air Mail and Ocean Mail Contracts, United States Senate, 73d Congress, 2d Session, pursuant to Senate Resolution 349, 72d Congress). Washington, D. C., 1933.

memorandum, referring to a certain senator as a persistent opponent, commented that the senator might listen if the existing demands for subsidy could be " developed from a whisper into a roar."

In developing the whisper into a roar, lists of all who had contracts for shipping materials were procured from the various shipyards. The concerns were divided into separate lines, such as electrical, steel, sanitary plumbing, and the other goods that went into ship construction. Stories were released to the trade papers in these lines calling attention to what shipbuilding had meant to employment. These releases were carried into the towns where substantial contracts had been placed with local industries; the material was also subdivided by states for local release.

Two middle-western outlets were used to funnel out the material. The Mississippi Valley Association (of St. Louis) and the Midwest Foreign Trade Association (the Cincinnati Chamber of Commerce) were each given expense accounts of five hundred dollars a month. The assistance of a propaganda bureau in Washington was obtained for a fee of a thousand dollars a month and an expense account of six hundred dollars a month, some of which was regularly paid to a woman's club lecturer in Washington. This publicity agency sought to " contact " the channels of general publicity. The bureau asserted that it had succeeded in having its material used by a lecturer on current affairs who spoke over a coast-to-coast radio broadcasting hook-up. It supplied material to writers for the magazines of large circulation, such as the *Saturday Evening Post* and the *National Geographic Magazine,* and furnished articles to the North American Newspaper Alliance and the Western Newspaper Union. Conferences were held with the newspaper correspondents of the principal press associations, newspaper chains, and individual journals. Speeches were written for notable public personages who were scheduled to participate in a merchant marine conference (including General Pershing, who was unable to attend, but whose speech was read into the record and used for publicity purposes).

Officials of the Steamship Owners' Association testified that they had been approached in 1930 by representatives of the American Farm Bureau Federation who asked for $94,000 to assist them in disseminating material favorable to the merchant marine. They asserted that the Federation was able to reach 1,250,000 farm families in the country, that it had 15,000 community units, 1,837 county farm bureau organizations, 10,000 volunteer leaders and workers in state organizations,

6,000 salaried employees, a national headquarters in Chicago and legislative headquarters in Washington. They said they had worked as propagandists for the National Electric Light Association, the National Lumbermen's Association, the Portland Cement Association, the Copper and Brass Research Association, and the National Automobile Chamber of Commerce. The Steamship Owners' Association considered the offer but finally decided to handle their own propaganda.

Among the several points to be noticed in this propaganda enterprise are the definiteness of the overt acts sought; the initial survey of active centers of hostility, friendship, and indifference; the initial survey of potential vested and sentimental interests; the functional specialization of special and general appeals; the choice and coordination of indirect outlets. The concentration of publicity in the districts of various congressmen exemplifies another strategic principle. The effort to create events (such as occasions for the speeches of distinguished persons) is in the best manner of modern propaganda.

This particular campaign does not illustrate certain other strategical and tactical considerations, such as the importance of dividing the opposition, which was one of the main purposes of anti-Kaiser and anti-monarchical propaganda fostered by the Allies during the World War. Nor does it vividly display the numerous modes of distracting attention from inconvenient matters. When a wave of pessimism was generated by the fall of Warsaw in the autumn of 1915, the Russian government announced the taking of the Dardenelles. Crowds gathered to thank God for this glorious victory. The next day, of course, there was general disappointment, but the population had been given a chance to "work off steam." Such procedures are of dubious value in the long run, of course. The use of reassuring language by the public leader of a movement while his subordinates do the "dirty work" is one of the most ancient devices of manipulation. This often prevents the hostile forces from gathering their full strength until it is too late. But the mail contracts case did furnish examples of counter-propaganda, since the shipowners complained continually of the British propaganda against the American merchant marine.

The high importance of coordinating propaganda with all other means of social control cannot be too insistently repeated. Quick fact-finding by spies or other informants is of obvious value. When propaganda is shrewdly timed with violence, as in the counter-offensive of the Entente after July, 1918, moods of pessimism and internal resentment can be greatly intensified.

The Organization of Propaganda

Propaganda that aims directly at the sacred symbols and practices of a ruling order requires men and women who are "sincere" in the sense that they are emotionally bound to the doctrines they spread. The risks are too great for propagandists of less than religious strength of conviction. Hence the wisdom of Lenin in insisting upon the decisive rôle of the professional devotee of the proletarian revolution.

For less fundamental purposes it is possible, and often wise, to rely upon the directing influence of those who are emotionally detached from the problem, and who make a profession of management. Much of the tragic waste of good intentions in social effort comes about from sheer lack of technical skill.

The choice of personnel in movements that look forward to revolutionary violence is restricted to those who are willing to endure personal danger and who sense the necessity of taking physical risks. The importance of this consideration is exhibited in the socialist movements of Germany and Russia. In Germany the trades unions and the socialist political parties found it possible, in the course of the nineteenth and twentieth centuries, to multiply their membership and in this sense to become mass organizations. Violent deterrents, such as were imposed upon the Russian movement, were much less frequently employed in Germany, and the organizations formed in the name of the proletariat became pacific and bureaucratic. By multiplying their insurance and cultural features the German organizations seemed to exercise an all-absorbing control over the lives of broad layers of the population. This seeming strength proved illusory; the copious tent of the proletarian vocabulary took in the camel of complacent comfort. Staffs of editors, membership secretaries, municipal councilors, and their associates made their living short of serious risk, and in the crisis they failed to seize the power; not so the Russians.

Propaganda organizations of all kinds find it important to arrange close personal connections with official agencies of policy formation. The appraisal of collective psychological conditions is not yet amenable to objective metersticks. Valuable propaganda openings are constantly lost, as they were during the World War, because the makers of policy become absorbed in the ponderables of men and guns, forgetting the less ponderable but no less contributory factors of emotions and men. After years of self-contradiction and ambiguity, the British government was prevailed upon by Crewe House to coordinate its diplomatic and propaganda policies toward the South Slavs and the Italians.

Under democratic forms of government the determiners of policy may not be quite so neatly hierarchized as under dictatorship. Hence the propaganda executive is constrained to remain sensitive to the sentiments of such agencies as legislatures, who are bound to cherish the liveliest suspicion of the propaganda departments. This can be mitigated by insuring the formal participation of the chief partisan groups, and by arranging for an unceasing stream of private explanation of what is afoot.

When propaganda must be carried on in secrecy, the utmost ingenuity may be shown in developing flexible and effective forms of organization and procedure. During the period of neutrality before the United States entered the World War, the English had six or eight different offices in the United States, so that no one man, in or out of the service, knew all the secrets. When a compromising document was of such importance that it could not be destroyed, it was marked "confidential, for the information of the U.S. Secret Service only." If it were seized, the plea could be made that it was the intention all along to communicate with the government.

Under conditions of secrecy, the use of funds is open to grave abuse. Sir William Wiseman, head of the British propaganda in the United States, is reported by George S. Viereck to have said that even under the most favorable conditions seventy-five per cent of all the money spent on secret service work is wasted. Most of the money the Germans paid to the Hindus for propaganda was immediately invested in real estate.

In the absence of highly objective measuring rods, propagandists are free to exaggerate the extent and the influence of their activities. In the course of the hearings devoted to mail subsidy propaganda, the head of a Washington publicity agency was compelled to admit that one of his own reports to his principal showed "an excess of zeal" in describing his work.

The Symbols and Styles of Propaganda

Since the distinctive means by which collective reactions are controlled in propaganda involve the use of representations, the principles governing their choice are peculiarly crucial. Some of the most grotesque errors into which propagandists have fallen have arisen from carelessness in searching for the precise meaning that is attached to words or intonations, pictures or tunes, by those who are presumed to be influenced by them. Through such negligence the Germans circulated a photogravure portrait of a native chief in European dress in

Moslem India for propaganda purposes, forgetting that true believers abhor photographs, stiff shirts, and starched collars.

Available dictionaries and lexicons are so highly generalized that the working propagandist is usually constrained to rely upon assistants whom he judges to be intimately conversant with local differences. Very recently certain technical aids have been employed, such as the questionnaire and even the free word-association test, in order to uncover the meanings attached to *Jew* and *monopoly* in different social classes and regions. Vocabularies of encomium and opprobrium have their variable constituents; a slang word of today, like *kibitzer,* is meaningless tomorrow. Certain words and stories persist through the centuries. A stock example is the tale of a tub filled with the eyes of prisoners taken by the Turks. This story has done duty in Europe since the First Crusade.

The propagandist recognizes that symbols of any kind become so intertwined with the whole personality integration of an individual that the study of their significance becomes a matter of the utmost complexity. By the use of the technique of free-fantasy, modern clinical psychology can probe the deeper meanings of the personality after the manner invented by Freud. Some meanings are found which are private and unshared by other individuals. Thus magenta may arouse the aggressive impulses of Mr. A, since clothes of this color were forced upon him by an eccentric mother in the face of the derision of the neighborhood. The pursuit of the long chains of association by means of psychoanalysis enables several thousand symbols to be located with respect to their capacity to arouse and to gratify certain component impulses of a given personality. Some are connected with anti-social impulses that are usually kept in check; some are bound up with the early compulsions and ideals; others are laden with no strong emotional charge.

A psychoanalytic system of classification can be adopted even though the technique of observation is more casual than the prolonged clinical interview. If the trained propagandist samples the reactions of representative members of a community, the symbol patterns of the whole community can be exposed. Symbols that arouse the anti-social impulses of most of the members of the community may be called the *counter-mores* patterns, such as the use of obscene or sacrilegious language. Those that arouse the fervently held and socially acceptable ideals and practices are the *mores* patterns; pious exhortations or pictures of the national hero are illustrations. The patterns of *expediency* are the expressions of matters-of-fact.

The task of the propagandist is to re-define the responses toward certain objects by the management of the available supply of symbols. The simplest way to make a devil of the Kaiser is to present the Kaiser in all the ways that are current for presenting a devil. If the propaganda problem is to foster revolution, this means that the task is to overcome the psychological processes that have embedded the symbols and practices of the ruling order within the personalities of the community as a whole. An established order guides emotional growth through family, school, and kindred agencies, so that the support of the public régime is a matter of private conscience. Hence the task of the revolutionist is to break up the ascendancy of the ruling symbols over the conscience, and literally to create crises of conscience by attaching pro-conscience symbols to the new, and anti-social symbols to the old. Hence the "injustices" of the old and the "justice" of the new become the cardinal themes; for example, the "selfishness and cruelties of capitalism" are contrasted with the "ethical superiority of the classless society." Aggressive tendencies must be turned against the former symbol of love and respect; affections must be deflected from the old to the new.

These considerations show why the psychological task of the revolutionist is far more difficult than that of the reformer, who keeps the central symbols intact and strives simply to recapture them as sanctions for a particular demand for war, or tariff protection, or national insurance.

A consideration of the diversity of meanings attached to specific symbols by particular persons shows why ambiguity is an aid to concerted action. A high degree of generality is essential to popular appeal; symbols must be sufficiently vague to enable the individual to transfer his private loves and hates and hopes and fears to the slogans and catchwords of the movement. It is significant that the triumphs of Marxist socialism in the nineteenth century were won with a symbolic structure which went to great length in analyzing the historical development of industrial society, but had very little to offer about the precise nature of the "classless society." This ambiguity was a propaganda advantage in competition with some of the earlier forms of wishful socialism which dwelt in detail upon the new society. In a rapidly changing social order in which the gas lights of yesterday's Utopia had to be succeeded by the electric lights of today's Utopia, ambiguity was a very special advantage. In more static communities, rather more concrete pictures of ultimate felicity can be employed successfully, a fact that has been shown by the success of detailed ideas of heaven in the propaganda of some missionary societies. Nonetheless, concerted action depends upon a high order of generality, since the persons, practices, and phrases of a movement are the polarization points for immense concentrations of private emotion.

The styles of presentation that arouse the masses to effective action are dynamic in the extreme. The dramatic art of the Russian Revolution was hyperdynamic. Theaters and posters depicted surging masses who groaned beneath the weight of crown and miter, then cast off their shackles with triumphant shouts and cries. All was stir, defiance, turmoil. With the consolidation of the new order of things, the style has lost much of its rapid tempo. The proletarian portrayed today by the Soviet artist or dramatist may stand in dignified repose. The theater is no longer constrained to reiterate the trauma of revolution. It retards and varies its pace, subdivides and hence enlarges its group figures, and even places conflict within a single breast, thus bordering upon the despised introspectionism of the " bourgeois theater." Decried by the revolutionary fundamentalists, these modifications in style evidence the security of the socialist state rather than its distintegration. Roberto Michels has drawn attention to the worshipful reverence of many monarchical hymns, like " God Save the King "; the accelerated tempo of the national songs which accompanied the growth of nationalism in western Europe; and the feverish speed, the satiric bitterness, and the bloodthirsty appeal of revolutionary music. The shifting insecurity level of the masses powerfully modifies the resonance of particular modes of appeal.

The Channels of Propaganda

The channels of propaganda available to the propagandist may be classified according to the intimacy of contact among those who use them and according to the number of persons affected. They may also be classified according to their availability for anti-authoritarian or pro-authoritarian propaganda.

Intimate forms of communication are necessarily adopted when vigilant authority threatens to visit serious penalties on the disseminator of ideas subversive of its ascendancy.

Many of the channels of more general contact strive to retain the compelling power of the more intimate kinds of talk; hence the pastoral letter, the neighborly voice on the radio, the informal close-up on the newsreel, the dialogue, and the importation of informal salutations into public addresses.

Another factor in conditioning the act of communication is the length of time necessary to the production of symbols prior to their dissemination. A vaudeville performer may improvise his joke and reach his audience instantly; a systematic theorist like Descartes may live in comparative seclusion for years in the preparation of a document of conscious propaganda value.*

In acute crises, when concerted action impends, considerations of speed in the preparation and dissemination of material take the upper hand. Hence the prominence of public speaking, especially in the form of the harangue rather than the heavily stylized oration. Hence the rôle of the poster, in the primitive form of writing on a wall, or in the more complicated shape of print on paper, during wars and revolutions. Hence the importance of rumor that can be circulated from mouth to mouth without the avowal of personal responsibility. Leaflets, tracts, and pamphlets often make great sacrifices to speed in mechanical production; extended argument is subordinated to exhortation, warning, and allied forms of excited discourse, designed to intensify mass excitement, or possibly to allay collective passion. Unless the hand of repression is too severe, collective gatherings and demonstrations abound, with all their restless milling or marching about, and with all their opportunities for shouts, songs, and gestures. At the very peak of crisis, letters no longer serve as media of persuasion but as coordinating signals between organizers of action.

When the task of crisis propaganda is to reach masses compactly segregated at a distance, and protected by all the devices of vigilant violence, much ingenuity is essential to the choice of successful channels. During the late spring and summer of 1918 the German armies in the West, numbering 3,700,000 men, were deluged with more than sixty-five million pieces of enemy propaganda; the leaflets were distributed by airplane and by balloons which could float in the prevailing westerly winds.

In times of stress, but of peace, the radio can be employed for propaganda at a distance. Moscow has been especially active in broadcasting programs in foreign languages. In the event of another general war, it seems probable that the effectiveness of the radio will be severely crippled by the use of technical means of interfering with transmission. Such contingencies illustrate again that the appropriateness of a channel of propaganda is not only a matter of its technical potentiality, its state of effective utilization, but also of its actual control.

If there is more time to infiltrate propaganda among those occupy-

* On the propagandistic rôle of Descartes, consult Franz Borkenau, *Der Übergang vom feudalen zum bürgerlichen Weltbild*, p. 340. Paris, 1934.

ing distant territory, ostensibly nonpartisan associations can be partially relied upon. Such channels are the stock in trade of irredentist and cultural unity propagandas, such as the post-war German efforts among German-speaking peoples in Austria and elsewhere. Singing societies, athletic associations, fraternal orders, and similar conduits constantly stimulate cultural sentiments which it is hoped will be easily directed to political ends, either in major crises or in ordinary commercial and diplomatic negotiations. The activity of foreign governments among people of alien origin in the United States has been very marked in connection with loans and debt settlements.

Albert Mousset, who has discussed the problem of French propaganda abroad, emphasizes the importance of selecting the most receptive channels. For cultural propaganda this would mean painting and academic missions in Poland and concerts in Czechoslovakia. Among the relatively permanent channels of propaganda are classed language courses, literary circles, and libraries. The occasional vehicles are missions, conferences, tournées, expositions, cinema, and sports. Information for the foreign press is constant. French experience is said to show that music internationalizes easily (Debussy, Faure, Ravel); the theater, the novel, poetry, and painting are less universal. Material of an historical, literary, or sociological character is prone to " disillusion and wound."

If the purpose of a propaganda is the slow promotion of creeds and dogmas, with no definite intention of reaching ultimate political goals, reliance can be put on personal work and service. The service features of the various religious propagandas have furnished them with successful avenues of approach to many alien peoples; hence the medical, technical, and literary work of the missionary societies. Personal persuasion and example may be subordinated to such indirect methods as those described by Paul Radin in connection with the spread of the peyote cult among the Winnebago Indians. A sick man, perhaps neglected by his relatives, would be tended by known members of the cult. If restored to health, he would feel under obligation to them, and it was implied that the best recompense would be affiliation with the cult.

If the problem is to reach those who are secluded within the influential circles of a given society, and whom it is desired to suborn to revolutionary attitudes, permeation may occur through personal contact among dinner guests, house guests, or salon visitors. Through the salons of the eighteenth century the cleavages in the ruling régime of France were widened by exposure to the freeze and thaw of controversy. Those who bear the complicated culture of a reading civilization can be reached by the discreet circulation of books whose content satisfies the critical standards of the time; hence the appeal value of the systematizing social critics to the middle-class intellectuals prior to the French and Russian revolutions.

When the goal is to incite the masses to ultimate revolutionary action, defensive violence by the ruling élite quickly drives the movement "underground," linking each new initiative to the long history of secret societies. Christianity was deeply influenced by the secret society technique of the East as it sought to survive the persecution of Roman authorities during the early years. The strong hold of masonic symbolism on the French revolutionists was the outcome of protective and offensive adaptation.

Changes in the channels of technical communication have had such diverse effects upon the spread of revolutionary and conformist symbols that it is difficult to appraise their net result. Before cheap printing and general literacy, before moving pictures and radio, the possibilities of applying stimuli simultaneously to masses were extremely restricted. The Greeks and Romans lived much in the open air, and their attention had to be captured at the congregating centers, such as the gymnasium, the temple, the theater, the forum, the marketing place, the highway. The *Acta Diurna* and *Acta Senatus* at Rome were put on walls, where they caught the eye of the strolling or lolling populace. Poets often read their offerings at the public baths. Crude processional choruses were produced by the peasants of Attica and by the Dorian communities at harvest festivals, in which the performers, dressed as goats or satyrs, amused their neighbors with sallies of rustic wit. The more elaborate derivatives of these humble beginnings were developed first at Athens, where comedy rather than tragedy became the most frequent medium of topical allusion.

Any effort to introduce simultaneity among the scattered congregating places of the listening-looking world depended upon somewhat laborious means of transmission. The *Acta Diurna* of Rome were copied for use in provincial cities and towns. Politicians and business men in classical and medieval times developed systems of newsletters and staffs of professional copyists. The newsletters of the Fugger banking house are perhaps the most famous examples. The popes sought to reach the remote corners of western Europe during the investiture controversy by means of traveling monks and merchants. Secular rulers frequently resorted to strolling players and poets.

The modern motion picture, however, has easily solved the engineering problems involved in reaching centers of assembly throughout vast territories with a minimum of time lag. The newsreel and " shorts " can be quickly made and spread. The radio is generally used in the western world to reach individuals in their dispersed dwellings; previously the word-of-mouth route was confined to congregating centers or to the administratively difficult personal canvass. Thus far both radio and motion picture installations have required substantial capital expenditure, and have been monopolized by the ruling few whenever they conceived their interests to be seriously threatened. The comparative ease of detection of radio and motion picture equipment has also played into the hands of the ruling classes.

The spread of cheap printing and of literacy has no doubt aided those desirous of fostering social innovation, despite the efforts of authority to control the production and distribution of books, pamphlets, and periodicals, and to monopolize the school. Although huge capital investments are needed for some kinds of publishing ventures, and the physical equipment is readily detectable and liable to confiscation, effective printing can also be carried on with cheaper and more mobile units. Printed matter is of special aid in coordinating protest groups which are dispersed throughout many districts. Since the printed document is generally, though not invariably, read in isolation, it may be used to nurture the growth of deviational attitudes among members of a community.

Printed propaganda has been especially prominent in connection with the rise of the middle classes. Crane Brinton has remarked that " the middle class was too large to gain its experience of politics directly by personal contact, by struggle and intrigue. It was obliged to learn indirectly from books." The Protestant sects valued enough learning to enable the individual to read the catechism and the creed, and the Catholics were compelled to follow suit. Improved methods of printing and the growth of the modern division of labor enabled book learning to escape from clerical hands. One feature of this development was the transformation of the vernaculars into literary languages. Early in the eighteenth century work in the social sciences was mainly in Latin; in the second half of the century it was in a modern language. The nineteenth century witnessed the rediscovery of many submerged cultures as an incident of the spread of nationalism and of proletarianism. Wider layers of the population were constantly being stimulated into political activity; thus reading circles started for manual workers in France or Great Britain by bourgeois humanitarians frequently became transformed into centers of anti-capitalism, joining with the trade union or the political party in demanding a reconstruction of society.

The rise of a new method of communicating did not lead to the abandonment of the older channels; witness the vitality of conversation in the salons of the eighteenth century, or in the taverns and cafés of many countries in the modern era.

The task of maintaining the ascendancy of a given élite requires the coordinated use of symbols, property, and violence. Propaganda may be devoted to extending and defending the ideology which preserves the existing methods of gaining wealth and distinction. In many times and places the symbols that sustain the existing distribution of values are transmitted with a minimum of premeditation, since they are deeply implanted in the culture. Under such conditions the ceremony is one of the most potent means of preserving the traditional order. In a given community true ceremonies exist only when the patterns are sustained by an unchallenged conviction of the importance of their performance for the welfare of the whole. Some of the potency of the ceremony is derived from the stereotyping of the forms that are invoked; observe the conservatism of sacred dances. Symbols of unity are brought to the focus of collective attention in a setting in which primitive emotional attitudes are reinstated and reaffirmed. The ceremonial is a reminder of continuity and permanence, offering the individual another opportunity to identify his own destiny with the imperishable. Any number of private emotional stresses may be extinguished in the personal revalidation of the symbols of the culture. The wounds of thwarted ambition and factional rivalry may be healed and forgotten in the rituals of reconciliation.

Since the essence of ceremonial potency is its acceptance as self-evident, it is no longer correct to speak of true ceremonies when conflict has resulted in the devaluation of the accepted forms. The former ceremonies are then debased to spectacles which divert, excite, or provoke. The spectacle may, of course, be a powerful means of preserving authority. Since the ruling élite typically has control of a large proportion of the material assets of the community, sporting events, dramatic pageants, or triumphal processions may be lavishly mounted. The spectacle can be combined with the distribution of goods and services, ranging all the way from simple souvenirs to generous barbecues and bread lines.

The true demonstration implies active participation rather than passive inspection. Some demonstrations are also ceremonials, but some of them may be simple spectacles for certain members of the community, who may look with interest at the floats of a parade but feel no urge to take part and no concern about the outcome. Protest demonstrations miss their goal when they are "good shows"; the patriotic demonstration can shade off to a mere spectacle without immediate danger to the ruling order.

Revolutionary groups are not without true ceremonies, evaluated from the standpoint of the group itself. Thus a conspirative group may face the zero hour with solemn handclasps, moments of devout meditation before the busts of departed heroes, and other somewhat stylized ways of coping with inner anxiety. Often these spring up spontaneously from forms borrowed from beyond the culture of the revolutionary group; but they may be unified and propagated as an integral part of its inner life.

The ruling and not the challenging élite typically has the benefit of architectural and plastic media of communication. Edifices serve the ends of psychological control no less than those of shelter or storage. The impression of irresistible might and immemorial solidity that is connected with pyramids, triumphal arches, obelisks, palaces, and gigantic sculptured figures is evident enough. More subtle perhaps is the psychological result of dwelling-house architecture. Socialized attitudes may be self-consciously fostered, as in the new apartment houses in the Soviet Union, by diverting activities from the seclusion of the small family to the constant interplay of the common playground, laundry, and kitchen. The urge of the landed proprietor to establish an aloof and compact island of authority was sufficiently well expressed in the country manor; the preoccupation of the merchant with safety and display was externalized in the carefully guarded piles erected in the turbulent commercial towns of Renaissance Italy. Frozen into brick, stone, and cement are past expectations which are constantly renewed in the experience of those who come in touch with them.

The Study of Propaganda

Many specific purposes have contributed to the body of systematic literature on propaganda. The venerable problem of success in war led to the earliest known systematic discussion of propaganda in the military classic of the East, *The Book of War* by Sun Tzu, dating from the fifth century B. C. " In night fighting," remarks the sage, "beacons and drums are largely used; in day fighting, a great number of banners and flags, and the enemy's eyes and ears are confounded." " When surrounding an enemy, allow him an outlet," he advises, and continues to comment shrewdly upon the attitudes of six countries known to him, and how to handle them. Sir Thomas More's *Utopia* portrays propaganda among the Utopians, who set up proclamations among the enemy offering rewards to the slayer of the enemy's prince, hoping thus to sow dissension through suspicion.

The whole problem of preserving the power of the prince in war and peace led to the analysis of symbol handling in Kautilya's *Arthaśāstra*, the Indian classic dating from 321 to 296 B.C. In Book X he says, "Astrologers and other followers of the king should infuse spirit into the army by pointing out the impregnable nature of the array of his army." Secret agents should circulate among the enemy and depress their morale by spreading rumors of their certain defeat. Book I discusses "Winning over Factions for or against an Enemy's Cause in an Enemy's State," and enumerates the various categories of the discontented and how they may be handled. Some are "provoked," some "alarmed," some "ambitious," and some "haughty."

The problem of political success motivated Quintus, the younger brother of Cicero, to write a handbook for those who wanted to be elected consul, stressing the ways of achieving popularity through what we call "gladhanding." How to indoctrinate children is considered in the earliest pedagogical writings. How to indoctrinate the heathen has been described by specialists in the propagation of the world's missionary religions. How to coalesce a national state through a shrewd prince was the problem of Machiavelli. How to lead masses to effective revolutionary action over large areas was the problem to which Lenin made signal contribution. How to deal with persons accused of crimes committed in excited crowds or mobs stimulated the work of Judge Tarde in France and of jurists in Italy. How to expose the evils of democracy by delineating the blind emotionalism of the crowd was the *tendence* of Le Bon. How to improve democracy by discovering the conditions of private and collective thought occupied Graham Wallas. How to make sales has instigated the production of the vast library on advertising. How to make propaganda, in general, has recently become a problem, both of practitioners and of those who seek to understand social processes.

Scanning the whole body of systematic reflection on propaganda, its connection becomes evident with periods of rapid social change in which the bonds of an older social order are in dissolution, leaving exposed both the presuppositions and the methods of political survival, and in which the focus of attention has been drawn to new geographical, historical, or class discoveries. Aristotle's contributions date from an epoch in which a new form of governmental organization, the empire, was crushing out the city state; and it is not surprising to discover that Machiavelli wrote in the stirring years of the Renaissance rather than in some bucolic interlude. Both men wrote when the horizon of men's minds had been widened through vivid contact with new peoples and new places, and with the remnants of ancient cultures. Likewise, they were living in turbulent days which had brought the "lower" strata of the population into the arena of active politics.

The study of propaganda has necessarily been bound up with the growth of social sciences in modern times. The direct effects of the voyages of discovery were even more influential on the social sciences than the rediscovery of the heliocentric universe, since they brought to the ears of Europe the tidings of ways of life far different from the classical inheritance. The veneration of classical literature, when coupled with the scientific habit of instrumented curiosity, eventually created a science of history, and archeology that brought the ancient world closer to the understanding of the critical mind. The canons of documentary criticism, first clearly formulated by Mabillon, built up dependable time perspectives in history. Increasing specialization expanded the range of dependable observations about oriental, primitive, classical, medieval, and ancient peoples; and, presently, a naturalistic approach to the study of the child and the mentally disordered revealed a startling body of symbolic data.

Despite the presence of the major conditions for the direct study of propaganda in the eighteenth century, the necessity of glorifying the will of the people rather than the will of the king was scarcely conducive to the objective study of ways and means of manipulating the common will. The specialists on the spinning of systematic theories were mainly concerned with justifications, and while plenty of ingenuity was shown in practical propaganda, there is no monumental treatise dating from the bourgeois revolution.

The main literary contributions came later, when certain members of the intellectual group, principally derived from the middle class, sought to arouse the masses to effective protest against capitalism. The sheer magnitude of the task, together with the colossal instance of the French Revolution as a case study, greatly stimulated the analysis of propaganda technique. Whenever the direct veneration of the creative potency of the mass was uppermost in revolutionary minds, the study of strategical and tactical issues was subordinated, as in many of the utopian socialist movements. When history was recaptured for revolutionary purposes by Marx, tactical questions connected with propaganda came frankly to the front.

It will be recalled that much of the scholarship of the reaction in Europe sought, by emphasizing the processes of historical continuity, and casting scorn upon "rationalistic" programs of change, to deflate the hopes of those who desired the reconstruction of society. The very data that had done duty to undermine the assumption of immutability in the eighteenth century were now turned to conservative purposes. It was Marx who so ingeniously turned this appeal to history into an appeal for revolution in a form that outdistanced his competitors in the following decades. Welding the metaphysics of Hegel to the time- and space-bound changes in the instrumentalities of production, Marx sought to reduce the reigning theology, philosophy, jurisprudence, and their popular projections to "ideologies" beneficial to the profit-takers, and bound to be supplanted by the contradictions generating within the system of capitalistic production.

Although this powerfully provocative treatment seemed to debase the historical rôle of ideas and to exalt the rôle of "material" conditions, such did not prove to be the case. It was stressed from the beginning that surviving ideologies could retard the emergence of a clarified self-consciousness on the part of the working class; hence one of the tasks of the fully class-conscious proletarian was to reflect on how to tear asunder the veil of the older ideologies. As the proletarian revolution was deferred from decade to decade, the potency of these older symbol structures became more and more manifest, side by side with the capacity for innovation which distinguished capitalistic modes of production. Serious tensions developed between revolutionary thinkers who were inclined to trust the "material" growth of society to put victory into their laps, and revolutionary thinkers who insisted upon the possible seizure of power in situations of general discontent by a band of determined and skilled professional revolutionists. Lenin, of course, became the most vigorous exponent of this theory and practice.

The Marxist analysis and the Marxist propaganda put the problem of the connection between "material" and "ideological" changes in the very center of social scientific inquiry, as gradually became more clear. The "Streit um Marx" as it developed in the ensuing years led to the generalization of the concept of "ideology" from a partisan term to a category of general applicability. The most influential line of development was through the "myth" of Sorel to the "derivations" of Pareto. It is safe to say that the theory of interaction between the "material" and the "ideological" (however defined and in whatever terminological equivalents) is generally accepted, and that the main issues are over the order of magnitude of these relationships. New technical devices have been applied to the study of these connections. The extent of the results obtainable by propaganda in given situations is obviously one of the principal questions of theoretical interest; hence the analysis of the rôle of propaganda has become increasingly pivotal for theories of social change that seek to state the reciprocal influence of the " material " and the " ideological."

The available terminologies for drawing distinctions within this general field of inquiry, together with the interest in its cognate problems, owe much to German romanticism. The emphasis upon the organic, totalistic unity of separate collective entities was an appeal to understand the distinctive personality of each, especially as disclosed in the cultural manifestations of the whole body of participants. Hence the avid pursuit of folk tales, dialects and folk art, the growth of philology, and the development of the psychology of peoples by Lazarus and Steinthal.* The romanticists created a profound respect for the non-reflective processes of society, paving the way for the popularity of the conceptions of a " collective unconscious," " creative energy," and " individual unconscious " which played so large a rôle in the " anti-rationalism " of the following years. They made much of the *Zeitgeist* and stimulated the formation of many words to convey collective psychological nuances. In the forties the German economists reacted against the " perpetualism " of the English classical school, which was preoccupied with stating the routines of the competitive market, and underlined the time- and convention-bound limitations upon the processes of economic life. Hence the rich monographic literature on the growth of institutions fostered by the German historical school, and the ease with which economists developed general conceptions of the whole historical and social process, signalized in the sociological writings of Schmoller, Sombart, and Oppenheimer. Saturated with the sense of unity, German sociology responded to the distinction drawn between folk culture and civilization by Tönnies; propaganda was unmistakably associated with *Gesellschaft* and not *Gemeinschaft*. Equivalent emphases are found in the psychological and cultural histories, such as those of Lamprecht and Dilthey. The reaction against the English classical school led to parallel discoveries of historical and psychological relativity in the work of Walter Bagehot in England, of Thorstein Veblen in the United States. The study of conflict groups,

* Lazarus, incidentally, said that his interest in differences went back to his childhood astonishment that the Christians of his town should be Protestants who spoke German and Catholics who spoke Polish. He was Jewish and his community of three thousand was equally divided between Poles and Germans. (See Alfred Leicht, *Lazarus der Begründer der Völkerpsychologie*, Leipzig, 1904.)

like trade unions and political parties, brought ideological issues firmly into the area of discussion.

As the specialization of research has proceeded in recent years, influential contributions to the understanding of psychological processes and the conditions of their control have been unearthed. The exciting phenomena of hypnotism and later of psychoanalysis and general clinical psychology, gave currency to various theories of *suggestion, imitation, infection, contagion, illusion,* and *delusion.* Practitioners and students of propaganda often borrowed the terms, and sometimes the concepts, of various physiologists, physicians, and psychologists. Thus the biologist Tschachotin, responsible for the "Three Arrow" propaganda of the German Socialists, used Pavlov's concept of the *conditioned reflex.* Other formulations have proceeded in terms of *instinct, habit, response, situation,* and *attitude.*

From the comparative ethnologists have come certain terms, like *pattern,* and certain mapping techniques for the handling of culture traits in relation to culture areas. Theories of diffusion have been reformulated in the light of these data, conferring new life upon the formal list of factors affecting the process of "imitation," drawn up by Tarde and other social and psychological systematists. The study of dynamic biological, psychological, and sociological processes has exposed the important rôle of deviational forms in diffusion; witness the mixed forms enumerated in Raoul de la Grasserie, *De l'hybridité mental et social: Étude de psychosociologie* (Paris, 1911). Many students of collective behavior, notably Robert E. Park, have protested against the over-generalization of the concept *crowd* in Le Bon, which included everything from revolutionary mobs to dull parliamentary debates, and have proposed supplementary concepts like *public.*

Combined with the newer psychological emphases, the constant reference of the idea to its setting that characterized the pragmatism of William James and John Dewey was widely influential. Graham Wallas pondered long whether he should name his *Human Nature in Politics,* "Pragmatic Politics"; and attributed much of his viewpoint to Ribot's psychology of the emotions and the sentiments, and to William James. Laboratory types of psychology have contributed extensively to the armory of techniques being adapted to the survey of the results of propaganda, a convergence that is reviewed in the summary by the Murphys of *Experimental Social Psychology.*

Propaganda and Social Equilibrium

The analysis of the relationship of propaganda to other social changes can proceed by examining it in connection with theories of social equilibrium and theories of social development. In order to stimulate the orientation of research in this field toward fundamental problems of social theory, certain tentative statements may be passed in review.

Thus it may be said that, in general, propaganda *increases with departures* from equilibrium. Individuals may believe that departure from equilibrium threatens them or affords them new opportunities for advancement. Thus insecurity among business interests during the "muckraking era" in the early twentieth century stimulated the hiring of press agents. Sensational examples of business and political success through resort to propaganda contributed to the use of this technique in the war and post-war years.

Another general statement is that the resort to propaganda increases the tension between *individualizing* and *collectivizing* tendencies. Research may confirm the interpretation that the extensive use of propaganda by individuals, firms, associations, unions, parties, and other groups in the modern world sharpened the cleavages within modern communities, produced much frustration through self-nullification, and stimulated the individual, from sheer necessity, to subordinate himself to movements in the name of large aggregates. Once collective crises of discontent have been resolved, of course, differentiating and individualizing tendencies re-emerge.

Another aspect of the same general process is the tendency of propaganda to heighten the tension between *localizing* and *universalizing* movements. Disaffected elements within any community are receptive toward symbols in the name of which they can sharpen their attacks upon the established order. Thus the socialist vocabulary was borrowed extensively by the wage earners of many countries; hence the resort to defensive propaganda on the part of the beneficiaries of the established order. Efforts to emphasize localism became so intense that many socialist parties minimized the international aspects of their movement, and sought to defend their patriotism in order to win middle-class support.

One consequence of intensive reliance upon propaganda may be such an intensification of the crisis that *other instruments* of social control are invoked, as in war and revolution. Still another general aspect to be considered is that in the long run propaganda plays into the hands of the enemies rather than the friends of established orders. Long before violence can be concentrated or economic instrumentalities assembled, subversive rumors can pass from mouth to mouth; some propaganda is both cheap and elusive.

Propaganda and Social Development

The function of propaganda may also be considered in the light of theories of the consequences of social development for the relative ascendancy of classes, skills, personalities, and attitudes. Thus from the French to the Russian Revolution the net effect of propaganda upon the emergence or the retardation of the " proletarian revolution " could be appraised. Contemporary events since the Russian Revolution might be construed in terms of a possible passage between the emergence of the intellectual workers who favored bureaucratic state systems in actual practice, and a possible next world revolution which marks the emergence of the manual toilers.*

Propaganda is itself a *skill,* and propagandists may be viewed as in competition with the wielders of other skills for income, safety, and deference. Hence the interest in examining the wealth and position of advertisers, missionaries, and publicity men of all degrees in various times and places.

Certain *personality* types may be more attracted to propaganda than other types, and hence the rise and fall of propaganda may contribute something to that often neglected historical dialectic which seals the relative fate of rival personality forms.

Likewise, some *attitudes* are fostered by the exercise of the techniques of propaganda which sharpen the inner contradiction between impulses toward survival and impulses toward sacrifice on behalf of aesthetic, moralistic, or contemplative ends. The poignancy of this inner struggle between " reasons of state " (" reasons of survival ") and other reasons is in some measure exhibited in the masterly review by Friedrich Meinecke of this historic conflict.

Propaganda, in common with other social processes, has its bearing upon the distribution of values, upon *who gets what, when, and how* in terms of class, skill, personality, and attitude.

* See, for example, Max Nomad, *Rebels and Renegades.*

BIBLIOGRAPHY

PART I. PROPAGANDA STRATEGY AND TECHNIQUE

A. THEORIES OF PROPAGANDA

Theories of how to conduct successful propaganda have been formulated by public relations counsels, advertisers, political scientists, social psychologists, sociologists, social workers, journalists, and publicists. In this section titles *of the most general interest* are included from the special fields. Less abstract or less important references are listed elsewhere.

ADAMS, HENRY FOSTER. *Advertising and Its Mental Laws.* New York: Macmillan, 1916. 333 pp.

"Advertising," *Encyclopedia of the Social Sciences.* (By Leverett S. Lyon.)

AKHUN, M. I., and PETROV, V. A. *Bolcheviki i Armiia v 1905–1917.* Leningrad: Krasnaia Gazeta, 1929. 348 pp.

History and technique of Bolshevik propaganda among the troops before and during the World War.

ALLISON, JAMES MURRAY. *First Essays on Advertising.* London: C. Palmer, 1926. 231 pp.

Connects advertising with labor policy, agency technique, shipping, life insurance, middlemen. Notes on "The Library of an Advertising Man," pp. 166–206.

————. *Second Essays on Advertising,* with an introduction by the Rt. Hon. Viscount Leverhulme. London: Benn, 1929. 135 pp.

ARREN, JULES. *Comment il faut faire de la publicité.* Paris: Lafitte, 1912. 307 pp.

How to handle publicity. Spanish edition: *La ciencia de la publicidad,* translated and adapted by J. M. Fernández. Second edition. Madrid: Editorial Labor, 1931. 205 pp.

————. *La Publicité, lucrative et raisonnée: Son rôle dans les affaires.* Paris: Bibliothèque des ouvrages practiques, 1909. 436 pp.

BAKER, ARCHIBALD G. *Christian Missions and a New World Culture.* Chicago and New York: Willett, Clark, 1934. 322 pp.

Chapter 8 undertakes to generalize for the benefit of missionaries the principal methods of influencing behavior.

BALABANOFF, ANGELICA. *Erziehung der Massen zum Marxismus.* Berlin: Laubsche Verlagsbuchhandlung, 1927. 164 pp.
Theory and technique of Socialist agitation advocating mass revolution.

BARTELS, RUDOLF. *Lehrbuch der Demagogik.* Berlin: Springer, 1905. 143 pp.

BASCHWITZ, KURT. *Der Massenwahn: Seine Wirkung und seine Beherrschung.* Munich: Beck, 1923. 275 pp.
How to control the illusions of the masses. Deals especially with war propaganda.

BEAGLEHOLE, B. F. "Some Aspects of Propaganda," *Australian Journal of Psychology and Philosophy,* June, 1928, pp. 93–110.

Behind the Scenes in Politics (anonymous). New York: Dutton, 1924. 308 pp.
A collection of rules of thumb for campaign strategists. Chapter 9 is on propaganda, chapter 10 on politicians and the press.

BEHRMANN, HERMANN. *Reklame.* Berlin: Spaeth und Linde, 1923. 283 pp.

BENNETT, CHARLES. *Scientific Salesmanship.* St. Louis: American Efficiency Bureau, 1933. 702 pp.
Appendix contains 314 selected articles on salesmanship.

BERNAYS, EDWARD L. *Crystallizing Public Opinion.* New York: Boni and Liveright, 1923. 218 pp.
By a leading public relations counsel.

————. *Propaganda.* New York: Liveright, 1928. 159 pp.

Bibliothek der kommunistischen Internationale. Hamburg: Hoym, 1920–22.
This series of books contains important writings on the theory and tactics of the Bolshevik party.

BIDDLE, WILLIAM W. "A Psychological Definition of Propaganda," *Journal of Abnormal and Social Psychology,* 26: 283–95 (October, 1931).
Bibliography, pp. 294–95.

BIRNBAUM, ALFRED. *Das Wesen der Propaganda: Eine psychologische Studie.* Berlin, 1920.
Psychological and psychopathological theory of the nature of propaganda.

BONNS, EDWARD, and CARRIER, C. E. *Putting it Over by Means and Methods of Exploitation.* New York: Siebel Publishing Corporation, 1925. 236 pp.
Propaganda, pp. 113–28.

BORDEN, NEIL HOPPER. *Problems in Advertising.* London, Chicago, and New York: A. W. Shaw, 1927. 677 pp.

Presentation of a wide variety of advertising problems and cases gathered by the Harvard Business School with the assistance of a group of advertising agencies and publishers.

BRADDOCK, ALBERT P. *Psychology and Advertising.* London: Butterworth, 1932. 246 pp.

CARR, C. F., and STEVENS, F. E. *How to Speak in Public: A Popular Guide to Fluency in Debate and to the Easy Mastery of the Art of Effective Self-Expression on All Public Occasions,* with an introduction by the Rt. Hon. T. P. O'Connor, M.P. Second edition. London: Sir I. Pitman, 1930. 117 pp.

CASSON, HERBERT NEWTON. *Ads and Sales: A Study of Advertising and Selling from the Standpoint of the New Principles of Scientific Management.* Chicago: McClurg, 1911. 167 pp.

CHAMBONNAUD, L., GAUTIER, ÉMILE, and THIBAUDEAU, F. *Les Affaires et l'annonce (La technique des affaires, méthodes françaises et étrangères,* vol. 7). Paris: Dunod, 1921. 548 pp.

CICERO, QUINTUS TULLIUS. "On Standing for the Consulship," in Marcus Tullius Cicero, *Treatises . . . on the Nature of the Gods . . . ,* translated by C. D. Yonge (Bohn's Classical Library, vol. 19), pp. 485–503. London, 1853.

Advice addressed by Quintus Cicero to his brother.

COSTE, CHARLES. *La Psychologie sociale de la guerre.* Nancy: Berger-Levrault, 1928. 112 pp.

Includes an analysis of the methods of moral mobilization, the technique of propaganda, and the value of psychological stimuli.

CRONAU, RUDOLPH. *Das Buch der Reklame — Geschichte, Wesen, und Praxis.* Ulm: Wohler, 1887. 492 pp.

Advertising technique.

CUNLIFFE, JOHN W. "The Case for Publicity," in Lawrence W. Murphy, *An Introduction to Journalism,* pp. 300–02. New York: Nelson, 1930.

DICKINSON, HOWARD WILLIAMS. *Crying Our Wares.* New York: John Day, 1929. 308 pp.

The technique of advertising.

DODGE, R. "Psychology of Propaganda," *Religious Education,* 15: 241–52 (October, 1920).

Frequently quoted.

"Drives, Money-Raising," *Encyclopedia of the Social Sciences.* (By Philip Klein).

DUNLAP, KNIGHT. *Civilized Life: The Principles and Applications of Social Psychology.* Baltimore: Williams and Wilkins, 1934. 392 pp. Revised edition of the author's *Social Psychology* (1925). See "Propaganda" in the Index.

DURSTINE, ROY SARLES. *This Advertising Business.* New York and London: Scribners, 1928. 331 pp. A general description of the advertising business, from the point of view of the agency, by a successful advertising man.

EASTMAN, MAX. *Marx, Lenin, and the Science of Revolution.* New York: Boni, 1927. 263 pp. Interprets from a materialist standpoint the place of propaganda in revolutionary planning and revolutionary crises.

ENGLISH, HORACE BIDWELL. "Emotional Short Circuiting of Thought," *Journal of Abnormal and Social Psychology,* 26: 402–04 (January, 1932).

ERDMANN, KARL OTTO. *Die Kunst Recht zu behalten: Methode und Kunstgriffe des Streitens und andere Aufsätze.* Fourth edition. Leipzig: H. Haessel, 1925. How to win arguments. By a distinguished logician.

FELLER, FRITZ MIROSLAV. *Gesammelte Schriften zur Einführung der Psychoanalyse in die Werkpraxis.* Berlin: Verlag des Archives für angewandte Psychologie, 1931, Buch 2. 160 pp. Applications of psychoanalysis.

FITE, WARNER. "New Essay in the Psychology of Advertising," *Unpopular Review,* 4: 110, 366 (July and October, 1915).

FÖLLMER, WILHELM. *Politische Versammlung und ihre Leitung.* Berlin, 1921. 15 pp. How to conduct political meetings.

FRARY, RAOUL. *Manuel du démagogue.* Paris: Cerf, 1884. 310 pp. Illustrations of "demagoguery."

FRIBOURG, ANDRÉ. *Les Semeurs de haine, leur oeuvre en Allemagne avant et depuis la guerre.* Paris: Berger-Levrault, 1922. 468 pp.

FRIEDLANDER, KURT THEODOR. *Der Weg zum Kaufer: Ein Theorie der praktischen Reklame.* Berlin: Springer, 1926. 197 pp.

FUERNBERG, F. *Where to Begin? How to Build a Mass Young Communist League.* New York: Youth International Publishers.

GOODE, KENNETH MACKARNESS. *Manual of Modern Advertising.* New York: Greenberg, 1932. 497 pp.

GRAVES, WILLIAM B., editor. *Readings in Public Opinion: Its Forma-*

tion and Control. New York and London: Appleton, 1928. 1281 pp.
Reprints much propaganda material. Bibliography at the end of each
chapter.

GREGO, EMILIO. *Come si lancia un prestito di guerra.* Milan: LIM,
1918. 105 pp.
A study in applied psychology and a documented history of official and
unofficial propaganda for war loans.

GUNDLACH, ERNEST THEODORE. *Facts and Fetishes in Advertising.* Chicago: Consolidated Book Publishers, 1931. 672 pp.
A "realistic" contemporary volume on advertising and sales promotion.

HADAMOWSKY, EUGEN. *Propaganda und Nationale Macht.* Oldenburg:
Gerhard Stalling, 1933. 153 pp.
Technique of propaganda in behalf of a National Socialist Germany.

HALL, SAMUEL ROLAND. *The Advertising Handbook: A Reference
Work Covering the Principles and Practice of Advertising.* Second
edition. New York: McGraw-Hill, 1930. 1046 pp.
An orthodox and comprehensive treatment of advertising procedure.

————. *Theory and Practice of Advertising: A Textbook Covering
the Development and Fundamental Principles of Advertising and
Methods of Principal Advertisers.* New York: McGraw-Hill, 1926.
686 pp.

HARRINGTON, E. "Writing with a Purpose," *Chicago English Journal*
(high school edition), 17: 660–66 (October, 1928).

HARTSHORNE, HUGH, MILLER, J. QUINTER, and others. *Community Organization in Religious Education.* New Haven: Yale University,
1932. London: Oxford University, 1933. 250 pp.
Experiments in New Haven. Bibliography, pp. 249–50.

HESS, HERBERT WILLIAM. *Advertising: Its Economics, Philosophy, and
Technique.* Philadelphia and London: Lippincott, 1931. 516 pp.
An academic approach to advertising.

HIGHAM, CHARLES FREDERICK. *Looking Forward: Mass Education
through Publicity.* London: Nisbet, 1920. 183 pp.
By a successful English advertising man.

HITLER, ADOLF. *Mein Kampf.* Munich: Franz Eber Nachfolger, 1932.
782 pp.
War propaganda, pp. 193 ff.; National Socialist propaganda, pp. 649 ff.
English translation: *My Battle.* Boston: Houghton Mifflin, 1933. 297 pp.

HOLLINGSWORTH, HARRY LEIR. *Advertising and Selling: The Principles
of Appeal and Response.* New York: Appleton, 1925. 313 pp.

HOTCHKISS, GEORGE BURTON. *An Outline of Advertising: Its Philosophy, Science, Art, and Strategy.* New York: Macmillan, 1933. 509 pp.

A standard volume. The outgrowth of a long and successful experience in teaching advertising. Bibliographies at the ends of chapters.

JERROLD, B. "On the Manufacture of Public Opinion," *Nineteenth Century,* 13:1080–92 (1883).

KAUTILYA. *Kautilya's Arthaśāstra,* translated by Dr. R. Shamasastry, with an introductory note by Dr. J. F. Fleet. Mysore: The Wesleyan Mission Press, 1929. 484 pp.

An Indian classic of political science dating from 321 to 296 B.C. See especially the sections on the treatment of dissension and disaffection.

KENT, FRANK RICHARDSON. *The Great Game of Politics.* Revised edition. Garden City: Doubleday, Doran, 1930. 346 pp.

Chapters on lobbies, campaign publicity, business men's movements, press agents, and other pressure devices.

KING, HERBERT F. *Practical Advertising.* New York: Appleton, 1933. 385 pp.

KITSON, HARRY DEXTER. *Manual for the Study of the Psychology of Advertising and Selling.* Philadelphia: Lippincott, 1920. 116 pp.

KLEPPNER, OTTO. *Advertising Procedure.* New York: Prentice-Hall, 1925. 539 pp.

A standard comprehensive textbook by a New York advertising agency man. Well-annotated reading suggestions, pp. 505–19.

KOENIG, THEODOR. *Reklame-Psychologie: Ihr gegenwärtiger Stand, ihre praktische Bedeutung.* Munich: R. Oldenbourg, 1924. 206 pp.

The psychology of advertising.

KONISHI, TETSUO. *Propaganda.* Tokyo: Heibonsha, 1930. 276 pp.

Written in Japanese. Similar to Lasswell's *Propaganda Technique.* No Japanese sources are cited in the bibliography.

KRACAUER, S. "Die Gruppe als Ideenträger," *Archiv für Sozialwissenschaft und Sozialpolitik,* 49:594–622 (1922).

The rôle of groups in the diffusion of ideas.

LASSWELL, HAROLD DWIGHT. *Propaganda Technique in the World War.* New York: Knopf, 1927. London: Kegan Paul, Trench, and Trubner, 1927. 233 pp.

Discusses propaganda organization, war guilt and war aims, satanism, the illusion of victory, preserving friendship, demoralizing the enemy, and results of propaganda.

———. "Theory of Political Propaganda," *American Political Science Review,* 21:627–31 (August, 1927).

"Propaganda is the management of collective attitudes by the manipulation of significant symbols [or representations]. The word *attitude* is taken to mean a tendency to act according to certain patterns of valuation."

LAUTERER, KARL. *Lehrbuch der Reklame: Einführung in das Werbewesen.* Vienna: Barth, 1923. 351 pp.

Advertising textbook. Bibliography, pp. 334–39.

LE BON, GUSTAVE. *The World Unbalanced.* London: Unwin, 1924. 256 pp.

See the section on "How to Reform the Mentality of a People."

LEE, IVY LEDBETTER. "The Art of Publicity," in Samuel Crowther, editor, *Book of Business,* 4:78–86. New York, 1920.

By a leading publicity man.

———. *Publicity.* New York: Industries Publishing Company, 1925. 64 pp.

Addresses given before the American Association of Teachers of Journalism in Chicago, the Advertising Club of New York, and the annual convention of the American Electric Railway Association. Includes also questions and answers relating to principles and methods. Publicity is defined and defended.

LENIN, VLADIMIR ILYICH. *Agitation und Propaganda: Ein Sammelband.* Vienna: Verlag für Literatur und Politik, 1929. 250 pp.

"Einzige autorisierte Ausgabe." Propaganda spreads belief; agitation exploits the passing emotional opportunity.

Library of Sales and Advertising. Chicago: A. W. Shaw, 1914. 4 vols.

LINK, HENRY CHARLES. *The New Psychology of Selling and Advertising.* New York: Macmillan, 1932. 293 pp.

LIPPERT, PETER. *Zur Psychologie des Jesuitenordens.* Second edition. Munich, 1923.

Psychology of the Jesuits, whose survival in the propaganda field deserves careful study.

LIPSKY, ABRAM. *Man, the Puppet: The Art of Controlling Minds.* New York: Frank-Maurice, 1925. 275 pp.

Popularly written.

LONG, JOHN CUTHBERT. *Public Relations: Handbook of Publicity.* New York: McGraw-Hill, 1924. 248 pp.

LUCAS, DARRELL B., and BENSON, CHARLES EMILE. *Psychology for Advertisers.* New York and London: Harpers, 1930. 351 pp.

An extremely elementary text, "to be used in . . . business." Bibliography, pp. 338–43.

LUKÁCS, GEORG. *Geschichte und Klassenbewusstsein: Studien über Marxistische Dialektik.* Berlin: Malik-Verlag, 1923. 342 pp.

See the last chapter, "Methodisches zur Organisationsfrage," for a dialectical analysis of propaganda and allied tactical questions.

LUMLEY, FREDERICK ELMORE. "Nature of Propaganda," *Sociology and Social Research,* 13: 315-24 (March, 1929).

————. *The Propaganda Menace.* New York: Century, 1933. 454 pp.

"Propaganda is promotion which is veiled in one way or another as to (1) its origin or sources, (2) the interests involved, (3) the methods employed, (4) the content spread, and (5) the results accruing to the victims — any one, any two, any three, any four, or all five." Describes propaganda in many fields. Bibliography, pp. 433-45.

MACPHERSON, WILLIAM. *The Psychology of Persuasion.* New York: Dutton, 1920. 256 pp.

First considers persuasion as a subjective mental process, then as a form of expression calculated to modify the conduct of others. "Wordless Persuasion"; "Verbal Persuasion"; and "Formal Persuasion in Speeches, Books, Novels, Drama."

MARBE, KARL. *Psychologie der Wertreklame.* Stuttgart: Poeschel, 1930. 33 pp.

The appeal of premiums and free services in creating attitudes favorable to a business or product.

MATAJA, VICTOR. *Die Reklame: Eine Untersuchung über Abkundigungswesen und Werbetätigkeit im Geschäftsleben.* Leipzig: Duncker und Humblot, 1910. 489 pp.

A standard advertising treatise. Bibliography, pp. 479-86.

MAYER, RAYMOND CHARLES. *How to do Publicity.* New York: Harpers, 1933. 258 pp.

Written by a publicity expert.

MEAD, EDWARD SHERWOOD. "The Work of the Promoter," *Annals of the American Academy of Political and Social Science,* 20: 559-70 (1902).

MERRIAM, CHARLES EDWARD. *The Making of Citizens: A Comparative Study of Methods of Civic Training.* Chicago: University of Chicago, 1931. 371 pp.

Summarizes the nine volumes of the *Civic Training Series,* dealing with the problem of civic education, the social composition of civic cohesion, and a comparison of techniques of civic training. Bibliographic footnotes.

MILLIOUD, M. "La Propagation des idées," *Revue philosophique,* 69: 589-600; 70: 168-91.

Modern Advertising: An Authoritative and Practical Guide to the Use of Every Form of Present-Day Publicity, Including Contribu-

tions by Upwards of 30 Leading Specialists, with a foreword by the Rt. Hon. Viscount Burnham. London: Sir I. Pitman, 1926. 2 vols.

MOUSSET, ALBERT. *La France vue de l'étranger, ou le déclin de la diplomatie et le mythe de la propagande.* Paris: L'Île de France, 1926. 222 pp.
General principles of propaganda discussed in relation to France's foreign reputation.

MUNSON, EDWARD LYMAN. *The Management of Men: A Handbook on the Systematic Development of Morale and the Control of Human Behavior.* New York: Holt, 1921. 801 pp.

ODEGARD, PETER H. *The American Public Mind.* New York: Columbia University, 1930. 308 pp.
A general study of public opinion by a specialist in propaganda research. Bibliography, pp. 280–91.

PEAR, T. H. "The Psychology of Advertising," in Bernard Muscio, editor, *Lectures on Industrial Administration (Delivered at Cambridge).* New York: Dutton, 1920.

PETERSON, JOSEPH, and DAVID, QUENTIN J. *The Psychology of Handling Men in the Army.* Minneapolis: Perine Book Company, 1919. 146 pp.

PHELPS, GEORGE HARRISON. *Tomorrow's Advertisers and Their Advertising Agencies.* New York and London: Harpers, 1929. 256 pp.

PIATNITSKY, A. *World Communists in Action.* New York: Workers' Library Publishers.

PLAUT, P. "Grundsätzliches zur Reklamepsychologie," *Zeitschrift für angewandte Psychologie,* 18: 225–49 (July, 1921).
Fundamentals of advertising psychology.

PLENGE, JOHANN. *Deutsche Propaganda: Die Lehre von den Propaganda als praktische Gesellschaftslehre.* Bremen: Angelsachsen Verlag, 1922. 78 pp.
Adversely critical of some phases of German propaganda. Proposes an "applied science."

POFFENBERGER, ALBERT THEODOR. *Psychology in Advertising.* Chicago and New York: A. W. Shaw, 1925. 632 pp.
A standard textbook. Bibliography, pp. 617–23.

"Propaganda," *Encyclopedia of the Social Sciences.* (By Harold D. Lasswell.)

"Propaganda," *Handbuch der Politik.* (By Bernhard Schwertfeger.)

QUIETT, GLENN C., and CASEY, RALPH D. *Principles of Publicity*. New York and London: Appleton, 1926. 420 pp.

By a public relations counsel and a professor of journalism. Discusses college, philanthropic, church, civic, school, and business publicity. How the publicity man makes use of the newspaper, newsreel, movie, and magazine. Has a thoroughgoing plan for "campaigns."

RAGEOT, G. "*Psychologie de la publicité,*" *L'Illustration*, 18:650–51 (June 23, 1928).

RASSAK, JULES. *Psychologie de l'opinion et de la propagande politique.* Paris: Rivière, 1927. 286 pp.

Psychology of political propaganda.

REICHENBACH, HARRY. *Phantom Fame: The Anatomy of Ballyhoo, as Told to David Freedman*. New York: Simon and Schuster, 1931. 258 pp.

By a master of publicity stunts.

Report of Conference on Pressure Groups and Propaganda, University of Chicago, May 2 and 3, 1931. 105 pp., mimeographed.

Specialists on research compare opinions and definitions of pressure groups and propaganda.

RHEINSTROM, CARROLL. *Psyching the Ads, the Casebook of Advertising: The Methods and Results of 180 Advertisements*. New York: Covici, Friede, 1929. 362 pp.

"The most outstanding examples from *Keyed Copy* have been selected as a nucleus for this book. . . . 126 concrete advertising cases . . . 57 different types of merchandise or services . . . illustrate the methods of 80 different advertising agencies." — *Introduction*.

RIEGEL, O. W. *Mobilizing for Chaos: The Story of the New Propaganda*. New Haven: Yale University, 1934. 231 pp.

How post-war nationalistic governments control agencies of communication. By a former American newspaper correspondent in Europe, now a professor of journalism. Bibliography, pp. 215–23.

RIIS, ROGER WILLIAM, and BONNER, CHARLES W., JR. *Publicity: A Study of the Development of Industrial News*. New York: J. H. Sears, 1926. 176 pp.

Written by publicity experts.

ROHWALDT, KARL. "Reklame-Psychologie," *Schweizer Schriften für rationnelles Wirtschaften,* no. 6, pp. 1–27 (1928).

ROUTZAHN, EVART G. *Elements of a Social Publicity Program*. New York: Russell Sage Foundation, 1920. 17 pp.

Paper read before the Division on the Organization of Social Forces at the New Orleans meeting of the National Conference of Social Work, April, 1920.

ROUTZAHN, EVART G., and ROUTZAHN, MARY SWAIN. *The A B C of Exhibit Planning*. New York: Russell Sage Foundation, 1918. 216 pp.

See especially chapters 10–12, on the "Organization of a Campaign," including a classified list of publicity methods.

ROUTZAHN, MARY SWAIN. *Travelling Publicity Campaigns*. New York: Russell Sage Foundation, 1920. 142 pp.

Educational tours of railroad trains and motor vehicles; methods of advance publicity; follow-ups. Illustrated.

RUBEN, PAUL, editor. *Die Reklame, ihre Kunst und Wissenschaft, unter Mitarbeit bekannter Fachleute, Juristen, und Künstler.* Berlin: H. Paetel, 1914. 2 vols.

RUXTON, ROBERT. *Twenty Pamphlets on Advertising*. Cambridge, Massachusetts: Harvard University, 1921–23. Total of 316 pp.

SAGARET, J. "L'Opinion," *Revue philosophique*, 86: 19–38 (1918).

The theory of how opinions may be diffused.

SCHOPENHAUER, ARTUR. *Parerga und Paralipomena: Kleine philosophische Schriften*. Berlin: A. W. Hahn, 1862. 2 vols.

Technique of argument. See "Zur Logik und Dialektik," in the second volume.

SCHULTZE-PFAELZER, GERHARD. *Propaganda, Agitation, Reklame: Eine Theorie des gesamten Werbewesens*. Berlin: Stilke, 1923. 231 pp.

General theory of propaganda, agitation, advertising.

SCOTT, WALTER DILL. *Influencing Men in Business*. New York: Ronald Press, 1911, 1914, 1916, 1928. 172 pp.

—————. *The Psychology of Advertising*. Boston: Small, Maynard, 1908, 1913, 1917, 1921, 1931. 1931 edition, 300 pp.

A standard textbook on the subject. Contains a bibliography.

—————. "Psychology of Advertising," *Atlantic Monthly*, 93: 29–36 (January, 1904).

SHELDON, GEORGE H. *Advertising Elements and Principles*. New York: Harcourt, Brace, 1925. 243 pp.

SNOW, ADOLPH JUDAH. *Psychology in Business Relations*. Chicago and New York: A. W. Shaw, 1925. 562 pp.

SOREL, GEORGES. *Réflexions sur la violence*. Paris: Rivière, 1912. 440 pp.

Stresses the rôle of myth in mass action. American edition: *Reflections on Violence*. New York: Huebsch, 1912. 299 pp.

STARCH, DANIEL. *Principles of Advertising*. Chicago and New York: A. W. Shaw, 1923. 998 pp.

Emphasis is on advertising research.

STERN-RUBARTH, EDGAR. *Die Propaganda als politisches Instrument.* Berlin:Trowitzsch, 1921. 116 pp.
Bibliography, p. 6.

STRONG, EDWARD KELLOGG. *The Psychology of Selling and Advertising.* New York:McGraw-Hill, 1925. 468 pp.

SWISHER, CARL BRENT. *Motivation and Political Technique in the California Constitutional Convention, 1878–79.* Claremont, California: Pomona College, 1930. 132 pp.
How to handle conventions. Bibliography, pp. 117–25.

THORNDIKE, EDWARD L. "Psychology and Advertising," *Scientific American,* 105:250–51 (September 16, 1911).

TIPPER, HARRY, and others. *Advertising:Its Principles and Practice.* Second edition. New York:Ronald Press, 1925. 473 pp.

TSCHACHOTIN, SERGEI. *Trepil Mod Hagekors.* Copenhagen:Frem-Vorlag, 1933. 111 pp.
Theory of the "Triple Arrow" propaganda of the German Social-Democrats.

TSCHACHOTIN, SERGEI, and MIERENDORFF, C. *Grundlagen und Formen politischer Propaganda.* Magdeburg: Bundesvorstand des Reichsbanners Schwarz-Rot-Gold, 1932. 48 pp.
Tschachotin, a Russian physiologist, applies theory of "conditioning" to propaganda. Developed "Triple Arrow" propaganda in opposition to National Socialists in Germany.

WALSER, FRANK. *The Art of Conference.* New York and London: Harpers, 1933. 305 pp.
Bibliography, pp. 288–95.

WEEKS, ARLAND DEYETT. *Control of the Social Mind:Psychology of Economic and Political Relations.* New York and London:Appleton, 1923. 263 pp.

WHITE, PERCIVAL. *Advertising Research.* New York and London: Appleton, 1927. 597 pp.

WILDER, ROBERT HOLMAN, and BUELL, KATHARINE LOVING. *Publicity: A Manual for Use of Business, Civic, or Social Service Organizations.* New York:Ronald Press, 1923. 271 pp.
Places emphasis on the part of the publicity counselor.

WITIES, BERNHARD. "Das Wirkungsprinzip der Reklame:Eine psychologische Studie," *Zeitschrift für Philosophie und philosophische Kritik,* 128:138–54 (1906).

WOOLBERT, CHARLES HENRY. *The Fundamentals of Speech.* New York and London: Harpers, 1927. 536 pp.
A textbook of delivery, with a section on speech composition and interpretative reading.

WREFORD, REYNELL J. R. G. "Propaganda, Evil and Good," *Nineteenth Century,* 93:514–24 (1923).
Defines propaganda as " the dissemination of interested information and opinion."

WRIGHT, QUINCY, editor. *Public Opinion and World Politics.* Chicago: University of Chicago, 1933, 237 pp.
Lectures by John W. Dafoe, Jules Auguste Sauerwein, Edgar Stern-Rubarth, Ralph Haswell Lutz, and Harold Dwight Lasswell, sponsored by the Norman Wait Harris Foundation at the University of Chicago.

YOUNG, KIMBALL, editor. *Source Book for Social Psychology.* New York: Knopf, 1927. 844 pp.
Chapter 27 deals with " Propaganda: The Manufacture of Opinion."

———. *Social Psychology: An Analysis of Social Behavior.* New York: Crofts, 1930. 674 pp.
See especially chapter 27, on " Propaganda," and chapter 16, on " Language, Thought, and Social Reality."

B. THEORIES OF CLOSELY RELATED METHODS OF COLLECTIVE MANAGEMENT

Propaganda is only one of the principal methods of controlling collective responses. Successful social and political management often depends upon a proper coordination of propaganda with coercion, violent or non-violent; economic inducement (including bribery); diplomatic negotiation; and other techniques. The entries in this section, devoted to methods marginal to the propaganda field, are very severely limited to suggestive and representative titles.

AGABEKOW, GREGOR A. *Die Tscheka bei der Arbeit,* translated into German by Dr. A. Chanoch. Stuttgart and Berlin: Union Deutsche Verlags-Gesellschaft, 1932. 207 pp.
Memoirs of a leading administrator of the Cheka. Illustrates the influence of the Cheka upon foreign policy.

ARISTOTLE. *Politics.*

"Assassination," *Encyclopedia of the Social Sciences.* (By Max Lerner.)
" The hidden fears of society are aroused and a revulsion of feeling is

awakened by the enormity of the act. Thinking himself a martyr, the assassin succeeds only in creating a martyr for the cause he hates."

"Blacklist," *Encyclopedia of the Social Sciences*. (By Walter Nelles.)

"Blacklist, Labor," *Encyclopedia of the Social Sciences*. (By John A. Fitch.)

The Book of War: The Military Classic of the Far East, translated from the Chinese by Captain Everard Ferguson Calthrop. London: John Murray, 1908. 132 pp.
By Sun Tzu, fifth century B.C.

"Bribery," *Encyclopedia of the Social Sciences*. (By Harold D. Lasswell.)

BROUSSEAU, ALBERT. *Essai sur la peur aux armées, 1914–1918*. Paris: Alcan, 1920.
The management of fear situations in the army.

BYWATER, HECTOR CHARLES, and FERRABY, H. C. *Intelligence Service (Mémoires, études, et documents pour servir à l'histoire de la guerre mondiale)*. Paris: Payot, 1932. 272 pp.

―――. *Strange Intelligence*. New York: Long and Smith, 1931. 308 pp.
An account of the working of the British naval intelligence before and during the War, by former members of the staff.

CASE, CLARENCE MARSH. *Non-Violent Coercion: A Study in Methods of Social Pressure*. New York and London: Century, 1923. 423 pp.

CASPARY, ADOLF. *Wirtschaftsstrategie und Kriegsführung*. Berlin: Mittler, 1932. 166 pp.

CHAMPERNOWNE, HENRY. *The Boss: An Essay upon the Art of Governing American Cities*. New York: G. H. Richmond, 1894. 243 pp.
Well-known exposition of the technique of being a "boss."

CLARK, EVANS, editor. *Boycotts and Peace*. New York: Harpers, 1932. 381 pp.
Some economic and political implications of the boycott.

"Conspiracy, Political," *Encyclopedia of the Social Sciences*. (By Joseph J. Senturia.)

CROOK, WILFRID HARRIS. *The General Strike: A Study of Labor's Tragic Weapon in Theory and Practice*. Chapel Hill: University of North Carolina, 1931. 649 pp.
Bibliography, pp. 625–36.

"Detective Agencies, Private," *Encyclopedia of the Social Sciences*. (By Robert W. Dunn.)
"Some agencies drop the word detective from their titles, calling them-

selves industrial service bureaus, corporation auxiliaries, audit, inspection, and efficiency companies, and personnel relations counselors."

"Diplomacy," *Encyclopedia of the Social Sciences.* (By C. Delisle Burns.)

"Direct Action," *Encyclopedia of the Social Sciences.* (By Lewis L. Lorwin.)

"Dual Unionism," *Encyclopedia of the Social Sciences.* (By David J. Saposs.)

ENGELS, FRIEDRICH, and LENIN, NICOLAI. *Militärpolitische Schriften* (*Elementarbücher des Kommunismus,* Bände 16 und 24). Berlin: Internationaler Arbeiterverlag. Band 2: Lenin, *Die Revolution von 1905 und der imperialistische Krieg.* 1930. 176 pp. Band 3: Lenin, *Die Oktoberrevolution und die Rote Armee.* 1932. 179 pp.
Organization and tactics of armed workers' uprisings under wartime conditions.

"Espionage," *Encyclopedia of the Social Sciences.* (By Richard Wilmer Rowan.)

"Excommunication," *Encyclopedia of the Social Sciences.* (By H. D. Hazeltine.)

"Ex-Intelligence Officer" (pseudonym). *The German Spy System from Within.* London, 1914.

"Fraternizing," *Encyclopedia of the Social Sciences.* (By Harold D. Lasswell.)

FREYTAG-LORINGHOVEN, FREIHERR VON. *Die Psyche der Heere.* Berlin: Mittler, 1923. 175 pp.
Military psychology.

"Guerrilla Warfare," *Encyclopedia of the Social Sciences.* (By Carleton Beals.)

HILLER, ERNEST THEODORE. *The Strike: A Study in Collective Action.* Chicago: University of Chicago, 1928. 304 pp.

HOORN, DIRK VAN. *Bijdrage tot de psychologie van den feldheer.* Groningen: M. de Vaal, 1910. 163 pp.
The command of a field army.

"Hunger Strikes," *Encyclopedia of the Social Sciences.* (By S. K. Ratcliffe.)

HUNT, EDWARD EYRE. *Conferences, Committees, Conventions, and How to Run Them.* New York and London: Harpers, 1925. 218 pp.
Bibliography, pp. 197–205.

INTER-PARLIAMENTARY UNION. *What Would Be the Character of a New War?* London: P. S. King, 1931. 411 pp.
A report drawn up by experts for the Inter-Parliamentary Union. Treats of the new weapons, and the psychological, demographic, financial, and general economic effects of war.

LAIDLER, HARRY WELLINGTON. *Boycotts and the Labor Struggle.* New York and London: John Lane, 1914. 488 pp.
Bibliography, pp. 473–80.

LANDAU, CAPTAIN HENRY. *All's Fair: The Story of the British Secret Service behind the German Lines.* New York: Putnam, 1934. 328 pp.

LEBAUD, PIERRE CHARLES ÉMILE. *Maniement moral de la troupe.* Paris: Lavanzelle, 1924. 108 pp.
The art of the commanding officer.

LENZ, J. *Proletarische Politik im Zeitalter des Imperialismus und der sozialistischen Revolution.* I Teil: *Grundbegriffe der Marxistisch-Leninistischen Strategie und Taktik.* Berlin: Internationaler Verlag, 1931. 186 pp.
Textbook on Marxist-Leninist strategy and tactics.

LETTOW-VORBECK, PAUL VON, and others, editors. *Die Weltkriegsspionage (Original Spionage-Werk). Authentische Enthüllungen über Entstehung, Art, Arbeit, Technik, Schliche, Handlungen, Wirkungen, und Geheimnisse der Spionage vor, während, und nach dem Kriege auf Grund amtlichen Materials aus Kriegs-, Militär-, Gerichts- und Reichs-Archiven. Vom Leben und Sterben, von den Taten und Abenteuren der bedeutendsten Agenten bei Freund und Feind.* Basel: Moro-Verlag, 1932. 688 pp.
Espionage during the World War in all countries.

LIMAN, PAUL. *Der politische Mord im Wandel der Geschichte: Eine historisch-psychologische Studie.* Berlin: A. Hofmann, 1912. 263 pp.
The efficacy of assassination.

LUMLEY, FREDERICK ELMORE. *Means of Social Control.* New York and London: Century, 1925. 415 pp.
Chapter 8 is entitled "Propaganda."

MACHIAVELLI, NICCOLÒ. *The Prince.*

MALAPARTE, CURZIO. *Coup d'état: The Technique of Revolution.* New York: Dutton, 1932. 251 pp.
By an Italian Fascist with experience in the seizure of power.

MAURICE, MAJOR GENERAL SIR FREDERICK BARTON. *Principles of Strategy: A Study of the Application of the Principles of War,* with an introduction by Field Marshal Sir G. Milne. New York: R. R. Smith, 1930. 243 pp.

An outstanding treatise.

Mühsam, Erich (?). "Propaganda der Tat," *Fanal* (Organ of the Anarchistische Vereinigung), 4: 1–11 (October, 1929).

Anarchist discussion of propaganda of the deed.

Netschajeff, Sergei. *The Diary of a Revolutionist.*

When, how, and whom to assassinate. German title: *Katechismus der Revolution.*

Neuberg, A. (pseudonym). *Der bewaffnete Aufstand: Versuch einer theoretischen Darstellung.* Zurich: Otto Meyer, 1928.

Secret literature of the Communist International published under a false imprint. An extended analysis of armed uprisings at Hamburg, Canton, and elsewhere. Contains bibliography.

Nicolai, Walter. *Geheime Mächte: Internationale Spionage und ihre Bekämpfung im Weltkrieg und Heute.* Leipzig: K. F. Koehler, 1925. 184 pp.

―――. *The German Secret Service.* London: Kegan Paul, Trench, and Trubner, 1924. 299 pp.

A systematic account by the chief of the intelligence service of the German general staff.

"Passive Resistance and Non-Cooperation," *Encyclopedia of the Social Sciences.* (By H. N. Brailsford.)

"Policing, Industrial," *Encyclopedia of the Social Sciences.* (By Horace B. Davis.)

"Political Police," *Encyclopedia of the Social Sciences.* (By Roger N. Baldwin.)

Posse, Ernst H. *Die politischen Kampfbünde Deutschlands.* Second edition. Berlin: Junker und Dünnhaupt, 1931. 103 pp.

A very compact survey of the militant political organizations of Germany.

Pouget, Émile. *Sabotage,* translated from the French by Arturo M. Giovannitti. Chicago: C. H. Kerr, 1913. 108 pp.

"Praetorianism," *Encyclopedia of the Social Sciences.* (By Frederick Mundell Watkins.)

Remer, Charles Frederick, and Palmer, William B. *A Study of Chinese Boycotts with Special Reference to Their Economic Effectiveness.* Baltimore: Walter Hines Page School of International Relations, 1933. 306 pp.

Ronge, Maximilian. *Kriegs- und Industrie-Espionage.* Vienna: Amalthea, 1930. 424 pp.
By the Austrian chief of military intelligence.

Ross, Edward Allsworth. *Social Control: A Survey of the Foundations of Order.* New York and London: Macmillan, 1901. 463 pp.
Bibliography, pp. 443–48.

Rowan, Richard Wilmer. *Spy and Counterspy: The Development of Modern Espionage.* New York: Viking, 1928. 322 pp.

Russell, Charles Edmund. *Espionage and Counter-Espionage, MI-4: A Series of Lectures Prepared for the Regular Army, National Guard, and Reserve Officers of the U.S.A. and Delivered before the Officers of the New York Corps Area by Major C. E. Russell; with an Appendix Containing a Chapter on Spies, Propaganda, Codes and Ciphers, and Espionage and Counter-Espionage in Government Departments.* Garden City: Published for the Cecero Book Club by Country Life Press, 1926. 263 pp.

"Sabotage," *Encyclopedia of the Social Sciences.* (By Paul F. Brissenden.)

Saposs, David Joseph. *Left Wing Unionism: A Study of Radical Policies and Tactics.* New York: International Publishers, 1926. 192 pp.

Schmitthenner, Paul. *Europäische Geschichte und Söldnertum* (Schriften der kriegsgeschichtlichen Abteilung im historischen Seminar der Friedrich-Wilhelms Universität, Berlin, vol. 5). Berlin: Junker und Dünnhaupt, 1933. 32 pp.
Mercenary soldiery in European history.

Schraudenbach, L. *Psyche und Organisation des "Volkskrieges."* Berlin, 1926.
The psyche and organization of irregulars.

"Secret Societies," *Encyclopedia of the Social Sciences.* (By Nathan Miller.)

Shalloo, Jeremiah P. *Private Police, with Special Reference to Pennsylvania* (Monograph Series of the American Academy of Political and Social Science, no. 1). Philadelphia: American Academy of Political and Social Science, 1934. 224 pp.
Discusses railroad police, coal and iron police, private detectives, and private watchmen. Contains bibliographies.

Spiridovitch, Aleksandr Ivanovitch. *Histoire du terrorisme russe, 1886–1917.* Paris: Payot, 1930. 672 pp.
Complete account of the terroristic activities of the Social Revolutionary group.

SWEENEY, WALTER CAMPBELL. *Military Intelligence: A New Weapon in War.* New York: Stokes, 1924. 259 pp.

TAYLOR, SIR HENRY. *The Statesman: An Ironical Essay on the Art of Succeeding.* London: Rees, Orme, Brown, Green, and Longman, 1836. 267 pp. Reprinted, Cambridge, England: W. Heffer, 1927. 191 pp.

TROTSKY, LEON. *Dictatorship vs. Democracy.* London: Labour Publishing Company, 1921. New York: Workers' Party, 1922. 191 pp.
A translation of *Terrorizm i Kommunizm* (Petrograd, 1921).

VIOLLE, JAMES NICHOLAS GABRIEL. *L'Espionnage militaire en temps de guerre* (thesis, University of Paris). Paris: Larose, 1903. 267 pp. Bibliography, pp. 261–64.

WARDLE, CAPTAIN M. K. "Notes on Fear in War," *Army Quarterly,* 2: 263–73 (1922).
How soldiers are controlled in situations involving threats to morale.

WHITE, LEONARD DUPEE. *Whitley Councils in the British Civil Service: A Study in Conciliation and Arbitration.* Chicago: University of Chicago, 1933. 357 pp.
By a United States Civil Service commissioner.

YARDLEY, HERBERT OSBORN. *The American Black Chamber.* Indianapolis: Bobbs-Merrill, 1931. 375 pp.
How the American government deciphered the secret codes of enemies and friends during the Great War.

C. THEORIES OF THE GENERAL PATTERNS OF COLLECTIVE RESPONSE

No theory of propaganda is adequate unless it has been formulated with reference to the main body of psychological, social-psychological, and general social scientific theory. The titles in this section sample the principal trends of theory and method in these several fields. Definitions of concepts like *crowd, public, opinion, suggestion, stimuli, response, collective representations, imitation,* and *myth* are included here, together with attempts to state general "laws of collective behavior."

I. BIBLIOGRAPHY

ESSERTIER, DANIEL. *Psychologie et sociologie: Essai de bibliographie critique* (Publications du centre de documentation sociale, l'École normale supérieure). Paris: Alcan, 1927. 234 pp.

Geck, Ludwig Heinrich Adolf. "Social Psychology in Germany: A Bibliographical Introduction," translated from the German by B. V. Norovkin, *Sociology and Social Research*, 13:504–16 (July, 1929); 14:108–29 (November, 1929).

―――. *Sozialpsychologie im Auslande: Eine Einführung in die ausländische Literatur, vorzüglich im Hinblick auf die sozialpsychologische Systematik.* Berlin: Dümmler, 1928. 119 pp.

Library of Congress. *List of Recent References on Labor Unrest with Special Reference to Psychology* (Select List of References no. 449). Washington, D. C., 1921. 4 folios, multigraphed.

―――. *List of References on Political and Social Psychology* (Select List of References no. 726). Washington, D. C., 1922. 7 folios, mimeographed.

Parker, Carleton Hubbell. *The Psychological Approach to Labor Problems.* New York: Public Affairs Information Service, 1920. 8 folios, typewritten.
Reading list by Carleton H. Parker, edited by Cornelia S. Parker.

Social and Industrial Psychology: A Selected Bibliography (Russell Sage Foundation Library Bulletin no. 61). October, 1923. 4 pp.

Stoltenberg, Hans L. "Neue Arbeiten zur Sozialpsychologie," *Zeitschrift für die gesamte Staatswissenschaft*, 87:136–48 (1929).

Young, Kimball. "The Field of Social Psychology," *Psychological Bulletin*, 24:661–91 (1927).

2. REFERENCES

Adler, Georg. *Die Bedeutung der Illusionen für Politik und soziales Leben.* Jena: Fischer, 1904. 55 pp.
Significance of illusions in political and social life.

"Agitation," *Encyclopedia of the Social Sciences.* (By Harold D. Lasswell.)
The term designates a phase of a social movement.

Allier, Raoul Scipion Philippe. *La Psychologie de la conversion chez les peuples non civilisés.* Paris: Payot, 1925. 2 vols.
Ethnological contribution to the psychology of conversion.

Allport, Floyd H. *Institutional Behavior: Essays toward a Reinterpretation of Contemporary Social Organization.* Chapel Hill: University of North Carolina, 1933. 539 pp.
Behavioristic social psychology. Denies "reality" to the concept *group*.

ANGELL, NORMAN. *The Public Mind: Its Disorders and Its Exploitation*. London: Douglas, 1926. 220 pp.

BECHTEREV, VLADIMIR MIKHAILOVITCH. *Die Bedeutung der Suggestion im sozialen Leben*. Wiesbaden: J. F. Bergmann, 1905. 142 pp.
French edition: *La Suggestion et son rôle dans la vie sociale, traduit et adapté du russe par le Dr. P. Keraval*. Paris: C. Boulangé, 1910. 276 pp.

―――. *General Principles of Human Reflexology: An Introduction to the Objective Study of Personality*. New York: International Publishers, 1932. 467 pp.
A Russian physiologist treats social control as "collective reflexology."

BEHRENDT, RICHARD. *Politischer Aktivismus*. Leipzig: C. L. Hirschfeld, 1932. 178 pp.
Theory of the conditions of the inauguration of political action.

―――. "Psychologie et sociologie du radicalisme politique," *Revue des sciences politiques*, 56:550–70 (October, 1933).

BENTHAM, JEREMY. *The Theory of Fictions*, with an introduction by C. K. Ogden (International Library of Psychology, Philosophy, and Scientific Method). London: Kegan Paul, Trench, and Trubner, 1932. 161 pp.

BERNARD, LUTHER LEE. *Introduction to Social Psychology*. New York: Holt, 1926. 651 pp.
Critical of "instinct" social psychologies. Bibliography, pp. 591–636.

BINKLEY, ROBERT C. "Concept of Public Opinion in the Social Sciences," *Social Forces*, 6:389–96 (March, 1928).

BIRNBAUM, KARL. *Soziologie der Neurosen: Die nervösen Störungen in ihren Beziehungen zum Gemeinschafts- und Kulturleben* (Sonderabdruck aus *Archiv für Psychiatrie*, Band 99). Berlin: Springer, 1933. 87 pp.
Neuroses treated as functions of civilization and culture.

BLONDEL, CHARLES A. *Introduction à la psychologie collective*. Paris: Colin, 1928. 210 pp.
By a psychopathologist. Partie 1: "La Psychologie selon Comte, Durkheim, Tarde"; Partie 2: "La Part du collectif dans la vie mentale."

BOGOSLOVSKY, BORIS B. *The Technique of Controversy: Principles of Dynamic Logic* (International Library of Psychology, Philosophy, and Scientific Method). New York: Harcourt, Brace. London: Kegan Paul, Trench, and Trubner, 1928. 266 pp.
Treatise on logic by an American pragmatist. Develops logical categories which might, of course, be employed in redefining propaganda theory or in presenting a cause to a public consisting largely of "intellectuals."

Böhmig, W. "Massenpsychologisches aus katholischer Kirche und Sozialdemokratie," *Archiv für Psychiatrie,* 70: 109–28 (1924).
Psychopathologist compares aspects of Catholic and Social-Democratic behavior.

Bryce, Viscount James. *Modern Democracies.* Revised edition. New York: Macmillan, 1927. 2 vols.
"Public opinion," vol. 1, chap. 15. "Propaganda," vol. 1, p. 155; vol. 2, pp. 459–60, 483–84.

Burrow, Trigant. *The Social Basis of Consciousness: A Study in Organic Psychology, Based upon a Synthetic and Societal Concept of the Neuroses* (International Library of Psychology, Philosophy, and Scientific Method). New York: Harcourt, Brace, 1927. 256 pp.
Undertakes to arrive at a means of assessing the effect of culture itself on psychology.

Cantril, Hadley. *General and Specific Attitudes* (Psychological Monographs, vol. 42, no. 5, whole no. 192). Princeton: Psychological Review Company, 1932. 109 pp.

Carr, Lowell J. "Public Opinion as a Dynamic Concept," *Sociology and Social Research,* 13: 18–29 (September, 1928).

Chadwick, Thomas. *The Influence of Rumour on Human Thought and Action.* Manchester, England: Sherratt and Hughes, 1932. 158 pp.

Chassériaud, R. *La Formation de l'opinion publique.* Paris: Rivière, 1914. 70 pp.
Considers especially public opinion and the press.

Christensen, Arthur. *Politics and Crowd Morality,* translated from the Danish by A. Cecil Curtis. London: Williams and Norgate, 1915. 270 pp.

Clark, Carroll D. "The Concept of the Public," *Southwestern Social Science Quarterly,* 13: 311–21 (March, 1933).

Colm, Gerhart. "Die Masse," *Archiv für Sozialwissenschaft und Sozialpolitik,* Band 54 (1924).

"Conversion, Religious," *Encyclopedia of the Social Sciences.* (By Joseph Jastrow.)
The psychology of conviction.

Conway, Martin. *The Crowd in Peace and War.* New York, 1915.

Cooley, Charles Horton. *Human Nature and the Social Order.* New York: Scribners, 1902. 413 pp.
See also the author's *Social Organization* (New York, 1909) and his *Social Process* (New York, 1918).

"Custom," *Encyclopedia of the Social Sciences.* (By Edward Sapir.)
Comments upon the circumstances under which customs are modified;
important for propaganda theory.

DAVENPORT, FREDERICK MORGAN. *Primitive Traits in Religious Revivals:
A Study in Mental and Social Evolution.* New York and London:
Macmillan, 1905. 323 pp.
Psychology of conviction. Expansion of a Ph. D. thesis at Columbia University.

DEHERME, GEORGES. *Les Forces à regler: Le nombre et l'opinion publique.* Third edition. Paris: Grasset, 1919. 258 pp.
The relation between public opinion and the size of political units.

DENISON, JOHN HOPKINS. *Emotion as the Basis of Civilization.* New
York: Scribners, 1928. 555 pp.
Stresses emotional factors in history; few technical psychological concepts. Bibliography, pp. 541–42.

DENNES, WILLIAM RAY. *The Method and Presuppositions of Group
Psychology* (University of California Publications in Philosophy,
vol. 6, no. 1). Berkeley: University of California, 1924. 182 pp.

DEWEY, A. GORDON. "On Methods in the Study of Politics," *Political
Scienee Quarterly,* 38:636–51 (1923); 39:218–33 (1924).
Analyzes contemporary interest groups.

DEWEY, JOHN. *Human Nature and Conduct.* Eleventh edition. New
York, 1930. 336 pp.
"The book sets forth a belief that an understanding of habit and of
different types of habit is the key to social psychology." — *Preface.*

DIMOND, SYDNEY GEORGE. *The Psychology of the Methodist Revival:
An Empirical and Descriptive Study.* London: Oxford University,
1926. 296 pp.
Bibliography, pp. 280–89.

DUPRAT, GUILLAUME L. *La Psychologie sociale: Sa nature et ses principales lois* (Bibliothèque de psychologie expérimentale, IV, 4). Paris:
G. Doin, 1920. 369 pp.
Proposes an extensive list of laws of social psychology. Bibliography, pp.
357–61.

DURKHEIM, ÉMILE. *Les Formes élémentaires de la vie réligieuse: Le
système totémique en Australie.* Paris: Alcan, 1912. 647 pp.
English edition translated from the French by J. W. Swain. London:
Allen and Unwin, 1915. New York: Macmillan, 1915. 456 pp. Applies
to the study of religion Durkheim's concept of "collective representations."

EDWARDS, LYFORD PATERSON. *The Natural History of Revolution*. Chicago: University of Chicago, 1927. 229 pp.
A sociological interpretation.

ELIOT, THOMAS D. "A Psychoanalytic Interpretation of Group Formation and Behavior." *American Journal of Sociology*, 26:333–52 (1920).

ELLIOTT, HARRISON SACKET. *The Process of Group Thinking*. New York: Association Press, 1928. 229 pp.
"Democratic participation" in the deliberations of groups, small and large. Bibliography, pp. 223–25.

"Ethnocentrism," *Encyclopedia of the Social Sciences*. (By George P. Murdock.)

FEUTER, EDUARD. "Individuen und Massen," *Jahrbuch für Soziologie*, 1926, Band 2, pp. 202 ff.

FILANGIERI, GAETANO. *The Science of Legislation*, translated from the Italian by Richard Clayton. London: Emery and Adams, 1806. 2 vols.
Emphasizes relations between legislation and public opinion.

FLUEGGE, G. "Zur Psychologie der Massen," *Preussische Jahrbücher*, 183:345–69 (1921).
Crowd psychology.

FOLSOM, JOSEPH KIRK. *Social Psychology*. New York: Harpers, 1931. 701 pp.
Has been well received as a working synthesis. Bibliography, pp. 664–77.

FREUD, SIGMUND. *Group Psychology and the Analysis of the Ego*, translated from the German by James Strachey. London: International Psychoanalytical Press, 1922. 134 pp.
The theory that groups form through "identification" in relation to a leader.

FROMM, ERICH. "Über Methode und Aufgabe einer analytischen Sozialpsychologie," *Zeitschrift für Sozialforschung*, 1:28–54 (1932).
A methodological statement of the relations of psychoanalysis to social psychology. Exemplified in the author's *Die Entwicklung des Christusdogmas* (Vienna, 1931).

————. "Die psychoanalytische Charakterologie und ihre Bedeutung für die Sozialpsychologie," *Zeitschrift für Sozialforschung*, 1:253–77 (1932).
Applies Freud's theory of personality types to social psychology.

GARTH, THOMAS R. *Race Psychology*. New York: McGraw-Hill, 1931. 260 pp.
One result of psychometric testing is the disclosure of cultural patterns.

GEIGER, THEODOR. *Die Masse und ihre Aktion: Ein Beitrag zur Soziologie der Revolutionen.* Stuttgart: Enke, 1926. 193 pp.
Geiger uses the term *crowd* to refer only to revolutions. Careful differentiation from other forms of collective action is undertaken. Has a bibliography of one page at the end.

GERSDORF, KARL VON. *Ueber den Begriff und das Wesen der öffentlichen Meinung.* 1846.
An early analysis of the concept and nature of public opinion.

GINSBERG, MORRIS. *Psychology of Society.* London: Methuen, 1921, 1928. New York: Dutton, 1922. 174 pp.

GLOVER, EDWARD. *War, Sadism, and Pacifism.* London: Allen and Unwin, 1933. 148 pp.
By the Director of Scientific Research, London Institute of Psychoanalysis.

GOLDHAMER, H. "Psychological Analysis of War," *Sociological Review,* 26: 249–67 (July, 1934).

GOTHEIN, EBERHARD. *Soziologie der Panik* (Schriften der Deutschen Gesellschaft für Soziologie, Band I). 1911.

HANDMAN, MAX. "The Bureaucratic Culture Pattern and Political Revolutions," *American Journal of Sociology,* 39: 301–14 (November, 1933).

HAR, KYUNG DURK. *Social Laws: A Study of the Validity of Sociological Generalizations.* Chapel Hill: University of North Carolina, 1930. 256 pp.
Collection and comparison of types of generalizations.

HARLAND, OSWALD HENRY. *Some Implications of Social Psychology.* London: Knopf, 1928. 104 pp.

HAYES, EDWARD C. "The Formation of Public Opinion," *Journal of Applied Sociology,* 10: 6–9 (1925).

HELLPACH, WILLY. *Elementares Lehrbuch der Sozialpsychologie.* Berlin: Springer, 1933. 165 pp.
General text on social psychology. The author, minister of education in Baden, has written many technical articles and books on the subject.

HENDRICH, FRANZ JOSIAS VON. *Über den Geist des Zeitalters und die Gewalt der öffentlichen Meinung.* 1797.
An early systematic analysis of public opinion.

HENTIG, HANS VON. *Über den Zusammenhang von kosmischen, biologischen, und sozialen Krisen.* Tübingen: Mohr, 1920. 105 pp.
A criminologist by profession speculates on relations between cosmic, biological, and social disturbances.

HOLTZENDORFF, FRANZ VON. *Wesen und Werth der öffentlichen Meinung*. Munich: M. Rieger'sche Universitäts-Buchhandlung, 1879. 159 pp.

Systematic statement of the nature and significance of public opinion.

"Honor," *Encyclopedia of the Social Sciences*. (By T. V. Smith.)

"Honor cannot be arbitrated, but it can be vindicated; apologies, wars, indemnities are the instruments for its protection."

HYNDMAN, HENRY MAYERS. *The Evolution of Revolution*. London: Richards, 1920. 406 pp.

JASPERS, KARL. *Psychologie der Weltanschauungen*. Third edition. Berlin: Springer, 1925. 486 pp.

By a philosopher and psychiatrist. Bibliographic footnotes.

JASTROW, JOSEPH. *The Psychology of Conviction: A Study of Beliefs and Attitudes*. Boston and New York: Houghton Mifflin, 1918. 387 pp.

JERUSALEM, FRANZ WILHELM. *Soziologie des Rechts*. Vol. 1: *Gesetzmässigkeit und Kollektivität*. Jena: Fischer, 1925.

Sociology of law.

JORDAN, ELIJAH. *Theory of Legislation: An Essay on the Dynamics of the Public Mind*. Indianapolis: Progress Publishing Company, 1930. 486 pp.

The act of legislation is the discovery of the symbol that elicits sufficient vested and sentimental interest to inaugurate stable institutional changes.

KANTOR, JACOB ROBERT. *An Outline of Social Psychology*. Chicago: Follett Publishing Company, 1929. 420 pp.

A synthesis obtained by the situational approach. Contains biblographies.

KARPF, FAY BERGER. *American Social Psychology: Its Origins, Development, and European Background*. New York: McGraw-Hill, 1932. 461 pp.

Bibliography, pp. 431–48.

KING, CLYDE L. "Public Opinion as Viewed by Eminent Political Theorists," *University of Pennsylvania Public Lectures*, 3:417–53 (1916).

KISTIAKOWSKI, THEODOR. *Gesellschaft und Einzelwesen: Eine methodologische Studie*. Berlin: O. Liebmann, 1899. 205 pp.

KOHT, HALVDAN. "The Importance of the Class Struggle in Modern History," *Journal of Modern History*, 1:353–61 (September, 1929).

KRAPPE, ALEXANDER HAGGERTY. *The Science of Folk-Lore*. New York: Dial Press, 1930. 344 pp.

Contains bibliographies.

Kraškovič, Ludwig, Jr. *Die Psychologie der Kollektivitäten,* translated from the Croatian original, which appeared in *Mjesecnik,* organ of the Juristiche Gesellschaft in Zagreb. Vukovar, 1915. 142 pp.
Extensive compilation of historical material exhibiting the emotionality of collective responses. Bibliography, pp. iii–iv.

Kraus, Herbert. "Prolegomena zum Begriff der öffentlichen Meinung," *Festschrift* (für Franz von Liszt, Berlin, 1911), pp. 148–67.
Compendium and critical analysis of terms related to *public opinion.*

Kroeber, Alfred Louis. "The Possibility of a Social Psychology," *American Journal of Sociology,* 23:623–50 (1918).
By a well-known anthropologist.

Krueger, Ernest Theodore, and Reckless, Walter C. *Social Psychology.* New York and London: Longmans, Green, 1931. 578 pp.
Emphasizes importance of life history document, following W. I. Thomas. Has bibliographies.

"Language," *Encyclopedia of the Social Sciences.* (By Edward Sapir.)

Lasswell, Harold Dwight. *World Politics and Personal Insecurity: A Contribution to Political Psychiatry.* New York: McGraw-Hill, 1935. 307 pp.
States and applies the configurative method of analysis, developing implications of the author's *Psychopathology and Politics* (Chicago, 1930). Bibliographic footnotes.

"Leadership," *Encyclopedia of the Social Sciences.* (By Richard Schmidt.)

Leopold, Lewis. *Prestige: A Psychological Study of Social Estimates.* London: Unwin, 1913. 352 pp.

Lippmann, Walter. *The Phantom Public.* New York: Harcourt, Brace, 1925. 205 pp.
"What the public does is not to express its opinions but to align itself for or against a proposal."

————. *Public Opinion.* New York: Harcourt, Brace, 1922. 427 pp.
First presented the now-popular concept *stereotype.*

Lorden, D. M. "Mob Behavior and Social Attitudes," *Sociology and Social Research,* 14:324–31 (1930).

Lowell, Abbott Lawrence. *Public Opinion and Popular Government.* New edition. New York: Longmans, Green, 1926. 415 pp.

————. *Public Opinion in War and Peace.* Cambridge, Massachusetts: Harvard University, 1923. 302 pp.

Lund, Frederick Hansen. *Psychology: An Empirical Study of Behavior.* New York: Ronald Press, 1933. 475 pp.

McDougall, William. *Introduction to Social Psychology*. Fourteenth edition. Boston: J. W. Luce, 1921. 418 pp.

A social psychology constructed on the basis of a list of instincts.

————. *The Group Mind: A Sketch of the Principles of Collective Psychology, with Some Attempt to Apply Them to the Interpretation of National Life and Character*. Second edition. Cambridge, England: Cambridge University, 1927. 304 pp.

A sequel to the author's *Introduction to Social Psychology*.

Maller, Julius Bernard. *Cooperation and Competition: An Experimental Study in Motivation* (Ph. D. thesis. Teachers College Contributions to Education, no. 384). New York: Columbia University, 1929. 176 pp.

An attempt to measure and compare the behavior of children under conditions of competition and cooperation. Bibliography, pp. 165–72.

Manheim, Ernst. *Die Träger der öffentlichen Meinung: Studien zur Soziologie der öffentlichen Meinung*. Brünn: R. M. Rohrer, 1933. 145 pp.

The carriers of public opinion.

Mannheim, Karl. *Ideologie und Utopie*. Bonn: Friedrich Cohen, 1929. 250 pp.

Systematic development of a sociology based upon Marx, Engels, Sorel, Pareto, and Max Weber. English translation is in preparation.

Markey, John F. *The Symbolic Process and Its Integration in Children* (International Library of Psychology, Philosophy, and Scientific Method). New York: Harcourt, Brace, 1928. 192 pp.

Bibliography, pp. 176–86.

Marr, Heinz. *Das Problem der Masse*. Stuttgart, 1920.

Martin, Everett Dean. *The Behavior of Crowds: A Psychological Study*. New York and London: Harpers, 1920. 311 pp.

Maurois, André. *The Next Chapter: The War against the Moon*. New York: Dutton, 1928. 46 pp.

An effective take-off on the belligerent instincts of man.

Mayreder, R. *Der typische Verlauf sozialer Bewegungen*. Second edition. Vienna, 1926.

Analyzes successive phases of social movements, from agitation to organization, from ideology to phraseology.

Michels, Roberto. *Corso d'Sociologia Politica*. Milan: De Marsico, 1926.

A course given by Michels in the University of Rome, dealing with the conception of the élite.

————. "Sociological Character of Political Parties," *American Political Science Review*, 21:753–73 (November, 1927).

MILLER, HERBERT ADOLPHUS. *Races, Nations, and Classes*. Philadelphia: Lippincott, 1924. 196 pp.
The analysis of collective responses to deprivation.

MINGUZZI, LIVIO. *La teoria della opinione publica nello stato constituzionale: Saggio*. Turin and Rome: Roux, 1893.
Theory of public opinion in the constitutional state.

"Mob," *Encyclopedia of the Social Sciences*. (By L. L. Bernard.)

MOEDE, WALTHER. *Experimentelle Massenpsychologie: Beiträge zur Experimentalpsychologie der Gruppe*. Leipzig: S. Hirzel, 1920. 239 pp.
Experimental social psychology.

"Morale," *Encyclopedia of the Social Sciences*. (By Harold D. Lasswell.)

MOSCA, GAETANO. *Elementi di scienza politica*. Second edition. Turin: Fratelli Bocca, 1923. 514 pp.

MOSER, HEINRICH. "Der Volkswille: Ein Beitrag zur Psychologie der öffentlichen Meinung" (unpublished dissertation, Heidelberg, 1922).

MOYSSET, HENRI. *L'Opinion publique*. Lyons, 1910.
The author was a distinguished propagandist of the French government during the World War.

MUKERJEE, RADHAKAMAL, and SEN-GUPTA, NARENDRA NATH. *Introduction to Social Psychology*. Boston and New York: Heath, 1928. 304 pp.

MÜLLER-FREIENFELS, RICHARD. *Allgemeine Sozial- und Kultur-psychologie*. Leipzig: J. A. Barth, 1930. 292 pp.
By a philosopher and psychoanalyst. Contains bibliographical notes at the end of each chapter.

MURCHISON, CARL ALLANMORE. *Social Psychology: The Psychology of Political Domination*. Worcester: Clark University, 1929. London: Oxford University, 1929. 210 pp.
Social differences are outcomes of individual differences.

MURPHY, GARDNER, and MURPHY, LOIS BARCLAY. *Experimental Social Psychology*. New York and London: Harpers, 1931. 709 pp.
Critical commentary on the voluminous literature in all modern languages.

NOTCH, FRANK K. *King Mob: A Study of the Present-Day Mind.* New York: Harcourt, Brace, 1930. 226 pp.

Graphic description of current phenomena of collective behavior, stimulated by the new mechanical means of communication.

"Öffentliche Meinung," *Politische Handwörterbuch.* (By Wilhelm Bauer.)

OGBURN, WILLIAM FIELDING. *Social Change with Respect to Culture and Original Nature.* Fifth printing. New York: Viking, 1928. 365 pp.

Concept of "social lag" between material and other social changes. Frequently cited.

OGDEN, CHARLES KAY. *Opposition: A Linguistic and Psychological Analysis* (Psyche Miniatures, General Series, no. 41). London: Kegan Paul, Trench, and Trubner, 1932. 103 pp.

OGDEN, CHARLES KAY, and RICHARDS, I. A. *The Meaning of Meaning: A Study of the Influence of Language upon Thought and of the Science of Symbolism* (International Library of Psychology, Philosophy, and Scientific Method). New York: Harcourt, Brace. London: Kegan Paul, Trench, and Trubner, 1925. 544 pp.

An influential analysis of the variable meaning of words.

"Opinion publique," *Dictionnaire général de la politique.* (By Maurice Bloch.)

PAGET, E. H. "Sudden Changes in Group Opinion," *Social Forces,* 7:438–74 (March, 1929).

PALMER, PAUL A. "The Concept of Public Opinion in the History of Political Thought."

In preparation at Harvard University.

PARETO, VILFREDO. *Trattato di sociologia generale.* Florence: G. Barbéra, 1916, 1923. 2 vols.

Pareto's concept of *dérivation* is of special interest to propagandists. French edition: *Traité de sociologie générale.* Paris: Payot, 1917–19. 2 vols. English translation has been announced by Harcourt, Brace.

PARK, ROBERT E. "Human Nature, Attitudes, and Mores," in Kimball Young, editor, *Social Attitudes,* pp. 17–45. New York: Holt, 1931.

―――. *Masse und Publikum: Eine methodologische und soziologische Untersuchung* (inaugural dissertation, Heidelberg). Bern: Lack und Grunau, 1904. 112 pp.

A critique of Le Bon, and an elaboration of the distinction between *crowd* and *public.*

PAVLOV, IVAN P. *Lectures on Conditioned Reflexes: Twenty-five Years*

of Objective Study of the Higher Nervous Activity (Behavior) of Animals. New York: International Publishers, 1928. 414 pp.
A Russian physiologist presents control of behavior as a problem of conditioning elementary reflexes.

PIERCE, FREDERICK. *Our Unconscious Mind and How to Use It.* New York: Dutton, 1922. 323 pp.
From a psychoanalytic point of view. Chapter 8 deals with " The New Psychology in Selling." Bibliography, pp. 321–23.

PLATT, CHARLES. *Psychology of Social Life: A Materialistic Study with an Idealistic Conclusion.* New York: Dodd, Mead, 1922. 284 pp.
" Written, on the whole, in the spirit of an old fashioned liberal." — EVERETT DEAN MARTIN, in the *New York Evening Post Literary Review,* July 29, 1922.

PRIVAT, EDMOND. *Le Choc des patriotismes: Les sentiments collectifs et la morale entre nations.* Paris: Alcan, 1931. 179 pp.

" Proletariat," *Encyclopedia of the Social Sciences.* (By Alfred Meusel.)

" Public Opinion," *Lalor's Encyclopedia of Political Science, etc.* (By Johann Kaspar Bluntschli.)

PUGLIESE, G. A. *La publica opinione.* Rivista di Giurisprudenza, 1898.

REICH, WILHELM. *Massenpsychologie des Faschismus: Zur Sexualökonomie der politischen Reaktion und zur proletarischen Sexualpolitik.* Copenhagen, Prague, and Zurich: Verlag für Sexualpolitik, 1933. 283 pp.
Psychoanalyst interprets Fascism and appraises Communist propaganda technique among workers and middle classes.

RIVERS, WILLIAM HALSE RIVERS. *Psychology and Politics and Other Essays* (International Library of Psychology, Philosophy, and Scientific Method). London: Kegan Paul, Trench, and Trubner, 1923. 180 pp.
Ethnologist modifies and applies psychoanalytic theories.

RODA RIVAS, ARCADIO. *Ensayo sobre la opinión pública.* Madrid, 1870.
Essay on public opinion.

ROMAGNOSI, GIOVANNI DOMENICO. *Dell'indole e dei fattori dell'incivilimento.* Third edition. Prato, 1835.
An early juristic interpretation of public opinion.

ROSENSTOCK, EUGEN. *Die europäischen Revolutionen.* Jena: Eugen Diederichs, 1931. 554 pp.
History viewed as a movement from one world revolution to the next. Defines *total* and *partial* revolutions. Analyzes five European revolutions.

Rossi, Pasquale. *Sociologia e psicologia collettiva.* Rome: C. Colombo, 1904. 237 pp.

History and methods of collective psychology.

Rumpf, Max. "Über Illusiongemeinschaften," *Schmöllers Jahrbuch,* Band 49, Heft 3 (1925).

Illusion as a basis of group formation.

Schank, Richard Louis. *A Study of a Community and Its Groups and Institutions Conceived of as Behaviors of Individuals* (Psychological Monographs Series). Princeton: Psychological Review Company, 1932. 133 pp.

Only the verbal behavior of this community is investigated.

Schneersohn, F. "Die Kritik der Lehre von psychischen Infektion (resp. psychischer Epidemie) und die objektive Aneignungstheorie," *Zeitschrift für Völkerpsychologie und Soziologie,* 2: 101–24.

A rigorous critique of theories of "psychological epidemics."

————. "Suggestion und Nachahmung als unfruchtbare Fiktion der individuellen und sozialen Psychologie," *Ethos,* 1: 414–39.

"*Suggestion* and *imitation* as fruitless fictions of individual and social psychology."

Schou, Hans Jakob. *Religiösitet og sygelige sindstilstande.* Second edition. Copenhagen, 1924.

English edition: *Religion and Morbid Mental States,* translated from the Danish by W. W. Worster. New York: Century, 1926. 217 pp.

Sedman, V. R. "Some Interpretations of Public Opinion," *Social Forces,* 10: 339–50 (March, 1932).

Sganzini, Carlo. *Die Fortschritt der Völkerpsychologie von Lazarus bis Wundt.* Bern, 1913.

History of social psychology from Lazarus to Wundt.

Shepard, Walter J. "Public Opinion," *American Journal of Sociology,* 15: 32–60 (1909).

Sieber, Siegfried. *Die Massenseele: Ein Beitrag zur Psychologie des Krieges, der Kunst, und der Kultur.* Dresden: "Globus," 1918. 128 pp.

Sighele, Scipio. *Psychologie des Auflaufs und der Massenverbrechern.* Dresden and Leipzig: C. Reissner, 1897. 216 pp.

An influential Italian contribution to the psychology of crowds and mobs.

Simmel, Georg. "Superiority and Subordination as Subject Matter of

Psychology," *American Journal of Sociology*, 2:167–89, 392–415 (1896–97).

A translation by Albion W. Small of chapter 3 of the author's *Soziologie*, entitled "Über- und Unterordnung."

SOLVAY, ERNEST. *Note sur des formules d'introduction à l'énergétique physio- et psycho-sociologie* (Instituts Solvay. Inst. de sociologie. Notes et mémoires, Fasc. 1). Brussels: Misch et Thron, 1906. 76 pp.

SOROKIN, PITIRIM ALEXSANDROVITCH. *Contemporary Sociological Theories*. New York and London: Harpers, 1928. 785 pp.

An exhaustive compendium of sociological thought. Note especially the vigorous criticism of subjectivistic theories in chapters 11, 12, and 13.

————. *The Sociology of Revolution*. Philadelphia and London: Lippincott, 1925. 428 pp.

By a sociologist who personally experienced a major revolution. See especially the chapters on "Transformation of Speech Reactions," "The Reactions of Authority and Subordination."

SOROKIN, PITIRIM ALEXSANDROVITCH, and BOLDYREFF, J. W. "An Experimental Study of the Influence of Suggestion on the Discrimination and Valuation of People," *American Journal of Sociology*, 37:720–38 (March, 1932).

Ninety-six per cent of 1,484 persons tested were found to agree with a "false dogmatic suggestion" concerning the merits of a musical selection; 58.9 per cent agreed with a "persuasive suggestion."

STEINER, JESSE FREDERICK. *The American Community in Action: Case Studies of American Communities*. New York: Holt, 1928. 392 pp. Bibliography, pp. 373–87.

STIELER, GEORG. *Person und Masse: Untersuchungen zur Grundlegung einer Massenpsychologie*. Leipzig: Felix Meiner, 1929. 239 pp.

Following Le Bon, this volume discusses the "fundamentally orgiastic, lyrical, and expressive" actions of public assemblies.

STOLTENBERG, HANS LORENZ. *Sozialpsychologie*. Berlin: K. Curtius, 1914–22. 2 vols.

Very formalistic.

STRATTON, GEORGE MALCOLM. *Social Psychology of International Conduct*. New York: Appleton, 1929. 387 pp.

Analysis, by a psychologist, of the origin and nature of racial prejudices and national mentalities.

SYMONDS, PERCIVAL MALLON. *Diagnosing Personality and Conduct*. New York: Century, 1931. 602 pp.

Bibliography, pp. 571–72, and at ends of chapters.

SZIRTES, ARTUR. *Zur Psychologie der öffentlichen Meinung.* Vienna and Leipzig: M. Perles, 1921. 100 pp.

TARDE, GABRIEL. *Études de psychologie sociale.* Paris: V. Giard et E. Brière, 1898. 326 pp.
The rôle of imitation.

————. *L'Opinion et la foule.* Paris: Alcan, 1901, 1922. 226 pp.
The influence of suggestion and imitation.

TAYLOR, JOHN LIONEL. *Social Life and the Crowd.* Boston: Small, Maynard, 1923.

TEMPLE, SIR WILLIAM. *Miscellanea.* Third edition. London: J. Tonson, 1691. 232 pp.
See the "Essay upon the Original and Nature of Government," dated 1672. An Englishman, reflecting upon affairs in France, discerned currents of public opinion.

THOMAS, DOROTHY SWAINE, LOOMIS, ALICE M., and ARRINGTON, RUTH E. *Social Behavior Patterns (Observational Studies of Human Behavior,* vol. 1). New Haven: Yale University Institute of Human Relations, 1933. 271 pp.
"The purpose of the authors is to formulate simple indices of social interaction and to define individual and group behavior in terms of these indices. This volume is a report on the development and present status of their program."

THOMPSON, GEORGE CARSLAKE. *Public Opinion and Lord Beaconsfield.* London: Macmillan, 1886. 2 vols.
The material is analyzed in terms of an elaborate conception of public opinion. Distinguishes *opinion* which is "predominant" from that which is "public"; defines *biasses, notions, policies, views.*

THOULESS, ROBERT H. *Social Psychology: A Textbook for Students of Economics.* London: W. B. Clive, 1925. 376 pp.
Bibliography, pp. 360–68.

THURNWALD, RICHARD. "Führerschaft und Siebung," *Zeitschrift für Völkerpsychologie und Soziologie,* 2: 1–18 (March, 1926).
Ethnologist discusses leadership and ordination.

TÖNNIES, FERDINAND. "Die grosse Menge und das Volk," *Soziologische Studien und Kritiken,* 2: 277–303. Jena: Fischer, 1925–26.

————. *Kritik der öffentlichen Meinung.* Berlin: Springer, 1922. 583 pp.
Standard history of theories of public opinion.

TROTSKY, LEON. *The Permanent Revolution,* translated by Max Schachtman. New York: Pioneer Publishers, 1931. 157 pp.

Trotter, William. *The Instincts of the Herd in Peace and War.* Fifth impression. London: Unwin, 1920. 264 pp.

Vergin, Fedor. *Subconscious Europe.* London: Cape, 1932. 381 pp.
German edition: *Das unbewusste Europa: Psychoanalyse der europäischen Politik.* Vienna and Leipzig: Hess, 1931. 342 pp. Psychoanalytic reviewers take exception to this author's use of psychoanalytic concepts.

Vico, Giovanni Battista. *Opere.* Naples: Stamperia de classici latini, 1858–65. 7 vols. in 4.
Early Italian sociologist. See volumes 4 and 5, *Principi di una scienza nuova.*

Vierkandt, A., editor. *Handwörterbuch der Soziologie.* Hrsg. in Verb. mit G. Briefs, F. Eulenburg, F. Oppenheimer, W. Sombart, F. Tönnies, A. Weber, L. v. Wiese. Stuttgart: Enke, 1931. 690 pp.

Visser, H. L. A. *De psyche der menigte: Bijdrage tot de studie der collectief psychologische verschijnselen.* Haarlem: H. D. Tjeenk Willink en Zoon, 1911. 232 pp.
Study of collective psychological phenomena. Bibliographic footnotes.

———. *De collectieve psyche in recht en staat.* Haarlem, 1916.

Vleugels, Wilhelm. "Der Begriff der Masse," *Jahrbuch für Soziologie,* 2: 176–201 (1926).

———. *Masse und Führer.* Cologne, 1921.

Wallas, Graham. *Human Nature in Politics.* Third edition. New York: Knopf, 1921. 313 pp.
Introduced modern psychological trend in political analysis. See also the author's *The Great Society* (New York, 1914).

Ward, Lester Frank. *The Psychic Factors of Civilization.* Second edition. Boston: Ginn, 1906. 369 pp.
Bibliography, pp. 333–52.

Weatherly, Ulysses Grant. *Social Progress: Studies in the Dynamics of Change.* Philadelphia and London: Lippincott, 1926. 388 pp.

Weber, Max. *Wirtschaft und Gesellschaft. Grundriss der Sozialökonomik,* III Abteilung. Second edition. Tübingen: Mohr, 1925. 840 pp.
Note the concept of *charisma.*

Wieser, Friedrich. *Das Gesetz der Macht.* Vienna: Springer, 1926. 562 pp.
Political theory of a competent Austrian economist.

———. "Machtpsychologie," *Zeitschrift für Volkswirtschaft und Sozialpsychologie,* N. S., 3: 1–30 (1923).
The psychology of power.

WILLIAMS, JAMES MICKEL. *Principles of Social Psychology as Developed in a Study of Economics and Social Conflict.* New York: Knopf, 1922, 1927. 459 pp.

Bibliography, pp. 431–52.

WILSON, FRANCIS G. "Concepts of Public Opinion," *American Political Science Review,* 27:371–92 (June, 1933).

WOLFE, ALBERT BENEDICT. *Conservatism, Radicalism, and Scientific Method.* New York: Macmillan, 1925. 354 pp.

Bibliography, pp. 335–38.

YOUNG, KIMBALL, editor. *Social Attitudes.* New York: Holt, 1931. 382 pp.

A volume dedicated to W. I. Thomas by fifteen former students and colleagues. Contains bibliographies.

ZNANIECKI, FLORIAN. *The Laws of Social Psychology.* Chicago: University of Chicago, 1925. 320 pp.

Emphasizes "the relative, historical character of all our values, even of reality itself."

PART II. PROPAGANDA CLASSIFIED BY THE NAME OF THE PROMOTING GROUP

A. NATIONAL GOVERNMENTS AND OFFICIAL INTERNATIONAL AGENCIES

I. IN PEACE

ALBERT-PETIT, A. "La Propagande allemande chez nous," *Journal des débats,* vol. 40, pt. 1, pp. 1028–29 (June 23, 1933).

AUSLANDSTELLE DES KRIEGSPRESSEAMTS [Germany]. *Handbuch der Auslandspresse,* 1918. Berlin: Mittler, 1918. 270 pp.
Official German press guide.

BAUSMAN, FREDERICK. "Under Which Flag?" *American Mercury,* 12: 195–203 (October, 1927).

BELINA-PODGAETSKI, N. "Soviet Propaganda in Foreign Ports," translated by M. Burr. *English Review,* 58: 701–06 (June, 1934).

BENOIST, J. "La Politique allemande aux frontières," *Revue des sciences politiques,* 50: 515–38 (October, 1927).
German propaganda in neighboring countries.

BERCHTOLD, WILLIAM E. "Press Agents of the New Deal," *New Outlook,* 164: 23–30 (July, 1934).

————. "The World Propaganda War," *North American Review,* 238: 421–30 (November, 1934).

BERNUS, P. "La Propagande allemande," *Journal des débats,* 39: 338–39 (March 4, 1932).

————. "La Propagande allemande et la paix," *Journal des débats,* 39: 493–95 (April 1, 1932).

————. "La Propagande française," *Journal des débats,* 40: 10–11 (January 6, 1933).

BRANDT, A. "Nazi International," *Catholic World,* 138: 394–404 (January, 1934).

BURON, E. "La Mémoire et l'oubli," *Mercure de France,* 254: 280–309 (September 1, 1934).
French report of German propaganda.

CALLENDER, HAROLD. "Europe's Propaganda Mills Keep Busy," *New York Times Magazine,* April 9, 1933.

"Chinese Official Publicity," *Far Eastern Review*, 27:206 (April, 1931).

COWELL, F. R. "Government Departments and the Press in the U. S. A.," *Public Administration*, April, 1931.

DARIAC, A. "La Propagande française à l'étranger," *Nouvelle revue*, May 1, 1933.
The organization of French propaganda abroad.

————. "Les pionniers de l'idée française," *Revue politique et littéraire*, 71:353–55 (June 17, 1933).

DIMOCK, MARSHALL EDWARD. "Selling Public Enterprise to the Public," *National Municipal Review*, 23:660–66 (December, 1934).

DUFFIELD, MARCUS. "Mussolini's American Empire: The Fascist Invasion of the United States," *Harper's Magazine*, 169:661–72 (November, 1929).

ECCARD, F. "La France doit organiser sa propagande," *Revue politique et littéraire*, 71:129–33 (March 4, 1933).

————. "La Propagande allemande," *Revue des deux mondes*, 8:44–60 (March 1, 1932).

EINZIG, PAUL. *Behind the Scenes of International Finance*. New York: Macmillan, 1931. 154 pp.
The foreign editor of the *Financial News* charges misuse of money power by the French government.

ESSARY, J. FRED. "Uncle Sam's Ballyhoo Men," *American Mercury*, 23:419–28 (August, 1931).
Press agents hired by government bureaus.

FLORENT-MATTER, EUGÈNE. *La France est-elle défendu? La propagande allemande, ses armes, ses méthodes, ses succès*. Paris: Tallandier, 1930. 224 pp.
Declares that France is not aware of the importance of foreign (German, Communist) propaganda efforts before, during, or since the World War.

"Free Trips for Journalists and Professors," *China Weekly Review*, 56:293–94 (May 2, 1931).
Free trips paid for by the Japanese government to improve its relations with intellectuals abroad.

"French Government Propaganda," *National Republic*, 21:8–9 (May, 1933).

GOT, A. "L'Organisation de la propagande allemande," *Mercure de France*, 173:598–612 (August 1, 1924).

HALLGREN, M. A. "La Propagande nazie en Amérique," *L'Europe nouvelle*, 17:827–29 (August 18, 1934).

"How Shall We Meet Nazi Propaganda?" *Nation*, 137:526 (November 8, 1933).
Discussion of this article appeared in the *Nation*, 137:707–08 (December 20, 1933), and 138:46 (January 10, 1934).

HOWARD, H. P. "Japanese Propaganda, History, and Journalism," *China Weekly Review*, 62:338 (October 22, 1932).

"International Labor Organization," *Encyclopedia of the Social Sciences*. (By Francis G. Wilson.)

INTERNATIONAL LABOUR OFFICE. *The International Labour Organization: The First Decade*. London: Allen and Unwin, 1931. 382 pp.

JACKSON, JUDITH, and KING-HALL, STEPHEN. *The League of Nations Yearbook, 1932*. New York: Macmillan, 1932. 604 pp.
The first annual issue of a handbook in English comparable to Ottlik's French publication. See the references to the Information Section, etc.

"Japan's Official Propaganda," *Literary Digest*, November 25, 1921.

JOXE, L. "Note sur l'effort allemand et l'effort italien en matière de propagande," *L'Europe nouvelle*, 16:83 (January 28, 1933).

KADEN, ERICH HANS, and SPRINGER, MAX. *Der politische Charakter der französischen Kulturpropaganda am Rhein*. Berlin: Vahlen, 1924. 107 pp.
The political implications of cultural propaganda.

KLOSS, H. "Französische Sprachpolitik," *Deutsche Rundschau*, 209: 184–89 (November, 1926).

LALLEMANDE, C. "Quelques sophismes de la propagande allemande," *Revue politique et littéraire*, 69:289–91 (May 16, 1931).
Condensed and translated in the *International Digest*, 1:33–35 (July, 1931).

LASSWELL, HAROLD DWIGHT. "The Status of Research on International Propaganda and Opinion," *American Journal of Sociology*, 32:198–209 (1926).

LEE, IVY LEDBETTER. *The Problem of International Propaganda: A New Technique Necessary in Developing Understanding between Nations*. New York: Ivy Lee, 1934. 37 pp.
An address delivered in London on July 3, 1934, before a private group of persons concerned with international affairs. Advocates the use of modern propaganda media by governments to explain their points of view to the masses in foreign countries.

LÉVY, R. "Propagande allemande en Chine," *L'Europe nouvelle*, 16: 527–28 (June 3, 1933).

LORE, LUDWIG. "Nazi Politics in America," *Nation*, 137:615–17 (November 29, 1933).
Reply by George Sylvester Viereck in the *Nation*, 137:708–09 (December 20, 1933).

MÉNABRÉA, A. "De l'utilité de la gloire," *Revue politique et littéraire*, 71:622–25 (October 21, 1933).
On French propaganda.

MERK, FREDERICK. "British Government Propaganda and the Oregon Treaty," *American Historical Review*, 40:38–62 (October, 1934).
Contains bibliography.

"National Council of Propaganda," *Canadian Forum*, 14:165 (February, 1934).

NIBB, J. "False Witness against Neighbor Nations," *Catholic World*, 138:716–21 (March, 1934).

PRICE, CLAIR. "Europe Wages a War of Electric Words," *New York Times Magazine*, September 10, 1933.
Political propaganda over the radio: "the newest form of armaments in the old ammunition box of Europe."

"Propagande nazie," *Journal des débats*, 40:368–69 (September 8, 1933).

"A Real Case of Tainted News," *Collier's Weekly*, 53:16 (June 6, 1914).
The Canadian government paid the Western Newspaper Union $42,000 a year to run articles about Canada's land openings.

REDMAN, H. V. "Anglophobia in Japan," *Quarterly Review*, 261:254–65 (October, 1933).
Allegation of anti-British propaganda.

RIVAUD, A. "Les Formes actuelles de la propagande allemande, à propos du livre 'Our Genial Enemy, France,' d'E. Schoonmaker," *Journal des débats*, 39:1092–94 (December 30, 1932).

RUSSELL, THOMAS. "How Advertising Was Used in the British Railroad Strike," *Printers' Ink*, 109:61–64 (October 16, 1919).

SCHMECKEBIER, LAWRENCE F., and WEBER, G. A. *The Bureau of Foreign and Domestic Commerce: Its History, Activities, and Organization*. Baltimore: Johns Hopkins University, 1924. 180 pp.
An important channel of business promotion under the Harding and Coolidge administrations.

SCOTT, KENNETH. "The Political Propaganda of 44–30 B. C.," *American Academy in Rome: Memoirs*, 11:7–49 (1933).

Smertenko, J. J. "Hitlerism Comes to America," *Harper's Magazine*, 167:660–70 (November, 1933).
National-Socialist propaganda in America.

"Spending Vast Sums to Influence World Opinion," *China Weekly Review*, 60:383–85 (May 21, 1932).
A Chinese allegation concerning Japanese propaganda.

Stowe, Lee. *Nazi Means War*. New York: McGraw-Hill, 1933. 142 pp.

Tallents, Sir Stephen G., and Whitehead, Harold. "Salesmanship in the Public Service: Scope and Technique," *Public Administration*, 11:259–76 (1933).

Taufflieb, Général. "La Propagande étrangère aux États-Units," *Revue politique et littéraire*, 71:257–59 (May 6, 1933).

"Une Impudente propagande allemande: La France en armes," *L'Illustration*, 183:506 (December 10, 1932).

United States Senate, Special Committee to Investigate Propaganda or Money Alleged to Have Been Used by Foreign Governments to Influence United States Senators, 70th Congress, 1st Session. David A. Reed, Chairman. *Hearings*. Washington, D. C.: Government Printing Office, 1927–28. In 4 parts, 341 pp.

Vehse, Otto. *Die amtliche Propaganda in der Staatskunst Kaiser Friedrichs II* (Forschungen zur mittelälterlichen und neueren Geschichte). Munich: Verlag der münchner Drucke, 1929. 247 pp.

Vogel, Rudolph. *Deutsche Presse und Propaganda des Abstimmungskampfes in Oberschlesien*. Beuthen: Oberschlesische Zeitung, 1931. 182 pp.
Detailed analysis of the German press campaign at the time of the Upper Silesian plebiscite. A contribution to the study of modern propaganda technique.

Witt-Guizot, F. de. "La Propagande allemande et l'Alsace," *Revue des deux mondes*, sér. 8, 12:341–56 (November 15, 1932).

2. IN WAR

A. BIBLIOGRAPHY

Hoover War Library, Stanford University. *Catalogue of Paris Peace Conference Delegation Propaganda in the Hoover War Library*. Stanford University, California: Stanford University, 1926. 96 pp.

Lutz, Ralph Haswell. "Studies of World War Propaganda, 1914–33," *Journal of Modern History*, 5:496–516 (December, 1933).
Professor Lutz is chairman of the directors of the Hoover War Library at Stanford University.

B. REFERENCES

ANTON, REINHOLD. *Die Lügenpresse: Der Lügenfeldzug unserer Feinde, nach eine Gegenüberstellung deutscher und feindlicher Nachrichten u. a. der W.T.B.-, Reuter-, Havas-, und P.T.A. Telegramme über den Weltkrieg, 1914–1916.* Leipzig: Zehrfeld, 1916. 112 pp.
An attempt to list all the lies in Allied propaganda.

ASHTON, SIR GEORGE. *"Propaganda—and the Father of It,"* Cornhill Magazine, N.S., 48:223–41 (1920).
Avers that Germany sired propaganda.

AVENARIUS, FERDINAND. *Das Bild als Verleumder: Beispiele und Bemerkungen zur Technik der Völkerverhetzung.* Munich: Callwey, 1915. 78 pp.
A list of faked pictures used by the Allies.

BAUDRILLART, ALFRED. *Une Campagne française.* Paris: Bloud et Gay, 1917. 272 pp.
The means used by the Catholic Committee to contribute to the French cause and French propaganda abroad, especially in Spain, during the World War. By the rector of the Institut catholique de Paris.

BEAVERBROOK, WILLIAM MAXWELL AITKEN, BARON. *Politicians and the War, 1914–16.* Garden City: Doubleday, 1928. 264 pp.
Lord Beaverbrook, proprietor of the *Daily Express,* was connected with British propaganda activities.

BENJAMIN, HAZEL C. *"Official Propaganda and the French Press during the Franco-Prussian War,"* Journal of Modern History, 4:214–30 (1932).

BENJAMIN, LEWIS S. *German Propagandist Societies* (65th Congress, 2d Session, Senate Document 278). Washington, D.C.: Government Printing Office, 1918. 15 pp.
An article by Lewis Melville (pseudonym) reprinted from the *London Quarterly Review* and the *Living Age.*

BERNSTORFF, JOHANN HEINRICH, GRAF VON. *My Three Years in America.* London: Skeffington and Son, 1920. 359 pp.
By the German ambassador to the United States, 1914–17.

BERTKAU, FRIEDRICH. *Das amtliche Zeitungswesen im Verwaltungsgebiet Ober-Ost. Beitrag zur Geschichte der Presse im Weltkrieg* (dissertation, Leipzig). Leipzig, 1928. 165 pp.
Bibliography, pp. 163–65.

BLANKENHORN, HEBER. *Adventures in Propaganda: Letters from an*

Intelligence Officer in France. Boston and New York: Houghton Mifflin, 1919. 166 pp.

An American propagandist abroad.

BLUMENTAL, F. *Burzhuaznaya Politrabota v Mirovuyu Voinu 1914–1918, Obrabotka Obschestvennogo Mneniya.* Moscow: GIZ, 1928. 168 pp.

Bourgeois political work during the World War. Contains a compendious study of Allied propaganda.

BORNECQUE, HENRI, and DROUILLY, JOSÉ GERMAIN. *La France et la guerre: Formation de l'opinion publique pendant la guerre.* Paris: Payot, 1921. 159 pp.

French propaganda during the World War.

BOURGEOIS, MAURICE. " La Propagande britannique et américaine dans les pays ennemis pendant la guerre," *Les Archives de la grande guerre,* 9: 157–71, 289–308 (1921).

BRIGGS, MITCHELL PIRIE. *George D. Herron and the European Settlement.* Stanford University, California: Stanford University, 1932. 178 pp.

Mr. Herron was special representative, interpreter, and propagandist of President Wilson in Switzerland.

BRUNTZ, GEORGE C. "Allied Propaganda and the Collapse of the German Empire."

In preparation at Hoover War Library, Stanford University.

————. "Propaganda as an Instrument of War," *Current History,* 32: 743–47 (July, 1930).

BUCHANAN, A. RUSSELL. "European Propaganda in the United States, 1914–1917."

In preparation at Hoover War Library, Stanford University.

BUNAU-VARILLA, PHILIPPE. *The Great Adventure of Panama, Wherein Are Exposed Its Relation to the Great War and Also the Luminous Traces of the German Conspiracies against France and the United States.* Garden City: Doubleday, Page, 1920. 267 pp.

By a French press proprietor.

BUSCH, MORITZ. *Bismarck in the Franco-German War, 1870–71.* New York: Scribners, 1879. 2 vols.

CHAFEE, ZECHARIAH, JR. "The Conscription of Public Opinion," in Norris F. Hall, editor, *The Next War.* Cambridge, Massachusetts: Harvard Alumni Bulletin Press, 1925.

CHARTERIS, BRIGADIER GENERAL JOHN. *At G.H.Q.* London: Cassell, 1931. 363 pp.

A chronological account of propaganda work at General Headquarters.

COMANDO SUPREMO DEL R. ESERCITO [Italy]. *Propaganda palese ed approcci clandestin per la pace, luglio 1917, nov. 1918*. Rome, 1918. An official investigation of German war propaganda.

COMMISSIONE D' INCHIESTA [Italy]. *Relazione della Commissione d' inchiesta r. d. 12 gennaio 1918 — n. 35. Dall'Isonzo al Piave 24 ottobre — 9 novembre 1917*. Rome, 1919. 2 vols. Results of an official investigation of German war propaganda.

COMMITTEE ON PUBLIC INFORMATION [United States]. *Complete Report of the Chairman of the Committee on Public Information, 1917, 1918, 1919*. Washington, D. C.: Government Printing Office, 1920. 290 pp.

COOK, SIR EDWARD TYAS. *The Press in War-Time, with Some Account of the Official Press Bureau*. London: Macmillan, 1920. 200 pp. Bibliographic footnotes.

CORPO D'ARMATA TERRITORIALE DI GENOA [Italy]. *Vade mecum a cura dell'ufficio stampa e propaganda*. Genoa, 1918.

CREEL, GEORGE. *How We Advertised America: The First Telling of the Amazing Story of the Committee on Public Information That Carried the Gospel of Americanism to Every Corner of the Globe*. New York and London: Harpers, 1920. 466 pp. By the head of the Committee on Public Information, the organization that directed the United States government news and publicity campaign during the World War.

CROZIER, JOSEPH. *In the Enemy's Country*, translated from the French by Forrest Wilson. New York: Knopf, 1931. 235 pp. French efforts to encourage defeatist elements in Germany.

DANIÉLOU, CHARLES. *Les Affaires étrangères*. Paris: Figuière, 1927. 255 pp. French war propaganda.

DANILOV, I. U. *Rossiya v Mirovoi Voine*. Berlin: Slovo, 1924. 396 pp. Russia in the World War. Memoirs of a Russian general, containing remarks on the efforts of the Imperial Government to create a war psychology.

DEMARTIAL, GEORGES. *La Guerre de 1914: Comment on mobilisa les consciences*. Paris: Éditions des cahiers internationaux, 1922. 325 pp. War propaganda and censorship in France.

DEMETER, KARL. "Die Filmspropaganda der Entente im Weltkriege," *Archiv für Politik und Geschichte*, 4: 214-31 (1925).

DE ROUX, MARIE. *Le Défaitisme et les manoeuvres pro-allemandes, 1914-1917*. Paris: Nouvelle librairie nationale, 1918. 128 pp. Activities of the French intelligence service in combating defeatism and pro-German maneuvers.

DESGRANGES, LIEUTENANT PIERRE, and DE BELLEVAL, LIEUTENANT. *En mission chez l'ennemi, 1915–1918.* Paris, 1930.
French efforts to encourage defeatist elements in Germany.

DROUILLY, JOSÉ GERMAIN, and GUÉRINON, E. *Les Chefs d'oeuvre de la propagande allemande.* Paris: Berger-Levrault, 1919. 277 pp.
Analyzes leading German propagandist writings.

EBBINGHAUS, THÉRÈSE. *Napoleon, England, und die Presse, 1800–1803.* Munich and Berlin: R. Oldenbourg, 1914. 211 pp.
Napoleon's propaganda technique, with special reference to England. Contains bibliographic footnotes, and bibliography, pp. xi–xv.

FALCKE, HORST P. *Vor dem Eintritt Amerikas in den Weltkrieg: Deutsche Propaganda in den Vereinigten Staaten von Amerika, 1914–1915.* Dresden: C. Reissner, 1928. 304 pp.
The former German consul-general in New York gives an unvarnished account of German propaganda activities. Bibliography, pp. 299–300.

FELGER, F. *Was wir vom Weltkrieg nicht wissen, im Auftrage der Weltkriegsbücherei herausgegeben.* Berlin: Andermann, 1929. 640 pp.
General history of World War propaganda.

FERRARA, ORESTES. *Tentatives de intervención Europea en América.* Havana: Editorial Hermes, 1933. 176 pp.
Analysis of the steps taken by and on behalf of Spain to crystallize the opposition to intervention by the United States in Cuba in 1898. Bibliographic footnotes.

FISHER, HAROLD HENRY. *The Defeatist Movement in Russia, 1914–1917.* Stanford University, California: Stanford University, 1934.

FORD, GUY STANTON. "America's Fight for Public Opinion," *Minnesota History Bulletin,* 3: 3–26 (1919).
A succinct account of the wartime activities of the Committee on Public Information.

FRAUENHOLZ, EUGEN VON. *Die antideutsche Propaganda durch das schweizer Gebiet im Weltkrieg, speziell die Propaganda in Bayern* (Münchener historische Abhandlungen, Series 2, no. 3). Munich: Beck, 1933.
Anti-German propaganda by way of Switzerland during the World War.

FYFE, HENRY HAMILTON. *Northcliffe: An Intimate Biography.* London: Allen and Unwin, 1930. 349 pp.

——. *The Making of an Optimist.* London: L. Parsons, 1921. 279 pp.
Close to Lord Northcliffe; war reminiscences.

GENERAL STAFF [Great Britain]. *Daily Review of the Foreign Press: Short Press Guide, September, 1917.* London, 1917. 31 pp.
Wartime press guide of Great Britain.

GERLACH, HELLMUT VON. *Die grosse Zeit der Lüge.* Charlottenburg: Verlag der Weltbühne, 1926. 109 pp.
German pacifist and liberal discusses war propaganda.

GLAISE-HORSTENAU, EDMUND VON. *Die Katastrophe, die Zertrummerung Oesterreichs-Ungarns, und das Werden der Nachfolgestaaten.* Zurich, etc.: Amalthea, 1929. 525 pp.
Austro-Hungarian war propaganda problems. Bibliography, pp. 492–98. English edition: *The Collapse of the Austro-Hungarian Empire.* London: Dent, 1930. New York: Dutton, 1930. 347 pp. Bibliography, pp. 339–44.

GORDON, G. O. "Nemetskaya Propaganda na Russkom Fronte," *Golos Minuvshago,* Moscow, 1918, nos. 4–6.
An account of German propaganda on the Russian front line, based on personal impressions and authentic documents.

GORE, JAMES HOWARD. *American Legionnaires of France.* Washington, D. C.: W. F. Roberts, 1920. 451 pp. Supplement, 1922, 274 pp.
A directory of Americans on whom France has conferred the Legion of Honor.

GRAUX, LUCIEN. *Les Fausses nouvelles de la grande guerre.* Paris: Édition française illustrée, 1918—. 7 vols.
Lists a vast amount of false information, the creation of the collective imagination as well as of the self-conscious propagandists.

GULICK, SIDNEY LEWIS. *Anti-Japanese War-Scare Stories.* New York and Chicago: Fleming H. Revell, 1917. 89 pp.

HALSALLE, HENRY DE. *A Secret Service Woman: Experiences of Olga von Kopf, the Famous International Spy.* London: T. W. Laurie, 1917. 192 pp.
Propaganda as well as espionage.

HANSI (pseudonym of Johann Jakob Waltz) and TONNELAT, E. *A travers les lignes ennemies: Trois années d'offensive contre le moral allemand.* Paris: Payot, 1922. 191 pp.
French propaganda offensive on the Western Front.

HARDIE, MARTIN, and SABIN, ARTHUR K. *War Posters Issued by Belligerent and Neutral Nations, 1914–1919.* 46 pp.
Plates, with brief description.

HENRY, ALBERT. *Études sur l'occupation allemande en Belgique.* Brussels: Lebègue, 1920. 465 pp.
Studies of the Activist movement, the deportations, and the work of the

Comité national, by the general secretary of the Comité national de secours.

HERMANN, CARL. *Geheimkrieg: Dokumente und Untersuchungen eines Polizeichefs an der Westfront.* Hamburg and Berlin: Hanseatische Verlagsanstalt, 1930. 214 pp.

Evidence as to the effectiveness of Allied propaganda against the German army.

HOLBROOK, FRANKLIN F., and APPEL, LIVIA. "The Fight for Public Opinion," in *Minnesota in the War with Germany,* 2: 64–88. St. Paul: Minnesota Historical Society, 1932.

A study of the measures taken to mobilize wartime attitudes within a single state.

HUBER, GEORG. *Die französische Propaganda im Weltkrieg gegen Deutschland.* Munich: Pfeiffer, 1928. 314 pp.

L'Imposture par l'image: Receuil de gravures falsifiées et calomnieuses publiées par la presse illustrée austro-allemande pendant la guerre (anonymous). Paris: Payot, 1917. 80 pp.

A list of faked pictures used by the Central Powers.

"Kadaver," *Nation* (London), 38: 171–72 (October 31, 1925).

A famous atrocity fake by Brigadier General Charteris.

KLOBUKOWSKI, ANTONY WLADISLAS. *Souvenirs de Belgique, 1911–1918.* Brussels: L'Éventail, 1928. 267 pp.

Former French ambassador to Belgium; head of French war propaganda.

KNESEBECK, LUDOLF GOTTSCHALK VON DEM. *Die Wahrheit über den Propagandafeldzug und Deutschlands Zusammenbruch.* Munich: Fortschrittliche Buchhandlung, 1927. 168 pp.

Deals especially with the part played by the press.

KOESTER, FRANK. *The Lies of the Allies: A Remarkable Collection of Facts, Proofs, and Documents of How England, the Anglo-Maniacs, and the "Big Dailies" Humbug the American People.* New York: Issues and Events, 1916. 48 pp.

KRIEGSPRESSEAMT [Germany]. *Handbuch deutscher Zeitungen, 1917, bearbeitet im Kriegspresseamt von D. Oskar Michel.* Berlin: O. Elsner, 1917. 440 pp.

The wartime press guide of Germany.

LANGEROCK, HUBERT. "The Flemish Demand for Autonomy," *Current History,* 18: 789–94 (August, 1923).

Reviews German efforts to promote Belgian disunity in the World War by means of the "Council of Flanders," a separatist organization.

LANGSAM, WALTER CONSUELO. *The Napoleonic Wars and German Nationalism in Austria* (Columbia University Studies in History, Economics, and Public Law, no. 324). New York: Columbia University, 1930. 241 pp.

The Austrian government carried on a campaign of propaganda designed to incite the peoples of both Austria and Germany to resist Napoleon.

LECHARTIER, GEORGES. *Intrigues et diplomaties à Washington, 1914–1917*. Paris: Plon, 1919. 302 pp.

Anti-German propaganda by a Frenchman. German activity in the United States.

LEQUEUX, WILLIAM, editor. *Bolo, the Super-Spy: An Amazing Exposure of the Traitor's Secret Adventures as a Spy in Britain and France Disclosed from Official Documents by Armand Méjan, Ex-Inspector of the Paris Sûrété Générale*. London: Odhams, 1918. 185 pp.

LEROUGE, GUSTAVE. *"La Gazette des Ardennes," son histoire, son organisation, ses collaborateurs*. Paris: Tallandier, 1919. 228 pp.

Lord Riddell's War Diary, 1914–1918. London: Ivor Nicholson and Watson, 1933. 387 pp.

Lord Riddell, a close personal friend of Mr. Lloyd George, was during the World War an intermediary between Fleet Street and the departments of state.

LOZOVSKY, A. (pseudonym). *Kak my izdavali vo vrmia voiny internatsionalisticheskiya gazety v Parizhe*, Moscow: Pechat i revolyutsiya, 1923, no. 5.

How internationalist and anti-patriotic newspapers were published in Paris during the World War.

LUDENDORFF, GENERAL ERICH VON. *Meine Kriegserinnerungen, 1914–1918*. Berlin: Mittler, 1919, 1920. 628 pp.

The German general stresses the effectiveness of Entente propaganda. English edition: *My War Memoirs, 1914–1918*. London: Hutchinson, 1919. 2 vols. American edition: *Ludendorff's Own Story*. New York and London: Harpers, 1920. 2 vols.

LUTZ, RALPH HASWELL, editor. *The Fall of the German Empire, 1914–1918*. Stanford University, California: Stanford University, 1932. London: Oxford, 1932. 2 vols.

Includes documents illustrating the rôle of propaganda.

MARCHAND, LOUIS. *L'Offensive morale*. Paris: Renaissance du livre, 1920. 338 pp.

A study of the *Gazette des Ardennes* and the *Bonnet rouge* to show how the German general staff attempted to undermine French morale.

MASSARD, ÉMILE NICOLAS. *Les Espions à Paris*. Paris: Michel, 1923. 252 pp.

MASSART, JEAN. *The Secret Press in Belgium*. New York: Dutton, 1918. 96 pp.
Covers the activities of the entire Belgian clandestine press.

MAYER, LIEUTENANT COLONEL EMIL. *La Psychologie du commandement*. Paris: Flammarion, 1924.
Analyzes the methods used by Pétain to restore French morale in 1917; relation of propaganda to other methods.

MÉLOT, JOSEPH. *La Propagande allemande et la question belge* (Les Cahiers belges, no. 1). Brussels and Paris: G. van Oest, 1917. 48 pp.

MILLACK, W. "Französische Propaganda in Danzig, 1807–13," *Westpreussischer Geschichtsverein Zeitschrift*, 65: 91–109 (1925).

MILLIS, WALTER. *The Martial Spirit: A Study of Our War with Spain*. Boston and New York: Houghton Mifflin, 1931. 427 pp.
A study of events of the Spanish-American War. Includes an account of the publicity tactics of the "yellow press." Bibliography, pp. 411–17.

MINISTÈRE DE LA GUERRE ET DES AFFAIRES ÉTRANGÈRES [France]. *Répertoire des journaux et périodiques utilisés dans les bulletins de presse étrangère à la date du 1er novembre 1917*. Deuxième tirage, revue augmenté; confidentiel. Paris, 1918. 50 pp.
Wartime press guide of France.

MINISTERO DELL'INTERNO [Italy]. *La propaganda all'estero dal novembre 1917 al diciembre 1918*. Rome, 1919.
Results of an official investigation of wartime propaganda.

MOGENS, VICTOR. "Politik, Propaganda, Presse, Publikum," *Deutsche Rundschau*, 54: 171–78 (December, 1927).

MOLL, SCHWESTER CLARA MARIA. *Französisch-revolutionäre Propaganda an der mittleren Saar zu Beginn des ersten Koalitionskrieges*. Saarlouis: Hausen, 1931. 59 pp.

MOYZISCHEWITZ, CAPTAIN (on the General Staff). *Propaganda*. "Als Handschrift gedruckt am 3. April, 1919." 10 pp.
Cited in R. H. Lutz, "Studies of World War Propaganda," *Journal of Modern History*, 5: 496–516 (December, 1933).

MÜHSAM, KURT. *Wie wir belogen wurden: Die amtliche Irreführung des deutschen Volkes im Weltkrieg*. Munich: A. Langen, 1918. 189 pp.
German anarchist protests against official propaganda; many instances cited.

NICHOLSON, IVOR. "Aspect of British Official Wartime Propaganda," *Cornhill Magazine,* 70:593–606 (May, 1931).

NICOLAI, WALTER. *Nachrichtendienst, Presse, und Volkstimmung in Weltkrieg.* Berlin: Mittler, 1920. 226 pp.
Espionage and propaganda against Germany.

NIEMANN, ALFRED. *Revolution von Oben — Umsturz von Unten.* Berlin: Verlag für Kulturpolitik, 1927. 448 pp.

OSZWALD, ROBERT PAUL. *Die Streit um den belgischen Franktireurkrieg.* Cologne: Gilde, 1931. 284 pp.
Digests the extensive literature of the controversy over civilian warfare in Belgium.

PARKER, SIR GILBERT. "The United States and the War," *Harper's Magazine,* 136:521–31 (1918).
By a British agent in the United States.

PÉRIVIER, ANTONIN. *Napoléon journaliste.* Paris: Plon-Nourrit, 1918. 434 pp.
Napoleon as a propagandist.

PHILIPSON, C. *Alsace-Lorraine.* 1918.
German control of former French schools in pursuance of the Germanization policy.

POKROVSKY, M. N. *Tsarskaya Rossiya i Voina.* Moscow: GIZ, 1924. 87 pp.
Contains an analysis of Imperial Russian propaganda and the related problems of censorship and espionage.

PONSONBY, ARTHUR A. W. H. *Falsehood in War-Time, Containing an Assortment of Lies Circulated throughout the Nations during the Great War.* New York: Dutton, 1928. 192 pp.
Tests authenticity of propaganda. Author active in Union of Democratic Control and in pacifist circles.

POSSE, PAUL. *Die Boches: Eine Culturschande in System. Eindrucksvoll vertieft durch Meisterwerke der künstlerischen Sektion für Bochologie (Völker Untereinander,* Band 1). Leipzig: G. Kummer, 1928. 195 pp.
A German presents ironically the propaganda against the "Boche." Bibliography, pp. 185–92.

POWELL, MAJOR EDWARD ALEXANDER. *The Army behind the Army.* New York: Scribners, 1919. 470 pp.
Propaganda and espionage; by a leader of Boy Scouts.

RECKTENWALD, FRIEDERIKE. *Kriegsziele und öffentliche Meinung Englands, 1914–16.* Stuttgart: W. Kohlhammer, 1929. 147 pp.
War aims and public opinion in England as revealed in a study of the press.

Report of the Central Committee for National Patriotic Organizations [England]. London: Buck and Wooton, 1916. 40 pp.
This British committee issued a flood of pamphlets through subcommittees and the University of Oxford.

ROUQUETTE, LOUIS. *Allemagne et Amérique: La propagande germanique aux États-Unis.* Paris: Chapelot, 1916. 154 pp.

RUBETTI, GUIDO. *Un'arma per la vittoria, la pubblicità nei prestiti italiani di guerra.* Milan: Risorgimento Grafico. Vol. 1, 1918; vol. 2, 1919.
Definitive study of war-loan propaganda. The second volume is a study of the propaganda of the fifth national war loan.

SCHÖNEMANN, FRIEDRICH. *Die Kunst der Massenbeeinflussung in den Vereinigten Staaten von Amerika.* Stuttgart: Deutsche Verlagsanstalt, 1924. 212 pp.
America's domestic propaganda during the World War.

SILBER, JULES CRAWFORD. *The Invisible Weapons.* London: Hutchinson, 1932. 288 pp.
Narrative of the experiences of a German secret service agent as an employee of the British postal censorship during the World War.

STREET, C. J. C. "Propaganda behind the Lines," *Cornhill Magazine,* 47: 488–99 (1919).
Entente propaganda.

STUART, SIR CAMPBELL. *Secrets of Crewe House: The Story of a Famous Campaign.* London and New York: Hodder and Stoughton, 1920. 240 pp.
British war propaganda described by a responsible official.

SUSLOV, P. V. *Politicheskoe Obespechenie Sovetsko-Pol'skoi Kampanii 1920 goda.* Moscow: Gosizdat, 1930. 174 pp.
A study of the political side of the World War, and especially of the work of the political agents with the Red Army.

THIMME, HANS. *Weltkrieg ohne Waffen.* Stuttgart: Cotta, 1932. 294 pp.
Based on German archival material. Analyzes Entente propaganda against Germany, particularly the pamphlet war on the troops.

TROMMER, HARRY. *Urkundenfälschung und Betrug im Weltkriege.* Leipzig: Wiegandt, 1928. 190 pp.
The author views wartime falsehood as a problem in criminology.

UNFER, LOUIS. "German War Propaganda in Germany Directed against Anglo-Saxon Countries" (unpublished M.A. thesis in history, University of Illinois, 1931).

UNITED STATES SENATE, COMMITTEE ON THE JUDICIARY. *Brewing and Liquor Interests and German and Bolshevist Propaganda* (report and hearings of a subcommittee of the Committee on the Judiciary, 65th Congress, 2d Session, pursuant to Senate Resolutions 307 and 439). Washington, D.C.: Government Printing Office, 1919. 3 vols.

————. *The National German-American Alliance* (hearings before a subcommittee of the Committee on the Judiciary, 65th Congress, 2d Session, on S. 3529). Washington, D.C.: Government Printing Office, 1918. 698 pp.

Die Ursachen des deutschen Zusammenbruchs im Jahre 1918. Berlin: Deutsche Verlagsgesellschaft für Politik und Geschichte, 1926–29. 12 vols.

Proceedings of the German parliamentary committee to investigate Germany's collapse.

VIERECK, GEORGE SYLVESTER. *Spreading Germs of Hate.* New York: Liveright, 1930. 327 pp.

By a German-American journalist active in pro-German propaganda.

VOLOTSKOI, I.A. *Ocherki po voyennoy: Rabote pechati.* Moscow: GIZ, 1928. 199 pp.

Sketches the military work of the Russian press during the World War.

WEILL, GEORGES. "Les Gouvernements et la presse pendant la guerre," *Revue d'histoire de la guerre mondiale,* 11:97–118 (1933).

WHITEHOUSE, VIRA (BOARDMAN). *A Year as a Government Agent.* New York and London: Harpers, 1920. 316 pp.

An American agent in Switzerland who operated publicly.

WIEHLER, RUDOLPH. *Deutsche Wirtschaftspropaganda im Weltkreig.* Berlin: Mittler, 1922. 74 pp.

Bibliography, pp. 69–74.

WILKERSON, MARCUS. *Public Opinion and the Spanish-American War: A Study of War Propaganda.* Baton Rouge: Louisiana State University, 1932. 141 pp.

The influence exerted by the press, especially the "yellow" newspapers.

C. LIST OF MAJOR COLLECTIONS OF WAR PROPAGANDA

Bibliothèque et musée de la guerre, Château de Vincennes (Seine), France.

Hoover War Library, Stanford University, California, U.S.A.

Imperial War Museum, South Kensington, S. W. 7, London, England.
Weltkriegsbücherei, Schloss Rosenstein, Stuttgart-Berg, Germany.

There is also a good collection in the Preussiche Staatsbibliothek, Berlin, and a comprehensive collection of American official propaganda at the Council of National Defense, Washington, D. C.

B. LOCAL INSTITUTIONS

State, provincial, municipal, and local governments; public (not necessarily official) agencies, such as hospitals, schools, and libraries.

I. BIBLIOGRAPHY

ALEXANDER, C. "Research in Educational Publicity," *Teachers College Record,* 29: 479–87 (March, 1928).

LIBRARY OF CONGRESS. *List of Publications on Publicity for the States* (Select List no. 107). Washington, D. C., March 3, 1916. 11 pp., typewritten.

Lists publications, by state chambers of commerce, bureaus of state government, etc., relative to natural resources, opportunities for development, and social conditions. Gives good clues to such promotional bodies. Relevant titles are included in the present bibliography.

MORRIS, L., and others. "Annotated Bibliography of Researches in Educational Publicity to June, 1927," *Teachers College Record,* 30: 40–45 (October, 1928).

MUNRO, WILLIAM BENNETT. *A Bibliography of Municipal Government in the United States.* Cambridge, Massachusetts: Harvard University, 1915. 472 pp.

2. REFERENCES

"Advertising School Bond Issues," *American School Board Journal,* 72: 94–96 (March, 1926).

ALEXANDER, CARTER. *School Statistics and Publicity* (Beverly Educational Series, edited by W. W. Charters). Boston and New York: Silver, Burdette, 1919. 332 pp.

Bibliography, pp. 317–21, and at ends of chapters.

ALEXANDER, CARTER, and THEISEN, W. W. *Publicity Campaigns for Better School Support.* Yonkers-on-Hudson: World Book Company, 1921. 164 pp.

Bibliography, pp. 151–58.

ARTHUR, J. N., and others. "A City Manager's Contact with the Public," *Public Management,* July–August, 1931.

BENNETT, E. "Dealing with the Newspapers," *American School Board Journal,* 72:47 (May, 1926).

BEYLE, HERMAN CAREY. *Governmental Reporting in Chicago.* Chicago: University of Chicago, 1928. 303 pp.
Analyzes the appeal value of reports of all governmental agencies. Bibliography, pp. 274–91.

BOLSER, C. M. "Have You a Director of Publicity in Your School?" *School and Society,* 12:513–17 (November 27, 1920).

BRISCOE, WALTER ALWYN. *Library Advertising:"Publicity" Methods for Public Libraries, Library Work with Children, Rural Library Schemes, etc., with a Chapter on the Cinema and the Library.* New York:H. W. Wilson, 1921. London:Grafton, 1921. 127 pp.

BUNNING, G. H. S. "Personal Relations of Officials and the Public," *Public Administration,* January, 1931.

CANNON, CARL L. *Publicity for Small Libraries.* Chicago:American Library Association, 1929. 34 pp.
Bibliography, pp. 32–34.

CHAPMAN, C. W. "Selling the High School to the Community," *High School Quarterly,* 12:76–80 (January, 1924).

"City Government's Advertising Opportunity:Why Don't Political Parties Show the Excellent Things Being Accomplished Now, without Waiting for the Next Election?" *Printers' Ink,* 3:41–42, 44 (May 6, 1920).

City Manager Yearbook, 1931. Chicago:International City Managers' Association, 1931.
Pages 105–339 are on government reporting.

COMMITTEE ON UNIFORM STREET AND SANITATION RECORDS, CHICAGO. *How to Prepare an Annual Public Works Report.* Chicago, 1933.
Represents a self-conscious effort to systematize the public relations of municipal agencies.

DEPARTMENT OF COMMERCE. *Advertising for Community Promotion.* Washington, D. C.:Government Printing Office, 1928. 47 pp.

DOUGLASS, HARL R. *Organization and Administration of Secondary Schools.* Boston:Ginn, 1932. 568 pp.
Chapter 20:"Utilizing Community Data and Relationships"; chapter 21; "High School Publicity."

FARLEY, BELMONT MERCER. *What to Tell the People about the Public Schools:A Study of the Content of the Public School Publicity Program* (Teachers College Contributions to Education, no. 355). New York:Columbia University, 1929. 136 pp.
Bibliography, pp. 133–36.

FOLEY, E. J., and FINER, HERMAN. "Officials and the Public," *Public Administration,* January, 1931.

FREEMAN, REV. JAMES E. *A Civic Opportunity.* Minneapolis: The Publicity Club, 1911. 15 pp.
   Address given before the Publicity Club. Chamber of Commerce urges city to spend money advertising "municipal improvement."

"Government Reporting," *Encyclopedia of the Social Sciences.* (By Wylie Kirkpatrick.)

GOVERNMENTAL RESEARCH ASSOCIATION. *Twenty Years of Municipal Research.* New York, 1927. 36 pp.
   What the municipal research movement in America is, where and how it operates, what it costs, and some of its achievements.

GRAVES, W. BROOKE. "Publicity by State Governments" (unpublished manuscript at Temple University).

HARGER, CHARLES M. "Publicity Does a State," *Independent,* 71: 478–81 (August 31, 1911).
   Discusses the publicity campaign of the Kansas Board of Agriculture.

HENDRICK, JOHN B. *Message to the 13th State Legislature [of Wyoming].* Cheyenne, Wyoming, 1915. 17 pp.
   A governor's recommendations for appropriation for a publicity campaign.

HOLT, H. Q. "Letting the Patrons Know What a School Is Doing," *Popular Education,* 42: 385 (March, 1925).

INDIANA STATE BUREAU OF LEGISLATIVE INFORMATION. *Digest of Laws Relating to State Publicity or State Advertising Activities.* Indianapolis, Indiana, 1914. 11 pp., typewritten.

KAUL, A. S. *Kommunalpolitik und Presse.* Heidelberg, 1933 (?). 112 pp.
   City government and the press.

KEELEY, M. P., and CARPENTER, W. W. "College Publicity in the Daily Papers," *Education,* 54: 49–53 (September, 1933).

KIRKPATRICK, WYLIE. "The Preparation of Public Reports: Telling Citizens How the Public Job Is Done," *American City,* 44: 113–15, 125–27 (April and May, 1931).

———. *Reporting Municipal Government* (Municipal Administration Service Publication no. 9). New York, 1928.

MACKAY, D. L. "Advertising a Medieval University," *American Historical Review,* 37: 515–16 (April, 1932).

MILLER, CLYDE R., and CHARLES, FRED. *Publicity and the Public School.* Boston and New York: Houghton Mifflin, 1924. 179 pp.

MINTO, JOHN. *A History of the Public Library Movement in Great Britain and Ireland* (The Library Association Series of Library Manuals, no. 4). London: Allen and Unwin, 1932. 366 pp.
Bibliography, pp. 343–44.

MISSOURI STATE BUREAU OF LABOR STATISTICS. *"Boost Missouri" and "Call to the Farm": A Pamphlet Which Gives Information Relative to the Work the Bureau of Labor Statistics Has Undertaken during 1913–14–15 to Make Known the Resources, Advantages, and Opportunities of Missouri.* Jefferson City, Missouri: Hugh Stephens Printing Company, 1913. 18 pp.

NATIONAL COMMITTEE ON MUNICIPAL REPORTING. *Public Reporting, with Special Reference to Annual, Departmental, and Current Reports of Municipalities.* New York: Municipal Administration Service, 1931. 158 pp.
Selected bibliography, p. 158.

PAIGE, ROBERT MYRON, compiler. *A Directory of Organizations in the Field of Public Administration.* Chicago: Public Administration Clearing House, 1934. 178 pp.
Lists national, state, and regional organizations in the United States and Canada. Makes a classification of national organizations by 56 fields of activity. Bibliography, pp. 174–75.

PETERSON, R. S. "Selling Your School to the Town," *American School Board Journal,* 74: 49–50 (June, 1927).

"Place of Humor in Advertising Water Works," *American City,* 44: 113–16 (June, 1931).

REED, P. I. "Publicity for Instructional Achievements in English," *Primary Education,* 32: 626 (December, 1924).

REYNOLDS, R. G. "Newspaper Publicity for the Public Schools," *Teachers College Record,* 26: 22–31 (September, 1924).

———. "Publicity for Public Schools," *Teachers College Record,* 25: 89–97 (March, 1924).

RYAN, C. T. "Psychology in School Publicity," *American School Board Journal,* May, 1933, pp. 27–28.

SHERMAN, NATHANIEL. At Yale University. Is gathering material for a book on educational publicity and propaganda.

STEVENSON, P. R. "Developing a Program for Continuous School Publicity," *American School Board Journal,* 70: 36 (April, 1925).

"Street Cars Carry Publicity for City Ordinances," *American City,* 24: 59 (January, 1921).

SUNDELSON, J. WILNER. "Felicitous Nomenclature," *Bulletin of the National Tax Association,* vol. 19, no. 1, p. 5 (October, 1933).
How taxes can be made acceptable by giving them a name with the right emotional appeal.

WALLER, JAMES FLINT. *Public Relations for the Public Schools: A Manual Based on a Study of Good Practice.* Trenton, New Jersey: Mac-Crellish and Quigley, 1933. 112 pp.

WARD, GILBERT OAKLEY. *Publicity for Public Libraries: Principles and Methods for Librarians, Library Assistants, Trustees, and Library Schools.* New York: H. W. Wilson, 1924. 315 pp.
Bibliography, pp. 299–309.

WHITE, LEONARD DUPEE. *The City Manager.* Chicago: University of Chicago, 1927. 355 pp.
See the index under "Public relations," "Press," "Publicity," etc., for discussions of the manager's problem of public relations.

WILLMOTT, J. F. "Public Reports and Public Opinion," *National Municipal Review,* 13: 421–25 (August, 1924).

WOODDY, CARROLL H. "Press Relations in City Management," *Public Management,* July–August, 1931.

C. POLITICAL PARTIES IN THE UNITED STATES

I. GENERAL DISCUSSIONS

BROOKS, SYDNEY. "English and American Elections," *Fortnightly Review,* N.S., 87: 246–56 (1910).

"Campaign, Political," *Encyclopedia of the Social Sciences.* (By Edward McChesney Sait.)

COHANE, DAVID B. *Practical Political Procedure: Guide for Party Workers.* Boston: Meador, 1932. 159 pp.

GOMPERZ, JULIAN. "Zur Soziologie des amerikanischen Parteiensystems," *Zeitschrift für Sozialforschung,* 1: 278–310 (1932).

GOSNELL, HAROLD FOOTE. "Political Meetings in the Chicago Black Belt," *American Political Science Review,* 28: 254–59 (April, 1934).

HAYNES, FREDERICK EMORY. *Social Politics in the United States.* Boston and New York: Houghton Mifflin, 1924. 414 pp.

HOLCOMBE, ARTHUR NORMAN. *The New Party Politics.* New York: Norton, 1933. 148 pp.
Professor of government at Harvard University foresees class lines replacing party lines in American politics.

KENT, FRANK RICHARDSON. *Political Behavior: The Heretofore Unwritten Laws, Customs, and Principles of Politics as Practiced in the United States*. New York: Morrow, 1928. 342 pp.

LEUTSCHER, G. D. *Early Political Machinery in the United States*. Philadelphia, 1903.

MADDOX, WILLIAM P. "Advisory Policy Committees for Political Parties," *Political Science Quarterly*, 49:253-68 (June, 1934).

MERRIAM, CHARLES EDWARD, and GOSNELL, HAROLD FOOTE. *The American Party System*. Revised edition. New York: Macmillan, 1929. 488 pp.

MUNRO, WILLIAM BENNETT. *The Invisible Government*. New York: Macmillan, 1928. 169 pp.

NEPRASH, JERRY ALVIN. *The Brookhart Campaigns in Iowa, 1920-1926: A Study in the Motivation of Political Attitudes* (Columbia University Studies in History, Economics, and Public Law, no. 336). New York: Columbia University, 1932. London: P. S. King, 1932. 128 pp.
Bibliography, pp. 124-26.

ORTH, SAMUEL PETER. *The Boss and the Machine: Chronicle of the Politicians and Party Organization*. New Haven, Connecticut: Yale University, 1919. 203 pp.

OSTROGORSKI, MOISEI YAKOVLEVITCH. *Democracy and the Party System in the United States*. Revised edition. New York: Macmillan, 1926. 469 pp.
Bibliography, pp. 457-61.

OVERACKER, LOUISE. "Campaign Funds in a Depression Year," *American Political Science Review*, 27:769-84 (October, 1933).

————. *Money in Elections*. New York: Macmillan, 1932. 472 pp.
The use of money in elections here and abroad. Discusses publicity of campaign expenditures.

PEEL, ROY VICTOR. "The Political Machine of New York City," *American Political Science Review*, 27:611-18 (August, 1933).

PEEL, ROY VICTOR, and DONNELLY, THOMAS CLAUDE. *The 1928 Campaign*. New York: New York University Bookstore, 1931. 129 pp. New York: R. R. Smith, 1931. 183 pp.
Bibliography, pp. 177-83.

POLLOCK, JAMES KERR. *Party Campaign Funds*. New York and London: Knopf, 1926. 296 pp.

PRINGLE, HENRY FOWLES. *Theodore Roosevelt: A Biography.* New York: Harcourt, Brace, 1931. 627 pp.
Bibliography, pp. 607–12.

SAIT, EDWARD McCHESNEY. *American Parties and Elections.* New York and London: Century, 1927. 608 pp.
See Part 5 on " Elections."

STANWOOD, EDWARD. *A History of the Presidency.* New edition, revised by Charles Knowles Bolton. New York and Boston: Houghton Mifflin, 1928. 2 vols.

TURNER, G. K. "Manufacturing Public Opinion," *McClure's Magazine,* July, 1912.

2. THE TWO MAJOR PARTIES

BARCLAY, T. S. "The Publicity Division of the Democratic Party, 1929–30," *American Political Science Review,* 25: 68–72 (1931).

BRIGHT, JOHN. *Hizzoner Big Bill Thompson.* New York: Cape and Smith, 1930. 302 pp.
Thompson's political progress from 1900 to 1927.

BROOKS, ROBERT CLARKSON. *Political Parties and Electoral Problems.* Third edition. New York and London: Harpers, 1933. 653 pp.
Gives details of campaign publicity at some length.

CASEY, RALPH D. "Propaganda Technique of the 1928 Presidential Campaign " (unpublished Ph. D. thesis, University of Wisconsin, 1929).

CROLY, HERBERT DAVID. *Marcus Alonzo Hanna.* New York: Macmillan, 1912. 495 pp.
Includes discussions of presidential campaign methods of 1896 and 1900.

DAVENPORT, WALTER. *The Power and the Glory: The Life of Boies Penrose.* New York: Putnam, 1931. 240 pp.

ERIKSSON, ERIK McKINLEY. "Official Newspaper Organs and the Presidential Elections of 1828, 1832, and 1836 " (unpublished Ph. D. thesis, University of Iowa, 1922).

GOSNELL, HAROLD FOOTE. *Boss Platt and His New York Machine.* Chicago: University of Chicago, 1924. 370 pp.
Bibliographic footnotes.

JOHNSON, CLAUDIUS O. *Carter Henry Harrison I.* Chicago: University of Chicago, 1928. 306 pp.
Methods of municipal campaigning in Chicago from 1879 to 1893.

KENT, FRANK RICHARDSON. *The Democratic Party: A History.* New York and London: Century, 1928. 568 pp.

Bibliography, p. 519.

LAFOLLETTE, ROBERT MARION. *LaFollette's Autobiography: A Personal Narrative of Political Experiences.* Madison, Wisconsin: The Robert M. LaFollette Company, 1913. 807 pp.

MERRIAM, CHARLES EDWARD. *Chicago: A More Intimate View of Urban Politics.* New York: Macmillan, 1929. 305 pp.

Describes municipal elections from 1909 to 1928, including Professor Merriam's own campaigns.

MYERS, GUSTAVUS. *History of Tammany Hall.* New York: The Author, 1901. 357 pp. New York: Boni and Liveright, 1917. 414 pp.

MYERS, WILLIAM STARR. *The Republican Party: A History.* New York and London: Century, 1931. 517 pp.

Republicans of New York: A Pictorial and Concise Biographical Record of the Republicans of the Empire State at the Beginning of the 20th Century, Published for Journalistic and Historical Reference. New York: Publishing Society of New York, 1906. 444 portraits, 295 pp.

SAYRE, WALLACE S. "Personnel of Republican and Democratic National Committees," *American Political Science Review,* 26: 360–63 (April, 1932).

Data on age, education, membership in fraternal, religious, and political organizations, and economic interests and alliances.

THOMAS, HARRISON COOK. *The Return of the Democratic Party to Power in 1884* (Columbia University Studies in History, Economics, and Public Law, vol. 89, no. 2). New York: Longmans, Green, 1919. 263 pp.

WHITE, WILLIAM ALLEN. *Politics: The Citizen's Business.* New York: Macmillan, 1924. 330 pp.

Mainly about the 1924 campaign. Has chapters on lobbies.

WOODDY, CARROLL HILL. *The Case of Frank L. Smith.* Chicago: University of Chicago, 1931. 393 pp.

"From the tangled threads of Illinois Republicanism, Mr. Wooddy weaves a tessellated tapestry of purchased politics." — PETER H. ODEGARD.

————. *The Chicago Primary of 1926: A Study in Election Methods.* Chicago: University of Chicago, 1926. 299 pp.

3. THIRD-PARTY MOVEMENTS

A. BIBLIOGRAPHY

Library of Congress Select List of References no. 1073. 232 titles.

B. REFERENCES

CLARK, JOHN BUNYAN. *Populism in Alabama* (Ph.D. thesis, New York University, 1926). Auburn, Alabama: Auburn Printing Company, 1927. 196 pp.

DOUGLAS, PAUL HOWARD. *The Coming of a New Party*. New York and London: McGraw-Hill, 1932. 236 pp.

FINE, NATHAN. *Labor and Farmer Parties in the United States, 1828–1928*. New York: Rand School of Social Science, 1928. 445 pp.

HAYNES, FREDERICK EMORY. *Third Party Movements since the Civil War, with Special Reference to Iowa: A Study in Social Politics*. Iowa City: State Historical Society of Iowa, 1916. 564 pp. Out of print.

HICKS, JOHN DONALD. *The Populist Revolt: A History of the Farmers' Alliance and the Peoples' Party*. Minneapolis: University of Minnesota, 1931. 473 pp.
Bibliography, pp. 445–64.

LAIDLER, HARRY WELLINGTON. *Socialism in Thought and Action*. New York: Macmillan, 1920. 546 pp.

LEAGUE FOR INDEPENDENT POLITICAL ACTION. Publishes pamphlets concerning its program and activities.

LEWIS, PAUL G. *A Short Treatise on Propaganda and Objections to the Socialist Party from a Technical Standpoint*. Milwaukee: Pabst Publishing Company, 1921. 35 pp.

MARTIN, ROSCOE COLEMAN. *The People's Party in Texas: A Study in Third Party Politics*. Austin: University of Texas, 1933. 280 pp.
Bibliography, pp. 269–74.

RUSSELL, CHARLES EDWARD. *The Story of the Non-Partisan League*. New York and London: Harpers, 1920. 332 pp.

D. POLITICAL PARTIES IN FOREIGN COUNTRIES

For communism throughout the world, see Part III, Section A, Subdivision 1; for communism in particular countries, see Part III, Section B, Subdivision 7.

"Action française," *Encyclopedia of the Social Sciences*. (By Carlton J. H. Hayes.)

ARMSTRONG, HAMILTON FISH. *Hitler's Reich: The First Phase.* New York: Macmillan, 1933. 73 pp.
Suggests that Germans are suffering from collective mental aberrations.

ARNESON, B. A. "Norway Moves toward the Right," *American Political Science Review,* 25: 152–57 (1931).

BACHEM, KARL. *Vorgeschichte, Geschichte, und Politik der deutschen Zentrumspartei, 1815–1914.* Cologne: J. P. Bachem, 1927–32. 9 vols.
Standard history of the German Center Party.

BEARD, CHARLES AUSTIN, and RADIN, GEORGE. *The Balkan Pivot: Yugoslavia.* New York: Macmillan, 1929. 325 pp.

BENOIST, CHARLES. *Les Lois de la politique française.* Paris: Fayard, 1928. 320 pp.
A well-known French historian attempts to determine the underlying principles that condition the conduct of French policies.

BERGSTRÄSSER, LUDWIG. *Geschichte der politischen Parteien in Deutschland.* Sixth edition. Mannheim: J. Bensheimer, 1932. 226 pp.
Bibliographic footnotes.

BISSON, T. A. "Ten Years of Kuomintang: Revolution vs. Reaction," *Foreign Policy Reports,* vol. 8, no. 25 (February 15, 1933).

BLAKENEY, R. B. D. "British Fascism," *Nineteenth Century,* 97: 132–41 (January, 1925).

BLAND, J. O. P. "Kuomintang Propaganda," *English Review,* 49: 582–90 (November, 1929).

BOURGIN, GEORGES, CARRÈRE, JEAN, and GUÉRIN, ANDRÉ. *Manuel des partis politiques en France.* Paris: Rieder, 1928. 304 pp.
A standard guide.

BRITISH LABOUR PARTY. Publishes annual reports of conferences.

BUXTON, CHARLES RODEN. *Electioneering Up-to-Date, with Some Suggestions for Amending the Corrupt Practices Act.* London: F. Griffiths, 1906. 90 pp.

CALLCOTT, WILFRID HARDY. *Liberalism in Mexico, 1857–1909.* Stanford University, California: Stanford University, 1931. London: Oxford University, 1931. 410 pp.
Bibliography, pp. 384–401.

CAMBRAY, PHILIP GEORGE. *The Game of Politics: A Study of the Principles of British Political Strategy.* London: John Murray, 1932. 194 pp.
Analysis of political propaganda by a member of the central office of the Conservative party.

CAPEK, EMANUEL. "The Background of Political Parties in Czechoslovakia," *Slavonic Review*, 10: 90–104 (1931).

CHAPMAN, CHARLES EDWARD. *History of the Cuban Republic*. New York: Macmillan, 1927. 685 pp.
Bibliography, pp. 657–75.

CHMELAŘ, JOSEF. *Political Parties in Czechoslovakia*. Prague: "Orbis," 1926. 102 pp.

CHRISTENSEN, JÖRGEN V. *Det radicale Venstre, 1905-1930*. Copenhagen, 1930.
The "Radical Left" in Denmark.

———. *Venstres Historie i Korteste Traek*. Second edition. Ringsted, Denmark, 1924.
"Brief History of the Left" in Denmark.

CLARKSON, JESSE DUNSMORE. *Labour and Nationalism in Ireland* (Columbia University Studies in History, Economics, and Public Law, no. 266). New York: Columbia University, 1925. 502 pp.
Bibliography, pp. 479–91.

COLEGROVE, K. W. "Labor Parties in Japan," *American Political Science Review*, 23: 329–63 (1929).

CONDLIFFE, JOHN BELL. *New Zealand in the Making*. London: Allen and Unwin, 1930. 524 pp.
See especially chapters 5 and 6. Bibliography, pp. 477–513.

———. "Political Parties and State Experiments, 1876–1921," *Cambridge History of the British Empire*, vol. 7, pt. 2, chap. 9.
Political parties in New Zealand.

CRANE, JOHN OLIVER. *The Little Entente*. New York: Macmillan, 1931. 222 pp.
Contains material on the political parties of the Succession States. Bibliography, pp. 214–15.

CUNOW, HEINRICH. *Die Parteien der grossen französischen Revolution und ihre Presse*. Second edition. Berlin, 1912.

DARRAS, M. "Les Partis en Tschécoslovaquie," *Monde slave*, 2: 294–308 (1925).

DEAKIN, FRANK B. *Spain Today*. New York: Knopf, 1924. 221 pp.

DJIRAS, A. C. *L'Organisation politique de la Grèce d'après la constitution républicaine* (thesis, Paris). Paris, 1927. 176 pp.
Bibliography, pp. 167–69.

EBERLEIN, GUSTAV WILHELM. *Der Faschismus als Bewegung*. Berlin: Scherl, 1929. 141 pp.

A scholarly monograph on the background of Fascism, its organization and leadership.

ESTOURNELLES DE CONSTANT, PAUL HENRI BENJAMIN, BARON D'. *L'Organisation de l'Union interparlementaire*. Paris: Delagrave, 1910. 52 pp.

FINER, HERMAN. *Representative Government and a Parliament of Industry, or a Study of the German Federal Economic Council*. London: Allen and Unwin, 1923. 273 pp.

Bibliographic footnotes.

―――. *The Theory and Practice of Modern Government*. New York: Dial Press, 1932. 2 vols.

Comparative survey of governments of England, France, Germany, and the United States. A revised edition in one volume appeared in 1934.

FLEINER, F. *Tradition, Dogma, Entwicklung als aufbauende Kräfte der schweizerischen Demokratie*. Zurich: Füssli, 1933(?). 31 pp.

Deals with presuppositions of political life in Switzerland.

FOURNOL, ÉTIENNE. *Manuel de politique française*. Paris, 1933.

FRANK, WALTER. *Hofprediger Adolf Stöcker und die Christlich-Soziale Bewegung*. Berlin: R. Hobbing, 1928. 450 pp.

GEYER, KURT. *Führer und Masse in der Demokratie*. Berlin.

GOSNELL, HAROLD FOOTE. *Why Europe Votes*. Chicago: University of Chicago, 1930. 247 pp.

Bibliographic footnotes.

GRAHAM, MALBONE W. *New Governments of Eastern Europe*. New York: Holt, 1927. 683 pp.

The governments of Germany, Hungary, Austria, and the Succession States.

GRAY, FRANK. *Confessions of a Candidate*. London: Hopkinson, 1925. 174 pp.

A Junior Liberal Whip writes candidly on British elections of 1923–24.

GRUENING, ERNEST HENRY. *Mexico and Its Heritage*. New York: Century, 1928. 728 pp.

Contains material on Mexican political parties. Bibliography, pp. 667–92.

GURIAN, WALDEMAR. "Zur Soziologie der Wahlpropaganda," *Archiv für Politik und Geschichte*, III, vol. 6, pp. 585–89 (June, 1925).

HAIDER, CARMEN. *Do We Want Fascism?* New York: John Day, 1934. 276 pp.
A comparative study of German and Italian Fascism. Bibliography, pp. 275–76.

HARING, C. H. "Chilean Politics, 1920–1928," *Hispanic American Historical Review*, 11: 1–26 (1931).

HEINBERG, JOHN G. "The Personnel of French Cabinets, 1871–1930," *American Political Science Review*, 25: 389–96 (May, 1931).
Emphasizes the fact that Cabinet changes merely rotate offices among members of the parliamentary élite.

HELFRITZ, HANS. *Staatskunst und Parteipolitik: Eine Skizze.* Berlin, 1923. 48 pp.

HEUSS, THEODOR. *Hitlers Weg.* Stuttgart: Union Deutsche Verlags-Gesellschaft, 1932. 167 pp.
An inquiry into the historical and political significance of the National Socialist movement.

HOFFMAN, FRIEDRICH. "Erscheinungen der Parteienideologie," *Kölner Vierteljahrshefte für Soziologie*, Band 5, Heften 1 und 2, pp. 62–72.
Phenomena of party ideology.

HOFFMANN, A. C. A., and others. *Onze politieke Partijen.* Second edition. Baarn, 1918.
Political parties in the Netherlands.

HOOVER, CALVIN B. *Germany Enters the Third Reich.* New York: Macmillan, 1933. 243 pp.
Suggests with much more emphasis than other commentators that German National Socialism approximates socialization.

IVANOVICH, ST. *V. K. P. Desiat' Let Kommunisticheskoi Monopolii.* Paris: Société d'éditions franco-slaves, 1928. 256 pp.
A critical history of the Communist party in the ten years after its victory.

JANSON, F. E. "Minority Governments in Sweden," *American Political Science Review*, 22: 407–13 (1928).

JOUVENEL, ROBERT DE. *La République des camarades.* Paris: Grasset, 1914. 270 pp.
Ironic characterizations of politics under the Third Republic.

KNAPLUND, P. "Norwegian Elections of 1927 and the Labor Government," *American Political Science Review*, 22: 413–16 (1928).

KOELLREUTTER, OTTO. *Die politischen Parteien im modernen Staate.* Breslau: F. Hirt, 1926. 96 pp.
Bibliography, p. 93.

"Kuomintang," *Encyclopedia of the Social Sciences.* (By M. Searle Bates and Frank Wilson Price.)

LAGARDELLE, HUBERT. "Die syndicalistische Bewegung in Frankreich," *Archiv für Sozialwissenschaft und Sozialpolitik,* 26:96–143, 606–48 (1908).

LASSWELL, HAROLD DWIGHT. "The Psychology of Hitlerism," *Political Quarterly,* 4:373–84 (July–September, 1933).

LAURENT, RAYMOND, and PRELOT, M. *L'Échiquier politique.* Paris, 1928.

————. *Manuel politique.* New edition. Paris, 1928.

LEWINSOHN, RICHARD. *Das Geld in der Politik.* Berlin, 1931. 367 pp.
Contains materials relating to the financial activities of parties and groups in politics. Also appeared as *L'Argent dans la politique.* Paris: Gallimard, 1931.

LIPINSKI, RICHARD. *Die Sozialdemokratie von ihren Anfängen bis zur Gegenwart.* Berlin, 1927. 2 vols.

LOEWENSTEIN, K. "Zur Soziologie der parliamentarischen Repräsentation in England vor der ersten Reformbill," *Archiv für Sozialwissenschaft und Sozialpolitik,* 51:614–708 (1923–24).
Contribution to the analysis of the social composition of the British Parliament.

LYNN, J. C. H. *Political Parties in China.* Peiping, 1930.

MACMAHON, ARTHUR W. "The British General Election of 1931," *American Political Science Review,* 26:333–45 (April, 1932).

MADDOX, WILLIAM P. *Foreign Relations in British Labour Politics: A Study of the Formation of Party Attitudes on Foreign Affairs, and the Application of Political Pressure Designed to Influence Government Policy, 1900–1924.* Cambridge, Massachusetts: Harvard University, 1934. 253 pp.
Chapter 6 is devoted to Labour propaganda and pressure activities. Bibliography, pp. 242–48.

MAGNUSSON, GERHARD. *Socialdemokratien i Sverige.* Stockholm: P. A. Norstedt, 1920–24. 3 vols.
Social Democratic movement in Sweden.

MALONE, A. E. "Party Government in the Irish Free State," *Political Science Quarterly,* 44:363–78 (1929).

MARTIN, R. *Idee und Partei: Eine Untersuchung ihrer Wechselwirkung im Sozialismus.* Vienna, 1926. 23 pp.

MARTOV, J. *Geschichte der russichen Sozialdemokratie. Mit Nachtrag von Th. Dan: Die Sozialdemokratie Russlands nach dem Jahre 1908.* Berlin: Dietz, 1926. 340 pp.

MEHRING, FRANZ. *Geschichte der deutschen Sozialdemokratie.* Twelfth edition. Stuttgart: J. H. W. Dietz, 1922. 4 vols.

MERTL, JAN. "Das politische Parteiwesen in der Tschechoslowakei," *Zeitschrift für Politik,* 20: 502–19 (1930).

MICHELS, ROBERTO. *Sozialismus und Fascismus als politische Strömungen in Italien: Historische Studien.* Munich: Meyer und Jessen, 1925. 323 pp.

————. *Zur Soziologie des Parteiwesens in der modernen Demokratie: Untersuchungen über die oligarchischen Tendenzen des Gruppenlebens.* Second edition. Leipzig: A. Kroner, 1925. 528 pp.
Influential analysis of oligarchical tendencies of political parties.

MIDDLETON, W. L. *The French Political System.* New York: Dutton, 1933. London: Benn, 1932. 296 pp.

MOON, PARKER THOMAS. *The Labor Problem and the Social Catholic Movement in France.* New York: Macmillan, 1921. 473 pp.

MORGAN, W. T. "The British Political Debacle in 1931: A Study of Public Opinion," *Southwestern Social Science Quarterly,* September, 1932.

MOSS, WARNER. *Political Parties in the Irish Free State.* New York: Columbia University, 1933. London: P. S. King, 1933. 233 pp.
Emphasizes the plight of the younger generation. Bibliographic footnotes.

NAUMANN, FRIEDRICH. *Die politischen Parteien.* Berlin: Buchverlag der "Hilfe," 1910. 107 pp.
Political parties in Germany.

NORDICUS (pseudonym). *Hitlerism, the Iron Fist in Germany.* New York: Mohawk Press, 1932. 243 pp.
A well-informed, fairly sober analysis of the Nazi movement.

OLIVEIRA VIANNA, F. J. "O problema dos partidos," in the author's *Problemas de politica objectiva,* pp. 103–45. São Paulo: Companhia editora nacional, 1930.
Political parties of Brazil.

ORIONE, F. "Los partidos políticas en teoría y en la práctica Argentina," *Revista Argentina de ciencias políticas,* 8: 70–88 (1914).

OSTROGORSKI, MOISEI YAKOVLEVITCH. *Democracy and the Organization of Political Parties,* translated from the French by F. Clarke. New York: Macmillan, 1902. 2 vols.

Partei und Klasse im Lebensprozess der Gesellschaft (Forschungen zur Völkerpsychologie und Soziologie, edited by Dr. Richard Thurnwald, Band 3). Leipzig, 1926. 119 pp.
Bibliographic footnotes.

PECCHIO, GIUSEPPE. *Un 'elezio di membri del parlamento en Inghliterra.* Lugano: Vanelli, 1826.
Comments on public opinion.

PERNOT, M. "La Politique et les partis en Hongrie," *Europe nouvelle,* 16: 675–77 (1933).

"Political Parties [of Esthonia]," *Estland* [Esthonian Yearbook], edited by Albert Pullerits, pp. 31–35. Tallinn: M. Minis, 1929.

"Political Parties in Poland," *Polish Handbook,* edited by Francis Bauer Czarnomski, pp. 34–42. London: Eyre and Spottiswoode, 1925.

POLLOCK, JAMES KERR. *Money and Politics Abroad.* New York: Knopf, 1932. 328 pp.
Campaign expenditures and their regulation by law in England, Ireland, Germany, and France.

POMBA, GIUSEPPE LUIGI, editor. *La civiltà Fascista illustrata nella dottrina e nelle opere.* Turin: Torinese, 1928. 685 pp.
This book consists of numerous authoritative articles surveying all aspects of Fascist thought and activity. Among the contributions may be mentioned those by Volpi on the historical development of the movement, by Morello on the dissolution of the old régime, by Gorgolini on the March on Rome, by Gentile on the essence of Fascism, by Cian on the precursors of Fascism, by Torre on the new spirit of Italian foreign policy, by Rollini on the colonial policy, by Alberti on finances. There are other essays on religion, art, legislation, agriculture, industry, the cooperatives, syndicalism, the labor code, etc. Contains a bibliographic essay, pp. 651–85.

QUIGLEY, HAROLD SCOTT. *Japanese Government and Politics.* New York and London: Century, 1932. 442 pp.
Bibliographic footnotes; references at ends of chapters.

REED, THOMAS HARRISON. *Government and Politics of Belgium.* Yonkers-on-Hudson: World Book Company, 1924. 197 pp.

REH, H. "Die belgische Volkschule im Parteikempf," *Pädagogisches Magazin,* 1919, no. 730.

REID, E. M. "The Rise of National Parties in Canada," Papers and Proceedings of the Canadian Political Science Association, 4: 187–200 (1932).

RÖNBROM, HANS-KRISTER. *Frisinnade landsföreningen 1902–1927.* Stockholm: Sapon og Lindström, 1929. 399 pp.
National Liberal Union of Sweden.

ROSENBAUM, L. *Beruf und Herkunft der Abgeordneten in den deutschen und preussischen Parlamenten, 1847–1919.* Frankfort, 1923.
Occupation and origin of deputies in the German and Prussian parliaments.

ROTH, PAUL. *Die Programme der politischen Parteien und die politische Tagespresse in Deutschland.* Halle, 1913.

ROUCEK, JOSEPH SLABEY. *Contemporary Roumania and Her Problems: A Study in Modern Nationalism.* Stanford University, California: Stanford University, 1932. London: Oxford University, 1932. 422 pp. Bibliography, pp. 383–411.

SALOMON, FELIX, editor. *Die deutschen Parteiprogramme.* New edition, revised by W. Mommsen and G. Franz. Leipzig, 1931–32. 3 vols.
Covers the literature of the German parties since 1844.

SALTS, A. *Die politischen Parteien Lettlands.* Riga, Latvia, 1926.

SALVEMINI, GAETANO. *Il partito populare e la questione romana.* Florence, 1922.

SCHENKER, ERNST. *Die sozialdemokratische Bewegung in der Schweiz von ihren Anfängen bis zur Gegenwart.* Appenzell, 1926. 224 pp. Bibliography, pp. 217–21.

SCHMIDT, RICHARD, and GRABOWSKY, ADOLF, editors. "Die Parteien: Urkunden und Bibliographie der Parteienkunde," *Zeitschrift für Politik, Beihefte,* Band 1, pts. 1–3 (1912–13).
Sources and bibliography for the study of German parties.

SCHNEIDER, HERBERT WALLACE. *Making the Fascist State.* New York: Oxford University, 1928. 403 pp.
In describing the Fascist state the author is careful to stress the lack of a concise program and to bring out the various viewpoints within the movement. Extensive appendices and bibliography.

SCHNEIDEWIN, MAX. "Wahlagitation im alten Rom," *Preussische Jahrbücher,* 130:259 ff. (1907).

SCHOVELIN, JULIUS. "Blade af Höjres Historie," *Det nye Denmark,* vol. 4, no. 10 (1931).
Pages from the history of the Danish parties of the "right."

SCHUMAN, FREDERICK LEWIS. "The Political Theory of German Fascism," *American Political Science Review,* 28:210–33 (April, 1934).

SEIPEL, I. "Christlichsoziale Partei in Österreich," in Hermann Sacher, editor, *Staatslexikon*, fifth edition, cols. 1270–73. Freiburg im Breisgau, 1926.

SERTOLI, M. "I partiti politici in Bulgaria," *Nuova Antologia*, 276:522–27 (1931).

SIEGFRIED, ANDRÉ. *Tableau des partis en France*. Paris: Grasset, 1930. 245 pp.

————. *Tableau politique de la France de l'ouest sous la troisième république*. Paris: Colin, 1913. 536 pp.

Exhaustive analysis of politics of western France.

SIGHELE, SCIPIO. *Contra il Parlamentarismo: Saggio di Psicologia Collettiva*. Milan, 1895.

See also the author's *Il Nazionalismo e i Partiti Politici*. Milan: Fratelli Treves, 1911. 259 pp.

SMOGORZEWSKI, CASIMIR. *Le Jeu complexe des partis en Pologne*. Paris: Gebethner et Wolff, 1928. 40 pp.

A convenient handbook.

SOKOLSKY, GEORGE E. "The Kuomintang," China Yearbook, 1928, chap. 28; 1929–30, chap. 26.

SOLTAU, ROGER HENRY. *French Parties and Politics, 1871–1930*. New York: Oxford University, 1930. 90 pp.

This is the latest edition of a well-known survey, now brought up to date.

SOUYUN, TCHÉOU. *L'Évolution de l'opinion publique depuis la révolution de 1911 et l'organisation des partis politiques actuels en Chine*. Nancy: De Granville, 1933. 192 pp.

SPAHN, MARTIN. *Das deutsche Zentrum (Kultur und Katholizismus, Band 5)*. Mayence: Kirchheim, 1907. 117 pp.

Bibliography, pp. 115–16.

SPENCER, HENRY RUSSELL. *Government and Politics of Italy*. Yonkers-on-Hudson: World Book Company, 1932. 307 pp.

STEVENS, DAVID HARRISON. *Party Politics and English Journalism, 1702–1742* (Ph. D. thesis, Chicago, 1914). Chicago: University of Chicago, 1916. 156 pp.

Bibliography, pp. 135–45.

STONE, SHEPARD. "Hitler's Showmen Weave a Magic Spell," *New York Times Magazine*, December 3, 1933.

STRICKER, F., editor. *Die politischen Parteien der Staaten des Erdballs*. Münster, 1923–24. 11 vols.

STUART, G. H. *The Governmental System of Peru.* Carnegie Institution Publication no. 370. Washington, D. C., 1925.
Chapter 8 is on parties.

STYRA, ROBERT. *Das polnische Parteiwesen und seine Presse.* Plauen: Verlag junges Volk, 1926. 169 pp.
A survey of Polish party alignment and the political affiliations of the press.

SULTAN, HERBERT. *Die Entwicklungsgeschichte der grossen politischen Parteien in Deutschland* (Schriften der Deutschen Gesellschaft für Politik an der Universität Halle). Bonn, 1922.

———. "Zur Soziologie des modernen Parteisystems," *Archiv für Sozialwissenschaft,* 55:91 ff. (1926).

SULZBACH, WALTER. *Die Grundlagen der politischen Parteibildung.* Tübingen: Mohr, 1921. 181 pp.
Sociological analysis of political parties.

SZIRTES, A. *Gazdasagpolitiken partok bejlödese.* Budapest, 1917.

THÖRNBERG, ERNST HERMAN. *Samhällsklasser och politiska partier i Sverige.* Stockholm: P. A. Norstedt, 1917. 170 pp.
Social classes and political parties in Sweden. Contains bibliographic footnotes.

TSCHACHOTIN, SERGEI. "Lehren der Wahlkämpfe," *Deutsche Republik,* 6:1131–36 (June 4, 1932).
Problems of Socialist propaganda.

———. "Die positive Seite unserer Niederlage," *Deutsche Republik,* 6:1093–97 (May 28, 1932).
Problems of Socialist propaganda.

UNDERHILL, F. H. "The Party System in Canada," Papers and Proceedings of the Canadian Political Science Association, 4:201–12 (1932).

VAN CALKER, FRITZ. *Wesen und Sinn der politischen Parteien.* Tübingen, 1928. 36 pp.

VANDERVELDE, ÉMILE. *Le Parti ouvrier belge.* Brussels: Maison nationale d'édition l'Églantine, 1925. 503 pp.

VÉRAN, JULES. *Comment on devient: Député, Sénateur, Ministre.* Paris: Bossard, 1924. 131 pp.
The technique of getting ahead in French politics.

WACHSMUTH, W. *Geschichte der politischen Parteiungen alter und neuer Zeit.* Brunswick, 1853–76.
Band 1, *Alterthum,* 1853. Band 2, *Mittelalter,* 1854. Band 3, Abtheilung

1, *Neuzeit, bis zur Mitte des 17 Jahrhundert,* 1856; Abtheilung 2, *Neuzeit, bis auf unsere Zeit,* 1876.

WAWRZINEK, KURT. *Die Entstehung der deutschen Antisemitenparteien, 1873–1890.* Berlin, 1927.
The rise of the German anti-Semitic parties.

WEBSTER, NESTA H. *The Socialist Network.* London: Boswell, 1926. 165 pp.
A survey of the Socialist organization in the various countries of Europe and in the United States.

WEILL, GEORGES. *Histoire du parti républicain en France, 1814–1870.* Paris: Alcan, 1900. 552 pp. Reprinted, 1928. 431 pp.
Bibliography, pp. 531–34 in the original edition; pp. 408–13 in the reprint.

————. "Die Sozialistische Partei (Parti Socialiste) in Frankreich, 1920–1928," *Archiv für die Geschichte des Sozialismus und der Arbeiterbewegung,* 14:67–87 (1929).

WOO, THOMAS TZE CHUNG. *The Kuomintang and the Future of the Chinese Revolution.* London: Allen and Unwin, 1928. 275 pp.

ZÉVAÈS, ALEXANDRE B. *Le Parti socialiste de 1904 à 1923.* Paris: Rivière, 1923.

ZINOVIEV, GRIGORII. *Geschichte der kommunistischen Partei Russlands (Bolschewiki): Abriss in 6 Vorträgen.* Hamburg: Verlag der kommunistischen Internationale, 1923. 230 pp.

ZURLINDEN, S. "Politische Parteien," in Naum Reichesberg, editor, *Handwörterbuch der schweizerischen Volkswirtschaft, Sozialpolitik, und Verwaltung,* Band 3, 1 Hälfte, pp. 254–94. Berne: Verlag Encyklopädie, 1903–11.

E. PROFESSIONAL GROUPS: AUTHORS, ENGINEERS, LAWYERS, PHYSICIANS, TEACHERS, AND OTHERS

ALEXANDER, CARTER. *Some Present Aspects of the Work of Teachers' Voluntary Associations in the United States* (Teachers College Contributions to Education, no. 36). New York: Columbia University, 1910. 109 pp.
Bibliography, pp. 101–03.

AUTHORS' LEAGUE OF AMERICA, INC. Publishes an annual pamphlet describing its activities. Promotes legislation on copyrights, plagiarism, censorship, corrupt publishers, etc.

CHASE, A. M. "The Author and Publicity," *Bookman,* 35: 161–63 (April, 1912).

CLINE, D. C. "Public Service Employees in Politics," *Social Forces,* 5: 127–32 (September, 1926).

COUNCIL ON LEGAL EDUCATION AND ADMISSIONS TO THE BAR [OF THE AMERICAN BAR ASSOCIATION], editors. *The Lawyer and the Public.* Chicago: University of Chicago, 1933. 180 pp.
Reprints of fifteen radio lectures given under the auspices of the National Advisory Council on Radio in Education.

EATON, W. P. "Footlight Fiction," *American Magazine,* 65: 164–73 (December, 1907).

HURST, EDWARD. *The Technical Man Sells His Services.* New York: McGraw-Hill, 1933. 239 pp.
How college-trained technicians may apply scientific methods to the problem of getting a job.

KANE, P. "Toot Your Horn," *Musician,* 31: 11 (January, 1926).
Advertising a musician.

LEAGUE OF WESTERN WRITERS. Annual meetings reported in the *Overland Monthly* (now the *Overland Monthly and Out West Magazine*).

————. "Constitution and By-Laws," *Overland Monthly,* N. S., 86: 328 (September, 1928).

"Making the Music Teacher's Advertising Pay," *Étude,* 50: 461–62 (July, 1932).

MARTIN, EDWARD M. "The Rôle of the Chicago Bar Association in Judicial Elections" (thesis in preparation, University of Chicago).

MEADE, CHARLES W. "Victory of Publicity," *Bookman,* 26: 95–98 (September, 1907).

MILLARD, B. "Authors and Publicity," *Bookman,* 34: 394–99 (December, 1911).

"New Ideas in Advertising," *Musician,* 22: 575 (August, 1917).
For musicians.

ORNSTEIN, MARTHA. *The Rôle of the Scientific Societies in the 17th Century.* Chicago: University of Chicago, 1928. 308 pp.
First published as a Ph. D. thesis, Columbia University, 1913. Bibliography, pp. 271–83.

Publicity Methods for Engineers. Chicago: American Association of Engineers, 1922. 187 pp.
Advocates the publicity man.

RUTHERFORD, LOUISE N. At the University of Pennsylvania. Now writing on activities of the American Bar Association.

SELLE, ERWIN S. *The Organization and Activities of the National*

Educational Association: A Case Study in Educational Sociology.
New York: Teachers College, Columbia University, 1932. 180 pp.

SHRYOCK, RICHARD H. "Public Relations of the Medical Profession in Great Britain and the United States, 1600–1870: A Chapter in the Social History of Medicine," *Annals of Medical History,* N. S., 2: 308–39.

THOMPSON, DONNA FAY. *Professional Solidarity among the Teachers of England* (Ph. D. thesis. Columbia University Studies in History, Economics, and Public Law, no. 288). New York: Columbia University, 1927. London: P. S. King, 1927. 338 pp.
Bibliography, pp. 333–34.

"Why You Should Advertise," *Musician,* 24: 10 (August, 1919).
Advertising a musician.

WINTERS, FRITZ. *Der deutscher Beamten-Bund: Seine Entstehung und Entwicklung.* 1931.
A survey of the historical development of the German civil servants' federation by one of its leading officials.

F. LABOR GROUPS

For revolutionary propaganda in the name of labor, see Part III, Section A, Subdivision 1, and Section B, Subdivision 7.

ADLER, GEORG. *Die Geschichte der ersten sozial-politischen Arbeiterbewegung in Deutschland, mit besonderer Rücksicht auf die einwirkenden Theorien.* Breslau: E. Trewendt, 1885. 333 pp.
Bibliography, pp. i–x.

"American Federation of Labor," *Encyclopedia of the Social Sciences.* (By John R. Commons.)

AMERICAN FEDERATION OF LABOR. *History, Encyclopedia, and Reference Book.* Washington, D. C., 1919–24. 2 vols.
Published by authority of the 1916 and 1917 conventions.

BARDOUX, JACQUES. *L'Ouvrier anglais d'aujourdhui* (Publié par la Société d'études et d'informations économiques). Paris: Hachette, 1921. 277 pp.

BECKNER, E. R. "The Trade-Union Educational League and the American Labor Movement," *Journal of Political Economy,* 33: 410–31 (August, 1925).

BUELL, RAYMOND LESLIE. *International Relations.* Revised edition. New York: Holt, 1929. 838 pp.
Chapter 7 is a discussion of international labor organizations. See especially the section on "Treaties against Propaganda."

CARROLL, MOLLIE RAY. *Labor and Politics: The Attitude of the American Federation of Labor toward Legislation and Politics.* Boston and New York: Houghton Mifflin, 1923. 206 pp.
Selected bibliography, pp. 199–201.

CASSAU, THEODOR. *Die Gewerkschaftsbewegung.* Halberstadt: H. Meyer, 1925. 355 pp.
By an experienced technical advisor of trade unions. Bibliography, pp. 347–50.

CHILDS, HARWOOD LAWRENCE. *Labor and Capital in National Politics* (Ph. D. thesis, University of Chicago). Columbus: Ohio State University, 1930. 286 pp.
A systematic comparison of the American Federation of Labor and the American Chamber of Commerce. Bibliography, pp. 271–79.

CUROE, PHILIP R. V. *Educational Attitudes and Policies of Organized Labor in the United States* (Teachers College Contributions to Education, no. 201). New York: Columbia University, 1926. 202 pp.

Der deutschnationale Handlungsgehilfen-Verband: Geschichte und Wirken (Publications of Division 17 of the Deutschnationale Handlungsgehilfen-Verband, no. 101 b). Berlin, 1930 (?). 35 pp.
Study of an association of clerical workers.

DOW, RICHARD SYLVESTER. *What Are the Demands of the Reform Agitator?* Cambridge, Massachusetts: Riverside Press, 1912. 83 pp.
Social problems of the Lawrence strike.

EDWARDS, CORWIN D. *The First International Workingmen's Association* (Abstract of a Ph. D. thesis). Ithaca, New York: Cornell University. 6 pp.

FAY, CHARLES NORMAN. *Labor in Politics, or Class versus Country.* Privately printed at Cambridge, Massachusetts, 1920. 284 pp.
Written from the point of view of a reactionary, in contrast with the socialistic volume of the same title by Robert Hunter.

FOSTER, WILLIAM ZEBULON. *The Great Steel Strike and Its Lessons.* New York: Huebsch, 1920. 265 pp.

———. *Misleaders of Labor.* Chicago: Trades Unions Educational League, 1927. 336 pp.
On "tainted labor journalism."

GOODRICH, CARTER. "The Australian and American Labor Movements," *Economic Record,* 4: 193–208 (1928).

"Guild Socialism," *Encyclopedia of the Social Sciences.* (By G. D. H. Cole.)

GUILLAUME, JAMES. *L'Internationale, documents et souvenirs, 1864–1878*. Paris: Société nouvelle de librairie et d'édition, 1905–1910. 4 vols.

HANSOME, MARIUS. *World Workers' Educational Movements: Their Social Significance* (Ph. D. thesis. Columbia University Studies in History, Economics, and Public Law, no. 338). New York: Columbia University, 1931. London: P. S. King, 1931. 594 pp.
Bibliography, pp. 562–65, 579–80.

HARDMAN, JACOB B. S., editor. *American Labor Dynamics in the Light of Post-War Developments: An Inquiry by Thirty-two Labor Men, Teachers, Editors, and Technicians*. New York: Harcourt, Brace, 1928. 432 pp.

HELD, ADOLF. *Die deutsche Arbeiterpresse der Gegenwart*. Leipzig: Duncker und Humblot, 1873. 196 pp.
The workers' press in Germany.

HUNTER, ROBERT. *Labor in Politics*. Chicago: Socialist Party of America, 1915. 202 pp.
Written from the point of view of a Socialist, in contrast with the more reactionary volume of the same title by Charles Norman Fay.

"Industrial Relations," *Encyclopedia of the Social Sciences*. (By Leo Wolman.)

"Industrial Workers of the World," *Encyclopedia of the Social Sciences*. (By Paul F. Brissenden.)

The International Labor Organization: The First Decade. Boston: World Peace Foundation, 1931. 382 pp.
By the staff of the office in Geneva.

Internationales Handwörterbuch des Gewerkschaftswesens, 1930.
Encyclopedia of trade unionism. Thus far volumes A–O have appeared; they contain a number of valuable articles dealing with different labor and employer groups.

KATAYAMA, SEN. *The Labor Movement in Japan*. Chicago: C. H. Kerr, 1918. 147 pp.
By the founder of the Japanese Communist movement.

KIRK, WILLIAM. *National Labor Federations in the United States* (Johns Hopkins University Studies in Historical and Political Science, Series 24, nos. 9–10). Baltimore: Johns Hopkins University, 1906. 150 pp.

"Knights of Labor," *Encyclopedia of the Social Sciences*. (By Mary R. Beard.)

"Labor Movement," *Encyclopedia of the Social Sciences.* (By John R. Commons.)

"Labor Parties," *Encyclopedia of the Social Sciences.* (By J. B. S. Hardman.)

LORWIN, LEWIS L., and FLEXNER, JEAN ATHERTON. *The American Federation of Labor: History, Policies, and Prospects.* Washington, D. C.: Brookings Institution, 1933. 573 pp.
Bibliography, pp. 548–55.

MERRITT, WALTER GORDON. *History of the League for Industrial Rights.* New York: League for Industrial Rights, 1925. 132 pp.

NESTRIEPKE, KARL. *Die Gewerkschaftsbewegung.* Stuttgart, 1923–25. 3 vols.
The first volume traces the movement to the outbreak of the World War; the second covers the war period; the third deals primarily with other groups closely connected with the free trade-union movement.

O'LEARY, JOHN W. "Strike Facts and Principles," *Open Shop Review,* 16: 381–98 (October, 1919).
On propaganda by unions.

"Organized Labor in National Politics," *Editorial Research Reports,* August 31, 1928.

PIPKIN, C. W. "Relations of the International Labor Office with the League of Nations," *Annals of the American Academy of Political and Social Science,* 166: 124–34 (March, 1933).

PORTUS, G. V. "The Labour Movement in Australia, 1788–1914," in Meredith Atkinson, editor, *Australia: Economic and Political Studies,* chap. 4. Melbourne, 1920.

REED, LOUIS SCHULTZ. *The Labor Philosophy of Samuel Gompers* (Ph. D. thesis. Columbia University Studies in History, Economics, and Public Law, no. 327). New York: Columbia University, 1930. 191 pp.
Bibliography, pp. 185–88.

RICE, STUART ARTHUR. *Farmers and Workers in American Politics* (Ph. D. thesis. Columbia University Studies in History, Economics, and Public Law, no. 253). New York: Columbia University, 1924. 233 pp.
Farmers and workers, the author finds, can combine on utilitarian questions but not on moral questions.

ROTHSTEIN, T. *From Chartism to Labourism: Historical Sketches of the English Working Class Movement.* New York: International Publishers, 1929. 365 pp.

SALVEMINI, GAETANO. *Movimento operaio italiano. Saggi critici.* Bologna: Cappelli, 1922.

SAPOSS, DAVID J. *The Labor Movement in Post-War France* (Social and Economic Studies of Post-War France, vol. 4). New York: Columbia University, 1931. 508 pp.
Bibliography, pp. 495–502.

SCHLÜTER, HERMANN. *Die Internationale in Amerika,* translated as *The First International in America.* Chicago: Deutschen Sprachgruppe der sozialistischen Partei, 1918. 527 pp.

SEIDEL, RICHARD. *Die Gewerkschaftsbewegung in Deutschland.* Amsterdam: Internationale Gewerkschafts-Bibliothek, 1931.
A history of the trade-union movement, with special emphasis upon free trade unions. The author is intimately associated with the movement. See his *The Trade Union Movement of Germany.* Amsterdam: International Federation of Trade Unions, 1928. 157 pp.

SPERO, STERLING DENHARD. *The Labor Movement in a Government Industry: A Study of Employee Organization in the Postal Service* (Ph. D. thesis, Columbia University, 1924). New York: Doran, 1924. 320 pp.

SPERO, STERLING DENHARD, and HARRIS, ABRAM L. *The Black Worker.* New York: Columbia University, 1931. 509 pp.
Economic setting of the wage-earner's attitude toward politics.

SUTCLIFFE, J. T. *A History of Trade-Unionism in Australia.* Melbourne and London: Macmillan, 1921. 226 pp.
Bibliography, pp. 215–18.

THIEL, OTTO. *Die Sozialpolitik der deutschnationale Handlungsgehilfen-Verband: Geschichte und Wirken.*
Study of an association of clerical workers.

WALLING, WILLIAM ENGLISH. *American Labor and American Democracy.* New York and London: Harpers, 1926. 2 vols.
" Primarily an account, by a sympathetic ' insider,' of the evolution of the fundamental policies of the American Federation of Labor." — *American Journal of Sociology.*

WARE, NORMAN J. *The Labor Movement in the United States, 1860–1895.* New York and London: Appleton, 1929. 409 pp.
Bibliography, pp. 393–97.

WEBER, ADOLF. *Der Kampf zwischen Kapital und Arbeit.* Fifth edition. Tübingen: Mohr, 1930. 547 pp.
Standard treatise dealing with the history, organization, fighting methods, and social and political significance of the struggle.

Wittvogel, K. A. " Die Grundlagen der chinesischen Arbeiterbewegung," *Archiv für die Geschichte des Sozialismus und der Arbeiterbewegung,* 15:238–69 (1930).

The bases of the Chinese labor movement, by an Austrian Marxist.

G. AGRARIAN GROUPS

"Agrarian Movements," *Encyclopedia of the Social Sciences.* (By various authors.)

"Agrarian Syndicalism," *Encyclopedia of the Social Sciences.* (By Louis G. Michael.)

Agresti, Olivia Rossetti. *David Lubin: A Study in Practical Idealism.* Boston: Little, Brown, 1922. 372 pp.

An important agricultural reformer.

"Agricultural Labor," *Encyclopedia of the Social Sciences.* (By J. A. Venn.)

"Agricultural Societies," *Encyclopedia of the Social Sciences.* (By Nelson Antrim Crawford.)

"Agriculture, Government Services for," *Encyclopedia of the Social Sciences.* (By Nelson Antrim Crawford.)

Atkeson, Thomas C. *Outlines of Grange History.* Washington: The National Farm News, 1928. 61 pp.

———. *Semicentennial History of the Patrons of Husbandry.* New York: Orange, Judd, 1916. 364 pp.

Barrett, Charles Simon. *The Mission, History, and Times of the Farmers' Union: A Narrative of the Greatest Industrial-Agricultural Organization in History and Its Makers.* Nashville, Tennessee: Marshall and Bruce, 1909. 419 pp.

———. *Uncle Reuben in Washington.* Washington, D. C.: Farmers' National Publishing Company, 1923. 218 pp.

"Written by an arch-lobbyist in picturesque style."—E. P. Herring. Mr. Barrett was president of the Farmers' Educational and Cooperative Movement of America.

Die Bauerninternationale. Berlin: Neues Dorf, 1926. 186 pp.

Twenty essays published by the International Peasant Council in Moscow, setting forth the agrarian problems of Europe from the Bolshevik standpoint.

Bücher, Karl. *Die Aufstande der unfreien Arbeiter, 143–129 v. Chr.* Frankfort, 1874. 132 pp.

An " agrarian movement " of ancient Greece and Rome.

BUCK, SOLON JUSTUS. *The Agrarian Crusade: A Chronicle of the Farmer in Politics* (Chronicles of America Series, vol. 45). New Haven: Yale University, 1921. 215 pp.

————. *The Granger Movement: A Study of Agricultural Organization and Its Political, Economic, and Social Manifestations, 1870–1880.* Cambridge, Massachusetts: Harvard University, 1913. 384 pp.
Bibliography, pp. 313–51.

CAPPER, ARTHUR. *The Agricultural Bloc* (The Farmer's Bookshelf Series). New York: Harcourt, Brace, 1922. 171 pp.

CIASCA, R. *L'Origine del programma per l'opinione nazionale italiana del 1847–48.* Rome, 1916.

CLAYTON, JOSEPH. *Robert Kett and the Norfolk Rising.* London: M. Secker, 1912. 275 pp.
Kett's Rebellion, 1549.

The Condition of Agriculture in the United States and Measures for Its Improvement: A Report by the Business Men's Commission on Agriculture. Washington, D.C.: United States Chamber of Commerce, 1927. New York: National Industrial Conference Board, 1927. 273 pp.

DONOVAN, HERBERT DARIUS AUGUSTINE. *The Barnburners: A Study of the Internal Movements in the Political History of New York State and of the Resulting Changes in Political Affiliation, 1830–1852* (Ph.D. thesis, New York University, 1917). New York: New York University, 1925.
Bibliography, pp. 127–34.

DUBROVSKY, SERGEI MITROFANICH. *Krestianstvo v. 1917 gody* (Publication of Mezhdunarodny Agrarny Institut, Moscow). Berlin: P. Parey, 1929. 206 pp.
Translated into German as *Die Bauernbewegung in der russischen Revolution, 1917.*

ELIOT, CLARA. *The Farmers' Campaign for Credit* (Ph.D. thesis, Columbia University, 1926). New York and London: Appleton, 1927. 312 pp.
Bibliographic footnotes.

"Farm Bloc," *Encyclopedia of the Social Sciences.* (By E. Pendleton Herring.)

"The Farm Issue in National Politics," *Editorial Research Reports,* July 17, 1928.

"Farmers' Alliance," *Encyclopedia of the Social Sciences.* (By Edward Wiest.)

"Farmers' Organizations," *Encyclopedia of the Social Sciences.* (By Carl C. Taylor.)

"Farmers' Union," *Encyclopedia of the Social Sciences.* (By Edward Wiest.)

GARGAS, SIGISMUND. *Die grüne Internationale.* Halberstadt: H. Meyer, 1927. 55 pp.
Outlines the organization, aims, and activities of the Peasant International.

"Grange," *Encyclopedia of the Social Sciences.* (By Solon J. Buck.)

HICKS, JOHN D., and BARNHART, JOHN D. "The Farmers' Alliance,' *North Carolina Historical Review,* 6: 254–80 (1929).

International Institute of Agriculture: General Policy and Activities. Statement presented to the General Assembly (Rome, 1926), by G. de Michelis, president.

JAHAN, PAUL. *Le Mouvement syndical agricole.* Bourges: Imprimerie des orphelins du centre, 1924. 116 pp.

KELLEY, OLIVER HUDSON. *Origin and Progress of the Order of the Patrons of Husbandry in the United States.* Philadelphia: J. A. Wagenseller, 1875. 441 pp.

KILE, ORVILLE MERTON. *The Farm Bureau Movement.* New York: Macmillan, 1921. 282 pp.

PEARSON, RAYMOND A. *Agricultural Organizations in European Countries* (New York State Department of Agriculture Bulletin no. 66). Albany, 1914.

PERIAM, JONATHAN. *The Groundswell: A History of the Origin, Aims, and Progress of the Farmers' Movement.* Cincinnati: E. Hannaford, 1874. Chicago: Hannaford and Thompson, 1874. 576 pp.

PHIPPS, HELEN. "The Agrarian Phase of the Mexican Revolution of 1910–20," *Political Science Quarterly,* 39: 1–18 (1924).

———. *Some Aspects of the Agrarian Question in Mexico* (Ph. D. thesis, Columbia University, 1925; University of Texas Bulletin no. 2515). Austin: University of Texas, 1925. 157 pp.
Bibliography, pp. 149–57.

PRATT, EDWIN A. *Agricultural Organization: Its Rise, Principles, and Practice Abroad and at Home.* London: P. S. King, 1912. 259 pp.
Evolution of the Agricultural Organization Society, pp. 88–139.

Representation and Organization of Agricultural Workers (International Labour Office Studies and Reports, Series K, no. 8). Geneva, 1928.

STOLZE, WILHELM. *Bauernkrieg und Reformation.* Leipzig: Eger und Sievers, 1926. 127 pp.
The Peasants' Revolt, 1524–25.

————. *Zur Vorgeschichte des Bauernkrieges* (Staats- und sozialwissenschaftliche Forschungen, Band 18, Heft 4). Leipzig: Duncker und Humblot, 1900. 57 pp.

SZEBERÉNYI. *Massenbewegungen in den Bauernstädten des Ungarischen Niederlandes.* Budapest, 1913.

TANNENBAUM, FRANK. *The Mexican Agrarian Revolution.* New York: Published by Macmillan for the Institute of Economics of the Brookings Institution, 1930. 543 pp.
Bibliography, pp. 536–38.

TAYLOR, CARL C. "Farmers' Movements as Psychosocial Phenomena," Papers and Proceedings of the American Sociological Society, 1928, pp. 153–62.

WIEST, EDWARD. *Agricultural Organization in the United States* (University of Kentucky Studies in Economics and Sociology, vol. 2). Lexington, Kentucky: University of Kentucky, 1923. 618 pp.
Selected references at the end of each chapter.

WIETH-KNUDSEN, K. A. "Entwicklungsgeschichte des Internationalen Landwirtschaftsinstituts in Rom," *Festschrift für Lujo Brentano zum 70 Geburtstag,* pp. 439–60. Munich, 1916.

WOOD, LOUIS AUBREY. *A History of Farmers' Movements in Canada.* Toronto: Ryerson Press, 1924. 374 pp.

H. SEX AND AGE GROUPS

I. WOMEN

ABENSOUR, LÉON. *La Féminisme sous le règne de Louis-Philippe et en 1848.* Paris: Plon-Nourrit, 1913. 337 pp.

————. *La Femme et la féminisme avant la révolution.* Paris: E. Leroux, 1923. 477 pp.
Bibliography, pp. 463–74.

ADDAMS, JANE, and others. *Women at The Hague: The International Congress of Women and Its Results.* New York: Macmillan, 1916. 171 pp.

BARNETT, AVROM. *Foundations of Feminism: A Critique.* New York: McBride, 1921. 245 pp.
Bibliography, pp. 225–36.

BÄUMER, GERTRUD. *Die Frau im neuen Lebensraum*. Berlin: Herbig, 1931. 285 pp.

BENNETT, HELEN CHRISTINE. *American Women in Civic Work*. New York: Dodd, Mead, 1915. 277 pp.
Sketches of eleven leading American women. First written for the *Pictorial Review* and the *American Magazine*.

BIRNEY, CATHERINE H. *The Grimké Sisters, Sarah and Angelina: The First American Women Advocates of Abolition and Women's Rights*. Boston: Lee and Shepard, 1885. 319 pp.

BOMAR, WILLIE MELMOTH. *The Education of Homemakers for Community Activities: A Study of the Community Interests and Activities of Representative Homemakers to Discover Certain Needs for Home Economics Education* (Ph. D. thesis. Teachers College Contributions to Education, no. 477). New York: Columbia University, 1931. 135 pp.

BRECKINRIDGE, SOPHONISBA PRESTON. "The Activities of Women outside the Home," *Recent Social Trends*, 1: 709–51. New York, 1933. The author has also published a monograph in the *Recent Social Trends* series, under the title *Political, Social, and Economic Activities of Women*.

CATT, CARRIE CHAPMAN, and SHULER, NETTIE ROGERS. *Woman Suffrage and Politics: The Inner Story of the Suffrage Movement*. Second edition. New York: Scribners, 1926. 504 pp.

DELL, FLOYD. *Women as World Builders: Studies in Modern Feminism*. Chicago: Forbes, 1913. 104 pp.

FAWCETT, MILLICENT, and TURNER, E. M. *Josephine Butler: Her Work and Principles and Their Meaning for the Twentieth Century*. London: Association for Moral and Social Hygiene, 1927. 164 pp.
"Her 'repeal movement' remains a remarkable and successful example of public agitation in the field of social reform." — EDITH ABBOTT in *Encyclopedia of the Social Sciences*. A list of Mrs. Butler's books and larger pamphlets is in the Appendix.

GRINBERG, SUZANNE. *Historique du mouvement suffragiste*. Paris, 1926.

HARPER, IDA HUSTED. *History of Woman Suffrage*. New York: Woman Suffrage Publishing Company, 1919. 32 pp.

———. *The Life and Work of Susan B. Anthony*. Indianapolis and Kansas City: Bowen-Merrill, 1898–1908. 3 vols.

HARRIMAN, FLORENCE JAFFRAY (MRS. J. BORDEN). *From Pinafores to Politics*. New York: Holt, 1923. 359 pp.

IRWIN, INEZ HAYNES. *The Story of the Woman's Party.* New York: Harcourt, Brace, 1921. 486 pp.

KOLLONTAY, A. M. *Die Arbeiterin und Bäuerin in Sowjet-Russland.* Leipzig: Franke, 1921. 46 pp.
The functions of women in building socialism through administration, education, political propaganda, etc.

LANGE, HELENE. *Die Frauenbewegung in ihren modernen Problemen.* Third edition. Leipzig: Quelle und Meyer, 1924.

――――. *Lebenserinnerungen.* Berlin, 1921.
A prominent pioneer among German feminists.

LANGE, HELENE, and BÄUMER, GERTRUD. *Handbuch der Frauenbewegung.* Berlin: W. Moeser, 1901–02. 4 vols.

MOORE, MILDRED. "A History of the Women's Trade-Union League of Chicago" (unpublished thesis, University of Chicago, Department of Practical Theology, 1915). 30 pp.

NATIONAL CIVIC FEDERATION, WOMAN'S DEPARTMENT. *The Woman Power of the Nation, a Problem of Adjustment: Facts and Factors in Movements of American Women to Meet Changing Conditions in the Economic, Social, and Civic Life of the Nation.* New York, 1932. 2 vols.

NATIONAL HUGHES ALLIANCE, WOMEN'S COMMITTEE. *Women in National Politics.* New York, 1916. 38 pp.

NATIONAL LEAGUE OF WOMEN VOTERS. *Explanation of the Program of the Department of Efficiency in Government, 1932–1934.* Washington, D. C., 1932. 22 pp.

――――. *Explanation of the Program of the Department of Social Hygiene, 1932–34.* Washington, D. C., 1932. 16 pp.

OWINGS, CHLOE. *Women Police: A Study of the Development and Status of the Women Police Movement.* New York: Hitchcock, 1925. 337 pp.
Written for the International Association of Policewomen.

PANKHURST, E. SYLVIA. *The Suffragette Movement.* London: Longmans, Green, 1931. 631 pp.

PHILLIPS, MARION, editor. *Women and the Labour Party.* London: Headley, 1918. New York: Huebsch, 1918. 110 pp.
A survey by various women writers of the activities of English women as trade unionists, " brain-workers," internationalists, etc.

PUCKETT, HUGH WILEY. *Germany's Women Go Forward.* New York: Columbia University, 1930. 329 pp.
Bibliography, pp. 315–24.

ROBERTSON-SCOTT, JOHN WILLIAM. *The Story of the Women's Institute Movement in England, Wales, and Scotland.* Idbury, Kingham, England: The Village Press, 1925. 289 pp.
The Women's Institute fosters "the organization of community clubs and organizations all over England."

SHAW, ANNA HOWARD. *The Story of a Pioneer.* School edition. New York and London: Harpers, 1929. 291 pp.
Miss Shaw's autobiography.

SMEDLEY, CONSTANCE. *Crusaders: The Reminiscences of Constance Smedley.* London: Duckworth, 1929. 265 pp.
The author founded the International Lyceum Club for women.

STANTON, ELIZABETH CADY, and others. *History of Woman Suffrage.* New York: Fowler and Wells, 1881–1922. 6 vols.

STEVENS, DORIS. *Jailed for Freedom.* New York: Boni and Liveright, 1920. 388 pp.
Graphic story told by a militant participant in the woman suffrage campaign.

STRACHEY, RAY (MRS. RACHEL CONN COSTELLOE). *The Cause: A Short History of the Women's Movement in Great Britain.* London: Bell, 1928. 429 pp.
Bibliography, pp. 419–21. American edition: *Struggle: The Stirring Story of Woman's Advance in England.* New York: Duffield, 1930.

USBORNE, MRS. H. M., editor. *Women's Work in Wartime: A Handbook of Employments.* London: T. W. Laurie, 1917. 174 pp.

WARD, MAY ALDEN. "The Influence of Women's Clubs in New England and in the Middle-Eastern States," *Annals of the American Academy of Political and Social Science,* September, 1906.

WATERMAN, WILLIAM RANDALL. *Frances Wright* (Ph.D. thesis, Columbia University, 1924). New York: Columbia University, 1924. 267 pp.
An early propagandist for women's rights. Bibliography, pp. 257–64.

WEBER, GUSTAVUS W. *The Women's Bureau: Its History, Activities, and Organization.* Baltimore: Johns Hopkins University, 1923. 31 pp.
A much-condensed summary of promotional activities lying behind the organization of the bureau.

Women in Public Life (*Annals of the American Academy of Political and Social Science,* vol. 56, no. 145). 1914. 194 pp.
Essays by various authors on the feminist movement, legislative influence of women, public activities of women, etc.

WOMEN'S EDUCATIONAL AND INDUSTRIAL UNIONS. Have published many studies of women's activities with special reference to their economic status.

2. CHILDREN'S GROUPS AND YOUTH MOVEMENTS

BARCLAY, LORNE WEBSTER. *Educational Work of the Boy Scouts* (Department of the Interior, Bureau of Education, Bulletin no. 41). Washington, D. C.: Government Printing Office, 1921. 10 pp.

BRYANT, LOUISE FRANCES. *Educational Work of the Girl Scouts* (Department of the Interior, Bureau of Education, Bulletin no. 46). Washington, D. C.: Government Printing Office, 1921. 14 pp.

DOGGETT, LAURENCE LOCKE. *History of the Y. M. C. A., 1844–1861.* New York: Association Press, 1916–22.

FISCHER, ZYRILL. *Bolschewistiche Kinder- und Jugendbewegung.* Vienna: Selbstverlag, 1931. 16 pp.

The Girl Reserve Movement: A Manual for Advisers. New York: Y. W. C. A., 1921. 825 pp.
Has bibliographies.

JACKSON, GLENN E. " The Hi-Y Movement," in *Y. M. C. A. Boys' Work Executives' Manual.* New York: Y. M. C. A.

JUNIOR ORDER UNITED MECHANICS OF THE UNITED STATES OF NORTH AMERICA. *A Short History of the J. O. U. A. M.* 1931 (?). Pamphlet.

LIFSCHITZ, ANNA. " Kinderorganisationen in Sowjetrussland," *Pädagogische Rundschau,* 6: 8–14 (1929–30).

SCHÜLLER, RICHARD. *Von den Anfängen der proletarische Jugendbewegung bis zur Gründung der kommunistische Jugend-Internationale.* Berlin: Verlag der Jugend-Internationale, 1931. 224 pp.

TOBEY, JAMES ALNER. *The Children's Bureau: Its History, Activities, and Organization* (Institute for Government Research, Service Monographs of the United States Government, no. 21). Baltimore: Johns Hopkins University, 1925. 83 pp.
Refers to the promotional demands lying behind the formation of the bureau. Bibliography, pp. 72–80.

TSCHITSCHERIN, G. *Skizzen aus der Geschichte der Jugendinternationale,* translated from the Russian by Hans Ruoff. Berlin: Verlag der Jugend-Internationale, n. d. 103 pp.
The workers' youth movement in Europe to the end of the World War.

WADE, E. K. *Twenty-one Years of Scouting: The Official History of the Boy Scout Movement from Its Inception.* London: Pearson, 1929. 288 pp.

WANG, TSI C. *The Youth Movement in China* (Ph. D. thesis, University of Chicago, 1925). New York: New Republic, 1927. 245 pp.

I. ECCLESIASTICAL AND COUNTER-ECCLESIASTICAL GROUPS

I. ECCLESIASTICAL

"American Churches in National Politics," *Editorial Research Reports,* August 15, 1928.

AMERICAN SUNDAY SCHOOL UNION. Annual Reports.

ASHLEY, W. B., compiler. *Church Advertising: Its How and Why.* Philadelphia: Lippincott, 1917. 200 pp.
Addresses given before the Associated Advertising Clubs of the World.

BECKMANN, JOHANNES. *Die katholische Missionsmethode in China in neuester Zeit, 1842–1912.* Immensee: Missionshaus Bethlehem, 1931. 202 pp.

BERGSTRÄSSER, LUDWIG, compiler. *Der politische Katholizismus: Dokumente seiner Entwicklung.* Munich: Drei Masken Verlag, 1921–23. 2 vols.

BRAITHWAITE, WILLIAM CHARLES. *The Beginnings of Quakerism.* London: Macmillan, 1912. 562 pp.

"Bray, Thomas," *Encyclopedia of the Social Sciences.* (By I. L. Kaudel.)
Founder of the Society for Promoting Christian Knowledge, 1698.

BROWN, MARIANNA CATHERINE. *Sunday-School Movements in America* (Ph. D. thesis, Columbia University, 1902). New York and Chicago: Revell, 1901. 269 pp.
Bibliography, pp. 246–57.

BROWN, WILLIAM ADAMS. *The Church in America: A Study of the Present Condition and Future Prospects of American Protestantism.* New York: Macmillan, 1922. 378 pp.

BURTON, JOHN WEAR. *A Missionary Survey of the Pacific Islands.* New York: World Dominion Press, 1930. 124 pp.

CANNON, FRANK JENNE, and O'HIGGINS, H. J. *Under the Prophet in Utah: The National Menace of a Political Priestcraft.* Boston: C. M. Clark, 1911. 402 pp.

CARLSON, H. E. "Winning Ads," *Homiletic Review,* 93: 386–87 (May, 1927).

CASE, FRANCIS HIGBEE. *Handbook of Church Advertising*. New York and Cincinnati: Abingdon Press, 1921. 186 pp.

"Catholic Emancipation," *Encyclopedia of the Social Sciences*. (By Dennis Gwynn.)

"Catholic Parties," *Encyclopedia of the Social Sciences*. (By Ludwig Bergsträsser.)

"Chassidism," *Encyclopedia of the Social Sciences*. (By Koppel S. Pinson.)

"Christian Science," *Encyclopedia of the Social Sciences*. (By Herbert W. Schneider.)

"Church Lobby," *Christian Century*, 46:674–76 (May 22, 1929).

COCHET, MARIE-ANNE. *Essai sur l'emploi du sentiment réligieux comme base d'autorité politique*. Paris, 1925. 144 pp.

COLE, STEWART GRANT. *The History of Fundamentalism*. New York: R. R. Smith, 1931. 360 pp.
Bibliography, pp. 341–50.

―――. "Psychology of the Fundamentalist Movement" (unpublished Ph. D. thesis, University of Chicago, 1929). 668 pp.
Gives some account of promotional effort within the denominations.

COOKE, RICHARD JOSEPH. *The Church and World Peace*. New York: Abingdon Press, 1920. 178 pp.

DOUGLASS, HARLAN PAUL. *Protestant Cooperation in American Cities*. New York: Institute of Social and Religious Research, 1930. 514 pp.
The activities of city-church federations.

DU PLESSIS, JOHANNES. *The Evangelization of Pagan Africa*. Capetown: Juta, 1930. 408 pp.
A standard work.

ENGEL, P. ALOIS. *Die Missionsmethode der Missionäre von Heiligen Geist auf dem afrikanischen Festland* (Missionswissenschaftliche Studien, N. S., nos. 3–4). Knechtsteden: Missionsdruckerei, 1932. 296 pp.
Methods of missionaries on the African continent.

FOREIGN MISSIONS CONFERENCE OF NORTH AMERICA. *Christian Education in China: A Study Made by an Educational Commission Representing the Mission Boards and Societies Conducting Work in China*. New York, 1922. 430 pp.

"Franciscan Movement," *Encyclopedia of the Social Sciences*. (By Helen Sullivan.)
The Franciscan Order " has, in general, attracted more recruits than any

other religious order of the church; and it has remained pre-eminently the order of the poor." — HELEN SULLIVAN.

FÜLÖP-MILLER, RENÉ. *The Power and Secret of the Jesuits,* translated from the German by F. S. Flint and D. F. Tait. New York: Viking, 1930. 523 pp.
Bibliography, pp. 491–514.

"Fundamentalism," *Encyclopedia of the Social Sciences.* (By H. Richard Neibuhr.)

GARRISON, WINFRED ERNEST. *Religion Follows the Frontier: A History of the Disciples of Christ.* New York and London: Harpers, 1931. 317 pp.

GOVE, FLOYD SHERMAN. *Religious Education on Public School Time* (Harvard Bulletin on Education no. 11). Cambridge, Massachusetts: Harvard University, 1926. 143 pp.
Bibliography, pp. 133–43.

GOYAU, GEORGES. *Les Prêtres des missions étrangères.* Paris: Grasset, 1932.

GRANVILLE, GRANVILLE G. LEVESON-GOWER, EARL OF. " The Vatican and the Press," *Contemporary Review,* 94: 650–65 (December, 1908).

GULICK, SIDNEY LEWIS. *The Winning of the Far East: A Study of the Christian Movement in China, Korea, and Japan* (report to the Federal Council of Churches of Christ in America, 1923). 185 pp.

GULICK, SIDNEY LEWIS, and MACFARLAND, CHARLES STEDMAN. *The Church and International Relations.* Missionary Education Movement, 1917. 3 vols.

GUY, H. N. "Development of Relations between Religious and Labour Organizations" (dissertation in preparation at Harvard University).

Handbook of the Churches: A Survey of the Churches in Action.
Annually, 1917—. A complete encyclopedia of religious organizations in the United States, together with a summary of contemporary religious developments.

HARTSHORNE, HUGH, and LOTZ, ELSA. *Case Studies of Present-Day Religious Teaching.* New Haven: Published by the Yale University Press for the Institute of Social and Religious Research, 1932. London: Oxford, 1932. 295 pp.

HARTSHORNE, HUGH, STEARNS, HELEN R., and UPHAUS, WILLARD E. *Standards and Trends in Religious Education.* New Haven: Published by the Yale University Press for the Institute of Social and Religious Research, 1933. London: Oxford, 1933. 230 pp.
Bibliography, pp. 227–30.

HOOKER, ELIZABETH R. *United Churches.* New York: Doran, 1927. 306 pp.

A study of the development of local church unions in rural America, showing the conditions that have led to union and describing the various types of united churches found.

HORODETZSKY, SAMUEL ABA. *Hachassiduth vehachassidim,* with complete bibliography. Berlin, 1923. 4 vols. Abridged translation by Maria Horodetzsky-Magasanik under the title *Leaders of Hassidism.* London, 1928.

A movement of the Jewish Reformation, which began in the eighteenth century.

HUMPHREYS, DAVID. *An Historical Account of the Incorporated Society for the Propagation of the Gospel in Foreign Parts, to the Year 1728.* London: J. Downing, 1730. 356 pp.

"Jesuits," *Encyclopedia of the Social Sciences.* (By Walter Goetz.)

JOINT COMMITTEE ON SURVEY OF CHRISTIAN LITERATURE FOR MOSLEMS. *The Power of the Printed Page in the World of Islam.* Cairo, Egypt, 1922. 221 pp.

Bibliographic footnotes.

JORGA, NICHOLAS. *My American Lectures.* Bucharest: State Printing Office of Roumania, 1932. 192 pp.

A series of addresses made by the Roumanian prime minister in the United States in 1929. Has a chapter on "Catholic Organizations and Propaganda in Southern Europe."

KELLEY, THE VERY REV. FRANCIS, editor. *The First Catholic Missionary Congress.* Chicago: J. S. Hyland, 1909.

LASKER, BRUNO. *Religious Liberty and Mutual Understanding: An Interpretation of the National Seminar of Catholics, Protestants, and Jews, Washington, D. C., March 7–9, 1932.* New York: National Conference of Jews and Christians, 1932. 76 pp.

LEACH, WILLIAM HERMAN. *Church Publicity: A Complete Treatment of Publicity Opportunities and Methods in the Local Church.* Nashville, Tennessee: Cokesbury Press, 1930. 270 pp.

Bibliography, pp. 262–63.

LEE, UMPHREY. *The Historical Background of Early Methodist Enthusiasm* (Columbia University Studies in History, Economics, and Public Law, no. 339). New York: Columbia University, 1931. London: P. S. King, 1931. 176 pp.

Bibliography, pp. 149–72.

LIMBERT, PAUL MOYER. *Denominational Policies in the Support and Supervision of Higher Education* (Ph. D. thesis. Teachers College

Contributions to Education, no. 378). New York: Columbia University, 1929. 242 pp.
Bibliography, pp. 237–42.

LINDQUIST, GUSTAVUS ELMER EMANUEL. *A Handbook for Missionary Workers among the North American Indians.* New York: Home Missions Council and Council of Women for Home Missions, 1932. 87 pp.
Bibliography, pp. 83–87.

McCLURE, EDMUND. *Two Hundred Years: The History of the Society for Promoting Christian Knowledge, 1698–1898.* London, 1898.

MACFARLAND, CHARLES STEDMAN. *The New Church and the New Germany.* New York: Macmillan, 1933. 207 pp.
A study of the church under the Hitler régime, by the general secretary emeritus of the Federal Council of the Churches of Christ in America.

"Missions," *Encyclopedia of the Social Sciences.* (By K. S. Latourette.)

MURPHY, JAMES. "Cardinal Gotti and the Propaganda," *Catholic World,* 76: 1–15 (1902).

NORTON, SISTER MARY AQUINAS. *Catholic Missionary Activities in the Northwest, 1818–1864* (Ph. D. thesis). Washington, D. C.: Catholic University of America, 1930. 154 pp.

NORTON, WILLIAM B. *Church and Newspaper.* New York: Macmillan, 1930. 271 pp.

PERNOT, MAURICE. *Le Saint-siège, l'église catholique et la politique mondiale.* Paris: Colin, 1924. 214 pp.
The activity of the church in world affairs during the last twenty-five years. Bibliography, pp. 213–14.

PHILIPSON, RABBI DAVID. *The Reform Movement in Judaism.* New edition. London and New York: Macmillan, 1931. 503 pp.

PIEPER, KARL. *Die Propaganda: Ihre Entstehung und religiöse Bedeutung.* Aachen, 1922. 30 pp.

PRATT, JAMES BISSETT. *The Pilgrimage of Buddhism.* New York: Macmillan, 1928. 758 pp.
Standard history of the diffusion of Buddhism in the Far East. Contains a chapter on present-day Buddhist propaganda. Bibliographic footnotes.

PRICE, MAURICE THOMAS. *Christian Missions and Oriental Civilizations, a Study in Culture Contact: The Reactions of Non-Christian Peoples to Protestant Missions from the Standpoint of Individual and Group Behavior; Outline, Materials, Problems, and Tentative*

Interpretations, with a foreword by Robert E. Park. Shanghai, China: Privately printed, 1924. 578 pp.
Bibliography, pp. 547–62.

RICHARDSON, NORMAN EGBERT, and LOOMIS, ORMOND E. *The Boy Scout Movement Applied by the Church.* New York: Scribners, 1915. 445 pp.

SANFORD, ELIAS BENJAMIN. *Origin and History of the Federal Council of the Churches of Christ in America.* Hartford, Connecticut: S. S. Scranton, 1916. 528 pp.

SCHWICKERATH, ROBERT. *Jesuit Education: Its History and Principles Viewed in the Light of Modern Educational Problems.* St. Louis: B. Herder, 1903, 1905. First edition, 687 pp.
Bibliography, pp. 662–70.

SHIPLEY, MAYNARD. *The War on Modern Science: A Short History of the Fundamentalist Attacks on Evolution and Modernism.* New York and London: Knopf, 1927. 415 pp.

SMITH, HERBERT HEEBNER. *Church and Sunday School Publicity: Practical Suggestions for Using the Printed Word to Extend the Influence of the Gospel.* Philadelphia: Westminster Press, 1922. 176 pp.
Bibliography, pp. 170–72.

STELZLE, CHARLES. *Principles of Successful Church Advertising.* New York and Chicago: Revell, 1908. 172 pp.

STRONG, JOSIAH. *Religious Movements for Social Betterment* (Monographs on American Social Economics, no. 14). New York: League for Social Service, 1900. 50 pp.
Prepared for the Department of Social Economy of the United States Commission to the Paris Exposition of 1900.

VERCESI, ERNESTO. *Il movimento cattolico in Italia, 1870–1922.* Florence: La Voce, 1923. 306 pp.

WINCHESTER, BENJAMIN SEVERANCE. *The Church and Adult Education.* New York: R. R. Smith, 1930. 181 pp.

WOODSON, CARTER G. *History of the Negro Church.* Washington, D. C.: Associated Publishers, 1921. 330 pp.

WORLD'S SUNDAY SCHOOL ASSOCIATION. Yearbook.

2. COUNTER-ECCLESIASTICAL

AMERICAN ASSOCIATION FOR THE ADVANCEMENT OF ATHEISM. Bulletin, 1926—. Annual Reports.

"Anticlericalism," *Encyclopedia of the Social Sciences.* (By J. Salwyn Schapiro.)

"Atheism," *Encyclopedia of the Social Sciences*. (By Morris R. Cohen and Oscar Jàszi.)

CONNORS, FRANCIS JOHN. "Samuel Finley Breese Morse and the Anti-Catholic Political Movements in the United States, 1791–1872," *Illinois Catholic Historical Review*, 10: 83–122.

FAIRHURST, ALFRED. *Atheism in Our Universities*. Cincinnati: Standard Publishing Company, 1923. 212 pp.

"Freethinkers," *Encyclopedia of the Social Sciences*. (By Robert Eisler.)

HERBIGNY, M. D'. "La Propagande soviétique antiréligieuse," *Revue des deux mondes*, 13: 573–601, 798–821 (February 1, 15, 1933).

JORDAN, WILBUR KITCHENER. *The Development of Religious Toleration in England from the Beginning of the English Reformation to the Death of Queen Elizabeth*. London: Allen and Unwin, 1932. 490 pp.
Bibliography, pp. 421–77.

MAUTHNER, FRITZ. *Der Atheismus und seine Geschichte im Abendlande*. Stuttgart: Deutsche Verlagsanstalt, 1920–23. 4 vols.

PUBLICITY BUREAU CONCERNING ROMAN CATHOLIC RULERS. *The Present Uprising against the Roman Catholic Hierarchy: An Open Letter to the Democratic National Committeemen and to the Democratic National Delegates by Publicity Bureau Concerning Activities of the Roman Catholic Rulers against the People's Rule*. Washington, D. C.: H. S. Burwell, 1911. 119 pp.

PUBLICITY BUREAU FOR THE EXPOSURE OF POLITICAL ROMANISM. *Stupendous Issues: The Case Stated and Evidence Presented by the Publicity Bureau for the Exposure of Political Romanism*. New York, 1916. 15 pp.

ROBERTSON, JOHN MACKINNON. *A History of Freethought in the Nineteenth Century*. London: Watts, 1929. 2 vols.

STIMSON, DOROTHY. *The Gradual Acceptance of the Copernican Theory of the Universe* (Ph. D. thesis, Columbia University). Hanover, New Hampshire: 1917. 147 pp.
Bibliography, pp. 130–44.

WILLIAMS, MICHAEL. *The Shadow of the Pope*. New York and London: McGraw-Hill, 1932. 329 pp.
Anti-Catholic agitations and campaigns in America.

ZIEGLER, ADOLPH. *Die russiche Gottlosenbewegung*. Munich: Kösel und Pustet, 1932. 248 pp.
Exhaustive study of the methodology and events of the religious struggle in all fields of social life.

J. MINORITIES AND RACIAL GROUPS

AMERICAN JEWISH COMMITTEE. Annual Reports.
This committee exists to protest discrimination against Jews in any part of the world; it conducts a Bureau of Jewish Social Research, which compiles the American Jewish Yearbook.

BAKER, PAUL E. *Negro-White Adjustment*. New York: Association Press, 1934.
The history, philosophy, and programs of the interracial agencies in America.

BALDENSPERGER, FERNAND. *Le Mouvement des idées dans l'émigration française (1789–1815)*. Paris: Plon-Nourrit, 1924. 2 vols.
The reactions of the *émigrés* toward their new environments, their interpretations of the calamity which they thought had befallen France, and their fresh conception of the future.

CHICAGO COMMISSION ON RACE RELATIONS. *The Negro in Chicago*. Chicago: University of Chicago, 1922. 672 pp.
Chapters 9 and 10, public opinion in race relations; chapter 9, current beliefs regarding Negroes on the part of white citizens, and opinions of Negroes on racial problems; chapter 10, "Instruments of Opinion Making"; the press; the Negro press; propaganda for and against the Negro.

DRAHN, ERNST. "Russische Emigration," *Zeitschrift für die gesamte Staatswissenschaft*, Jahrgang 89, Heft 1, pp. 124–30 (1930).

FEDERATION OF POLISH JEWS IN AMERICA, NEW YORK OFFICE. *Our Aims and Purpose*.
Pamphlet.

FOREIGN LANGUAGE INFORMATION SERVICE. *Foreign Language Publications in the United States*. New York, 1926–30, 2 vols.
Classified by groups and by states.

"Jewish Emancipation," *Encyclopedia of the Social Sciences*. (By Salo Baron.)

Jewish Yearbook. London, 1896 —.

JOHNSON, CHARLES SPURGEON. *The Negro in American Civilization: A Study of Negro Life and Race Relations in the Light of Social Research*. New York: Holt, 1930. 538 pp.
Bibliography, pp. 485–509.

LASKER, BRUNO. *Filipino Immigration*. Chicago: University of Chicago, 1931. 445 pp.

LEWINSON, PAUL. *Race, Class, and Party: A History of Negro Suffrage and White Politics in the United States*. New York and London: Oxford, 1932. 302 pp.
Bibliography, pp. 289–92.

Lindquist, Gustavus Elmer Emanuel. *The Red Man in the United States: An Intimate Study of the Social, Economic, and Religious Life of the American Indian.* New York: Doran, 1923. 461 pp.
Bibliography, pp. 442–47.

Locke, Alain. *The New Negro.* New York: Boni, 1925. 446 pp.

McKenzie, Roderick Duncan. *Oriental Exclusion: The Effect of American Immigration Laws, Regulations, and Judicial Decisions upon the Chinese and Japanese on the American Pacific Coast.* Chicago: University of Chicago, 1928. 200 pp.
A report prepared for the Institute of Pacific Relations.

Mears, Elliot Grinnell. *Resident Orientals on the American Pacific Coast.* Chicago: University of Chicago, 1928. 545 pp.

Millis, Harry Alvin. *The Japanese Problem in the United States.* New York: Macmillan, 1915. 334 pp.

National Association for the Advancement of Colored People. *National Association for the Advancement of Colored People: Its History, Achievements, Purposes.* New York, 1926.
The Association also publishes an annual report.

——. *The First Line of Defense: A Summary of Twenty Years' Civil Rights Struggle for American Negroes.* New York, 1929(?).

Negro Yearbook. Tuskegee Institute, Alabama, 1912—.

Noel-Buxton, Noel Edward, and Conwil-Evans, T. P. *Oppressed Peoples and the League of Nations.* London: Dent, 1922. New York: Dutton, 1922. 230 pp.
How minorities air their grievances. Bibliography, p. 218.

Nowlin, William F. *The Negro in American National Politics.* Boston: The Stratford Company, 1931. 148 pp.

Ovington, Mary White. *How the National Association for the Advancement of Colored People Began.* New York, 1923.

Rimscha, Hans von. *Der russische Bürgerkrieg und die russische Emigration, 1917–1921.* Jena: Frommann, 1924. 170 pp.
A factual study of the history and the socio-political composition of the *émigrés* from Russia.

——. *Russland jenseits der Grenzen.* Jena: Frommann, 1927. 238 pp.
A study of Russian emigration, its groups, organizations, and activities.

Schmidt, Carl E. *Aims and Purposes of the Steuben Society of America.* New York: Steuben Society, 1925.

SCHRADER, FREDERICK FRANKLIN. *1683–1920.* New York: Concord Publishing Company, 1920. 250 pp.

Discusses the Steuben Society of America, pro- and anti-German propaganda in the United States during the World War, etc.

————. *The Germans in the Making of America.* Boston: The Stratford Company, 1924. 274 pp.

Bibliography, pp. 259–64.

YOUNG, DONALD RAMSEY. *American Minority Peoples: A Study in Racial and Cultural Conflicts in the United States.* New York and London: Harpers, 1932. 621 pp.

A systematic sociological treatment. Bibliography, pp. 594–607.

YOUNG, DONALD RAMSEY, editor. *The American Negro.* Philadelphia: American Academy of Political and Social Science, 1928. 359 pp. Also appeared as a volume of the *Annals* of the Academy, November, 1928.

See especially the sections on " Organizations for Social Betterment " and " Race Relations in Other Lands."

K. BUSINESS GROUPS

Most commercial advertising titles are included in this section. Some of the treatises on method are given in Part I, Section A; references on the general function of advertising in society and on the problem of control are listed in Part VII.

I. BIBLIOGRAPHICAL AND REFERENCE TITLES

" Books for the Advertising Man," *Bulletin of the Advertising Federation of America,* January, 1931.

CALKINS, EARNEST ELMO. *Advertising* (American Library Association, Reading with a Purpose Series, no. 51). Chicago: American Library Association, 1929. 32 pp.

COWAN, FRANCES M. *Sales Executives' List of References to Principal Articles, Books, Reports, and Data Published Since 1916 Relative to Sales Management and Advertising.* Chicago: Dartnell Corporation, 1925. 108 pp.

Fowler's Publicity: An Encyclopedia of Advertising and Printing. New York: Publicity Publishing Company, 1897. 1016 pp.

PHELPS, E. M., editor. " National Advertising: Bibliography," *University Debaters Annual, 1928–29,* pp. 387–426.

2. BUSINESS ASSOCIATIONS

AGNEW, HUGH ELMER. *Cooperative Advertising by Competitors.* New York: Harpers, 1926. 246 pp.
"Promoting a whole industry by combined efforts in advertising."

BONNETT, CLARENCE ELMORE. *Employers' Associations in the United States.* New York: Macmillan, 1922. 594 pp.
Gives specific instances of influence on legislation. Contains bibliographies.

BRETTNER, HANS WILHELM P. A. *Die Organisation der industriellen Interessen in Deutschland unter besonderer Berücksichtigung des "Reichsverband der deutschen Industrie."* Berlin: Organisation Verlagsgesellschaft, 1924. 64 pp.
Most extensive book on the principal German industrialists' association. Bibliography, pp. 57–60.

BRITISH LABOUR PARTY, LABOUR RESEARCH DEPARTMENT. *The Federation of British Industries* (Studies in Labour and Capital, vol. 5). London: Labour Publishing Company, 1923. 64 pp.
Contains descriptions of many employers' associations.

BUECK, HENRY AXEL. *Der Centralverband deutscher Industrieller, 1876–1901.* Berlin: Deutscher Verlag, 1902–05. 3 vols.
The most complete study of this period in the history of this leading association of German industrialists.

"Chambers of Commerce," *Encyclopedia of the Social Sciences.* (By Paul Studenski.)

CHILDS, HARWOOD LAWRENCE. *Labor and Capital in National Politics* (Ph. D. thesis, University of Chicago). Columbus: Ohio State University, 1930. 286 pp.
A systematic comparison of the American Federation of Labor and the American Chamber of Commerce. Bibliography, pp. 271–79.

DROSSINIS, C. G. *Les Chambres de commerce à l'étranger.* Paris, 1921.

ELLIOT, J. M. Is studying trade associations at Harvard Graduate School of Business Administration.

"Employers Associations," *Encyclopedia of the Social Sciences.* (By Clarence Elmore Bonnett.)

"Expanding the Market for Concrete Masonry through National Co-operative Advertising," *Concrete,* 35: 16 (July, 1929).

FITZPATRICK, F. STUART. *A Study of Business Men's Associations.* Olean, New York: Olean Times Publishing Company, 1925. 177 pp.

HERRING, EDWARD PENDLETON. "Chambres de commerce in France," *American Political Science Review,* 25: 689–700 (August, 1931).

INTERNATIONAL LABOUR OFFICE. "Employers' Organizations," *International Labour Directory*, 1925, pt. 2.

JONES, FRANKLIN DANIEL. *Trade Association Activities and the Law*. New York: McGraw-Hill, 1922. 360 pp.

KAUFMANN, EMIL. *Die Organisation der freien Interessenvertretungen des deutschen Einzelhandels*. Berlin, 1931.
A critical study of the organizational problems of the shopkeepers in Germany.

KEPPEL, FREDERICK PAUL. *The International Chamber of Commerce*. New York: Association for International Conciliation, 1922. 24 pp.
Also appeared as an article in *International Conciliation*, no. 174, pp. 187–210 (1922).

LIBRARY OF CONGRESS. *Select List of References on Employers' Associations* (Select List of References no. 343). Washington, D.C.: Government Printing Office, 1919.

MINISTRY OF LABOUR [GREAT BRITAIN]. *Directory of Employers' Associations, Trade Unions, Joint Associations, etc.* London: H.M. Stationery Office, 1932. 197 pp.

MOST, OTTO. *Selbstverwaltung der Wirtschaft in den Industrie- und Händelskammern*. Jena: Fischer, 1927. 168 pp.
Authoritative description of the work of chambers of commerce in Germany.

MÜFFELMANN, LEOPOLD. *Die wirtschaftlichen Verbände*. Leipzig: G.J. Göschen, 1912. 125 pp.
History and activities of the various economic organizations. Valuable for the information it gives concerning the Bund der Industrieller and the Centralverband deutscher Industrieller.

NATIONAL ASSOCIATION OF COMMERCIAL ORGANIZATION SECRETARIES. Publishes pamphlets, etc., containing material on structure, methods, and aims of business associations.

NATIONAL ASSOCIATION OF MANUFACTURERS. Publishes bulletins and statements of its aims.
A leading trade association.

———. *National Trade Associations*. 1922.
Contains answers to a questionnaire on association activities.

NATIONAL INDUSTRIAL CONFERENCE BOARD. *Trade Associations: Their Economic Significance and Legal Status*. New York, 1925. 388 pp.

NAYLOR, EMMET HAY. *Trade Associations*. New York: Ronald Press, 1921. 389 pp.
Handbook on organization and management. Bibliography, pp. 321-26.

POWELL, LEONA MARGARET. *A History of the United Typothetae of America.* Chicago: University of Chicago, 1926. 219 pp.
Leading trade association in the commercial and periodical branches of the printing industry. Bibliography, pp. 189–91.

STURGES, KENNETH. *American Chambers of Commerce.* New York: Williams College, 1915. 278 pp.
Bibliography, pp. 265–68.

TAYLOR, ALBION GUILFORD. *Labor Policies of the National Association of Manufacturers* (Ph. D. thesis, University of Illinois). Urbana, Illinois: University of Illinois, 1928. 184 pp.

TRADE ASSOCIATION EXECUTIVES IN NEW YORK CITY. *Year Book, List of Members, and Book of Information.* New York, 1922–23 to 1930–31. (No issue for 1927–28.)

UNITED STATES CHAMBER OF COMMERCE. Publishes, among other things: (1) *The Nation's Business;* (2) *General Bulletin* (weekly); (3) *Legislative Bulletin* (weekly during sessions of Congress); (4) *Weekly Business Statistics;* (5) *Monthly Business Indicator*; (6) specially requested information; (7) referenda on opinions of members; (8) statements on policies of the Chamber of Commerce.

UNITED STATES DEPARTMENT OF COMMERCE. *Trade Association Activities* (Domestic Commerce Series, no. 20). Revised edition. Washington, D. C.: Government Printing Office, 1927. 381 pp.
Reviews points of contact between business organizations and federal bureaus. Bibliography, pp. 346–65.

WILLIAMS, A. H. Is studying trade associations at Wharton School, University of Pennsylvania.

WOLFE, A. J. Series of articles on commercial organization in Germany, France, Switzerland, and the United Kingdom, in United States Department of Commerce, Bureau of Foreign and Domestic Commerce, Special Agents Series, nos. 78, 98, 101, and 102. Washington, D. C.: Government Printing Office, 1915.

ZIMAND, SAVEL. *The Open Shop Drive : Who Is behind It and Where Is It Going?* New York: Bureau of Industrial Research, 1921. 61 pp. Bibliography, pp. 50–54.

3. ADVERTISING METHODS IN THE UNITED STATES

A. BOOKS

Advertising (Library of Business Practice, vol. 6). Chicago: A. W. Shaw, 1914. 216 pp.
A collection of articles.

"Advertising," in R. H. Montgomery, editor, *American Business Manual*, 2:511–60. New York, 1911.

Advertising and Publicity: Addresses Delivered at the 16th Annual Journalism Week at the University of Missouri, May 4–8, 1925 (University of Missouri Bulletin, vol. 26, no. 26; Journalism Series, no. 35). Columbia, Missouri: University of Missouri, 1925. 32 pp.

AGNEW, HUGH ELMER. *Advertising Media: How to Weigh and Measure*. New York: Van Nostrand, 1931. 426 pp.

———. *Co-operative Advertising by Competitors*. New York: Harpers, 1926. 246 pp.
"Promoting a whole industry by combined efforts in advertising."

ASPLEY, JOHN CAMERON. *What a Salesman Should Know about Advertising*. Chicago: Dartnell Corporation, 1921. 119 pp.

Attracting and Holding Customers: How Publicity Can Bring Customers (Shaw Retailing Series). Chicago: A. W. Shaw and Company, 1919. 230 pp.

AUDIT BUREAU OF CIRCULATIONS. *Scientific Space Selection*. Chicago, 1921. 167 pp.
A textbook on the selection of advertising media, for advertising managers, space buyers, agency account executives, and other advertising specialists.

AUMUELLER, FERDINAND O. *Mechanics of Advertising*. Milwaukee: Cramer-Krasselt, 1922. 95 pp.

AYMAR, GORDON CHRISTIAN. *An Introduction to Advertising Illustration*. New York and London: Harpers, 1929. 236 pp.

AZOY, ANASTASIO CARLOS MARIANO. *A Primer of Advertising*. New York and London: Harpers, 1930. 178 pp.

BALMER, EDWIN. *The Science of Advertising*. Chicago: Wallace Press, 1909. 64 pp.

BARNARD, WILLIAM FRANCIS. *The Buying Impulse and How to Lead It*. Cleveland: International Displays Company, 1920. 39 pp.

Better Business. Philadelphia: N. W. Ayer, 1914. 45 pp.

BLACKMAN COMPANY (ADVERTISING AGENCY). *Advertising and Salesmanship*. New York, 1924–27. 2 vols., mimeographed.
A collection of pamphlets.

BOWMAN, NEAL BOWERS. *Advertising Principles*. Philadelphia: Birnbaum, Jackson, 1931. 153 pp.

———. *Advertising Simplified*. Philadelphia: N. Bowman, 1927. 104 pp.

BRENISER, ROSS DALBEY. *Is It Capital You Need? or, How to Sell a Business of Idea.* Philadelphia, 1913. 76 pp.

CHASE, STUART, and SCHLINK, F. J. *Your Money's Worth: A Study in the Waste of the Consumer's Dollar.* New York: Macmillan, 1927. 285 pp.

————. *Schemes back of the Ads.* Philadelphia: R. D. Breniser, 1914. 36 pp.

CHERINGTON, PAUL T. *The Consumer Looks at Advertising,* with an introduction by Stanley Resor. New York and London: Harpers, 1928. 196 pp.

CLIFFORD, WILLIAM GEORGE. *Building Your Business by Mail: Direct Advertising Campaign from the Experience Records of 361 Firms in Every Line of Business.* Chicago: Business Research Publishing Company, 1914. 448 pp.

CODY, SHERWIN. *How to Deal with Human Nature in Business.* New York: Funk and Wagnalls, 1915. 488 pp.

COLLINS, KENNETH. *The Road to Good Advertising.* New York: Greenberg, 1932. 217 pp.
A realistic volume by the former advertising manager of Macy's, now with Gimbels.

CONFERENCE ON INDUSTRIAL ADVERTISING AND SELLING, May 10, 1929, at Washington, D. C. Report. Wilmington, Delaware, 1929. 79 pp.
A conference held under the auspices of the National Industrial Advertisers' Association, the Industrial Committee of Association of National Advertisers, and the United States Department of Commerce.

COOLIDGE, CALVIN. *Address of President Coolidge before the American Association of Advertising Agencies, Washington, D. C., October 27, 1926.* Washington, D. C.: Government Printing Office, 1926. 7 pp.

DE BOWER, HERBERT FRANCIS. *Advertising Principles.* New York: Alexander Hamilton Institute, 1917. 330 pp.
"Prepared as a part of the modern business course and service of the Alexander Hamilton Institute." — *Title page.*

DE WEESE, T. A. "Keeping a Dollar at Work: Fifty Talks on Newspaper Advertising," *New York Evening Post,* 1915.

————. *The Principles of Practical Publicity: Being a Treatise on the Art of Advertising.* Philadelphia: G. W. Jacobs, 1908. 250 pp.

DICKINSON, HOWARD WILLIAMS. *A Primer of Promotion.* New York: John Day, 1927. 85 pp.

DIPPY, ALBERT W. *Advertising Production Methods.* New York: McGraw-Hill, 1929. 318 pp.

DONOVAN, HOWARD McCORMICK, and MITCHELL, GEORGE. *Advertising Response: A Research into the Influences That Increase Sales*. Philadelphia and London: Lippincott, 1924. 195 pp.

DOYLE, KITCHEN, AND McCORMICK, INC. *Waste Places in Advertising*. New York, 1929. 60 pp.

DUNLAP, ORRIN ELMER. *Radio in Advertising*. New York and London: Harpers, 1931. 383 pp.

DURSTINE, ROY SARLES. *Making Advertisements and Making Them Pay*. New York: Scribners, 1920. 264 pp.

DUTCHER, LE GRAND. *5555 Result-Producing Advertising, Selling Phrases*. Philadelphia: Dewey and Eakins, 1912. 140 pp.

EADS, GEORGE W., HUSE, N. A., and LINN, M. P. *Problems of Advertising: Addresses Delivered in Journalism Week, 1918* (University of Missouri Bulletin, vol. 19, no. 27). Columbia, Missouri: University of Missouri, 1918. 20 pp.

EDGAR, ALBERT E. *How to Get More Business*. Columbus, Ohio: The Advertising World, 1921. 142 pp.
See part 1, "Advertising."

ELLISON, C. E. *How to Make Advertisements Appealing*. New York: International Textbook Company, 1927.

FITT, A. B. *The Human Instincts in Business*. Melbourne: Lothian Book Company, 1922. 99 pp.

FOX, IRVING P. *One Thousand Ways and Schemes to Attract Trade, Gathered from Actual Experiences of Successful Merchants; Illustrated with Hundreds of Half-Tone and Line Cuts Suitable for Advertising Purposes*. Fifth edition. Boston: Spatula Publishing Company, 1927. 165 pp.

FREDERICK, CHRISTINE McGAFFEY. *Selling Mrs. Consumer*. New York: The Business Bourse, 1929. 405 pp.

FREEMAN, WILLIAM COOLBAUGH. *One Hundred Advertising Talks*. New York: Winthrop Press, 1912. 228 pp.

FRENCH, GEORGE. *Twentieth Century Advertising*. New York: Van Nostrand, 1926. 588 pp.

GALLOWAY, LEE, and HARMON, G. HOWARD. *Advertising, Selling, and Credits*. New York: Alexander Hamilton Institute, 1912. 651 pp.
"Especially prepared for the Alexander Hamilton Institute course in accounts, finance, and management." — *Title page*.

GAUSS, CHESTER A., and WIGHTMAN, LUCIUS I. *Sales and Advertising: A Practical Treatise on Selling Problems*. Chicago: American Technical Society, 1922. 2 vols.

GILES, RAY. *The Sales Expansion Question Book*. New York and London: Harpers, 1930. 161 pp.

GOODE, KENNETH MACKARNESS, and POWEL, HARFORD, JR. *What about Advertising?* New York and London: Harpers, 1927. 399 pp.

GOODE, KENNETH MACKARNESS, and RHEINSTROM, CARROLL. *More Profits from Advertising and More Advertising from Profits*. New York and London: Harpers, 1931. 275 pp.

GREER, CARL RICHARD. *Advertising and Its Mechanical Production*. New York: Crowell, 1931. 474 pp.

————. *The Buckeye Book of Direct Advertising*. Hamilton, Ohio: Beckett Paper Company, 1925. 222 pp.
Mechanics of production of direct mail material.

GRISELL, THOMAS OLEN. *Budgetary Control of Distribution*, with a foreword by Bruce Barton. New York and London: Harpers, 1929. 99 pp.

GROUCHO (pseudonym). *What Groucho Says: The Almost Amiable Growls of a Hard Working Advertising Man*. New York and London: Harpers, 1930. 266 pp.

GUNDLACH, ERNEST THEODORE. *Old Sox on Trumpeting*. Second edition. Chicago: Consolidated Book Publishers, 1928. 379 pp.
" Satire, attacking the alleged bunk in advertising." — *Publishers' preface*.

HAASE, ALBERT E. *Advertising Appropriation: How to Determine It and How to Administer It*. New York and London: Harpers, 1931. 181 pp.

HALL, S. ROLAND. *Mail Order and Direct-Mail Selling*. New York: McGraw-Hill, 1928. 494 pp.

HAWLEY, RAYMOND, and ZABIN, JAMES BARTON. *Understanding Advertising*. New York and Chicago: Gregg Publishing Company, 1931. 150 pp.

HOBBS, FRANKLYN. *Excerpts from His Scrapbook, Comprising Important Advertising Information as Composed by Franklyn Hobbs Himself, and His Staff*. Chicago: The Author, 1907. 16 pp.

HOOVER, HERBERT. *Remarks of President Hoover at the Dinner of the Association of National Advertisers, Washington, D. C., November 10, 1930*. Washington, D. C.: Government Printing Office, 1930. 2 pp.

HOPKINS, CLAUDE C. *My Life in Advertising*. New York and London. Harpers, 1927. 206 pp.
Contains a discussion of patent medicine advertising.

HOTCHKIN, WILLIAM ROWLAND. *Making More Money in Advertising.* New York: The Author, 1926. 273 pp.

HOTCHKISS, GEORGE BURTON, and FRANKEN, RICHARD BENJAMIN. *The Leadership of Advertised Brands: A Study of 100 Representative Commodities Showing the Names and Brands That Are Most Familiar to the Public.* New York: Doubleday, Page, 1923. 256 pp.

HURST, JOHN F. *The Universal Question:" Can We Stay in Business?"* Chicago: Privately printed, 1927. 34 pp.
Alternate pages are samples of posters.

In Behalf of Advertising: A Series of Essays Published in National Periodicals from 1919 to 1928. Philadelphia: N. W. Ayer, 1929. 266 pp.

INTERNATIONAL CORRESPONDENCE SCHOOLS. *The Advertisers' Handbook: A Book of Reference, Dealing with Plans, Typography, Illustration, Mediums, Management, and Other Details of Advertising Practice.* First edition, 52d thousand, 8th impression. Scranton, Pennsylvania: International Correspondence Schools, c. 1910. 413 pp.

JAMES, FRANCIS BACON. *Advertising and Other Addresses.* Cincinnati: Robert Clarke, 1907. 136 pp.

JOHNSON, A. P. *Library of Advertising: Fundamental Principles, Advertising Mediums.* Chicago: Cree Publishing Company, 1911. 6 vols.

KASTOR, ERNEST H. *Advertising.* Chicago: LaSalle Extension University, 1918. 317 pp.

KETTERING, CHARLES F. *Can Engineering Principles Be Applied to Advertising?* Hamilton, Ohio: The Champion Coated Paper Company, 1927. 32 pp.
Address given before the Association of National Advertisers, Detroit, May 9, 1927.

KITSON, HARRY DEXTER. *Scientific Advertising.* New York: Codex Book Company, 1926. 73 pp.

KITTREDGE, W. A. *The Advertising Conference* (" By the Goswoggii "). Chicago: Lakeside Press, 1927. 13 pp.

LE BLANC, NOVELL E. *Rudiments of Newspaper Advertising Construction.* Lake Charles, Louisiana: N. E. Le Blanc, 1921. 28 pp.

LEWIS, ELIAS ST. ELMO. *Preliminaries to Efficient Advertising.* New York: Alexander Hamilton Institute, 1914. 48 pp.
One of a series of Modern Business lectures especially prepared for the Alexander Hamilton Institute.

Lewis, Norman. *Samples, Demonstration, and Packaging: Their Use.* New York: Ronald Press, 1928. 250 pp.

Lowndes, William G., Chenery, Edward D., and Wiltshire, George J., compilers. *Advertising and Selling Digest: A Digest of 36 Lectures Given by Leading Authorities under the Auspices of the Advertising Club of New York.* New York: Advertising Club of New York, 1926. 249 pp.

MacGregor, Theodore Douglas. *Pushing Your Business: A Textbook of Advertising, Giving Practical Advice on Advertising for Banks, Trust Companies, Safe Deposit Companies, Investment Brokers, Real Estate Dealers, Insurance Agents, and All Interested in Promoting Their Business by Judicious Advertising.* Fifth edition. New York: Banker's Publishing Company, 1913. 202 pp.

MacManus, Theodore F. *The Sword Arm of Business.* New York: Devin-Adair, 1927. 188 pp.

McMurtrie, Douglas Crawford. *Modern Typography and Layout.* Chicago: Eyncourt Press, 1929. 190 pp.

Mahin, John Lee. *Advertising: Selling the Consumer.* Garden City: Doubleday, Page, 1914. 260 pp.; 1919 reprint, 98 pp.
Published for Associated Advertising Clubs of the World. Bibliography at the end of each chapter.

————. "Commercial Value of Advertising." University of Chicago, Publications of the College of Commerce and Administration, 1: 175–202 (1904).

————. *Lectures on Advertising.* Chicago: Privately printed, 1912. 5 pp.

Miller, George Laflin. *Aesop Glim, Advertising Fundamentalist.* New York: Prentice-Hall, 1930. 237 pp.

Morrow, Marco. *Things to Tell the Merchant: Address Delivered at Kansas Newspaper Week, under the Auspices of the Department of Journalism, University of Kansas, May 10–14, 1914* (University of Kansas News Bulletin, vol. 15, no. 7). Lawrence, Kansas: University of Kansas, 1914. 8 pp.

Mulhall, Walter F. (pseudonym of Franklin B. Evans). *Two Men in a Pullman.* New York: A. H. Vela, 1931. 30 pp.

Munsey, Frank. "Advertising in Some of Its Phases," *Munsey's Magazine,* 20: 476–86 (1898).

Nesbit, Wilbur Dick. *First Principles of Advertising.* New York and Chicago: Gregg Publishing Company, 1922. 111 pp.

Orman, Felix. *A Vital Need of the Times: A Symposium of Views and Comments Expressed by Leaders of American Economic Thought, and a Collection of Letters to the Author.* New York: F. Orman, 1918. 149 pp.

OSBORN, ALEXANDER FAICKNEY. *Brass Tacks of Advertising: An Unmysterious Analysis of the Practical Phases of the Kind of Advertising Which Analyzes.* Buffalo, New York: Published by the Hansauer-Jones Printing Company, under the auspices of the Buffalo Ad Club, 1915. 135 pp.

OSWALD, JOHN CLYDE. *How to Buy Printing Profitably.* New York: Employing Printers' Association, 1927. 134 pp.

PAGE DAVIS CORRESPONDENCE SCHOOL OF ADVERTISEMENT WRITING. *Prospectus.* Chicago, 1901. 64 pp.

PARSONS, FLOYD W. *American Business Methods for Increasing Production and Reducing Costs in Factory, Store, and Office.* New York and London: Putnam, 1921. 373 pp.

PRESBREY, FRANK. *History and Development of Advertising.* Garden City: Doubleday, Doran, 1929. 642 pp.

RAMSAY, ROBERT E. *Effective Direct Advertising: The Principles and Practice of Producing Direct Advertising for Distribution by Mail or Otherwise.* New York and London: Appleton, 1928. 560 pp.

RICHARDSON, A. O. *The Power of Advertising.* New York: Lambert, 1913. 300 pp.

RORTY, JAMES. *Our Master's Voice: Advertising.* New York: John Day, 1934. 394 pp.
Criticism of advertising as a handmaiden of American "pseudo-culture."

ROWSE, EDWARD JAMES, and FISH, LOUIS JOSEPH. *The Fundamentals of Advertising.* Cincinnati: Southwestern Publishing Company, 1926. 223 pp.

ST. JOSEPH, MISSOURI, PUBLIC LIBRARY. *Mr. Advertiser, Do You Know —? Facts the Library Can Furnish about Advertising.* St. Joseph, Missouri: Combe Printing Company, 1912. 2 pp.

SAMPSON, HENRY. *A History of Advertising from the Earliest Times.* London: Chatto and Windus, 1875. 616 pp.

SCHERMERHORN, JAMES. *Advertising: The Light That Serves and Saves.* New York and Chicago: Published by Doubleday, Page for the Educational Committee of the A. A. C. of A., 1914. 30 pp.

SHAW, A. W., AND COMPANY. *Bulletin for Advertisers Who Sell to Business Men.* 1916–21, 43 issues.

SHERBOW, BENJAMIN. *Effective Type Use for Advertising.* New York: Benjamin Sherbow, 1922. 139 pp.

SHRYER, WILLIAM A. *Analytical Advertising*. Detroit: Business Service Corporation, 1912. 228 pp.

TAYLOR, HENRY C. (pseudonym). *What an Advertiser Should Know: A Handbook for Everyone Who Advertises*. Chicago: Brown and Howell, 1914. 95 pp.

The Third Ingredient in Selling: A Brief, Practical Explanation of Some Fundamental Principles of Marketing under Present-Day Conditions. New York: James F. Newcomb and Company, 1927. 51 pp.

THOMSON, WILLIAM A. *Making Millions Read and Buy*. New York: William Drey, 1934. 248 pp.

VAILE, ROLAND SNOW. *Economics of Advertising*. New York: Ronald Press, 1927. 183 pp.

WADSWORTH, GERALD BERTRAM. *Principles and Practice of Advertising*. New York: G. B. Wadsworth, 1913. 271 pp.

WALDO, RICHARD H. *The Second Candle of Journalism: Address at Kansas Newspaper Week, under the Auspices of the Department of Journalism, University of Kansas, May 10–14, 1914* (University of Kansas News Bulletin, vol. 14, no. 15). Lawrence, Kansas: University of Kansas, 1914. 6 pp.

WILSON, WOODROW. *Address of President Wilson to the Associated Advertising Clubs, Philadelphia, Pennsylvania, June 29, 1916*. Washington: Government Printing Office, 1916. 6 pp.

WOODWARD, WARREN OLMSTEAD. *Selling Service with the Goods*. New York: McCann, 1921. 187 pp.
Psychology of window displays.

WOOLF, JAMES DAVIS. *Writing Advertising*. New York: Ronald Press, 1926. 287 pp.

B. ARTICLES

AD MAN (pseudonym). "Do You Believe in Ads?" *Outlook*, 143: 475–77 (August 4, 1926).

ADAMS, H. F. "Why We Buy," *Scribner's*, 67: 608–16 (May, 1920).

ADAMS, HENRY C. "What Is Publicity?" *North American Review*, 175: 895–904 (1902).

ALLEN, F. L. "Success: An Up-to-Date Advertisement," *Independent*, 115: 498 (October 31, 1925).

BABSON, R. W. "Worth Your Money," *Colliers*, 81: 8–9 (January 28, 1928).

BASSETT, W. R. "Taking the Guess Out of Business," *Forbes Magazine*, 12: 425 (July 5, 1924).

Batten, H. A. "An Advertising Man Looks at Advertising," *Atlantic,* 150:53–57 (July, 1932).

Beasley, N. "Breaking into Advertising," *Saturday Evening Post,* 200: 35 (July 30, 1927).

Bliven, Bruce O. "Mobilizing the Ad," *Harper's Weekly,* 62:199 (February 26, 1916).

Breneiser, S. G. "Illustrative Advertising Designs," *School Arts Magazine,* 28:10–11 (September, 1928).

Brigance, W. N. "Wisdom While You Wait," *North American Review,* 226:751–57 (December, 1928).

Brisco, N. A. "Mediums of Advertising," *Economics of Business,* 1910–14, pp. 282–306.

———. "Principles of Advertising," *Economics of Business,* 1910–14, pp. 260–81.

Bruhn, A. J. "Magazines and the Advertiser," *Western Advertising,* August, 1924, p. 21.

———. "Non-Standard Advertising Mediums," *Western Advertising,* December, 1924, p. 29.

Burnett, V. "Ten Simple Rules for Improving Direct Advertising," *Advertising and Selling,* 3:22 (August 13, 1924).
The author is secretary of the Institutional Advertising Committee, General Motors Corporation.

Calkins, Earnest Elmo. "Advertising's New Rôles," *Rotarian,* 43:6–9 (October, 1933).

———. "Does It Pay to Advertise?" *Century,* 107:851–60 (April, 1924).

———. "Now Is the Time to Advertise," *Review of Reviews,* 81: 52–56 (March, 1930).

———. "The Passing Procession of Magic Formulas," *Advertising and Selling,* 4:24 (November 19, 1924).

———. "What Advertising Really Is," *Woman's Home Companion,* 56:14 (March, 1929).

Chase, S. "Putting Halitosis on the Map," *Survey,* 61:127–29 (November 1, 1926).

Clark, N. M. "Making Wisecracks Is Charlie Archbold's Business," *American Magazine,* 100:68 (November, 1925).
The use of epigrams as a means of advertising a product.

Cline, M. S. "Advertising World," *English Journal,* 17:446–54 (June, 1928).

COOK, A. B. "Advertising in Its Relation to Profits," *Bankers Magazine*, 115:213–17 (August, 1927).

COULTEE, D. W. "Compelling Success through Mail Order Advertising," *Advertising and Selling*, 2:10 (October 6, 1923).

CRAIN, G., JR. "Fundamentals of Reference Mediums," *Class*, August, 1921.

CUSHING, C. P. "Enjoying the Want Ad," *Colliers*, 49:27 (July 13, 1912).

"Daily Reminders," *Atlantic Monthly*, 139:714–15 (May, 1927).

DELL, R. "Advertisements," *New Statesmen*, 24:592–93 (February 28, 1925).

DENNIS, C. H. "Millions for Ideas," *Forbes Magazine*, 24:42 (July 15, 1929).

DE WEESE, T. A. "The Job That Is Facing the Advertiser Today," *Advertising and Selling*, 13:30 (June 12, 1929).

DIGGES, I. W. "Refinement of Outdoor Advertising," *National Municipal Review*, 14:613–17 (October, 1925).

ECKHARDT, H. "Deadly Generalities Opposed to Vivid Word-Pictures," *Advertising and Selling*, 3:21 (October 8, 1924).

EMERSON, G. "Publicity as a Recognized Business Force," *Nation*, 106:367–68 (March 28, 1918).

FOLLETT, W. "The Tenth Muse," *Virginia Quarterly Review*, 5:346–62 (July 1, 1929).

GASS, A. D. "Advertising, Read It and Chuckle," *Forum*, 80:955–57 (December, 1928).

GILES, R. "111 Product Questions That Point the Way to Increased Sales," *Advertising and Selling*, 13:17–18 (July 10, 1929).

———. "To a Portfolio of Advertisements That Didn't Pay," *Advertising and Selling*, 13:28 (June 12, 1929).

GOODE, K. M. "Review of Rheinstrom's 'Psyching the Ads,'" *Advertising and Selling*, 13:36 (June 12, 1929).

GOODMAN, M. "The Humanness of Advertising," *Harper's Weekly*, 62:362 (April 8, 1916).

GRAY, G. W. "Yankee Shrewdness and Wit Put This Store on the Map," *American Mercury*, June, 1926.

GUNDLACH, E. T. "Three Principles of Mail Order Advertising," *Class*, June, 1924, p. 38.

HACKETT, CATHERINE ISABEL. "The New Deal and Advertising," *Forum*, 91:98–104 (February, 1934).

HALL, J. "Humanizing Technical Advertising," *Class*, November, 1923, p. 11.

HANET-ARCHAMBAULT, G. "La 'Publicity' en Amérique," *Mercure de France*, 149:673–85 (1921).

"Indirect Advertisement," *Outlook*, 69:485–87 (October 26, 1901).

"It Has Always Paid to Advertise," *Mentor*, 15:65 (May, 1927).

JENKINS, M. "Human Nature and Advertising," *Atlantic Monthly*, 94:393–401 (September, 1904).

JENNINGS, D. W. "The One Measure of a Copy-Writer's Success," *Western Advertising*, May, 1924, p. 14.

JOHNSON, NUNNALLY. "They Laughed!" *Harper's Magazine*, 166:119–22 (December, 1932).

JONES, D. D. "Advertising Has Some Foot Rules," *Nation's Business*, 17:55–56 (September, 1929).

JONES, EDWARD D. "Publicity as a Policy," *Annals of the American Academy of Political and Social Science*, 85:314–20 (September, 1919).

KELLEY, L. "Shape, Size, and Wording of Coupons and Replies," *Advertising Fortnightly*, December 19, 1923, p. 25.

KENWOOD, P. "Locating the Soft Spots in a List of Media," *Advertising Fortnightly*, February 13, 1924, p. 11.

KENYON, BERNICE LESBIA. "A Housewife Looks at Advertising," *American Mercury*, 29:181–89 (June, 1933).
Discussion on this article appeared in the *American Mercury*, 29:500–01 (August, 1933) and 30:117 (September, 1933).

KINGSBURY, N. C. "National Advertising," *Overland*, 68:327–31 (October, 1916).

KISER, S. E. "Always Too Much Copy," *Advertising and Selling*, 13:24 (August 7, 1929).

KISS, J. A. "Type Has Become a Dominant Part of the Advertising Picture," *Inland Printer*, 83:49–52 (July, 1929).

LAING, W. T. "What Is the Value of Position in Publication Advertising?" *Advertising Fortnightly*, February 27, 1924, p. 15.

LEIGH-BENNETT, D. "Business and Advertising," *World Today*, 47:215–19 (February, 1926).

LESSER, H. A. "White Space vs. Black Space Is the Advertiser's Problem," *Inland Printer*, 83:91–92 (August, 1929).

LOCKWOOD, R. B. "Putting the Trade Character to Work," *Class*, September, 1923, p. 58.

LYND, R. "Advertising," *New Statesman*, 29:472–73 (July 23, 1927).

MacCARTHY, D. "Art of Advertisement," *New Statesman*, 12:12–13 (October 5, 1918).

MacFARLAND, J. H. "Reform of Outdoor Advertising," *National Municipal Review*, 15:20–22 (January, 1926).

Magazines devoted almost entirely to this subject and not indexed here include: *Printed Salesmanship; Printer's Ink; Printer's Ink Monthly; Sales Management Magazine.*

MARQUIS, J. C. "Advertising as an Aid to Direct Selling," *Annals of the American Academy of Political and Social Science*, 50:197–202 (November, 1913).

NORWOOD, GILBERT. "Advertisements," *English Review*, 38:477–81 (April, 1924).
Reply by J. M. Allison in the same journal, 38:727–31 (May, 1924).

OLSHAUSEN-SCHÖNBERGER, K. "American Advertising through German Eyes," *Living Age*, 344:277–78 (May, 1933).

O'NEILL, H. "On Reading American Magazines: Advertising Section," *Living Age*, 324:301–03 (February 7, 1925).

PARSONS, F. W. "Putting Novelty into Selling," *Gas Age*, 63:865–66 (June 22, 1929).

PERSHALL, J. R. "Slide Rules for Advertising," *Gas Age*, 64:67–68 (July 13, 1929).

PORTER, L. S. "Are You Convincing?" *Harper's Weekly*, 155:518–20 (September, 1927).

POWERS, M. K. "Story Form Copy," *Advertising Fortnightly*, February 13, 1924, p. 15.

PUBLICITY DEPARTMENT OF WESTERN ELECTRIC COMPANY. "Practical Psychology and the O.K.," *Advertising and Selling*, 3:24 (July 30, 1924).

RANKIN, W. H. "Advertising Opens a Golden Door," *World Review*, 3:30 (September 27, 1926).

RENDALL, V. "Fame and the Advertiser," *Saturday Review*, 146:113–14 (July 28, 1928).

"Repetition is Reputation," *New Republic*, 51:127 (August 3, 1927).

RESOR, S. "Dollar-a-Year Graduate School: Part Advertising Plays as a Guide to Buying," *Pictorial Review*, 30:8 (June, 1929).

RHODES, H. K. "Analysis of Some Advertisements," *School Science and Mathematics*, 19:458–60 (May, 1919).

RORTY, JAMES. "Advertising and the Depression," *Nation*, 137:703–04 (December 20, 1933).

————. "I Was an Ad-Man Once," *New Republic*, 73:290–93 (January 25, 1933).

ROWE, B. "Defence of Advertising," *Hibbert Journal*, 24:136–42 (October, 1925).

ST. CLAIR, L. "Is Your Advertising Ailing?" *Nation's Business*, 17:19–21 (August, 1929).

SCHLINK, F. J. "Bear Oil: Old Magic for New Times," *New Republic*, 59:277–79 (July 31, 1929).

SNEAD, W. H. "But That's Merely a Detail!" *Advertising and Selling*, 13:34 (August 7, 1929).

STOKES, C. W. "Simple Life, and How Advertising Will Sell Anything," *New Republic*, 59:203–05 (July 10, 1929).

SURREY, R. "How Many Shoddy Words Do You O.K. in Your Advertising?" *Automotive Industries*, June 12, 1924, p. 1274.

"Those Remarkable Human Beings in the Ad Pictures," *Literary Digest*, 64:54–57 (February 28, 1920). Reprint from *Advertising and Selling*.

UPDEGRAFF, R. R. "First and Last Steps in Advertising," *Advertising and Selling*, 3:19 (August 27, 1924).

————. "High Cost of Mediocrity in Advertising," *Advertising Fortnightly*, January 16, 1924, p. 11.

"Vision in Advertising," *Scientific American*, 119:456 (December 7, 1918).

WAGNER, P. "Cigarettes vs. Candy," *New Republic*, February 13, 1929, pp. 343–45.

WALLACE, R. "Lucky or a Sweet or Both!" *Nation*, 128:305–07 (March 13, 1929).

WAXMAN, P. "Power and Cheapness of Good Advertising," *American Magazine*, 81:50 (March, 1916).

WEAVER, L. "Place of Advertising in Industry," *Quarterly Review*, 250:113–27 (January, 1928).

WHITE, E. B. "Where Do the New Eras Go?" *Magazine of Business,* 54:505 (November, 1928).

WILCOX, CLAIR. "Brand Names, Quality, and Price," *Annals of the American Academy of Political and Social Science,* 173:80–85 (May, 1934).

WILKINSON, C. "Tell It in Pictures," *Outlook,* January 8, 1927, p. 28.

WILLIAMS, F. H. "The Right Sort of Publicity for the Plant," *Industrial Management,* 61:32 (January, 1921).

WISEMAN, M. "From behind the Advertising Looking-Glass," *Survey,* 61:130–32 (November 1, 1928).

WOODFORD, J. "Help Wanted," *American Mercury,* 15:491–96 (December, 1928).

"Words That Sing to Your Pocketbook," *Atlantic Monthly,* 124:572–75 (October, 1919).

YOUNGREEN, C. "Advertising as a World Force," *Advertising and Selling,* 13:25 (August 21, 1929).

4. ADVERTISING METHODS ABROAD

GENERAL

BARTLETT, D. "Advertising as an Aid to Export Trade," *Annals of the American Academy of Political and Social Science,* 127:186–90 (September, 1926).

WYMAN, W. F. "Helping Foreign Merchants to Sell American Goods," *World's Work,* 30:730–32 (October, 1915).

AFRICA

JANSSEN, FRANS. *Le Réclame commercial et le placement des produits belges au Congo.* Brussels: R. Weverbergh, 1925. 20 pp.

ARGENTINA

SANGER, JESSE WILLIAM. *Advertising Methods in Argentina, Uruguay, and Brazil* (United States Bureau of Foreign and Domestic Commerce, Special Agents Series, no. 190). Washington, D. C.: Government Printing Office, 1920. 119 pp.

BOLIVIA

SANGER, JESSE WILLIAM. *Advertising Methods in Chile, Peru, and Bolivia* (United States Bureau of Foreign and Domestic Commerce, Special Agents Series, no. 185). Washington, D. C.: Government Printing Office, 1919. 56 pp.

Brazil

Brown, Harold McD. *Advertising and Merchandising in Brazil*. New York: Export Committee, Association of National Advertisers, 1921. 58 pp., mimeographed.

Sanger, Jesse William. *Advertising Methods in Argentina, Uruguay, and Brazil* (United States Bureau of Foreign and Domestic Commerce, Special Agents Series, no. 190). Washington, D. C.: Government Printing Office, 1920. 119 pp.

Chile

Sanger, Jesse William. *Advertising Methods in Chile, Peru, and Bolivia* (United States Bureau of Foreign and Domestic Commerce, Special Agents Series, no. 185). Washington, D. C.: Government Printing Office, 1919. 56 pp.

China

Chew, K. S. " Chinese Papers as Advertising Mediums," *China Weekly Review*, 46: 15–20 (September 1, 1928).

" Engineering Advertising in the Far East," *Far Eastern Review*, 27: 76 (February, 1931).

Ling, C. P. " Effective Advertising in China," *China Weekly Review*, 46: 171 (October 10, 1928).

Sanger, Jesse William. *Advertising Methods in Japan, China, and the Philippines* (United States Bureau of Foreign and Domestic Commerce, Special Agents Series, no. 209). Washington, D. C.: Government Printing Office, 1921. 107 pp.

" Some British Advertising Practices in China," *China Weekly Review*, 56: 408–10 (May 23, 1931).

" Survey Shows Growth of Chinese Newspaper Advertising," *China Weekly Review*, 36: 200–01 (April 24, 1926).

Wang, Y. P. *The Rise of the Native Press in China*. New York: Columbia University, 1924. 50 pp.

Chapter 4 gives an account of advertising groups, methods, and expenditures in the native press of China. " In relying on patent medicine advertising as a chief source of income, native newspapers, until they can find a substitute, simply have to accept and print them."

Colombia

Propaganda Commercial, Medillín, Colombia. New York: Schilling Press, 1923 (?). 271 pp.

Cuba

Sanger, Jesse William. *Advertising Methods in Cuba* (United States Bureau of Foreign and Domestic Commerce, Special Agents Series, no. 178). Washington, D. C.: Government Printing Office, 1919. 47 pp.

CZECHOSLOVAKIA

SUTNAR, M., and others. " O dobrou reklamu," *Masarykova akad. práce, Ustavu pro vědeckou organisaci obchodu,* 4: 1–79 (1930).

DENMARK

HANSEN, MAX KJAER. *Den danske Presse: Dansk Annoncerings-Haandbog.* Copenhagen: S. Hasselbalch, 1928. 144 pp.

――――. *Haandbog i Reklame: Til Brug ved Handelsundervisning.* Copenhagen: G. E. C. Gads, 1926. 130 pp.

KORVIL, N. *Annonceteknisk Haandbog om Annonceopsaetning, Arrangement, Placering.* Copenhagen: A. Busck, 1927. 95 pp.

EUROPE

MAYERINGH, P. W. " Selling to Europe," *Advertising and Selling,* 13: 19–20 (September 4, 1929).

FRANCE

ANGÉ, LOUIS. " Du rôle de la publicité dans la technique commerciale," *Grande revue,* 105: 113–26 (1921).

――――. *Pour bien faire sa publicité* (La Culture méthodique des affaires). Paris: J. Oliven, 1930. 270 pp.

BROCKMAN, LÉON E. *Des Millions gaspillés en annonces* (Études sur les affaires, no. 6). Paris: Nouvelle librairie commerciale, 1931. 266 pp.

" De la publicité," *L'Illustration,* vol. 86, pt. 1, p. 21 (March 17, 1928).

ELVINGER, FRANCIS, and ANGIER, LUCIEN. *Méthodes modernes de vente* (Études sur les affaires, no. 1). Paris: Nouvelle librairie commerciale, 1930. 219 pp.

HERVIER, PAUL LOUIS. " L'Humour dans la publicité," *Nouvelle revue,* N. S., 46: 301–16 (1907).

MONSANTO, C. M. *Catalogue d'exportation illustré de MM. les commissionaires-exportateurs.* Paris: C. M. Monsanto, 191(?). 2 vols.

" Publicité," *Annales politiques et littéraires,* 83: 139–40 (August 10, 1924).

" La Publicité moderne," *L'Illustration,* vol. 86, pt. 2, p. 11 (August 18, 1928).

GERMANY AND AUSTRIA

" Die Ahnen Reklamemarke," *Illustrierte Zeitung,* 143: vii–xii (1914).

DANNENBERG, WILLIBALD. *Reklame die Gewinn bringt: Praktische Einführung in die Werbekunst, besonders auch für Kleinfirmen, zug-*

leich als Leitfaden für Werbekurse in Kaufmanns-Schulen. Hamburg: Hanseatische Verlagsanstalt, 1928. 281 pp.

FRIESENHAHN, P. *Handbuch der Reklame, für Kaufleute, Industrieller, Gewerbetreibende Handlungsgehilfen, und Reklamefachmänner.* Second edition. Stuttgart: W. Violet, 1914(?). 312 pp.

GUGGENBUEHL, ADOLF. *Reklame in Amerika und bei uns.* Zurich: Verlag Organisator, 1928. 28 pp.

HARTUNGEN, CHR. VON. *Psychologie der Reklame.* Stuttgart, 1921.

LAUTERER, KARL. *Die Reklame von Morgen.* Zurich: Verlag Organisator, 1929. 36 pp.

MAYER, FRITZ. *Das Publizitätsproblem in der Wirtschaft* (Erlangen Universität, Staatswissenschaftliches Seminar, Abhandlungen, Heft 9). Leipzig: R. Noske, 1930. 441 pp.
Publicity problems in business.

Nachrichtdienst, Schriftverkehr, und Reklame, bearbeitet von Prof. Dr. Hellauer, Prof. Dr. Jaederholm, Prof. Dr. Zeitler, Dozent Dr. Runkel, Prof. Dr. Isaac, Prof. Dr. Mahlberg, Privatdozent Dr. Scheller, Privatdozent Dr. Lyzinski (*Grundriss der Berufswirtschaftslehre,* Band 13). Leipzig: G. A. Gloeckner, 1928. 538 pp.
Contains bibliographies.

PANETH, ERWIN. *Grundriss der kaufmännischen Reklame und des Reklamerechts in Deutschland und Oesterreich.* Munich: R. Oldenbourg, 1927. 240 pp.
Bibliography, pp. xv–xvi.

SANDER, FRIEDRICH KARL. *Verkaufs-Organisation und Geschafts-Reklame.* Leipzig: Thalacker und Schöffer, 1913. 314 pp.

SCHMIEDCHEN, JOHANNES, editor. *Neues Handbuch der Reklame, mit zahlreichen, teils mehrfarbigen Beilagen und Abbildungen, unter Mitwirkung namhafter Autoren und Fachleute.* Berlin-Lichterfelde: R. Wichert, 1929. 616 pp.

SCHUBERT, WALTER F. *Die deutsche Werbegraphik.* Berlin: Francken und Lang, 1927. 252 pp.

SEIDT, FRANZ. *Neues Handbuch der Reklame zum praktischen. Gebrauch für Kaufleute.* Berlin: R. Wichert, 1914. 384 pp.

GREAT BRITAIN

BOARDMAN, W. J. " William Wagstaffe, Humanitarian," *World Today,* 44: 417–20 (October, 1924).

BRIDGEWATER, HOWARD. *Advertising, or the Art of Making Known* (Pitman's Practical Primers of Business). London: Sir I. Pitman, 1910. 102 pp.

BULL, ALBERT E. *The Business Man's Guide to Advertising.* London: Sir I. Pitman, 1922. 124 pp.

"Coupons and the Advertiser," *Saturday Review,* 146:567–68 (November 3, 1928).

CRAWFORD, SIR WILLIAM, and others. *Advertising and the Man in the Street.* Leeds: Yorkshire Evening News, 1929. 88 pp.

DERRICK, PAUL E. *How to Reduce Selling Costs: A Warning and Suggestion Concerning a Matter of Vital Importance to Every Manufacturer.* London: G. Newnes, 1916. 231 pp.

DICKINSON, G. LOWES. "Publicity in Industrial Accounts, with a Comparison of English and American Methods," *Journal of the Royal Statistical Society,* N. S., 87:342–91 (May, 1924).

DUFFIELD, E. N. "Salesmanship That Isn't: The Weak Spot of the British Motor Car Business," *World Today,* 45:438–45 (April, 1925).

FREER, CYRIL C. *The Inner Side of Advertising: A Handbook for Advertisers, Those Engaged in Advertising, and Students.* London: Library Press, 1921. 247 pp.

FRY, ROGER ELLIOT. *Art and Commerce* (Hogarth Essays, no. 16). London: L. and V. Woolf, 1926. 22 pp.

GREENLY, A. J. *Psychology as a Sales Factor.* London: Sir I. Pitman, 1927. 214 pp.

HERD, HAROLD. *Bigger Results from Advertising.* London: Allen, 1926. 163 pp.

HOLE, E. S., and HART, J. *Advertising and Progress: A Defense by E. S. Hole and a Challenge by J. Hart.* London: Review of Reviews, 1914. 271 pp.

HUGHES, ELWYN O. *An Outline of Advertising.* London: Chapman and Hall, 1929. 161 pp.
Bibliography, pp. 157–60.

JONES, CHRISTOPHER. *Handbook of Advertising: A Manual for Those Who Wish to Become Acquainted with the Principles and Practice of Advertising.* London: Sir I. Pitman, 1912. 133 pp.

KAUFMANN, HERBERT. *The Clock That Had No Hands, and Nineteen Other Essays about Advertising.* London: Hodder and Stoughton, 1912. 116 pp.

LAWRENCE, T. B., editor. *What I Know about Advertising: A Series of Lectures Given at the International Advertising Exhibition, 1920, Promoted by the Thirty Club of London, and Made into a Book for the Benefit of Students of Business by Fourteen Leading Experts.* London: Spottiswoode, Ballantyne, 1921. 246 pp.

MAXWELL, EDWARD LEWIS. "A Matter-of-Fact Talk on Advertising," *Magazine of Commerce,* 4: 117–21 (1904).

MORAN, CLARENCE. *The Business of Advertising.* London: Methuen, 1905. 192 pp.

MORTON, J. B. "On a Candle Lit by an Elephant," *Spectator,* 146:342–43 (March 7, 1931).

PRAIGG, NOBLE T., editor. *Advertising and Selling, by 150 Advertising and Sales Executives.* London: Sir I. Pitman, 1924. 483 pp.

PRESTON, JOHN F., and ARCH, ERIC. *Advertising, Printing, and Art in Commerce.* London: Chapman and Hall, 1927. 301 pp.

PRIESTLEY, J. B. "The Magic City," *Saturday Review,* 148: 316–17 (September 21, 1929).

RUSSELL, THOMAS. "The Economic Soundness of Commercial Advertising," *International Review,* 1:817–34 (1914).

SHEPHERD, A. F. *Business First Principles: An Exposition in Simple Terms of the Force Which Germinates All Activity, All Progress, and All Achievement.* London: Business Builders, Ltd., 1923. 48 pp.

STIRRUP, CHARLES HOLT. "The £-s-d of Advertising," *Chambers' Journal,* Series 7, 20: 777–79 (1930).

STREET, EDMUND, and JACKSON, LIONEL. "Advertising," *Royal Society of Arts Journal,* 61: 247–57 (1913).

TEILHET, D. L. "England Advertises," *Advertising and Selling,* 13: 19–20 (August 7, 1929).

UNITED STATES BUREAU OF FOREIGN AND DOMESTIC COMMERCE. *Shipment of Samples and Advertising Matter to the British Empire* (Trade Reference Bulletin no. 122). Washington, D. C.: Government Printing Office, 1923. 16 pp.

"The Uses of Advertisement," *Spectator,* 123: 168, 240–41 (August 9, 23, 1919).

WEAVER, LAWRENCE. "The Place of Advertising in Industry," *Quarterly Review,* 250: 113–27 (1928).

HOLLAND

STEENHOFF, W. "De reclameplaat," *Elsevier's Geillustreerd Maandschrift,* 76: 1–6 (1928).

INDIA

RENSHAW, DONALD, and SPOFFORD, C. B., JR. *Advertising in India* (Bureau of Foreign and Domestic Commerce, Trade Information Bulletin no. 318). Washington, D. C.: Government Printing Office, 1925. 28 pp.

ITALY

Annuario della pubblicità italiana: La collezione del più bello materiale pubblicitario italiano dell'anno. Bolzano: " Casa Reclame," 1929 —. Consists of mounted colored plates, preceded by brief descriptive text in English, French, German, Italian, and Spanish.

CAVALLI, PIO. *La spada dell'America: La pubblicità in teoria e nella tecnica.* Milan: Fratelli Treves, 1919. 400 pp.

JAPAN

BERLINER, ANNA. *Japanische Reklame in der Tageszeitung.* Stuttgart: Poeschel, 1925. 108 pp.

" Engineering Advertising in the Far East," *Far Eastern Review,* 27: 76 (February, 1931).

JOHNSON, ALFONSO. "Advertising Foreign Goods in Japan," *Trans-Pacific,* 1:29–34 (December, 1919).

SANGER, JESSE WILLIAM. *Advertising Methods in Japan, China, and the Philippines* (United States Bureau of Foreign and Domestic Commerce, Special Agents Series, no. 209). Washington, D. C.: Government Printing Office, 1921. 107 pp.

KOREA

" How to Advertise in Korea," *Trans-Pacific,* 12:6 (June 13, 1925).

LATIN-AMERICA

AUGHINBAUGH, WILLIAM EDMUND. *Advertising for Trade in Latin-America* (Century Foreign Trade Series). New York: Century, 1922. 282 pp.

DEL MAR, ALEX. "How to Sell Latin-America," *Engineering Magazine,* 50: 341–56 (1915).

WAKEFIELD, ROBERTA P. *Shipment of Samples and Advertising Matter to Latin-America and the West Indies* (United States Bureau of Foreign and Domestic Commerce, Trade Information Bulletin no. 250). Washington, D. C.: Government Printing Office, 1924. 54 pp.

NORWAY

MILLAR, ROBERT. *The Uncharted Amazon: A Study of the Science of Publicity with a Purpose.* Oslo: Some and Company, 1924. 59 pp.

PALESTINE

"The Gentle Art of Suasion in Palestine," *Near East,* 34:745 (December 20, 1928).

SOUTH AFRICA

Trade and Advertising in South Africa. London: Argus South African Newspapers, Ltd., 1916–19. 2 vols. January, 1916: "American Edition."

URUGUAY

SANGER, JESSE WILLIAM. *Advertising Methods in Argentina, Uruguay, and Brazil* (United States Bureau of Foreign and Domestic Commerce, Special Agents Series, no. 190). Washington, D. C.: Government Printing Office, 1920. 119 pp.

U. S. S. R.

"Inreklama, Russian State Bureau for Foreign Advertising," *Business Week,* p. 26, December 9, 1933.

5. CAMPAIGNS OF SELECTED BUSINESS GROUPS

A. BANKS AND SECURITIES COMPANIES

ALBIG, W. ESPEY. *A History of School Savings Banks in the United States and Its European Beginnings.* New York: American Bankers Association, 1928.

ALLEN, V. D. "Making a Bank Opening Yield New Business," *Bankers Magazine,* 114:471–77 (March, 1927).

ALVERSON, M. "Aiding the Securities Salesman," *Bankers Magazine,* 120:49–51 (January, 1930).

"American Bank Advertising," *Bankers Magazine,* 108:182–83 (February, 1924).

"The Art of Unloading," *Nation,* 75:145–46 (August 21, 1902).

AURACHER, C. E. "Educating the Savings Prospects," *Bankers Magazine,* 112:256–57 (February, 1926).

"Bank Advertising of a Century Ago That Brought Results," *Bankers Magazine,* 117:447 (September, 1928).

BARTLETT, J. T. "Poster Idea for Selling Bank Advertising Literature," *Bankers Magazine,* 111:356–57 (September, 1925).

BOURNE, C. E. "Advertising a Canadian Bank with 900 Branches," *Bankers Magazine,* 117:1031–36 (December, 1928).

BRANDEIS, LOUIS D. *Other People's Money and How the Bankers Use It.* New York: Stokes, 1914. 233 pp.
Summary of the findings of the Pujo Commission.

BROWNE, SCRIBNER. *Tidal Swings of the Stock Market.* New York: Magazine of Wall Street, 1918. 113 pp.

BRYSON, A. E. "Appraisal of Financial Advertising," *Bankers Magazine,* 116:648–51 (May, 1928).

————. "A Banker's View of Advertising," *Bankers Magazine,* 119: 31–37 (July, 1929).

"Campaign of Civic Advertising by the Union Trust Company of Cleveland," *Bankers Magazine,* 118:209–17 (February, 1929).

CHAMBLISS, L. A. "Should Banks Advertise to Banks?" *Bankers Magazine,* 123:13–17 (July, 1931).

————. "Stimulating Unprofitable Commercial Accounts," *Bankers Magazine,* 118:557–63 (April, 1929).

CHASE, M. E. "Lobby Displays as an Aid to New Business," *Bankers Magazine,* 118:922–28 (June, 1929).

CLARKE, B. C. "Business-Building Advertising Stressed at Financial Advertisers' Meeting," *Bankers Magazine,* 113:162–64 (August, 1926).

COOK, A. B. "Trust Advertising Media," *Bankers Magazine,* 122:611–17 (May, 1931).

COOPER, FRANCIS (pseudonym). *Financing an Enterprise: A Manual of Information and Suggestions for Promoters, Investors, and Business Men.* Fourth edition. New York: Ronald Press, 1915. 524 pp.

COSTE, PIERRE. *La Lutte pour la suprématie financière.* Paris: Payot, 1932. 224 pp.
Reviews the triangular struggle for control between the London, Paris, and New York money markets.

DE BEBIAN, A. M. "Advertising the Foreign Banking Department of a Large Bank," *Bankers Magazine,* 114:821–25 (June, 1927).

DEVLIN, W. E. "Banks Should Advertise for Business, Not Merely Good Will," *Bankers Magazine,* 110:1002–03 (June, 1925).

DONOVAN, J. "Use of Direct Mail in Selling Trust Services: Excerpts," *Bankers Magazine,* 122:115–22 (January, 1931).

DURHAM, R. F. "Largest Gathering of Financial Advertisers on Record Hears Splendid Program at Columbus," *Bankers Magazine,* 111:729–44 (November, 1925).

————. "What Gets Financial Advertising Copy Read?" *Bankers Magazine,* 113:833–38 (December, 1926).

EASTON, J. M. "Advertising Your Safe Deposit Vault," *Bankers Magazine,* 116:641–44 (May, 1928).

ELLSWORTH, F. W. "Advertising for Trust Business," *Bankers Magazine*, 116:667–71 (May, 1928).

FINANCIAL ADVERTISERS ASSOCIATION. Publishes proceedings of its annual conventions, which are also reported in *Bankers Magazine*. 1930 convention (Louisville, Kentucky), *Bankers Magazine*, 121:551–66 (October, 1930); 1931 convention (Boston), *Bankers Magazine*, 123:599–635 (October, 1931).

———. *Advertising Investment Securities.* New York: Prentice-Hall, 1928. 312 pp.
On the technique of indirect advertising and merchandising methods, media, preparation of copy, car cards, inquiry copy, newspaper space selection, "trademarked bonds," etc. Contains many reproductions of successful layouts. Prepared by the Investment Research Committee of the Financial Advertisers Association at the suggestion of the Education Committee of the Investment Bankers Association of America.

———. "Financial Advertisers Challenge the Next Decade," *Bankers Magazine*, 118:27–32 (January, 1929).

"Financial Advertisers Challenge the Next Decade," *Bankers Magazine*, 120:891–92 (June, 1930).

FUCHS, F. "How We Made a Long Story Short," *Bankers Magazine*, 111:312 (September, 1925).

GOULD, G. O. "Movies as Bank Lobby Displays," *Bankers Magazine*, 122:603–09 (May, 1931).

GREIG, M. M. "Trust Business through Posters," *Bankers Magazine*, 117:545–47 (October, 1928).

GRIMM, H. B. "Selling Trust Company Services through Personal Salesmanship," *Bankers Magazine*, 114:565–67 (April, 1927).

HAYES, WILLIAM. "Can a Trust Company Successfully Administer a Great Newspaper?" *Bankers Magazine*, 111:709–13 (November, 1925).

"How Banks Are Advertising." Series beginning in *Bankers Magazine*, June, 1926.

KIDDY, A. W. "Banking and Democracy: Greater Publicity Desirable," *Spectator*, 141:91–92 (July 21, 1928).

KITTREDGE, E. H. "What Financial Advertising Has Accomplished," *Bankers Magazine*, 110:271–75 (February, 1925).

KNAPP, G. P. "Art in Financial Advertising," *Bankers Magazine*, 108:229 (February, 1924).

———. "Developing the Savings Business through Cultivation of the Existing Customer," *Bankers Magazine,* 110:635–40 (April, 1925).

———. "What Makes Bank Publicity Good?" *Bankers Magazine,* 112:685–86 (May, 1926).

KNOX, W. E. "Savings Banks and Advertising," *Bankers Magazine,* 109:1071–74 (December, 1924).

KUNKEL, F. E. "Electrical Advertising for Banks," *Bankers Magazine,* 116:835–39 (June, 1928).

"Luring the Small Investor into Speculation," *World's Work,* 13:8715–18 (April, 1907).

McCLEISH, E. E. "Direct Mail Advertising for Banks," *Bankers Magazine,* 115:635–37 (November, 1927).

———. "Newspaper Looks at Trust Advertising," *Bankers Magazine,* 123:827–28 (December, 1931).

MacGREGOR, T. D. "New Business Ideas and Suggestions," *Bankers Magazine,* 117:199–202 (August, 1928).

McKNIGHT, T. "Wall Street Marries Broadway," *Scribners,* 86:164–68 (August, 1929).

MEREDITH, L. D. "What's in a Name?" *Bankers Magazine,* 123:317–21 (September, 1931).

MORSE, G. S. "Financial Advertising," *Bankers Magazine,* 109:95–97 (July, 1924).

MURPHY, C. D. "Bank Advertising and the Charge of Negligence in Public Relations," *Bankers Magazine,* 124:13–18 (January, 1932).

NEEDHAM, E. T. "Luring Tired Eyes at Christmas," *Bankers Magazine,* 109:1099–1100 (December, 1924).

"Oh, Mercy NO!" *Bankers Magazine,* 111:349–51 (September, 1925).

PATTON, JAMES. *Manual for the Instruction of "Rings," Railroad and Political, with a Short History of the Chicago and Northwestern "Ring" and the Secret of Its Success in Placing an Over-Issue of Twenty Millions with a Margin of Three Millions, in Three Years.* Abridged edition. New York: American News Company, 1866. 76 pp.

PRINCE, A. R. "Advertising Plays an Important Rôle in Security Values," *Magazine of Wall Street,* 44:620–22 (August 10, 1929).

PROCHNOW, H. V. "Knowing Their Stuff," *Bankers Magazine,* 111:352–54 (September, 1925).

"A Promoter at Work: First-Hand Stories of Experience in Bringing

Opportunities and Investors Together; Legitimate Schemes and Frauds; the Profits of Promoting. By a Promoter." *World's Work,* 9:5876–78 (February, 1905).

Ross, R. E. "Human Interest Campaign to Sell Investments," *Bankers Magazine,* 120:487–90 (April, 1930).

Shields, A. A. "Making Type Alone Tell the Story," *Bankers Magazine,* 112:253–56 (February, 1926).

Thieme, W. L. "New Business Problem for the Average-Sized Bank," *Bankers Magazine,* 117:233–38 (August, 1928).

Weldon, T. T. "Complete Campaign for New Trust Business," *Bankers Magazine,* February, April, July, October, December, 1925.

————. "Hastening the Trust Prospect's Final Action," *Bankers Magazine,* 115:551–53 (November, 1927).

————. "Helping Trust Prospects toward Self-Persuasion," *Bankers Magazine,* 118:725–28 (May, 1929).

————. "Keeping the Lawyer in Mind in Trust New Business Effort," *Bankers Magazine,* 114:683–87 (May, 1927).

————. "Plan for Spending $10,000 in Trust New Business Effort," *Bankers Magazine,* 115:279–90 (September, 1927).

————. "Public Relationship of Trust Companies," *Bankers Magazine,* 114:11–13, 478–80 (January and March, 1927).

————. "Trust Prospect Costs," *Bankers Magazine,* 119:347–51 (September, 1929).

"Where Does the Bank Advertising Manager Fit?" *Bankers Magazine,* 113:37–38 (July, 1926).

Wilson, E. B. "Budget before Investing in Advertising," *Bankers Magazine,* 109:1031 (November, 1924).

————. "Where Premiums May Be at a Discount," *Bankers Magazine,* 109:410 (September, 1924).

Winsor, H. B. "Getting Ahead with Headlines," *Bankers Magazine,* 109:593 (October, 1924).

————. "One Hundred Trust Ads Analyzed," *Bankers Magazine,* 115:817–19 (December, 1927).

————. "What Do Trust Advertisements Do?" *Bankers Magazine,* 117:27–32 (July, 1928).

————. "What Questions Make Good Headlines?" *Bankers Magazine,* 113:378–82 (September, 1926).

WRIGHT, A. F. "How Massachusetts Savings Banks Cooperate to Get New Deposits," *Bankers Magazine*, 110:45-47 (January, 1925).

————. "What Counts Most in Attracting New Customers," *Bankers Magazine*, 113:468-70 (October, 1926).

B. UTILITIES COMPANIES

COCHRAN, C. B. "Privately Owned Utilities in Ohio and Their Efforts to Perpetuate Themselves" (unpublished M. A. thesis, Ohio State University, 1932).

FEDERAL TRADE COMMISSION. *Hearings on Utilities Corporations* (Senate Document no. 92, 70th Congress, 1st Session). Washington, D. C.: Government Printing Office, 1928.

GIANT POWER BOARD [State of Pennsylvania]. *Report to the Governor of Pennsylvania, December 7, 1926.* Harrisburg, Pennsylvania, 1927. 183 pp.

GRUENING, ERNEST. *The Public Pays: A Study of Power Propaganda.* New York: Vanguard, 1931. 273 pp.
Based on the Federal Trade Commission investigation.

HOUSE MILITARY AFFAIRS COMMITTEE. *Hearing on Muscle Shoals* (H. R. 16396, H. R. 16614), January 25 to March 1, 1927. Washington, D. C.: Government Printing Office, 1927. 4 pts., 741 pp.

KINGSBURY, N. C. "Influence of Publicity in Establishing Relations between Utilities and the Public," American Gas Association, Report of Proceedings of 1st Annual Convention, General Session, 1919, pp. 130-45.

LEE, IVY LEDBETTER. *Publicity for Better Service Corporations.* New York, 1916(?). 27 pp.
Substance of an address before the annual convention of the American Electric Railway Association, Atlantic City, October 10, 1916. See also "Discussion Following Address of I. Lee on 'Publicity,'" Proceedings of the American Electric Railway Association, 1916 convention.

LEVIN, JACK. *Power Ethics: An Analysis of the Activities of the Public Utilities in the United States, Based on a Study of the United States Federal Trade Commission Records,* with an introduction by Dr. John H. Gray. New York: Knopf, 1931. 191 pp.

MULLANEY, BERNARD J. *Nine Years of the Illinois Committee on Public Utility Information.* Chicago, 1928.
Organized in 1919 by Samuel Insull "to make the public better acquainted with . . . the public utility industry." The Committee publishes a *News Bulletin* and a *Speakers' Bulletin.*

NATIONAL ELECTRIC LIGHT ASSOCIATION. *The Radical Campaign against*

American Industry, as Shown by the Brief and Exhibits Offered to the Federal Trade Commission in Its Investigation into Public Utilities. Washington, D.C.: National Electric Light Association, 1930. 96 pp.

The National Electric Light Association became the "Edison Institute" in 1933. The officials and offices remain the same.

NORRIS, SENATOR GEORGE W. *The Power Trust and the Press* (Public Ownership League of America, Bulletins nos. 55 and 55-A), 1929.

A speech made on May 20, 1929.

"Prostitution of the Daily Press by the Public Service Corporations," *Arena,* 34: 93-95 (July, 1905).

Gives facsimiles of headings in several newspapers publishing the advertisements.

RAUSHENBUSH, HILMAR S. *High-Power Propaganda.* New York: New Republic, 1928. 89 pp.

Based upon the findings of the Federal Trade Commission.

SELIGMAN, EDWIN R. A. "Academic Obligations: A Report on the Public Utility Propaganda to the Committee on Ethics of the American Association of University Professors," in Bulletin of American Association of University Professors, vol. 16, May, 1930.

THOMPSON, CARL D. *Confessions of the Power Trust.* New York: Dutton, 1932. 670 pp.

There are twenty chapters on "Propaganda Methods" and fourteen on "The War on Public Ownership."

WEBBINK, PAUL. "Public Utilities Propaganda in the Schools," *Editorial Research Reports,* June 28, 1928.

C. MISCELLANEOUS

American Railways, December 15, 1919 —.

The Association of Railroad Executives established a newspaper and said in it: "The purpose of this journal is the dissemination among the American people of correct information about the railroads to the end that their future operation may be for the greatest benefit to the public as a whole."

BAKER, R. S. "How Railroads Make Public Opinion," *McClure's,* 26: 535-49 (March, 1906).

BAUER, W. W. "Antisepticonscious America," *American Mercury,* 29: 323-26 (July, 1933).

BETTER SCHOOLS LEAGUE, INC., 176 W. Adams, Chicago. *Publicity Material for School Bond Campaigns.* Chicago, 1928. Pamphlet.

————. *Seven Years of Service to the School Children of America.* Chicago, 1931.
Organized in 1923. "A group of farsighted, broadminded executives in the school supply and equipment industry."

BROWN, MARGARET LOUISE. *Asa Whitney and His Pacific Railroad Publicity Campaign* (Ph. D. thesis, University of Michigan, 1931). Cedar Rapids, Iowa: Torch Press, 1933. Also in *Mississippi Valley Historical Review*, vol. 20, no. 2 (September, 1933).

"Bubbles, Speculative," *Encyclopedia of the Social Sciences.* (By Willard L. Thorp.)

CHIATI, MAHMOUD BADAWI. *Les Ententes industrielles internationales.* Paris: Montparnasse, 1928. 199 pp.
An examination of the objects, limitations, and effects of international understandings.

COLE, A. H. "Agricultural Crazes," *American Economic Review,* 16: 622–39 (1926).

"Company Unions," *Encyclopedia of the Social Sciences.* (By William M. Leiserson.)

Congressional Record, 63d Congress, 2d Session, May 12, 1914, pp. 8859 ff.
How railroads made public opinion. See page 8865 for chart showing the paths of influence from the railroads to the Interstate Commerce Commission. See pages 8866–9224 for exhibits entitled "Proof of Efforts to Control Decision of Interstate Commerce Commission in Advance Rate Cases."

CONSUMERS' RESEARCH, INC. Confidential reports.
May be used for clues to new publicity campaigns.

COOK, R. C. "A Consumer Study of Hosiery Advertising," *Journal of Home Economics,* 21: 905–08 (December, 1929).

CORPORATION OF FOREIGN BONDHOLDERS, London. Publishes occasional reports on its endeavours to collect on defaulted foreign investments held in England.

DAHL, J. O. *Selling Public Hospitality: A Handbook of Advertising and Publicity for Hotels, Restaurants, and Apartment Houses.* New York and London: Harpers, 1929. 357 pp.

DAMERON, KENNETH. *Men's Wear Merchandising* (Ph. D. thesis, Columbia University, 1930). New York: Ronald Press, 1930. 566 pp.

DAVENPORT, E. H., and COOKE, SIDNEY RUSSELL. *The Oil Trusts and Anglo-American Relations.* London: Macmillan, 1923. 272 pp.

ELLIOT, HOWARD. *Minnesota, the Railways, and Advertising: Address . . . before Minnesota Federation of Commercial Clubs in Annual Convention, St. Paul, January 26, 1911.* St. Paul: McGill, Warner, 1911. 16 pp.

————. *The Relation of the Railway to the Community and State-wide Advertising: Address before the Oregon Development League, Salem, November 29, 1910.* 14 pp.

HAMILTON, WALTER IRVING. *Promoting New Hotels: When Does It Pay?* with an introduction by James S. Warren. New York and London: Harpers, 1930. 158 pp.

HEBB, RICHARD D. *Fundamentals of Company Publicity* (General Management Series, no. 111). New York: American Management Association, 1930. 16 pp.

HERRING, EDWARD PENDLETON. "Special Interests and the Interstate Commerce Commission," *American Political Science Review,* 27: 738–52, 899–918 (October and December, 1933).

"How Publicity Paid Edison," *Literary Digest,* 58: 34–35 (July 6, 1918).

HUSBAND, J. "Building and Advertising: How Advertisements Can Help a Man," *House Beautiful,* 39: 180 (May, 1916).

LEWINSOHN, RICHARD. *Wie sie gross und reich werden: Lebensbilder erfolgreicher Männer.* Berlin: Ullstein, 1927. 287 pp.
Rockefeller, the Rothschilds, Nobel, Morgan, the Krupps, Edison, Ford, Ballin, Leverhulme, Stinnes.

"Light on the Film Trade: Publicity and the Picture," *Saturday Review,* 149: 219–21 (February 22, 1930).

"Modern Coffee Propaganda Methods," *Bulletin of the Pan-American Union,* 62: 603–05 (June, 1928).

MORSE, S. "Trusts Now Speak through Authorized Press Agents," *American Magazine,* 62: 457–63 (September, 1906).

MUNSON, M. S. "Data File Gets Attention of Architects," *Class,* October, 1924, p. 24.

MYERS, GUSTAVUS. *History of the Great American Fortunes.* Chicago: C. H. Kerr, 1911. 3 vols.

NATIONAL CLEAN UP AND PAINT UP CAMPAIGN BUREAU, 3713 Washington Avenue, St. Louis, Missouri. *Clean Up and Paint Up Blue Book.* St. Louis, 1921. 31 pp.
Suggestions for local campaigns.

OLIVIER, M. *La Politique du charbon, 1914–1921.* Paris: Alcan, 1922. 301 pp.

PARKER, T. H. "How a Fifty-Cent Advertisement Disposed of 50,000 Canteloupes," *Country Life,* 23:140 (March, 1913).

PUBLICITY PUBLISHING COMPANY. Circular advertising "Fowler's Publicity." New York: Publicity Publishing Company, 1897(?).
Scroll wound on roller in box in New York Public Library. An early exhibit of publicity for publicity writers.

QUIETT, GLENN C. *They Build the West.* New York: Appleton-Century, 1934. 541 pp.
Includes accounts of promotional efforts of Western railroads and of Far Western cities.

REDDALL, ARTHUR R. *Publicity Methods for Life Underwriters.* New York: Crofts, 1927. 356 pp.
"Approved by the National Association [of Life Underwriters] and the Life Underwriters Association of Canada."

Report of Testimony before the Joint Committee at the New York State Insurance Hearing (1908).
See 2: 1738–65; 3: 2110 ff.; 4: 3192–94.

RIPLEY, WILLIAM ZEBINA. *Railroads: Rates and Regulation.* New York: Longmans, Green, 1912. 659 pp.
Pages 496–98 describe in detail the railways' propaganda in 1906 against the Hepburn Amendments.

SCHÖNEMANN, FRIEDRICH. *Die Kunst der Massenbeeinflussung in den Vereinigten Staaten von Amerika.* Stuttgart: Deutsche Verlagsanstalt, 1924. 212 pp.
Chapter 8 is on business as a carrier of propaganda; pages 190–91 on the Chemical Foundation and the German Dye Industry.

"Secret Remedies and the Press," *World Today,* 44:336–39 (September, 1924).

"The Seventeen Plans," *Drug Trade News,* September 18, 1933.
Seventeen-point program of the United Manufacturers of Proprietary Medicine for defeating a federal pure food and drugs bill.

SINSHEIMER, ALLEN. *Retail Advertising of Men's and Boys' Wear.* New York: Harpers, 1926. 271 pp.

SMITH, F. F. "What Shall a Man Believe? Dentifrice, Mouth, Antiseptic, and Patent Medicine Advertisings," *Hygeia,* 12:216–17 (March, 1934).

UNITED STATES SENATE. *Alleged Activities at the Geneva Conference* (hearings before a subcommittee of the Committee on Naval Af-

fairs, 71st Congress, 1st Session, pursuant to Senate Resolution 114).
Washington, D. C.: Government Printing Office, 1930. 699 pp.

Shows how business interests engaged in publicity campaigns supporting
a big navy.

————. *Hearings before a Special Committee on Investigation of Air
Mail and Ocean Mail Contracts,* 73d Congress, 2d Session, pursuant
to Senate Resolution 349 (72d Congress) and Senate Resolution 143
(73d Congress). Washington, D. C.: Government Printing Office,
1933–34. In nine parts, total 4180 pp.

VAN NAME, W. G. "Anti-Conservation Propaganda," *Science,* 61:
415–16 (April 17, 1925).

Variety (weekly). New York: Variety Publishing Company.

Devoted to theatrical and motion picture news.

WARREN, L. L. " Propaganda in Industrial Relations," *Industrial Management,* 55: 197–98 (March, 1918).

" Zoning Plan," *New York Evening Post,* June 28, 1918; *New York
Times,* June 18, 1918; *Outlook,* January 1, 1919.

Zoning plan for postal rates meant ruin to agricultural publication business, said agricultural publishers.

PART III. PROPAGANDA CLASSIFIED BY THE RESPONSE TO BE ELICITED

Studies that emphasize the objective sought by the propagandist are listed here.

A. RESPONSE TOWARD SYMBOLS OF PERSONS AND GROUPS

I. THE WORLD AS A WHOLE : INTERNATIONALISM AND PROLETARIANISM

Propagandas for world unity in the name of such symbols as *humanity, mankind,* or *proletariat.* For communism throughout the world, see Part III, Section A, Subdivision 1; by country, Part III, Section B, Subdivision 7.

AUBERT, T. "Bolshevism as a World Menace," *Current History.* 30: 225–30 (May, 1929).

CLAPARÈDE, JEAN LOUIS. *L'Enseignement de l'histoire et l'esprit internationale.* Paris: Presses universitaires, 1931. 105 pp.

"Communist Parties," *Encyclopedia of the Social Sciences.* (By Lewis L. Lorwin.)

DUNN, ARTHUR W. "Education for World Understanding through the Junior Red Cross," *Progressive Education.*

EICKHOFF, RICHARD. *Die interparliamentarische Union 1889 bis 1914: Der Vorläufer des Völkerbundes.* Berlin, 1921.

FELLOWSHIP OF RECONCILIATION. *Statement of Purpose.* Pamphlet.

FISHER, HAROLD HENRY. "The Origin of the Third International, 1902–1919." In preparation at Hoover War Library, Stanford University.

FLORINSKY, MICHAEL T. *World Revolution and the USSR.* New York: Macmillan, 1933. 264 pp.
The first two chapters deal with the period of the World War.

GUREVICH, A. *Vozniknovenie i Razvitie Kommunisticheskogo Internatsionala.* Kharkov: Gosizdat, 1925. 224 pp.
The origin and development of the Third International.

GURIAN, WALDEMAR. *Bolschewismus: Einführung in Geschichte und Lehre.* Second edition. Freiburg: Herder, 1932. 338 pp.
English edition: *Bolshevism : Theory and Practice,* translated by E. I. Watkin. New York: Macmillan, 1932. 402 pp.

HARLEY, JOHN EUGENE. *International Understanding: Agencies Educating for a New World.* Stanford University, California: Stanford University, 1931. London: H. Milford, 1931. 604 pp.
Descriptive inventory of organizations.

HOERNLE, EDWIN. *Grundfragen der proletarischen Erziehung.* Berlin: Verlag der Jugend-Internationale, 1929. 209 pp.
Basic questions of proletarian education.

HUDSON, MANLEY O. "Effect of the Present Attitude of the United States toward the League of Nations," *Annals of the American Academy of Political and Social Science,* 120: 112–14 (July, 1925).

INTERNATIONAL INSTITUTE OF INTELLECTUAL COOPERATION. *Bulletin de la coopération intellectuelle.* Official monthly. Paris, 1931 —.
Succeeds *La Coopération intellectuelle,* which began publication in 1929.

The International Institute of Intellectual Cooperation. Paris: League of Nations, 1927. 32 pp.

"Internationale," *Handwörterbuch der Staatswissenschaften.* Fourth edition, 5: 473–77. (By Conrad Schmidt.)
A brief history of all three Internationals.

KURELLA, ALFRED. *Gründung und Aufbau der kommunistischen Jugend-Internationale.* Berlin: Verlag der Jugend-Internationale, 1930. 253 pp.
History of the Communist Youth International.

LASKI, HAROLD J. "The Position and Prospects of Communism," *Foreign Affairs,* 11: 93–106 (October, 1932). League of Nations societies in many countries publish bulletins and reports of their activities.

LENZ, J. *The Second and Third Internationals.* New York, 1931.

LORWIN, LEWIS L. *Labor and Internationalism.* New York: Published by Macmillan for the Institute of Economics of the Brookings Institution, 1929. 682 pp.
Bibliography, pp. 625–46.

MILIUKOV, PAVEL NIKOLAEVICH. *Bolshevism: An International Danger.* London: Allen, 1920. 303 pp.
An exposition of Bolshevik propaganda throughout the world, by a member of the Kerensky government.

MÜNZENBERG, WILLI. *Die dritte Front: Aufzeichnungen aus 15 Jahren proletarischer Jugendbewegung.* Berlin: Neuer deutscher Verlag, 1930. 389 pp.
Continues the history of the Communist Youth movement. Bibliography, pp. 381–89.

————. *Solidarität: Zehn Jahre Internationale Arbeiterhilfe*. Berlin: Neuer deutscher Verlag, 1931. 527 pp.
The Communist auxiliary for workers' aid.

NASH, P. C. "Scholars' International," *Current History*, 34:905–06 (September, 1931).
On the League of Nations Committee on Intellectual Cooperation.

PIATNITSKY, O. *The Organization of a World Party*. London: The Dorrit Press, 1928. 94 pp.

POSTGATE, RAYMOND WILLIAM. *The Workers' International*. London: Swarthmore Press, 1920. New York: Harcourt, Brace, 1920. 125 pp. Bibliography, pp. 117–21.

"Prize Contests of the League of Nations Association," *School and Society*, 31:111–12 (January 25, 1930).

PRUDHOMMEAUX, M. J. *Enquête sur les livres scolaires d'après-guerre*. Paris: Dotation Carnegie, 1923.

RAYMONT, T. "Schools and the League of Nations Union," *Educational Review*, 73:262–63 (May, 1927).

ROCHESTER, ANNA. "Communism: A World Movement," *World Tomorrow*, 13:16–23 (January, 1930).

ROTHBARTH, MARGARETE. *Geistige Zusammenarbeit im Rahmen des Voelkerbundes*. Münster: Aschendorff, 1931. 195 pp.
The first monographic treatment of the League's work in intellectual cooperation, written by a woman closely associated with the League's activities.

SOMBART, WERNER. *Proletarische Sozialismus*. Jena: Fischer, 1924. 2 vols.
Proletarian socialism. Volume 1 is on doctrine, volume 2 on the movement.

STALIN, JOSIF VISSARIONOVICH. *Leninism*. New York: International Publishers, 1928. 472 pp.
The translation of a collection of speeches and articles expressing the views of the Russian leader.

STEKLOFF, G. M. *History of the First International*. London: Martin Lawrence, 1928. 463 pp.

STOKER, SPENCER LONGSHORE. *The Schools and International Understanding*. Chapel Hill: University of North Carolina, 1933. 243 pp. Bibliography, pp. 221–38.

TER MEULEN, JAKOB. *Der Gedanke der Internationalen Organisation in seiner Entwicklung*. The Hague, 1917, 1929.
Analysis of proposals for international organization by the librarian of the Peace Palace at The Hague.

Troisième congrès international d'éducation morale. *L'Esprit International et l'enseignement de l'histoire.* Paris: Delachaux et Niestle, 1923.

TROTSKY, LEON. *L'Internationale communiste après Lénine.* Paris: Rieder, 1930. 438 pp.

————. *Piat' Let Kominterna.* Second edition. Moscow: Gosizdat, 1925. 660 pp.
Five years of the Third International; a detailed account of its organization and work.

————. *La Révolution permanente.* Paris: Rieder, 1932. 340 pp.
Expanded treatment of the theory that proletarian revolution must take place in all countries.

————. *Voina i Revoliutsiia.* Second edition. Moscow: Gosizdat, 1923. 2 vols.
The breakdown of the Second International and the beginnings of the Third.

VANDERVELDE, ÉMILE. "Is Communism Spreading?" *Foreign Affairs,* 8: 84–98 (October, 1929).

WALDECKER, BURKHART. *Die Stellung der menschlichen Gesellschaft zum Völkerbund: Versuch einer Darstellung des Kampfes um die Weltorganisation.* Berlin: Heymann, 1931. 374 pp.
Heavily documented book giving a comprehensive survey of the attitude of various social groups to the idea of international organization generally and to the League of Nations in particular. Discusses the attitudes of parties, social classes, professions, religious groups, countries, etc. Bibliography, pp. 347–74.

WHITE, LYMAN CROMWELL. *The Structure of Private International Organizations* (Ph.D. thesis, Columbia University, 1933). Philadelphia: George S. Ferguson, 1933. 327 pp.
Bibliography, pp. 324–26.

ZINOV'EV, GRIGORII. *L'Internationale communiste au travail.* Paris: Librairie de l'humanité, 1923. 187 pp.
A statement of the aims and activities of the Third International, by one of its leading figures.

2. PAN-NATIONALISM AND PAN-CONTINENTALISM

BÜCHI, ROBERT. *Die Geschichte der pan-amerikanische Bewegung.* Breslau: J. V. Kern, 1914. 189 pp.
Bibliography, pp. xiii–xvi.

BUELL, RAYMOND LESLIE. *International Relations.* Revised edition. New York: Holt, 1929. 838 pp.
A textbook. Chapter 4 summarizes movements for "racial nationalism" (Pan-Germanism, Pan-Turanism, etc.).

————. *Japanese Immigration* (World Peace Foundation Pamphlets, vol. 7, nos. 5–6).

"Following the passage of the Japanese Exclusion Law by the American Congress in 1924, journalists in Japan advocated the convention in Tokyo of a Conference of Colored Races and the formation of a League of Yellow Peoples."

COUDENHOVE-KALERGI, RICHARD NIKOLAUS. *Pan-Europe.* New York: Knopf, 1926. 234 pp.

By the leading protagonist of the Pan-European idea.

DEAKIN, F. B. "Spain and Hispano-Americanism," *Contemporary Review,* May, 1924.

DELAPOSSE. "Le Congrès panafricain," *Afrique française,* 1919, p. 53.

DE WARNAFFE. "Le Mouvement pan-nègre aux États-Unis et ailleurs," *Congo,* May, 1922.

DUBOIS, WILLIAM EDWARD B. "Back to Africa," *Century,* 105: 539–48 (1923).

On the Pan-African movement.

EASTWOOD, REGINALD ALLEN. *The Organization of a Britannic Partnership.* New York: Longmans, Green, 1922. 148 pp.

A discussion of forces making for a reorganization of the imperial machinery. The author suggests a conference of premiers, the appointment of resident dominion ministers, and an imperial court of appeal.

FERRARA, ORESTES. *El panamericanismo y la opinión europea.* Paris: Le Livre libre, 1930. 302 pp.

A survey of the evolution of European opinion on Pan-Americanism, with special reference to the Santiago and Havana conferences and their work, by the Cuban delegate to the League of Nations.

FISCHEL, ALFRED. *Der Panslavismus bis zum Weltkrieg.* Stuttgart and Berlin: Cotta, 1919. 590 pp.

Standard history of Pan-Slavism to the World War. Bibliography, p. vi.

GARVEY, MARCUS. "The Negro's Greatest Enemy," *Current History,* 18: 951–57 (September, 1923).

By the leader of the Universal Negro Improvement Association and American chief of the Pan-African movement of 1923–24. See also *Negro World,* August 16, 1924.

HACKETT, C. W. "How Plans for a Pan-American League of Nations Miscarried," *Current History,* 27: 529–34 (January, 1928).

HERRIOT, ÉDOUARD. *The United States of Europe.* New York: Viking, 1930. 330 pp.

After outlining the past history of the idea of European solidarity, the French radical statesman analyses the contemporary problem.

Höijer, O. *Le Scandanivisme dans le passé et dans le présent.* Paris, 1919.
A book immediately preceding the inception of the Norden movement.

Hutchinson, Paul. *The United States of Europe.* Chicago: Willett, Clark, and Colby, 1929. 225 pp.
An account of the origin of the idea, with a description of tendencies and obstacles.

Leger, Louis Paul Marie. *Le Panslavisme et l'intérêt français.* Paris: Flammarion, 1917. 360 pp.
By the historian of *Le Monde slave.*

Lewin, I. "Die panturanische Idee," *Preussische Jahrbücher,* 231: 58–69 (January, 1933).

Lote, R. "Le Germanisme d'après-guerre dans l'est de l'Europe," *Université de Grenoble, annales,* N. S., 1926, Lett. 3, pp. 13–26.
Post-war Germanism in eastern Europe.

Molisch, Paul. *Geschichte der deutschnationalen Bewegung in Oesterreich von ihren Anfängen bis zum Verfall der Monarchie.* Jena: Fischer, 1926. 278 pp.
A standard history of the German nationalist movement in Austria to 1918.

"Norden," *American Scandinavian Review,* August, 1923.
The Norden movement is mainly educational and cultural, according to this summary of its activities.

Ossendowski, Ferdinand. "King of the World," *Century,* 107: 246–56 (December, 1923).
Current Asiatic legend of "a yellow sovereign with divine power who is to come and rule over the world in the name of the yellow people." May figure in Pan-Asiatic symbolism in the future.

Paller, Heinz von. *Der grossdeutsche Gedanke.* Leipzig: Hofstetter, 1928. 163 pp.
A history of the Greater German idea, with special reference to the question of *Anschluss.*

"Pan-Turanianism," *Encyclopedia Britannica,* twelfth edition.

Rippy, J. Fred. "Pan-Hispanic Propaganda in Hispanic America," *Political Science Quarterly,* 37: 395 (March, 1922).

Sarolea, Charles. "Bolshevism and World Revolution," *Current History,* 19: 721–29 (February, 1924).
Discusses the possibility of Russian leadership of a Pan-Asiatic movement.

Snouck-Hurgronje. "Islam and Turkish Nationalism," *Foreign Affairs,* September 15, 1924.

Stoddard, T. L. "Pan-Turanism," *American Political Science Review,* 11:12 (1917).

Von Sosnosky. "The New Pan-Germanism," *Quarterly Review,* 240: 308 (1923).

Wertheimer, Mildred Saiz. *The Pan-German League, 1890–1914* (Columbia University Studies in History, Economics, and Public Law, vol. 112, no. 2). New York: Columbia University, 1924. 256 pp.
Discloses that this famous nationalist league drew its support from small bourgeois intellectuals and merchants.

Wilgus, Alva Curtis. "James G. Blaine and the Pan-American Movement" (unpublished Ph. D. thesis, University of Wisconsin, 1922).

Wuorinen, John Henry. "Efforts to Form a Union of Baltic States," *Current History,* 20:609–14 (July, 1924).

"X" (pseudonym). "Le Panislamisme et le pan-Turquisme," *Revue du monde musulman,* 22:179 (1913).

3. INDEPENDENCE NATIONALISM

Struggles in the name of a national symbol to become or to remain a state.

Andrea, U. d'. *Corradini e il nazionalismo.* Rome: Augustea, 1928. 111 pp.
A study of the origins of Italian nationalism in the pre-war years; useful for an understanding of Fascist backgrounds.

Armstrong, P. C. "Forces of Disunion in Canada," *Current History,* 20:601–06 (July, 1924).
Discusses a "separatist movement" in Quebec and the Maritime Province.

Banerjee, Sir Surendranath. *A Nation in the Making.* New York: Oxford University, 1925. 435 pp.
A history of Indian national development in the last half century, by a man long active in public life.

Beach, Thomas Miller. *Twenty-five Years in the Secret Service, by Henri Le Carone (pseudonym).* Fifth edition. London: W. Heinemann, 1892. 311 pp.
Mainly an account of the author's connection with the Fenian and other Irish movements in the United States and Canada.

Benda, Julien. *Esquisse d'une histoire des français dans leur volonté d'être une nation.* Paris: Gallimard, 1932. 270 pp.

BENES, EDVARD. *Svetova Valka a Nase Revolucie*. Prague:" Orbis," 1927–28. 3 vols.

A detailed study of the Czech movement for independence during the World War. The memoirs of Masaryk's chief lieutenant; one of the fundamental sources. French edition of volumes 1 and 2: *Souvenirs de guerre et la révolution*. Paris: Leroux, 1928–29. German edition: *Der Aufstand der Nationen*. Berlin: Cassirer, 1928. 755 pp. Somewhat abridged. English edition: *My War Memoirs*. London: Allen and Unwin, 1928. 512 pp. Considerably abridged.

BERGER, JULIUS. *Die Propaganda für den Keren Kajemeth*. Jerusalem, 1925. 36 pp.

The propaganda for Zionism.

BOEHM, MAX HILDEBERT. *Europa Irredenta: Eine Einführung in das Nationalitätenproblem der Gegenwart*. Berlin: R. Hobbing, 1923. 335 pp.

See also the *Ethnopolitischer Almanach,* founded in 1931 and published in Vienna and Leipzig, of which Boehm is co-editor with Otto Junghann.

BÖHM, ADOLF. *Die zionistische Bewegung*. Berlin, 1920.

BRODA, RUDOLF. " The Revival of Nationalities in the Soviet Union," *American Journal of Sociology*, 37: 82–94 (July, 1931).

BROUCKE, JEANNE. *L'Empire Arabe d'Ibn Seoud*. Brussels: Falk, 1929. 89 pp.

Arab nationalism.

La Catalogne rebelle. Paris: Agence mondiale, 1927.

A volume containing documents on the Catalan nationalist movement.

CLOUGH, SHEPARD BANCROFT. *A History of the Flemish Movement in Belgium*. New York: R. R. Smith, 1930. 316 pp.

Contains bibliography.

" Comitadji " (Interior Macedonian Revolutionary Society), *Encyclopedia of the Social Sciences*. (By Albert Sonnichsen.)

CYNN, HUGH HEUNG WO. *The Rebirth of Korea*. New York: Abingdon Press, 1920. 272 pp.

A statement of the aims of the independence movement, by a native Christian leader.

DAWSON, HENRY BARTON. *The Sons of Liberty in New York*. Poughkeepsie, New York: Platt and Schram, 1859. 118 pp.

EGGEN VAN TERLAN, J. L. *Contribution à l'histoire du mouvement flamand pendant la guerre*. Brussels: L'Églantine, 1931. 96 pp.

The account of an active Flemish agitator.

EICHSTÄDT, VOLKMAR. *Die deutsche Publizistik von 1830: Ein Beitrag zur Entwicklungsgeschichte der konstitutionellen und nationalen Tendenzen.* Berlin: Ebering, 1933. 209 pp.

ELVIKEN, ANDREAS. *Die Entwicklung des norwegischen Nationalismus* (Historische Studien, edited by Dr. E. Ebering, Heft 198). Berlin: Ebering, 1930. 132 pp.

ERGANG, ROBERT REINHOLD. *Herder and the Foundations of German Nationalism* (Ph. D. thesis, Columbia University). New York: Columbia University, 1931. London: P. S. King, 1931. 288 pp.
Bibliography, pp. 267–82.

FALNES, OSCAR JULIUS. *National Romanticism in Norway* (Columbia University Studies in History, Economics, and Public Law, no. 386). New York: Columbia University, 1933. London: P. S. King, 1933. 398 pp.
Bibliography, pp. 373–84.

GANDHI, MOHANDAS KARAMCHI. *Young India, 1919–1922, with a Brief Sketch of the Non-Cooperative Movement by Babu Rajendra Prasad.* New York: Huebsch, 1923. 1199 pp.
Now published by the Viking Press.

GEORGES-GAULIS, BERTHE. *Angora, Constantinople, Londres: Moustafa Kemal et la politique anglaise en Orient.* Paris: Colin, 1922. 257 pp.
The rise and success of the Turkish nationalist movement.

GILCHRIST, ROBERT NIVEN. *Indian Nationality.* New York: Longmans, Green, 1920. 246 pp.
A study of race, language, religion, and caste as factors in the making of Indian nationalism.

GIURATI, GIOVANNI. *La vigilia.* Milan: Mondadori, 1930. 318 pp.
The Fascist leader and former president of the Trento and Trieste Society tells the story of the Society's irredentist activity and agitation in the period from January, 1913, until Italy's entrance into the World War.

GRIFFIN, MARTIN IGNATIUS JOSEPH. *Catholics and the American Revolution.* Ridley Park, Pennsylvania: The Author, 1907–11. 3 vols.

HAUSER, HENRI. *Le Principe des nationalités: Ses origines historiques.* Paris: Alcan, 1916. 30 pp.

HAYES, CARLTON J. H. *Essays on Nationalism.* New York: Macmillan, 1926. 279 pp.
Nationalism is viewed as a substitute for declining religion. Bibliography, pp. 277–79.

————. *The Historical Evolution of Modern Nationalism.* New York: R. R. Smith, 1931. 327 pp.
An ideological study, intended to supplement the author's *Essays on Nationalism.*

HUMPHREY, EDWARD FRANK. *Nationalism and Religion in America, 1774–1789.* Boston: Chipman Law Publishing Company, 1924. 536 pp.
Bibliography, pp. 517–32.

HUNTER, EARLE LESLIE. *A Sociological Analysis of Certain Types of Patriotism: A Study of Certain Patriotic Attitudes, Particularly as These Appear in Peacetime Controversies in the United States* (Ph. D. thesis, Columbia University, 1932). New York: Paul Maisel, 1932. 263 pp.

"Irredentism," *Encyclopedia of the Social Sciences.* (By Max Hildebert Boehm.)

JOAD. "The Spanish Separatists," *Foreign Affairs,* May, 1924.
On the Catalan independence movement.

JOHANNET, RENÉ. *Le Principe des nationalités.* New edition. Paris: Nouvelle librairie nationale, 1923. 454 pp.

JOHNSEN, JULIA EMILY, compiler. *Independence for the Philippines.* New York: H. W. Wilson, 1924. 99 pp.
Debate material for and against the independence movement.

KOCH, D. M. G. *Herleving.* Weltevreden: Kolff, 1922. 486 pp.
A detailed history of the national movement in India, by a Dutch East-Indian publicist.

KOHN, HANS. *A History of Nationalism in the East* (translated from the German by Margaret M. Green). New York: Harcourt, Brace, 1929. 476 pp.
Bibliography, pp. 433–58. The German edition was entitled *Geschichte der Nationalen Bewegung im Orient.* Berlin-Grunewald: K. Vowinckel, 1928. 377 pp. Bibliography, pp. 343–58.

————. *Nationalism and Imperialism in the Hither East.* New York: Harcourt, Brace, 1932. 339 pp.
First published in German as *Nationalismus und Imperialismus im vorderen Orient.* Frankfort-on-the-Main: Societäts-Verlag, 1931. 455 pp.

————. *Nationalism in the Soviet Union.* London: Routledge, 1933. 164 pp.
First published in German as *Der Nationalismus in der Sowjetunion.* Frankfort-on-the-Main: Societäts-Verlag, 1932. 150 pp.

————. *Nationalismus: Über die Bedeutung des Nationalismus in*

Judentum und in der Gegenwart. Vienna and Leipzig: Löwit, 1922. 128 pp.
Stresses the rôle of nationalism as " secular religion."

KUSTER, R. *Die polnische Irredenta in West-Oberschlesien.* Berlin: Hallig, 1931. 178 pp.
An account of Polish propaganda by a man long resident in the disputed area. The book quotes extensively from the Polish press.

LOVETT, SIR HARRINGTON VERNEY. *A History of the Indian Nationalist Movement.* London: John Murray, 1920. 285 pp.
The earlier development of the movement, written by an official of long experience.

MACCALLUM, ELIZABETH PAULINE. *The Nationalist Crusade in Syria.* New York: Foreign Policy Association, 1928. 299 pp.
Bibliography, pp. 278-90.

MARGOLIN, ARNOL'D DAVIDOVICH. *Ukraine i Politika Antany.* Berlin: Efron, 1922. 397 pp.
An account of the Ukrainian movement and of the efforts made by Ukrainian groups to secure action from the Powers.

MICHELS, ROBERTO. *Der Patriotismus: Prolegomena zu seiner soziologischen Analyse.* Munich and Leipzig: Duncker und Humblot, 1929. 269 pp.
Chapter 4 is on the sociology of national anthems.

————. " Zur historischen Analyse des Patriotismus," *Archiv für Sozialwissenschaft und Sozialpolitik,* 36: 14-43, 394-449 (1913).
Influential sketch of the history of patriotism.

MITSCHERLICH, WALDEMAR OSKAR EILHARD. *Nationalismus: Die Geschichte einer Idee.* Leipzig: C. L. Hirschfeld, 1929.
Emphasizes the economic foundations of nationalism.

MOTVANI, K. L. "Propaganda in Mahatma Gandhi's Movement," *Social Forces,* June, 1930.

OSTROROG, LEON HRABIA. *The Angora Reform.* London: University of London, 1928. 99 pp.
Three lectures in which the author reviews the rise of Turkish nationalism resulting from the treaty of Sèvres, discusses the reasons for the overthrow of the Sultanate, and surveys the great reforms.

PAVLOVICH, M. (pseudonym of Mikhail Vel'tman), GURKO-KRIAZHIN, V. A., and VEL'TMAN, L. *Indiia v Bor'be za Nezavisimost'.* Moscow: Nauchnaia Assotsiatsiia Vostokovedeniia, 1925. 117 pp.
A brief survey of the nationalist movement by Bolshevik writers, one of them the editor of *Novyi Vostok.*

PERGLER, CHARLES. *America in the Struggle for Czechoslovak Independence.* Philadelphia: Dorrance, 1926. 112 pp.

PIEPER, E. H. "The Fenian Movement" (unpublished Ph. D. thesis, University of Illinois, 1931).
The Irish nationalist movement.

PINSON, KOPPEL S. *Bibliographical Introduction to Nationalism.* Announced. New York: Columbia University.

Propaganda cubana por la Independencia. New York: A. W. Howes, 1897. 76 pp.

REISS, RODOLPHE ARCHIBALD. *The Comitadji Question in Southern Serbia.* London: Hazell, 1924. 156 pp.
An account, by a Swiss professor friendly to the Serbian cause, of the Macedonian Revolutionary Organization and its post-war activities.

RENAUT, FRANCIS P. *La Politique de propagande des Américains durant la guerre d'indépendance.* Paris: Graouli, 1922—. 2 vols.
American propaganda abroad during the War for Independence. Bibliography, 1: 341–42.

RICE, DIANA. "The Free Isle of St. Louis," *New York Times Magazine,* August 24, 1924.
"In the spring of 1924 the Isle St. Louis, located in the Seine River at Paris, is said to have appealed to the League of Nations for autonomy, saying, 'High Magistrates of the Planet, Great Judges of the World Court, Guardians of the Pact of Nations, Protectors of all small oppressed peoples forgotten or wronged, l'île St. Louis hurls toward you a cry of appeal and protestation.'" — R. L. BUELL in *International Relations* (1929), p. 45.

SABRY, MOUSTAPHA. "La Genèse de l'esprit national égyptien, 1863–1882." Paris, 1924. 288 pp.
A dissertation based not only upon printed books and newspapers but also upon the unpublished memoirs of Arabi Pasha and of Mohammed Abduh, the intellectual leader of the earlier national movement. Bibliography, pp. 233–36.

SCHLESINGER, ARTHUR MEIER. *The Colonial Merchants and the American Revolution, 1763–1776.* (Columbia University Studies in History, Economics, and Public Law, no. 182). New York: Columbia University, 1918. 647 pp.
Bibliography, pp. 614–29.

SFORZA, CARLO. "Italy and Fascism," *Foreign Affairs,* 3: 358–70 (1924).

SMOGORZEWSKI, CASIMIR. *L'Union sacrée polonaise.* Paris: Gebethner et Wolff, 1929. 71 pp.
The story of the Polish organization during the war, based on unpublished material.

SROKOWSKI, KONSTANTY. *N. K. N. Zarys Historji Naczelnego Komitetu Narodowego.* Cracow: Krakowska Spolka Wydawnicza, 1923. 380 pp.

History of the National Supreme Committee, by its secretary-general. The author covers the period to the autumn of 1915 and throws much light on the activity of the Polish-Austrian group.

SULZBACH, WALTER. *Nationales Gemeinschaftsgefühl und wirtschaftliches Interesse.* Leipzig, 1929.

SYMONS, M. TRAVERS. *Britain and Egypt: The Rise of Egyptian Nationalism.* London: C. Palmer, 1925. 331 pp.

A history of the nationalist movement since the days of Arabi. Lays stress upon the importance of the University of Cairo as well as upon Arabi Pasha.

TETBY, P. "Fascism Today and Tomorrow," *Communist Review,* Series 3, 1:116–22 (February, 1929).

Survey of Fascism from a Communist viewpoint.

TURUK, F. *Belorusskoe Dvizhenie.* Moscow: Gosizdat, 1921. 145 pp.

An outline of the history of the White Russian movement in its national and revolutionary aspects.

VAN GENNEP, ARNOLD. *Traité comparatif des nationalités,* vol. 1. Paris, 1922.

Belgian ethnologist studies nationalisms as trait-complexes.

WEBSTER, JAMES BENJAMIN. *Christian Education and the National Consciousness in China.* New York: Dutton, 1923. 321 pp.

From an historical and sociological point of view.

WEILL, GEORGES JACQUES. *L'Éveil des nationalités et le mouvement libéral, 1815–1848* (Peuples et civilisations, vol. 15). Paris: Alcan, 1930. 592 pp.

WUORINEN, JOHN HENRY. *Nationalism in Modern Finland* (Ph.D. thesis, Columbia University, 1931). New York: Columbia University, 1931. 302 pp.

Makes use of a mass of material, unpublished and published, in Swedish and Finnish, bearing on the evolution of the national movement in the nineteenth and twentieth centuries. Bibliography, pp. 281–94.

ZIEGLER, HEINZ O. *Die moderne Nation: Ein Beitrag zur politischen Soziologie.* Tübingen: Mohr, 1931. 308 pp.

A critical review of sociological theories of nationalism.

B. RESPONSE TOWARD SYMBOLS OF POLICY

I. LOCAL CIVIC POLICY

Unofficial propaganda to modify the policy and organization of local official agencies, and of local institutions performing public functions.

AMERICAN CONSTRUCTION COUNCIL. *The Rebuilding of Slum Districts* (preliminary report). 1930. 5 pp.

The Council proposes a national movement for the rebuilding of slum districts by regional planning agencies working cordially with limited dividend corporations and municipal authorities.

BELLOWS, H. W. *Historical Sketch of the Union League Club.* New York, 1879.

GOVERNMENTAL RESEARCH CONFERENCE. *Twenty Years of Municipal Research: A Brief Discussion of the Municipal Research Movement in America.* New York, 1927. 36 pp.

MILLS, W. H., editor. *The Manchester Reform Club, 1871–1921.* Manchester, 1922.

NATIONAL ASSOCIATION OF CIVIC SECRETARIES. *City Clubs.* 1922.

REFORM CLUB OF NEW YORK. *Officers and Committees.* Issued by the Club from time to time since 1889.

General description of the officers and committees of the Club, its constitution, etc. The Club is interested in the tariff, the subways, "sound currency," New York Port problems, "some reprehensible practices of American government," etc. It has issued broadsides, pamphlets, and annual report, and a semi-monthly journal called *Tariff Reform.*

SPACKMAN, BARBARA. "The Woman's City Club of Chicago: A Civic Pressure Group" (unpublished A. M. thesis, University of Chicago, 1930. 156 pp.).

WARNER, EARL E. "The Activities of Citizen Organizations in the State Administration of Ohio."

In preparation at Ohio State University.

WEBER, GUSTAVUS ADOLPHUS. *Organized Efforts for the Improvement of Methods of Administration in the United States.* New York and London: Published by Appleton for the Institute of Government Research, 1919. 391 pp.

2. HUMANITARIAN AND WELFARE POLICY

A. BIBLIOGRAPHY

EATON, ALLEN, in collaboration with HARRISON, SHELBY M. *A Bibliog-*

raphy of Social Surveys. New York: Russell Sage Foundation, 1930. 467 pp.

By subjects, this index covers the state of every imaginable social institution from "Accidents" to "Zoning," including "Poliomyelitis" and Chinese churches. By areas it covers the United States (by states and cities) and certain European and Asiatic localities.

LIBRARY OF CONGRESS. *Brief List of References on the Historical Development of Charity and Social Work* (Select List of References no. 553). Washington, D. C.: Government Printing Office, 1921.

MUSCIO, B. *Vocational Guidance: A Review of the Literature* (Industrial Fatigue Research Board Report no. 12). London: H. M. Stationery Office, 1921.

ROUTZAHN, EVART G., and ROUTZAHN, MARY SWAIN. *Publicity Methods Reading List.* New York: Russell Sage Foundation, 1924. 48 pp.

Select references on publicity in social work and kindred fields.

ROUTZAHN, MARY SWAIN. "Six-Book Shelf on Publicity Methods," *Family,* 5: 35 (April, 1924).

WATSON, GOODWIN BARBOUR, and BIDDLE, DELIA H. *A Year of Research: 1927.* Chicago: Religious Education Association, 1929. 82 pp.

" Some investigations published between January 1, 1927, and January 1, 1928, bearing upon the program of religious, educational, and social agencies." Annotated bibliography, pp. 25–82.

WILCOX, JEROME KEAR. "The Adult Education Work of the United States Government, with a Selected Bibliography of Resultant Publications" (unpublished M. A. thesis, University of Illinois, 1928). 242 pp.

Bibliography, pp. 83–230.

ZIMAND, SAVEL. *Modern Social Movements: Descriptive Summaries and Bibliographies.* New York: H. W. Wilson, 1921. 260 pp.

Prepared under the auspices of the Bureau of Industrial Research.

B. REFERENCES

ABBOTT, GRACE. "History of the Juvenile Court Movement throughout the World," in Jane Addams and others, *The Child, the Clinic, and the Court,* pp. 267–73. New York, 1925.

"Abolition," *Encyclopedia of the Social Sciences.* (By Frank J. Klingberg.)

AMERICAN SCENIC AND HISTORIC PRESERVATION SOCIETY. Annual Reports. Albany, 1899 —.

"Animal Protection," *Encyclopedia of the Social Sciences.* (By William J. Schultz.)

BACH, ADOLF. "Kampf gegen die deutschen Spielbanken des neunzehnten Jahrhunderts," *Schmöllers Jahrbuch,* 46: 785–811 (1922). Anti-gambling propaganda.

BACON, ALBION FELLOWS. *Beauty for Ashes.* New York: Donald, Mead, 1914. 360 pp.
"Story of the winning of the Indiana State Housing Law by the woman who did it."

BALDWIN, W. H. "Publicity as a Means of Social Reform," *North American Review,* 173: 845–53 (1901).

BARNES, GILBERT HOBBS. *The Anti-Slavery Impulse, 1830–1844.* New York: D. Appleton–Century Company, 1934. 298 pp.
The author, a professor of economics, denies the adequacy of economic interpretations of the anti-slavery movement, and finds its motivation in a wave of moral impulses. Contains bibliographies.

BARTON, WILLIAM ELEAZER. *The Life of Clara Barton.* Boston and New York: Houghton Mifflin, 1922. 2 vols.
Founder of the American Red Cross.

BEST, HARRY. *Blindness and the Blind in the United States.* New York: Macmillan, 1933. 714 pp.
Standard treatise; deals extensively with movements for prevention of blindness and for the betterment of the condition of the blind.

Better Times.
Periodical about money-raising for philanthropic purposes. Starting with the October, 1923, issue, it includes a bi-monthly supplement on publicity, money-raising, and administrative methods.

BREITENBAEG, H. P. "Converting Wartime Experiments in Publicity to Community Use," Proceedings of the National Conference of Social Work, 1919, pp. 683–89.

BROCKWAY, ZEBULON REED. *Fifty Years of Prison Reform: An Autobiography.* New York: Charities Publication Committee, 1912. 437 pp.
Mr. Brockway was superintendent of the Elmira Reformatory from 1876 to 1900.

BROWN, J. R. "Publicity vs. Propaganda in Family (Social) Work," *Family,* 7: 75–79 (May, 1926).

BUELL, RAYMOND LESLIE. *International Relations.* Revised edition. New York: Holt, 1929. 838 pp.
Chapter 12 is on "International Humanitarianism."

BURKE, JOHN. "Publicity and Social Reform," *Catholic World,* 91: 198–211 (May, 1910).

CAULFIELD, ERNEST. *The Infant Welfare Movement in the Eighteenth Century.* New York: Paul B. Hoeber, 1931. 203 pp.

Bibliography, pp. 190–95.

CHEYNEY, EDWARD POTTS. *Modern English Reform, from Individualism to Socialism.* Philadelphia: University of Pennsylvania, 1931. London: Oxford, 1931. 223 pp.

Discusses the whole reform movement in Great Britain in the nineteenth century from the viewpoint of the special interests and agitators.

CHICAGO COUNCIL OF SOCIAL AGENCIES. *Financing of Social Agencies.* Chicago, 1924. 190 pp.

" Christian Socialism," *Encyclopedia of the Social Sciences.* (By Maurice B. Reckitt and Vida D. Scudder.)

CLARKSON, THOMAS. *The History of the Rise, Progress, and Accomplishment of the Abolition of the African Slave-Trade by the British Parliament.* London: Longman, Hurst, Reese, and Orm, 1808. 2 vols.

COLEMAN, SYDNEY H. *Humane Society Leaders in America, with a Sketch of the Early History of the Humane Movement in England.* Albany: American Humane Association, 1924. 270 pp.

COUPLAND, R. *The British Anti-Slavery Movement.* London: Butterworth, 1933. 256 pp.

Cruelties of Civilization. London: Humanitarian League Publications, 1895–97. 3 vols.

See especially volume 1, pages 3–27, "Humanitarianism: Its General Principles and Progress," by H. S. Salt, editor of the series.

CULPIN, EWART G. *The Garden City Movement Up-to-Date.* London: Garden Cities and Town Planning Association, 1913. 82 pp.

DIXON, WILLIAM HEPWORTH. *John Howard and the Prison-World of Europe.* Third edition. New York: R. Carter, 1850. London: Jackson and Walford, 1850. 401 pp.

DU BOIS, W. E. BURGHARDT. *The Suppression of the African Slave-Trade.* New York: Longmans, Green, 1896. 335 pp.

Encyclopedia of Social Reform. Third edition. New York and London: Funk and Wagnalls, 1910. 1321 pp.

Covers "all social reform movements and activities." Written by social workers, social scientists, and statisticians.

" Ethical Culture Movement," *Encyclopedia of the Social Sciences.* (By Herbert W. Schneider.)

" The ethical culture societies have initiated or actually promoted such movements as tenement house reform, abolition of child labor, visiting nurse associations, settlement houses . . . and legal aid bureaus. In Germany they have promoted public libraries and numerous charitable enterprises. The founding of the Secular Education League in England in 1907, the Universal Peace Congress in 1911, and the International Congresses on Moral Education also deserve mention. The movement originally sponsored the publication of the *Ethical Record* (1888–90) which was succeeded by the *International Journal of Ethics* (1890)."

EVANS, ALVA DELBERT, and HOWARD, L. G. REDMOND. *The Romance of the British Hospital Movement.* London: Hutchinson, 1930. 360 pp.

EVANS, RICHARDSON. *An Account of the Scapa Society.* London: Constable, 1926. 374 pp.

A society founded in 1893 to prevent or check the abuses of public advertising, especially billboards. Has offices near and cooperates with the National Trust for Places of Historic Interest and the Commons and Footpaths Preservation Society.

FAIRHOLME, EDWARD GEORGE, and PAIN, WELLESLEY. *A Century of Work for Animals: The History of the R.S.P.C.A., 1824–1924,* with a foreword by H.R.H. the Prince of Wales, and an introduction by Lord Lambourne. London: John Murray, 1924. 298 pp.

"Friendly Societies," *Encyclopedia of the Social Sciences.* (By W. H. Dawson.)

FRIMODT-MÖLLER, C. "Work of Medical Missions," *International Review of Missions,* 17: 186–97 (January, 1928).

"Garden Cities," *Encyclopedia of the Social Sciences.* (By Thomas Adams.)

GARDNER, A. R. L. *The Place of John Howard in Penal Reform* (Howard League Pamphlets, N.S., no. 9). London: Howard League, 1926.

GRIES, JOHN M., and FORD, JAMES, editors. *Housing Objectives and Programs.* Washington, D. C.: The President's Conference on Home Building and Home Ownership, 1932. 345 pp.

HARRIS, JOHN H. *A Century of Emancipation.* London: Dent, 1933. 287 pp.

On the protection of aborigines.

HART, ALBERT BUSHNELL. *Slavery and Abolition, 1831–1841.* New York and London: Harpers, 1906. 360 pp.

Bibliography, pp. 324–43.

HOPKINS, C. C. "Psychology of Advertising as Applied to Social Work," *Proceedings of the National Conference of Social Work,* 1910, pp. 547–55.

"Humanitarianism," *Encyclopedia of the Social Sciences.* (By Crane Brinton.)

IMMIGRANTS' PROTECTIVE LEAGUE OF CHICAGO. Annual Reports, 1909—. See also *The Immigrants' Protective League in 1930,* published by the League. 60 pp.

JACOBS, LEO. *Three Types of Practical Ethical Movements of the Past Half Century.* New York: Macmillan, 1922. 184 pp.
Contents: (1) The religious ethical movement; (2) the social ethical movement; (3) the ethical culture movement. Bibliography, pp. 175–81.

JENKS, CAMERON. *The Development of Governmental Forest Control in the United States.* Baltimore, 1928.
Conservation of natural resources as a means to the conservation of human resources.

JOHNSON, OLIVER. *William Lloyd Garrison and His Times, or, Sketches of the Anti-Slavery Movement.* New edition. Boston: B. B. Russell, 1881. 432 pp.

JONES, DORSEY D. *Edwin Chadwick and the Early Public Health Movement in England* (University of Iowa Studies in the Social Sciences, vol. 9, no. 3). Iowa City: University of Iowa, 1931. 160 pp.

KERWIN, JEROME GREGORY. *Federal Water Power Legislation* (Columbia University Studies in History, Economics, and Public Law, no. 274). New York: Columbia University, 1926. 396 pp.
The interplay of interest groups.

KLINGBERG, FRANK JOSEPH. *The Anti-Slavery Movement in England: A Study in English Humanitarianism* (Ph. D. thesis, Yale University, 1926). New Haven: Yale University, 1926. London: Oxford University, 1926. 390 pp.
Bibliography, pp. 309–20.

LANE-CLAYPON, JANET ELIZABETH. *The Child Welfare Movement.* London: Bell, 1920. 341 pp.

LINDEMANN, K. H. "Gartenstadtbewegung, Stadtverwaltung und Bodenreform," *Schmöllers Jahrbuch,* 15: 225–80 (1931).

LIPPMANN, WALTER. *The Campaign against Sweating.* New York: National Consumers' League, 1915. 29 pp. Reprinted from the *New Republic,* March 27, 1915.

LUCAS, W. P. "History of the Child Welfare Movement," *Nelson's Loose-Leaf Living Medicine* (New York, 1928), vol. 7, chap. 2.

McCREA, ROSWELL CHEYNEY. *The Humane Movement: A Descriptive Survey, Prepared on the Henry Bergh Foundation for the Promo-*

tion of Humane Education in Columbia University. New York: Columbia University, 1910. 444 pp.

Bibliography, pp. 279–319.

MacFayden, Dugald, compiler and writer. *Sir Ebenezer Howard and the Town Planning Movement*. Manchester: University of Manchester, 1933. 166 pp.

Biography of a shorthand reporter in the House of Commons who, under the influence of Edward Bellamy's *Looking Backward,* founded the garden-city movement in England.

Mandel, Arch. "What Shall We Tell the Public: A Critical Examination of Social Work Publicity," Proceedings of National Council of Social Work, 1932, pp. 565–74.

Manson, John. *The Salvation Army and the Public: A Religious, Social, and Financial Study*. Second edition. London: Routledge, 1908. New York: Dutton, 1908. 376 pp.

Mathieson, William Law. *British Slavery and Its Abolition, 1823–1838*. New York and London: Longmans, Green, 1926. 318 pp.

"Inquiry is confined to the West Indian group of colonies, including British Guiana and British Honduras." — *Preface.*

Middaugh, B. "After Unemployment Publicity — What?" *Family,* 12: 73–75 (May, 1931).

Morgan, J. E. "Propaganda: Its Relation to the Child Labor Issue," *Education,* 46:51–54 (September, 1925).

National Child Labor Committee. This group, organized in 1904, has published numerous reports, bulletins, drafts of proposed legislation, etc.

National Civic Federation. Carries on a program designed to improve relationships between capital and labor; combats Communistic and Socialistic attempts to win support of American labor unions; publishes pamphlets, leaflets, news releases, and reports of its numerous committees of inquiry.

National Consumers League. Publishes a long series of books and booklets on child labor legislation, women's hours of work, minimum wages, comments on Supreme Court decisions, and a bibliography on Women in Industry (Women in Industry Series, no. 5).

National Housing Association. *Housing Betterment,* official organ (quarterly) through 1927. *Housing,* official organ since 1928.

National Safety Council, Washington, D. C. Transactions and reports.

Norton, William John. *The Co-operative Movement in Social Work* (Social Welfare Library). New York: Macmillan, 1927. 373 pp.

PARMELEE, MAURICE. "The Rise of Modern Humanitarianism," *American Journal of Sociology*, 21:345–59 (1915).

PEASE, EDWARD REYNOLDS. *History of the Fabian Society.* Second edition. London: Fabian Society, 1925. 306 pp.
Complete list of Fabian publications, 1884–1924, pp. 289–302.

"Propaganda Methods of Opponents of Protective Labor Legislation," *American Labor Legislation Review*, 15:106–21 (June, 1925).
Symposium.

PROUTT. "Publicity: Before and After," *Family*, 10:301–05 (February, 1930).
Publicity for social work.

PUBLIC OWNERSHIP LEAGUE OF AMERICA. *Public Ownership.* January, 1921 —.
Organ of the League. Also publishes annual reports, some sixty bulletins, miscellaneous newspaper releases, etc., in support of municipal ownership of utilities, etc.

RAINWATER, CLARENCE ELMER. *The Play Movement in the United States* (Ph.D. thesis, University of Chicago). Chicago: University of Chicago, 1921. 371 pp.
Bibliography, pp. 356–65.

Reform Bulletin. Albany: Published by the Rev. O. R. Miller, January, 1910 —.
Weekly report concerning moral reform in the state of New York. The Rev. Miller is state superintendent of the New York Civic League.

ROUTZAHN, EVART G. *Elements of a Social Publicity Program.* New York: The Russell Sage Foundation, 1920. 17 pp.
Paper read before the Division on the Organization of Social Forces at the New Orleans meeting of the National Conference of Social Work, April, 1920.

ROUTZAHN, MARY SWAIN. "Using Case Stories in Newspaper Publicity," *Family*, 6:168–70 (October, 1925).

ROUTZAHN, MARY SWAIN, and ROUTZAHN, EVART G. *Publicity for Social Work.* New York: Russell Sage Foundation, 1928. 392 pp.

SALT, HENRY STEPHENS. *Animals' Rights Considered in Relation to Social Progress.* Revised edition. New York and London: Macmillan, 1894. London: Bell, 1922. 124 pp.
Bibliography, pp. 117–21.

SALTER, FRANK REYNER. *Some Early Tracts on Poor Relief,* with a preface by Sidney Webb. London: Methuen, 1926. 128 pp.

SHAW, GEORGE BERNARD. *The Fabian Society: Its Early History* (Fabian Tract no. 41). London, 1892.

SHULTZ, WILLIAM JOHN. *The Humane Movement in the United States* (Columbia University Studies in History, Economics, and Public Law, no. 252). New York: Columbia University, 1924. 319 pp.
Appendix I, Summary of Laws for Animal Protection. Appendix II, Summary of Laws for Child Protection.

SMITH, HERBERT HEEBNER. *Publicity and Progress: Twentieth Century Methods in Religious, Educational, and Social Activities.* New York: Hodder and Stoughton, 1915. 228 pp.
Bibliography, pp. 226–28.

SQUIRE, IRVING, and WILSON, K. A. *Informing Your Public.* New York: Association Press, 1924. 158 pp.
Technique of Y. M. C. A. publicity.

STILLMAN, CHARLES C. *Social Work Publicity: Its Message and Its Method* (Social Workers Library). London and New York: Century, 1927. 254 pp.

STREET, ELWOOD. " Current Methods of Social Service Publicity," Proceedings of the National Conference of Social Work, 1919, pp. 670–82.

STREITZ, RUTH. *Safety Education in the Elementary School: A Technique for Developing Subject Matter* (Ph. D. thesis, Columbia University). New York: National Bureau of Casualty and Surety Underwriters, 1926. 143 pp.
Bibliography, pp. 140–42.

STUBBS, CHARLES WILLIAM. *Charles Kingsley and the Christian Social Movement.* London: Blackie and Son, 1899. 199 pp.

TIFFANY, FRANCIS. *Life of Dorothea Lynde Dix.* Boston: Houghton Mifflin, 1890. 392 pp.
Pioneer crusader for better treatment of the insane.

TOUSLEY, C. M. " Focussed Publicity," Proceedings of the National Conference of Social Work, 1931, pp. 592–96.

TWENTIETH CENTURY FUND. *American Foundations and Their Funds.* New York, 1931, 1932.
Ninety-one foundations reported in 1931, 102 in 1932.

UNITED STATES CHAMBER OF COMMERCE, CIVIC DEVELOPMENT DEPARTMENT. *A Playground Handbook for Chamber of Commerce Executives.* Washington, D. C., 1929.

WAGNER, DONALD OWEN. *The Church of England and Social Reform Since 1854* (Columbia University Studies in History, Economics,

and Public Law, no. 325). New York: Columbia University, 1930. London: P. S. King, 1930. 341 pp.
Bibliography, pp. 328-36.

WAGNER, DONALD OWEN, editor. *Social Reformers: Adam Smith to John Dewey,* with a foreword by Carlton J. H. Hayes. New York: Macmillan, 1934. 749 pp.
"The pertinent passages from the writings of a variety of social reformers . . . " — *Foreword.* Each of the chapters is prefaced by an introductory essay by the editor and a list of references.

WHIPPLE, L., GRAVES, W. B., and TODD, A. J. "Social Work Publicity," Proceedings of the National Conference of Social Work, 1930, pp. 569-606.

3. GOVERNMENT ORGANIZATION AND FISCAL POLICY

Propagandas to modify the framework of national governments (short of revolution); to modify tariff, subsidy, and taxation policies.

"Anti-Corn Law League," *Encyclopedia of the Social Sciences.* (By W. H. Dawson.)

BARNES, DONALD GROVE. *A History of the English Corn Laws, 1660-1846.* New York: Crofts, 1930. 331 pp.

COMER, JOHN PRESTON. *Legislative Functions of National Administrative Authorities* (Columbia University Studies in History, Economics, and Public Law, no. 289). New York: Columbia University, 1927. London: P. S. King, 1927. 274 pp.
Chapters 7 and 8 deal with "Group Opinion in the Framing of Legislation."

EITEMAN, WILFORD J. "The Rise and Decline of Orthodox Tariff Propaganda," *Quarterly Journal of Economics,* 45: 22-39 (November, 1930).

FOULKE, WILLIAM DUDLEY. *Fighting the Spoilsmen.* New York and London: Putnam, 1919. 348 pp.
Reminiscences of the Civil Service Reform movement.

GARIS, ROY LAWRENCE. *Immigration Restriction: A Study of the Opposition to and Regulation of Immigration into the United States.* New York: Macmillan, 1927. 376 pp.
Bibliography, pp. 355-71.

HUNTER, MERLIN HAROLD. *The Development of Corporation Taxation in the State of New York* (Ph. D. thesis, Cornell University). Urbana, Illinois: The Author, 1917. 177 pp.
Bibliography, pp. 175-77.

JORDAN, H. D. "The Political Methods of the Anti-Corn Law League," *Political Science Quarterly*, 42: 58–76 (1927).

LOBINGIER, CHARLES SUMNER. *The People's Law, or Popular Participation in Law Making.* New York: Macmillan, 1909. 429 pp. Bibliography, pp. 395–409.

MERRIAM, CHARLES EDWARD, and LASSWELL, HAROLD DWIGHT. "Current Public Opinion and the Public Service Commissions," in Morris Llewellyn Cook, editor, *Public Utility Regulation,* chap. 15. New York: Ronald Press, 1924. 310 pp.

OBERHOLTZER, ELLIS PAXSON. *The Referendum in America.* New edition. New York: Scribners, 1911. 533 pp.

PRENTICE, ARCHIBALD. *History of the Anti-Corn Law League.* London: W. and F. G. Cash, 1853. 2 vols.

RATNER, SIDNEY. "The Income Tax of 1894: A Study of the Economic and Social Forces Underlying Its Legislative and Judicial History." In preparation at Columbia University.

"Reformism," *Encyclopedia of the Social Sciences.* (By Horace M. Kallen.)

"Regional Planning," *Enyclopedia of the Social Sciences.* (By John Nolen.)

STEWART, FRANK MANN. At University of Texas. Has unpublished manuscript of a study of the National Municipal League.

———. *The National Civil Service Reform League: History, Activities, and Problems.* Austin: University of Texas, 1929. 304 pp. Bibliography, pp. 278–93.

———. "Propaganda Methods of the National Civil Service Reform League," *Southwest Political and Social Science Quarterly,* 9: 15–37 (June, 1928).

VOLWILER, ALBERT TANGEMAN. "Tariff Strategy and Propaganda in the United States, 1887–1888," *American Historical Review,* 36: 76–96 (October, 1930).

WHITE, LEONARD DUPEE. *Introduction to Public Administration.* New York: Macmillan, 1926. 495 pp. See chapters 2, "The External Relationships of Public Administration," and 19, "Control of Administration: Legislature and Electorate."

WIGMORE, JOHN HENRY. "The Movement for International Assimilation of Private Law: Recent Phases," *Minor's Law Review,* 20: 42–60 (1925–26).

Young, Arthur Nichols. *A History of the Single Tax Movement in the United States* (Ph. D. thesis, Princeton University, 1914). Princeton, New Jersey: Princeton University, 1916. 340 pp. Bibliography, pp. 325–28.

4. MILITARIST AND PACIFIC FOREIGN POLICY

Comparative studies concerning the world as a whole are in Part III, Section A, Subdivision 1.

A. BIBLIOGRAPHY

"International Cooperation for Peace: A Bibliography," *Publishers' Weekly,* 116: 2910–13 (December 28, 1929).
Compiled by the American Library Association and the World Peace Foundation.

B. REFERENCES

Abad, C. H. "The Munitions Industry in World Affairs," *Scribners,* 94: 176–79 (September, 1933).

Allen, Devere. *The Fight for Peace.* New York: Macmillan, 1930. 751 pp.
A broad history of the American peace movement during the last century, followed by an analysis of the problem in our own day and the organizations working for its solution.

American Peace Society. *The Advocate of Peace through Justice.*
The Society publishes annual reports and a quarterly.

American School Citizenship League. *Eleven-Year Survey of Activities of the American School Peace League from 1908 to 1919.* Boston, 1919. 55 pp.
Before 1919 the School Citizenship League was called the School Peace League. See also its *Yearbook,* 1911—.

"Anti-Militarism," *Encyclopedia of the Social Sciences.* (By Lewis L. Lorwin.)

Barnes, Roswell P. *Militarizing Our Youth: The Significance of the Reserve Officers Training Corps in Our Schools and Colleges.* New York: Committee on Militarism in Education, 1927. 47 pp.

Beales, Arthur Charles Frederick. *The History of Peace.* New York: Dial Press, 1931. London: Bell, 1931. 355 pp.
History of the peace movement and peace organizations in the nineteenth century. A standard and comprehensive work.

Beard, Charles Austin. *The Navy: Defense or Portent?* New York: Harpers, 1932. 198 pp.
A study of big navy propaganda.

BLIVEN, BRUCE ORMSBY. "Let's Have More Propaganda!" *World To-morrow*, 9:254–55 (December, 1926).

"Bloch, Jean de," *Encyclopedia of the Social Sciences.* (By Merle E. Curti.)

> Influential Russian pacifist. See his seven-volume work, *The Future of War,* translated in part by R. C. Long (New York, 1899). Complete translations are available in French and German.

BOECKEL, FLORENCE BREWER. *Between War and Peace.* New York: Macmillan, 1928. 601 pp.

> A handbook for peace workers, reviewing what has been done and what can be done to promote international goodwill.

BOSANQUET, MRS. HELEN (DENDY). *Free Trade and Peace in the 19th Century.* London: Williams and Norgate, 1925. 155 pp.

> Examines the effects of commercial interests on peace.

Building International Goodwill. New York: Macmillan, 1927. 258 pp.

> A series of essays prepared under the auspices of the World Alliance for International Friendship, in which recognized authorities discuss obstacles to peace and examine methods for preserving it.

"Conscientious Objectors," *Encyclopedia of the Social Sciences.* (By Clarence Marsh Case.)

COULTON, GEORGE GORDON. *The Main Illusions of Pacifism: A Criticism of Mr. Norman Angell and of the Union of Democratic Control.* Cambridge, England: Bowes and Bowes, 1916. 295 pp.

CURTI, MERLE EUGENE. *The American Peace Crusade, 1815–1860,* vol. 1 (Ph.D. thesis in history, Harvard University). Durham, North Carolina: Duke University, 1929. 250 pp. Vol. 2 in preparation.

> Bibliography, pp. 230–41. Of the forthcoming continuation of the study the author, who is at Smith College, writes, "Since the peace movement became much more extensive in this late period, I hope to correlate it with economic, social, and cultural forces working toward internationalism, and to gauge the influence of pacifists and internationalists in breaking down the American tradition of isolation." He is also studying "Promotional Activities of Pacifist and Militarist Pressure Groups in Relation to Opinion and Action since 1900," and has himself made much progress on the work.

———. *Bryan and World Peace* (Smith College Studies in History, vol. 16, nos. 3-4, pp. 111–262). Northampton, Massachusetts: Smith College, 1931.

DETZER, DOROTHY, executive secretary of the Women's International League for Peace and Freedom. Is making a comparative study of the methods used by contemporary American and European peace pressure groups.

DOREN, ALICE MACARTNEY. "Some Phases of the Peace Movement in America, 1898 to 1923" (unpublished M.A. thesis, University of Chicago, 1923).

ENGELBRECHT, H. C., and HANIGHEN, F. C. *Merchants of Death*. New York: Dodd, Mead, 1934. 308 pp.
The armament industry as a world-wide promotional group. Bibliography, pp. 285–96.

FEDERAL COUNCIL OF CHURCHES OF CHRIST IN AMERICA, COMMISSION ON INTERNATIONAL JUSTICE AND GOODWILL. *The Churches of America Mobilizing for World Justice and World Peace* and *The Churches of America and the World Court of Justice*.
Two pamphlets issued about 1923–24.

FOX, HENRY WATSON, editor. *The Religious Basis of World Peace*. London: Williams and Norgate, 1929. 167 pp.
A collection of articles stressing the influence of the church in the work for peace.

FUCHS, GUSTAV. *Der deutsche Pazifismus im Weltkrieg (Beiträge zur Geschichte der nachbismarckischen Zeit und des Weltkrieges*, Heft 4). Stuttgart: W. Kohlhammer, 1928. 76 pp.
German pacifism since Bismarck.

GULICK, SIDNEY LEWIS. *The Christian Crusade for a Warless World*. New York: Federal Council of Churches of Christ in America, 1923. New York: Macmillan, 1922. 197 pp.
Program for removal of causes of international friction.

HAAS, REV. FRANCIS J. *American Agriculture and International Affairs*. Washington, D.C.: Catholic Association for International Peace, 1930. 33 pp.

HANSEN, SYLVA. "Educational Policies of Some Prominent Peace and Religious Organizations, 1918–1927" (unpublished M.A. thesis, University of Iowa, 1927).

HARD, WILLIAM. Has an unpublished manuscript in his office in Washington, D. C., on the fight for and against the League of Nations, the pressure groups involved, and the men who mobilized the Republican organization against it.

HEMMENWAY, JOHN. *Apostle of Peace: Memoir of William Ladd*. Boston: American Peace Society, 1872. 272 pp.

INTERNATIONAL ANTI-MILITARIST BUREAU. *Organization and Program of the Anarcho-Syndicalist Anti-Militarists*. The Hague, 1925.

JAMES, WILLIAM. *The Moral Equivalent of War*. New York: American Association for International Conciliation, 1910. 20 pp.

A distinguished American pragmatist suggests a civic program to make peace as exciting to youth as war.

KEHR, ECKART. *Schlachtflottenbau und Parteipolitik, 1894–1901: Versuch eines Querschnitts durch die innenpolitischen, sozialen, und ideologischen Voraussetzungen des deutschen Imperialismus*. Berlin: Ebering, 1930. 464 pp.

German Navy League propaganda.

KOBLER, FRANZ, editor. *Gewalt und Gewaltlösigkeit*. Zurich: Rotapfel, 1928. 388 pp.

Anthology of articles on the movement of active pacifism from Penn to the World War.

"Ladd, William," *Encyclopedia of the Social Sciences*. (By Merle E. Curti.)

Ladd founded the American Peace Society in 1828.

LANE, R. P. "The Naval Building Policy of the United States."

In preparation. One of the Causes of War Series prepared under the supervision of Quincy Wright, professor of international law, University of Chicago.

LEE, GERALD STANLEY. *We: A Confession of Faith for the American People during and after War; a Study of the Art of Making Things Happen; a Recommendation of the First Person Plural for Men and Nations*. Garden City: Doubleday, Page, 1916. 728 pp.

Discusses peace propaganda, especially that of Andrew Carnegie.

LEHMANN-RUSSBÜLDT, OTTO. *Der Kampf der deutschen Liga für Menschenrechte, vormals Bund neues Vaterland, für den Weltfrieden, 1914–1927*. Berlin: Meusel, 1927. 190 pp.

A survey of the activities of the German Peace League from 1914 to 1927. Bibliography, pp. 133–36.

———. *War for Profits*, translated and with an introduction by Pierre Loving. New York: A. H. King, 1930. 175 pp.

Translation of *Die Blütige Internationale* (Hamburg: Fackelreiter Verlag, 1929), a study of post-war armament activities, the armament industry, and public opinion. Bibliography, pp. 171–75.

LEWINSOHN, RICHARD. *The Mystery Man of Europe: Sir Basil Zaharoff*. Philadelphia and London: Lippincott, 1929. 241 pp.

Propaganda of armament manufacturers.

LIPPMANN, WALTER. "Public Opinion and the Renunciation of War," Proceedings of the Columbia University Academy of Political Science, 13: 243–47 (January, 1929).

LOCHNER, LOUIS PAUL. *America's Don Quixote: Henry Ford's Attempt to Save Europe,* with a preface by Maxim Gorki. London: Kegan Paul, Trench, and Trubner, 1924. 240 pp.

MARVIN, FRED RICHARD. *Ye Shall Know the Truth.* New York, 1926. 93 pp.
"Exposé" of pacifist activities.

NATIONAL COUNCIL FOR THE PREVENTION OF WAR, Washington, D. C. Publishes a *News Bulletin,* reports of the Executive Secretary, and research bulletins.

NICKOLAUS, GÜNTER. *Die Milizfrage in Deutschland von 1848 bis 1933.* Berlin: Junker und Dünnhaupt, 1933. 196 pp.
The question of compulsory military service and the right to bear arms in Germany, 1848–1933.

Organizations in the United States That Promote Better International Understanding and World Peace. Washington, D. C.: National Council for Prevention of War, 1927.

"Peace Movements," *Encyclopedia of the Social Sciences.* (By Norman Angell.)

Peace Statements of Recent Popes. Washington, D. C.: National Catholic Welfare Conference, 1930.

Peace Yearbook. London: National Peace Council, 1910 —.

PHELPS, CHRISTINA. *The Anglo-American Peace Movement in the Mid-Nineteenth Century* (Columbia University Studies in History, Economics, and Public Law, no. 330). New York: Columbia University, 1930. London: P. S. King, 1930. 230 pp.
Bibliography, pp. 214–23.

PRUDHOMMEAUX, JULES JEAN. *Le Centre européen de la dotation Carnegie pour la paix internationale, 1911–1921.* Paris: Vve. Charier-Rousseau, 1921. 109 pp.

RODIN, ERNST V. *The Navy League and the Peace Movement.* Washington, D. C.: Navy League of the United States. Pamphlet.

SELDES, GEORGE. *Iron, Blood, and Profits: An Exposure of the World-Wide Munitions Racket.* London and New York: Harpers, 1934. 397 pp.
Bibliography, pp. 329–32.

———. "The New Propaganda for War," *Harpers,* 169: 540–55 (October, 1934).

STONE, WILLIAM T. "The Munitions Industry: An Analysis of the Senate Investigation, September 4–21, 1934," *Foreign Policy Reports,* 10: 250–68 (December 5, 1934).

Union of Democratic Control. *The Secret International Armament Firms at Work*. London, 1932. 48 pp.

United States Senate, Special Committee Investigating the Munitions Industry. *Hearings before the Special Committee Investigating the Munitions Industry,* 73d Congress, 3d Session, pursuant to S. Res. 206. Washington, D. C.: Government Printing Office, 1934. The "Nye Committee."

Waldman, Seymour. *Death and Profits: A Study of the War Policies Commission*. New York: Brewer, Warren, and Putnam, 1932. 156 pp.

What Makes Up My Mind on International Questions? Five Outlines for Leaders and Members of Discussion Groups. New York: Association Press, 1916. 92 pp.
Assumption : if there is discussion, there will be peace. Bibliography, pp. 90–92.

Women's International League for Peace and Freedom. Reports of its Congresses.

World Alliance for Promoting International Friendship through the Churches. *Handbook of the World Alliance*. New York, 1925.

World Peace Foundation. Annual Reports, documents, pamphlets, etc.

5. IMPERIALIST AND ANTI-IMPERIALIST POLICY

Imperialist propaganda defends political control over people of alien culture. Where imperialist control is of recent date, anti-imperialism may take the form of independence nationalism (Part III, Section A, Subdivision 3).

"L'Agitation communiste et antifrançaise en Indochine," *Journal des débats,* 32: 472–73 (September 18, 1925).

"Anti-British League Would Defend Asia," *Trans-Pacific,* 21: 10 (May 11, 1933).

"Anti-Religion Movement," *Chinese Recorder,* 53: 145 (1922).
A part of the general anti-foreign wave of 1922 in China.

Barnouw, A. J. "Communist Revolts in Java," *Current History,* 25: 834–48 (March, 1927).

Blumberger, Petrus. *Le Communisme aux Indes Néerlandaises*. Paris: Éditions du monde nouveau, 1929. 190 pp.
A Java official sets forth the serious labor problem in the Dutch colonies.

BLUMENTAL, F. *Lenin ob Imperialisticheskoy Voine.* Moscow: GIZ, 1929. 271 pp.
Principal statements of Lenin concerning the Imperialist (World) War.

BODELSEN, CARL ADOLF GOTTLIEB. *Studies in Mid-Victorian Imperialism* (doctoral thesis, Copenhagen, 1924). Copenhagen, London, etc.: Gyldendal, Nordisk Vorlag, 1924. 226 pp.
Bibliography, pp. 215–22.

BUKHARIN, NIKOLAI IVANOVICH. *Imperialism and World Economy.* New York: International Publishers, 1929. 173 pp.
English translation of an influential Bolshevist indictment of imperialism.

CHATTOPADHYAYA, V. "Faked Indian Statistics as Imperialist Propaganda," *Labour Monthly,* 12:539–45 (September, 1930).

COLLET, OCTAVE. *L'Évolution de l'esprit indigène aux Indes Orientales Néerlandaises.* Brussels: Falck, 1921. 138 pp.
Native problems in the Dutch possessions.

"Communist Attempts in the Dutch East Indies," *Literary Digest,* 94: 17 (August 20, 1927).

"Communists in Java," *Living Age,* 332:298–301 (February 15, 1927).

DORSENNE, J. "L'Organisation du parti communiste," *Journal des débats,* 38:909–11 (December 4, 1931).
Communist party in French Indo-China.

———. "Le Péril rouge en Indochine," *Revue des deux mondes,* 8: 519–56 (April 1, 1932).

DOZER, D. M. At Harvard; is studying the anti-imperialist movement in the United States.

ETHERTON, PERCY THOMAS. *In the Heart of Asia.* London: Constable, 1925. 305 pp.
The British consul-general and political agent in Chinese Turkestan discusses Soviet agitation in that region.

GÉRAUD, A. "La Gravité particulière du coup de force tenté en Indochine les 9–10 février: Les intrigues de Moscou," *Journal des débats,* 37:350–52 (February 28, 1930).
Attempted Communist *coup de force* in French Indo-China.

GODCHOT, S. M. "Moscou et l'Afrique du Nord," *Journal des économistes,* 84:196–204, 328–41 (May, 1926); 85:51–62 (July, 1926).

GROSSMANN, HENRYK. *Das Akkumulations- und Zusammenbruchsgesetz des kapitalistischen Systems* (Schriften des Instituts für Sozialforschung, Frankfort-on-the-Main). Leipzig: C. L. Hirschfeld, 1929. 628 pp.

This volume developed in part from Rosa Luxemburg's *Die Akkumulation des Kapitals*. Bibliographic footnotes.

GUCHKOV, A. "The Third International and Colonial Propaganda," *Slavonic Review*, 10: 509–24 (April, 1932).

HAUSER, HENRI. *L'Impérialisme américain*. Paris: "Pageslibres," 1905. 125 pp.

Bibliography, p. 125.

HIGH, S. "Moscow in Java," *Asia*, 27:644–49 (August, 1927).

HILFERDING, RUDOLF. *Das Finanzkapital: Eine Studie über die jüngste Entwicklung des Kapitalismus* (Marx-Studien, Band 3). Third edition. Vienna: Wiener Volksbuchhandlung, 1925. 477 pp.

"Imperialism," *Encyclopedia of the Social Sciences*. (By Julius Moritz Bonn.)

KLEINSCHMIT VON LENGEFELD, WILHELM. *Der geistige Gehalt im britischen Imperialismus*. Marburg: Elwert, 1928. 176 pp.

British imperialism as it appears from the writings in the *Round Table*.

LAWRENCE, JAMES COOPER. *The World's Struggle with Rubber, 1905–1931*. New York: Harpers, 1931. 151 pp.

A general systematic study of the rubber problem and the evolution of international efforts to find a solution.

LEGENDRE, A. "Où va la Chine? Comment la sauver d'elle même?" *Mercure de France*, 233:513–32 (February 1, 1932).

Suggestions for organizing anti-Communist activity in China.

LE NEVEU, C. A. "Le Communisme aux Indes Néerlandaises," *Journal des débats*, 36:743–46 (November 8, 1929).

LENIN, NICOLAI. *Imperialism kak Noveyshiy Etap Kapitalisma*. Petrograd, 1917.

Diagnosis of the era of imperialism and world wars. American edition: *Imperialism: The Latest Stage in the Development of Capitalism*, translated by J. T. Kozlowski. Detroit: Marxian Educational Society, 1924. 136 pp.

LUXEMBURG, ROSA. *Die Akkumulation des Kapitals: Ein Beitrag zur ökonomischen Erklärung des Imperialismus*. Leipzig: Franke, 1921. 2 vols.

How the inherent instability of the profits system leads to imperialism.

MOON, PARKER THOMAS. *Imperialism and World Politics*. New York: Macmillan, 1926. 583 pp.

Standard English-language work on imperialist history. Bibliographic footnotes.

Ocherki Revolutsionnoge Dvizheniia v Srednei Azii. Moscow: Nauchnaia Assotsiatsiia Vostokovedeniia, 1926. 152 pp.
A series of essays on the revolutionary movement in central Asia.

PAVLOVICH, M. (pseudonym of Mikhail Vel'tman). *The Foundations of Imperialist Policy.* London: Labour Publishing Company, 1922. 159 pp.
A translation of the first volume of the next title.

————. *Sobranie Sochinenii. Imperializm i Mirovaia Politika Poslednikh Desiatiletii.* Leningrad: Gosizdat, 1925. 4 vols.
A course of lectures by a leading communist writer on the history of imperialism. Volume 1: *Imperialism.* Volume 2: *Imperialism and the Struggle for Control of Railways and Waterways.* Volume 3: *The Struggle for Asia and Africa.* Volume 4: *The World War, 1914–1918.*

"La Politique coloniale et le bolchévisme," *Revue des deux mondes,* May 15, 1930, 7 per. 57, pp. 241–64.

POOLEY, A. M. *Japan's Foreign Policies.* New York: Dodd, Mead, 1920.
Evaluates the White Peril propaganda of 1913.

SALZ, ARTHUR. *Das Wesen des Imperialismus.* Leipzig and Berlin: Teubner, 1931. 201 pp.

SCROGGS, WILLIAM OSCAR. *Filibusters and Financiers: The Story of William Walker and His Associates.* New York: Macmillan, 1916. 408 pp.
American expedition to Nicaragua.

STEIGER, GEORGE NYE. *China and the Occident: The Origin and Development of the Boxer Movement.* New Haven: Yale University, 1927. London: Oxford University, 1927. 349 pp.
Bibliography, pp. 317–33.

TOWNSEND, MARY EVELYN. *Origins of Modern German Colonialism, 1871–1885* (Ph.D. thesis. Columbia University Studies in History, Economics, and Public Law, no. 223). New York: Columbia University, 1921. 207 pp.
Bibliography, pp. 197–201.

"La IIIᵉ Internationale contre la France et ses colonies," *Correspondant,* 299: 321–39 (May 10, 1925).

WEINBERG, ALBERT K. "Manifest Destiny: A Study of Nationalist Expansionism in American History."
In preparation at the Walter Hines Page School of International Relations, Johns Hopkins University.

WIEREGOED, A. J. "Recent Communist Disturbances in the Netherlands Indies and Their Significance," *Asiatic Review,* 23:385–92 (July, 1927).

WOOLF, LEONARD SIDNEY. *Economic Imperialism.* London: Swarthmore Press, 1920. New York: Harcourt, Brace, and Howe, 1920. 111 pp. Contains bibliographies.

————. *Empire and Commerce in Africa: A Study in Economic Imperialism.* London: Allen and Unwin, 1919. 374 pp.

6. INSTITUTIONAL DEFENSE (HYPER-PATRIOTISM, COUNTER-REVOLUTION)

ALLIED PATRIOTIC SOCIETIES, New York. *Civics versus Bolshevism.* Pamphlet.

Advocates " that children be so taught by the schools in presentation of what the government does for its citizens that it will be unnecessary ' to pass drastic laws to suppress the so-called doctrine of the " Reds." ' " — BESSIE L. PIERCE, in *Citizens' Organizations,* p. 13.

AMERICAN DEFENSE SOCIETY. Annual Report and Program.

"American Legion," *Encyclopedia of the Social Sciences.* (By A. A. Berle, Jr.)

AMERICAN LEGION. *Facts about the American Legion.* Revised edition. New York, 1930.

————. Proceedings of Annual Conventions.

Printed at government expense as House Documents. All the committees report their activities in full to the convention.

AMERICAN LEGION, AMERICANISM COMMISSION. See *The Huddle,* a magazine issued at irregular intervals; *Handbook on Americanism;* material on the observance of Armistice Day, etc.

American Legion Monthly. Indianapolis: Legion Publishing Corporation, July, 1926 — .

AMERICAN LEGION NEWS SERVICE. *Manual for American Legion Speakers.* New York, 1921. 68 pp.

AMERICAN LEGION, STATE DEPARTMENTS. Histories, proceedings, pamphlets, school texts, etc.

There are also departments for Continental Europe (Paris), Cuba (Havana), Mexico (Tampico), and the Philippine Islands (Manila).

American Legion Weekly. July 4, 1919–June 18, 1926.

Superseded by the *American Legion Monthly.*

"Anti-Radicalism," *Encyclopedia of the Social Sciences.* (By Alvin Johnson.)

BISSON, T. A. "The Rise of Fascism in Japan," *Foreign Policy Reports,* vol 8, no. 17 (October 26, 1932).

Gives list of organizations such as Kokuhonsha (National Foundation Society), Kenkokukai (Empire Foundation Society), Kokusuikai (Essence of National Culture Association), Dai Nihon Seisanto (Great Japan Production Society), etc.

BOHN, FRANK. "The Ku Klux Klan Interpreted," *American Journal of Sociology,* 30: 385-407 (January, 1925).

CONSTITUTION ANNIVERSARY SOCIETY, Chicago. Bulletin, 1923 —.

CURTIUS, ERNST ROBERT. *Maurice Barrès und die geistingen Grundlagen des französischen Nationalismus.* Bonn: Friedrich Cohen, 1922. 255 pp.

Discusses the ultra-nationalism of Barrès and the League of Patriots.

DAUGHTERS OF THE AMERICAN REVOLUTION. *Annual Reports* (1890—); Proceedings of "Continental Congresses" (conventions); reports of state chapters.

————. *History of the Daughters of the American Revolution: Their Patriotic Purposes and the Work They Have Accomplished towards Preserving and Commemorating the Heroic Deeds of the Builders of the Nation.* [n. p]: World's Progress Publishing Company, 1906. 342 pp.

DESCENDANTS OF THE SIGNERS OF THE DECLARATION OF INDEPENDENCE. Report of Annual Congress, 1908 —.

DUFFIELD, MARCUS. *King Legion.* New York: Cape and Smith, 1931. 330 pp.

On associations and organization of war veterans. "Little has been published in book form about the organization. There are two histories that cover only the early years; beyond that point the story must be pieced out of the Legion's records and other source material. The effort of this book is to allow the organization to tell its own story, as far as possible in direct quotations." — *Foreword.* Bibliography, pp. 317-19.

Les Faussaires contre les Soviets. Paris: Librairie du travail. 140 pp.

An exposé of anti-Bolshevik propaganda, especially in the matter of the Zinoviev letter.

FERNOW, MARY ALICE. "Educational Policies of Important Fraternal and Patriotic Organizations, 1918-1927" (unpublished M. A. thesis, University of Iowa, 1927).

FROST, STANLEY. *The Challenge of the Klan.* Indianapolis: Bobbs-Merrill, 1924. 302 pp.

FRY, HENRY PECK. *The Modern Ku Klux Klan.* Boston: Small, Maynard, 1922. 259 pp.

GURIAN, WALDEMAR. *Der Integrale Nationalismus in Frankreich.* Frankfort-on-the-Main, 1932. 131 pp.

The Action Française movement and the theories of its leader, Charles Maurras, in opposition to liberal parliamentarism.

HAPGOOD, NORMAN, editor. *Professional Patriots: An Exposure of the Personalities, Methods, and Objectives Involved in the Organized Effort to Exploit Patriotic Impulse in These United States during and after the Great War.* New York: A. and C. Boni, 1927. 210 pp.

HUNTER, EARLE LESLIE. *A Sociological Analysis of Certain Types of Patriotism* (Ph. D. thesis, Columbia University, 1932). New York, 1932. 263 pp.

Peacetime controversies over patriotism. Bibliography, pp. 252–63.

JAMES, MARQUIS. *A History of the American Legion.* 1923.

The Kourier.
Organ of the Knights of the Ku Klux Klan.

"Ku Klux Klan," *Encyclopedia of the Social Sciences.* (By Max Sylvius Handman.)

MECKLIN, JOHN MOFFATT. *The Ku Klux Klan: A Study of the American Mind.* New York: Harcourt, Brace, 1924. 244 pp.

NAVY LEAGUE OF THE UNITED STATES. Annual Reports of the Executive Secretary.

POST, LOUIS FREELAND. *The Deportations Delirium of 1920.* Chicago: C. H. Kerr, 1923. 338 pp.

POWELL, GARLAND W. *Service: A Handbook on Americanism.* Indianapolis: Cornelius Printing Company, 1924. 151 pp.

Mr. Powell was national director of the American Legion's Americanism Commission.

"Revolution and Counter-Revolution," *Encyclopedia of the Social Sciences.* (By Alfred Meusel.)

SENTINELS OF THE REPUBLIC. *Articles of Incorporation and By-Laws as Amended September, 1925.* Washington, D. C., 1925.

SIMPSON, BERTRAM LENOX. *Chang Tso-lin's Struggle against the Communist Menace.* Shanghai: Kelly and Walsh, 1927. 167 pp.

Anti-Communist activities of the war lord of North China.

SMITH, LE ROY F., and JOHNS, E. B. *Pastors, Politicians, Pacifists.* Chicago: Constructive Education Publishing Company, 1927. 422 pp.

Defends R. O. T. C. activities, deplores anti-militarism. Attacks the Federal Council of Churches of Christ in America.

The Sons of the American Revolution Magazine. Quarterly, 1912—.
See also the reports of this society's conventions and state chapters.

Stars and Stripes. Official publication of the American Legion during the Paris convention, issued September 17-25, 1927. Reproduced by the Chicago *Tribune* and the New York *Daily News.*

"A Study of Patriotic Propaganda," Federal Council of Churches of Christ in America, *Information Service,* May 5, 1928 (vol. 7).
An analysis of the literature attacking persons and organizations who seek to promote international peace through the churches.

VAN TYNE, CLAUDE HALSTEAD. *Loyalists in the American Revolution.* New York and London: Macmillan, 1902, 1929. 360 pp.

WHEAT, GEORGE S. *The Story of the American Legion.* New York and London: Putnam, 1919. 272 pp.
An account of the organization of the veterans at the St. Louis caucus, May, 1919.

WRIGHT, L. B. "Henry Roberts, Patriotic Propagandist and Novelist," University of North Carolina Studies in Philosophy, 29:176-99 (April, 1932).

7. INSTITUTIONAL ATTACK (REVOLUTION)

Includes communism by countries; for the world movement, see Part III, Section A, Subdivision 1.

ADAMIC, LOUIS. *Dynamite: The Story of Class Violence in America.* Revised edition. New York: Viking, 1934. 495 pp.
Bibliography, pp. 481-86.

ALAZARD, JEAN. *Communisme et "Fascio" en Italie.* Paris: Bossard, 1922. 117 pp.

ARSCHINOFF, P. *Geschichte der Machno-Bewegung (1918-1921).* Berlin: Der freie Arbeiter, 1923. 315 pp.
The author is a "convinced" anarchist, and a comrade-in-arms of Machno.

BAUDIN, LOUIS. "Propagande communiste au Peron," *Correspondant,* March 10, 1931.

BEALS, CARLETON. "Mexico and the Communists," *New Republic,* 62: 10-12 (February 19, 1930).
Historical notes on the Communist party of Mexico.

BENEDEK, C. "Among French Communists," *Living Age,* 332:875-78 (May 15, 1927).
Labor unions and leadership in the French Communist movement.

BERNUS, P. "Les Alliés français du bolchévisme," *Journal des débats,* 39: 661–62 (October 21, 1932).

BISSON, T. A. "The Communist Movement in China," *Foreign Policy Reports,* vol. 9, no. 4 (April 26, 1933).
"Steady propaganda carried on by the peasants among the troops occupying villages in Soviet areas was chiefly responsible for desertions from the government armies."

BÖHM, WILHELM. *Im Kreuzfeuer zweier Revolutionen.* Munich: Verlag für Kulturpolitik, 1924. 552 pp.
Bolshevism in Hungary.

"Le Bolchévisme et l'armée," *Revue des deux mondes,* May 15, 1929, 7 per. 51, pp. 266–90.

BOUCHOT, J. "L'Imperialisme soviet en Chine," *Correspondant,* 300: 641–65 (September 10, 1925).

BRISSENDEN, PAUL FREDERICK. *The I.W.W.: A Study of American Syndicalism* (Columbia University Studies in History, Economics, and Public Law, no. 193). Second edition. New York: Columbia University, 1920. 438 pp.
Bibliography, pp. 387–428.

"British Communism and Its Leaders," *English Review,* 45: 279–91 (September, 1927).
History, organization, development, funds, and personalities of the British Communist movement.

BYAS, HUGH. "Communist Movement in Japan," *Contemporary Review,* 141: 190–97 (February, 1932).

CASHMAN, JOSEPH T. *America Asleep: The Menace of Radicalism.* New York: National Security League, 1925.

CHAMBERLIN, W. H. "The Soviet Shadow in the East," *Literary Digest,* 88: 38–45 (March 13, 1926).
Covers China, India, and Japan.

CHAPMAN, HERBERT OWEN. *The Chinese Revolution, 1926–7: A Record of the Period under Communist Control as Seen from the Nationalist Capital, Hankow.* London: Constable, 1928. 310 pp.
The period when Communists almost gained control of South China. Bibliography, pp. 297–98.

CLEINOW, GEORGE. *Neu-Siberien (Sib-krai): Eine Studie zum Aufmarsch der Sowjetmacht in Asien.* Berlin: R. Hobbing, 1928. 426 pp.

"Communism in China," *Foreign Affairs,* 9: 310–16 (January, 1931).

"Communism in Great Britain," *Literary Digest,* 82: 13–19 (August 9, 1924).

"Communist Drive on Latin America," *Literary Digest,* 86: 18–19 (August 1, 1925).

"Communist Movement in Japan," *China Weekly Review,* 63: 382 ff. (January 28, 1933).
Number of Communists arrested in Japan in 1932; who goes " red " in Japan.

The Communist Party of Great Britain. London: Communist Party, 1928. 195 pp.
Report of the British Commission of the Ninth Plenum of the Comintern.

La Conspiration bolchéviste contre la Bulgarie. Sofia: Imprimerie de la cour, 1925. 108 pp.
A government publication, with documents and opinions to prove the seriousness of the Communist menace.

CREUTZBURG, A. *Die Organisations-Arbeit der kommunistische Partei Deutschlands.* Hamburg and Berlin: Hoym, 1931. 121 pp.
Social composition and tactics of the German Communist party, analyzed by a Communist.

"Crushing Communism," *Literary Digest,* 112: 16 (February 6, 1932).
Report of a Communist uprising in Salvador.

DAVIDSON, PHILIP G. "Whig Propagandists of the American Revolution," *American Historical Review,* 39: 442–53 (April, 1934).

DENNETT, TYLER. "Red Menace in China," *Current History,* 36: 758–60 (September, 1932).

DENNIS, A. L. P. "Germany and the Third International," *North American Review,* 217: 455–70 (October, 1923).

DILLING, ELIZABETH (Mrs. Albert W.). *The Red Network: A " Who's Who" and Handbook of Radicalism for Patriots.* Chicago: The Author, 1932. 352 pp.

DOBB, M. "The Crisis in Germany, with Text of the Appeal of the Central Committee of the Communist Party of Germany," *Labour Monthly,* 13: 491–98 (August, 1931).

FISH, HAMILTON, JR. "The Menace of Communism," *Annals of the American Academy of Political and Social Science,* 156: 54–61 (July, 1931).

GAMBS, JOHN SAKÉ. *The Decline of the I. W. W.* (Columbia University Studies in History, Economics, and Public Law, no. 361). New

York: Columbia University, 1932. London: P. S. King, 1932. 268 pp.
An analysis of the causes, economic and psychological, of the disintegration of the I. W. W., from 1917 to 1931. Supplements the history written by Paul F. Brissenden. Bibliography, pp. 241–61.

GAMMAGE, ROBERT GEORGE. *History of the Chartist Movement, 1837–1854.* New and revised edition. Newcastle-on-Tyne: Browne and Browne, 1894. 438 pp.
First published in 1854.

GISBORNE, F. A. W. "Communist Offensive in Australia," *English Review,* 51:59–71 (July, 1930).

GUYOT, Y. "L'Encerclement bolchévik en Asie et en Afrique," *Journal des économistes,* 83: 1–24 (January, 1926).

————. "Mainmise du Bolchévisme sur la Chine," *Journal des économistes,* 86: 3–20 (January, 1927).

HACKETT, C. W. "Communist Uprising in Salvador," *Current History,* 35: 843 (March, 1932).

HAMMOND, JOHN LAWRENCE, and HAMMOND, BARBARA. *The Age of the Chartists, 1832–1854.* New York and London: Longmans, Green, 1930. 386 pp.

HARDMAN, J. B. S. "Communism in America," *New Republic,* 64: 34–37, 63–67, 94–97, 120–22 (August 27–September 17, 1930).
Articles summarizing the findings of the Fish investigation.

HOUGH, EMERSON. *The Web: A Revelation of Patriotism.* Chicago: Published by Reilly and Lee, by authority of the national directors of the American Protective League, 1919. 511 pp.
Exposes "red" and pacifist activities.

HOVELL, MARK. *The Chartist Movement* (University of Manchester Historical Series, no. 116), posthumously edited and completed by Professor T. F. Tout. London: University of Manchester, 1918. 327 pp.
Bibliography, pp. 313–17 and footnotes.

HURD, A. "Communist Offensive by Sea," *Fortnightly Review,* 124: 696–708 (November, 1925).
A Communist strike in the British shipping industry.

IAROSLAVSKII, E. *Aus der Geschichte der kommunistischen Partei der Sowjet-Union.* Berlin: Hoym, 1929–31. 2 vols.
The German translation of a standard history of the party. These volumes cover the period from the Populists to about 1921. A third volume, bringing the history down to 1930, is to follow.

————. *Partiia Bol'shevikov v 1917 Godu.* Moscow: Gosizdat, 1927. 107 pp.
The Bolshevik group during the Revolution until its seizure of power.

KAAS, ALBERT. *Bolshevism in Hungary.* London: Richards, 1931. 410 pp.

KAIN, R. S. "The Communist Movement in the United States," *Current History,* 32: 1079–84 (September, 1930).

KARAKHAN, L. M. "Propaganda War in China," *Nation,* 123: 138 (August 11, 1926).

KELEMEN, B. "Soviet Strategy in Bulgaria," *Living Age,* 327: 407–11 (November 21, 1935).

KOMMUNISTISCHE PARTEI DEUTSCHLANDS. *Zwei Jahre und Kampf: Bericht des Zentralkomitees der kommunistischen Partei Deutschlands an den 12 Parteitag.* Berlin: Internationaler Verlag, 1929. 410 pp.
A statistical audit of the party.

KORSCH, K. "Die spanische Revolution," *Neue Rundschau,* vol. 42, pt. 2, pp. 289–302 (1931).

"Kuomintang versus Soviets," *Labour Monthly,* 14: 450–58, 514–20 (July–August, 1932).
Revolutionary activities of the Chinese Communist party.

LANDAU, MARK ALEXANDROVITCH. *Deux révolutions.* Paris: Union, 1921. 119 pp.
Compares the French and Russian revolutions, with emphasis on social aspects, tactics, and foreign policy.

LASKI, H. J. "Great Britain and the Communists," *New Republic,* 45: 183–84 (January 6, 1926).

LEDERER, L. "Bolshevism in Poland," *Living Age,* 305: 212–15 (April 24, 1920).

LEGENDRE, A. "Chine, Japon, et Bolchévisme," *Mercure de France,* 227: 320–40 (April 15, 1931).

"Lenin's Attempt to Capture Islam," *New Europe,* 15: 212–15 (June 10, 1920).

LÉWANDOWSKI, M. "Le Bolchévisme en Chine: Sun Yat-Sen, fondateur de la république chinoise," *Revue des deux mondes,* April 15, 1926, 7 per. 32, pp. 800–23.

————. "La Menace bolchéviste en Chine," *Revue des deux mondes,* June 1, 1925, 7 per. 27, pp. 629–49.

LOBANOV-ROSTOVSKY, A. "Bolshevism and Asia," *Edinburgh Review,* 248:349–57 (October, 1928).
Discussion of policy of the Third International in the East.

MARTCHENKO, GENERAL. "Le Communisme en France," *Correspond-ant,* 308:744–49 (September 10, 1927).

MARVIN, FRED RICHARD. *Are These Your Friends? An Exposé of the Plans and Purposes of the Socialists, Communists, I. W. W., and Non-Partisan League, and Showing the Close Relationship That Exists between the Leaders of These and All Other Radical Organizations of This Country.* Denver: The Author, 1922. 30 pp.

————. *Our Government and Its Enemies.* New York: Educational Committee of the American Coalition of Patriotic Societies, 1932. 244 pp.

MARX, KARL, and ENGELS, FRIEDRICH. *Germany: Revolution and Counter-Revolution* (Marxist Library, vol. 13). New York: International Publishers, 1933. 155 pp.
Discussion of the tactics of the proletarian elements in the German revolution of 1848, written in 1851 for the *New York Daily Tribune.*

MASON, EDWARD S. *The Paris Commune: An Episode in the History of the Socialist Movement.* New York: Macmillan, 1930. 386 pp.
"The causes of the revolution were only indirectly and very tenuously related to conscious and expressed desires for a socialist society." Yet "Socialism has taken the Commune from the history of France and has made it a battle cry for the proletariat of the world."

MELVILLE, C. F. "Red Imperialism," *Fortnightly Review,* 125:303–14 (March, 1922).
Organization of the Balkan Comintern.

MENG, C. Y. W. "Red Imperialism in Outer Mongolia," *China Weekly Review,* 56:470 ff. (May 30, 1931).
Communist leaders in Outer Mongolia and the organizations they represent.

MINISTRY OF FOREIGN AFFAIRS [China]. *Documents with Reference to the Sino-Russian Dispute.* Nanking: Far Eastern Information Bureau, 1929.
Contains a section on Bolshevism in China.

MITAREVSKII, N. *World-Wide Soviet Plots.* Tientsin: Tientsin Press, 1928. 211 pp.
The activities of the Soviet agents in Asia, as they appear from the documents seized in the Russian Embassy in Peiping.

MONTFORT, H. DE. "Le Peuple de Finlande contre le communisme," *Mercure de France,* 223:575–93 (November 1, 1930).

Mowry, Arthur May. *The Dorr War*. Providence, Rhode Island: Preston and Rounds, 1901. 420 pp.
The constitutional struggle in Rhode Island, 1842. Bibliography, pp. 400–06.

Nettlau, Max. *Der Vorfrühling der Anarchie: Ihre historische Entwicklung von den Anfängen bis zum Jahre 1864*. Berlin: "Der Syndikalist," F. Kater, 1925. 240 pp.
By an eminent anarchist scholar. Bibliographic footnotes.

Ombiaux, M. des. "Les Effets du Bolchévisme en Belgique," *Mercure de France*, January 15, 1923, 1 per. 61, pp. 327–43.

Oneal, James. *American Communism: A Critical Analysis of Its Origin, Development, and Programs*. New York: Rand Book Store, 1927. 256 pp.

Parker, Carleton. *The Casual Laborer*. New York: Harcourt, Brace, 1920. 199 pp.
Stresses sexual deprivation in lumber camps as a cause of radicalism.

"Le Parti communiste en Allemagne," *Journal des débats*, vol. 39, pt. 2, pp. 59–60 (July 8, 1932).

Party Organizer. New York: Communist Party of the U.S.A., 1930—.

Pease, Theodore Calvin. *The Leveller Movement: A Study in the History and Political Theory of the English Great Civil War* (Ph.D. thesis, University of Chicago, 1914). Washington: American Historical Association, 1916. Baltimore: Williams and Wilkins, 1916. 406 pp.

Pick, Eugene (pseudonym). *China in the Grip of the Reds: Sketches of the Extravagant Effort Made by the Soviet Russia to Set Up and Control a Red Regime in China, with Strong Light upon the Ruthless Character of Borodin and His Efforts*. Shanghai: North China Daily News, 1927. 46 pp.

Price, M. T. "Communist Policy and the Chinese Nationalist Revolution," *Annals of the American Academy of Political and Social Science*, 152: 229–40 (November, 1930).

"Les Progrès du communisme," *Journal des débats*, vol. 32, pt. 2, pp. 497–98.
Communism in Great Britain.

Rea, George Bronson. "Communist Menace in Manchuria," *Far Eastern Review*, 27: 461–64 (August, 1931).

Rechberg, A. "La Propagande soviétique en Chine et l'Angleterre," *Journal des débats*, vol. 36, pt. 1, pp. 580–81 (April 12, 1928).

"Revolution and Counter-Revolution," *Encyclopedia of the Social Sciences.* (By Alfred Meusel.)

RICE, S. "Communism in India," *Nineteenth Century,* 102:38–47 (July, 1927).

ROSENBLATT, FRANK FERDINAND. *The Chartist Movement in Its Social and Economic Aspects* (Columbia University Studies in History, Economics, and Public Law, no. 171). New York: Columbia University, 1916. 249 pp.

ROY, MANABENDA NATH. *Revolution und Konterrevolution in China.* Berlin: Soziologische Verlagsanstalt, 1930. 480 pp.
By a professional revolutionary who claims to have had experience in India, the Philippines, the Dutch East Indies, Mexico, and China.

ROYSE, M. W. "Eastern Europe and Its Communists," *Outlook,* 140: 327–30 (July 1, 1925).

RUST, W. "Communist Party Congress," *Labour Monthly,* 14:737–42 (December, 1932).
Communist Party of Great Britain.

SHANLEY, J. R. "War Front in the East," *Labour Monthly,* 14:356–61 (June, 1932).
On the Communist movement in China.

SLOSSON, PRESTON WILLIAM. *The Decline of the Chartist Movement* (Columbia University Studies in History, Economics, and Public Law, no. 172). New York: Columbia University, 1916. 216 pp.
Bibliography, pp. 211–14.

SMEDLEY, AGNES. "Germany's Red Front," *Nation,* 127:116–17 (August 1, 1928).
An account of the German Communist Party Congress.

SNOW, E., and SWEETLAND, R. E. "Strength of Communism in China," *Current History,* 33:521–29 (January, 1931).

TANG LEANG-LI, editor. *Suppressing Communist Banditry in China.* Shanghai: China United Press, 1934. 110 pp.
Systematic account of the development of Communism in China and the efforts of the Nanking government to suppress it.

TOPALOVIC, Z. "Ten Years' Communism in the Balkans," *Living Age,* 334:28–32 (January 1, 1928).
Discussion of background conditions of Communist activity in the Balkans.

TRICOCHE, GEORGE NESTLER. "La Crise du radicalisme aux États-Unis," *Action nationale,* N.S., 13:62–76 (1920).

TROTSKY, LEON. *Problems of the Chinese Revolution*. New York: Pioneer Publishers, 1932. 432 pp.

――――. *La revolución española*. Madrid: Publicaciones Treivos, 1931. 69 pp.

――――. *What Next? Vital Questions for the German Proletariat*. New York: Pioneer Publishers, 1932. 192 pp.

――――. *Whither England?* New York: International Publishers, 1925. 191 pp.
A forecast of the future of England, in terms of world revolution.

"Turkey's War on Communism," *Literary Digest*, 95: 15–16 (December 31, 1927).
Leaders and organization of the Communist movement in Turkey.

UNITED STATES DEPARTMENT OF JUSTICE. *Red Radicalism Described by Its Own Leaders*. Washington, D. C.: Government Printing Office, 1920. 83 pp.
Collection of alleged Bolshevist propaganda.

UNITED STATES HOUSE OF REPRESENTATIVES. *Investigation of Communist Propaganda* (hearings before a Special Committee on Communist Activities in the United States, 71st Congress, 2d Session, pursuant to House Resolution 220). Washington, D. C.: Government Printing Office, 1931. 22 vols.
Investigation of Communists by Congressman Fish. The official report of this committee, also entitled *Investigation of Communist Propaganda*, was condensed to about a hundred pages (Washington, D. C.: Government Printing Office, 1931).

UNITED STATES SENATE, COMMITTEE ON FOREIGN RELATIONS. *Russian Propaganda* (hearings before a subcommittee of the Committee on Foreign Relations, 66th Congress, 2d Session, pursuant to Senate Resolution 263). Washington, D. C.: Government Printing Office, 1920. 504 pp.
Investigation of Ludwig C. A. K. Martens, who claimed to be a representative of the U. S. S. R.

UNITED STATES SENATE, COMMITTEE ON THE JUDICIARY. *Bolshevik Propaganda* (hearings before a subcommittee of the Committee on the Judiciary, 65th Congress, 3d Session and thereafter, pursuant to House Resolutions 439 and 469). Washington, D. C.: Government Printing Office, 1919. 1265 pp.

WATKINS, G. J. "Revolutionary Communism in the United States," *American Political Science Review*, 14: 14–23 (February, 1920).

WERLIN, JOSEPH SIDNEY. "Russian Social-Democracy in the Period of its First Three Congresses" (unpublished Ph.D. thesis in history, University of Chicago, 1931).

WEST, JULIUS. *A History of the Chartist Movement.* London: Constable, 1920. Boston and New York: Houghton Mifflin, 1920. 316 pp. Bibliography, pp. 297–99.

WHITNEY, RICHARD MERRILL. *Reds in America: The Present Status of the Revolutionary Movement in the United States, Based on Documents Seized by the Authorities in the Raid upon the Convention of the Communist Party at Bridgman, Michigan, August 22, 1922; together with Descriptions of Numerous Connections and Associations of the Communists among the Radicals, Progressives, and Pinks.* New York: Beckwith Press, Inc., 1924. 287 pp.

Appeared in part in the *Boston Transcript.* Has a list of "radical publications and literature," pp. 71–84.

WOLF, D. E. "Communism in America," *Current History,* 33:916–17 (March, 1931).

YAKHONTOFF, VICTOR A. *The Chinese Soviets.* New York: Coward-McCann, 1934. 310 pp.

General account of the sovietized areas in China.

YARROS, VICTOR S. "Contemporary American Radicalism," *International Journal of Ethics,* 31:351–69 (1921).

C. PRACTICES

Propagandas that emphasize the direct modification of the habits of the masses, with or without legislative or administrative action.

I. HEALTH HABITS

AMERICAN MEDICAL ASSOCIATION. *Propaganda for Reform in Proprietary Medicines.* Fifth edition. Chicago, 1908. 296 pp.

ANDERSON, D. S. "Publicity and the Public Health Nurse," *Public Health Nurse,* 21:29–32 (January, 1929).

ARMSTRONG, DONALD B., M.D. "The Public Health Movement in the Light of Modern Psychology," *Modern Medicine,* 2:810–13 (December, 1920), 3:57–60 (January, 1921).

Discusses the application to health publicity of the idea that action usually results from emotion rather than from reason.

BACHE, LOUISE FRANKLIN. *Health Education in an American City.* New York: Doubleday, Doran, 1934.

Detailed outline of the technique used in the Syracuse health demonstration to publicize its objectives.

————. "Health Education Program in a City of 100,000," *American Journal of Public Health,* 18:581–86 (1928).

BEATTIE, N. R. "Public Health Propaganda," *Public Health,* 41:246–52 (1927–28).

BEERS, CLIFFORD. *The Mental Hygiene Movement.* New York: National Committee for Mental Hygiene, 1923. 411 pp.

————. *A Mind That Found Itself: An Autobiography.* Sixth edition. Garden City: Doubleday, Doran, 1932. 399 pp.
By the founder of the mental hygiene movement.

BERGER, HEINRICH, and EBNER, FRANZ. "Der gegenwärtige Stand und die Organisation der hygienischen Volksbelehrung." Berlin: Veröffentlichungen aus dem Gebiete der Medizinalverwaltung, vol. 28, pt. 1 (1929).

CARLTON, B. L. "Publicity as a Means of Promoting Efficiency in Public Health Work," *American City,* 23:53–57 (July, 1920).

CLARKE, F. C. "Combining against Tuberculosis," *Public Health Nurse,* 21:522–25 (October, 1929).

DALEY, W. A., and VINEY, HESTER. *Popular Education in Public Health.* London, 1926.

DUNHAM, G. C. "The International Exhibition," *American Journal of Public Health,* 21:1–10 (1931).

"Educational Services of the Massachusetts Tuberculosis League," *American Physical Education Review,* 30:452–53 (October, 1925).

ESTILL, C. L. "Publicity as an Essential in a Public Health Program," *Public Health Nurse,* 16:568–71 (November, 1924).

FEDERATION OF WOMEN'S CLUBS. "Suggested Program for the Tuberculosis Committee," *Public Health Nurse,* 19:135–36 (March, 1927).

HAMBERT, F. "Public Health Education in the Orient," *World's Health,* 8:454–58 (1927).

"Health Education," *Encyclopedia of the Social Sciences.* (By Iago Galdston.)

INTERNATIONAL LABOR OFFICE [Geneva]. *Encyclopedia of Industrial Hygiene.* 3 vols.
Discusses propaganda methods used among workers to secure their co-operation in international hygienic measures.

KENWOOD, HENRY, and JAMESON, W. W. "The Central Council for Health Education," *Public Health,* 42:118–24 (1928–29).

LANDIS, H. R. M. "Tuberculosis Problem and the Negro," *Public Health Nurse,* 19:25–26 (January, 1927).

"La Lutte contre la tuberculose en France," *Journal des débats,* vol. 37, pt. 1, p. 785 (May 16, 1930).

LYER, S. "La Lutte contre la tuberculose en Tschécoslovaquie," *Revue politique et littéraire,* 69:515 (December 3, 1931).

MACMASTER, J. "Local Newspapers as a Means of Publicity," *Public Health Nurse,* 19:452–55 (September, 1927).

MOINE, M. "Le Développement de l'organisation anti-tuberculeuse en France," *Journal de la société de statistique de Paris,* 67:58–68 (February, 1926).

MÖLLERS, BERNARD. *Gesundheitswesen und Wohlfahrtspflege im deutschen Reiche.* Second edition. Berlin, 1930.

MYERS, J. A. "Future Sound Development for Tuberculosis Societies," Proceedings of the National Conference of Social Work, 1931, pp. 126–35.

NATIONAL COMMITTEE FOR MENTAL HYGIENE. *Mental Hygiene,* a quarterly published since 1917. *Mental Hygiene Bulletin,* a monthly published since 1917. See also Proceedings of Mental Hygiene Conferences.

PUELMA, H. O. "Another Phase of the War on Tuberculosis," *National Municipal Review,* 20:377–88 (June, 1931).

RENIS, E. J. "Houston Anti-Tuberculosis League," *Public Health Nursing,* 24:150–51 (March, 1932).

ROOT, A. DE A. "New Partnership for Children's Health: Public and Private Forces Combine in the East Harlem District," *Child Health,* 5:93–96 (March, 1924).

ROUTZAHN, MARY SWAIN. "The Aim of Social Hygiene Publicity," *Journal of Social Hygiene,* 15:65–70 (February, 1929).

SHELLEY, H. J. "Local Publicity Use of Statistics from National and State Sources" (with reply by B. R. Rickards), *American Journal of Public Health,* 24:331–35 (April, 1934).

SHRYOCK, RICHARD H. "The Origins and Significance of the Public Health Movement in the United States," *Annals of Medical History,* N. S., 1:645–65.

STERN, BERNHARD JOSEPH. *Should We Be Vaccinated? A Survey of the Controversy in Its Historical and Scientific Aspects.* New York and London: Harpers, 1927. 146 pp.

"Symposium on How to Further Progress in Health Education and Publicity," *American Journal of Public Health,* 12:279–89 (1922).

"Tuberculosis Prevention in Schools," *Public Health Nurse,* 18: 496–97 (September, 1926).

VAUGHAN, H. F. "Established Points in a Community Program of Health Education," *American Journal of Public Health,* 20: 351–56 (1930).

WEBER, J. J. "The Motor Truck as a Travelling Health Clinic," *Modern Hospital,* 16: 261–67 (March, 1921).

WILLIAMS, E. G. "Preaching Health on the Highways," *American Journal of Public Health,* 7: 179–81 (February, 1917).

WINSLOW, CHARLES EDWARD AMORY. *The Evolution and Significance of the Modern Public Health Campaign.* New Haven: Yale University, 1923. 65 pp.

———. "Organizing a State Campaign on Public Health Education," *American Journal of Public Health,* 6: 805–13 (1916).

A World Panorama of Health Education. Geneva: World Federation of Education Associations, Health Section, 1929.

<h3 style="text-align:center">2. BIRTH CONTROL</h3>

<h4 style="text-align:center">A. BIBLIOGRAPHY</h4>

HIMES, NORMAN EDWIN. *A Guide to Birth Control Literature.* London: Douglas, 1931. 46 pp.

<h4 style="text-align:center">B. REFERENCES</h4>

ACHARD, M. "L'Avortement et la propagande anticonceptionnelle: Examen critique des projets soumis au Parlement" (unpublished thesis, University of Toulouse, 1917). 141 pp.

AMERICAN BIRTH CONTROL LEAGUE. Pamphlets on legal and ethical aspects, outlines of birth control methods, etc.

"Birth Control," *Encyclopedia of the Social Sciences.* (By Frank H. Hankins.)

Birth Control Review. New York, 1917 —.
"Dedicated to the cause of voluntary motherhood."

DUBLIN, LOUIS I. "Fallacious Propaganda for Birth Control," *Atlantic,* 137: 186–94 (February, 1926).

FIELD, JAMES ALFRED. *Essays on Population and Other Papers,* compiled and edited by Helen Fisher Hohman. Chicago: University of Chicago, 1931. 440 pp.
Includes an essay on "The Early Propagandist Movement in English Population Theory."

———. "Publicity by Prosecution: A Commentary on the Birth Control Propaganda," *Survey,* 35: 599–601 (1916).

"Gandhi on Birth Control," *Nation*, 121:243 (August, 1926).

GARRAUD, PIERRE, and LABORDE-LACOSTE, MARCEL. *La Répression de la propagande contre la natalité: La loi du 31 juillet 1920 réprimant la provocation à l'avortement et la propagande anti-conceptionnelle* (Extrait des Annales de l'Université d'Aix, N. S., tôme 8). Aix-en-Provence: Imprimerie Nicollet, 1921. 88 pp.

GAYLORD, E. "Restrictions in Regard to Regulation of Birth Imposed by Laws of the Various Civilized Nations," Proceedings of the National Conference of Social Work, 1931, pp. 136–42.

HIMES, NORMAN EDWIN. "The Birth Control Handbills of 1823," *Lancet*, August 6, 1927, pp. 313–16.

————. "McCulloch's Relation to the Neo-Malthusian Propaganda of His Time: An Episode in the History of English Neo-Malthusianism," *Journal of Political Economy*, 37:73–86 (February, 1929).

INTERNATIONAL NEO-MALTHUSIAN AND BIRTH CONTROL CONFERENCE, 1925. Proceedings. New York: American Birth Control League, 1925. 4 vols.
Sixth Conference. See Section 4, "Religious and Ethical Aspects." The Seventh Conference published an international survey of contraceptive practices.

RATTI, ACHILLE (Pope Pius XI). *On Christian Marriage*, New York: Barry-Vail Corporation, 1931.
Anti-birth control argument.

ROBINSON, VICTOR. *Pioneers of Birth Control in England and America*. New York: Voluntary Parenthood League, 1919. 107 pp.

SANGER, MARGARET. "Birth Control Steps Out: A Note on the Senate Hearing," *People*, 1:27–28 (April, 1931).

————. *My Fight for Birth Control*. New York: Farrar and Rinehart, 1931. London: Faber, 1932. 360 pp.

————. *The Pivot of Civilization*. New York: Brentano, 1922. 284 pp.
"Principles and aims of the American Birth Control League," pp. 277–84.

UNITED STATES SENATE, COMMITTEE ON THE JUDICIARY. *Birth Control* (hearings before a subcommittee of the Committee on the Judiciary, 72d Congress, 1st Session, on S. 4436). Washington, D. C.: Government Printing Office, 1932. 151 pp.

————. *Birth Control* (hearings before a subcommittee of the Committee on the Judiciary, 73d Congress, 2d Session, on S. 1842, a bill to amend sections . . . of the criminal code). Washington, D. C.: Government Printing Office, 1934. 175 pp.

VREELAND, FRANCIS McL. " The Process of Reform with Especial Reference to Reform Groups in the Field of Population " (unpublished Ph. D. thesis, University of Michigan, 1929).

"War against Birth Control," *American Mercury,* 2:231–36 (June, 1924).

3. TEMPERANCE AND PROHIBITION

"Anti-Saloon League," *Encyclopedia of the Social Sciences.* (By Peter H. Odegard.)

" Bankers Favor Prohibition Repeal," *Bankers Monthly,* 124:582 (May, 1932).

CARTER, HENRY. *The English Temperance Movement: A Study in Objectives.* Volume 1: The Formative Period, 1830–1899 (The Beckby Social Service Lectures, 1932). London: Epworth Press, 1933. 269 pp.

CHERRINGTON, ERNEST H., editor. *The Anti-Saloon League Yearbook.* Westerville, Ohio: The Anti-Saloon League, 1909–29.

————. *Education, the Only Solution of the Alcohol Problem: A Report of Educational Work in the Movement against Beverage Alcohol in the United States of America, Conducted through the World League against Alcoholism and the Anti-Saloon League of America, 1928–1929* (Pamphlets on Prohibition in the United States, no. 143). Westerville, Ohio, n. d. 23 pp.

See also no. 144 in the series, on the same theme.

————. *The Evolution of Prohibition in the United States: A Chronological History of the Liquor Problem and the Temperance Reform in the United States from the Earliest Settlements to the Consummation of Prohibition.* Westerville, Ohio: American Issue Press, 1920. 384 pp.

————. *History of the Anti-Saloon League.* Westerville, Ohio: American Issue Press, 1913. 160 pp.

————. *A New Plan of Campaign in the Interest of National Prohibition.* Westerville, Ohio: American Issue Press, 1919.

DARROW, CLARENCE S., and YARROS, VICTOR S. *The Prohibition Mania.* New York: Boni and Liveright, 1927. 254 pp.

GILFORD, DUFF. "That Squelched Prohibition Pamphlet," *New Republic,* 59:257–59 (July 24, 1929).

GLASSMAN, LEO M. " Russia's Campaign to Keep Ivan Sober," *New York Times Magazine,* March 5, 1933.

" How propaganda has replaced prohibition in the Soviet effort to change the drinking habits of the peasants."

GORDON, ERNEST BARRON. *When the Brewer Had the Stranglehold*. New York: Alcohol Information Committee, 1930. 276 pp.

JENSEN, H. E. "Propaganda and the Anti-Prohibition Movement," *South Atlantic Quarterly*, 32: 254–65 (July, 1933).

KELLY, H. H. "Prohibition and the Medical Fraternity," *North American Review*, 222: 53–57 (September, 1925).

KROUT, JOHN ALLEN. *The Origin of Prohibition* (Ph. D. thesis, Columbia University, 1925). New York: Knopf, 1925. 339 pp.
Bibliography, pp. 305–28.

LEWIS, B. G. "Does the Racketeer Want Prohibition?" *Review of Reviews*, 86: 30–31 (August, 1932).

MITCHELL, J. "Wet Strategy at the Polls," *Outlook*, 156: 332 (October 29, 1930).

NATIONAL WOMEN'S CHRISTIAN TEMPERANCE UNION. Reports of Annual Conventions.

"No Propaganda in the Schools," *Literary Digest*, 102: 11–12 (July 20, 1929).

ODEGARD, PETER H. *Pressure Politics: The Story of the Anti-Saloon League*. New York: Columbia University, 1928. 299 pp.
A standard work on propaganda technique.

ROOT, GRACE C. *Women and Repeal: The Story of the Women's Organization for National Prohibition Reform*, authorized by Mrs. Charles H. Sabin. New York: Harpers, 1933. 217 pp.
One of the leading groups promoting repeal of the Eighteenth Amendment.

STODDARD, CORA FRANCES. *Our One Hundred and Thirty-five Years of Temperance Struggle*. Revised edition. Evanston, Illinois: Woman's Christian Temperance Union.

UNITED STATES SENATE, COMMITTEE ON THE JUDICIARY. *Brewing and Liquor Interests and German Propaganda* (report and hearings of a subcommittee of the Committee on the Judiciary, 65th Congress, 2d Session, 1918, pursuant to Senate Resolutions 307 and 439). Washington, D. C.: Government Printing Office, 1919. 3 vols.
Often called the Overman Report.

"Who, How, Why of the Association against the Prohibition Amendment," *United States National Commission on Law Observance and Enforcement*, 5: 275–86 (1931).

WOMAN'S CHRISTIAN TEMPERANCE UNION. Reports of Annual Conventions, 1886—.
> State organizations of the W. C. T. U. also issue convention reports and other publications.

ZAHNISER, CHARLES R. "Pulpit, Press, and Public Opinion," *Christian Century*, 47:1411 (November 19, 1930).

4. UNIVERSAL LANGUAGE AND CALENDAR REFORM MOVEMENTS

"Calendar," *Encyclopedia of the Social Sciences*. (By Martin P. Nilsson.)
> Discusses calendar reform movements.

COUTURAT, LOUIS, and LEAU, LEOPOLD. *Histoire de la langue universelle*. Paris, 1907. 576 pp.

ESPERANTO ASSOCIATION OF NORTH AMERICA. *Amerika Esperanto*.
> Official organ of the Association.

GUÉRARD, ALBERT LÉON. *Short History of the International Language Movement*. New York: Boni and Liveright, 1922. London: Unwin, 1922. 268 pp.
> Bibliography, pp. 211–15.

Journal of Calendar Reform. New York: World Calendar Association, 1932—.

OGDEN, CHARLES KAY. *The System of Basic English*. New York: Harcourt, Brace, 1934. 320 pp.
> Advocates and explains the use of a basic English vocabulary of 850 selected words. One of several works by the leading promoter of the Basic English movement.

SHENTON, HERBERT NEWHARD, SAPIR, EDWARD, and JESPERSEN, OTTO. *International Communication*. London: Kegan Paul, 1931. 120 pp.
> Symposium on the problems of an international language.

STILES, MEREDITH NEWCOMB. *The World's Work and the Calendar*. Rochester, New York: The International Fixed Calendar League, 1934. 181 pp.
> A study advocating replacement of the Julian-Gregorian calendar with one of thirteen months.

5. CONSUMER'S COOPERATION (BUYING HABITS)

A. BIBLIOGRAPHY

"Cooperative Movement: A Select Bibliography," *Monthly Labor Review*, 31:782–801 (1930).

B. REFERENCES

"Consumers' Leagues," *Encyclopedia of the Social Sciences.* (By George Soule.)

Des Laudres, Maurice Charles E. *L'Acheteur, son rôle économique et social: Les Ligues sociales d'acheteurs.* Paris: Alcan, 1911. 510 pp.

Gaumont, Jean. *Histoire générale de la coopération en France, les idées et les faits, les hommes, et les oeuvres.* Paris: Fédération nationale des coopératives de consommation, 1923–24. 2 vols. Bibliographic footnotes.

Howe, Frederick Clemson. *Denmark, a Cooperative Commonwealth.* New York: Harcourt, Brace, 1921. 203 pp.

Nathan, Maud. *The Story of an Epoch-Making Movement.* Garden City: Doubleday, Page, 1926. 245 pp.

National Consumers' League. *The First Quarter Century, 1899–1924.* New York: National Consumers' League, 1925. 16 pp.

Poisson, Ernest. *La Politique du mouvement co-opératif français.* Paris: Presses universitaires, 1929. 253 pp.

Totomianz, Vakham Fomich. *Theorie, Geschichte und Praxis der Konsumentenorganisation.* Second edition. Berlin, 1929. 296 pp. Bibliographic footnotes.

6. MISCELLANEOUS

Baby Week Campaigns. Washington, D. C.: United States Department of Labor, Children's Bureau, 1917. 152 pp.

"Back-to-the-Land Movements," *Encyclopedia of the Social Sciences.* (By Carle C. Zimmerman.)

Cahill, Marion Cotter. *Shorter Hours: A Study of the Movement since the Civil War* (Columbia University Studies in History, Economics, and Public Law, no. 380). New York: Columbia University, 1932. London: P. S. King, 1932. 300 pp. Bibliography, pp. 289–293.

Carey, M. "American Colonization Society," *North American Review,* 35: 118–65 (1832). Proposed formation of colonies for free Negroes on the African coast.

Cheyney, Edward Potts. *The Anti-Rent Agitation in the State of New York, 1839–1846.* Philadelphia: Porter and Coates, 1887. 64 pp.

"Country Life Movement," *Encyclopedia of the Social Sciences.* (By Carl C. Taylor.)

Drury, Aubrey, compiler. *World Metric Standardization: An Urgent Issue.* San Francisco: World Metric Standardization Council, 1922. 524 pp.
Cites views of a long list of authorities and agencies who are promoting the metric system. Bibliography, pp. 403–503.

"Free Love," *Encyclopedia of the Social Sciences.* (By Robert Biffault.)

Le Rohu, Pierre. "Le Premier congrès international contre le duel," *Correspondant,* 231: 1204–14 (1908).

"Producers' Cooperation," *Encyclopedia of the Social Sciences.* (By David J. Saposs.)

Swift, H. G. *A History of Postal Agitation from Eighty Years Ago till the Present Day,* Book 1. New and revised edition. London: Percy Brothers, 1930. 302 pp.

Thomas, Norman. *The Conscientious Objector in America.* New York: Huebsch, 1923. 299 pp.
History of conscientious objection during the World War.

United States Senate, Committee on Manufactures. *The Metric System* (hearings before a subcommittee of the Committee on Manufactures, 67th Congress, 1st and 2d Sessions, on S. 2267, a bill to fix the metric system . . . as the single standard of weights and measures for certain uses). Washington, D. C.: Government Printing Office, 1922. 439 pp.

Waterman, Willoughby Cyrus. *Prostitution and Its Repression in New York City* (Columbia University Studies in History, Economics, and Public Law, no. 352). New York: Columbia University, 1932. London: P. S. King, 1932. 164 pp.
A chronological recitation of efforts to suppress prostitution in New York City through legislation, police action, specialized court procedure, and private law-enforcing agencies. Bibliography, pp. 160–62.

PART IV. THE SYMBOLS AND PRACTICES OF WHICH PROPAGANDA MAKES USE OR TO WHICH IT ADAPTS ITSELF

A propagandist is both helped and handicapped by the symbols and practices of the community. His skill consists in maneuvering successfully within the limits imposed by current vocabularies, prejudices, and practices. This section includes genetic studies of collective attitudes toward persons, groups, policies, doctrines, institutions, and practices.

A. HISTORICAL-ANALYTIC STUDIES OF COMPOSITE COLLECTIVE RESPONSES

Histories that emphasize the collective symbols of the time. In some instances systematic comparisons are made between region and region, epoch and epoch, culture and culture; data are assembled from the work of students of contemporary civilizations, from the historians of civilization, and from social anthropologists.

I. GENERAL HISTORY OF PUBLIC OPINION AND SYMBOLS

ALLEN, FREDERICK LEWIS. *Only Yesterday: An Informal History of the Nineteen-Twenties.* New York: Harpers, 1931. 370 pp.
Graphic presentation of minor fads and stereotypes. Social scientists might develop more formal methods of analyzing such material.

BABEAU, ALBERT. "L'Appel à l'opinion publique de l'Europe au milieu du XVIIIme siècle." Paris: Institut de France, Académie des sciences morales et politiques, Séances et travaux, 1904, N.S., vol. 62, pp. 161–78.

BAUER, WILHELM. *Die öffentliche Meinung in der Weltgeschichte.* Wildpark-Potsdam: Athenaion, 1930. 403 pp.
Lavishly illustrated. Standard treatise on history of public opinion by a professor of modern history in the University of Vienna. Bibliography, pp. 396–98.

———. *Die öffentliche Meinung und ihre geschichtlichen Grundlagen.* Tübingen: Mohr, 1914. 335 pp.
Without illustrations.

————. "Das Schlagwort als sozialpsychologische und geistesge-schichtliche Erscheinung," *Historische Zeitschrift,* Band 122, Heft 2, pp. 212–23.

BÖDDEKER, K. *Die öffentliche Meinung in England und ihr Ausdruck im 16.–17. Jahrhundert.* Heidelberg, 1886.

BORKENAU, FRANZ. *Der Übergang vom feudalen zum bürgerlichen Weltbild: Studien zur Geschichte der Philosophie der Manufaktur-periode* (Schriften des Instituts für Sozialforschung, Band 4). Paris: Alcan, 1934. 559 pp.

DAVIS, JEROME. *Contemporary Social Movements.* New York: Century, 1930. 901 pp.
A general text, treating of such subjects as Socialism, Communism, Fascism, and the peace movement.

DELAISI, FRANCIS. *Political Myths and Economic Realities.* A translation of *Les Contradictions du monde moderne.* London: Douglas, 1927. 409 pp. New York: Viking, 1927. 446 pp.

HALPHEN, LOUIS. *L'Essor de l'Europe, XIe–XIIIe siècles* (Peuples et civilisations, tôme 6). Paris: Alcan, 1932. 609 pp.
A treatise on the twelfth century. Pages 309 ff. analyse the means and agencies through which the papacy endeavored to control the life and thought of Western Christendom.

HUIZINGA, JOHAN. *The Waning of the Middle Ages: A Study of the Forms of Life, Thought, and Art in France and the Netherlands in the XIVth and XVth Centuries,* translated from the Dutch by F. Hopman. London: E. Arnold, 1924. 328 pp.
Bibliography, pp. 309–18. Sociology of the late Middle Ages. German edition: *Herbst des Mittelalters: Studien über Lebens- und Geistesfor-men des 14. und 15. Jahrhunderts in Frankreich und in den Nieder-landen.* Munich: Drei Masken, 1931. 556 pp. Bibliography, pp. 486–529; bibliographic footnotes. This volume is also available in the original Dutch (*Herfsttij der Middeleeuwen.* Haarlem: Tjeenk Willink, 1921) and in Spanish (*El Otoño de la Edad media.* Madrid: Revista de occi-dente, 1930—).

JESPERSEN, JENS OTTO HARRY. *Language: Its Nature, Development, and Origin.* London: Allen and Unwin, 1922. New York: Holt, 1928. 448 pp.
Standard work; some indications of dynamic principles.

KULKE, EDUARD. *Zur Entwicklungsgeschichte der Meinungen.* Leipzig, 1891.

KYDD, SAMUEL. *A Sketch of the Growth of Public Opinion.* London, 1888.

LEHMAN, B. H. *Carlyle's Theory of the Hero, Its Sources, Develop-ment, History, and Influence upon Carlyle's Work: A Study of a Nineteenth Century Idea.* Durham, North Carolina: Duke University, 1928. 212 pp.
Confucius' Superior Man is signalized, as well as Plato's Philosopher King, the Hebrew Messiah, Plutarch's Politician, Machiavelli's Prince, etc., tracing the Great Man's relation to the process of social change.

LILIENCRON, FREIHERR ROCHUS VON. *Mitteilungen aus dem Gebiete der öffentlichen Meinung in Deutschland während der 2ten Hälfte des 16ten Jahrhunderts.* Munich, 1874–75. 2 vols.

LILLY, WILLIAM SAMUEL. *On Shibboleths.* London: Chapman and Hall, 1892. 261 pp.
On public opinion and contemporary social questions.

"Literacy and Illiteracy," *Encyclopedia of the Social Sciences.* (By Helen Sullivan.)

"Literature," *Encyclopedia of the Social Sciences.* (By Max Lerner and Edwin Mims, Jr.)

MACKINNON, W. A. *History of Civilization and Public Opinion.* London: Longman, Brown, Green, and Longman, 1846. 2 vols.
A rifacimento of the author's *On Public Opinion in Great Britain and Other Parts of the World,* issued anonymously in 1828. Like many oth-ers in this field, this book distinguishes between "popular clamor" and "public opinion."

MARTIN, ALFRED VON. *Soziologie der Renaissance: Zur Physiognomik und Rhythmik bürgerlicher Kultur.* Stuttgart: Enke, 1932. 135 pp.

MIRBT, KARL. *Die Publizistik im Zeitalter Gregors VII.* Leipzig: J. C. Hinrich, 1894. 629 pp.
Bibliographic footnotes.

PLAYNE, CAROLINE ELISABETH. *The Neuroses of the Nations.* London: Allen and Unwin, 1925. New York: Seltzer, 1925. 468 pp.
This author finds that the World War grew out of collective neurotic states.

REICHENSPERGER, AUGUST. *Phrasen und Schlagwörter: Ein unentbehr-liches Noth- und Hülfsbüchlein für Zeitungsleser.* Paderborn, 1862.

ROBINSON, JAMES HARVEY. *The Mind in the Making.* New York: Harp-ers, 1921. 235 pp.
Essay on "intellectual history."

SCHNEIDER, HERBERT WALLACE. *The Puritan Mind.* New York: Holt, 1930. 301 pp.
Bibliography, pp. 265–97.

SCHOLZ, RICHARD. *Die Publizistik zur Zeit Philipps des Schönen und Bonifaz VIII.* (Kirchenrechtliche Abhandlungen, vols. 6–8). Stuttgart: Enke, 1903. 528 pp.

THOMPSON, JAMES WESTFALL. *Feudal Germany.* Chicago: University of Chicago, 1928. 710 pp.

Pages 249–60 discuss the war of investiture, when, according to the author, " for the first time in medieval history all classes of society from bishops and abbots and barons down to the lower classes of the people, even the servile peasantry, were interested in a common matter."

TROTSKY, LEON. *Literature and Revolution.* New York: International Publishers, 1925. 256 pp.

An extended critical essay discussing Russian literature, and literature in general, as an effect and an instrumentality of revolutionary movements.

URQUHART, DAVID. *Public Opinion and Its Organs.* London: Trübner, 1855. 94 pp.

VOSSLER, KARL. *Geist und Kultur in der Sprache.* Heidelberg, 1925. 267 pp.

Bibliographic footnotes. English edition: *The Spirit of Language in Civilization* (International Library of Psychology, Philosophy, and Scientific Method). London: Kegan Paul, Trench, and Trubner, 1932. 247 pp.

WARTHIN, ALFRED SCOTT. *The Physician of the Dance of Death: A Historical Study of the Evolution of the Dance of Death Mythus in Art.* New York: Paul B. Hoeber, 1931. 142 pp.

In its earliest form the dance of death was a didactic religious device for social control.

WOOLF, LEONARD SIDNEY, and WOOLF, VIRGINIA. *After the Deluge: A Study of Communal Psychology.* London: L. and V. Woolf, 1931. New York: Harcourt, Brace, 1931.

" The first volume of what is intended to be a full-length study of the psychology of man in the mass. . . . The deluge was the war . . .; the opening chapter examines its psychological causes."

2. ATTITUDES OF CLASSES AND SKILL-GROUPS

"Aristocracy," *Encyclopedia of the Social Sciences.* (By L. T. Hobhouse.)

BAKKE, E. WIGHT. *The Unemployed Man.* London: Nisbet, 1933. 308 pp.

BARTLETT, F. C. *Psychology and the Soldier.* Cambridge, England: Cambridge University, 1927. 223 pp.

"Bourgeoisie," *Encyclopedia of the Social Sciences*. (By Carl Brinkmann.)

BRENTANO, LUJO. *Der Unternehmer: Vortrag gehalten am 3. Januar 1907, in der Volkswirtschaftlichen Gesellschaft in Berlin* (Volkswirtschaftliche Zeitfragen, Vorträge und Abhandlungen, Heft 225). Berlin: Simion, 1907. 30 pp.

BRINKMANN, CARL. "Die Aristokratie im kapitalistischen Zeitalter," *Grundriss der Sozialökonomik,* Band 9, Teil 1: 22–34.

BRODA, RUDOLPH, and DEUTSCH, J. *Le Prolétariat international: Étude de psychologie sociale.* Paris: V. Girard et É. Brière, 1912. 254 pp.

BUISSON, FERDINAND. "La Morale professionelle: L'Homme politique," *Revue du mois,* 3: 277–97 (1907).

"Bureaucracy," *Encyclopedia of the Social Sciences*. (By Harold J. Laski.)

"Captain of Industry," *Encyclopedia of the Social Sciences*. (By Helen R. Wright.)

CARRÉ, HENRI PIERRE MARIE FRÉDÉRIC. *La Noblesse de France et l'opinion publique au XVIII᷎ siècle.* Paris: Champion, 1920. 650 pp. Bibliography, pp. 629–50.

CARRINGTON, HEREWARD. "The Mind of the Soldier: A Study in the Psychology of the Combatant, Based on First-Hand Documents and Interviews," *Forum,* 55: 49–68 (1916).

CLAGUE, EWAN, COUPER, WALTER J., and BAKKE, E. WIGHT. *After the Shutdown.* New Haven: Yale University Institute of Human Relations, 1934. 153 pp.
The readjustment of factory workers displaced by plant shutdowns.

CLEMENS, SEVERUS. *Der Beruf des Diplomaten.* Berlin: Deutsche Verlagsgesellschaft für Politik und Geschichte, 1926. 107 pp.
A pioneer essay on the psychology of the diplomat, by a former member of the German diplomatic service.

CONSIGLIO, P. "Alcune noti di psicologia militare," *Atti del V Congresso Internazionale di Psicologia,* pp. 594–606. Rome: Forzani, 1905.

CORBIN, JOHN. *The Return of the Middle Class.* New York: Scribners, 1922. 353 pp.
Bibliographic notes, last chapter.

DEMETER, KARL. *Das deutsche Offizierkorps in seinen historischsoziologischen Grundlagen.* Berlin: Hobbing, 1930. 369 pp.

EDWARDS, ALBERTO. *La fronda aristocrática en Chile.* Santiago: Imprenta Nacional, 1928. 308 pp.
A series of articles on the rôle of the Chilean aristocracy in politics since 1810.

EULENBURG, FRANZ. *Phantasie und Wille des wirtschaftenden Menschen.* Tübingen: Mohr, 1931. 47 pp.
Fantasy and will in economic activity.

FAHLBECK, PONTUS ERLAND. *Die Klasse und die Gesellschaft.* Jena: Fischer, 1922. 348 pp.
Bibliographic footnotes.

FRANZEN-HELLERSBERG, LISBETH. *Die jugendliche Arbeiterin: Ihr Arbeitswesen und Lebensform.* Tübingen: Mohr, 1932. 144 pp.
The working girl.

GAMIO, MANUEL, compiler. *The Mexican Immigrant.* Chicago: University of Chicago, 1931. 288 pp.
Application of anthropological technique to analysis of reaction patterns of an immigrant group. Contains autobiographical documents.

GECK, L. H. AD. *Die sozialen Betriebsverhältnisse im Wandel der Zeit: Geschichtliche Einführung in die Betriebssoziologie.* Berlin: Springer, 1931. 173 pp.
Occupational sociology.

GROETHUYSEN, BERNHARD. *Origines de l'esprit bourgeois en France.* Vol. 1: L'Église et la bourgeoisie. Third edition. Paris: Gallimard, 1927.

GROVES, ERNEST RUTHERFORD. *The Rural Mind and Social Welfare.* Chicago: University of Chicago, 1922. 205 pp.

HALBWACHS, MAURICE. "Beitrag zu einer soziologischen Theorie der Arbeiterklasse," *Jahrbuch für Soziologie,* 2: 366–85 (1926).

————. *La Classe ouvrière et ses niveaux de vie: Récherches sur la hiérarchie des besoins dans les sociétés industrielles contemporaines.* Paris: Alcan, 1913. 495 pp.

Handbook of Rural Social Resources, edited by Benson Young Landis. Chicago: University of Chicago, 1926.
Includes "the programs of national agencies engaged in rural social work."

HELLEN, OBERST G. VON DER. *Die Erziehung zum Soldaten: Eine vergleichende Studie über die in Deutschland, England, Frankreich, Italien, Österreich, und Russland dafür geltenden Bestimmungen sowie eine Anleitung für die Gestaltung des Unterrichts.* Graz: Leuschner und Lubensky, 1931.

A comparative study of the education of soldiers in the principal European countries.

JOSEPHSON, MATTHEW. *The Robber Barons: The Great American Capitalists, 1861–1901.* New York: Harcourt, Brace, 1934. 474 pp. Bibliography, pp. 455–60.

JÜNGST, HILDEGARD. *Die jugendliche Fabrikarbeiterin: Ein Beitrag zur Industriepädagogik.* Paderborn: Ferdinand Schöningh, 1929. 136 pp. The factory girl.

KELCHNER, MATHILDE. *Kummer und Trost jugendlicher Arbeiterinnen: Eine sozialpsychologische Unterschung an Aufsätzen von Schülerinnen der Berufsschule* (Forschungen zur Völkerpsychologie und Soziologie, Band 6). Leipzig: C. L. Hirschfeld, 1929. 90 pp. Attitudes of working girls.

LASSWELL, HAROLD DWIGHT. " The Moral Vocation of the Middle Income Skill Group," *International Journal of Ethics,* 45: 127–37 (January, 1935).

" The common factor in the seeming political confusion of our times is . . . [that] . . . in the name of the ' proletariat' the middle-income skill groups are rising to power at the expense of aristocracy and plutocracy."

LAZARSFELD, M., and ZEISL, H. "Die Arbeitslosen von Marienthal," *Psychologische Monographien,* 5: 123 (1933).

A study of the effect of unemployment lasting for two years or more was made in a village of 1,486 inhabitants. Complete information on each of the inhabitants was gathered. A historical review of the sociographic survey method is appended.

MANN, FRITZ K. " Finanzsoziologie," *Kölner Vierteljahreshefte für Soziologie,* vol. 12, no. 1, pp. 1–20 (August, 1933).

An effort to study the influence of all financial facts upon social life as a whole.

MEAD, EDWARD SHERWOOD. *The Work of the Promoter* (Publications of the American Academy of Political and Social Science, no. 359). 1903.

MELTZER, HYMAN. *Children's Social Concepts: A Study of Their Nature and Development* (Teachers College Contributions to Education, no. 192). New York: Columbia University, 1925. 91 pp.

An interview study of thirty-three students from the fourth grade through high school to determine the meanings they attached to certain social concepts. Bibliography, pp. 90–91.

MERRILL, FRANCIS E., and CLARK, CARROLL D. "The Money Market as a Special Public," *American Journal of Sociology,* 39:626–36 (March, 1934).

Very specialized types of information concerning social events enter the focus of attention of active participants in the money markets; this article analyzes some of the consequences.

MICHELS, ROBERTO. "Beitrag zur Lehre von der Klassenbildung," *Archiv für Sozialwissenschaft,* 49:561–93 (1922).

Contribution to the theory of class attitudes.

————. *Umschichtungen in den herrschenden Klassen nach dem Kriege.* Stuttgart: Kohlhammer, 1934.

————. "Zum Problem der Internationalen Bourgeoisie," in his *Probleme der Sozialphilosophie* (Leipzig and Berlin: Teubner, 1914. 208 pp.).

"Middle Classes," *Encyclopedia of the Social Sciences.* (By Alfred Meusel.)

OGBURN, WILLIAM FIELDING, and PETERSON, DELVIN. "Political Thought of the Social Classes," *Political Science Quarterly,* 31:300–17 (June, 1916).

OPPENHEIMER, FRANZ. "Käufer und Verkäufer: Ein Beitrag zur wirtschaftlichen Kollektivpsychologie," *Jahrbuch für Gesetzgebung,* 24:1369–1418 (1900).

"Plantation," *Encyclopedia of the Social Sciences.* (By George McCutchen McBride.)

"Proletariat," *Encyclopedia of the Social Sciences.* (By Alfred Meusel.)

"Proletariat," *Handwörterbuch für Soziologie,* pp. 441–58. (By Goetz Briefs.)

Religion among American Men, as Revealed by a Study of Conditions in the Army. New York: Association Press, 1920.

A study of the religious life and thought of a group of young men in the national army.

SANFORD, JOHN LANGTON, and TOWNSEND, MEREDITH. *The Great Governing Families of England.* Edinburgh: W. Blackwood, 1865. 2 vols.

SCHWIEDLAND, EUGEN. *Zur Soziologie des Unternehmertums.* Leipzig: C. L. Hirschfeld, 1933. 52 pp.

A book concerned with the problem of the control of business for the common good.

SHARP, WALTER RICE. *The French Civil Service: Bureaucracy in Transition.* New York: Macmillan, 1931. 588 pp.

Contains a section on organizations of civil service employees.

SOMBART, WERNER. *Der Bourgeois: Zur Geistesgeschichte des modernen Wirstschaftsmenschen.* Second edition. Munich and Leipzig: Duncker und Humblot, 1920. 540 pp.

An earlier edition was translated by M. Epstein as *The Quintessence of Capitalism.* London: Unwin, 1915. New York: Dutton, 1915. 400 pp.

SPENDER, JOHN ALFRED. *The Public Life.* New York: Cassell, 1925. 2 vols.

The reflections of one of the leading English publicists on politics and politicians, democracy, public opinion, and the press.

STEINHAUSEN, S. "Fachmenschentum und Arbeitsmenschentum als geistige Typen des letzten Menschenalters," *Preussische Jahrbücher,* Band 204, Heft 3, pp. 288–304.

Specialists and workers as contemporary cultural formations.

STODDARD, THEODORE LATHROP. *Social Classes in Post-War Europe.* New York and London: Scribners, 1925. 178 pp.

TAUSSIG, FRANK WILLIAM, and JOSLYN, C. S. *American Business Leaders.* New York: Macmillan, 1932. 319 pp.

THOMAS, WILLIAM ISAAC, and ZNANIECKI, FLORIAN. *The Polish Peasant in Europe and America.* Second edition. New York: Knopf, 1927. 2 vols., 2250 pp.

Original edition 5 volumes; introductions to volumes 1 and 3 were historically influential in American social psychology, developing concepts of *value* and *object.* Introduced the life history document in sociological research.

THÜRAUF, ULRICH. *Geschichte der öffentlichen Meinung in Ansbach-Bayreuth, 1789–1815.* Ausbach, 1918.

"The War Mind, the Business Mind, and a Third Alternative," *Sociological Review,* 12: 113–36 (1920).

WEBER, MAX. "Politik als Beruf," in his *Gesammelte politische Schriften,* pp. 396–451 (Munich: Drei Masken Verlag, 1921).

Sociological analysis of the official.

WILLIAMS, JAMES MICKEL. *Human Aspects of Unemployment and Relief.* Chapel Hill: University of North Carolina, 1933. 235 pp.

WRIGHT, LOUIS B. "The Elizabethan Middle-Class Taste for History," *Journal of Modern History,* 3: 175–98 (June, 1931).

"The faith in the didactic value of history . . . did . . . coincide so precisely with the bourgeois conception of the utility of learning that histories were hailed as the perfect literature of that class."

3. ATTITUDES OF COMMUNITIES: NATIONS, CULTURES, LOCALITIES

BARCK, OSCAR THEODORE, JR. *New York City during the War for Independence* (Columbia University Studies in History, Economics, and Public Law, no. 357). New York: Columbia University, 1931. London: P. S. King, 1931. 267 pp.

Has a section on the "Press and Public Opinion." Bibliography, pp. 254–62.

BERTAUT, JULES. *L'Opinion et les moeurs* (La Troisième république; 1870 à nos jours, vol. 9). Paris: Éditions de France, 1931. 488 pp.

Opinion and custom under the Third Republic.

BETTS, T. J. "Chinese Public Opinion," *Foreign Affairs*, 11:470–77 (April, 1933).

BEVAN, EDWYN ROBERT. *Thoughts on Indian Discontents*. London: Allen and Unwin, 1929. 178 pp.

The psychological side of the Anglo-Indian problem.

BLEGEN, THEODORE C. "Minnesota Pioneer Life as Revealed in Newspaper Advertisements," *Minnesota History*, 7:99–121 (June, 1926).

Advertising itself reflects the culture of a community.

BLUMENTHAL, ALBERT. *Small Town Stuff*. Chicago: University of Chicago, 1932. 416 pp.

Description of a small Western mining town.

BRIGHAM, CARL CAMPBELL. *A Study of American Intelligence*. Princeton, New Jersey: Princeton University, 1923. 210 pp.

Distribution of responses measured by certain intelligence tests.

CABLE, MILDRED, and others. *The Challenge of Central Asia*. New York: World Dominion Press, 1929. 136 pp.

A survey of Tibet, Mongolia, and Turkestan for missionary purposes, with stress on the possibility of Bolshevik domination.

CALVERTON, V. F. (pseudonym). *The Liberation of American Literature*. New York: Scribners, 1932. 500 pp.

A historical-sociological study, from a Marxian point of view.

CURTIUS, ERNST ROBERT, and BERGSTRÄSSER, ARNOLD. *Frankreich*. Stuttgart: Deutsche Verlagsanstalt, 1930. 2 vols.

A book comparable to Dibelius' *England*, surveying the cultural and economic-political life of France. Reviews French politics, finance, industry, and international relations.

DABNEY, VIRGINIUS. *Liberalism in the South*. Chapel Hill: University of North Carolina, 1932. 456 pp.

The fields covered in this historical survey are politics, religion, education, race relations, industry, literature, journalism, and emancipation of women. The bibliography, pp. 429–41, cites more than three hundred titles.

DENISON, JOHN HOPKINS. *Emotional Currents in American History.* New York: Scribners, 1932. 420 pp.
An attempt to show how ideas and emotions have swept the American people along in certain channels.

DIBELIUS, WILHELM. *England.* New York: Harpers, 1930. 569 pp.
A German scholar's study of contemporary English life, institutions, and problems.

DICEY, ALBERT VENN. *Lectures on the Relation between Law and Public Opinion in England in the Nineteenth Century.* London and New York: Macmillan, 1905. 503 pp.
States that nineteenth-century English opinion was united on "destructive" measures, disunited on "constructive" measures.

DIESEL, EUGEN. *Germany and the Germans.* New York: Macmillan, 1931. 315 pp.
Surveys the geographical, biological, and climatic characteristics of Germany, discusses the people, their mode of life, their activities, and their mentality. The last section the author devotes to the complex problems of Germany's collapse and resurrection, the industrial changes, the new psychology, and the new political organizations.

DOBIE, E. "Looking at Oregon Territory through Advertisements," *Washington Historical Quarterly,* 18: 103–09 (April, 1927).
Advertisements as a source for historical research.

FÜLÖP-MILLER, RENÉ. *The Mind and Face of Bolshevism: An Examination of Cultural Life in Soviet Russia.* London and New York: Putnam, 1927. 308 pp.
Bibliography, pp. 291–99.

GEIGER, THEODOR. *Die soziale Schichtung des deutschen Volkes.* Stuttgart: Enke, 1932. 142 pp.
Social structure of Germany quantitatively analyzed.

GRANET, MARCEL. *Chinese Civilization.* New York: Knopf, 1930. 444 pp.
Analyzes the propaganda that promoted filial piety and certain other traits of Chinese culture, pp. 310 ff.

GUÉRARD, ALBERT LÉON. *The Life and Death of an Ideal: France in the Classical Age.* New York: Scribners, 1928. 391 pp.

HART, HORNELL NORRIS. "Changing Social Attitudes and Interests," in *Recent Social Trends,* 1: 382–443. New York, 1933.
Based on a quantitative study of newspapers and periodicals in the United States.

HARVEY, EDWIN D. *The Mind of China*. New Haven: Yale University, 1933. 321 pp.
By a former professor of sociology at Yale-in-China.

HINDUS, M. G. "The Jew as Radical," *Menorah Journal,* 13: 367–79 (August, 1927).

HOFFMANN-KRAYER, EDUARD, and BÄCHFOLD-STÄUBLI, H., editors. *Handwörterbuch des deutschen Aberglaubens (Handwörterbücher zur deutschen Volkskunde,* pt. I, vols. 1–3). Berlin, 1927–31.
On German superstitions.

INSTITUTE OF PACIFIC RELATIONS. Publications.
"A self-governing and self-directing body concerned with promoting the best relations between the Pacific peoples. . . . Originally called 'Conference on Problems of the Pacific Peoples.'" Publishes a series of books and mimeographed documents, and *Pacific Affairs,* a monthly magazine.

JOHNSON, G. B. "Newspaper Advertisements and Negro Culture," *Journal of Social Forces,* 3: 706–09 (May, 1925).
Culture reflected in advertising.

KOELLE, WILLIAM. *Englische Stellungnahme gegenüber Frankreich in der Zeit von deutsch-französicher Krieg 1870/71 bis zur Besetzung Ägyptens durch England 1882: Ein Beitrag zur Vorgeschichte des Weltkrieges.* Berlin: Ebering, 1934. 137 pp.
Bibliography, pp. 5–8. Appendix, pp. 94–137, consists mostly of press citations.

LÉGER, BERNARD M. E. *Les Opinions politiques des provinces françaises: Caractères principaux des divers partis politiques français et " géographie électorale" de la France* (Collection des réformes politiques et sociales). Paris: J. Gamber, 1933. 268 pp.
Factual study of contemporary French politics, based partly on election statistics.

LEWIS, LAWRENCE. *The Advertisements of the Spectator, Being a Study of the Literature, History, and Manners of Queen Anne's England as They Are Reflected Therein, as Well as an Introduction to the Origins of the Art of Advertising.* Boston: Houghton Mifflin, 1909. 307 pp.
Advertising as a source for cultural history.

LUDKE, GERHARD, and MACKENSEN, LUTZ. *Deutscher Kulturatlas.* Berlin: De Gruyter, 1928—.
The complete atlas will contain 500 maps, illustrating every phase of German history.

LUETKENS, CHARLOTTE. "Demokratie und öffentliche Meinung in den

Vereingten Staaten," in *Soziologische Studien* . . . , dedicated to Alfred Weber, pp. 190–206. Potsdam, 1930.

LYND, ROBERT S., and LYND, HELEN MERRELL. *Middletown: A Study in Contemporary American Culture.* New York: Harcourt, Brace, 1929. 550 pp.
Anthropological technique developed in the study of primitive cultures is applied in a case study of a complex contemporary culture.

MADARIAGA, SALVADOR DE. *Englishmen, Frenchmen, and Spaniards,* with an introductory note by A. E. Zimmern. London: Oxford University, 1928. 256 pp.
Typical of the best impressionistic interpretations of culture contrasts.

MASARYK, THOMAS GARRIGUE. *The Spirit of Russia.* New York: Macmillan, 1919. 2 vols.
Russian intellectual history and life, viewed in its religious, philosophical, social, and political aspects, by a scholar-statesman. Contains a discussion of Russian Socialism and the Revolutionary movement.

MAYO, KATHERINE. *Mother India.* New York: Harcourt, Brace, 1927. 454 pp.
Probably the most discussed book about India since the World War. Among the many replies published may be mentioned C. S. Ranga Iyer, *Father India* (London: Selwyn, 1927); Dhan Gopal Mukerji, *A Son of Mother India Answers* (New York: Dutton, 1928); Ernest Wood, *An Englishman Defends Mother India* (New York: Tantrik, 1930); K. Natarajan, *Miss Mayo's Mother India* (Madras: Natesan, 1928); Lajpat Raya, *Unhappy India* (Calcutta: Banna, 1928); Syam S. Chakravarty, *My Mother's Picture* (London: Thacker, 1930); Dalip Singh Saund, *My Mother India* (Los Angeles: Wetzel, 1930); J. A. Chapman, *The Character of India* (Oxford: Blackwell, 1928). These and other criticisms have been examined and the argument of Miss Mayo restated by Harry H. Field, *After Mother India* (New York: Harcourt, Brace, 1929).

———. *Volume Two.* New York: Harcourt, Brace, 1931. 313 pp.
More evidence to support the contentions of Miss Mayo's previous book.

MENCKEN, HENRY LOUIS. *The American Language: A Preliminary Inquiry into the Development of English in the United States.* Third edition. New York: Knopf, 1923. 489 pp.
Bibliography, pp. 436–67.

MICHELS, ROBERTO. *Italian von Heute.* Zurich: Füssli, 1930. 410 pp.
The well-known German-Italian sociologist reviews the evolution of modern Italy.

NATHAN, GEORGE JEAN, and MENCKEN, HENRY LOUIS. *The American Credo: A Contribution toward the Interpretation of the National Mind.* New York: Knopf, 1920. 191 pp.

Ogle, Bladen. "Social Ideas in American Literature since 1920" (unpublished M. A. thesis, Ohio State University, 1932).

O'Higgins, Harvey, and Reede, E. H. *The American Mind in Action.* New York and London: Harpers, 1924. 336 pp.

Parrington, Vernon Louis. *Main Currents in American Thought: An Interpretation of American Literature from the Beginnings to 1920.* New York: Harcourt, Brace, 1927–30. 3 vols.
Bibliography at end of each volume.

Paullin, Charles O. *Atlas of the Historical Geography of the United States,* edited by John K. Wright. Washington: Carnegie Institution, 1932. New York: American Geographical Society, 1932. 162 pp., 166 plates.
Plates 102–22 are on "Political Parties and Opinion, 1788–1930," plates 123–32 on "Political, Social, and Educational Reforms, 1775–1931."

Playne, Caroline Elisabeth. *The Pre-War Mind in Britain: An Historic Review.* London: Allen and Unwin, 1928. 444 pp.

Plekhanov, Georgy Valentinovich. "Das französische Drama und die französische Malerei im achtzehnten Jahrhundert," translated from the Russian by J. Herzmark in *Neue Zeit,* vol. 29, pt. 1, pp. 542–51, 572–83 (1911).
The aesthetics of a distinguished historical materialist theoretician.

Pott, William S. Appleton. *Chinese Political Philosophy.* New York: Knopf, 1925. 110 pp.
Indicates sources of Chinese resistance to Western types of political propaganda.

Price, Maurice T. *Christian Missions and Oriental Civilizations: A Study in Culture Contact; the Reactions of Non-Christian Peoples to Protestant Missions from the Standpoint of Individual and Group Behavior,* with a foreword by Robert E. Park. Shanghai: Privately printed, 1924. 578 pp.
Bibliography, pp. 547–62.

Santayana, George. *Character and Opinion in the United States, with Reminiscences of William James and Josiah Royce, and Academic Life in America.* New York: Scribners, 1920. 233 pp.

Siegfried, André. *France: A Study in Nationality.* New Haven: Published by Yale University for the Institute of Politics, 1930. London: Oxford University, 1930. 122 pp.

Strunsky, Simeon. "Jones, His Opinions and Politics," *Atlantic Monthly,* 148:479–88 (October, 1931).

TURNER, FREDERICK JACKSON. *The Frontier in American History.* New edition. New York: Holt, 1926. 375 pp.
Bibliographic footnotes.

———. *The Significance of Sections in American History.* New York: Holt, 1933. 347 pp.
"Declaring that the 'significance of the section in American history is that it is the faint image of a European nation and that we need to re-examine our history in the light of this fact,' Turner carefully defined his terms and elaborated an objective methodology for the re-examination which he advocated." — MERLE E. CURTI.

VATTIER, GEORGES. *Essai sur la mentalité canadienne française.* Paris: Champion, 1928. 381 pp.
A heavily documented dissertation on national psychology.

VETH, CORNELIS. *De Humor in de moderne Nederlandsche Literatur.* Amsterdam: Nederlandsche Uitgevers-Maatschap, 1929. 207 pp.

WOODBURN, JAMES ALBERT. "Western Radicalism in American Politics," *Mississippi Valley Historical Review,* 13: 143–68 (1926–27).

WOODBURY, MARGARET. *Public Opinion in Philadelphia, 1789–1801* (Ph.D. thesis, Bryn Mawr College). Durham, North Carolina: Seeman Printery, 1919. Northampton, Massachusetts: Smith College, 1920. 138 pp.
Bibliography, pp. 133–38. ·

ZWIEDINECK-SÜDENHORST, H. VON. *Die öffentliche Meinung in Deutschland im Zeitalter Ludwigs XIV.*

4. ATTITUDES DURING CRISES : DISASTER, WAR AND BALANCING OF POWER, REVOLUTION

BLEY, WULF, editor. *Revolutionen der Weltgeschichte: 2 Jahrtausende Revolutionen und Bürgerkriege.* Munich: Moser, 1933. 991 pp., 843 original photographs, and documents.

BROWN, WILLIAM ADAMS. *The Groping Giant.* New Haven: Yale University, 1920. 204 pp.
A study, largely psychological, of Russian social groups — the masses, the Bolsheviki, the intelligentsia — by a member of the American Committee on Public Information.

CARROLL, EBER MALCOLM. *French Public Opinion and Foreign Affairs, 1870–1914.* New York: Century, 1931. 356 pp.
A detailed study of public opinion and its currents, based on newspapers, documents, and periodical literature.

CARTER, J. D. *The Attitude of France in the Austro-Serbian Conflict, 1914.* Toulouse: Privat, 1927.

CLARK, DORA MAY. *British Opinion and the American Revolution.* New Haven: Yale University, 1930. London: Oxford, 1930. 308 pp. Bibliography, pp. 281–89.

DROZ, JACQUES. *L'Opinion publique dans la Province Rhénane au cours du conflit Austro-Prussien 1864–66* (Rheinisches Archiv, no. 22). Bonn: Röhrscheid, 1932. 54 pp.

ELBERTZHAGEN, HUGO. "Der Einfluss grosser Katastrophen in Natur- und Völkergeschehen auf Weltanschauung und Glauben," *Deutsche Rundschau,* 47: 200–13 (1921).
Psychological consequences of natural and social catastrophes.

ENGERAND, LOUIS. *L'Opinion publique dans les Provinces Rhénanes et en Belgique, 1789–1815.* Paris, 1919. 183 pp. Bibliographic footnotes.

EVERTH, ERICH. *Die Öffentlichkeit in der Aussenpolitik von Karl V. bis Napoleon.* Jena: Fischer, 1930. 500 pp.

GRÜNING, IRENE. *Die russische öffentliche Meinung und ihre Stellung zu den Grossmächten, 1878–1894.* Königsberg and Berlin: Ost-Europa Verlag, 1929. 219 pp. Bibliography, pp. 207–15.

HALLAYS, ANDRÉ. *L'Opinion allemande pendant la guerre, 1914–1918.* Paris: Perrin, 1919. 268 pp.

HINKHOUSE, FRED JUNKIN. *The Preliminaries of the American Revolution as Seen in the English Press, 1763–1775* (Columbia University Studies in History, Economics, and Public Law, no. 276). New York: Columbia University, 1926. London: P. S. King, 1926. 216 pp. Bibliography, pp. 206–11.

HOLCOMBE, ARTHUR NORMAN. *The Chinese Revolution: A Phase in the Regeneration of a World Power.* Cambridge, Massachusetts: Harvard University, 1930. 401 pp.

JORDAN, DONALDSON, and PRATT, EDWIN J. *Europe and the American Civil War,* New York: Houghton Mifflin, 1931. London: Oxford University, 1931. 300 pp.

JUSSERAND, JEAN ADRIEN ANTOINE JULES. *Le Sentiment américain pendant la guerre.* Paris: Payot, 1931. 157 pp.

JUX, ANTON. *Der Kriegsschrecken des Frühjahrs 1914 in der europäischen Presse.* Berlin-Charlottenburg: H. W. Hendriock, 1929. 248 pp.

KANTOROWICZ, HERMANN. *The Spirit of British Policy and the Myth of the Encirclement of Germany,* revised by the author and translated by W. H. Johnston. New York: Oxford University, 1932. 541 pp.

LAMPMANN, THEOPHIL. *Die Entwicklung der öffentlichen Meinung in Westfalen zur Zeit der französischen Revolution* (inaugural dissertation, Münster). Witten, 1914. 86 pp.
Bibliography, two pages at the beginning.

LEFÈBVRE, GEORGES. *La Grande Peur de 1789.* Paris: Colin, 1932. 282 pp.
The spread of anxiety after the fall of the Bastille.

LOKKE, CARL LUDWIG. *France and the Colonial Question: A Study of Contemporary French Opinion, 1763–1801* (Columbia University Studies in History, Economics, and Public Law, no. 365). New York: Columbia University, 1932. London: P. S. King, 1932. 254 pp.
Bibliography, pp. 236–46.

MACDONALD, HELEN GRACE. *Canadian Public Opinion on the American Civil War* (Columbia University Studies in History, Economics, and Public Law, no. 273). New York: Columbia University, 1926. London: P. S. King, 1926. 237 pp.
Bibliography, pp. 224–32.

MARRARO, HOWARD ROSARIO. *American Opinion on the Unification of Italy, 1846–1861.* New York: Columbia University, 1932. 345 pp.
Based largely on the study of a large number of New York newspapers and magazines, with a few from other cities. Bibliography, pp. 320–32.

MARTIN, KINGSLEY. "Public Opinion: The English Press and the Manchurian Dispute," *Political Quarterly,* 3:117–24 (January, 1932).

————. "Shanghai in the British Press," *Political Quarterly,* 3:281–88 (April, 1932).
Opinion following the Japanese bombardment of the Chinese city.

MAY, ARTHUR JAMES. *Contemporary American Opinion on the Mid-Century Revolutions in Central Europe* (Ph. D. thesis, University of Pennsylvania). Philadelphia, 1927. 135 pp.
Bibliography, pp. 129–35.

MAZON, ANDRÉ. *Lexique de la guerre et de la révolution en Russie, 1914–1918.* Paris: Champion, 1920. 65 pp.
Mazon studied the formation of the new Russian language on the spot during the war period.

MESSER, AUGUST. "Studien zur Psychologie des Krieges," *Preussiche Jahrbücher,* February, 1917.

MITTELSTAEDT, ANNA. *Der Krieg von 1859, Bismarck und die öffentliche Meinung in Deutschland.* Stuttgart, 1904.

NAFZIGER, RALPH O. "The Newspapers and Public Opinion in the United States concerning the War in Europe, 1914–1917" (unpublished Ph. D. thesis, University of Wisconsin, 1933).

PLAYNE, CAROLINE ELISABETH. *Britain Holds On, 1917, 1918.* London: Allen and Unwin, 1933. 440 pp.
Miss Playne continues her study of British Liberal reactions to the war.

————. *Society at War, 1914–1916.* Boston: Houghton Mifflin, 1931. 380 pp.
A study in national psychology, dealing with British opinion in the first years of the war.

PRICE, MAURICE T. "The Nanking Road Incident, May 30, 1925."
In preparation at Walter Hines Page School of International Relations, Johns Hopkins University. Partly a psychological study.

PRINCE, SAMUEL HENRY. *Catastrophe and Social Change: Based upon a Sociological Study of the Halifax Disaster* (Columbia University Studies in History, Economics, and Public Law, no. 212). New York: Columbia University, 1920. 153 pp.

RAYMOND, DORA NEILL. *British Policy and Opinion during the Franco-Prussian War* (Columbia University Studies in History, Economics, and Public Law, no. 227). New York: Columbia University, 1921. 435 pp.
Bibliography, pp. 406–12.

SCHULTHESS, HERMANN. *Die Anteilnahme der schweizerischen öffentlichen Meinung an den Verhandlungen der europäischen Kongresse 1814–1816.* Zurich: Leemann, 1928. 77 pp.

STERN, ALFRED. *Der Einfluss der französischen Revolution auf das deutsche Geistesleben.* Stuttgart and Berlin: Cotta, 1928. 248 pp.
Contains bibliography.

STERN, WILLIAM, editor. *Jugendliches Seelenleben und Krieg: Materialien und Berichte; unter Mitwirkung der breslauer Ortsgruppe des Bundes für Schulreform* (Beihefte zur Zeitschrift für angewandte Psychologie und psychologische Sammelforschung). Leipzig: Barth, 1915. 181 pp.
Children's reactions to war, described by the "differential" psychologist.

TOSTI, AMEDEO. *Come ci vide l'Austria Imperiale.* Milan: Mondadori, 1930. 312 pp.
A detailed study of Austrian opinion of Italy during the war, based on examination of the Vienna archives, parliamentary debates, newspapers, and memoirs.

TROTSKY, LEON. *The History of the Russian Revolution.* New York: Simon and Schuster, 1932. 3 vols.

Vic, Jean. *La Littérature de guerre: Manuel méthodique et critique des publications de langue française, 2 août 1914–11 novembre 1918.* Paris: Presses françaises, 1923. 5 vols.

Methodological and critical bibliography of all publications of the War period in the French language, with summaries of the most general critical opinion at the time of the appearance of each work.

Wilkerson, Marcus M. *Public Opinion and the Spanish-American War.* Baton Rouge: Louisiana State University, 1932. 137 pp.

The influence of the New York *Journal,* New York *World,* and other newspapers in arousing war sentiment. Bibliography, pp. 132–37.

Willis, Irene Cooper. *England's Holy War: A Study of English Liberal Idealism during the Great War.* New York: Knopf, 1928. 398 pp.

How Liberals reverbalized the war to themselves. Bibliography, p. 379.

B. SYMBOLS OF PERSONS

Examples of studies devoted to the analysis of collective attitudes toward particular persons.

Albjerg, Esther Marguerite (Hall). "The New York Press and Andrew Johnson" (unpublished Ph. D. thesis, University of Wisconsin, 1925).

Czarnowski, Stefan. *Le Culte des héros et ses conditions sociales: Saint Patrick, héros national de l'Irlande.* Paris: Travaux de l'année sociologique, publiés sous la direction de M. É. Durkheim, 1919. 369 pp.

Bibliographic footnotes.

Dechamps, Jules. *Sur la légende de Napoléon.* Paris: Champion, 1931. 276 pp.

A study of the nature and origin and some manifestations of the legend, primarily from a literary rather than an historical angle.

"Diabolism," *Encyclopedia of the Social Sciences.* (By Maximilian Rudwin.)

Historical analysis of the Devil.

Ellis, F. *The Case of Sacco and Vanzetti from Cartoons in the Daily Worker.* New York: The Daily Worker, 1927.

Faÿ, Bernard. *The Two Franklins: Fathers of American Democracy.* Boston: Little, Brown, 1933. 397 pp.

Bibliography, pp. 363–77.

Fraenkel, Osmond K. *The Sacco-Vanzetti Case.* New York: Knopf, 1932. 550 pp.

A definitive history of the case, heavily documented.

FROMM, ERICH. *Die Entwicklung des Christusdogmas.* Vienna: Internationaler psychoanalytischer Verlag, 1931. 72 pp.
Marxian and Freudian concepts are used in this study of the diffusion of Christianity during the first century.

GRAF, ARTURO. *The Story of the Devil,* translated from the Italian by Edward Noble Stone. New York: Macmillan, 1931. 296 pp.
Primarily narrative rather than analytic or evaluative.

GUÉRARD, ALBERT LÉON. *Reflections on the Napoleonic Legend.* New York: Scribners, 1924. 276 pp.

HAGEN, MAXIMILIAN VON. *Das Bismarckbild in der Literatur der Gegenwart.* Berlin: Heymann, 1929. 80 pp.

HARDY, F. H. "The Making of a President," *Fortnightly Review,* August, 1896.

"Hero Worship," *Encyclopedia of the Social Sciences.* (By Gottfried Salomon.)

HOOVER, HERBERT CLARK. Has a collection of 20,000 cartoons and caricatures of himself.

These cartoons, clipped from the press of Germany, England, U. S. S. R., Japan, and France, cover the period from war days until the present. When Hoover was President they were stored in a room in the White House, to which he refers as his " Chamber of Horrors."

LANGE, KARL. *Bismarcks Sturz und die öffentliche Meinung in Deutschland und im Auslande.* Stuttgart: Deutsche Verlagsanstalt, 1927. 78 pp.
Bibliography, pp. 77–78.

LINGLEY, CHARLES RAMSDELL. "Official Characteristics of President Cleveland," *Political Science Quarterly,* 33: 255–65 (June, 1918).

LYONS, EUGENE. *The Life and Death of Sacco and Vanzetti.* New York: International Publishers, 1927. 208 pp.

MARTIN, KINGSLEY. "Public Opinion: The Assassin of M. Doumer," *Political Quarterly,* 3: 428–33 (July, 1932).

―――. *The Triumph of Lord Palmerston.* London: Allen and Unwin, 1924. 259 pp.

MOMMSEN, WILHELM. *Bismarcks Sturz und die Parteien.* Stuttgart: Deutsche Verlagsanstalt, 1924. 206 pp.
The relation of the parties and the press to Bismarck's fall.

ROBBINS, HELEN PEABODY. "Public Opinion concerning Theodore Roosevelt, 1900–1901 " (unpublished M. A. thesis, University of Illinois, 1933).

RUDWIN, MAXIMILIAN JOSEF. *The Devil in Legend and Literature.* Chicago and London: Open Court, 1931. 354 pp.

SINGER, ARTHUR. *Bismarck in der Literatur: Ein bibliographischer Versuch*. Second edition. Wurzburg: C. Kabitzsch, 1909. Vienna: E. Stülpnagel, 1912. 340 pp.

STODDARD, HENRY LUTHER. *As I Knew Them: Presidents and Politics from Grant to Coolidge*. New York: Harpers, 1927. 571 pp.

THOMPSON, GEORGE CARSLAKE. *Public Opinion and Lord Beaconsfield*. London: Macmillan, 1886. 2 vols.

The material is analyzed in terms of an elaborate conception of public opinion.

WEITENKAMPF, FRANK. *Christ in Art: Notes on the John Powell Lenox Collection*. New York Public Library, 1920. 8 pp.

The Lenox collection consists of several thousand pictures, mounted in fifteen volumes and presented to the Art and Prints Division of the New York Public Library.

WHITTEMORE, FRANCES DAVIS. *George Washington in Sculpture*. Boston: Marshall Jones, 1933. 203 pp.

"All the sculptural representations of Washington that are of consequence."

C. SYMBOLS OF GROUPS

Studies devoted to the analysis of collective attitudes toward particular social groups.

1. BIBLIOGRAPHY

FOREIGN LANGUAGE INFORMATION SERVICE. *The Immigrant Portrayed in Biography and Story: A Bibliography*. New York, 1925.

2. REFERENCES

ALBIG, WILLIAM. "Opinions concerning Unskilled Mexican Immigrants," *Sociology and Social Research*, 15: 62–72 (1930).

"Antisemitism," *Encyclopedia of the Social Sciences*. (By Benjamin Ginzburg.)

BERNSTEIN, HERMAN. *The History of a Lie: The Protocols of the Wise Men of Zion*. New York: J. S. Ogilvie, 1921. 84 pp.

The forgery of the "Protocols of the Elders of Zion" as a technique of anti-semitic propaganda.

BRAWLEY, BENJAMIN GRIFFITH. *The Negro in Literature and Art in the United States*. Third edition. New York: Duffield, 1929. 231 pp. Bibliography, pp. 213–28.

BROCHER, HENRI. *Le Mythe du héros et la mentalité primitive*. Paris: Alcan, 1932. 126 pp.

BROMBACHER, KUNO. *Der deutsche Bürger im Literaturspiegel von Lessing bis Sternheim.* Munich: Musarion, 1920. 146 pp.

BUCK, CARL DARLING. "Language and the Sentiment of Nationality," *American Political Science Review,* 10:44–69 (1916).

BUEL, ELIZABETH C. BARNEY. *Manual of the United States for the Information of Immigrants and Foreigners.* Washington, D.C.: Daughters of the American Revolution, 1923. 95 pp.
Has been translated into several languages.

CARTER, EDWARD CLARK, editor. *China and Japan in Our University Curricula.* New York: American Council, Institute of Pacific Relations, 1929. 183 pp.
A survey of Far Eastern studies in American institutions.

CATTANI, PAUL. *Die Medizin in der politischen Presse: Eine sozialmedizinische Studie.* Staus, 1913.
Study of press handling of doctors, quacks, public hygiene movements, epidemics, legal control of medicine, etc.

CLARK, CUMBERLAND. *Shakespeare and National Character: A Study of Shakespeare's Knowledge and Dramatic and Literary Use of the Distinctive Racial Characteristics of the Different Peoples of the World.* London: Hamlin, 1932. 308 pp.

CONTRERAS, FRANCISCO. *Le Chili et la France.* Paris: Bossard, 1919. 164 pp.
A brief survey of Chile's affairs and problems, with special treatment of her sympathies for France and the possibilities of further French propaganda.

COOK, J. G. *Anglophobia.* Boston: Four Seas, 1919. 138 pp.
An English analysis of the anti-British prejudices current in the United States.

DESCOURT, JACQUEAU. "La Médicine au théâtre dans les temps modernes" (dissertation, Paris, 1905).

DETWEILER, FREDERICK GERMAN. "The Rise of Modern Race Antagonisms," *American Journal of Sociology,* 37:738–48 (March, 1932).
The origins in history of the race antagonisms existing in the modern world are shown to date from the period of the discoveries. Ancient civilizations such as Greece and Rome had very little social distinction based on color or race.

DICKINSON, BURRUS SWINFORD. "The Newspaper and Labor: An Inquiry into the Nature and Influence of Labor News and Comment in the Daily Press" (unpublished Ph.D. thesis, University of Illinois, 1930).

FAIRSWORTH, J. "How Anti-American Sentiment Is Fostered in Japan," *China Weekly Review*, 63: 475 (February 18, 1933).

FINOT, JEAN. *Le Préjugé des races*. Paris: Alcan, 1905. 518 pp.

GAZLEY, JOHN GEROW. *American Opinion of German Unification, 1848–1871* (Columbia University Studies in History, Economics, and Public Law, no. 267). New York: Columbia University, 1926. 583 pp.
Bibliography, pp. 567–75.

GEORGE, HENRY. "The Kearney Agitation in California," *Popular Science Monthly*, 17: 433–53 (1880).
Excitement over the Chinese exclusion propaganda.

GIST, NOEL P. "Race Attitudes in the Press," *Sociology and Social Research*, 17: 25–36 (1932).
A study of the attitudes of whites toward Negroes, as represented by seventeen white daily newspapers.

GOOCH, GEORGE PEABODY. *Germany and the French Revolution*. London and New York: Longmans, Green, 1920. 543 pp.

GRASS, FRIEDRICH. *Die Liquidation des Stinnes-Konzerns und ihre Behandlung in der Presse*. Heidelberg, 1928.

HERTZ, FRIEDRICH OTTO. *Race and Civilization*. New York: Macmillan, 1928. London: Kegan Paul, Trench, and Trubner, 1928. 328 pp.
Collection of symbolisms regarded as indicative of racial superiority. Contains bibliographic notes.

HICKS, G. "Wanted — Non-Radicals," *Christian Century*, 43: 1452–53 (November 25, 1926).
"Plus" use of the term *radical*.

HILL, PRINCESS ENOLA. "Public Opinion and the Labor Disorders of the '70's" (unpublished M. A. thesis, University of Illinois, 1932).

HOLLÄNDER, EUGEN. *Die Karikatur und Satire in der Medizin*. Stuttgart: Enke, 1905. 354 pp. 223 illustrations.
Bibliography, pp. xiii–xv.

———. *Die Medizin in der klassischen Malerei*. Second edition. Stuttgart: Enke, 1913. 477 pp.
Contains bibliography.

HOYLER, AUGUST. *Gentleman-Ideal und Gentleman-Erziehung mit Besonderer Berücksichtigung der Renaissance*. Leipzig: Meiner, 1933. 223 pp.

HU SHIH. *The Promotion of Cultural Relations between China and Great Britain*. London: The Universities China Committee, 1927 (?). 15 pp.

Synopses of three lectures by Dr. Hu in the British universities, November and December, 1926.

INTER-CHURCH WORLD MOVEMENT, COMMISSION OF INQUIRY. *Public Opinion and the Steel Strike.* New York: Harcourt, Brace, 1921. 341 pp.
"Opinion" as influenced by press, civil government, actions of workers, reports of spies, and conceptions or misconceptions of foreign language communities.

LACOURBE, P. DE. "La Médicine et la grande presse" (unpublished dissertation, Paris, 1907).

LASKER, BRUNO. *Jewish Experiences in America.* New York: The Inquiry, 1930. 309 pp.
"This book, which is intended for Jewish study groups, provides discussion materials and methods for the analysis of the racial prejudice against the Jews in America and its causes." Part 5 discusses attitude testing. Reading list in Part 3.

LEVINGER, LEE JOSEPH. *Anti-Semitism in the United States: Its History and Causes* (Ph. D. thesis, University of Pennsylvania, 1925). New York: Bloch, 1925. 120 pp.
Bibliography, pp. 119–20.

LIPPMANN, WALTER. "Why Social Work Is Not Popular," *Better Times,* May, 1923, pp. 7–8.

MEYER, EDWARD STOCKTON. *Machiavelli and the Elizabethan Drama* (inaugural dissertation, Heidelberg). Weimar: E. Felber, 1897. 180 pp.

MINARD, RALPH DAY. *Race Attitudes of Iowa Children* (Ph. D. thesis. University of Iowa Studies, N. S., no. 217). Iowa City: University of Iowa, 1931. 101 pp.
Bibliography, p. 66.

MOHL, RUTH. *The Three Estates in Medieval and Renaissance Literature* (Columbia University Studies in English and Comparative Literature). New York: Columbia University, 1933. 425 pp.
Bibliography, pp. 391–400.

NAUMANN, J. W., editor. *Die Presse und der Katholik.* Augsburg, 1932.

NERMAN, TURE. *Folkhatet: En vardskrigs studie.* Stockholm, 1918.

OLBRICH, KARL. *Die Freimaurer im deutschen Volksglauben; die im Volke umlaufenden Vorstellungen und Erzählungen von den Freimaurern.* Breslau: Marcus, 1930. 142 pp.
Bibliography, pp. 131–36.

Ordway, Samuel Hanson, Jr. *An Elegant History of New York Society for Young Persons of Quality, with a Glossary and Certain Examples of Armorial Bearings.* New York: Elegant History Publishing Company, 1926. 82 pp.

————. *An Elegant History of Political Parties.* New York: Duffield, 1928. 72 pp.

Peirce, Walter Thomson. *The Bourgeois from Molière to Beaumarchais: The Study of a Dramatic Type* (abridgement of Ph. D. thesis, Johns Hopkins University). Columbus, Ohio: F. J. Heer, 1907. 88 pp.
Bibliography, pp. 83–85.

Perkins, Mary Hallowell. *The Servant Problem and the Servant in English Literature.* Boston: R. G. Badger, 1928. 186 pp.
"The English servant as he appeared in English literature since the sixteenth century . . . through the eighteenth." — *Introduction.* Bibliography, pp. 183–86.

Phayre, Ignatius (pseudonym of William George Fitz-Gerald). " The British Press and the United States," *Quarterly Review,* 259: 229–44 (October, 1932).

Philipson, Rabbi David. *The Jew in English Fiction.* New revised edition. Cincinnati: Robert Clarke, 1911. 207 pp.
From Marlowe's *Jew of Malta* to Israel Zangwill's *Children of the Ghetto.*

Pierce, Bessie Louise, and Norris, Joe L. *As Others See Chicago: Impressions of Visitors, 1673–1933.* Chicago: University of Chicago, 1933. 540 pp.
A brief sketch of the author's life precedes each selection. Bibliography, pp. 518–23.

Pinnow, Hermann, editor. *Deutschland im Lichte ausländischer Schulbücher der Nachkriegszeit; im Auftrage des Verbandes deutscher Geschichtslehrer.* Berlin: Verlag für Kulturpolitik, 1927. 109 pp.
"Germany in the light of foreign post-war school books."

Radczun, Willi. *Das englische Urteil über die Deutschen bis zur Mitte des 17. Jahrhunderts.* Berlin: Ebering, 1933. 220 pp.
English opinion on the Germans to the middle of the seventeenth century.

Rice, Stuart Arthur. "Stereotypes," *Journal of Personnel Research,* 5: 267–76 (1926).
Discusses experimental methods for determining common stereotypes concerning the appearance of various classes of persons.

RODES, JEAN. *Les Chinois: Essai de psychologie ethnographique.* Paris: Alcan, 1923. 233 pp.
A French writer on China studies the characterizations given by early travelers and then attempts to analyze the modern Chinese mind.

ROUTZAHN, MARY SWAIN. "Interpreting the Social Worker to the Public," *Proceedings of the National Conference of Social Work,* 1931, pp. 541–50.

SCHIEBER, CLARA EVE. *The Transformation of American Sentiment toward Germany, 1870–1914.* Boston: Cornhill, 1923. 294 pp.
A study of the changes in the attitude of the United States toward Germany since the Franco-German War as reflected in newspaper comments.

SPARGO, JOHN. *The Jew and American Ideals.* New York and London: Harpers, 1921. 147 pp.

STAUFFER, VERNON. *New England and the Bavarian Illuminati* (Columbia University Studies in History, Economics, and Public Law, no. 191). New York: Columbia University, 1918. 374 pp.
Summarizes the history of the Illuminati Order in Bavaria and the spread to America in 1798 of the myth of their continued existence. Bibliography, pp. 361–74.

THOMAS, WILLIAM ISAAC. "Race Psychology: Standpoint and Questionnaire, with Particular Reference to the Immigrant and the Negro," *American Journal of Sociology,* 17: 725–75 (1912).

TUPPER, ELEANOR. "American Sentiment toward Japan, 1904–1924" (unpublished Ph. D. thesis, Clark University).

VETH, CORNELIS. *Der Advokat in der Karikatur.* Berlin: O. Stollberg, 1927. 119 pp.
The lawyer in cartoon.

———. *Der Arzt in der Karikatur.* Berlin: O. Stollberg, 1927. 153 pp.
The physician in cartoon.

VOEGELIN, ERICH. *Die Rassenidee in der Geistesgeschichte von Ray bis Carus.* Berlin: Junker und Dünnhaupt, 1933. 160 pp.

WALLGREN, ABIAN A. *The A. E. F. in Cartoon, from The Stars and Stripes, Official Newspaper of the A. E. F.* Philadelphia: Dan Sowers, 1933. 76 pp.

WATSON, HAROLD FRANCIS. *The Sailor in English Fiction and Drama, 1550–1800* (Columbia University Studies in English and Comparative Literature). New York: Columbia University, 1931. 241 pp.
Bibliography, pp. 220–30.

WHITE, ELIZABETH BRETT. *American Opinion of France from Lafayette to Poincaré* (in part a Ph. D. thesis, Clark University). New York: Knopf, 1927. 346 pp.
Bibliography, pp. 315–30.

WHITE, LEONARD DUPEE. *Further Contributions to the Prestige Value of Public Employment.* Chicago: University of Chicago, 1932. 88 pp.
Method: free word association.

————. *Prestige Value of Public Employment in Chicago.* Chicago: University of Chicago, 1929. 183 pp.
Prestige value of public employment is assessed by means of questionnaires, rating scales, word association, and newspaper analysis.

WIECKING, EMMA. "France as Depicted in Literature for American Children, with Special Reference to Nationalism and Internationalism" (unpublished M. A. thesis, Columbia University, 1928).

D. SYMBOLS OF POLICIES AND DOCTRINES

Studies devoted to the analysis of collective attitudes toward particular policies and doctrines.

BAILEY, THOMAS A. "The West and Radical Legislation, 1890–1930," *American Journal of Sociology,* 38:603–12 (January, 1933).

BEARD, CHARLES AUSTIN. *An Economic Interpretation of the Constitution of the United States.* New York: Macmillan, 1913. 330 pp.

————. *The Idea of National Interest: An Analytical Study in American Foreign Policy.* New York: Macmillan, 1934. 583 pp.

BECKER, CARL LOTUS. *The Declaration of Independence: A Study in the History of Political Ideas.* New York: Harcourt, Brace, 1922. 286 pp.

BENTWICH, NORMAN. *The Religious Foundations of Internationalism: A Study in International Relations throughout the Ages.* London: Allen and Unwin, 1933. 288 pp.

BOETTIGER, L. A. "Organic Theory of Social Reform Movements," *Journal of Social Forces,* 3:60–64 (November, 1924).

BRAMELD, THEODORE BURGHARD HURT. *A Philosophic Approach to Communism* (Ph. D. thesis, University of Chicago). Chicago: University of Chicago, 1933. 242 pp.
Bibliography, pp. 225–35.

BURY, JOHN BAGNELL. *The Idea of Progress: An Inquiry into Its Origin and Growth.* London: Macmillan, 1920. 377 pp. New York: Macmillan, 1932. 357 pp.

CHAMBERLAIN, JOHN RENSSELAER. *Farewell to Reform, Being a History of the Rise, Life, and Decay of the Progressive Mind in America.* New York: Liveright, 1932. 333 pp.

CHINARD, GILBERT. *La Doctrine de l'Américanisme.* Paris: Hachette, 1919. 90 pp.
This survey of the historical evolution of the American tradition contains a discussion of American nationalism and internationalism.

CLARK, MARY V. "The Passing of the County Farm," *Survey,* 43: 624–25 (1919).
The "County Farm" is being rechristened.

CLOUGH, N. P. *Beiträge zur Beurteilung der Oesterreichischen Anschlussfrage in der öffentlichen Meinung der Vereinigten Staaten Nordamerikas.* Heidelberg: Meistr, 1933 (?). 77 pp.

DAHLIN, EBBA. *French and German Public Opinion on Declared War Aims, 1914–1918* (Stanford University Publications in History, Economics, and Political Science, vol. 4, no. 2). Stanford University, California: Stanford University, 1933. London: Oxford University, 1933. 168 pp.
Reveals many problems of the home propaganda. Bibliography, pp. 154–62.

DEMARTIAL, GEORGES. *Le Mythe des guerres de légitime défense.* Paris: Rivière, 1931. 164 pp.

FARNAM, H. W. "The Psychology of Reform," *Unpopular Review,* 11: 150–66 (1919).

FEIERTAG, SISTER LORETTA CLARE. *American Public Opinion on the Relations between the United States and the Papal States (1847–1867)* (Ph. D. thesis, Catholic University of America). Washington, D. C.: Catholic University of America, 1933. 188 pp.
Bibliography, pp. 177–81.

FOERSTER, NORMAN, editor. *Humanism and America: Essays on the Outlook of Modern Civilization.* New York: Farrar and Rinehart, 1930. 294 pp.
Symposium presenting opposed viewpoints on the American literary humanist movement. Bibliography, pp. 291–94.

GAIN, PAUL HENRY. *La Question du tunnel sous la manche.* Paris: Rousseau, 1932. 289 pp.
A study of the proposal to build a tunnel between England and France.

GAY, J. *Les Deux Romes et l'opinion française: Les Rapports franco-italiens depuis 1915.* Paris: Alcan, 1931. 248 pp.

GRATTAN, CLINTON HARTLEY. *Why We Fought.* New York: Vanguard, 1929. 468 pp.

GRATTAN, CLINTON HARTLEY, editor. *The Critique of Humanism.* New York: Brewer and Warren, 1930. 364 pp.
Symposium presenting opposite viewpoints of the American literary humanist movement.

GUIGNEBERT, CHARLES ALFRED HONORÉ. *L'Évolution des dogmes.* Paris: Flammarion, 1910, 1917. 351 pp.
A standard treatise on comparative religion.

GURIAN, WALDEMAR. *Die politischen und sozialen Ideen des französischen Katholizismus, 1789–1914.* Munich-Gladbach: Volksverein-Verlag, 1928. 330 pp.

HARDING, SAMUEL BANNISTER. *The Contest over the Ratification of the Federal Constitution in the State of Massachusetts* (Harvard Historical Studies, vol. 2). New York and London: Longmans, Green, 1896. 194 pp.

HARPER, HEBER REECE. *What European and American Students Think on International Problems* (Ph. D. thesis. Studies of the International Institute of Teachers College, no. 12). New York: Columbia University, 1931. 255 pp.
A digest of opinion.

HAYWORTH, DONALD. "An Analysis of Speeches in the Presidential Campaigns from 1884 to 1920," *Quarterly Journal of Speech,* 16: 35–42 (February, 1930).
From a Ph. D. thesis, University of Wisconsin, 1929.

HEATH, VERNON LAWRENCE. "Newspaper Reports of Legislative Proceedings in the *New York Times* and *London Times*" (unpublished M. A. thesis, University of Illinois, 1929).

HERKENBERG, KARL OTTO. *The Times und das deutsch-englische Verhältnis im Jahre 1898,* with an introduction by Martin Spahn. Berlin: Deutsche Verlagsgesellschaft für Politik und Geschichte, 1925. 143 pp.
London *Times* and Anglo-German relations in 1898. Bibliography, p. 143.

HOUGHTON, N. D. "Public Opinion and International Policies. Summary of Round Table." Berkeley: Proceedings of the Institute of International Relations, 5: 182–84 (1930).

JOHNSON, ALVIN W. *The Legal Status of Church-State Relationships in the United States, with Special Reference to the Public Schools.* Minneapolis: University of Minnesota, 1934.
Part 1 deals with state legislation and court decisions pertaining to Bible

reading in the public schools. Part 2 deals with other sectarian influences in the schools. Part 3 is on "Sunday" legislation, citing cases on the question of its constitutionality.

KALLEN, HORACE MEYER, editor. *Freedom in the Modern World.* New York: Coward, McCann, 1928. 304 pp.

Lectures delivered at the New School for Social Research by Walton H. Hamilton, Rev. John A. Ryan, F. J. Foakes-Jackson, and others.

KASSEL, C. "Natural History of Reform," *Open Court,* 42:414-24 (July, 1928).

KEESECKER, WARD W. *Legal Status of Bible Reading and Religious Instruction in the Public Schools* (United States Bureau of Education Bulletin no. 14). Washington, D. C., 1930. 29 pp.

By a specialist on school legislation.

KERBY, W. J. "The Natural History of a Reform Law," *Catholic World,* 102:147-59 (1915-16).

KOLSTAD, ARTHUR. *A Study of Opinions on Some International Problems as Related to Certain Experiences and Background Factors* (Teachers College Contributions to Education, no. 555). New York: Columbia University, 1933. 95 pp.

Five hundred Teachers College students were tested, and "background factors" were compared. Bibliography, pp. 94-95.

LANGE, CHRISTIAN LOUS. "Histoire de la doctrine pacifique et de son influence sur le développement du droit international," *Académie de droit international, recueil des cours,* 13:171-426 (Paris, 1927).

Bibliography, pp. 173-74.

LEUPOLT, ERICH. *Die Aussenpolitik in den bedeutendsten politischen Zeitschriften Deutschlands, 1890-1909* (Das Wesen der Zeitung, vol. 2, no. 3). Leipzig: Reinicke, 1933. 181 pp.

LIPPMANN, WALTER, and SCROGGS, WILLIAM O. *The United States in World Affairs.* New York and London: Published by Harpers, for the Council on Foreign Relations, 1932 —.

An annual that includes summaries of opinions.

LOCKHART, EARL GRANGER. "The Attitudes of Children toward Law" (unpublished Ph. D. thesis, University of Iowa, 1930. 61 pp.).

Quantitative.

MCCULLOCH, ROBERT W. "Question Time in the British House of Commons," *American Political Science Review,* 27:971-78 (December, 1933).

MCGEE, JOHN EDWIN. *A Crusade for Humanity: The History of Or-*

ganized Positivism in England (Ph. D. thesis, Columbia University, 1931). London: Watts, 1931. 249 pp.
"Organized positivism" was a small group interested in Comte's *Religion of Humanity*. Bibliography, pp. 235–49.

McRae, M. A. "Public Opinion and International Policies," Proceedings of the Institute of International Relations, 5: 170–73 (1930).

Meinecke, Friedrich. *Die Idee der Staatsräson in der neueren Geschichte*. Munich and Berlin: Oldenbourg, 1925. 546 pp.

Mencken, Henry Louis. *Notes on Democracy*. New York: Knopf, 1926. 212 pp.
Example of anti-democratic symbolism.

Moyer, George Samuel. *Attitude of the United States towards the Recognition of Soviet Russia*. Philadelphia: University of Pennsylvania, 1926. 293 pp.
A carefully documented doctoral thesis analyzing the American recognition policy, the attitude of the government, Congress, and public opinion toward Soviet Russia, the experiences of England and France, etc. The author's conclusions are adverse to recognition. Bibliography, pp. 287–93.

Nathan, Marvin. *The Attitude of the Jewish Student in the Colleges and Universities towards His Religion*. Philadelphia: Marvin Nathan, 1932. 264 pp.
Based on 1,500 replies to 3,700 schedules sent to 57 colleges throughout the country.

National Council for the Prevention of War. *International Affairs as Presented in Fifty Leading Periodicals*. Monthly. Washington, D. C., 1923—.

Nevins, Allan. *American Press Opinion, Washington to Coolidge: A Documentary Record of Editorial Leadership and Criticism, 1785–1927*. Boston and New York: Heath, 1928. 598 pp.

——. "Why America Rejected the League." *Current History*, 36: 20–26 (April, 1932).

Paasche, Frau Elise (Faber). *Männer Wehrlos, Frauen Schutzlos: Unsere Propagandareise gegen die Schuldlüge*. Neckargemund: Im Selbstverlage, 1927. 102 pp.
A study of propaganda against the "lie" of Germany's war responsibility.

Pataa, M. *L'Attitude des divers partis politiques anglais à l'égard du problème du chômage*. Paris: Lavergne, 1933. 360 pp.
Attitude of English political parties toward unemployment.

"Radicalism," *Encyclopedia of the Social Sciences.* (By Horace M. Kallen.)

RECKTENWALD, FRIEDERIKE. *Kriegsziele und öffentliche Meinung Englands, 1914–1916.* Stuttgart: Kohlhammer, 1929. 147 pp.

SCHUMAN, FREDERICK LEWIS. *American Policy toward Russia since 1917.* New York: International Publishers, 1928. 399 pp.
A scholarly study of Russian-American relations since March, 1917, with an extended analysis of the reasons advanced for withholding recognition, such as propaganda, financial claims, etc.

"Social Evangelism's Recession," *American Federationist,* 32: 189–91 (March, 1925).

TRENHOLME, LOUISE IRBY. *The Ratification of the Federal Constitution in North Carolina* (Columbia University Studies in History, Economics, and Public Law, no. 363). New York: Columbia University, 1932. London: P. S. King, 1932. 282 pp.
Bibliography, pp. 250–67.

TURNER, LORENZO DOW. *Anti-Slavery Sentiment in American Literature Prior to 1865* (Ph. D. thesis, University of Chicago). Washington, D. C.: Association for Study of Negro Life and History, 1929. 188 pp.
Bibliography, pp. 153–82.

UNDERHILL, F. H. "Canada's Relations with the Empire as Seen by the Toronto *Globe, 1857–67,*" *Canadian Historical Review,* 10: 106–28 (1929).

WERNER, DOROTHY LEEDS. *The Idea of Union in American Verse* (Ph. D. thesis, University of Pennsylvania, 1931). Philadelphia, 1932. 108 pp.
Bibliography, pp. 94–108.

WHITE, WILLIAM ALLEN. *Masks in a Pageant.* New York: Macmillan, 1928. 507 pp.

WILLIS, IRENE COOPER. *England's Holy War.* New York: Knopf, 1928. 399 pp.
Traces the evolution of English Liberalism from confirmed pacifism to the crusading spirit of the World War. The evidence is taken primarily from the files of the leading Liberal newspaper, the *Daily News,* and the story covers the period through the peace settlements.

ZIMMERN, ALFRED. "The Influence of Public Opinion in Foreign Policy," in Geneva Institute of International Relations, *Problems of Peace,* Series 3, pp. 299–300. London, 1929.

E. SYMBOLS OF INSTITUTIONS

I. PRO-INSTITUTIONAL SYMBOLS

Analyses of how loyalty to the principal symbols of the established order is inculcated. Some titles on detailed techniques will be found in Part III, Section B, Subdivision 6.

ADAMSON, JOHN WILLIAM. *English Education, 1789–1902.* Cambridge, England: Cambridge University, 1930. 519 pp.

ALCANTARA, SISTER M. *A Course in Civics for Use in the Parochial Schools.* Washington, D.C.: National Catholic Welfare Conference, 1923.

AMERICAN HISTORICAL ASSOCIATION, COMMISSION ON THE SOCIAL STUDIES. *Conclusions and Recommendations.* Announced for 1935.

AMERICAN POLITICAL SCIENCE ASSOCIATION. *Report of the Committee on Policy,* pp. 127–72 (Supplement to the *American Political Science Review,* February, 1930).
An effort to determine objectives and curriculum content in civic education.

AMERICAN POLITICAL SCIENCE ASSOCIATION, COMMITTEE ON HIGH SCHOOL CIVICS. " The Study of Civics," *American Political Science Review,* 16: 116–25 (1922).

"Americanization," *Encyclopedia of the Social Sciences.* (By Read Lewis.)

ARNETT, CLAUDE E. *The Social Beliefs and Attitudes of American School Board Members.* Emporia, Kansas: Emporia Gazette Press, 1932. 235 pp.
Sponsored by the Commission on the Investigation of the Social Studies in the Schools.

BEARD, CHARLES AUSTIN. *A Charter for the Social Sciences* (Report of the Commission on the Social Studies, American Historical Association). New York: Scribners, 1932. 122 pp.

BILLINGS, NEAL. *A Determination of Objectives Basic to the Social Studies Curriculum* (Ph.D. thesis, Columbia University). Baltimore: Warwick and York, 1929. 289 pp.
An " objective " technique (based on a questionnaire) is employed for the identification of " frontier thinkers " and the selection of 888 " basic generalizations " from their works. In a similar fashion, " central themes " were selected " around which can be woven the data of the social studies." — C. E. MERRIAM. Bibliography, pp. vii–viii, 274–76.

BROOKS, ROBERT CLARKSON. *Civic Training in Switzerland: A Study of*

Democratic Life (Civic Training Series). Chicago: University of Chicago, 1930. 436 pp.
Bibliographic footnotes.

CHARTERS, WERRETT WALLACE. *The Teaching of Ideals.* New York: Macmillan, 1927. 372 pp.
A textbook dealing with the techniques of character education. Bibliography, pp. 359–65.

COE, GEORGE ALBERT. *Educating for Citizenship: The Sovereign State as Ruler and as Teacher.* New York: Scribners, 1932. 205 pp.

COUNTS, GEORGE SYLVESTER. *The American Road to Culture: A Social Interpretation of Education in the United States.* New York: John Day, 1930. 194 pp.

COUNTS, GEORGE SYLVESTER, and BEARD, CHARLES AUSTIN. *Education in an Industrial Age* (Report of the Commission on the Social Studies, American Historical Association). Announced.

DICKERSON, ROY E. "Suggested Program for Educational Day," *De Molay Councilor,* 3:3 (August, 1924).

DRINKWATER, JOHN. *Patriotism in Literature.* New York: Holt, 1924. London: Williams and Norgate, 1924. 255 pp.

ECKERT, CHRISTIAN. "Staatsbürgerliche Erziehung," *Jahrbuch für Gesetzgebung, Verwaltung und Volkwirtschaft im deutschen Reich,* 36:1321–63 (1912).

ELDRIDGE, SEBA. *The New Citizenship: A Study of American Politics.* New York: Crowell, 1929. 357 pp.
"A sociological analysis explaining the impotence of the citizen as a factor in American politics in terms of the relatively greater significance to the individual of his primary group relationships which are largely non-civic as compared with his secondary group relationships in the community and nation. A reorganization of political life upon the basis of primary groups is the proposed panacea." — C. E. MERRIAM.

EURICH, ALVIN C., editor. *The Changing Educational World.* Minneapolis: University of Minnesota, 1931. 311 pp.
Essays concerned with developments of the last twenty-five years.

FISHER, S. G. "The Legendary and Myth-Making Process in Histories of the American Revolution," *Proceedings of the American Philosophical Society,* 51:53–76 (1912).

GAUDIG, HUGO. "Schulstimmung — eine psychologische Analyse," *Zeitschrift für pädagogische Analyse,* 16:262–69 (1915).

GAUS, JOHN M. *Great Britain: A Study of Civic Loyalty* (Civic Training Series). Chicago: University of Chicago, 1929. 329 pp.
Bibliography, pp. xv–xx.

HARPER, SAMUEL NORTHRUP. *Civic Training in Soviet Russia* (Civic Training Series). Chicago: University of Chicago, 1929. 401 pp.

————. *Making Bolsheviks.* Chicago: University of Chicago, 1931. 167 pp.

Abridgment of the author's *Civic Training in Soviet Russia.*

HART, JOSEPH KINMONT. *Democracy in Education: A Social Interpretation of the History of Education.* New York: Century, 1918. 418 pp. Bibliography, pp. 410–16.

HAYES, CARLTON J. H. *France, a Nation of Patriots.* New York: Columbia University, 1930. 487 pp.

Appendices: A. Digest of typical textbooks in French schools for instruction in history, morals and civics, geography, and reading. B. Guide to teacher societies. C. Select list of French periodicals (other than dailies). D. Guide to daily newspapers of Paris. E. Guide to leading daily newspapers of provincial France.

HESSEN, SERGIUS. *Die Entwicklung des Schulwesens in Sowjetrussland in den Jahren 1926–1929.* Leipzig: Quelle und Meyer, 1930. Reprinted from *Die Neue Erziehung,* pp. 629 ff., 701 ff.

————. "Das kommunistische Bildungsideal und seine Wandlungen," Neue Jahrbücher für Wissenschaft und Jugendbildung, 1930, pp. 705–19.

————. *Kritische Vergleichung des Schulwesens der andern Kulturstaaten.* Langensalza: Beltz, 1928. Reprint from *Handbuch der Pädagogik,* edited by Nohl-Pallat, 4 vols., Abschnitt 3.

Compares the school life of Soviet Russia with that of other civilized countries.

HORNE, CHARLES L. *The Story of Our American People.* New York: United States History Publishing Company, 1926. 2 vols.

The history book written especially for the children of the seventh and eighth grades by request of the American Legion. "Not one man's work but the nation's." Excerpt: "The fact that our continent lay so long unused has seemed to many earnest thinkers one of the world's most striking manifestations of the Divine Purpose of God" (page 6).

JACHINSON, J. "Grundrisse der Sowjetischen Pädologie," *Die Neue Erziehung,* 11: 378–84.

JACKSON, JEROME CASE, and MALMBERG, CONSTANTINE F. *Religious Education and the State.* Garden City: Doubleday, Doran, 1928. 195 pp. Bibliography, pp. 189–95.

JÁSZI, OSCAR. *The Dissolution of the Hapsburg Monarchy* (Civic Training Series). Chicago: University of Chicago, 1929. 488 pp. Bibliography, pp. 461–80.

JERSCHOW, A. "Das System der kommunistischen Erziehung und Bildung in den sozialistischen Städten," *Das werdende Zeitalter,* 9–10: 508–20.

JOHNSON, HENRY. *An Introduction to the History of the Social Sciences in the Schools* (Report of the Commission on the Social Studies, American Historical Association, pt. 2). New York: Scribners, 1932. 145 pp.

KALASCHNIKOFF. "Erziehung im Lichte der Marxistischen Soziologie," *Die Neue Erziehung,* 10: 174 ff., 342 ff., 509 ff.
A professor in the Second University in Moscow considers pedagogy as a socio-biological discipline.

KOSOK, PAUL. *Modern Germany* (Civic Training Series). Chicago: University of Chicago, 1933. 348 pp.

LEWIN, J. "Die Volksbildung in Sowjetrussland," *Preussische Jahrbücher,* 210: 34–52 (October, 1927).

LINDABURY, RICHARD VLIET. *A Study of Patriotism in the Elizabethan Drama* (Ph. D. thesis. Princeton Studies in English, no. 5). Princeton, New Jersey: Princeton University, 1931. 218 pp.
Bibliography, pp. 203–12.

LUNATCHARSKI, ANATOLI VASILIEVITCH. "Die Ziele der Sowjetschule," *Europäische Revue,* Jahrg. 3, 6, pp. 426–36.

MAHAN, THOMAS JEFFERSON. *An Analysis of the Characteristics of Citizenship* (Teachers College Contributions to Education, no. 315). New York: Columbia University, 1928. 44 pp.
A determination of the "duties," "difficulties," and "qualities" of citizenship by questionnaire and interview. Civics textbooks are checked against the findings. Bibliography, p. 44.

MAKOWSKI, ERICH. *Staatsbürgerliche Erziehung der Schuljugend in den Vereinigten Staaten von Nordamerika.* Paderborn: Ferdinand Schöningh, 1932. 92 pp.

MARRARO, HOWARD ROSARIO. *Nationalism in Italian Education.* New York: Italian Digest and News Service, 1927. 161 pp.
Bibliography, pp. 147–61.

———. "The New Education in Italy," *Current History,* 37: 571–77 (February, 1933).

MARSHALL, LEON CARROLL. *A Social Process Approach to Curriculum-Making in the Social Studies* (Report of the Commission on the Social Studies, American Historical Association). Announced.

MAYHEW, ARTHUR INNES. *The Education of India: A Study of British Educational Policy in India, 1835–1920, and Its Bearing on the Na-*

tional Life and Problems in India Today. London: Faber and Gwyer, 1926. 306 pp.
Bibliography, pp. 287–89.

MERRIAM, CHARLES EDWARD. *Civic Education in the United States* (Report of the Commission on the Social Studies, American Historical Association, pt. 6). New York: Scribners, 1934. 196 pp.
Bibliography, pp. 187–93.

————. *The Making of Citizens: A Comparative Study of the Methods of Civic Training.* Chicago: University of Chicago, 1931. 371 pp.
Professor Merriam summarizes and discusses the findings of the ten volumes in the Civic Training Series, of which he was the editor. Bibliographic footnotes.

NATIONAL COUNCIL OF JEWISH WOMEN, DEPARTMENT OF IMMIGRANT AID. *Suggestions for Stimulating Naturalization among the Foreign Born.* New York, 1925.

NIESSEL, A. "La Propagande politique dans l'armée rouge," *Revue politique et littéraire,* 70: 129–30 (March 5, 1932).

NORWOOD, CYRIL. *The English Tradition of Education.* London: John Murray, 1926. 340 pp.

NÖTZEL, KARL. *Soziale Bewegung in Russland: Ein Einführungsversuch auf Grund der russischen Gesellschaftslehre.* Stuttgart, Berlin, and Leipzig: Deutsche Verlagsanstalt, 1923. 556 pp.

"Patriotism," *Encyclopedia of the Social Sciences.* (By Francis W. Coker.)

PEAKE, CYRUS HENDERSON. *Nationalism and Education in Modern China* (Ph. D. thesis, Columbia University). New York: Columbia University, 1932. 240 pp.
A history of the efforts made by Chinese officials and government educators between 1860 and 1929 to modernize the training of youth. Contains digests of Chinese textbooks. Bibliography, pp. 211–35.

PIERCE, BESSIE LOUISE. *Citizens' Organizations and the Civic Training of Youth.* New York: Scribners, 1933. 428 pp.
Thoroughgoing analysis of citizens' groups that attempt to influence civic training in the United States.

————. *Civic Attitudes in American School Textbooks* (Civic Training Series). Chicago: University of Chicago, 1930. 297 pp.
Analyzes the manner of presenting historical events in four hundred texts.

REISNER, EDWARD HARTMAN. *Historical Foundations of Modern Education.* New York: Macmillan, 1927. 513 pp.

————. *Nationalism and Education since 1789: A Social and Political History of Modern Education.* New York: Macmillan, 1922. 575 pp.

RUGG, EARLE UNDERWOOD. *Curriculum Studies in the Social Sciences and Citizenship: An Investigation into Educational Values.* Greeley, Colorado: Colorado State Teachers College, 1928. 214 pp.
" Summarizes most of the ' objective ' studies of citizenship problems, socially valuable facts in the social sciences, and of activities, abilities, and traits demanded of citizens. These criteria are employed in an evaluation of the secondary social science–citizenship curriculum." — C. E. MERRIAM. Bibliography, pp. 204–14.

RUGG, HAROLD ORDWAY. *Building a Science of Society for the Schools.* New York, 1934. 35 pp.
Contains a description of the procedure followed in formulating Professor Rugg's Social Science Pamphlets, which have been widely used in the schools, and lists the many influential works of the author.

RUSSELL, BERTRAND. *Education and the Modern World.* New York: W. W. Norton, 1932. 245 pp.
Published in England as *Education and the Social Order.*

RYBNIKOFF, N. " Die Ideologie des russischen Schulkindes der Gegenwart," *Zeitschrift für angewandte Psychologie,* 32:213–19.

SCHNEIDER, HERBERT WALLACE, and CLOUGH, SHEPARD B. *Making Fascists* (Civic Training Series). Chicago: University of Chicago, 1929. 211 pp.
Bibliography, p. 205; bibliographic footnotes.

SCOTT, JONATHAN FRENCH. *The Menace of Nationalism in Education.* London: Allen and Unwin, 1926. 223 pp.

————. *Patriots in the Making.* New York: Appleton, 1916. 262 pp.
Studies of pre-war militaristic education in Germany, France, and Switzerland.

SHARP, W. H. *The Educational System of Japan* (Office of the Director-General of Education in India, Occasional Reports, no. 3). Bombay: Government Central Press, 1906. 523 pp.

SLOANE, WILLIAM H. *Die politische Erziehung des jungen Amerikaners* (Schriften der Wheeler-Gesellschaft zur Erörterung von Fragen des deutschen und ausländischen Bildungswesens, no. 1). Berlin, 1914.

SMITH, HENRY LESTER, and LITTELL, HAROLD. *Education in Latin America.* New York and Cincinnati: American Book Company, 1934. 431 pp.
Bibliography, pp. 413–24.

SNEDDEN, DAVID SAMUEL. *Civic Education; Sociological Foundations and Courses.* Yonkers-on-Hudson: World Book Company, 1922. 333 pp.
A volume addressed primarily to teachers, containing many suggestions with respect to teaching and an exposition of the sociological approach to civic education. Bibliography, p. 330.

————. *Educations for Political Citizenship: A Critical Analysis of Certain Unsolved Problems of School Educations towards Superior Memberships in Democratic Political Societies.* New York: Columbia University, 1932. 196 pp.
Bibliography, pp. 193–94.

The Social Studies in Secondary Education (Report of the Committee on Social Studies of the Commission on the Reorganization of Secondary Education, United States Bureau of Education, Bulletin no. 28). Washington, D. C.: Government Printing Office, 1916.

STEWART, GEORGE. *The Story of Scottish Education.* London: Sir I. Pitman, 1927. 164 pp.
Bibliography, pp. 163–64.

STRONG, ANNA LOUISE. " Making Bolshevists of Central Asians," *Asia,* 29:870–75 (November, 1929).
Sovietization of Turkestan.

The Teaching of Community Civics (Report of a Special Committee of the Commission on the Reorganization of Secondary Education, United States Bureau of Education, Bulletin no. 23). Washington, D. C.: Government Printing Office, 1915.

TROW, WILLIAM C., editor. *Character Education in Soviet Russia.* Ann Arbor, Michigan: Ann Arbor Press, 1934. 199 pp.
An editor's introduction and five translated articles written for the instruction of leaders of the " Young Pioneers," communistic organization for ten- to fifteen-year-olds.

TRYON, ROLLA MILTON. *The Social Studies as School Subjects* (Report of the Commission on the Social Studies, American Historical Association). Announced.

UNITED STATES WAR DEPARTMENT. *Citizenship Training Manual 2000–25.* Washington, D. C.: Government Printing Office, November 30, 1928.
Prepared under the direction of the Chief of Staff. Supersedes the *Manual of Citizenship Training.*

UNITED STATES WAR DEPARTMENT, ADJUTANT GENERAL'S OFFICE. *Studies in Citizenship for Citizens in Military Training Camps*

(Army Training Manual, nos. 1–4). Washington, D. C.: Government Printing Office, 1922–24.

WEBER, ELIZABETH ANNE. *The Duk-Duks: Primitive and Historic Types of Citizenship* (Civic Training Series). Chicago: University of Chicago, 1929. 142 pp.
Bibliography, pp. 135–39.

WEILL, GEORGES JACQUES. *Histoire de l'enseignement secondaire en France.* Paris: Payot, 1921. 253 pp.
Bibliography, pp. 241–46.

Whither America? The Menace of Americanism and How to Overcome It (United States Patriotic Society, Inc., Americanization Series, no. 2).

WOODY, THOMAS. *New Minds: New Men?* New York: Macmillan, 1932. 528 pp.
Civic training in the Soviet Union.

WOOLSTON, HOWARD. "Propaganda in Soviet Russia," *American Journal of Sociology,* 38: 32–41 (July, 1932).

2. ANTI-INSTITUTIONAL SYMBOLS

Systems of symbolic protest against the principal features of the established order. For details of technique, see Part III, Section B, Subdivision 7.

A. UTOPIAN SYMBOLISM

"Anarchism," *Encyclopedia of the Social Sciences.* (By Oscar Jászi.)

BECKER, CARL LOTUS. *The Heavenly City of the Eighteenth-Century Philosophers.* New Haven: Yale University, 1932. 168 pp.

"Communistic Settlements," *Encyclopedia of the Social Sciences.* (By Dorothy W. Douglas and Katharine DuPre Lumpkin.)

ELTZBACHER, PAUL. *Anarchism,* translated by Steven T. Byington. New York: B. R. Tucker, 1908. 309 pp.
Available also in French, German, Russian, Yiddish, etc.

"Fourier and Fourierism," *Encyclopedia of the Social Sciences.* (By Edward S. Mason.)

GERLICH, FRITZ. *Der Kommunismus als Lehre des tausendjähriges Reiches.* Munich, 1920.

GHIO, PAUL. *L'Anarchisme aux États-Unis.* Paris: Colin, 1903. 196 pp.

GIDE, CHARLES. *Communist and Co-operative Colonies,* translated by Ernest F. Row. New York: Crowell, 1930. 224 pp.
An account of nearly all the important modern examples of socialist, communist, anarchist, and cooperative colonies.

HERTZLER, JOYCE ORAMEL. *The History of Utopian Thought.* New York: Macmillan, 1923. 321 pp.
Bibliographic footnotes.

HOLDEN, ARTHUR CORT. *The Settlement Idea: A Vision of Social Justice.* New York: Macmillan, 1922. 213 pp.
Bibliography, pp. 207–13.

"Messianism," *Encyclopedia of the Social Sciences.* (By Hans Kohn.)

MÜHSAM, ERICH. *Revolution, Kampf-Marsch, und Spottlieder.* Berlin: Verlag der Freie Arbeiter, 1925. 55 pp.

MUMFORD, LEWIS. *The Story of Utopias.* New York: Boni and Liveright, 1922. 315 pp.
Bibliography, pp. 309–15.

PRUDHOMMEAUX, JULES. *Icarie et son fondateur, Étienne Cabet: Contribution à l'étude du socialisme expérimental.* Paris: E. Cornély, 1907. 688 pp.
Bibliography, pp. xiii–xl.

PRYS, J. *Der Staatsroman des 16. und 17. Jahrhunderts und sein Erziehungsideal.* Würzburg, 1913.

B. OTHER SYMBOLISM

"Apostasy and Heresy," *Encyclopedia of the Social Sciences.* (By John W. Herring.)

BRINTON, CLARENCE CRANE. "Revolutionary Symbolism in the Jacobin Clubs," *American Historical Review,* 32:737–52 (1926–27).

DAVIDSON, PHILIP GRANT, JR. "Revolutionary Propaganda in New England, New York, and Pennsylvania, 1763–1776" (Ph.D. thesis, University of Chicago, 1929. 269 pp.).
Bibliography, pp. 252–69.

ELTON, GODFREY. *The Revolutionary Idea in France, 1789–1871.* Second edition. London: E. Arnold, 1931. New York: Longmans, Green, 1931. 191 pp.
Bibliography, pp. 182–85.

FAŸ, BERNARD. *L'Esprit révolutionnaire en France et aux États-Unis à la fin du XVIIIme siècle.* Paris: Champion, 1925. 378 pp.
Bibliography, pp. 345–62. English edition: *The Revolutionary Spirit in France and America,* translated by Ramon Guthrie. New York: Harcourt, Brace, 1927. 613 pp. Bibliography, pp. 575–600.

GRAHAM, MARCUS, editor. *An Anthology of Revolutionary Poetry,* with an introduction by Ralph Cheyney and Lucia Trent. New York: The Active Press, 1929. 353 pp.

I. W. W. Songs: Songs of the Workers. Twenty-third edition. Chicago: Industrial Workers of the World, 1928. 96 pp.

KARMIN, O. "L'Influence du symbolisme maçonnique sur le symbolisme révolutionnaire," *Revue historique de la révolution française,* 1 (1910).

LANDAU, MARK ALEKSANDROVITCH. *Deux révolutions.* Paris: Union, 1921. 119 pp.

Comparison of the French and Russian revolutions.

MAXE, JEAN (pseudonym). *L'Anthologie des défaitistes.* Paris: Bossard, 1925. 2 vols.

A collection of extracts to illustrate the defeatist propaganda, especially the red propaganda in France.

MICHELS, ROBERTO. "Psychologie der antikapitalistischen Massenbewegungen," *Grundriss der Sozialökonomik,* Band 9 (1925).

MORANGE, G. *Les Idées communistes dans les sociétés secrètes et dans la presse sous la monarchie de juillet.* Paris, 1905.

ORTEGA Y GASSET, JOSÉ. *The Revolt of the Masses.* New York: W. W. Norton, 1932. 204 pp.

The professor of philosophy at the University of Madrid asserts that our era is characterized by the revolt of the mediocre masses against aristocratism.

POSTGATE, RAYMOND WILLIAM. *Revolution from 1789 to 1906: Documents Selected and Edited with Notes and Introduction.* London: Richards, 1920. 399 pp.

Contains bibliographies.

Red Cartoons from the Daily Worker, *the* Worker's Monthly, *and the* Liberator. New York: The Daily Worker, 1927.

SEIFERT, JOSEF LEO. *Die Weltrevolutionäre, von Bogomil über Hus zu Lenin.* Zurich, Leipzig, and Vienna: Amalthea, 1930. 480 pp.

Bolshevism is but a new stage in the great sectarian movements of the Slavs, says this author.

WELSCHINGER, HENRI. *Le Théâtre de la révolution, 1789–1799, avec documents inédits.* Paris: Charavay, 1880. 524 pp.

French fantasy-life during a revolutionary decade, as depicted on the stage.

F. PRACTICES AND SYMBOLS OF PRACTICES

The overt habit patterns of the community as revealed in studies of voting, buying, giving, ceremonializing, and cognate behavior. These studies are closely connected with analyses of the symbols of the overt practices that are current in the community. Several market analyses are cited in order to bring these minute studies to the attention of a larger number of social scientists.

Advertisers' Cyclopedia of Selling Phrases: A Collection of Advertising Short Talks as Used by the Most Successful Merchants and Advertisement Writers; Classified and Arranged so as to Facilitate the Expression of Ideas and Assist Merchants in General Lines of Business and Specialists in Special Lines in the Preparation and Compilation of Advertising Copy. New York: Advertisers' Cyclopedia Company, 1909. 1360 pp., illustrated.

"Amateur," *Encyclopedia of the Social Sciences.* (By Elizabeth Todd.)

The Anti-Saloon Song Book. Westerville, Ohio: Anti-Saloon League of America.

ASSOCIATION OF NATIONAL ADVERTISERS. *An Analysis of 285 National Advertising Budgets, 1932–33, Including a Comparison with Budget Figures for the Years 1929 and 1930.* New York, 1933. 135 pp.
A study of the market for advertising.

BEAGLEHOLE, ERNEST. *Property, a Study in Social Psychology* (Studies in Political Science and Sociology, no. 1). London: Allen and Unwin, 1931. 327 pp.
Bibliography, p. 322.

BRANDT, LILLIAN. *How Much Shall I Give?* New York: Frontier Press, 1921. 153 pp.
"An analysis and description of the motives which influence givers in deciding to what causes, and how much, they will give."

CALVERTON, V. F. (pseudonym). "The Compulsive Basis of Social Thought, as Illustrated by the Varying Doctrines as to the Origins of Marriage and the Family," *American Journal of Sociology,* 36: 689–721 (March, 1931).

"Ceremony," *Encyclopedia of the Social Sciences.* (By C. Delisle Burns.)

CHAMBERLAIN, ARTHUR H. *Thrift Education: Course of Study Outline for Use in Years One to Eight.* Chicago: American Society for Thrift, 1928.

CORBETT, E. "American Legend: Emerson, the Mouse-Trap, and Advertising," *Century,* 117: 303–10 (January, 1929).

COZENS, M. L. *A Handbook of Heresies.* London, 1928.

CRITCHFIELD AND COMPANY. *Digest of Merchandising and Advertising Information.* Chicago, 650 pp.
Newspapers, population, industries, magazines, rates, radio stations, number of passenger cars on farms, etc.

CROWELL PUBLISHING COMPANY. *Fifty Manufacturers: Leading American Business Enterprises Report Their Methods of Distribution and Market Analysis.* New York, 1925. 38 pp.

CURTIS PUBLISHING COMPANY. *The Farm Market.* Philadelphia, 1918. 68 pp.

DEARBORN, GEORGE VAN NESS. *The Psychology of Clothing* (Psychological Review Monographs, vol. 26, no. 1, whole no. 112). Princeton, New Jersey, and Lancaster, Pennsylvania: Psychological Review Company, 1918. 72 pp.
Bibliography, pp. 71–72.

DICKERSON, ROY E. "Suggested Program for Defense Day and Roosevelt's Birthday," *De Molay Councilor,* September, 1924, p. 3.

————. "Suggested Program for Parent's Day," *De Molay Councilor,* October, 1924, p. 3.

————. "Suggestions for the Observance of Patriot's Day," *De Molay Councilor,* April, 1925, p. 15.

"Efficiency," *Encyclopedia of the Social Sciences.* (By Sumner H. Slichter.)
Discusses origin and diffusion of the emphasis upon efficiency.

FICK, H. *Der deutsche Militarismus der Vorkriegszeit: Ein Beitrag zur Soziologie des Militarismus.* Potsdam: Protte, 1932. 103 pp.
Militarism in pre-war Germany.

FRANK, ALBERT, AND COMPANY. *The Albert Frank Investment Survey; Why and How People Invest.* New York, 1922. 62 pp.

GOSNELL, HAROLD FOOTE. *Why Europe Votes.* Chicago: University of Chicago, 1930. 247 pp.
Bibliographic footnotes.

GRAVES, WILLIAM BROOKE. *Uniform State Action.* Chapel Hill, North Carolina: University of North Carolina, 1934. 368 pp.
Digests material relating to a large number of agencies whose work tends to bring about some measure of uniformity in the governmental practices of the American states. Appendixes list about 150 organizations of state administrative officers.

GRAY, WILLIAM S., and MUNROE, RUTH. *The Reading Interests and Habits of Adults.* New York: Macmillan, 1929. 305 pp.
A digest of the investigations of reading and related subjects that have a bearing on adult education, with case studies of about three hundred adults representing various social groups, to determine their reading habits. Bibliography, pp. 275–98.

HAMLIN, CHARLES H. *The War Myth in United States History*. New York: Association to Abolish War, 1927. 93 pp.
Bibliographies at ends of most chapters.

"Holy Places," *Encyclopedia of the Social Sciences*. (By Robert Briffault.)

HUNTLEY, FRANK LIVINGSTONE. "Attitudes toward War in Nineteenth and Twentieth Century English Fiction" (unpublished M. A. thesis, University of Chicago, 1926).

INTERNATIONAL MAGAZINE COMPANY, New York. *Drug Jobbing Map*.

————. *Dry Goods Jobbing Map*.

————. *Electrical Jobbing Map*.

————. *Grocery Jobbing Map*.

————. *Hard and Soft Water Map*.

————. *Trading Area System of Sales Control*.
These market analyses, published in 1929, suggest division of the country into 632 trading areas.

JEWISH WELFARE BOARD [New York]. *Bulletin on the Observance of Lincoln's Birthday*.

————. *Bulletin on the Observance of Washington's Birthday*.
These bulletins were issued to constituent societies in January, 1927.

KIEHL, ARMIN. *System der Markt-Analyse: Die Praxis kontinentaler Untersuchungen*. Lübeck: C. Coleman, 1929. 192 pp.

KU KLUX KLAN. Has published a catalog of official robes and banners, a *Katechism,* a song book, and reports of its "Kloncilium."

MCGRAW-HILL BOOK COMPANY. *Industrial Marketing: A Survey of the Buying Habits of Industry*. New York, 1925. 58 pp.

MARTIN, ROSCOE C. "The Municipal Electorate: A Case Study," *Southwestern Social Science Quarterly,* December, 1933.
A study of non-voting.

MAY, HERBERT LOUIS, and PETGEN, DOROTHY. *Leisure and Its Use: Some International Observations*. New York: A. S. Barnes, 1928. 268 pp.

NATIONAL SOCIETY OF SONS OF THE AMERICAN REVOLUTION. *Suggestions for Celebrations of Constitution Day*. Washington, D. C., 1926.

NATIONAL WOMAN'S CHRISTIAN TEMPERANCE UNION. *Songs for the Loyal Temperance Legion*. Evanston, Illinois, 1929(?).

————. *Subjects and Suggestions for Contests or Class Work Plans*. Evanston, Illinois, 1929–30.

NUSSBAUM, FREDERICK L. *A History of the Economic Institutions of Modern Europe: An Introduction to* Der Moderne Kapitalismus *of Werner Sombart.* New York: Crofts, 1933. 448 pp.

"The author has undertaken . . . the almost superhuman task of condensing into one volume the whole of Sombart's *Der Moderne Kapitalismus.*"

PAINTER, W. "Give Moses a Chance: Bible Quotations in Advertising," *Collier's,* 75:29 (January 10, 1925).

"Persecution," *Encyclopedia of the Social Sciences.* (By Horace M. Kallen.)

PORRITT, ARTHUR, editor. *The Causes of War, Economic, Industrial, Racial, Religious, Scientific, and Political.* New York: Macmillan, 1932. 235 pp.

PORTER, KIRK HAROLD. *History of Suffrage in the United States* (Ph. D. thesis, University of Chicago). Chicago: University of Chicago, 1918. 260 pp.

RICE, EMMETT AINSWORTH. *A Brief History of Physical Education.* New York: A. S. Barnes, 1926. 276 pp.

Bibliography at ends of chapters.

SALTER, SIR ARTHUR, and others. *The Causes of War.* New York: Macmillan, 1932. 235 pp.

Since there were thirteen diverse *rapporteurs,* each writing a somewhat specialized report, this collection of essays represents a wide variety of current rationalizations of the practice of war.

"Sex Education and Sex Ethics," *Encyclopedia of the Social Sciences.* (By M. A. Bigelow.)

"Short Ballot Movement," *Encyclopedia of the Social Sciences.* (By William B. Munro.)

"Short Hours Movement," *Encyclopedia of the Social Sciences.* (By Selig Perlman.)

SIMIAND, FRANÇOIS. *Le Salaire, l'évolution sociale et la monnaie: Essai de théorie expérimentale du salaire.* Paris: Alcan, 1932. 3 vols.

"Wages." Exemplifies the view that social science does not require hypotheses but the enumeration of factors whose interrelationships are corroborated by the comparison of their function during selected time intervals along a continuum in a given place.

SPARLING, EDWARD J. *Do College Students Choose Vocations Wisely?* (Teachers College Contributions to Education, no. 561). New York: Columbia University, 1933. 110 pp.

Vocational attitudes of freshman, sophomore, and junior students at Long Island University. Less than 3 per cent of the fathers of these students are engaged in teaching, medicine, law, and dentistry; nearly 95 per cent of the sons and daughters intend to engage in these professions.

STEWART, PAUL WILLIAM. *Market Data Handbook of the United States* (United States Department of Commerce, Domestic Commerce Series, no. 30). Washington, D. C.: Government Printing Office, 1929. 535 pp.

STODDART, ALEXANDER. *Great Markets of America: A Study of 54 Trading Areas in 36 States East of the Rocky Mountains.* New York: General Outdoor Advertising Company, 1929. 400 pp.

STREITZ, RUTH. *Safety Education in the Elementary School: A Technique for Developing Subject Matter* (Ph. D. thesis, Columbia University). New York: National Bureau of Casualty and Surety Underwriters, 1926. 143 pp.
Bibliography, pp. 140–42.

STRIEDER, JACOB. *Studien zur Geschichte kapitalistischer Organisationsformen; Monopole, Kartelle und Aktiengesellschaften im Mittelalter und zu Beginn der Neuzeit.* Munich and Leipzig: Duncker und Humblot, 1914. 486 pp.
Study of capitalistic forms of organization and indication of their cultural setting. Bibliography, pp. xxii–xxix.

SUMNER, W. A. "Reading Interests and Buying Habits of the Rural and Village Subscribers of a Daily Newspaper," *Journalism Quarterly,* 9: 182–90 (June, 1932).
A questionnaire study.

THOMPSON, J. WALTER, COMPANY. *Population and Its Distribution.* Fifth edition. New York and London: Harpers, 1931. 617 pp.
A compendium of useful information for advertisers, based on national and local censuses and other current data.

————. *Retail Shopping Areas: A Suggested Grouping of Counties about 683 Principal Shopping Centers, with 642 Sub-Centers Indicated.* New York, 1927. 299 pp.

TIBBITTS, CLARK. "Majority Votes and the Business Cycle," *American Journal of Sociology,* 36: 596–607 (January, 1931).
Confirms the suspicion that when an election follows a business expansion the party in power will receive a greater proportion of the vote than when an election occurs in a period of severe business depression.

VETERANS OF FOREIGN WARS OF THE UNITED STATES. *The Star-Spangled Banner: A Brief Story of the Song, Its Growth in Popularity and the Campaign Conducted by the Veterans of Foreign Wars of the United States Which Resulted in Its Adoption as Our National Anthem by Act of Congress.* Kansas City, 1932. 8 pp.

The Voice of the Church. Official Utterances of the Second Christian Denominations and Religious Organizations on the Question of Prohibition. Westerville, Ohio: American Issue Publishing Company.

WAGNER, DONALD OWEN. *The Church of England and Social Reform Since 1854* (Columbia University Studies in History, Economics, and Public Law, no. 325). New York: Columbia University, 1930. London: P. S. King, 1930. 341 pp.
Bibliography, pp. 328–36.

WAMBAUGH, SARAH. *Plebiscites Since the World War, with a Collection of Official Documents.* Washington: Carnegie Endowment for International Peace, 1933. 2 vols.
By an official of the League of Nations. Has sections on propaganda during plebiscites. Bibliography, 1:557–603.

WAPLES, DOUGLAS. "Community Studies in Reading," *Library Quarterly,* 3: 1–20 (1933).
Reading habits of the lower East Side of New York.

WHITNEY, RICHARD. *Public Opinion and the Stock Market.* Address before the Boston Chamber of Commerce, January 29, 1931. Pamphlet.
The wide distribution of our securities " is fraught with danger unless this vast mass of investors can be taught to look at the real value of the property they own, and not to rely on tips, rumors, and hopes." The president of the New York Stock Exchange analyzes the investor's imagination.

WILSON, FRANCIS G. "The Pragmatic Electorate," *American Political Science Review,* 24: 16–37 (February, 1930).

YOUNG, CHARLES. *Military Morale of Nations and Races.* Kansas City, Missouri: Franklin Hudson, 1912. 273 pp.

Y. P. B. Song Book. Evanston, Illinois: Young People's Branch, Woman's Christian Temperance Union.

PART V. THE CHANNELS OF PROPAGANDA

A. BIBLIOGRAPHY

No inclusive bibliography on the channels of propaganda has yet appeared. Some specialized bibliographies appear below, in Sections C and D.

B. GENERAL TREATMENTS

Willey, Malcolm MacDonald, and Rice, Stuart Arthur. *Communication Agencies and Social Life.* New York and London: McGraw-Hill, 1933. 229 pp.

Apparently this is the only volume surveying this field inclusively.

C. AGENTS WHO SPECIALIZE IN THE MANAGEMENT OF PROPAGANDA

1. ADVERTISING MEN AND ADVERTISING FIRMS

See Part II, Section K.

2. PRESS AGENTS, PUBLICITY MEN, PUBLIC RELATIONS COUNSELS

"Advertising Agents Condemn Free Publicity," *Printers' Ink,* 111:196 (1920).

Discusses press agents.

"Advertising Agents Wake Up to the Menace of the Press Agent," *Printers' Ink,* 110:19–20 (March 4, 1920).

"Autobiography of a Theatrical Press-Agent," *American Magazine,* April, May, and June, 1913.

Beatty, Jerome. "Dexter Fellows, the Master of Ballyhoo," *American Magazine,* 109:62–67 (March, 1930).

Bernays, Edward L. "The Press Agent Has His Day," *Printers' Ink,* 110:107–08 (February 26, 1920).

Bruno, Howard A., and Blythe, Richard R. *The Modern Torchbearers.* New York: "Printed for presentation" by Bruno and Blythe, Public Relations Counsels, New York, 1928. 25 pp.

Brief glorification of the public relations counsel, with an account of methods used in publicity for "one of the largest states of the union."

CARTER, JOHN. "Unseen Empire," *Independent*, 121: 6–8, 30–32 (July 7, 14, 1928).

E. Hofer and Sons, publishers and public utility propagandists.

CARY, HAROLD. "Deadbeating the Editors," *Collier's*, 74: 21 (November 15, 1924).

"Confessions of a Literary Press-Agent," *Bookman*, 24: 335–39 (December, 1906).

"Examples of Press-Agent Activity," *Printers' Ink*, 110: 8 (March 11, 1920).

FLYNN, JOHN T. "Edward L. Bernays: The Science of Ballyhoo," *Atlantic Monthly*, 149: 562–71 (May, 1932).

FRANKLIN, B. "Theatrical Press-Agent," *Overland Monthly*, N. S., 53: 89–98 (February, 1909).

HARRISON, WALTER MUMFORD. *The Public Relations Man and the Editor: An Address before the Convention of the American Gas Association, October 10, 1928*. New York: Ivy Lee, 1928. 29 pp.

IRWIN, WILLIAM. "The Press-Agent: His Rise and Decline," *Collier's Weekly*, 48: 24–25 (December 2, 1911).

KOFOED, JACK. "The Inside Story of Fight Ballyhoo," *Editor and Publisher*, vol. 63, no. 6, p. 13 (June 28, 1930).

Free publicity.

MANNING, GEORGE H. "Defunct Foshay Interests Obtained Free Space Worth Millions," *Editor and Publisher*, vol. 63, no. 6, p. 22 (June 28, 1930).

———. "Insull Propaganda Operations Told," *Editor and Publisher*, vol. 66, no. 33, pp. 5, 34 (December 30, 1933).

Report of testimony at Federal Trade Commission hearings.

"Massachusetts Press Asks Agents to Change Publicity Practices," *Editor and Publisher*, May 17, 1930, p. 20.

One of a series of references in this periodical on the free publicity problem.

MAUÉ, D. R. "Fame While It's Hot," *Outlook*, 149: 462–63 (July 18, 1928).

MULLETT, MARY B. "Beating the Broadway Drum," *American Magazine*, 101: 18–19 (April, 1926).

NATHAN, GEORGE J. "Press Agents of Royalty," *Harper's Weekly*, 53: 27 (December 11, 1909).

"Newspaper Publishers Affronted by Increasing Bold Assaults from

Free Space Grafting Army," *Western Publisher,* 26:5 (June 14, 1930).

PRINGLE, HENRY F. "Mass Psychologist," *American Mercury,* 19:155–62 (February, 1930).
On Edward L. Bernays.

"Publicity, Public Opinion, and the Wily Press Agent," *Literary Digest,* 67:58–62 (October 2, 1920).

"Publisher's View of the Press Agent," *Printers' Ink,* 110:25–27 (March 25, 1920).

SOBEL, BERNARD. "Theatrical Press-Agentry," *Bookman,* 66:257–61 (November, 1927).

"Theatrical Press-Agent's Confession and Apology," *Independent,* 59:191–96 (July 27, 1905).

TURNER, GEORGE K. "Manufacturing Public Opinion," *McClure's Magazine,* 39:316–27 (July, 1912).

WALKER, STANLEY. *City Editor.* New York: Stokes, 1934. 336 pp.
"Maestros with Brasses and Wood-Winds" deals with press agents.

————. "Men of Vision," *American Mercury,* 10:89–93 (January, 1927).

WILSON, F. W. "How Dare the Publishers Discriminate against the Press-Agent?" *Printers' Ink,* 110:132–33 (March 18, 1920).

3. INTELLECTUALS: EDUCATORS, CLERGYMEN, LAWYERS

The modern expansion of technology has afforded abundant new opportunities for specialization in the use of symbols. One result has been the increasing prominence of the "intellectual" in modern society; he often appears as reporter, interpreter, and advocate.

ABRAMS, RAY HAMILTON. *Preachers Present Arms: A Study of the War-Time Attitudes and Activities of the Churches and the Clergy in the United States, 1914–1918* (Ph. D. thesis, University of Pennsylvania, 1931). Philadelphia: Ray H. Abrams, 1933. 297 pp.
Bibliography, pp. 281–88.

BAGLEY, WILLIAM C., FORD, GUY STANTON, and others. *The Selection and Training of the Teacher* (Report of the Commission on the Social Studies, American Historical Association). Announced.

BALDWIN, ALICE MARY. *The New England Clergy and the American Revolution.* Durham, North Carolina: Duke University, 1928. 222 pp.
Bibliography, pp. 190–209.

BARNARD, HENRY. *American Educational Biography: Memoirs of Teachers, Educators, and Promoters and Benefactors of Education, Science, and Literature.* Syracuse, New York: C. W. Bardeen, 1874. 526 pp.

BECKER, HOWARD. "Space Apportioned Forty-eight Topics in *The American Journal of Sociology, 1895–1930,*" *American Journal of Sociology,* 38:71–79 (July, 1932).
Focus of attention of specialized students of society.

BONNER, ROBERT JOHNSON. *Lawyers and Litigants in Ancient Athens: The Genesis of the Legal Profession.* Chicago: University of Chicago, 1927. 276 pp.

CAMPBELL, REV. REGINALD JOHN. *Thomas Arnold.* New York and London: Macmillan, 1927. 242 pp.

CARR-SAUNDERS, ALEXANDER MORRIS, and WILSON, P. A. *The Professions.* Oxford, England: Clarendon Press, 1933. 536 pp.
Survey of all the professions in England and Wales except the church and the army; their history, character, and relations with society.

CAVERT, REV. SAMUEL MCCREA. *Securing Christian Leaders for Tomorrow: A Study in Present Problems of Recruiting for Christian Life Service.* New York: Doran, 1926. 179 pp.

COENEN, P. "Zur Geschichte der Lehrerbewegung in Russland," *Preussische Lehrerzeitung,* 1926, nos. 111–16.

COT, PIERRE. "Les Avocats et les universitaires dans la politique," *Revue politique et parlementaire,* 124:202–22 (1925).
Discusses the parliamentary shortcomings and talents of two types: lawyers and academicians.

CURTI, MERLE EUGENE. *Social Ideas of American Educators* (Report of the Commission on the Social Studies, American Historical Association). Announced.

DAVIS, JEROME. "A Study of Protestant Church Boards of Control," *American Journal of Sociology,* 38:418–32 (November, 1932).

"Ethics in the Teaching Profession," *Research Bulletin of the National Education Association,* 9:1–92 (1931).
Contains selected bibliography.

"Expert," *Encyclopedia of the Social Sciences.* (By George E. G. Catlin.)

GOOCH, GEORGE PEABODY. *History and Historians in the Nineteenth Century.* Fourth impression. London and New York: Longmans, Green, 1928. 604 pp.

HARPER, MANLY H. *Social Beliefs and Attitudes of American Educators* (Teachers College Contributions to Education, no. 294). New York: Columbia University, 1927. 91 pp.
Tested three thousand "teachers and other educators" throughout the country on seventy-one controversial statements.

"Learned Societies," *Encyclopedia of the Social Sciences*. (By Frederic A. Ogg.)

"Legal Profession and Legal Education," *Encyclopedia of the Social Sciences*. (By H. D. Hazeltine, Max Radin, and A. A. Berle, Jr.)

LEWIS, SINCLAIR. *Elmer Gantry*. New York: Harcourt, Brace, 1927. New York: Grosset and Dunlap, 1929. 432 pp.
Realistic novel about a clergyman.

MAAS, F. "Über die Herkunftsbedingungen der geistigen Führer," *Archiv für Sozialwissenschaft und Sozialpolitik,* 41:144–86 (1916).
Social origins of intellectual leaders.

MAN, HENDRIK DE. *Die Intellektuellen und der Sozialismus*. Jena: Eugen Diederichs, 1926. 37 pp.

———. *Massen und Führer*. Potsdam, 1932.

MOFFETT, M'LEDGE. *The Social Background and Activities of Teachers College Students* (Teachers College Contributions to Education, no. 375). New York: Columbia University, 1929. 133 pp.
A questionnaire analysis of over a thousand students in fifteen teachers' colleges. Bibliography, pp. 129–33.

POWDERMAKER, HORTENSE. "Leadership in Central and Southern Australia," *Economica,* 8:168–90 (1928).
A study in terms of "functional anthropology."

SINGER, RABBI ARNOLD. *The Jewish Educator*. Jamaica, Long Island, 1932. 83 pp.

SPAHR, WALTER EARL, and SWENSON, RINEHART JOHN. *Methods and Status of Scientific Research*. New York: Harpers, 1930. 553 pp.
Propaganda may appear as "research." This volume discusses standard practices in the gathering, preparation, and marketing of social science materials, and describes personnel and institutions so engaged. Bibliographic footnotes.

STEPHENS, H. M. "Nationality and History," *American Historical Review,* 21:225 ff. (1916).
Discusses historians as creators of nationalistic prejudices.

VAN TYNE, C. H. "Influence of the Clergy, and of Religious and Sectarian Forces on the American Revolution," *American Historical Review,* 19:44–64 (1913).

WHITRIDGE, ARNOLD. *Dr. Arnold of Rugby.* London: Constable, 1928. 243 pp.

4. INTELLECTUALS: AGITATORS AND PROPHETS, POLITICIANS, POPULARIZERS AND WRITERS

For biographies and studies of newspaper personnel, see Part V, Section D, Subdivision 1 B.

ALLEN, B. S. "Minor Disciples of Radicalism in the Revolutionary Era," *Modern Philosophy,* 21:277–301 (February, 1924).

ANSTICE, E. H. "China's Student Politicians," *Pacific Affairs,* August, 1932.

BÄUMER, GERTRUD. *Sinn und Formen geistiger Führung.* Berlin, 1930.

BELLESSORT, ANDRÉ. *Les Intellectuels et l'avènement de la troisième république (1871–1875).* Paris: Grasset, 1931. 255 pp.

BENDA, JULIEN. *La Trahison des clercs.* Paris: Grasset, 1927. 188 pp.
Thesis: modern intellectuals forsake "truth" to pursue "power." Translated by R. Aldington as *The Great Betrayal.* London, 1928. American edition: *The Treason of the Intellectuals.* New York: Morrow, 1928.

BERNARD, J. "Political Leadership among the North American Indians," *American Journal of Sociology,* 34:296–315 (1928–29).

BOLITHO, WILLIAM. "The Anarchy of Sister Claudia," *Outlook* (London), 53:24–25 (January 12, 1924).

BORN, WOLFGANG. "Die Kunst im Lebensraum des neuen Russlands," *Kunst und Künstler,* 31:330–38 (September, 1932).
The function of the artist in present-day Russia is the evocation of "social energy."

BRAILSFORD, HENRY NOEL. *Shelley, Godwin, and Their Circle.* New York: Holt, 1913. 256 pp.
Study of "The French Revolution in England."

BRIN, HENNOCH. *Zur Akademiker- und Intellektuellenfragen in der Arbeiterbewegung.* Strasbourg, 1928.

BROUN, HEYWOOD, and LEECH, MARGARET. *Anthony Comstock, Roundsman of the Lord.* New York: Literary Guild, 1927. 285 pp.

CHASE, STUART. *Are Radicals Crazy? An Analysis of Their Main Tenets in the Light of Modern Science.* New York: League for Industrial Democracy, 1926. 12 pp.

CHITAMBAR, JASHWANT RAO. *Mahatma Gandhi: His Life, Work, and Influence.* Philadelphia and Chicago: John C. Winston, 1933. 266 pp. Bibliography, pp. 261–62.

CLARK, L. PIERCE. *Lincoln: A Psycho-Biography.* New York and London: Scribners, 1933. 570 pp.
A psychoanalytic interpretation of Abraham Lincoln.

"Clarté Movement," *Encyclopedia of the Social Sciences.* (By H. W. L. Dana.)
"An attempt to organize writers and scientists both of the Allies and of the Central Powers into 'a league of intellectual solidarity for the triumph of the international cause.'"

COLE, GEORGE DOUGLAS HOWARD. *The Life of William Cobbett.* London: W. Collins, 1924. 458 pp.
"England's last peasant leader." — JOHN LAWRENCE HAMMOND. Bibliography, pp. 438–48.

COLLINS, A. S. *The Profession of Letters: A Study of the Relation of Author to Patron, Publisher, and Public.* London, 1928. 279 pp.
Bibliography, pp. 270–73.

COWLEY, W. S. "Three Distinctions in the Study of Leadership," *Journal of Abnormal and Social Psychology,* vol. 33, no. 2 (July–September, 1928).

DA COSTA, CHARLES. *Les Blanquistes.* Paris, 1912.

DAKIN, EDWIN FRANDEN. *Mrs. Eddy: The Biography of a Virginal Mind.* New York and London: Scribners, 1929. 553 pp.
Bibliography, pp. 525–37.

DART, RUFUS. *The Puppet-Show on the Potomac.* New York: McBride, 1934. 266 pp.
The use of ghost writers by public figures.

DESPRÉS, ARMAND. *Manuel du parfait radical.* Paris: A. Savine, 1896. 36 pp.

DESTLER, CHESTER McA. "The Influence of Edward Kellogg upon American Radicalism, 1865–96," *Journal of Political Economy,* 40: 338–65 (1932).

DICKINSON, J. J. "Theodore Roosevelt, Press Agent," *Harper's Weekly,* 51: 1410 (September 28, 1907).

DRAHN, ERNST. *Lenin, Vladimir Il'ic Ul'janov: Eine Bio-Bibliographie.* Second edition. Berlin: Prager, 1925. 77 pp.
Bibliography of works by and concerning Lenin in all languages.

EASTMAN, MAX. *Artists in Uniform: A Study of Literature and Bureaucratism.* New York: Knopf, 1934. 261 pp.
The artist as propagandist.

"Encyclopédistes," *Encyclopedia of the Social Sciences.* (By René Hubert.)

FLEURY, ÉDOUARD. *Études révolutionnaires: Camille Desmoulins et Roch Marcandier. La Presse révolutionnaire.* Second edition. Paris, Didier, 1851. 2 vols.

GANDHI, MOHANDAS KARAMCHAND. *The Story of My Experiments with Truth.* Ahmedabad: Navajivan Press, 1927–29. 2 vols.
Mr. Gandhi's autobiography.

GARRISON, W. P., and GARRISON, F. J. *William Lloyd Garrison: The Story of His Life as Told by His Children.* New York, 1885–89. 4 vols.

GEFFROY, GUSTAVE. *L'Enfermé.* Paris, 1897.
On Louis Auguste Blanqui.

GOLDMAN, EMMA, "Johann Most," *American Mercury,* 8: 158–66 (June, 1926).

———. *Living My Life.* New York: Knopf, 1931. 2 vols.

HAAS, JAKOB DE. *Theodor Herzl.* Chicago, 1927. 2 vols.
About the Viennese journalist who became promoter of Zionism.

HALL, GRANVILLE STANLEY. *Jesus, the Christ, in the Light of Psychology.* Garden City: Doubleday, Page, 1917. 2 vols.

HAMMOND, JOHN LAWRENCE, and HAMMOND, BARBARA. *James Stansfeld: A Victorian Champion of Sex Equality.* New York and London: Longmans, Green, 1932. 311 pp.
Bibliography, pp. 297–300.

HARDEN, MAXIMILIAN. *I Meet My Contemporaries,* translated from the German by W. C. Lawton, with an introduction by H. E., Mr. James W. Gerard. New York: Holt, 1925. 287 pp.

HARLOW, RALPH VOLNEY. *Samuel Adams: Promoter of the American Revolution: A Study in Psychology and Politics.* New York: Holt, 1923. 363 pp.
Uses psychoanalytic concepts.

HECKMAN, DAYTON. "Political Leadership in Ohio" (unpublished M. A. thesis, Ohio State University, 1931).
A study of the physical characteristics, fraternal affiliations, etc., of successful candidates.

HIBBEN, PAXTON. *Henry Ward Beecher: An American Portrait.* New York: Doran, 1927. 390 pp.
Bibliography, pp. 357–67.

HIBBEN, PAXTON, and GRATTAN, C. HARTLEY. *The Peerless Leader: William Jennings Bryan.* New York: Farrar and Rinehart, 1929. 446 pp.
Bibliography, pp. 409–19.

HOBSON, J. A. *Richard Cobden, the International Man.* London: Unwin, 1919. New York, Holt. 415 pp.

HOLL, KARL. *Thomas Chalmers und die Anfänge der Kirchlich-sozialen Bewegung.* Tübingen, 1913.

HOPKINS, PRYNCE. *Father or Sons? A Study in Social Psychology* (thesis, University of London). London: Kegan Paul, Trench, and Trubner, 1927. 252 pp.

A student of J. C. Flügel collects examples of the Oedipus complex among the acts and writings of political, economic, and religious "leaders." Bibliographic footnotes.

HOWE, FREDERIC CLEMSON. *Confessions of a Reformer.* New York: Scribners, 1925. 352 pp.

"Intellectuals," *Encyclopedia of the Social Sciences.* (By Roberto Michels.)

JOHNSON, D. C. *Pioneers of Reform: Cobbett, Owen, Place, Shaftesbury, Cobden, Bright,* with a preface by Sidney Webb. London: Methuen, 1929. 189 pp.

JOSEPHSON, MATTHEW. *Zola and His Time: The History of His Martial Career in Letters, with an Account of His Circle of Friends, His Remarkable Enemies, Cyclopean Labors, Public Campaigns, Trials, and Ultimate Glorification.* New York: Macaulay, 1928. 558 pp. Bibliography, pp. 551–52.

KASTEIN, JOSEF. *The Messiah of Ismir: Sabbitai Zevi.* New York: Viking Press, 1931. 346 pp.

"Biography of a seventeenth-century Jew of Smyrna who became head of the most extensive Messianic movement that has occurred in Judaism since the time of Christ." — LYFORD P. EDWARDS.

KENNEDY, WILLIAM DORSEY, editor. *The Free-Lance Writer's Handbook.* Cambridge, Massachusetts: The Writer Publishing Company, 1926. 395 pp.

Discusses conditions under which the free-lance writer operates. "The Magazine Market," pp. 249–364. "The Book Publishers," pp. 364–78.

KINCHELOE, SAMUEL CLARENCE. "The Prophet: A Study in the Sociology of Leadership" (unpublished Ph.D. thesis, University of Chicago, 1929). 264 pp. Bibliography, pp. 242–64.

KÜNKEL, FRITZ. *Grundzüge der politischen Charakterkunde.* Berlin: Junker und Dünnhaupt, 1931. 118 pp.

Analysis of political personalities from the standpoint of Alfred Adler.

LANGE-EICHBAUM, WILHELM. *Genie-Irrsinn und Ruhm.* Munich: E. Reinhardt, 1928. 498 pp.

"Genius-Insanity and Fame." Abstracts of pathographies of many historical characters. Bibliography, pp. 437–96. See also the author's *The Problem of Genius,* translated by Eden and Cedar Paul. London: Kegan Paul, Trench, and Trubner, 1931. 187 pp.

LASSWELL, HAROLD DWIGHT. *Psychopathology and Politics.* Chicago: University of Chicago, 1930. 285 pp.

Chapters 6 and 7 are on political agitators. Bibliography, pp. 268–76.

"Leadership," *Encyclopedia of the Social Sciences.* (By Richard Schmidt.)

LOGGINS, VERNON. *The Negro Author: His Development in America* (Ph.D. thesis, Columbia University, 1931). New York: Columbia University, 1931. 480 pp.

Bibliography, pp. 408–57.

LOTE, RENÉ. *Les Intellectuels dans la société française de l'ancien régime à la démocratie.* Paris: Alcan, 1918. 215 pp.

McDONOUGH, R. "Propaganda and the Writer," *Commonweal, 20:* 35–37 (May 11, 1934).

MASON, J. S. "Blanqui and Communism," *Political Science Quarterly,* 44: 498–527 (1929).

MERRIAM, CHARLES EDWARD. At University of Chicago. Is preparing a summary of his studies in political leadership.

MICHELS, ROBERTO. "La psicologia sociale della bohème e il proletariato intelletuale." Accademia di Scienze Morali e Politiche della Società Reale di Napoli, *Atti,* 54: 181–99 (1931).

The social psychology of the bohemian and the intellectual proletariat.

MORLEY, JOHN. *Diderot and the Encyclopédistes.* London: Chapman and Hall, 1878. 2 vols.

MUNRO, WILLIAM BENNETT. *Personality in Politics: A Study of Three Types in American Public Life.* New and revised edition. New York: Macmillan, 1933. 121 pp.

Up-to-date edition of a standard work on the reformer, the boss, and the political leader in the United States.

NAVILLE, PIERRE. *La Révolution et les intellectuels: Mieux et moins bien, 1927. Que peuvent faire les surréalistes?"* Paris: Gallimard (Éditions de la Nouvelle revue française), 1928. 148 pp.

NETTLAU, MAX. *Michael Bakunin: Eine Biographie.* 3 vols. Reproduced by autocopyist, London, 1896–1900.

An abridgement of this work appeared as: *Michael Bakunin: Eine biographische Skizze* (Berlin: Pawlowitsch, 1901. 64 pp.).

NOMAD, MAX. *Rebels and Renegades*. New York: Macmillan, 1932. 430 pp.
Historical analysis of the rôle of the intellectual in proletarian movements. Discusses competition of the intellectuals with manual workers, plutocracy, and aristocracy. Bibliography, pp. 407–16.

PATON, S. "The Psychology of the Radical," *Yale Review*, October, 1921.
According to Paton, "the radical is a person in whom the self, herd, and sex instinct . . . are not gratified. Just what these instincts are and how their lack of balance is apprehended, he fails to enlighten us." — G. B. VETTER, *Journal of Abnormal and Social Psychology*, 25: 32.

PENG-PAI. "Memoirs of a Chinese Communist," *Living Age*, 344: 117–29 (April, 1933).

PERLMAN, SELIG. *A Theory of the Labor Movement*. New York: Macmillan, 1928. 321 pp.
Stresses the rôle of the intellectuals in the labor movement.

PHILLIPSON, COLEMAN. *Three Criminal Law Reformers: Beccaria, Bentham, Romilly*. London and Toronto: J. M. Dent, 1923. New York: Dutton. 344 pp.
Bibliography, pp. xv–xvi; bibliographic footnotes.

RAPPOPORT, CHARLES. *Jean Jaurès: L'homme — le penseur — le socialiste*. Second edition. Paris: L'Émancipatrice, 1916. 434 pp.

RINALDO, JOEL. *Psychoanalysis of the "Reformer."* New York: Lee, 1921. 137 pp.
Argues, without supporting cases, that the reformer is always a meddling hysteric.

ROBINSON, JAMES HARVEY. *The Humanizing of Knowledge*. New York: Doran, 1923. 119 pp.
The rôle of popularizers. "Urges scientists and other specialists to express their discoveries and conclusions in a form which will appeal to the great mass of readers."

ROCKER, RUDOLPH. *Johann Most, das Leben eines Rebellen*. Berlin: "Der Syndikalist," F. Kater, 1924. 482 pp.

ROOT, W. T. "The Psychology of Radicalism," *Journal of Abnormal and Social Psychology*, 19: 342–54.
Radicals have a low "emotional breaking point."

ROSSMAN, JOSEPH. *The Psychology of the Inventor: A Study of the Patentee*. New and revised edition. Washington, D. C.: Inventors Publishing Company, 1931. 252 pp.
Provides statistics on the traits of inventors, their occupations, motives,

source of livelihood, fathers' occupations, marital status, etc. Contains bibliographies.

RÜHLE, OTTO. *Karl Marx, Leben und Werk.* Hellerau bei Dresden: Avalun-Verlag, 1928. 476 pp.
From the standpoint of Alfred Adler. Bibliography, p. 474. English edition: *Karl Marx: His Life and Work,* translated by Eden and Cedar Paul. New York: Viking, 1929. 419 pp. Bibliography, pp. 401–02.

SCHROEDER, THEODORE. "Conservative, Liberal, and Radical," *Psychoanalytic Review,* 1920, pp. 376–84.
"There are neurotic and psychotic radicals, . . . liberals, and conservatives."

SMITH, VINCENT ARTHUR. *Asoka.* Third edition. Oxford, England: Clarendon Press, 1920. 278 pp.
Life of the most distinguished propagandist of *ahimsa* and *dharma.*

SPARGO, JOHN. *The Psychology of Bolshevism.* New York: Harpers, 1919. 150 pp.
"Spargo, a former Socialist, anxious to reestablish his reputability during the years of open season on radicals following the World War, wrote a whole book . . . delineating the character, motivation, and personalities of 'radicals' in terms of 'psychoneuroses,' 'hysterical hyperaesthesia,' 'fixed ideas,' and the mechanisms of crowd behavior." — G. B. VETTER, *Journal of Abnormal and Social Psychology,* 25: 33.

STEUART, JUSTIN. *Wayne Wheeler, Dry Boss: An Uncensored Biography.* New York and Chicago: Revell, 1928. 304 pp.
Mr. Wheeler died in 1927. Mr. Steuart had been his confidential secretary.

STRACHAN-DAVIDSON, JAMES LEIGH. *Cicero and the Fall of the Roman Republic.* New York: Putnam, 1903. 446 pp.

TAIT, W. D. "The Menace of the Reformer," *Journal of Abnormal and Social Psychology,* vol. 21, p. 343.
"This species of human suffers from 'hypertrophy of the parental instinct,' which irresistably prompts him to over-protect the poor and the bad." — G. B. VETTER, *Journal of Abnormal and Social Psychology,* 25: 34.

TAN SHIH-HUA. *A Chinese Testament: The Autobiography of Tan Shih-Hua, as told to S. Tretiakov.* New York: Simon and Schuster, 1934. 316 pp.
The life of a student revolutionary.

TAO, L. K. "Unemployment among Intellectual Workers in China," *Chinese Social and Political Science Review,* 13: 251–61 (1929).

TIFFANY, FRANCIS. *Life of Dorothea Lynde Dix.* Eighth edition. New York and Boston: Houghton Mifflin, 1892. 392 pp.

TROTSKY, LEON. *Lenin*. New York: Minton, Balch, 1925. 236 pp.
Somewhat unsystematic reminiscences.

————. *My Life*. New York: Scribners, 1930. 613 pp.

VAUGHAN, WAYLAND FARRIES. *The Lure of Superiority* (Ph. D. thesis, Harvard University). New York: Holt, 1928. 307 pp.
"'Compensation for inferiority' is the key to most radicals." Bibliography, pp. 297–99.

VERNADSKY, GEORGII VLADIMIROVICH. *Lenin, Red Dictator*. New Haven: Yale University, 1931. 351 pp.
A standard biography of Lenin.

VILLARD, OSWALD GARRISON. *Prophets True and False*. New York: Knopf, 1928. 355 pp.

WEBB, BEATRICE. *My Apprenticeship*. New York and London: Longmans, Green, 1926. 442 pp.

WELLS, HERBERT GEORGE. *The Open Conspiracy: Blue Prints for a World Revolution*. Revised edition. London: Hogarth Press, 1930. 243 pp.
World revolution by the popularizers.

WOLFE, A. B. "The Motivation of Radicalism," *Psychological Review*, vol. 28 (1921).

ZÉVAÈS, A. B. *Auguste Blanqui*. Paris, 1920.

ZINK, HAROLD. *City Bosses in the United States*. Durham, North Carolina: Duke University, 1930. 371 pp.
Domestic and social characteristics of twenty municipal bosses.

5. LOBBYISTS

A. BIBLIOGRAPHY

LIBRARY OF CONGRESS. *Select List of References on Lobbying*. Washington, D. C., 1912. 4 pp., typewritten.

B. REFERENCES

BOYCE, WILLIAM A., JR. "Women as Lobbyists," *National Municipal Review*, 16: 571–76 (September, 1927).

BUSBEY, L. WHITE. *Uncle Joe Cannon*. New York: Holt, 1927. 362 pp.
A biography that "casts light on the activities of the lobby." Mr. Busbey was for twenty years Mr. Cannon's private secretary.

CONSUMERS' RESEARCH. *General Bulletin*.
Published quarterly. Not to be confused with the confidential reports on specific products published by the same organization. Often reports lobbying activities of commercial groups.

Essary, J. Fred. *Covering Washington: Government Reflected to the Public in the Press, 1822–1926.* Boston and New York: Houghton Mifflin, 1927. 280 pp.
See the chapter on "The Evolution of the Lobby."

Foley, John. *Andrew H. Green and Thomas C. Fields; Secret Management of the Central Park Commission; John Foley's Letters (as Chairman of a Committee of the Reform Association of New York) to Mayor Havemeyer and the Taxpayers of New York.* New York: J. Polhemus, 1874. 40 pp.

Gilbert, Clinton Wallace. *Behind the Mirrors: The Psychology of Disintegration.* New York and London: Putnam, 1922. 236 pp.
By the author of *The Mirrors of Washington.* Includes a chapter on lobbies.

Hard, William. *The Lawyer as a Lobbyist* (address). Pennsylvania Bar Association Reports, 35: 267–77 (1929).

Herring, Edward Pendleton. "Great Britain Has Lobbies Too," *Virginia Quarterly Review,* 6: 342–55 (July, 1930).

———. "Group Participation in Federal Administration." In preparation.

———. *Group Representation before Congress* (Institute for Government Research, Studies in Administration, vol. 22). Baltimore: Johns Hopkins University, 1929. 309 pp.
Thoroughgoing study of lobbying. Annotated bibliography, pp. 292–304.

———. "Scotching the Veterans' Lobby," *North American Review,* 236: 48–54 (July, 1933).

King, Judson. "Political Lawyers," National Popular Government League, *Bulletin* (February 10, 1928).

———. "Who's Who in the Super-Power Lobby in Washington and Out," National Popular Government League, *Bulletin* (November 25, 1927).

"Lobby," *Encyclopedia of the Social Sciences.* (By E. Pendleton Herring.)

Logan, Edward B. *Lobbying (Annals of the American Academy of Political and Social Science,* Supplement to vol. 144, July, 1929. 91 pp.).
Succinct and thorough.

Lowry, E. G. "Propaganda of Special Interests," *Saturday Evening Post,* 192: 5 (January 31, 1920).

More Merry-Go-Round (Anonymous). New York: Liveright, 1932.
482 pp.
Chapter 13 is on "Lobbies."

MULLER, HELEN MARIE, compiler. *Lobbying in Congress.* New York:
H. W. Wilson, 1931. 122 pp.
Debate materials, briefs, bibliography, and reprints of selected articles
on the lobby. Bibliography, pp. 13–17.

POLLOCK, JAMES K. "Auxiliary and Non-Party Organizations in England," *Southwestern Political and Social Science Quarterly,* 11:393–
407 (March, 1931).
Contains bibliography.

POORE, BEN PERLEY. *Perley's Reminiscences of Sixty Years in the National Metropolis.* Tecumseh, Michigan: A. W. Mills, 1886. 2 vols.
Graphic account of the old-time lobby.

REINSCH, PAUL S., editor. *Readings on American State Government.*
Boston and New York: Ginn, 1911. 473 pp.
Has articles on the lobby by Robert M. La Follette and William E.
Russell.

SCHAFFNER, MARGARET A. *Lobbying* (Wisconsin Free Library Commission, Legislative Reference Department, Comparative Legislation Bulletin no. 2). Madison, Wisconsin, 1906.

SIEGFRIED, ANDRÉ. *America Comes of Age.* New York: Harcourt,
Brace, 1927, 1928. 358 pp.
Has chapters on lobbies, etc.

TANNER, HUDSON C. *"The Lobby" and Public Men from Thurlow
Weed's Time.* Albany, New York: G. MacDonald, 1888. 422 pp.

UNITED STATES HOUSE OF REPRESENTATIVES, SELECT COMMITTEE ON
LOBBY INVESTIGATION. *Charges against Members of the House, and
Lobby Activities of the National Association of Manufacturers and
Others* (hearings before the Select Committee, 63d Congress, 2d
Session, pursuant to H.R. 198). Washington, D.C.: Government
Printing Office, 1913. 4 vols., 2974 pp.

UNITED STATES SENATE, COMMITTEE ON THE JUDICIARY. *Alleged Dye
Monopoly* (hearings before a subcommittee of the Committee on
the Judiciary, 67th Congress, 2d Session, pursuant to S. Res. 77,
creating a special committee to investigate expenditures made in
behalf of various propaganda and in the maintenance of lobbies in
Washington). Washington, D.C.: Government Printing Office,
1922. 1485 pp.

———. *Lobby Investigation* (hearings before a subcommittee of the
Committee on the Judiciary, 71st Congress, 1st, 2d, and 3d Ses-

sions, and 72d Congress, 1st Session, pursuant to S. R. 20 and S. R. 475, resolutions to investigate the activities of lobbying associations in and around Washington). Washington, D. C.: Government Printing Office, 1929–32. 5088 pp.

Issued in 11 parts and an index. Hearings from October 15, 1929, to November 24, 1931.

————. *Maintenance of a Lobby to Influence Legislation* (hearings before a subcommittee of the Committee on the Judiciary, 63d Congress, 1st Session, pursuant to S. R. 92). Washington, D. C.: Government Printing Office, 1913. 4 vols., 4657 pp.

United States Senate, Ship-Purchase Bill Special Committee. *Maintenance of a Lobby to Influence Legislation on the Ship-Purchase Bill* (hearings pursuant to S. R. 543). Washington, D. C.: Government Printing Office, 1915. 485 pp.

Virginia State Library. *Legislative Reference List, 1912.* Richmond, Virginia, 1911.

Pages 41–43 are on "lobbying and legislative procedure."

Warner, Earl. "Law Making through Interest Groups in Ohio" (unpublished M. A. thesis, Ohio State University, 1929).

Zellar, Belle. "Pressure Groups and the New York Legislature" (dissertation in preparation at Columbia University).

D. AGENCIES UTILIZED IN THE DISSEMINATION OF PROPAGANDA

I. THE PRESS

A. INFLUENCES AFFECTING THE PRESS; THE INFLUENCE OF THE PRESS

(I.) BIBLIOGRAPHY

N. W. Ayer and Sons Company. *Directory of Newspapers and Periodicals.* Philadelphia, annually.

A guide to publications printed in the United States and possessions, Canada, Bermuda, Cuba, and the West Indies. Continues the *American Newspaper Annual and Directory,* which began publication in 1869.

Bömer, Karl. *Bibliographisches Handbuch der Zeitungswissenschaft.* Leipzig: O. Harrassowitz, 1929.

Bömer, Karl, and Rochlin, R. *Internationale Bibliographie des Zeitungswesens.* Leipzig: Published for Deutsche Institut für Zeitungskunde by O. Harrassowitz, 1932. 373 pp.

Cannon, Carl L. *Journalism: A Bibliography.* New York: New York Public Library, 1924. 360 pp.

CASEY, RALPH D. *Annotated Bibliography of Articles on Journalistic Subjects in American Magazines.*
Appears from time to time in *Journalism Quarterly*. See especially the entries under Public Opinion, Propaganda, Publicity, Censorship, etc.

MOTT, FRANK LUTHER. *Selected Lists of Books on Journalism.* Iowa City: University of Iowa, 1932. 27 pp.

Newspaper Press Directory and Advertiser's Guide. London: Mitchell, annually 1846 to date.
Contains full particulars of every newspaper, magazine, review, and periodical published in the British Isles, a newspaper map of the United Kingdom, the continental, American, Indian, and colonial papers, and a directory of class papers and periodicals.

PARK, ROBERT E. "Topical Summaries of Current Literature: The American Newspaper," *American Journal of Sociology, 32: 806–13.*

SCOTT, JONATHAN FRENCH. "Review Article: The Press and Foreign Policy," *Journal of Modern History, 3: 627–38* (December, 1931).

The Times (London). *Tercentenary Handlist of English and Welsh Newspapers, Magazines, and Reviews, 1620–1920.* London: The Times, 1920. 212 pp.

(2.) REFERENCES

The literature on the press is so voluminous that the compilers have attempted to prepare only a narrowly selected list of citations. For current developments in journalism readers are referred to specialized publications devoting their contents to articles on the newspaper and periodical. The following journals in this field may be cited: *American Press, Editor and Publisher, Guild Reporter, Journalist* (London), *Journalism Quarterly, National Printer Journalist, Matrix, Newsdom,* and *Quill.*

ABBOT, WILLIS J. "Dragon's Teeth: The Press and International Misunderstandings," *Virginia Quarterly Review,* vol. 4, no. 3 (July, 1928).
The responsibility of both the foreign correspondent and the newspaper he represents.

————. "Proportion in the News," *Journalism Quarterly, 8: 100–07* (March, 1931).

————. *Watching the World Go By.* Boston: Little, Brown, 1934. 358 pp.
A good deal of attention is paid to political party conventions, campaigns, and party appeals.

ACKERMAN, CARL W. "Leadership of the Press," *National Printer Journalist,* 52: 42–43, 68 (February, 1934).

ALLEN, CHARLES LAUREL. *Country Journalism.* New York: Thomas Nelson's Sons, 1928.
Chapter 14 deals with editorial policy and editorial influence.

ALLEN, ERIC W. "Economic Changes and Editorial Influence," *Journalism Quarterly,* 8: 342–59 (September, 1931).

————. "International Origins of the Newspapers: The Establishment of Periodicity in Print," *Journalism Quarterly,* 7: 307–19 (December, 1930).

ALLEN, FRANK HERDEE. "Government Influence on News in the United States during the World War" (unpublished Ph. D. thesis, University of Illinois, 1934).
A study of the Committee on Public Information and its dealings with the press.

ANGELL, NORMAN (pseudonym). *The Press and the Organization of Society.* London: Labour Publishing Company, 1922. 123 pp.
Discussion of the problem of the press in its general social aspect and from the special point of view of the Labor movement.

ARBIB-COSTA, ALFONSO. "Journalism in Italy, 1933," *Journalism Quarterly,* 10: 289–91 (December, 1933).

ARENDT, P. *Elektro-Weltnachrichtendienst und Presse* (Münster Universität, Institut für Wirtschafts- und Sozialwissenschaften, Zeitungs-Seminar, Publications, no. 2). 1930.

BAILEY, LOA EVELYN. "An Examination of the Influences Affecting the Policies of the Press" (unpublished master's essay, Columbia University, 1921).

BAKER-CROTHERS, HAYES, and HUDNUT, WINIFRED. *Problems of Citizenship.* New York: Holt, 1924. 514 pp.
Chapters 2 and 3 are on the influence of the press. Bibliography, pp. 471–506.

BARNHART, THOMAS F. "Newspaper Leadership in Times of Depression," *Journalism Quarterly,* 10: 1 ff. (March, 1933).
The achievements of the rural newspaper in guiding opinion for constructive social action.

BASSETT, WARREN L. "Editors Vote Lindbergh Feat Best Story; Pulitzer Greatest Editor," *Editor and Publisher,* 67: 60, 266, 270 (July 21, 1934).

BASTIAN, GEORGE C. (Revised by Leland D. Case.) *Editing the Day's News.* New York: Macmillan, 1932. 252 pp.

BAUMGARTNER, APOLLINARIS WILLIAM. *Catholic Journalism: A Study of Its Development in the United States, 1789–1930* (M. S. thesis in journalism, Columbia University). New York: Columbia University, 1931. 113 pp.
Bibliography, pp. 105–07.

BEACH, STEWART. "Leadership and Journalism," *Outlook,* 152:290–93 (June 19, 1929).

BEAVERBROOK, WILLIAM MAXWELL AITKEN, BARON. *Politicians and the Press.* London: Hutchinson, 1925. 127 pp.
In 1918 the author was British Minister of Information.

BEAZELL, WILLIAM P. "The Party Flag Comes Down," *Atlantic,* 147: 366–72 (March, 1931).
Newspapers are said to be exhibiting less political partisanship.

———. "Tomorrow's Newspaper," *Atlantic,* 146:24–30 (July, 1930).

BELLOC, HILAIRE. "The English Revolution and the Press," *Harper's,* 151:367–73 (August, 1925).

———. *The Free Press.* London: Allen and Unwin, 1918. 102 pp.
The capitalist press vitiates and misinforms public opinion. Its correction lies in the formation of small independent organs.

BENÉT, STEPHEN VINCENT. "The United Press," *Fortune,* 7:67 ff. (May, 1933).
An account of the development of a great news agency, with special reference to its foreign contacts.

BENNETT, IRA ELBERT. *Editorials from the Washington Post, 1917–1920.* Washington: Washington Post Company, 1921.
Discussions of great issues at the close of the War.

BENT, SILAS. *Ballyhoo: The Voice of the Press.* New York: Boni and Liveright, 1927. 398 pp.
"Perhaps the best and most comprehensive of the several books devoted to criticism of the modern newspaper and its ways. Highly controversial and undefendable, but stimulating." — FRANK L. MOTT.

———. "The Future Newspaper," *Century,* 117:342–48 (January, 1929).

———. "Scarlet Journalism," *Scribner's,* 84:563–69 (November, 1928).

———. *Strange Bedfellows: A Review of Politics, Personalities, and the Press.* New York: Boni and Liveright, 1928. 347 pp.
Chapter 11 discusses the rôle of the press in foreign affairs; chapter 14, Hearst and the Mexican forgeries; chapter 17, the power lobby and propaganda.

————. "Two Kinds of News," *Yale Review*, n. s., 16: 691–709 (July, 1927).

BERNHARD, L. *Der "Hugenberg-Konzern": Psychologie und Technik einer Grossorganisation der Presse*. Berlin, 1928.

BERTKAU, FRIEDRICH. "Tendencies toward Financial Concentration in the International Newspaper Field," *Journalism Quarterly*, 10: 109–24 (June, 1933).

BERTKAU, FRIEDRICH, and BÖMER, KARL. *Der wirtschaftliche Aufbau des deutschen Zeitungsgewerbes*. Berlin: Duncker, 1932. 207 pp. Bibliography, pp. 205–07.

BETHLÉEM, L. *La Presse*. Paris: Revue des lectures, 1928.

BICKEL, KARL AUGUST. *New Empires: The Newspaper and the Radio*. Philadelphia: Lippincott, 1930. 112 pp.
Chapter 2 contains a brief discussion of international news communication and the pressure that national states exert to control the flow of news through "official" and "semi-official" news agencies.

BILLY, ANDRÉ, and PIOT, JEAN. *Le Monde des journaux: Tableau de la presse française contemporaine*. Paris: G. Crès, 1924. 239 pp.

BLEYER, WILLARD GROSVENOR. "The Beginnings of English Journalism," *Journalism Quarterly*, 8: 317–28 (September, 1931).

————. "Does Press Merit Privileged Places?" *Editor and Publisher*, 67: 214, 216, 309 (July 21, 1934).

————. "Freedom of the Press and the New Deal," *Journalism Quarterly*, 11: 22–35 (March, 1934).

————. "Journalism in the United States, 1933," *Journalism Quarterly*, 10: 296–301 (December, 1933).

————. *Main Currents in the History of American Journalism*. Boston and New York: Houghton Mifflin, 1927. 464 pp.
A standard history. Pages 420–22 discuss the newspaper and propaganda. Bibliography, pp. 431–41.

————. *Newspaper Writing and Editing*. Boston: Houghton Mifflin, 1932. 482 pp.

————. *The Profession of Journalism*. Boston: Atlantic Monthly Press, 1918. 292 pp.
A collection of articles from the *Atlantic Monthly*. Bibliography, pp. 279–89.

BOESCH, WALTER. *Zur Geschichte der politischen Presse im Kanton Luzern von 1848–1914*. Zurich: Leeman, 1931. 149 pp.

Bömer, Karl. "German Journalism in 1931," *Journalism Quarterly,* 8: 435–45 (December, 1931).

The *Gruppenpresse* — the press designed for social and political groups — dominated journalism in Germany in 1931, although some of the newspapers, for the sake of circulation, called themselves "non-partisan."

Bömer, Karl, editor. *Handbuch der Weltpresse, 1931.* Berlin: Duncker, 1931.

A publication of the German Institute of Journalism. The section on American newspapers is not comprehensive.

Bose, P. N., and Moreno, H. W. B. *A Hundred Years of the Bengali Press, Being a History of the Bengali Newspapers from Their Inception to the Present Day.* Calcutta: H. W. B. Moreno, 1920. 129 pp.

Botscharow, J. *Die Entwicklungswege der russischen Presse, 1621–1928.* Moscow, 1928.

Bourdon, Georges, and others. *Le Journalisme d'aujourd'hui.* Paris: Delagrave, 1931.

A series of lectures by journalists, presenting a picture of contemporary French journalism.

Bourne, Henry Richard Fox. *English Newspapers.* London: Chatto and Windus, 1877. 2 vols.

Historical sketches for the period 1860–77.

Bowman, William Dodgson. *The Story of the Times.* New York: Dial Press, 1931. 342 pp.

History of the London *Times.*

Brisbane, Arthur. *Editorials from the Hearst Newspapers.* New York: Albertson Publishing Company, 1906. 402 pp.

A representative Brisbane collection.

Britton, Roswell S. *The Chinese Periodical Press, 1800–1912.* Shanghai: Kelly and Walsh, 1933. 151 pp. and 24 plates.

Bush, Chilton Rowlette. *Editorial Thinking and Writing.* New York and London: Appleton, 1932. 453 pp.

Contains much information on editorial policy.

————. *Newspaper Reporting of Public Affairs: An Advanced Course in Newspaper Reporting and a Manual for Professional Newspaper Men.* New York and London: Appleton, 1929. 406 pp.

An exposition of courts and official departments as news sources. Bibliography, pp. 389–95.

Butler, Charles R. "Recent Economic Trends in Newspaper Publishing," *Journalism Quarterly,* 9: 66–68 (March, 1932).

CAIN, J. M. "American Portraits: The Editorial Writer," *American Mercury*, 1: 196–200, 433–38 (February and April, 1924).

――――. "Are Editorials Worth Reading?" *Saturday Evening Post* 200: 21 (December 24, 1927).

CALDWELL, M. G. "Sensational News in the Modern Metropolitan Newspapers," *Journal of Criminal Law and Criminology*, July-August, 1932.

CARLÉ, W. *Weltanschauung und Presse*. Leipzig, 1931.

CARR, C. F., and STEVENS, F. E. *Modern Journalism*. London and New York: Pitman, 1931. 238 pp.
English newspaper practice.

CARR, PHILIP. "French Journalism," *Contemporary Review*, 137: 760–64 (June, 1930).

CASEY, RALPH D. "The Present Status of Journalistic Literature," *Journalism Quarterly*, 8: 125–36 (March, 1931).

――――. "Scripps-Howard Papers in the 1928 Presidential Campaign," *Journalism Quarterly*, 7: 210–31 (September, 1930).
A study in chain newspaper editorial control from the center.

CASEY, RALPH D., and BARNHART, THOMAS F. "Rural Press Kept Pace with Nation," *Editor and Publisher*, 67: 56–57, 254, 256, 258 (July 21, 1934).
The development and influence of weekly journalism over a fifty-year period.

CASON, CLARENCE E. "Journalism in Liberal Education," *Journalism Quarterly*, 8: 141–52 (March, 1931).

A Century of Journalism: The Sydney Morning Herald and Its Record of Australian Life, 1831–1931. Sydney: John Fairfax, 1931. London: Australian Book Company, 1931. 805 pp.

CHALONER, S. R. *Die britische Presse vom Standpunkt der Zeitungsindustrie, und ihrer Finanzierung* (Münster Universität, Institut für Wirtschafts- und Sozialwissenschaften, Zeitungs-Seminar, Publications, no. 1). 1929.

CHAMBERLAIN, JOSEPH EDGAR. *The Boston Transcript: A History of Its First Hundred Years*. Boston: Houghton Mifflin, 1930, 241 pp.

CHAMBERS, J. "Press and the Public Official," *Forum*, 44: 14–25 (January, 1910).

CHAO, THOMAS MING-HENG. *The Foreign Press in China*. Shanghai, 1931.

"The Chicago *Tribune*," *Fortune*, 9: 101–13, 180–88, 201–13 (May, 1934).
> Part 1: "McCormick and the *Tribune*," p. 101; Part 2: "Circulation," p. 201; Part 3: "Advertising," p. 211. Contains an estimate of the annual earnings of the *Tribune*.

CHICAGO *Tribune* STAFF. *The W G N: A Handbook of Newspaper Administration — Editorial, Advertising, Production, Circulation*. Chicago: The Chicago Tribune, 1922. 302 pp.
> Issued as a 75th anniversary book.

CHILD, RICHARD WASHBURN. "Do Propagandists Color News?" *American Press*, vol. 48, no. 9, p. 3 (June, 1930).

CLARK, CARROLL DEWITT. "News: A Sociological Study" (unpublished Ph.D. thesis, University of Chicago, 1931). 464 pp.

————. "Yellow Journalism as a Mode of Urban Behavior," *Southwestern Social Science Quarterly*, December, 1933.

COGGESHALL, REGINALD. "Diplomatic Implications in International News," *Journalism Quarterly*, 11: 141–59 (June, 1934).

COHEN, B. "South American Journalism in 1931," *Journalism Quarterly*, 8: 429–34 (December, 1931).

COLE, V. L. *The Newspaper and Crime* (University of Missouri Bulletin, vol. 28, no. 4).

"Comic History," *Saturday Review of Literature*, 10: 108 (September 16, 1933).
> Analysis of the newspaper comic strip.

Conference on the Press, under the Auspices of the School of Public and International Affairs, Princeton University, April 23–25, 1931. Washington, D. C.: Printing Corporation of America, 1931. 145 pp.
> Quotes views held by newspapermen concerning their profession. Important contributions on the press and the government, and the press in international affairs.

"Confession of an Editorial Writer," *New Republic*, 46: 294–98 (April 28, 1926).

"Confession of an Editorial Writer (a Reply)," *New Republic*, 47: 256–57 (July 21, 1926).

COOK, ELIZABETH CHRISTINE. *Literary Influences in Colonial Newspapers, 1704–1750*. New York: Columbia University, 1921. 279 pp.

COOPER, KENT. "Whence the News?" *Saturday Evening Post*, August 16, 1930, pp. 34 ff.
> An account by the general manager of the Associated Press of the news-gathering methods of his association.

COSMIN, S. (pseudonym of S. P. PHOCAS-COSMETATOS). *Diplomatie et presse dans l'affaire grècque, 1914-1916.* Paris: Société mutuelle d'édition, 1921. 313 pp.
The story of events in Greece during the war, expounded by a partisan of King Constantine.

CRAWFORD, NELSON ANTRIM, and ROGERS, CHARLES ELKINS. *Agricultural Journalism.* New York: Knopf, 1926. 300 pp.
Writing for farm papers, the community weekly, bulletins, etc.

CROSMAN, RALPH L. "Freedom of the Press in 1930," *Journalism Quarterly,* 8: 108-24 (March, 1931).

―――. "Freedom of the Press in 1931," *Journalism Quarterly,* 9: 149-69 (June, 1932).

CROWELL, CHESTER T. "American Journalism Today," *American Mercury,* 2: 197-204 (June, 1924).

DASCALAKIS, AP. *La Presse néohelénnique.* Paris: Gamber, 1930. 124 pp.

DAVIS, ELMER HOLMES. *History of the New York Times, 1815-1921.* New York: New York Times, 1921. 434 pp.

DAVIS, HALLAM WALKER. *The Column.* New York and London: Knopf, 1926. 166 pp.

DELL, ROBERT. "The Corruption of the French Press," *Current History,* 35: 193-98 (November, 1931).
By the Paris correspondent of the *Manchester Guardian.*

DETWEILER, FREDERICK GERMAN. *The Negro Press in the United States* (Ph. D. thesis, University of Chicago, 1922). Chicago: University of Chicago, 1922. 274 pp.
Bibliography, pp. 270-72.

DICKEY, C. B. "The Truth about Newspapers," a series of articles in *World's Work,* vols. 48 and 49.

DICKINSON, BURRUS. "The Influence of the Press in Labor Affairs," *Journalism Quarterly,* 9: 269-80 (September, 1932).

DOAN, EDWARD N. "Chain Newspapers in the United States," *Journalism Quarterly,* 9: 329-38 (December, 1932).

DOUGLASS, PAUL F. *The Newspaper and Responsibility.* Cincinnati: Caxton Press, 1929. 114 pp.
The newspaper is said to assume "an anomalous, semi-official, vital, circumjacent, though irresponsible and non-compulsory position in relation to the state." This study concludes that with the organization of the newspaper craft into a profession, newswriters will become devoted to the cause of improving human relations.

DOUGLASS, PAUL F., and BÖMER, KARL. " The Press as a Factor in International Relations," *Annals of the American Academy of Political and Social Science,* 162: 242–72 (July, 1932).
A highly factual description of current central European news systems.

DRESLER, ADOLF. *Geschichte der italienische Presse.* Vol. 1: *Von den Anfängen bis 1815.* Munich: R. Oldenbourg, 1931. 184 pp.

―――. *Über die Anfänge der römischen Zeitungspresse: Der Zeitungsdrucker Ludwig Grignani.* Munich: Südost-Verlag, 1930. 25 pp.

" Editorials for Every Man," *Commonweal,* 9: 333–34 (January 23, 1929).

ELLARD, ROSCOE. " Slump Revitalized Editorial Pages," *Editor and Publisher,* 66: 11, 34 (January 6, 1934).

ELTZBACHER, PAUL. *Die Presse als Werkzeug der auswärtigen Politik.* Jena: Eugen Diederichs, 1918. 161 pp.
Bibliography, pp. 149–52.

EMIN, AHMED. *The Development of Modern Turkey as Measured by Its Press* (Columbia University Studies in History, Economics, and Public Law, no. 142). New York: Columbia University, 1914. 143 pp.
Bibliography, pp. 141–42.

ESSARY, J. FRED. *Covering Washington: Government Reflected to the Public in the Press, 1822–1926.* Boston and New York: Houghton Mifflin, 1927. 280 pp.
Chatty reflections by the Washington correspondent of the Baltimore *Sun,* on newspaper personnel, and on interviews with the President, the Supreme Court, the diplomats, the lobbyists, and congressmen. Has a chapter on " The Evolution of the Lobby."

―――. " Democracy and the Press," *Annals of the American Academy of Political and Social Science,* 169: 110–20 (September, 1933).
Included is a criticism of the press for its failure to point out the flaws in the " prosperity " economy in the Harding-Coolidge era.

ESTER, KARL D'. *Zeitungswesen.* Breslau: Hirt, 1928.
A brief treatment of journalism by a leading German scholar in this field.

EVERTH, E. " Die Zeitung im Dienste der Öffentlichkeit," *Archiv für Buchgewerbe und Gebrauchsgraphik,* vol. 65, no. 4, pp. 1–30 (1928).

FATTORELLO, FRANCESCO. *Le origini del giornalismo in Italia.* Udine: Del Bianco e figlio, 1929. 201 pp.

FAY, SIDNEY BRADSHAW. "Der Einfluss der Vorkriegspresse in Europa," *Berliner Monatshefte,* May, 1932.

FAŸ, BERNARD. *Notes on the American Press at the End of the Eighteenth Century.* New York: The Grolier Club, 1927. 29 pp.

———. "The Influence of the Pre-War Press in Europe," Proceedings of the Massachusetts Historical Society, vol. 64 (March, 1931).

———. "Prewar Diplomacy and the European Press," *Current History,* 33:212–17 (November, 1930).

FENTON, FRANCES. *The Influence of Newspaper Presentations upon the Growth of Crime and Other Anti-Social Activity* (Ph. D. thesis, University of Chicago, 1911). Chicago: University of Chicago, 1911. 96 pp.

FERGUSON, FRED S. "Covering the 'War Beat' in France," *Editor and Publisher,* 67:150, 154 (July 21, 1934).

FISCHER, LOUIS. "Lies about Russia," *New Republic,* 67:94–96, 199–202 (June 10 and July 8, 1931).
A criticism of the handling of Russian news by the Chicago *Tribune.*

FLINT, LEON NELSON. *The Conscience of the Newspaper: A Case Book in the Principles and Problems of Journalism.* New York and London: Appleton, 1925. 470 pp.
Included in the volume are comments on the press and propaganda. The case method is applied to questions of newspaper ethics.

———. *The Editorial, with Case Material and Assignments.* New York and London: Appleton, 1928. 319 pp.
The case method is applied.

FORD, EDWIN H. "Books for Your Journalism Library," *Quill,* 21:6 (December, 1933).

"Foreign Language Press," *Encyclopedia of the Social Sciences.* (By Caroline F. Ware.)

FORT, FRÁNA L. "Polský tisk, jeho vývoj a prítomnost," *Casopis Svobodne Skoly Politických Nauk v Praze,* vol. 5, no. 6, pp. 183–86 (March, 1933).
"The Polish Press, Its Development and Present."

FRANKLIN, FABIAN. "Newspaper Possibility," *Saturday Review of Literature,* 7:689–90 (March 28, 1931).

GARR, MAX. *Die wirtschaftlichen Grundlagen des modernen Zeitungswesens* (Wiener Staatswissenschaftlichen Studien, vol. 10, pt. 3). 1912.

GAUVREAU, ÉMILE. *Hot News.* New York: Macaulay, 1931. 316 pp.
Fictionized reminiscences and success formulae of a prominent editor of New York tabloids.

GERALD, J. EDWARD. "Aspects of Journalism in South Africa," *Journalism Quarterly,* 8: 213–24 (June, 1931).

————. "Journalism in South America, 1933," *Journalism Quarterly,* 10: 302–08 (December, 1933).

GIVEN, JOHN LA PORTE. *Making a Newspaper.* New York: Holt, 1907. 325 pp.

GOSNELL, CULLEN B., and NIXON, RAYMOND B., editors. *Public Opinion and the Press.* Atlanta: Emory University, 1933. 177 pp.
Some twenty addresses and discussions at the sixth annual Institute of Citizenship.

GROSSE, O. *Der Beamte und die Zeitung.* Jena, 1927.

GROTH, OTTO. *Die Zeitung: Ein System der Zeitungskunde.* Mannheim: J. Bensheimer, 1928–30. 4 vols.
A treatise on the science of journalism. Bibliography, vol. 4, pp. 343–549.

GUNTHER, JOHN. "Funneling the European News," *Harper's Magazine,* 160: 635–47 (April, 1930).
A short account of the work of the foreign correspondent by the Vienna representative of the Chicago *Daily News.*

HALE, ORON JAMES. *Germany and the Diplomatic Revolution: A Study in Diplomacy and the Press, 1904–1906.* Philadelphia: University of Pennsylvania, 1931. London: Oxford University, 1931. 233 pp.
Contains critical discussion of editors, press agencies, and writings on the press question. Bibliography, pp. 214–26.

————. "Nationalism in Press, Films, and Radio," *Annals of the American Academy of Political and Social Science,* 175: 110–16 (September, 1934).

HAMILTON, W. P. "The Case for Newspapers," *Atlantic,* 105: 646–54.

HANAZONO, KANESADA. *The Development of Japanese Journalism.* Osaka: Osaka Mainichi, 1924. 110 pp.

————. "Journalism in Japan, 1933," *Journalism Quarterly,* 10: 309–15 (December, 1933).

HATFIELD, THEODORE M. "John Dunton's Periodicals," *Journalism Quarterly,* 10: 209–25 (September, 1933).

HATIN, EUGÈNE. *Histoire politique et littéraire de la presse en France.* Paris, 1861. 8 vols.

HEATON, JOHN LANGDON. *Cobb of The World*. New York: Dutton, 1924. 397 pp.
Reprint of the best editorials written by Frank I. Cobb of the New York *World* from 1908 to 1921.

————. *The Story of a Page: Thirty Years of Public Service and Public Discussion in the Editorial Columns of the New York World*. New York and London: Harpers, 1913. 364 pp.

HELLWIG, W. *Unternehmungsformen der deutschen Tagespresse (Das Wesen der Zeitung*, vol. I, pt. 4). Leipzig, 1929.

HENNING, ALBERT F. *Ethics and Practices in Journalism*. New York: Long and Smith, 1932. 204 pp.
A textbook treatment of the ethics and folkways of journalism.

HOLMES, J. S. "Crime and the Press," *Journal of Criminal Law and Criminology*, 20: 60–69 (1929).

HOOKER, RICHARD. *The Story of an Independent Newspaper*. New York: Macmillan, 1924. 237 pp.
A history of the Springfield *Republican*. The nation-wide influence of a provincial paper in political affairs.

HUDSON, FREDERIC. *Journalism in the United States from 1690 to 1872*. New York: Harpers, 1873. 789 pp.
An early work by a New York *Herald* staff member who worked for James Gordon Bennett, Sr. Marred by historical inexactitude.

HYDE, GRANT M. "Public Opinion and the Press," *Journalism Quarterly*, 8: 73–83 (March, 1931).

————. "United States Journalism in 1931," *Journalism Quarterly*, 8: 419–28 (December, 1931).

INDEPENDENT LABOUR PARTY. *The Capitalist Press: Who Owns It and Why*.

IRWIN, WILL. Series of articles describing the practices in modern journalism in *Collier's Weekly*, vols. 46, 47, and 48.
Historical, with important analyses of the practices of individual newspapers.

ISAACS, GEORGE ALFRED. *The Story of the Newspaper Printing Press*. London: Co-operative Printing Society, Ltd., 1931. 287 pp.

JOHNSON, GERALD WHITE. *What Is News?* New York and London: Knopf, 1926. 98 pp.
An editorial writer on the Baltimore *Sun* defines news as "an account of such events as a first-rate newspaperman, acting as such, finds satisfaction in writing and publishing."

Jones, Kennedy. *Fleet Street and Downing Street*. London: Hutchinson, 1920. 363 pp.
By an associate of Lord Northcliffe.

Journalism Quarterly. Contains articles and bibliographies on all topics of journalistic interest. Published by the Association of Schools and Departments of Journalism and the American Association of Teachers of Journalism.

Jubin, Georges. " Journalism in France," *Journalism Quarterly*, 10:273–82 (December, 1933).

Just, Arthur W. *Die Presse der Sowjetunion: Methoden diktatorischer Massenführung*. Berlin: Duncker, 1931. 304 pp.
Prepared under the auspices of the German Institute for Journalism. Contains bibliographies.

Jux, Anton. *Die Kriegsschrecken des Frühjahrs 1914 in der europäischen Presse*. Berlin-Charlottenburg: H. W. Hendriock, 1929. 248 pp.

Kantorowicz, Ludwig. *Die sozialdemokratische Presse Deutschlands*. Tübingen: Mohr, 1922. 112 pp.
Bibliography, pp. 111–12.

Kästner, A. *Die spanische Presse*.

Kawabe, Kisaburo. *The Press and Politics in Japan* (Ph. D. thesis, University of Chicago, 1919). Chicago: University of Chicago, 1921. 190 pp.
Bibliography, pp. 169–78.

Kellogg, Paul U. " How News of a Great Battle Is Gathered," *New York Evening Post*, Magazine Section, March 30, 1918.

Kent, Frank Richardson. *The Great Game of Politics*. Garden City: Doubleday, Doran, 1930. 346 pp.
See especially chapters 32 and 33, " Why the Newspapers Do Not Print All the Facts," and " The Newspaper's Political Policy."

King, Marion Reynolds. " One Link in the First Newspaper Chain, *The South Carolina Gazette*," *Journalism Quarterly*, 9:257–68 (September, 1932).

Kisch, Egon Erwin. *Klassicher Journalismus*. Berlin: R. Kaemmerer, 1923. 163 pp.
Anthology of German journalistic masterpieces.

Kleinpaul, Johannes. *Das Nachrichtwesen der deutschen Fürsten im 16. und 17. Jahrhundert: Ein Beitrag zur Geschichte der geschriebenen Zeitungen*. Leipzig: Klein, 1930. 178 pp.

KRASSOV, VLADIMIR. "Journalism in Russia, 1933," *Journalism Quarterly*, 10: 292–95 (December, 1933).

KROCK, ARTHUR, editor. *The Editorials of Henry Watterson*. New York: Doran, 1923. 430 pp.

LABOUR RESEARCH DEPARTMENT. *The Press*. London: Labour Publishing Company, 1923. 47 pp.

LAUZANNE, STÉPHANE JOSEPH VINCENT. *Sa majesté la presse*. Paris: Fayard, 1925. 253 pp.
A famous essay by one of the best-known Parisian journalists.

LEE, ALFRED McCLUNG. "Fifty Years of Daily Newspapers," *Editor and Publisher*, 67: 50–51, 294–95 (July 21, 1934).

————. "Trends in the American Daily Newspaper Industry" (unpublished Ph. D. thesis, Yale University, 1933).
Dr. Lee has published articles on newspaper trends in *Editor and Publisher* for December 2 and 16, 1933, and for March 10 and 17 and April 21, 1934.

LEE, JAMES MELVIN. *The History of American Journalism*. Boston and New York: Houghton Mifflin, 1917. 462 pp.
Factual, with little attention to the effects of social change on the press.

LEECH, HARPER, and CARROLL, JOHN C. What's the News? Chicago: Covici, Friede, 1926. 183 pp.

LEVRAULT, LÉON. *Le Journalisme*. Paris: Mellottée, n. d.
A one-volume history of French journalism, of recent date.

LEVY, RAPHAEL. "The Daily Press in France," *Modern Language Journal*, 13: 294–303 (January, 1928).

LIPPMANN, WALTER. *Liberty and the News*. New York: Harcourt, Brace, 1920. 104 pp.
Three papers from the *Atlantic Monthly*.

————. *The Phantom Public*. New York: Harcourt, Brace, 1925. 205 pp.

————. "The Press and Public Opinion," *Political Science Quarterly*, 46: 161–70 (June, 1931).

————. *Public Opinion*. New York: Macmillan, 1929. 427 pp.
Part 7, "Newspapers."

LIPPMANN, WALTER, and MERZ, CHARLES. "A Test of the News," Supplement to *New Republic*, August 4, 1920.
Questions the handling of the New York *Times* Russian news from 1917 to 1920.

LLOYD, ALFRED HENRY. "Newspaper Conscience: A Study in Half

Truths," *American Journal of Sociology,* 27:197–210 (September, 1921).

LÖBL, EMIL. *Kultur und Presse.* Leipzig, 1903.

LUCE, HENRY R. "The Press Is Peculiar," *Saturday Review of Literature,* 7:646–47 (March 7, 1931).
Publishers of newspapers are free from interlocking financial relationships with other business corporations.

LÜDDECKE, THEODOR. *Die Tageszeitung als Mittel der Staatsführung.* Hamburg: Hanseatische Verlagsanstalt, 1933. 216 pp.
The daily paper as a tool of the state.

LUNDBERG, GEORGE A. "The Newspaper and Public Opinion," *Journal of Social Forces,* 4:709–15 (1926).

McCLURE, S. S. "And McClure Tells How He Did It," *Editor and Publisher,* 67:82, 90 (July 21, 1934).
McClure's account of the origin of his newspaper syndicate.

MacDOUGALL, CURTIS D. *A College Course in Reporting for Beginners.* New York: Macmillan, 1932. 536 pp.

McGEEHAN, W. O. "Our Changing Sports Page," *Scribner's,* 84:56–60 (July, 1928).
By the former sports editor of the New York *Herald-Tribune.*

McKENZIE, VERNON. *Behind the Headlines.* New York: Cape and Smith, 1931. 286 pp.
Fourteen reporters' accounts of how certain news stories were obtained.

McMURTRIE, DOUGLAS C. "American Journalism 245 Years Old," *Editor and Publisher,* 67:59, 260, 262 (July 21, 1934).

———. "The Beginning of the Press in South Dakota," *Journalism Quarterly,* 10:125–31 (June, 1933).

———. "The Pioneer Press in Montana," *Journalism Quarterly,* 9:170–81 (June, 1932).

———. Is preparing a history of the press in the United States. Separate accounts of the pioneer press in various states have been published in the *National Printer Journalist* in 1933 and 1934.

McNITT, V. V. "Sam McClure Started Something," *Editor and Publisher,* 67:80, 84, 86, 90 (July 21, 1934).
Origin of the newspaper syndicate.

MAHIN, HELEN O., editor. *The Editor and His People.* New York: Macmillan, 1924. 380 pp.
Collection of editorials written by William Allen White, and published in the *Emporia Gazette.*

MANNING, GEORGE H. " Bennett Fight Opened Senate to Press," *Editor and Publisher*, 67: 116, 118 (July 21, 1934).
Recognition of right of reporters to record news of Congress.

MANSFIELD, F. J. *Sub-Editing: A Book Mainly for Young Journalists.* London: Sir I. Pitman, 1932. 248 pp.
General exposition of English newspaper methods. Bibliography, p. 231.

MARQUIS, DON[ALD ROBERT PERRY]. " Men Who Make Newspapers," *Yale Review*, n. s., 16: 45–56 (October, 1926).

MARTIN, FRANK L. " The Journalism of Japan," *University of Missouri Bulletin*, 19: 10, Journalism Series, 16 (April, 1918).

MARTIN, KINGSLEY. " Public Opinion; Rationalization of the Press and Democracy," *Political Quarterly*, 1: 428–35 (July-September, 1930).
Editorial policies and crusades of important London newspapers.

————. " The Russian Press," *Political Quarterly*, 4: 116–20 (January, 1933).

MAVITY, NANCY BARR. *The Modern Newspaper*. New York: Holt, 1930. 308 pp.
An introductory text by a newspaper woman.

MENCKEN, HENRY LOUIS. *Making a President: A Footnote to the Saga of Democracy.* New York: Knopf, 1932. 186 pp.
Mr. Mencken's dispatches from the Republican and Democratic conventions in Chicago, 1932. The preface gives interesting sidelights on how reporting is carried on at national conventions.

MERZ, CHARLES. " The American Press," *Century*, 113: 103–10 (November, 1926).

————. " The Big News of 1926," *New Republic*, 49: 213–14 (January 12, 1927).

————. *The Great American Band Wagon.* New York: John Day, 1928. 263 pp.
See chapter 6.

————. " What Makes a First Page Story," *New Republic*, 45: 156–58 (December 30, 1925).

MEYER, KARL H. *Die geistige Haltung Russlands und die Sowjetpresse* (Münster Universität, Institut für Wirtschafts- und Sozialwissenschaften, Zeitungs-Seminar, Publications, no. 3). 1931. 32 pp.

MILLS, JOHN SAXON. *The Press and Communications of the Empire.* London: W. Collins, 1924. 289 pp.
British cable control and supremacy.

MILLS, W. HASLAM. *The Manchester Guardian: A Century of History.* New York: Holt, 1922. 146 pp.

A reprint from the *Guardian's* centenary number.

Missouri Crime Survey. New York: Macmillan, 1920. 587 pp.

See Part 10, pp. 299–430.

MOHR, MARTIN. *Zeitungskunde und Zeitungswissenschaft.* Leipzig, 1927.

MORGAN, J. E. "Youth and the Crisis in American Life, with Particular Reference to College Journalism," *School and Society,* 39: 193–98 (February 17, 1934).

MORISON, STANLEY. *The English Newspaper.* Cambridge, England: Cambridge University, 1932. 335 pp.

MOSCHOPOULOS, NICÉPHORE. *Histoire de la presse grècque.* Paris: Presses universitaires de France, 1930.

————. *La Presse dans la renaissance balkanique.* Athens: Messager d'Athènes, 1931. 149 pp.

MOTT, FRANK LUTHER. *Country Correspondence in Iowa Weekly Newspapers* (University of Iowa School of Journalism Series, no. 1). Iowa City: University of Iowa, 1928. 28 pp.

MÜNZER, GERHARD. *Öffentliche Meinung und Presse.* Karlsruhe, 1928.

MURPHY, LAWRENCE WILLIAM. *An Introduction to Journalism: Authoritative Views on the Profession.* New York: Nelson, 1930. 399 pp.

An anthology.

NASH, VERNON. "Chinese Journalism in 1931," *Journalism Quarterly,* 8: 446–52 (December, 1931).

————. "Journalism in China, 1933," *Journalism Quarterly,* 10: 316–22 (December, 1933).

NATHAN, GEORGE JEAN. "Tabloids," *American Mercury,* 7: 363–64 (March, 1926).

NEVINS, ALLEN. *American Press Opinion from Washington to Coolidge.* New York: Heath, 1928. 598 pp.

An extensive anthology of newspaper editorials.

————. *The Evening Post: A Century of Journalism.* New York: Boni and Liveright, 1922. 590 pp.

The standard history of the New York *Evening Post.*

NEVINSON, HENRY WOODD. *Last Changes, Last Chances.* New York: Harcourt, Brace, 1928. 361 pp.

Observations and experiences of a well-known journalist, covering the war and post-war period, the Irish situation, and the Ruhr occupation.

NEW YORK *Sun* EDITORS. *Casual Essays of the Sun.* New York: R. G. Cooke, 1905. 422 pp.
Lighter editorials by Dana, Church, and others.

O'BRIEN, FRANK MICHAEL. *The Story of the Sun, 1833–1928.* New York and London: Appleton, 1928. 305 pp.
The standard history of the New York *Sun.*

OCKHAM, DAVID. *Stentor, or the Press of Today and Tomorrow* (Today and Tomorrow Series). New York: Dutton, 1928. 69 pp.

OGDEN, ROLLO. "Journalism and Public Opinion," *American Political Science Review,* 7: 194–200 (February, 1913, Supplement).

ORTON, WILLIAM C. "News and Opinion," *American Journal of Sociology,* 33: 80–93 (July, 1927).

PARK, ROBERT EZRA. *The Immigrant Press and Its Control.* New York: Harpers, 1922. 487 pp.
Part I: The Foreign-Born in America in Their Relation to the Press. Part II: Contents of the Foreign-Language Press (contains in translation many quotations from advertisements, news, and editorials). Part III: Natural History of the Immigrant Press. Part IV: Control of the Press.

———. "Natural History of the Newspaper," *American Journal of Sociology,* 29: 273–89.

———. "Topical Summaries of Current Literature: The American Newspaper," *American Journal of Sociology,* 32: 806–13.

PARK, ROBERT E., and BURGESS, E. W. *The City.* Chicago: University of Chicago, 1925. 239 pp.
Chapter 4, "The Natural History of the Newspaper."

PATTERSON, DON DENHAM. *The Journalism of China* (University of Missouri Journalism Series, Bulletin no. 26). Columbia, Missouri, 1922. 89 pp.
List of Chinese newspapers, pp. 79–89.

PAYNE, GEORGE HENRY. *History of Journalism in the United States.* New York and London: Appleton, 1920. 453 pp.
Main tendencies in the institutional development of journalism, with little emphasis upon biographies. Bibliography, pp. 399–427.

PENN, IRVINE GARLAND. *The Afro-American Press and Its Editors.* Springfield, Massachusetts: Willey and Company, 1891. 565 pp.

PERRY, STUART HOFFMAN, and WHITE, EDWARD J. *Newspapers and the Courts* (University of Missouri Bulletin, vol. 29, no. 28). Columbia, Missouri, 1928. 24 pp.

PEW, MARLEN. "Public Service Journalism," *Journalism Quarterly*, 8: 89–99 (March, 1931).

———. "Twenty-five Millions for News," *Editor and Publisher*, 67: 78, 248, 252 (July 21, 1934).
Expenditures in the publishing of newspapers.

"Philippson, Ludwig," *Encyclopedia of the Social Sciences*. (By Trude W. Rosmarin.)
About the "creator of Jewish journalism."

PORRITT, EDWARD. *The Unreformed House of Commons: Parliamentary Representation before 1832*. Cambridge, England: Cambridge University, 1903. 2 vols.
Volume 1, pages 584–96, are on "The House of Commons and the Press." Bibliography, 2: 531–56.

POTAPOV, N. *Pechat i voina*. Moscow: GIZ, 1926. 82 pp.
Attitudes of the Russian press during the World War.

"Press," *Encyclopedia of the Social Sciences*. (By Dexter Merriam Keezer.)

"Press and Public Opinion," *American Political Science Review*, 7: 201–03 (February, 1913).

"Problems of Journalism," Proceedings of the American Society of Newspaper Editors. Annually, 1925 —.

PROVIDENCE *Journal* STAFF. *Half Century with the Providence Journal*. Providence, R. I.: The Journal Company, 1904. 235 pp.
A memorial of Richard Henry Davis, secretary of the company.

RADDER, NORMAN JOHN. *Newspapers in Community Service*. New York: McGraw-Hill, 1926. 269 pp.
"Socially useful" achievements of the press, with citations on many cases.

RECOULY, RAYMOND. "Journalism and International Politics," *Harper's Magazine*, 146: 99–106 (December, 1922).

REGIER, CORNELIUS C. *The Era of the Muckrakers* (Ph. D. thesis). Chapel Hill: University of North Carolina, 1932. 254 pp.
Bibliography, pp. 217–41.

"Research Problems and Newspaper Analysis," *Journalism Bulletin*, vol. 1, no. 1, pp. 17–22.

RIETSCHEL, M. *Der Familienbesitz in der deutschen politischen Tagespresse (Das Wesen der Zeitung*, vol. 1, pt. 1). Leipzig, 1928.

ROBB, ARTHUR. "Chain Journalism in Sixth Decade," *Editor and Publisher*, 67: 74, 222, 224, 226, 228, 230, 232 (July 21, 1934).

————. "Modern Presses Begin in Eighties," *Editor and Publisher,* 67: 198–208, 299–300 (July 21, 1934).

ROGERS, CHARLES E. "The Social Justification of the Business Press," *Journalism Quarterly,* 11: 235–45 (September, 1934).
The economic place and justification of trade and class periodicals.

ROGERS, JAMES EDWARD. *The American Newspaper.* Chicago: University of Chicago, 1909. 213 pp.

ROSE, DONALD F. "The Great American Editorial," *Forum,* 80: 427–31 (September, 1928).

ROSENTHAL, J. *Zeitungen und Relationen des 15–18. Jahrhunderts.* Munich: Rosenthal, 1928. 146 pp.

ROSEWATER, VICTOR. *History of Co-operative Newsgathering in the United States.* New York and London: Appleton, 1930. 430 pp.
A history of the Associated Press, with chapters on the United Press and the International News Service. Bibliography, pp. 411–16; bibliographic footnotes.

ROWLANDS, JOHN. "Science and the Front Page," *Technology Review,* 32: 82–85 (December, 1929).

RUSSELL, CHARLES EDWARD. "The Radical Press in America," *Bookman,* 49: 513–18 (July, 1919).

SALMON, LUCY MAYNARD. *The Newspaper and Authority.* New York: Oxford University, 1923. 505 pp.
A scholarly examination of newspaper "trustworthiness."

————. *The Newspaper and the Historian.* New York: Oxford University, 1923. 566 pp.
An extensive study of the newspaper as historical source material. Reviews the literature of caricature, cartoon, and illustration during the World War, pp. 381 ff. Bibliography, pp. 493–566; bibliographic footnotes.

SALOMON, LUDWIG. *Geschichte des deutschen Zeitungswesens, von den ersten Anfängen bis zur Wiederaufrichtung des deutschen Reiches.* Oldenbourg and Leipzig: Schulze, 1900. (Revised, 1906.) 3 vols.
Standard history of German journalism.

SAMKALDEN, H. *Publieke Meening, Pers en Staat: Een Bijdrage tot de Sociologie van het Dagbladwesen.* Leiden: J. Ginsberg, 1932. 218 pp.
"Public Opinion, Press, and State: A Contribution to the Sociology of the Newspaper."

SCARBOROUGH, HAROLD E. "The British Press," *Foreign Affairs,* 12: 508–19 (April, 1934).

SCHOEN, CURT. *Der Vorwärts und die Kriegserklärung. Vom Fürstenmord in Serajewo bis zur Marneschlacht, 1914.* Berlin: H. W. Hendriock, 1929. 124 pp.

SCHOENFELD, AMRAM. "The Laugh Industry," *Saturday Evening Post*, 202: 12–13 (February 1, 1930).
The making and syndication of comic strips.

SCHÖTTLE, HERMANN. *Die "Times" in der ersten Marokkokrise, mit besonderer Berücksichtigung der englisch-deutschen Beziehungen* (Historische Studien, no. 196). Berlin: Ebering, 1930. 239 pp.

SCHWEDLER, W. *Die Nachricht im Weltverkehr.* Berlin: Deutsche Verlagsgesellschaft für Politik und Geschichte, 1922. 133 pp.
An account of the international news apparatus, with an appeal for a higher type of service free from propaganda.

SCOTT, JONATHAN FRENCH. *Five Weeks: The Surge of Public Opinion on the Eve of the Great War.* New York: John Day, 1927. 305 pp.
Analysis of newspapers in a crisis. Bibliography, pp. 281–98.

―――――. "Review Article: The Press and Foreign Policy," *Journal of Modern History*, 3: 627–38 (December, 1931).

SCOTT-JAMES, ROLFE ARNOLD. *The Influence of the Press.* London: S. W. Partridge, 1913. 320 pp.
One of the best known books on the subject. The subject is treated historically.

"Sell the Papers! The Malady of American Journalism," *Harper's*, 151: 1–9 (June, 1925).

SHAABER, MATTHIAS ADAM. *Some Forerunners of the Newspaper in England, 1476–1622* (Ph.D. thesis, University of Pennsylvania). Philadelphia: University of Pennsylvania, 1929. London: Oxford University, 1929. 368 pp.
Bibliography, pp. 329–33.

SIEBERT, FREDRICK S. "Contemporary Regulations of the British Press," *Journalism Quarterly*, 8: 235–56 (June, 1931).

―――――. "International Protection of Rights in News," *Journalism Quarterly*, 9: 290–303 (September, 1932).

SINCLAIR, UPTON. *The Brass Check: A Study of American Journalism.* Pasadena: The Author, 1919. 445 pp.
Highly controversial "exposé" of the press.

―――――. *Money Writes.* New York: Boni, 1927. 227 pp.

SMITH, CARROLL E. "A Century of Journalism, 1784–1884," *Editor and Publisher*, 67: 68, 272, 274, 276 (July 21, 1934).

SPENCER, MATHEW LYLE. *Editorial Writing*. Boston: Houghton Mifflin, 1924. 364 pp.

SPENDER, J. A. "The Press and International Affairs," *Yale Review*, 17: 485–98 (April, 1928).

STEFFENS, LINCOLN. "How I Made a Crime Wave," *Bookman*, 68: 416–19 (December, 1928).

STEINER, JESSE FREDERICK. "The Rural Press," *American Journal of Sociology*, 33: 412–23 (November, 1927).

STERN, J. DAVID. "The Renaissance of the Editorial Page," *Literary Digest*, 116: 9 (August 26, 1933).
The effect of the depression on the editorial page.

STONE, MELVILLE ELIJAH. "The Associated Press," *Century Magazine*, N. S., 47: 299–310; N. S., 48: 143–51, 299–310 (1905).
By the general manager of this press association.

————. *Fifty Years a Journalist*. Garden City: Doubleday, Page, 1921.
Includes an account of the building up of the foreign contacts of the Associated Press.

STUTTERHEIM, KURT VON. *Die englische Presse von ihren Anfängen bis zur Gegenwart (Zeitung und Zeit*, vol. 6). Berlin: Duncker, 1933. 139 pp.

SURY D'ASPREMONT, PAUL DE. *La Presse à travers les âges: France, Allemagne, Angleterre, États-Unis*. Paris and Bruges: Desclée, de Brouwer, et Cie., 1929. 268 pp.

TAEUBER, IRENE BARNES. "Changes in the Content and Presentation of Reading Material in Minnesota Weekly Newspapers, 1860–1929," *Journalism Quarterly*, 9: 281–89 (September, 1932).

THAYER, FRANK. *Newspaper Management*. New York and London: Appleton, 1926. 481 pp.
Business management of the newspaper.

THOMAS, CHARLES M. "The Publication of Newspapers during the American Revolution," *Journalism Quarterly*, 9: 358–73 (December, 1932).

THOMAS, ISAIAH. *The History of Printing in America*. Worcester: Isaiah Thomas, 1810. (Later edition, Albany: American Antiquarian Society, 1874, 2 vols.)
Later historians made use of this source. Contains biographies of printers and histories of leading newspapers and magazines.

THOMPSON, W. A. *National Advertising and the Newspaper*. New York: Association Business Papers, Inc., 1921.

THORPE, MERLE H., editor. *The Coming Newspaper*. New York: Holt, 1915. 323 pp.
A collection of speeches and articles devoted to discussion of editorial methods and newspaper influence.

TRAUB, HANS KARL THEODOR. *Grundbegriffe des Zeitungswesens: Kritische Einführung in die Methode der Zeitungswissenschaft*. Stuttgart: Poeschel, 1933. 184 pp.
Bibliographic footnotes.

———. *Zeitungswesen und Zeitungsleser*. Dessau, 1928.

TREUE, W. "Presse und Politik in Deutschland während des Burenkrieges," *Berliner Monatshefte*, August, 1933.
Press and politics in Germany during the Boer War.

TUNIS, JOHN ROBERT. *Sports: Heroics and Hysterics*. New York: John Day, 1928. 293 pp.
Study of sports reporting.

TURNBULL, GEORGE. "Early Oregon Newspaper History," *Frontier and Midland* (May, 1931).

UNIVERSITY OF MISSOURI SCHOOL OF JOURNALISM. Bulletin series on journalism subjects from 1912 to 1930.

VAN DOREN, CARL. "Day In and Day Out," *Century*, 107: 308 (December, 1923).
On columnists and columns.

VILLARD, OSWALD GARRISON. "Are the Tabloids a Menace? " *Forum*, 77: 485–501 (April, 1927).

———. *The Press of Today*. New York: The Nation, 1930. 96 pp.
The press is weighed on the value-scale of a distinguished liberal.

———. "Sex, Art, Truth and Magazines," *Atlantic*, 137: 388–98 (March, 1926).

———. "Two Kinds of Journalism," *Saturday Review of Literature*, 1: 393–94 (December 20, 1924).

———. "The Waning Power of the Press," *Forum*, 86: 141–45 (September, 1931).

WALCH, ERICH. "Die innere Technik der Sowjetpresse," *Zeitungswissenschaft*, 6: 455–58 (1931).
Technique of influencing the masses by means of " stylistic principles inherent in the Soviet system."

WALKER, STANLEY. *City Editor*. New York: Stokes, 1934. 336 pp.
By the former city editor of the New York *Herald-Tribune*, now on the New York *Mirror*.

WANG, Y. P. *The Rise of the Native Press in China.* New York: Columbia University, 1924. 50 pp.

"There are now over 1,000 dailies, weeklies, and monthlies published in China. . . . Almost every class of people has its own organ. For example, there is a paper for beggars in Canton, another for the sing-song girls of the same city, and among the latest in the field the *Chinese Druggist,* a monthly of Shanghai, and the *Labour Weekly* of Canton."

The War from This Side: Editorials from the Philadelphia North American. Philadelphia: Lippincott, 1915. 410 pp.

WARREN, CARL N. *News Reporting: A Practice Book.* New York: Harpers, 1929. 263 pp.

A textbook.

WEITENKAMPF, FRANK. "The Inwardness of the Comic Strip," *Bookman,* 61: 574-77 (July, 1925).

WHEELHOUSE, MARY E. At Minnesota Historical Society, St. Paul. Is preparing a study of James M. Goodhue, founder and editor of the *Minnesota Pioneer,* 1849-52, and compiling a representative selection of his editorials, including many addressed to prospective immigrants.

WHITE, WILLIAM ALLEN. "Good Newspapers and Bad," *Atlantic,* 153: 581-86 (May, 1934).

The commercialized newspaper versus the public service newspaper.

WICKWAR, WILLIAM HARDY. *The Struggle for the Freedom of the Press, 1819-1832.* London: Allen and Unwin, 1928. 325 pp.

Bibliography, pp. 316-22.

WIESE, LEOPOLD VON, editor. *Verhandlungen des siebenten deutschen Soziologentages.* Tübingen: Mohr, 1922. 293 pp.

Proceedings of the Seventh German Sociological Conference. A session was devoted to "The Press and Public Opinion."

WILDES, HARRY EMERSON. *Social Currents in Japan, with Special Reference to the Press* (Ph. D. thesis, University of Pennsylvania, 1927). Chicago: University of Chicago, 1927. 390 pp.

Analysis of press tendencies, the censorship, and international news agencies. Bibliography, pp. 363-71.

WILKERSON, MARCUS M. "The Press and the Spanish-American War," *Journalism Quarterly,* 9: 129-48 (June, 1932).

WILLEY, MALCOLM MACDONALD. *The Country Newspaper: A Study of Socialization and Newspaper Content* (Ph. D. thesis, Columbia University, 1926). Chapel Hill: University of North Carolina, 1926. London: Oxford University, 1926. 153 pp.

The thirty-five country newspapers of Connecticut were selected for this study. Bibliography, pp. 129-33.

————. "The Influence of Cultural Change upon Newspaper Style," *Sociology and Social Research,* vol. 13, no. 1 (September, 1928).

WILLEY, MALCOLM, and WEINFELD, WILLIAM. "The Country Weekly and the Emergence of 'One-Newspaper Places,'" *Journalism Quarterly,* 11:246–57 (September, 1934).

————. "The Country Weekly: Trends in Numbers and Distribution, 1900–1930," *Social Forces,* 13:51–56 (October, 1934).

WILLIAMS, J. B. *History of English Journalism to the Foundation of the Gazette.* New York: Longmans, Green, 1908. 293 pp.

WILLIAMS, J. EMLYN. "Journalism in Germany, 1933," *Journalism Quarterly,* 10:283–88 (December, 1933).

WILLIAMS, WALTER. *A New Journalism in a New Far East* (University of Missouri Bulletin, vol. 29, no. 45). Columbia, Missouri, 1928. 19 pp.

————. "The Press and the Bar," *Journalism Quarterly,* 7:320–27 (December, 1930).

WILLIAMS, WALTER, editor. *The Press Congress of the World in Hawaii, 1922. The Press Congress of the World in Switzerland, 1928.* Columbia, Missouri: E. W. Stephens Publishing Company.

Two volumes of proceedings illustrating comparative journalism.

WILMER, LAMBERT A. *Our Press Gang.* Philadelphia: T. B. Peterson, 1859. 395 pp.

A severe arraignment of the press.

WILSON, JAMES HARRISON. *The Life of Charles A. Dana.* New York: Harpers, 1907. 544 pp.

WISEHART, M. K. "The Ten Great News Stories of 1930," *American Magazine,* 111:46–51 (January, 1931).

WUTTKE, H. *Die deutschen Zeitschriften und die Entstehung der öffentlichen Meinung.* Third edition. Leipzig, 1875.

YOST, CASPER SALATHIEL. *The Principles of Journalism.* New York and London: Appleton, 1924. 170 pp.

Useful to the layman who wishes to understand the newspaper man's point of view. Written by the editorial editor of the St. Louis *Globe-Democrat.*

ZIMMERMANN, WALTER. *Die englische Presse zum Ausbruch des Weltkrieges.* Charlottenburg: Hochschule und Ausland, 1928. 269 pp.

B. NEWSPAPER PERSONNEL

ABBOT, WILLIS J. *Watching the World Go By.* Boston: Little, Brown, 1934. 358 pp.

By a former editor of the *Christian Science Monitor.*

ALLEN, ERIC W. "Medical Schools, Law Schools and Schools of Journalism," *Journalism Quarterly*, 8: 196–211 (March, 1931).

ATKINS, JOHN BLACK. *The Life of William Howard Russell*. London: John Murray, 1911. 806 pp. 2 vols.
Life of a great foreign correspondent of the London *Times*.

BARRETT, JAMES W. *The World, the Flesh and Messrs. Pulitzer*. New York: Vanguard, 1931. 117 pp.

BLEYER, WILLARD GROSVENOR. "What Schools of Journalism Are Trying to Do," *Journalism Quarterly*, 8: 35–44 (March, 1931).

BLYTHE, SAMUEL G. *The Making of a Newspaper Man*. Philadelphia: Henry Altemus, 1912. 239 pp.
A reporter's experiences.

BOETTIGER, JOHN. *Jake Lingle; or Chicago on the Spot*. New York: Dutton, 1931. 235 pp.

BLUMENFELD, R. D. *The Press in My Time*. London: Rich and Cowan, 1933. 253 pp.
By the former editor of the London *Daily Express*.

BRAZELTON, ETHEL M. COLSON. *Writing and Editing for Women*. New York: Funk and Wagnalls, 1927. 258 pp.

BOND, F. FRASER. *Mr. Miller of the Times*. London and New York: Scribners, 1931. 264 pp.
The life story of the man who for more than forty years was at the editorial helm of the New York *Times*.

BULLARD, FREDERICK LAURISTON. *Famous War Correspondents*. Boston: Little, Brown, 1914. 437 pp.

CASEY, RALPH D. "Journalism, Technical Training and the Social Sciences," *Journalism Quarterly*, 9: 31–45 (March, 1932).

CHAPIN, CHARLES E. *Charles Chapin's Story*. New York and London: Putnam, 1920. 334 pp.
A newspaperman's autobiography.

CLARKE, TOM. *MY Northcliffe Diary*. New York: Cosmopolitan Book Corporation, 1931. 301 pp.

CLIFT, ROMA D. "Some of the Criteria of Journalistic Ability" (unpublished M. A. thesis, University of Chicago, 1929).

COCHRAN, NEGLEY D. *E. W. Scripps*. New York: Harcourt, Brace, 1933. 315 pp.
Contains Scripps's memoranda on newspaper-making, and directions to his staff.

Conditions of Life and Work of Journalists (International Labour Office, Studies and Reports, Series L, no. 2). Geneva, 1928.

A painstaking analysis of working conditions in various countries. A study of trade union organizations of journalists, and associations of mutual welfare.

CONGDON, CHARLES T. *Reminiscences of a Journalist.* Boston: James R. Osgood, 1880. 393 pp.

An older journalistic autobiography by a New York *Tribune* man.

CORTISSOZ, ROYAL. *The Life of Whitelaw Reid.* New York: Scribners, 1921. 2 vols.

Official biography of a famous *Tribune* editor.

CRANFIELD, W. T., editor. *Journalism as a Career: Plain Counsels by Leading Journalists on the Qualifications and Training Needed, the Duties and Conditions of Work, and the Monetary and Other Rewards That May Be Expected.* London and New York: Sir I. Pitman, 1930. 100 pp.

Discusses *types* of journalists: the editor, the special correspondent, the foreign correspondent, the parliamentary correspondent, the technical writer, etc.

CREELMAN, JAMES. *On the Great Highway.* Boston: Lothrop, Lee and Shepard, 1907. 418 pp.

By the roving European correspondent of the New York *Herald* and New York *Journal* correspondent.

DARK, SIDNEY. *The Life of Sir Arthur Pearson.* London: Hodder and Stoughton, 1922. 228 pp.

Biography of the founder of *Pearson's Weekly* and the London *Daily Express.*

DASENT, ARTHUR I. *John Thadeus Delane, Editor of the Times.* New York: Scribners, 1908. 2 vols.

Standard life of the editor of the London *Times.*

DAVIS, RICHARD HARDING. *The Notes of a War Correspondent.* New York: Scribners, 1911. 263 pp.

DEBLOWITZ, HENRI STEPHAN. *My Memoirs.* London: Edward Arnold, 1903. 358 pp.

Life of the Paris correspondent of the London *Times.*

DENNIS, CHARLES H. *Eugene Field's Creative Years.* Garden City: Doubleday, Page, 1924. 332 pp.

Life of a newspaper columnist and poet.

———. "Lawson and Stone Hailed as Pioneers," *Editor and Publisher,* 67: 52, 295 (July 21, 1934).

Careers of noted journalists.

Dosch-Fleurot, Arno. *Through War to Revolution.* London: John Lane, 1931. 242 pp.
Experiences of an American newspaper correspondent.

Dovifat, Emil. "Education for Journalism in Germany and the Deutsche Institut für Zeitungskunde," *Journalism Quarterly,* 7: 232–35 (September, 1930).
Draws striking contrasts between the training of a prospective journalist in Germany and his training in the United States. Describes the elaborate researches of the Institut für Zeitungskunde.

Downey, Fairfax. *Richard Harding Davis: His Day.* New York and London: Scribners, 1933. 321 pp.

Dreiser, Theodore. *A Book about Myself.* New York: Boni and Liveright, 1922. 502 pp.
Dreiser's newspaper experiences.

Drewry, John E. "The Journalist's Inferiority Complex," *Journalism Quarterly,* 8: 12–23 (March, 1931).

Elton, Oliver. *C. E. Montague.* Garden City: Doubleday, Doran, 1929. 319 pp.
Memoir of a *Manchester Guardian* leader writer and man of letters.

Escott, Thomas Hay Sweet. *Masters of English Journalism: A Study of Personal Forces.* London: Unwin, 1911. 368 pp.

Faÿ, Bernard. *Franklin, the Apostle of Modern Times.* Boston: Little, Brown, 1929. 547 pp.

―――. *The Two Franklins: Fathers of American Democracy.* Boston: Little, Brown, 1933. 397 pp.
Benjamin Franklin and Benjamin Franklin Bache.

Fine, Barnett. "First Journalism Schools Scorned," *Editor and Publisher,* 67: 160, 200 (July 21, 1934).
The development of education for journalism in the United States.

―――. *A Giant of the Press.* New York: Editor and Publisher, 1933. 108 pp.
Biography of Carr Van Anda, managing editor of the New York *Times,* 1904–32.

Forrest, Wilbur. *Behind the Front Page.* New York: Appleton-Century, 1934. 350 pp.
War and foreign correspondence by a former United Press and later a New York *Tribune* reporter.

Fowler, Gene. *Timber Line.* New York: Covici, Friede, 1933. 480 pp.
The Denver *Post* and its former proprietors, Bonfils and Tammen.

FRANKLIN, BENJAMIN. *The Autobiography of Benjamin Franklin*. New York: Harcourt, Brace, 1926. 218 pp.
There are many editions of this autobiography.

FYFE, HAMILTON. *Northcliffe, an Intimate Biography*. New York: Macmillan, 1930. 349 pp.

GARDNER, GILSON. *Lusty Scripps*. New York: Vanguard, 1932. 274 pp.
A biography of the founder of the Scripps chain, informal in tone.

GAVIT, JOHN PALMER. " The Career of an Ideal Journalist," *American Press*, 52: 7 (February, 1934).

GIBBS, SIR PHILIP. *Adventures in Journalism*. New York: Harpers, 1923. 363 pp.
Journalistic reminiscence.

GODWIN, PARKE. *A Biography of William Cullen Bryant*. New York: Appleton, 1883. 854 pp. 2 vols.
The official biography by Bryant's son-in-law and successor on the New York *Evening Post*.

GRATTAN, C. HARTLEY. *Bitter Bierce*. Garden City: Doubleday, Doran, 1929. 291 pp.
Life of a newspaper columnist and essayist.

GREELEY, HORACE. *Recollections of a Busy Life*. New York: J. B. Ford, 1868. 624 pp.
This autobiography is standard, but should be supplemented by Don Seitz's biography.

HAMMOND, J. L. *C. P. Scott of the Manchester Guardian*. New York: Harcourt, Brace, 1934. 365 pp.

HAPGOOD, NORMAN. *The Changing Years*. New York: Farrar and Rinehart, 1930. 321 pp.
By a former editor of *Collier's, Harper's Weekly,* and *Hearst's International Magazine*.

HARRIS, JOEL CHANDLER, editor. *Life of Henry W. Grady, Including His Writings and Speeches*. New York: Cassell, 1890. 628 pp.
A memorial volume by Grady's associates on the Atlanta *Constitution*.

HARRIS, JULIA COLLIER, editor. *Joel Chandler Harris*, Chapel Hill, North Carolina: University of North Carolina, 1931. 429 pp.
Life of an editor, essayist, and literary man.

HOWE, EDGAR WATSON. *Plain People*. New York: Dodd, Mead, 1929. 317 pp.
Autobiography of the former editor and proprietor of the Atchison (Kansas) *Daily Globe*.

HUTCHEON, W. *Gentlemen of the Press: Memoirs and Friendships of Forty Years*. London: John Murray, 1933. 239 pp.

IRELAND, ALLEYNE. *Joseph Pulitzer: Reminiscences of a Secretary*. New York: Mitchell Kennerley, 1914. 236 pp.

JAMES, LIONEL. *Times of Stress*. London: John Murray, 1929. 320 pp.
By a former correspondent of the London *Times*.

KANSAS CITY *Star* STAFF. *William Rockhill Nelson*. Cambridge: Riverside Press, 1915.
Life of the former publisher of the Kansas City *Star*.

LEE, ALFRED McCLUNG. "Dunlap and Claypool: Printers and News-Merchants of the Revolution," *Journalism Quarterly*, 11: 161–178 (June, 1934).

LEE, JAMES MELVIN. *Opportunities in the Newspaper Business*. New York and London: Harpers, 1919. 100 pp.

LORD, CHESTER. *The Young Man and Journalism*. New York: Macmillan, 1926. 221 pp.

McCLURE, SAMUEL S. *My Autobiography*. New York: Stokes, 1914.
Recollections of the founder of *McClure's Magazine* and of the McClure newspaper syndicate.

McRAE, MILTON A. *Forty Years in Newspaperdom: The Autobiography of a Newspaper Man*. New York: Brentano, 1924. 496 pp.
Autobiography of one of the founders of the Scripps-McRae League.

MARCOSSON, ISAAC FREDERICK. *Adventures in Interviewing*. New York: John Lane, 1920. 314 pp.
A skillful interviewer at work in many parts of the world.

―――. *David Graham Phillips and His Times*. New York: Dodd, Mead, 1932. 308 pp.
Life of a former New York *Sun* reporter.

MAVERICK, AUGUSTUS. *Henry J. Raymond and the New York Press for Thirty Years: Progress of American Journalism from 1840 to 1870*. Hartford: A. S. Hale, 1870. 501 pp.

MERRIAM, GEORGE SPRING. *The Life and Times of Samuel Bowles*. New York: Century, 1931. 2 vols. 938 pp.

MILLIS, WALTER. "Hearst," *Atlantic*, 148: 696–709 (December, 1931).

MITCHELL, EDWARD PAGE. *Memoirs of an Editor*. New York: Scribners, 1924. 458 pp.
Commentary on New York journalism, especially the *Sun*.

MURPHY, LAWRENCE W. "Professional and Non-Professional Teaching of Journalism," *Journalism Quarterly*, 9: 46–59 (March, 1932).

OGDEN, ROLLO, editor. *Life and Letters of Edwin Lawrence Godkin.* New York: Macmillan, 1907. 2 vols.
Official biography of the founder of *The Nation* and one-time editor of the New York *Evening Post.*

OLDER, FREMONT. *My Own Story.* New edition. New York: Macmillan, 1926. 340 pp.
By the former crusading editor of the San Francisco *Bulletin;* now editor of the *Call-Bulletin.*

OSWALD, JOHN CLYDE. *Benjamin Franklin Printer.* Garden City: Doubleday, Doran, 1917. 244 pp.

PEFFER, NATHANIEL. "The Newspaper Correspondent in China," in Lewis Hodous, editor, *Careers for Students of Chinese Language and Civilization,* pp. 23–27. Chicago: Published by the University of Chicago Press for the American Council of the Institute of Pacific Relations, 1933.
"Under existing conditions, no special qualification is demanded of a newspaper correspondent in China except that he be a good newspaperman."

PEMBERTON, MAX. *Lord Northcliffe: A Memoir.* London: Hodder and Stoughton, 1922. 250 pp.

PERRY, JOHN W. "Fanny Fern: Mother of Sob Sisters," *Editor and Publisher,* 67: 98, 110 (July 21, 1934).

POSTGATE, R. W. *That Devil Wilkes.* New York: Vanguard, 1929. 275 pp.

RAMSAYE, TERRY. "The Saga of James Keeley," *Editor and Publisher,* 67: 128, 190 (July 21, 1934).
Biography of former managing editor of Chicago *Tribune.*

ROGERS, CHARLES ELKINS. *Journalistic Vocations.* New York and London: Appleton, 1931. 354 pp.
Information for those who wish to enter vocational fields connected with journalism. Bibliography, pp. 327–34.

ROSEBAULT, CHARLES J. *When Dana Was the Sun: A Story of Personal Journalism.* New York: R. M. McBride, 1931. 294 pp.

ROSS, VIRGILIA PETERSON. "Master Thinker," *Outlook and Independent,* 155: 603–06 (August 20, 1930).
Brisbane's career and his viewpoint on important questions.

SEITZ, DON CARLOS. *Horace Greeley, Founder of the New York Tribune.* Indianapolis: Bobbs-Merrill, 1926. 433 pp.

———. *The James Gordon Bennetts.* Indianapolis: Bobbs-Merrill, 1928. 405 pp.

————. *Joseph Pulitzer: His Life and Letters*. New York: Simon and Schuster, 1924. 478 pp.

————. *Training for the Newspaper Trade*. Philadelphia: Lippincott, 1916. 163 pp.

SHAABER, MATTHIAS A. "Coleridge as a Journalist," *Journalism Quarterly*, 7:236–50 (September, 1930).

SMITH, HENRY JUSTIN. "Chicago Boys Have Gone Far and High," *Editor and Publisher*, 67:58, 286 (July 21, 1934).
Brief sketches of well-known writers and editors.

SPENDER, JOHN ALFRED. *Life, Journalism and Politics*. New York: Stokes, 1927. 2 vols. 475 pp.
By a distinguished English journalist.

STEED, HENRY WICKHAM. *Through Thirty Years*. New York: Doubleday, Page, 1924. 2 vols.
Reminiscences of an active life spent in Paris, Berlin, London, Rome, and Vienna in the service of the London *Times*.

STEFFENS, LINCOLN. *The Autobiography of Lincoln Steffens*. New York: Harcourt, Brace, 1931. 2 vols.
The life story of a journalist who covered many of the " big " stories of his time; also an account of his private life.

STEWART, GEORGE R. *Bret Harte, Argonaut and Exile*. Boston: Houghton Mifflin, 1931. 385 pp.
Early chapters deal with Harte's journalistic career.

STONE, MELVILLE ELIJAH. *Fifty Years a Journalist*. Garden City: Doubleday, Page, 1921. 371 pp.
Mr. Stone was for twenty-eight years general manager of the Associated Press.

TRENT, WILLIAM P. *Defoe, How to Know Him*. Indianapolis: Bobbs-Merrill, 1916. 329 pp.

TUCKERMAN, GUSTAVUS, JR. *Duranty Reports Russia*, New York: Viking, 1934. 401 pp.
The twelve-year record of the reporting of affairs in the U. S. S. R. by the correspondent of the New York *Times*.

ULRICH, CHARLES KENMORE. "Romance at the Golden Gate in 1884," *Editor and Publisher*, 67:100, 126 (July 21, 1934).
Careers of San Francisco reporters and editors.

VILLARD, OSWALD GARRISON. *Some Newspapers and Newspapermen*. Revised edition. New York: Knopf, 1926. 335 pp.

WATTERSON, HENRY. *Marse Henry: An Autobiography*. New York: Doran, 1919. 2 vols.

Autobiography of the former publisher of the Louisville *Courier-Journal*.

WEED, HARRIET A., editor. *Autobiography of Thurlow Weed*. Boston: Houghton Mifflin, 1883.

A second volume, titled *A Memoir of Thurlow Weed,* by his grandson, Thurlow Weed Barnes, fills out the record. The two volumes are given the cover title *The Life of Thurlow Weed*.

WEST, GEORGE P. "Hearst, a Psychological Note," *American Mercury,* 21: 298–308 (November, 1930).

WHYTE, FREDERIC. *Life and Letters of W. T. Stead*. Boston: Houghton Mifflin, 1925; London: Jonathan Cape. 1925. 713 pp. 2 vols.

WILL, ALLEN SINCLAIR. *Education for Newspaper Life*. Newark, N. J.: Essex Press, 1931. 314 pp.

WILLIAMS, TALCOTT. *The Newspaperman*. New York: Scribners, 1922. 209 pp.

WILLIAMS, WALTER. *Organization of Journalists in Great Britain* (University of Missouri Bulletin, vol. 30, no. 47). Columbia, Missouri, 1929. 39 pp.

WINKLER, JOHN KENNEDY. *William Randolph Hearst: An American Phenomenon*. New York: Simon and Schuster, 1928. 354 pp.

List of publications owned by Mr. Hearst, p. 319.

2. THE EDUCATIONAL SYSTEM

"Agricultural Education," *Encyclopedia of the Social Sciences*. (By A. R. Mann.)

AMERICAN HISTORICAL ASSOCIATION, COMMISSION ON THE SOCIAL STUDIES. *Investigation of the Social Studies in the Schools*.

This series contains volumes by William C. Bagley, Charles A. Beard, Howard K. Beale, Isaiah Bowman, George S. Counts, Merle E. Curti, Ernest Horn, Henry Johnson, Truman L. Kelley, A. C. Krey, Leon C. Marshall, Charles E. Merriam, Jesse H. Newlon, Bessie Louise Pierce, and others.

ANDREWS, FANNIE FERN. "The Teacher as an Agent of International Good Will," *School and Society,* 26: 121–30 (July 30, 1927).

ARCHDEACON, JOHN PHILIP. *The Week-Day Religious School* (Ph.D. thesis, Catholic University of America, 1927). Washington, D.C.: Catholic University of America, 1927. 90 pp.

Bibliography, pp. 85–89.

BEALE, HOWARD KENNEDY. *Freedom of Teaching in the Schools* (Report of the Commission on the Social Studies, American Historical Association). Announced.

BEGTRUP, HOLGER, LUND, HANS, and MANNICHE, PETER. *The Folk High Schools of Denmark and the Development of a Farming Community.* New edition. London: Oxford University, 1929. Copenhagen: A. Busck, 1929. 176 pp.

BÖRNEMANN, R. *Die französische Schulpropaganda das Haupthindernis der Völkerversöhnung.* Berlin, 1924.
"French school propaganda the principal impediment to international reconciliation."

BROCK, HENRY IRVING. "Six Books That Helped Mold the Nation," *New York Times Magazine,* February 25, 1934.
McGuffey's readers; famous texts for the elementary grades.

BUTTERWORTH, JULIAN EDWARD. *The Parent-Teacher Association and Its Work.* New York: Macmillan, 1928. 149 pp.
Bibliography, pp. 137–41.

CARR, WILLIAM G. "The School Child and Propaganda," Proceedings of the National Conference of Social Work, 1931, pp. 597–605.
Discusses the task of the schoolmaster in determining which civic and special groups may properly make their appeals to pupils in the schools.

"Co-education," *Encyclopedia of the Social Sciences.* (By Willystine Goodsell.)

"Correspondence Schools," *Encyclopedia of the Social Sciences.* (By Herbert Solow.)

COUNTS, GEORGE SYLVESTER. *The Social Composition of Boards of Education: A Study in the Social Control of Public Education.* Chicago: University of Chicago, 1927. 100 pp.

D'IRSAY, STEPHEN. *Histoire des universités françaises et étrangères depuis les origines jusqu'à nos jours.* Paris: Picard, 1933. 2 vols.

FLEXNER, ABRAHAM. *Universities, American, English, German.* New York: Oxford University, 1930. 381 pp.

"Folk High Schools," *Encyclopedia of the Social Sciences.* (By Joseph K. Hart.)

HART, ALBERT BUSHNELL. "School Books and International Prejudices," *International Conciliation,* January, 1911, no. 38.

HARTSHORNE, HUGH, and EHRHART, EARLE V. *Church Schools of To-day.* New Haven: Published by the Yale University Press for the Institute of Social and Religious Research, 1933. London: Oxford, 1933. 260 pp.

HEARNSHAW, F. J. C. "History as a Means of Propaganda," *Fortnightly Review,* August, 1923.

HOLT, W. STULL. *The Federal Board for Vocational Education: Its History, Activities, and Organization.* Baltimore: Johns Hopkins University, 1922. 74 pp.

"Industrial Education," *Encyclopedia of the Social Sciences.* (By H. S. Person.)

"Industrial education is the systematic and institutionalized effort of society to promote by educational methods the adaptation of its members to the changing conditions of livelihood activity."

JEZOWA, K. *Politische Propaganda in der deutschen Geographie.* Danzig, 1933(?). 80 pp.

JOHNSON, HENRY. *An Introduction to the History of the Social Sciences in Schools* (Report of the Commission on the Social Studies, American Historical Association, Part 2). New York: Scribners, 1932.

LITTLE, A. G. "Educational Organization of the Mendicant Friars in England," Transactions of the Royal Historical Society, N. S., 8: 49–70 (1894).

MERRIAM, CHARLES EDWARD, editor. *Studies in the Making of Citizens.* Chicago: University of Chicago, 1929–33. 9 vols.

World-wide study of methods of civic training. *France: A Nation of Patriots,* by Carlton J. H. Hayes (New York: Columbia University, 1930) is also a part of this series.

MILLER, CHARLES G. *The Poisoned Loving Cup: United States School Histories Falsified through Pro-British Propaganda in the Sweet Name of Amity.* Chicago: National Historical Society, 1928. 208 pp.

MÖHRING, N. "Die Lehrerbildung in Österreich, der Schweiz, und der russischen Sowjet-Republik," *Zeitschrift für den gesamten Schulwesen,* 1:603–19.

NATIONAL EDUCATION ASSOCIATION OF THE UNITED STATES, COMMITTEE ON PROPAGANDA. "Report of the Committee on Propaganda: Abstract," in Addresses and Proceedings of the National Education Association, 1929, pp. 204–17.

NATIONAL SOCIETY FOR THE STUDY OF EDUCATION. *Twenty-fifth Yearbook,* Part II, "Extra-Curricular Activities." Bloomington, Illinois: Public School Publishing Company, 1926.

An "assembly of materials descriptive of current practices and opinion" relative to extra-curricular activities, prepared by a committee with Leonard V. Koos as chairman.

NEWLON, JESSE H. *School Administration and Educational Leadership*

(Report of the Commission on the Social Studies, American Historical Association. New York: Scribners. Announced.

ORVIS, M. B. *The Application of Commercial Advertising Methods to University Extension* (United States Bureau of Education Bulletin no. 51). Washington, D. C., 1919.

PIERCE, BESSIE LOUISE. *Public Opinion and the Teaching of History in the United States* (Ph. D. thesis, University of Iowa, 1923). New York: Knopf, 1926. 380 pp.
See also Dr. Pierce's other writings on public opinion and civic training. Bibliography, pp. 337–54.

PRESCOTT, DANIEL ALFRED. *Education and International Relations.* Cambridge, Massachusetts: Harvard University, 1930. 177 pp.

REISNER, EDWARD HARTMAN. *The Evolution of the Common School.* New York: Macmillan, 1930. 590 pp.

ROBERTSON, D. A. "International Educational Relations of the United States, with a List of Organizations Interested," *Educational Record,* 6: 91–150 (April, 1925).

ROGER, I. E. "School System as a Publicity Agent," *Popular Education,* 42: 308–09 (February, 1925).

RÜHLMANN, P. "Seelische Abrüstung; ein Beitrag zu dem Kapitel: Politik durch das Schulbuch," *Preussische Jahrbücher,* 211: 203–15 (February, 1928).
"Mental and moral disarmament" may be furthered by textbooks.

RUSSELL, BERTRAND. *On Education, Especially in Early Childhood.* London: Allen and Unwin, 1926. 254 pp.

RUSSELL, H. L. "Agricultural Education in the Orient and Australia," Proceedings of the 40th Annual Convention of the Association of Land Grant Colleges, pp. 108–24. Washington, D. C., 1926.

SINCLAIR, UPTON. *The Goose Step: A Study of American Education.* Pasadena: The Author, 1924. 488 pp.

SMITH, DARRELL HEVENOR. *The Bureau of Education: Its History, Activities, and Organization.* Baltimore: Johns Hopkins University, 1923. 157 pp.

SYMONS, FARRELL. *Courses on International Affairs in American Colleges, 1930–1931.* Boston: World Peace Foundation, 1931. 353 pp.
Contains also a list indicating the status of international documentation in various libraries.

"The Textbook in American Education," 30th Yearbook of the National Society for the Study of Education, pt. 2. Bloomington, Illinois: Public School Publishing Company, 1931. 364 pp.

THORNDIKE, EDWARD LEE. *The Psychology of Arithmetic*. New York: Macmillan, 1922. 314 pp.

Shall the examples used in arithmetic books propagandize the business man by playing upon "profit and loss, rate of discount, compound interest, and bond yields?" Or shall they involve digging cellars, papering walls, and shoveling coal?

TRUE, A. C. *A History of Agricultural Education in the United States* (United States Department of Agriculture Miscellaneous Publications, no. 36). Washington, D. C.: Government Printing Office, 1929.

UENODA, S. "Examples of the Anti-Japanese Propaganda in Chinese Schools," *Trans-Pacific,* 19 : 4 (December 10, 1931).

VEBLEN, THORSTEIN B. *The Higher Learning in America*. New York: Huebsch, 1918. 286 pp.

"Where the alumni have a voice in the naming of a college president, the successful business men have the deciding voice."

WALLER, JAMES FLINT. *Outside Demands and Pressures on the Public Schools* (Teachers College Contributions to Education, no. 542). New York: Columbia University, 1932. 151 pp.

WARE, EDITH E. *International Relations in the United States: Survey for 1934*. New York: Published by Columbia University for the American National Committee on Intellectual Cooperation of the League of Nations, 1935. 503 pp.

Part 1 lists and describes agencies, foundations, organizations engaged in studies of international affairs. Part 2 analyzes the subject matter of such studies.

3. MOVING PICTURES AND THEATER

ALEXANDER FILM COMPANY, Colorado Springs, Colorado. *Motion Picture Advertising*. Colorado Springs, 1929. 36 pp.

Audience reaction.

————. *Nationwide Motion Picture Publicity for National Advertisers*. Colorado Springs, 1929.

Anbruch: Monatsschrift für moderne Musik.

Special issues devoted to the Russian theater: June–July, 1922; March, 1925; November–December, 1931.

BAB, JULIUS. *Das Theater im Lichte der Soziologie* (Zeitfragen aus dem Gebiete der Soziologie, 4th series, vol. 1). Leipzig: C. L. Hirschfeld, 1931. 227 pp.

BROWN, JOHN MASON. "Propagandist Theatres," *Theatre Arts Monthly,* 13 : 129–42 (1929).

CECIL-SMITH, E. "The Workers' Theatre in Canada," *Canadian Forum,* 14:68–70 (November, 1933).

CHENEY, SHELDON. *The Theatre: Three Thousand Years of Drama, Acting, and Stagecraft.* New York and London: Longmans, Green, 1929. 558 pp.
A standard historical treatise.

CROY, HOMER. *How Motion Pictures Are Made.* New York and London: Harpers, 1918. 365 pp.

DENCH, ERNEST ALFRED. *Advertising by Motion Pictures.* Cincinnati: Standard Publishing Company, 1916. 255 pp.

DEVEREUX, FREDERICK LEONARD, and others. *The Educational Talking Picture.* Chicago: University of Chicago, 1933. 222 pp.

DYSINGER, WENDELL STUART, and RUCKMICK, CHRISTIAN A. *Emotional Response of Children to the Motion-Picture Situation* (Ph. D. thesis, University of Iowa, 1933). New York: Macmillan, 1933. 122 pp.
A Payne Fund study.

FÜLÖP-MILLER, R., and GREGOR, JOSEF. *Das russische Theater.* Vienna: Amalthea-Verlag, 1927. 140 pp.
History of the Russian theater, with especial emphasis upon the period of the Revolution.

GIDONI, ALEXANDER. "Das russische Theater nach der Revolution," *Die Volksbühne,* 4:560–67 (1930).

HAMPTON, BENJAMIN BOWLES. *History of the Movies.* New York: Covici, Friede, 1931. 456 pp.

HÉRISSAY, JACQUES. *Le Monde des théâtres pendant la Révolution, 1789–1800.* Paris: Perrin, 1922. 444 pp.

HOLITSCHER, ARTUR. *Das Theater im revolutionären Russland.* Berlin: Volksbühnen-Verlag, n. d.
Brief introduction to the Soviet theater up to 1922.

HOLODAY, P. W., and STODDARD, G. D. *Getting Ideas from the Movies.*

JOHNSON, FREDERICK G. *The Press Agent's Handbook: How to Advertise a Play.* Chicago: T. S. Dennison, 1916. 68 pp.
For amateur entertainers.

KAISER, ERWIN. "Theater in der Sowjet-Union," *Die Weltbühne,* 28:240–43, 284–87 (1932).
The Russian theater in 1931.

Koon, Clive Morgan. *Motion Pictures in Education in the United States.* Chicago: University of Chicago, 1934. 114 pp.
Report compiled for international Congress of Educational and Instructional Cinematography held in Rome in 1934. Bibliography, pp. 83–89.

Lapierre, Marcel. *Le Cinéma et la paix.* Paris: Valois, 1932. 128 pp.

Lewis, Howard Thompson. *Cases on the Motion Picture Industry, with Commentaries* (Harvard Business Reports, vol. 8). New York and London: McGraw-Hill, 1930. 687 pp.

——. *The Motion Picture Industry.* New York: Van Nostrand, 1933. 454 pp.
Bibliography, pp. 435–37.

Lukács, Georg von. "Zur Soziologie des Modernen Dramas," *Archiv für Sozialwissenschaft und Sozialpolitik,* 38: 303–45, 662–706 (1914).

Marchand, René, and Weinstein, Pierre. *Le Cinéma.* Paris: Rieder, 1927. 176 pp.

Martin, H. "Moral and Religious Values of the Motion Picture," *Religious Education,* 22: 1008–14 (December, 1927).

Messel, Rudolph. "The Film in Russia," in *Twelve Studies in Soviet Russia,* edited for the New Fabian Research Bureau by Margaret I. Cole. London: Gollancz, 1933.

Motion Picture Almanac. Annual, 1929—.
Statistics and interpretation of trends in the motion picture industry.

Münsterberg, Hugo. *The Photoplay: A Psychological Study.* New York: Appleton, 1916. 232 pp.

Nicoll, Allardyce. *The Development of the Theatre: A Study of Theatrical Art from the Beginning to the Present Day.* London and New York: Harcourt, Brace, 1927. 246 pp.

Perry, Clarence Arthur. *The Work of the Little Theatres.* New York: Russell Sage Foundation, 1933. 228 pp.

Raiborn, R. A., and Davis, R. L. "Motion Pictures as an Aid to Business," series of articles in *Management and Administration,* March, April, May, June, 1923.

Ramsaye, Terry. *A Million and One Nights: A History of the Motion Picture.* New York: Simon and Schuster, 1926. 2 vols.

Rulon, Philip Justin. *The Sound Motion Picture in Science Teaching* (Harvard Studies in Education, vol. 20). Cambridge, Massachusetts: Harvard University, 1933. 236 pp.
Bibliography, pp. 109–10.

Seabury, William Marston. *Motion Picture Problems: The Cinema and the League of Nations.* New York: Avondale Press, 1929. 426 pp.

————. *The Public and the Motion Picture Industry.* New York: Macmillan, 1926. 340 pp.

SINCLAIR, UPTON. *Upton Sinclair Presents William Fox.* Los Angeles: The Author, 1933. 377 pp.
Biography of a leader of the cinema industry.

TAIROFF, ALEXANDER. *Das entfesselte Theater.* Potsdam: Kiepenheuer, 1927. 112 pp.
Theory of the modern Russian theater.

TRAUB, H. *Der Film als politisches Machtmittel..* Munich: Münchener Druck, 1933. 36 pp.

UNITED STATES BUREAU OF FOREIGN AND DOMESTIC COMMERCE. *The Motion Picture Industry in Continental Europe in 1931* (Trade Information Bulletin no. 797). Washington, D.C.: Government Printing Office, 1932.

————. *The Motion Picture Industry in Continental Europe in 1932* (Trade Information Bulletin no. 815). Washington, D.C.: Government Printing Office, 1933.

————. *The Motion Picture Industry in the United Kingdom in 1931* (Trade Information Bulletin no. 801). Washington, D.C.: Government Printing Office, 1932.

UNITED STATES DEPARTMENT OF COMMERCE. *British Film Showings and Trade* (Report no. 7, February 15, 1932). *The European Film Market* (Report no. 4, October 12, 1931). *Australian Imports and Censorship of Films* (Report no. 16, April 18, 1932). Washington, D.C.: Government Printing Office.
See also nos. 26 and 42.

UNITED STATES HOUSE OF REPRESENTATIVES, COMMITTEE ON INTERSTATE AND FOREIGN COMMERCE. *Hearings on H.R. 6097, to Provide for Inspecting, Classifying, and Cataloging Motion Pictures and ... to Create a Federal Motion Picture Commission* (73d Congress, 2d Session). Washington, D.C.: Government Printing Office, 1934. 76 pp.

4. RADIO, TELEPHONE, TELEGRAPH, CABLE, POSTAL SYSTEM, TELEVISION

A. BIBLIOGRAPHY

A Bibliography on Broadcasting. New York: Columbia Broadcasting System, 1934. 9 pp., mimeographed.

LINGEL, ROBERT. *Educational Broadcasting: A Bibliography.* Chicago: University of Chicago, 1932. 162 pp.

Radio Bibliography. New York: Printers' Ink, 1933.

B. REFERENCES

ALBERT, ARTHUR LEMUEL. *Electrical Communication.* New York: J. Wiley and Sons, 1934. London: Chapman and Hall, 1934. 448 pp. Bibliography at ends of chapters.

American Broadcasting. Ventura, California: Ventura Free Press, 1933. 15 pp.
An analytical study of one day's output of 206 commercial radio stations.

American Press. See this publication for continued development of newspaper and radio communication.

ARNOLD, FRANK ATKINSON. *Broadcast Advertising.* Second edition. New York: John Wiley and Sons, 1933. London: Chapman and Hall, 1933. 284 pp.
Includes a section on television.

ASSOCIATION OF NATIONAL ADVERTISERS. *The Advertiser Looks at a Radio.* New York, 1930. 120 pp.

BATSON, LAWRENCE DEARBORN. *Radio Markets of the World.* Washington, D. C.: Government Printing Office, 1931. 112 pp.

BECKMANN, FRITZ. *Die Organisationsformen des Weltfunkverkehrs.* Bonn: Marcus und Weber, 1925. 166 pp.
Radio as an international problem.

"Behind the Radio Battle on the Austrian Front," *Literary Digest,* 116:11 (September 2, 1933).

BENT, SILAS. "Radio Steals the Press' Thunder," *Independent,* July 9, 1927.

"Better Newspapers Urged to Combat Radio," *Pennsylvania Newspaper Publishers Association Bulletin,* vol. 2, no. 8, p. 1 (June 28, 1930).

BICKEL, KARL AUGUST. *New Empires: The Newspaper and the Radio.* Philadelphia: Lippincott, 1930. 112 pp.

BLOM, EDWARD CHARLES. *Radio and Electric Power Supply Equipment for Schools* (Teachers College Contributions to Education, no. 409). New York: Columbia University, 1930. 188 pp.
Apparatus for bringing the radio into the schools. Bibliography, pp. 160–63.

Broadcasting and Broadcast Advertising. See this publication for continued development of radio activities.

Broadcasting companies (NBC, CBC, BBC, etc.). Special reports of listeners' habits, advertisers' practices, etc.

BUEHLER, EZRA CHRISTIAN, compiler. *American vs. British System of Radio Control.* New York: H. W. Wilson, 1933. 361 pp.
Bibliography, pp. 25–50.

BUREAU INTERNATIONAL DE L'UNION TÉLÉGRAPHIQUE. *Journal télégraphique.* Berne, 1880–1933.
Superseded by *Journal des télécommunications.*

CARNEAL, GEORGETTE. *Conqueror of Space: An Authorized Biography of Lee DeForest.* New York: Liveright, 1930. 296 pp.

CHARTERS, WERRETT WALLACE. *Research Problems in Radio Education.* New York: National Advisory Council on Radio in Education Information Series, no. 4, pp. 1–17 (1931).

CLARK, KEITH. *International Communications: The American Attitude.* New York: Columbia University, 1931. 261 pp.
The evolution of international posts, telegraphs, and wireless, with an analysis of American policy in the organization of those services.

CLARKSON, RALPH PRESTON. *The Hysterical Background of Radio.* New York: J. H. Sears, 1927. 257 pp.

CODELL, MARTIN. " Crisis Develops in Radio-Press Relations," *Broad casting and Broadcast Advertising,* 8: 5–6 (March 1, 1935).
The coverage of news by Press-Radio Bureau and Transradio Press Service.

———. *Radio and Its Future.* New York: Harpers, 1930. 349 pp.
By the editor of *Broadcasting and Broadcast Advertising.*

DETROIT, UNIVERSITY OF. *Radio Advertising. A Survey of [Radio] Listeners' Preferences.* Detroit, Michigan, n. d.

DUNLAP, ORRIN ELMER, JR. *The Outlook for Television.* New York and London: Harpers, 1932. 297 pp.

———. *Radio in Advertising.* New York and London: Harpers, 1931. 383 pp.

———. " When Roosevelt Goes on the Air," *New York Times Magazine,* June 18, 1933.
The President's remarkable radio technique.

Editor and Publisher. See this publication for continued development of newspaper and radio communications.

Education by Radio. Organ of the National Committee on Education by Radio, Washington, D. C.
Weekly from February, 1931, to March, 1932; semimonthly from April to July, 1932; monthly since August, 1932.

Education on the Air (First Yearbook of the Institute for Education by Radio). Columbus: Ohio State University, 1930. 400 pp.
Papers delivered by men with years of experience in the field of educational broadcasting.

Education on the Air (Second Yearbook of the Institute for Education by Radio). Columbus: Ohio State University, 1931. 301 pp.

FEDERAL RADIO COMMISSION. Publishes hearings and annual reports.

FELIX, EDGAR HERBERT. *Television: Its Methods and Uses.* New York and London: McGraw-Hill, 1931. 272 pp.

———. *Using Radio in Sales Promotion.* New York: McGraw-Hill, 1927. 386 pp.

FELLNER, FREDERICK. *Communications in the Far East.* London: P. S. King, 1934. 370 pp.
A factual study of communications, especially in Japan and China.

FISHER, BEN S. "Radio and the Newspaper: An Analysis of Their Relationships," *Oregon Exchanges,* 14:5 (October, 1930).
By the attorney for the Federal Radio Commission.

"Five Point Program Urged on Radio," *Editor and Publisher,* 65:14 (April 29, 1933).
American Newspaper Publishers Association offers newspaper-radio adjustment plan.

GALLUP, GEORGE. "Survey Shows Radio Advertisers Reach But Small Portion of Public," *Editor and Publisher,* 63:28 (January 3, 1931).

GILMORE, W. S. "Radio Serves This Newspaper," *Quill,* 19:3 (June, 1931).
How the Detroit *News* handles broadcasting of news and advertising.

GOLDSMITH, ALFRED N., and LESCARBOURA, AUSTIN C. *This Thing Called Broadcasting.* New York: Holt, 1930. 362 pp.

HAMMARGREN, RUSSELL. "The Impact of Radio on the Newspaper: A Study of Developing Conflict between Two Agencies of Mass Impression, 1920–1934" (unpublished master's thesis, University of Minnesota, 1934).

HARD, WILLIAM. "Europe's Air and Ours," *Atlantic Monthly,* 150: 499–509 (October, 1932).

HARRIS, E. H. "New Radio Control System Needed," *Editor and Publisher,* 66:15 (June 10, 1933).
By the chairman of the radio committee of the American Newspaper Publishers Association.

———. "News Broadcasting Serious Problem," *American Press,* 5:6 (April, 1933).

HEARST, WILLIAM RANDOLPH. "Radio No Menace to Press," *Editor and Publisher,* 64: 17 (April 18, 1931).

HEDGES, WILLIAM S. "Enemies or Allies?" *Quill,* 19: 5 (February, 1931).
By the president of the Chicago *Daily News* broadcasting station.

―――. "What Television Will Mean to Newspapers, Explained by Chicago News Broadcast Chief," *American Press,* vol. 48, no. 10, p. 5 (July, 1930).

HOGAN, JOHN VINCENT LAWLESS. *Radio Facts and Principles Limiting the Total Number of Broadcasting Stations Which May Operate Simultaneously in the United States.* Washington, D. C.: Government Printing Office, 1928. 21 pp.
Testimony of a consulting radio engineer before the Federal Radio Commission.

INSTITUTE OF RADIO ENGINEERS. Yearbook. New York, 1916―.

KEATING, ISABELLE. "Pirates of the Air," *Harper's Magazine,* 169: 463–72 (September, 1934).
The developments that led up to the newspaper-radio truce on the broadcasting of news.

KERWIN, JEROME GREGORY. *The Control of Radio* (Public Policy Pamphlets, no. 10). Chicago: University of Chicago, 1934. 27 pp.
Discusses whether private enterprise in radio can endure.

KIRKPATRICK, CLIFFORD. *Report of a Research into the Attitudes and Habits of Radio Listeners.* St. Paul, Minnesota: Webb Publishing Company, 1933. 63 pp.
By a professor of sociology.

KOON, CLIVE MORGAN. *The Art of Teaching by Radio* (United States Office of Education Bulletin no. 4). Washington, D. C.: Government Printing Office, 1933. 91 pp.
By a government specialist in education by radio.

LINDSTROM, SIEGFRIED. "Millions of Japanese Listen In," *Asia,* 33: 592–99 (December, 1933).
A survey of the use of the radio in Japan.

"Local Broadcasts Not a Menace to Newspapers, Managers Say," *Editor and Publisher,* vol. 63, no. 5, p. 20 (June 21, 1930).

McNAMEE, GRAHAM (in collaboration with Robert Gordon Anderson). *You're on the Air!* New York: Harpers, 1926. 207 pp.

MANNING, GEORGE. "Radio News Service Demands Equal Rights in Press Galleries," *Editor and Publisher,* 66: 6 (November 4, 1933).

MORECROFT, JOHN HAROLD. "How the Propagandists Work in Radio," *Radio Broadcast,* July, 1925.

MORECROFT, JOHN HAROLD, PINTO, A., and CURRY, WALTER ANDREW. *Principles of Radio Communication.* Third edition, revised. New York: J. Wiley and Sons, 1933. London: Chapman and Hall, 1933. 1084 pp.

MOSELEY, SYDNEY A. *Who's Who in Broadcasting.* New York: Pitman Publishing Corporation, 1933.
"A biographical record of the leading personalities of the microphone in Great Britain."

MOYER, JAMES AMBROSE, and WORSTREL, JOHN F. *The Radio Handbook, Including Television and Sound Motion Pictures.* New York: McGraw-Hill, 1931. 886 pp.

MULLER, HELEN MARIE, compiler. *Education by Radio.* New York: H. W. Wilson, 1932. 175 pp.
Bibliography, pp. 13–20.

"National Broadcasting Company," *Fortune,* 2:70 (December, 1930).
Growth and development of broadcasting service.

NATIONAL RESEARCH COUNCIL OF JAPAN, RADIO RESEARCH COMMITTEE. *Report of Radio Research in Japan.* Tokyo, 1931—.
Includes bibliographies, abstracts, and references.

"Plan to End Radio News Competition Formed at New York Conferences," *Editor and Publisher,* 66: 3 (December 16, 1933).
Press, radio, and news services arrive at cooperative method to control dissemination of press news on the air.

PLANAS-SUÁREZ, SIMÓN. *La Sociedad de las Naciones y la Conferencia de Barcelona.* Lisbon: Centro Tipográfico Colonial, 1922. 149 pp.
Summary of the Barcelona Conference of 1921 on communications and transit.

"Postal Service," *Encyclopedia of the Social Sciences.* (By J. C. Hemmeon.)

POSTGATE, R. W. "Radio, Press, and Publishing," in *Twelve Studies in Soviet Russia,* edited for the New Fabian Research Bureau by Margaret I. Cole. London: Gollancz, 1933.

The Press-Radio Plan. New York: Press-Radio Committee, 1934. 8 pp., mimeographed.
Nine-point plan designed to end competition and friction between radio and the press.

"Radio," *Encyclopedia of the Social Sciences.* (By Howard T. Lewis, William A. Orton, and Harry Shulman.)

"Radio Advertising," *Fortune*, 2:65 (December, 1930).
Radio advertising costs and the listening public.

"Radio at Convention Cut Dailies' Sales," *Editor and Publisher*, 65:5 (August 13, 1932).
Total sales of Chicago newspapers reduced as result of broadcasting of Democratic and Republican conventions.

"Radio in Russia," *Review of Reviews*, 83:59 (February, 1931).
Broadcast of court proceedings in trial of eight Russian engineers.

The Radio Industry: The Story of Its Development, as Told by Leaders of the Industry to the Students of the Graduate School of Business Administration, Harvard University. Chicago, New York, and London: A. W. Shaw, 1928. 330 pp.

"Radio Not Newspaper's Competitor — Williamson," *United States Publisher and Printer*, vol. 8, no. 6, p. 12 (June, 1930).

"Radio Serious Competitor, Says O'Donnell," *Pennsylvania Newspaper Publishers Association Bulletin*, vol. 2, no. 9, p. 1 (July 5, 1930).

RADIO STATION WCCO, Minneapolis. *Broadcasting as an Advertising Medium*, n. d.
Analysis of the hours of the day and the kinds of people listening in at each hour.

RAYMOND, ALLEN. "Coming Fight over News," *New Outlook*, 161:13 (June, 1933).

————. "Static Ahead!" *New Outlook*, 162:17 (July, 1933).

RIEGEL, O. W. *Mobilizing for Chaos: The Story of the New Propaganda.* New Haven: Yale University Press, 1934. 231 pp.
Contains factual and interpretative material on effects of national influence over cables, radio, and press.

RINGLAND, MRS. A. "The League of Women Voters, the Voters, and the Radio; Voters' Campaign Information Service," *Woman's Journal*, N. S., 13:30 (September, 1928).

RISTOW, ALFRED. *Die Internationale Entwicklung und Bedeutung der Funkentelegraphie.* Königsberg: Ebering, 1926. 132 pp.
Dissertation surveying the development and present international status of radio.

ROBB, ARTHUR. "Radio Is Still Unproved Sales Medium Though Its Advertising Use Grows," *Editor and Publisher*, vol. 62, no. 50, p. 5 (May 3, 1930).

ROCHE, JOHN F. "Radio Program Space Is Increasing," *Editor and Publisher*, vol. 62, no. 52, p. 9 (May 17, 1930).

Rogers, Walter A. "International Electrical Communications," *Foreign Affairs*, December, 1922.

Rutherford, Geddes W. "Radio as a Means of Instruction in Government," *American Political Science Review*, 27:264–74 (April, 1933). Discusses several contemporary American projects in civic education by air.

Schmeckebier, Laurence Frederick. *The Federal Radio Commission: Its History, Activities, and Organization*. Washington, D. C.: Brookings Institution, 1932. 162 pp.
Bibliography, pp. 135–57.

Stewart, Irvin, editor. *Radio* (supplement to vol. 142 of *Annals of the American Academy of Political and Social Science*). Philadelphia, 1929. 107 pp.

Stockbridge, Frank Parker. "Newspapers Called on to Suppress Broadcasting Frauds," *American Press*, 48:1 (August, 1930).

Taylor, F. E. "Civic Education by Radio," *National Municipal Review*, 16:683–84 (November, 1927).

Tribolet, Leslie Bennett. *International Aspects of Electrical Communications in the Pacific Area* (Ph. D. thesis, Johns Hopkins University, 1928). Baltimore: Johns Hopkins University, 1929. London: Oxford University, 1929. 282 pp.
Bibliography, pp. 271–75.

Tunis, John R. "Forecasting Broadcasting," *Elks Magazine*, 9:26 (November, 1930).
An analysis of the future of the radio.

Tuthill, D. S. "How Radio Advertising Creates Additional Linage for Dailies," *American Press*, vol. 48, no. 10, p. 5 (July, 1930).

United States Department of Commerce. *Radio Activities of the Department of Commerce*. Washington, D. C.: Government Printing Office, 1931. 34 pp.
"Important events in radio, 1827 to 1930," pp. 22–34.

United States Department of Commerce, Bureau of Foreign and Domestic Commerce, Transportation Division, Communications Section. *Foreign Communication News*. Washington, D. C., 1929—.
Government bulletin, issued at irregular intervals.

United States Department of Commerce, Radio Division. *Commercial and Government Radio Stations of the United States*. Washington, D. C.: Government Printing Office, 1913—.

United States Federal Radio Commission. *Broadcasting Radio Stations of the United States.* Washington, D. C.: Government Printing Office, 1931—.

————. *Rules and Regulations.* Washington, D. C.: Government Printing Office, 1934. 186 pp.

The Voice of Experience. New York: Dodd, Mead, 1933. 367 pp.
" This book . . . contains the replies to fifty of the most frequently asked questions submitted to me during my years of broadcasting." — The Author.

Willey, Malcolm M., and Rice, Stuart A. *Communication Agencies and Social Life.* New York and London: McGraw-Hill, 1933. 229 pp.

5. BOOKS, PERIODICALS, SPECIAL PRINTED MEDIA, GRAPHIC ARTS, CARICATURE

Audin, Marius. *Histoire de l'imprimérie.* Paris: Jonquières, 1929. 2 vols.

Avenarius, Ferdinand. *Das Bild als Narr: Die Karikatur in der Völkerverhetzung, was sie aussagt, was sie verrät.* Munich: Callwey, 1918. 254 pp.
A study of the part played by caricature in campaigns of hate.

Averill, Ethel. *History of French Children's Books, 1750–1900.* Boston: Bookshop for Boys and Girls, 1934.

Beerbohm, Max. *A Book of Caricatures.* London: Methuen, 1907. 3 leaves and 48 plates.

————. *Cartoons: The Second Childhood of John Bull.* London: Swift, 1911. 19 leaves and 15 color plates.

Bengough, J. W. *A Caricature History of Canadian Politics.* Toronto: Grip Printing and Publishing Company, 1886. 2 vols. 962 pp.

Bishop, Joseph Bucklin. *Our Political Drama; Conventions, Campaigns, Candidates.* New York: Scott-Thaw, 1904. 236 pp.
Attention paid to political caricature.

Brenner, Anita. " Art's Storied Debate Renewed," *New York Times Magazine,* February 25, 1934.
Destruction of Rivera's murals at Rockefeller Center raises problems of art and propaganda.

Carter, John. " Propaganda — as Seen in Recent Books," *Outlook and Independent,* 155: 471 (July 23, 1930).

Cartoons from Punch. London: Bradbury, Agnew, 1906. 4 vols. 1832 pp.
Cartoons cover years 1841 to 1901.

CAUER, EDUARD. *Über die Flugschriften Friedrichs des Grossen aus der Zeit des siebenjährigen Krieges.* Potsdam, 1865.

CLEINOW, GEORG. "Das deutsche Buch in der Sowjetunion," *Der Auslandsdeutsche,* 1930, pp. 709–16.

DAHL, SVEND. *Histoire du livre de l'antiquité à nos jours.* Paris: Lamarre, 1933. 326 pp.

DARTON, FREDERICK JOSEPH HARVEY. *Children's Books in England: Five Centuries of Social Life.* Cambridge: Cambridge University, 1932. 359 pp.

"Davenport, Homer Calvin," in *Dictionary of American Biography.* (By Jean MacKinnon Holt.)
The life of the celebrated cartoonist of the New York *Journal.*

DAVIDSON, JO. "Now, Like Greece, We Foster Art," *New York Times Magazine,* March 18, 1934.
Civil Works Administration hires artists to adorn public buildings.

DUFFIELD, MARCUS. "The Pulps: Day Dreams of the Masses," *Vanity Fair,* 40: 26 ff. (June, 1933).
At the height of prosperity the "pulps" were said to have had an aggregate monthly sale of twenty million.

DUFFUS, ROBERT LUTHER. *Books: Their Place in a Democracy.* Boston and New York: Houghton Mifflin, 1930. 225 pp.
"A study, undertaken for the Carnegie Corporation, into the publication and distribution of serious, non-technical books."

EVERITT, GRAHAM. *English Caricaturists and Graphic Humorists of the 19th Century.* London: S. Sonnenschein, 1893. 427 pp.

FLEURY, JULES (CHAMPFLEURY, pseudonym). *Histoire de la caricature antique.* Third edition. Paris: E. Dentu, 1879. 347 pp.

————. *Histoire de la caricature au moyen-âge et sous la Renaissance.* Second edition. Paris: E. Dentu, 1875. 351 pp.

————. *Histoire de la caricature moderne.* Third edition. Paris: E. Dentu, 1885. 322 pp.

————. *Histoire de la caricature sous la Réforme et la Ligue — Louis XIII à Louis XVI.* Paris: E. Dentu, 1880. 323 pp.

————. *Histoire de la caricature sous la République, l'Empire, et la Restauration.* Second edition. Paris: E. Dentu, 1877. 363 pp.

————. *Histoire de l'imagérie populaire.* Second edition. Paris: E. Dentu, 1886. 286 pp.

————. *Le Musée secret de la caricature.* Paris: E. Dentu, 1888. 249 pp.

FLOWER, B. O. " Homer Davenport," *Arena,* 34: 58–69 (July, 1905).

FOX, W. *Printers, Press, and Profits.* London: Labour Research Department, 1933.

HOPKINS, DOROTHY JUNE. *Hop of the Bulletin.* Sydney: Angus and Robertson, 1929. 247 pp.
The work of a celebrated cartoonist of the Sydney *Bulletin.*

ISAACS, L. W. " Music and Politics," *Bookman,* 34: 484–88 (January, 1912).

KIRBY, ROLLIN. *Highlights: A Cartoon History of the 1920's.* New York: William Farquhar Payson, 1931. 140 pp.
A selection of Kirby's cartoons in the New York *World,* with a foreword by Walter Lippmann.

KÖSTER, HERMANN. *Geschichte der deutschen Jugendliteratur.* Fourth edition. Brunswick, Berlin, and Hamburg: Georg Westermann, 1927. 478 pp.

LOW, DAVID. *The Best of Low.* London: J. Cape, 1930. 211 pp.
A selection of drawings, originally published in the London *Evening Standard.*

LÖWIS OF MENAR, AUGUST VON. " Deutsche Bücher im fremdem Gewande: Russland " (continued by Charlotte Bauschinger), *Börsenblatt für den deutschen Buchhandel,* 1929, pp. 449–63; 1930, pp. 681–91; 1932, pp. 53–60, 81–86.
Bibliography of translations from German into Russian, with explanatory remarks.

LYNCH, JOHN GILBERT BOHUN. *A History of Caricature.* London: Faber and Gwyer, 1926. 126 pp.

McDOUGALL, WALTER HUGH. *THIS Is the Life!* New York: Knopf, 1926. 330 pp.
Autobiography of a well-known New York and Philadelphia cartoonist.

MARTIN, HELEN. " Nationalism and Children's Books " (unpublished Ph. D. thesis, University of Chicago, 1934).

MAURICE, ARTHUR BARTLETT, and COOPER, FREDERIC TABER. *A History of the Nineteenth Century in Caricature.* New York: Dodd, Mead, 1904. 363 pp.

MORGAN, MATTHEW SOMERVILLE. *The American Civil War Cartoons of Matt Morgan and Other English Artists.* London: Chatto and Windus, 1874. 224 pp.

MOTT, FRANK LUTHER. *A History of American Magazines, 1741–1850.* New York and London: Appleton, 1930. 848 pp.
Chronological list of magazines, pp. 785–809; bibliographic footnotes.

A second volume is in preparation covering the period from 1850 to the present.

Mr. Punch's Victorian Era. London: Punch, 1887–88. 3 vols. 994 pp.
An illustrated chronicle of 50 years of the reign of Queen Victoria.

MUMBY, FRANK ARTHUR. *Publishing and Bookselling: A History from the Earliest Times to the Present Day.* London: J. Cape, 1930. 480 pp.
Bibliography of publishing and bookselling, pp. 419–59.

Las Obras de José Guadalupe Posada, Grabador Mejicano, with an introduction by Diego Rivera. Mexico City: Published by Talleres Gráficos de la Nación for *Mexican Folkways,* 1930. 215 pp.
A celebrated social cartoonist. "Of the 15,000 cuts that Posada is said to have made for the leading publishing house of popular literature, Vanegas Arroyo, all that were not worn out, or stolen during the years of revolution are, so far as is known, published here." — *Foreword.*

OLBRICH, WILHELM. *Einführung in die Verlagskunde.* Leipzig: Hiersemann, 1932. 254 pp.

PAINE, ALBERT BIGELOW. *Th. Nast, His Period and His Pictures.* New York: Macmillan, 1904. 583 pp.
Life of the cartoonist who helped expose the Tweed Ring in New York.

PARTON, JAMES. *Caricature and Other Comic Art in All Times and Many Lands.* New York: Harpers, 1877. 340 pp.

"Printing and Publishing," *Encyclopedia of the Social Sciences.* (By R. L. Duffus.)

PUTNAM, GEORGE HAVEN. *Authors and Their Public in Ancient Times: A Sketch of Literary Conditions and of the Relations with the Public of Literary Producers, from the Earliest Times to the Fall of the Roman Empire.* New York: Putnam, 1894. 309 pp.
Bibliography, pp. xiii–xvii.

————. *Books and Their Makers during the Middle Ages: A Study of the Production and Distribution of Literature from the Fall of the Roman Empire to the Close of the Seventeenth Century.* New York: Putnam, 1896–97. 2 vols.
Bibliography, 1: xvii–xxvii.

RAEMAEKERS, LOUIS. *Kultur in Cartoons.* New York: Century, 1917. 316 pp.

RE, L. *La satira patriottica nelle scritte murali del risorgimento.* Brescia: Vannini, 1932. 250 pp.

RENARD, GEORGES FRANÇOIS. *Les Travailleurs du livre et du journal, 1925-26.* Paris: O. Doin, 3 vols.

RICHARDSON, LYON N. *A History of Early American Magazines, 1741–1789.* New York: Nelson, 1931. 414 pp.

ROBINSON, BOARDMAN. *Cartoons on the War.* New York: Dutton, 1915. 75 pp.

Selections from cartoons published in the New York *Tribune* and *Harper's Weekly.* "They represent the emotions evoked by the news from day to day, and make no pretense to a philosophic viewpoint. They do seek to express, however, a deep conviction that Germany is chiefly to blame for the war." — Selection from prefatory note by the artist.

TENNIEL, SIR JOHN. *Cartoons from Punch.* London: Bradbury and Evans, 187(?). 2 vols.

Subjects date from 1853 to 1870.

THORPE, JAMES. *Phil May, Master-Draughtsman and Humorist, 1864–1903.* London: G. G. Harrap, 1932. 210 pp.

ULRICH, F. "Formen und Methoden der russischen Literatur-Propaganda im Westen," *Börsenblatt für den deutschen Buchhandel,* 1930, pp. 957–59, 967–68.

Translated from *Na kniznom fronte,* 1929, no. 9. On Russian propaganda in Western Europe through newspapers and literary publications.

Vanity Fair, June-October, 1933. Series of five articles on American magazines.

VETH, CORNELIS. *Comic Art in England.* London: E. Goldston, 1930. 206 pp.

Bibliography, pp. 201–02.

WALKER, E. "Das russische Buchhandelsnetz," *Börsenblatt für den deutschen Buchhandel,* 1930, pp. 983–85.

WAPLES, DOUGLAS, and TYLER, RALPH W. *What People Want to Read About: A Study of Group Interest and a Survey of Problems in Adult Reading.* Chicago: University of Chicago, 1931. 312 pp.

WARD, LESLIE. *Forty Years of "Spy."* London: Chatto and Windus, 1915. 351 pp.

WEITENKAMPF, FRANK. *American Graphic Art.* Second edition. New York: Macmillan, 1924. 328 pp.

Chapter 12 on caricature, chapter 13 on the comic paper and the daily press. Bibliography, pp. 291–98.

6. FOUNDATIONS AND ENDOWMENTS

"Endowments and Foundations," *Encyclopedia of the Social Sciences.* (By William A. Orton.)

KEPPEL, FREDERICK PAUL. *The Foundation: Its Place in American Life. An Account of the Development of Philanthropic Endowments and Their Present Activities in Relation to Education and Scientific and Social Progress.* New York: Macmillan, 1930. 113 pp.

TWENTIETH CENTURY FUND. *American Foundations and Their Funds.* 1931, 1932.
"A general survey of the flow of funds from philanthropic foundations into various fields in this country," for the guidance of the Twentieth Century Fund in distributing the funds placed at its disposal by Edward A. Filene. Ninety-one foundations reported in 1931; 102 in 1932. From this report the student of gift propaganda may gain some idea of the scope and number of philanthropic activities to be investigated.

7. FAIRS, EXPOSITIONS, MUSEUMS

"Agricultural Fairs," *Encyclopedia of the Social Sciences.* (By Edward Wiest.)

AMERICAN ASSOCIATION OF MUSEUMS. Publications, including reports on museum attendance, behavior of visitors to museums, museum apparatus, and a *Handbook of American Museums* (Washington, D. C., 1932. 779 pp.).

BERKELEY, WILLIAM NOLAND. *The Small-Community Museum: Why It Is Entirely Feasible, Why It Is Extremely Desirable.* Lynchburg, Virginia: J. P. Bell, 1932. 88 pp.

BRIGHAM, WILLIAM TUFTS. *Report of a Journey around the World to Study Matters Relating to Museums.* Honolulu: Bishop Museum, 1913. 320 pp.

"Expositions, International," *Encyclopedia of the Social Sciences.* (By Guy Stanton Ford.)

"Fairs," *Encyclopedia of the Social Sciences.* (By Joseph Kulischer.)

GREAT BRITAIN, BOARD OF EDUCATION. *Memorandum on the Possibility of Increased Cooperation between Public Museums and Public Educational Institutions.* London: H. M. Stationery Office, 1931. 45 pp.

MURRAY, DAVID. *Museums: Their History and Their Use.* Glasgow: J. MacLehose, 1904. 3 vols.
List of museums in the United Kingdom, 1: 292–312. Bibliography, vols. 2 and 3.

NEURATH, OTTO. "Museums of the Future," *Survey Graphic,* 22: 459–63 (September, 1933).
By an official of the Social and Economic Museum of Vienna.

REA, PAUL MARSHALL. *The Museum and the Community*. Lancaster, Pennsylvania: Science Press, 1932. 259 pp.
A statistical study of the use of museums, prepared for the use of their executives.

RUBINOW, S. G. *Fairs and Their Educational Value* (North Carolina Agricultural Extension Service, Circular 69). Chapel Hill, North Carolina, 1918.

SMITH, RALPH CLIFTON. *A Bibliography of Museums and Museum Work*. Washington, D. C.: American Association of Museums, 1928. 302 pp.

8. THE SALON AND TAVERN

ALLEN, ROBERT JOSEPH. *The Clubs of Augustan London* (Harvard Studies in English, vol. 7). Cambridge, Massachusetts: Harvard University, 1933. 305 pp.
Coffee houses in the early eighteenth century.

ANDERSON, WALTER. " The Speakeasy as a National Institution," *Current History*, 36: 417–23 (July, 1932).

BOYNTON, PERCY H. *London in English Literature*. Chicago: University of Chicago, 1913. 346 pp.
Taverns as centers of opinion diffusion.

BURKE, THOMAS. *The English Inn*. London: Longmans, Green, 1930. 175 pp.
Describes wayside inns and town taverns of past and present England as "a focal point for observation of men and manners."

CLERGUE, HELEN. *The Salon: A Study of French Society and Personalities in the XVIII Century*. New York and London: Putnam, 1907. 359 pp.

GUILLOIS, ANTOINE. *Le Salon de Madame Helvétius*. Paris: Calmann-Lévy, 1894. 340 pp.

TINKER, CHAUNCEY BREWSTER. *The Salon and English Letters . . . in the Age of Johnson*. New York: Macmillan, 1915. 290 pp.

TORNIUS, VALERIAN HUGO. *Salons 1400–1900: A Pageant of Beauty and Wit*. London: Butterworth, 1929. New York: Cosmopolitan Book Corporation, 1929. 318 pp.
Bibliography, pp. 315–18.

9. CHAUTAUQUAS AND INSTITUTIONS FOR ADULT EDUCATION

" Extension Work, Agricultural," *Encyclopedia of the Social Sciences*. (By William Allison Lloyd.)

HAMILTON, JOHN. *Agricultural Instruction for Adults in Continental Countries* (United States Department of Agriculture, Office of Experiment Stations, Bulletin no. 163). Washington, D. C.: Government Printing Office, 1905.

―――. *Agricultural Instruction for Adults in the British Empire* (United States Department of Agriculture, Office of Experiment Stations, Bulletin no. 155). Washington, D. C.: Government Printing Office, 1905.

HURLBUT, JESSE LYMAN. *The Story of Chautauqua.* New York and London: Putnam, 1921. 429 pp.

KEPPEL, FREDERICK PAUL. *Education for Adults, and Other Essays.* New York: Columbia University, 1926. 94 pp.

LORIMER, FRANK. *The Making of Adult Minds in a Metropolitan Area.* New York: Macmillan, 1931. 245 pp.
Evaluates the various types of education undertaken by the city of Brooklyn and draws composite pictures showing the foci of attention in the adult education movement.

MARTIN, OSCAR BAKER. *The Demonstration Work: Dr. Seaman A. Knapp's Contribution to Civilization.* Boston: Stratford, 1921. 269 pp.
Novel techniques in agricultural education.

NOFFSINGER, JOHN SAMUEL. *Correspondence Schools, Lyceums, Chautauquas.* New York: Macmillan, 1926. 145 pp.

PEARSON, P. M. " The Chautauqua Movement," *Annals of the American Academy of Political and Social Science,* 40: 211–16 (1912).

TRUE, A. C. *A History of Agricultural Extension Work in the United States, 1785–1923* (United States Department of Agriculture, Miscellaneous Publications, no. 15). Washington, D. C.: Government Printing Office, 1928.

VINCENT, JOHN HEYL. *The Chautauqua Movement.* Boston: Chautauqua Press, 1886. 308 pp.

WORLD ASSOCIATION FOR ADULT EDUCATION. *International Handbook of Adult Education.* London, 1929. 476 pp.
Contains brief accounts and bibliographies of the adult education movement in the more important countries.

10. CLUBS, FRATERNITIES, SECRET SOCIETIES

BAIRD, GEORGE W. " Great Men Who Were Masons." Series of some two dozen popular biographies in *The Builder,* vols. 10 and 12 (1924 and 1926).

BERNHEIMER, CHARLES SELIGMAN, and COHEN, JACOB M. *Boys' Clubs*. New York: Baker and Taylor, 1914. 136 pp.

"Boys' and Girls' Clubs," *Encyclopedia of the Social Sciences*. (By W. I. Newstetter.)

BRINTON, CLARENCE CRANE. *The Jacobins: An Essay in New History*. New York: Macmillan, 1930. 319 pp.
Bibliography, pp. 281–98.

BROOKS, R. C. "Political Clubs in Prussian Cities," *Municipal Affairs*, 4: 375–84 (1900).

BUCHNER, MAX. "Zum Geheimbundwesen in alter und neuer Zeit," *Gelbe Hefte*, 3: 801–39 (1927).

CALHOUN, GEORGE MILLER. *Athenian Clubs in Politics and Litigation* (Ph.D. thesis, University of Chicago, 1911). Austin, Texas, 1913. 172 pp.
Bibliography, pp. 149–52.

CHALLAMEL, AUGUSTIN. *Les Clubs contre-révolutionnaires, cercles, comités, sociétés, salons, réunions, cafés, restaurants, et librairies*. Paris: Cerf, 1895. 633 pp.
"Collection de documents rélatifs à l'histoire de Paris pendant la révolution française."

"Clubs," *Encyclopedia of the Social Sciences*. (By Crane Brinton.)

"Clubs, Political," *Encyclopedia of the Social Sciences*. (By Joseph McGoldrick.)

COCHIN, AUGUSTIN. *Les Sociétés de pensée et la démocratie: Études d'histoire révolutionnaire*. Paris: Plon-Nourrit, 1921. 300 pp.

———. *Les Sociétés de pensée et la révolution en Bretagne (1788–1789)*. Paris: Champion, 1925. 2 vols.
Reading clubs, societies, and Masonic lodges are found by M. Cochin to have been so highly organized that "they gained the effectiveness of an American political machine . . . and carried into effect ideas utterly foreign to the genius of the French people." Bibliography, pp. 457–66.

DITO, ORESTE. *Massoneria, carboneria ed altre società segrete nella storia del risorgimento italiano*. Turin and Rome: Roux e Viarengo, 1905. 441 pp.
Masonry, carbonari, and other secret societies in the Italian Risorgimento.

EGAN, MAURICE FRANCIS, and KENNEDY, JOHN B. *The Knights of Columbus in Peace and War*. New Haven: Knights of Columbus, 1920. 2 vols.

Escott, Thomas Hay Sweet. *Club Makers and Club Members.* New York: Sturgis and Walton, 1914. 352 pp.

Fagan, Louis Alexander. *The Reform Club (1836–1886): Its Founders and Architect.* London: B. Quaritch, 1887. 143 pp.

"Fraternal Orders," *Encyclopedia of the Social Sciences.* (By Frank H. Hankins.)

Gumbel, Emil Julius. *Verschwörer.* Berlin: Malik Verlag, 1924. 224 pp.
A study of German nationalist secret societies.

Hartson, Louis D. "A Study of Voluntary Associations, Educational and Social, in Europe during the Period from 1100 to 1700," *Pedagogical Seminary,* 18: 10–31 (1911).

Heckethoon, Charles William. *Secret Societies of All Ages and Countries: A Comprehensive Account of Upwards of 160 Secret Organizations — Religious, Political, and Social — from the Most Remote Ages Down to the Present Time.* New edition. London: G. Redway, 1897. 2 vols.
Bibliography, 1: xix–xxvii; 2: xi–xvi.

Heron, Lepper. *Les Sociétés secrètes de l'antiquité à nos jours.* Paris: Payot, 1933. 320 pp.

Jonet, Alphonse. *Les Clubs: Leur histoire et leur rôle depuis 1789.* Paris, 1891.

Lantoine, Albert. *L'Histoire de la franc-maçonnerie française.* Second edition. Paris: Nourry, 1930. 332 pp.

Lennhoff, Eugen. *Politische Geheimbünde.* Zurich and Vienna: Amalthea, 1930. 560 pp.
Secret political associations throughout history.

Lewis, Harve Spencer. *Rosicrucian Questions and Anwers, with Complete History of the Rosicrucian Order.* San José, California: Rosicrucian Press, AMORC College, 1929. 300 pp.
Bibliography, pp. 60–68.

Lieberman, Willy. *Zur Geschichte und Organisation des römischen Vereinswesens.* Leipzig, 1890.
Roman clubs.

Londres, Albert. *Les Comitadjis.* Paris: Michel, 1932. 256 pp.
Anecdotal sketch of the Interior Macedonian Revolutionary Organization and its influence in Bulgarian politics. By a French journalist.

Luzio, Alessandro. *La massoneria e il risorgimento italiano.* Bologna, 1925, 2 vols.

MacBride, A. S. *Speculative Masonry: Its Mission, Its Evoluton, and Its Landmarks*. New York: George H. Doran, 1924. 254 pp.

Mackey, Albert Gallatin. *An Encyclopedia of Freemasonry and Its Kindred Sciences*. Revised and enlarged edition. Chicago, Toronto, etc.: Masonic History Company, 1929. 2 vols.

McKown, Harry Charles. *School Clubs, Their Organization, Administration, Supervision, and Activities*. New York: Macmillan, 1929. 498 pp.

Martin, Gaston. *La Franc-maçonnerie française et la préparation de la révolution*. Paris: Presses universitaires de France, 1926. 294 pp.
After sketching the history of the Masons in France, the author undertakes to define their attitude toward the philosophical ideas of the age. Bibliography, pp. 285–92.

————. *Manuel d'histoire de la franc-maçonnerie française*. Paris: Presses universitaires de France, 1929. 278 pp.
Contains bibliographies.

"Masonry," *Encyclopedia of the Social Sciences*. (By Frank H. Hankins.)

Molinari, Gustave de. *Les Clubs rouges pendant le siège de Paris*. Paris: Garnier frères, 1871. 390 pp.

"The Pitt Clubs of Great Britain," *New Monthly Magazine*, 5:430–39 (1816).

Preuss, Arthur, compiler. *A Dictionary of Secret and Other Societies*. St. Louis and London: B. Herder, 1924. 543 pp.

Robbins, Sir Alfred. *English-Speaking Freemasonry*. London: Benn, 1930. 367 pp.

Roth, Philip A. *Masonry in the Formation of Our Government, 1761–1799*. Milwaukee: Atlas Printing Company, 1927. 187 pp.

Russell, Charles E., and Rigby, Lilian M. *Working Lads' Clubs*. London: Macmillan, 1908. 445 pp.

Schneider, Ferdinand Josef. *Die Freimaurerei und ihr Einfluss auf die geistige Kultur in Deutschland am Ende des XVIII. Jahrhunderts*. Prague: Taussig und Taussig, 1909. 234 pp.
Freemasonry and German culture at the end of the eighteenth century.

Sweeney, Mark J. *Educational Work of the Knights of Columbus* (United States Department of the Interior, Bureau of Education, Bulletin no. 22). Washington, D. C., 1923.

Timbs, John. *Clubs and Club Life in London from the Seventeenth Century to the Present Time*. First edition, 17 vols., "extra illustrated." London: L. Bentley, 1866. New edition, Chatto and Windus, 1908. 544 pp.

WAITE, ARTHUR EDWARD. *The Doctrine and Literature of the Kabalah*. London: Theosophical Publishing Company, 1902. 508 pp.

————. *Emblematic Freemasonry and the Evolution of Its Deeper Issues*. London: Rider, 1925. 301 pp.
Bibliographic footnotes.

————. *A New Encyclopedia of Freemasonry (ars magna latomorum) and of Cognate Instituted Mysteries: Their Rites, Literature, and History*. London: Rider, 1921. 2 vols.

————. *The Real History of the Rosicrucians, Founded on Their Own Manifestoes, and on Facts and Documents Collected from the Writings of the Initiated Brethren*. London: G. Redway, 1887. New York: Bouton, 1888. 446 pp.

WEBSTER, HUTTON. *Primitive Secret Societies*. New York: Macmillan, 1932. 243 pp.
The first edition appeared in 1908.

WEBSTER, MRS. NESTA H. *Secret Societies and Subversive Movements*. London: Boswell Printing and Publishing Company, 1924. 419 pp.

II. ORAL COMMUNICATION

BROCK, HENRY IRVING. "The Great Fairy Tale Propaganda," *New York Times Magazine,* March 23, 1924.
Irish propaganda against British oppression, through fairy tales told to children.

DOLMAN, JOHN. *A Handbook of Public Speaking*. Revised edition. New York: Harcourt, Brace, 1934. 165 pp.
Bibliography, pp. 154–65.

DUBOIS, WARREN COUTANT. *Hints for the Political Speaker*. New York: LaPidus Printing Company, 1921. 111 pp.

HAYWORTH, DONALD. "An Analysis of Speeches in Presidential Campaigns from 1884 to 1920," *Quarterly Journal of Speech,* 16: 35–42 (February, 1930).
Mr. Hayworth wrote a Ph. D. thesis on this subject at the University of Wisconsin (1929).

HIGGINS, HOWARD HUBERT. *Influencing Behavior through Speech*. Boston: Expression Company, 1930. 346 pp.
Psychology of oratory. Bibliography, pp. 339–42.

HOFFMAN, WILLIAM G. *Public Speaking for Business Men*. Second edition. London and New York: McGraw-Hill, 1931. 383 pp.

HOLLISTER, RICHARD DENNIS TEALL. *Speech Making*. Ann Arbor, Michigan: George Wahr, 1918. 386 pp.

McGEE, JOHN A. *Persuasive Speaking*. New York: Scribners, 1929. 300 pp.

NEIL, C. EDMUND. *Sources of Effectiveness in Public Speaking: Psychological Principles Practically Used*. New York, Chicago, etc.: Hinds, Hayden, and Eldridge, 1920. 590 pp.

NEWBOLT, SIR HENRY. "The Roaring Boys," *Saturday Review of Literature,* July 30, 1927.
Singing as a medium of propaganda.

ORR, FREDERICK WESLEY. *Essentials of Effective Speaking: A Handbook for a Beginning Course in Speaking*. New York: Macmillan, 1931. 305 pp.

PATRIZI, MARIANO. *L'oratore: Saggio sperimentale*. Milan: Treves, 1912.
Experimental psychology of oratory.

PHELPS, ARTHUR STEVENS. *Speaking in Public*. Cleveland: F. M. Barton, 1930. 232 pp.
Bibliography, pp. 231–32.

Quarterly Journal of Speech. Contains articles by scientific students of the subject, analyzing selected speeches, speakers, and types of audiences.

ROBINSON, FREDERICK BERTRAND. *Effective Public Speaking*. Revised edition. Chicago: LaSalle Extension University, 1926. 467 pp.

SCOTT, WALTER DILL. *Psychology of Public Speaking, Adapted for Use as a Text Book in High Schools and Colleges*. New York: Noble and Noble, 1926. 233 pp.
Bibliography, pp. 217–33.

SHURTER, EDWIN DUBOIS, and MARSH, CHARLES ALMER. *Practical Public Speaking: The Extempore Method*. New York and Boston: Houghton Mifflin, 1929. 247 pp.

SIMRELL, V. E. "Oratory of the 1928 Presidential Campaign," *Quarterly Journal of Speech,* April, 1929 (vol. 15).

WEST, ROBERT WILLIAM. *Purposive Speaking*. New York: Macmillan, 1924. 182 pp.
A college text.

WILLIAMSON, ARLEIGH BOYD. *Speaking in Public*. New York: Prentice-Hall, 1929. 412 pp.

WINANS, JAMES ALBERT. *Public Speaking: Principles and Practice*. New York: Century, 1917. 526 pp.

Woolbert, Charles Henry, and Weaver, Andrew Thomas. *Better Speech: A Textbook of Speech Training for Secondary Schools.* Revised edition. New York: Harcourt, Brace, 1929. 463 pp.

12. HOUSE ORGANS

Burnett, Verne Edwin. "How Workers React to Propaganda," *Industrial Management,* 65: 250–53 (April, 1923).

Carpenter, Charles E. "Industrial Publicity and the House Organ," *Industrial Management,* 61: 247–49 (April, 1921).

Feather, W. "House Organs for Year Around Publicity," *Survey,* 56: 472 (July 15, 1926).

Flexner, J. A. "Selling the Company," *New Republic,* 38: 171–74 (April 9, 1924).

Hall, Samuel Roland. *Business Writing.* New York: McGraw-Hill, 1924. 222 pp.
Section 3, "Copy for House Organs."

Hamilton, Walter Irving. *Employer-Employee Relations in Hotels.* Baltimore: Williams and Wilkins, 1925. 158 pp.
Chapter 4 is entitled "House Organs an Aid to Management." Bibliography, pp. 144–45.

Hyde, Dorsey William, Jr. "House Organs as a Factor in Library Service," *Library Journal,* 45: 199–203 (March 1, 1920).

Kingsley, G. G. "How the Employee's Magazine Promotes Safety," *Industrial Management,* 62: 242–43 (October, 1921).

Klarwill, Victor von, editor. *The Fugger Newsletters, Being a Selection of Unpublished Letters from the Correspondents of the House of Fugger during the Years 1568–1605.* London: John Lane, 1924. 284 pp.
A second series of letters was published by the same editor in 1926. Bibliography, pp. 283–84.

Lee, James Melvin. *Business Writing.* New York: Ronald Press, 1920. 611 pp.
Chapter 33 is entitled "The House Organ." Bibliography, pp. 591–600.

McMahon, T. J. "Story of Our Social Magnet," *Industrial Management,* 57: 159 (February, 1919).

Mills, John, and Thompson, A. R. *Cost of Representative Employee Magazines.* New York: American Management Association, 1926.

More Business through House Organs (More Business Series no. 4). Boston: S. D. Warren Company. 44 pp.
Discusses format, typography, editorial content, reader interest, etc.

O'SHEA, PETER FRANCIS. *Employees' Magazines.* New York: Wilson, 1920. 122 pp.

"Promoting Better Home Ideals in the Department Store," *Builder's Age,* 47: 106–07 (April, 1925).

QUIETT, GLENN C., and CASEY, RALPH D. *Principles of Publicity.* New York and London: Appleton, 1929. 420 pp.
Chapter 8 is on "House Organs." Bibliography, pp. 399–410.

RAMSAY, ROBERT E. *Effective House Organs: Principles and Practice.* New York and London: Appleton, 1920. 361 pp.

TOWNSEND, CHARLES E. *Facts on the House Organ Field.* New York: Barron G. Collier, 1929.

TOWNSEND, GEORGE W. "Vitalizing the Plant Magazine," *Industrial Management,* 64: 12–14 (July, 1922).

VANDERCOOK, D. C. "Facts or Bunk — Which?" *Factory,* 34: 591–93 (April, 1925).

―――――. "What the Personnel Publication Can Do for the Worker," *Industrial Management,* 66: 307–10 (November, 1923).

VORHEES, ROBERT. "Factory Newspaper," *Industrial Management,* 55: 145 (February, 1918).

WENTZ, W. M. "How the Pennsylvania Sells Service and Loyalty to Its Employees," *Printed Salesmanship,* 52: 229–30 (November, 1928).

WINANS, W. R. R. "What Employee Publications Are Doing to Improve Industrial Relations," *Industrial Management,* 69: 212–14 (April, 1925).

13. LIBRARIES

AMERICAN LIBRARY ASSOCIATION. *A Survey of Libraries in the United States.* Chicago, 1926–27. 4 vols.

BOSTWICK, ARTHUR ELMORE. *The American Public Library.* Fourth edition. New York: Appleton, 1929. 471 pp.
Standard treatise. Bibliography, pp. 429–41.

BOSTWICK, ARTHUR ELMORE, editor. *Popular Libraries of the World.* Chicago: American Library Association, 1933. 316 pp.

CANNONS, HARRY GEORGE TURNER. *Bibliography of Library Economy, 1876–1920.* Chicago: American Library Association, 1927. 680 pp.

DUFFUS, ROBERT LUTHER. *Our Starving Libraries: Studies in Ten*

American Communities during the Depression Years. Boston: Houghton Mifflin, 1933. 148 pp.

Raises the question whether the Government is obliged to "guard the citizens against intellectual starvation" as well as physical starvation.

ESDAILE, ARUNDELL JAMES KENNEDY. *National Libraries of the World.* London, 1933.

ESDAILE, ARUNDELL JAMES KENNEDY, editor. *The Year's Work in Librarianship.* Published annually in London since 1929.

INTERNATIONAL INSTITUTE OF INTELLECTUAL COOPERATION. *Bibliothèques populaires et loisirs ouvriers.* Paris: League of Nations, 1933. 333 pp.

Study of the utilization of public libraries by the working classes during their leisure hours.

Leads (occasional mimeograph bulletin). Chicago: American Library Association.

MILKAU, FRITZ, editor. *Handbuch der Bibliothekswissenschaft.* Leipzig, 1931—.

WALTER, FRANK K. *The Library's Own Printing.* Chicago: American Library Association, 1934. 108 pp.

14. MISCELLANEOUS

ACHESON, ARTHUR. "Trademark Advertising as an Investment," *New York Evening Post,* 1: 10–46 (1917).

BEECHER, M. "Making the Name Plate a Salesman," *Advertising and Selling,* 2: 8 (September, 1923).

Doll Messengers of Friendship. New York: Commission on International Justice and Goodwill of Federal Council of Churches of Christ in America, n. d.

"Farmers' Social Organizations," *Cyclopedia of American Agriculture,* edited by L. H. Bailey. New York, 1907–09. 4 vols.

GIFFORD, A. G. "The Convention as a Method of Bringing Independent Opinion to Bear on the Government during the Nineteenth Century" (dissertation in preparation at the University of Wisconsin).

Handbook of Commercial and Financial Services. Providence, Rhode Island: Special Libraries Association, 1931. 95 pp. First supplement appeared in New York in 1932.

Private information services.

HILL, G. F. *Commemorative Medals as Instruments of German Propaganda.* London: Longmans, Green, 1917. 32 pp.

A study of 580 varieties of medals of German propaganda which penetrated neutral countries during the World War. By the keeper of coins and medals in the British Museum.

"International Advisers," *Encyclopedia of the Social Sciences.* (By Raymond Leslie Buell.)

PREVITE-ORTON, C. W. "Political Satire in English Poetry," *Living Age,* 265:298–301 (April 30, 1910).

SEYMOUR, H. M. "Appeal of Political Poetry," *Dial,* 56:11–12 (January 1, 1914).

SINCLAIR, UPTON. *Mammon Art.* Pasadena: The Author, 1925. 390 pp.
Even "art" may be propaganda for "big business."

"Sky-Painting with Light Gun," *Scientific American,* 137:143 (August, 1927).

SWAIN, BARBARA. *Fools and Folly during the Middle Ages and Renaissance.* New York: Columbia University, 1932. 234 pp.
The fool was frequently used as a means of bringing social criticism before the ruler.

WIEGAND, CHARMION VON. "In the Soviet Circuses, Fun Goes Serious," *New York Times Magazine,* November 26, 1933.
Propaganda via circuses in the U.S.S.R.; "the clown uses satire for social ends."

PART VI. THE MEASUREMENT OF THE EFFECTS OF PROPAGANDA

A. MEASUREMENT BY THE SCALING PROCEDURES OF L. L. THURSTONE

Professor L. L. Thurstone of the University of Chicago and his students have constructed scales, which may be obtained from the University of Chicago Press, concerning attitudes toward many subjects, including the following:

Birth Control
Capital Punishment
Censorship
Chinese
Church
Communism
Evolution
Germans
God
Law
Militarism-Pacifism

Movies
Negroes
Professional Training of
  Social Workers
Prohibition
Races
Sunday Observance
Treatment of Criminals
United States Constitution
War

Methodological discussions by Professor Thurstone and students whom he has influenced include:

DROBA, DANIEL D. "Methods Used in Measuring Public Opinion," *American Journal of Sociology*, 37:410–23 (1931).

————. "Political Parties and War Attitudes," *Journal of Abnormal and Social Psychology*, 24:468–72 (January, 1934).

JOHNSON, CHARLES S. "Measurement of Racial Attitudes," American Sociological Society Publications, 25:150–53 (1931).

PETERSON, RUTH C., and THURSTONE, L. L. "The Effect of a Motion Picture Film on Children's Attitudes toward Germans," *Journal of Educational Psychology*, 23:241–46 (1932).

RUSSELL, JAMES T., and WRIGHT, QUINCY. "National Attitudes on the Far Eastern Controversy," *American Political Science Review*, 27:555–77 (August, 1933).

STOUFFER, SAMUEL A. "Experimental Comparison of a Statistical and a Case History Technique of Attitude Research," *American Sociological Society Publications*, 25:154–56 (1931).

Discovers a close relation between the results by questionnaire procedures and by certain case study methods. Mr. Stouffer's dissertation at the University of Chicago was entitled "An Experimental Comparison of Statistical and Case History Methods of Attitude Research."

THURSTONE, LOUIS LEON. "Influence of Motion Pictures on Children's Attitudes," *Journal of Social Psychology*, 2:291–305 (August, 1931).

————. "The Measurement of Opinion," *Journal of Abnormal and Social Psychology*, 22:415–30 (1928).

————. "The Measurement of Social Attitudes," *Journal of Abnormal and Social Psychology*, 26:249–69 (1931).

————. "Rank Order as a Psychophysical Method," *Journal of Experimental Psychology*, 14:187–201 (1931).

THURSTONE, LOUIS LEON, and CHAVE, ERNEST JOHN. *The Measurement of Attitude: A Psycho-Physical Method and Some Experiments with a Scale for Measuring Attitude toward the Church*. Chicago: University of Chicago, 1929. 96 pp.

B. MEASUREMENT BY SCALING, QUESTIONNAIRE, PSYCHO-LOGICAL, AND OTHER METHODS CLOSELY RELATED TO "A"

I. BIBLIOGRAPHY

BAIN, READ. "An Attitude on Attitude Research," *American Journal of Sociology*, 33:940–57 (1928).

A general review of literature on attitudes and opinions, quoting 261 references.

DROBA, DANIEL D. "Methods for Measuring Attitudes," *Psychological Bulletin*, 29:309–24 (May, 1932).

Some 125 attitude studies are examined, and it is found that there are six methods in use now.

————. "Social Attitudes," *American Journal of Sociology*, 39:513–25 (January, 1934).

An article summarizing current literature. Lists 104 titles.

EDWARDS, A. S. "Experimental Social Psychology," *Journal of Abnormal Psychology*, 26:349–54 (January, 1932).

Bibliography.

GOSNELL, HAROLD FOOTE. "Statisticians and Political Scientists," *American Political Science Review*, 27:392–403 (June, 1933).

Reviews the current measurement studies in politics.

MURPHY, GARDNER, and MURPHY, LOIS BARCLAY. *Experimental Social Psychology.* New York and London: Harpers, 1931. 709 pp.
Chapters 10 and 11 discuss the literature of the measurement of personality and of attitudes.

SHERMAN, MANDEL. "Theories and Measurement of Attitudes," *Child Development.* 3: 15–28 (1932).
Quotes 88 sources.

2. REFERENCES

ALEXANDER, HERBERT B. "Negro Opinion and Amos and Andy," *Sociology and Social Research,* 16: 345–54 (1932).
Based on interviews with fifteen educated Negroes.

ALLPORT, F. H., and HARTMAN, D. A. "The Measurement and Motivation of Atypical Opinion in a Certain Group," *American Political Science Review,* 19: 735–60 (1925).
A precursor of the Thurstone method of grading a large number of possible attitudes toward a single issue.

————. "A Technique for the Measurement and Analysis of Public Opinion," American Sociological Society Publications, 20: 241–44 (1926).

ALLPORT, GORDON W. "The Composition of Political Attitudes," *American Journal of Sociology,* 35: 220–38 (1929).

ANDERSON, W. A. "The Occupational Attitudes and Choices of a Group of College Men," *Social Forces,* 6: 278–83 (1927); 6: 467–73 (1928).
"Found remarkable agreement of . . . comparative ratings of desirability . . . in the different occupational groups. . . . Taken in a Southern school, the occupation of preacher usually topped the lists, with bankers and manufacturers next in order of excellence." — G. B. VETTER, *Journal of Abnormal and Social Psychology,* vol. 25, p. 26 (1930).

ANNIS, A. D., and MEIER, N. C. "Induction of Opinion through Suggestion by Means of Planted Content," *Journal of Social Psychology,* 5: 68–81 (February, 1934).
Stories in a college paper were controlled and reactions studied.

ARNETT, CLAUDE E., DAVIDSON, H. H., and LEWIS, H. H. "Prestige as a Factor in Attitude Changes," *Sociology and Social Research,* 16: 49–55 (1931).

BAIN, READ. "Religious Attitudes of College Students," *American Journal of Sociology,* 32: 762–70 (1927).

————. "Stability in Questionnaire Response," *American Journal of Sociology,* 37: 445–53 (1931).

————. "Theory and Measurement of Attitudes and Opinions," *Psychological Bulletin*, 27: 357–79 (1930).

BARTLETT, LESTER W., and WHITE, WILBUR W. *Measurement of Goodwill: A Study of Goodwill in Non-Commercial Institutions as Represented by the Y.M.C.A.* New York: Association Press, 1932. 153 pp.
Utilizes indices of membership, membership persistence, the distance members come, the contributions members make, contribution persistence, outside activities, newspaper space, cooperative activities, etc.

BAUMGARTEN, F., and CRESCOTT, D. A. "Why Children Hate: An Experimental Investigation of the Reactions of School Children of Poland to the Enemy Occupation," *Journal of Educational Psychology*, 19: 303–12 (1928).
Eight different questions were asked of seven hundred Polish school children during the German occupation of Poland.

BETTS, GEORGE HERBERT. *The Beliefs of 700 Ministers and Their Meaning for Religious Education.* New York: Abingdon Press, 1929. 74 pp.

————. "Social Code of 54 Graduate Students," *Educational Trends*, January, 1932, pp. 25–39.

BEYLE, HERMAN CAREY. "The Editor Votes," *American Political Science Review*, 27: 597–611 (August, 1933).
Editors in American cities having a population of 30,000 or more were asked to answer a questionnaire on the "New Deal."

————. "A Scale for the Measurement of Attitude toward Candidates for Elective Governmental Office," *American Political Science Review*, 26: 527–44 (June, 1932).

BIDDLE, WILLIAM W. *Propaganda and Education* (Teachers College Contributions to Education, no. 531). New York: Columbia University, 1932. 84 pp.
"The development of skepticism should be one of the great educational aims of our time. . . . On the basis of an analysis of present-day methods of propaganda, a series of nine lessons was developed for experimentation. . . . Gullibility was measured by scoring the responses of students to a series of articles in a test given before and after the teaching with the nine lessons. Control groups were tested also, for comparison. The improvement of the experimental students over the controls was quite significant, statistically" (page 69). Bibliography, pp. 83–84.

BINNEWIES, W. G. "Measurement of Community Spirit," *Sociology and Social Research*, 12: 264–67 (1928).

————. "Measuring Changes in Opinion," *Sociology and Social Research*, 16: 143–48 (November, 1931).

————. "A Method of Studying Rural Social Distance," *Journal of Applied Sociology,* 10:239–42 (1926).

BLANCHARD, PHYLLIS MARY, and MANASSES, CARLYN. *New Girls for Old.* New York: Macaulay, 1930. 281 pp.
Tabulated answers to questions on what the girl of today thinks concerning sex relationships, marriage *vs.* a career, employment for women, companionate marriage, drinking, smoking, attitude of parents, etc.

BOGARDUS, EMORY STEPHEN. "American Attitudes toward Filipinos," *Sociology and Social Research,* 14:59–69 (1929).

————. "Filipino Immigrant Attitudes," *Sociology and Social Research,* 14:469–79 (1930).

————. "Mutations of Social Distance," *Journal of Applied Sociology,* 11:77–84, 272–87 (1926).

————. "Occupational Distance," *Sociology and Social Research,* 13:73–81 (1928).

————. "Sex Differences in Racial Attitudes," *Sociology and Social Research,* 12:279–85 (1928).

————. "Social Distance and Its Origin," *Journal of Applied Sociology,* 9:216–26, 299–308, 372–81 (1925).
A report of a social distance experiment carried on at the suggestion of Robert E. Park. "Among the later investigators who have applied the [case] method in a more limited and probably more accurate sense, Bogardus stands out as the best representative." — D. D. DROBA, *Psychological Bulletin,* May, 1932, p. 311.

————. "Social Distance in the City," American Sociological Society Publications, 20:40–46 (1926).

BUSCH, H. M. "Race Attitudes of Children," *Religious Education,* 21:277–81 (1926).

CALKINS, DOROTHY M. "Social Situations and Religious Attitudes," *Sociology and Social Research,* 14:249–55 (1930).

CANTRIL, HADLEY. *General and Specific Attitudes* (Psychological Monographs Series). Princeton, New Jersey: Psychological Review Company, 1932. 109 pp.

CARR, L. J. "The Measurement of Efficiency of Tuberculosis Publicity," Transactions of the Twenty-fourth Meeting of the National Tuberculosis Association, 1929.

CARTER, T. M. "Ethical Attitudes of 623 Men and Women," *International Journal of Ethics,* 43:279–94 (April, 1933).
A rating scale was used to evaluate verbal reactions to fifty-eight "ethical" situations.

CAVAN, R. T., and CAVAN, J. T. "The Attitudes of Young Business Women toward Home and Married Life," *Religious Education,* 22:817–20 (1927).

CHEN, KÊ-CHING. *The Influence of Oral Propaganda Material upon Students' Attitudes* (Ph. D. thesis, Columbia University. Archives of Psychology, no. 150). New York, 1933. 43 pp.
Bibliography, p. 39.

CLARK, W. W. "The Measurement of Social Attitudes," *Journal of Applied Sociology,* 8:345–54 (1924).

COE, G. A. "What Teachers of Secondary Education Think of Military Training in High Schools," *School and Society,* 26:174–78 (1927).

CUTLER, T. H., JR. "Effectiveness of Page Size in Magazine Advertising," *Journal of Applied Psychology,* 14:465–69 (October, 1930).

DAVIS, J. "Testing the Social Attitudes of Children in the Government Schools in Russia," *American Journal of Sociology,* 32:947–52 (1927).

DROBA, DANIEL D. "Methods Used for Measuring Public Opinion," *American Journal of Sociology,* 37:410–24 (November, 1931).

DUDYCHA, GEORGE J. "The Moral and Popular Beliefs of College Freshmen," *School and Society,* 32:69–72 (1930).

———. "The Religious Beliefs of College Freshmen," *School and Society,* 31:206–08 (1930).

———. "The Social Beliefs of College Freshmen," *School and Society,* 32:846–49 (1930).

———. "The Social Beliefs of College Seniors," *American Journal of Sociology,* 37:775–81 (March, 1932).
Results of a questionnaire presenting twenty-five propositions to seniors are compared with those previously obtained from freshmen. The results are very similar.

FEARING, FRANKLIN. "The Experimental Study of Attitude, Meaning, and the Processes Antecedent to Action, by N. Ach and others in the Würzburg Laboratory," *Methods in Social Science,* pp. 715–30. Chicago: University of Chicago, 1931.

FLORENCE, PHILIP SARGANT. *The Statistical Method in Economics and Political Science.* New York: Harcourt, Brace, 1928. London: Kegan Paul, Trench, and Trubner, 1929. 521 pp.

FORMAN, HENRY JAMES. *Our Movie-Made Children,* with an introduction by W. W. Charters. New York: Macmillan, 1933. 288 pp.
An investigation of the effects of movies on children, made by the Payne Fund at the request of the Motion-Picture Research Council.

FOWLER, O. F. "Civic Attitudes of High School Sophomores," *School Review,* 36: 25-37 (January, 1928).

FREDERICK, R. "An Investigation into Some Social Attitudes of High School Pupils," *School and Society,* 25: 410-12 (1927).

FREYD, M. "The Graphic Rating Scale," *Journal of Educational Psychology,* 14: 83-102 (1923).

GALLUP, GEORGE. "A Scientific Method for Determining Reader-Interest," *Journalism Quarterly,* 7: 1-13 (March, 1930).
An explanation of the so-called "Gallup method" of determining the interest of a reader in the news and feature material in a daily newspaper.

————. *Survey of Reader Interest in Saturday Evening Post, Liberty, Collier's, Literary Digest.* Evanston, Ill.: George Gallup, 1931. 63 pp.
Includes reader interest in both editorial matter and advertisements.

————. *Survey of Reader Interest in the Various Sections of the Sunday Newspapers.* Neenah, Wisconsin: Kimberly-Clark Corporation. 32 pp.

————. "What Do Newspaper Readers Read?" *Advertising and Selling,* 18: 22-23, 51 (March 31, 1932).
Survey of 40,000 readers of 14 metropolitan newspapers.

GARRISON, K. C., and MANN, MARGARET. "A Study of the Opinions of College Students," *Journal of Social Psychology,* 2: 168-78 (1931).

GOODWIN, E. H. *The Referendum System of the Chamber of Commerce of the United States* (International Chamber of Commerce, Digest no. 7).

GRIFFITH, C. R. "A Comment upon the Psychology of the Audience," *Psychological Monographs,* 30: 36-47 (1921).
Study of the focus of attention in a classroom.

GUILFORD, J. P. "The Method of Paired Comparisons as a Psychometric Method," *Psychological Review,* 35: 494-506 (1928).

————. "Racial Preferences of 1,000 American University Students," *Journal of Social Psychology,* 2: 179-204 (1931).

————. "Some Empirical Tests of the Method of Paired Comparisons," *Journal of General Psychology,* 5: 64-67 (1931).

GUTHRIE, E. R. "Measuring Student Opinion of Teachers," *School and Society*, 25: 175–76 (1927).

HARPER, HEBER REECE. *What European and American Students Think on International Problems: A Comparative Study of the World-Mindedness of University Students* (Ph. D. thesis, Columbia University, 1931. Studies of the International Institute of Teachers College, no. 12). New York: Columbia University, 1931. 255 pp.

HART, HORNELL NORRIS. *Progress Report on a Test of Social Attitudes and Interests* (University of Iowa Studies in Child Welfare, vol. 2, no. 4). Iowa City: University of Iowa, 1923. 40 pp. and tables. Bibliography, pp. 39–40.

HARTSHORNE, HUGH, MAY, M. A., and others. *Testing the Knowledge of Right and Wrong* (Religious Education Association Monograph no. 1). Chicago, 1927. 72 pp.
Studies of relative influence of parents, friends, Sunday-school teachers, and club leaders in the formation of knowledge of "right" and "wrong." Appeared serially in *Religious Education*, February, 1926–May, 1927.

HEVNER, KATE. "A Comparative Study of Three Psychophysical Methods," *Journal of General Psychology*, 4: 191–212 (1930).

HIGHFILL, R. D. "Effects of News of Crime and Scandal upon Public Opinion," *Journal of Criminal Law*, 17: 40–103 (May, 1926). Also in the *American Law Review*, 62: 13–93 (January, 1928).
Discusses the findings of criminologists such as Lombroso, Ferri, and Parmelee. Reviews a University of Chicago study on the same topic. Analyzes a mass of social facts that have appeared in the newspapers. Suggests the "criminal news expert" as a solution of the difficulties discovered.

HOTCHKISS, GEORGE BURTON, and FRANKEN, RICHARD B. *Newspaper Reading Habits of Business Executives and Professional Men in New York*. New York: Bureau of Business Research, New York University, 1922. 24 pp.

———. *Newspaper Reading Habits of College Students*. New York: Bureau of Business Research, New York University, 1920. 15 pp.

HYPES, J. L. "The Social Distance Score-Card as a Teaching Device," *Social Forces*, 7: 234–37 (1928).

JASPER, H. H. "Optimism and Pessimism in College Engineers," *American Journal of Sociology*, 34: 856–73 (1929).

JONES, E. S. "Opinions of College Students," *Journal of Applied Psychology*, 10: 427–36.
"E. S. Jones studied the opinions of college students on 25 items, po-

litical, religious, domestic and moral. The more intelligent students, as measured by tests, were slightly more 'radical' (as judged by the experimenter's criterion), more positive, and less suggestible (as measured by tendency to agree with statements as given)." — G. B. VETTER, *Journal of Abnormal and Social Psychology*, vol. 25, p. 28.

KATZ, DANIEL, and ALLPORT, FLOYD, with the cooperation of Margaret Babcock Jenness. *Students' Attitudes: A Report of the Syracuse University Reaction Study.* Syracuse: Craftsman Press, 1931. 408 pp. Bibliography, pp. 398–402.

KELLOWAY, W. F. "Young Peoples' Attitudes toward Worship," *Religious Education*, 25: 303–05 (1930).

KIMMINS, C. W. "The Special Interests of Children in the War at Different Ages," *Journal of Experimental Pedagogy*, vol. 3, no. 3 (December, 1915).

KIRKPATRICK, CLIFFORD. "A Tentative Study in Experimental Social Psychology," *American Journal of Sociology*, 38: 194–207 (September, 1932).
Belief in and transmission of rumor.

KOOS, LEONARD VINCENT. *The Questionnaire in Education.* New York: Macmillan, 1928. 178 pp.
Bibliography, pp. 168–74.

KORNHAUSER, ARTHUR W. "Changes in the Information and Attitudes of Students in an Economics Course," *Journal of Educational Research*, 22: 288–98 (1930).
A check-up on the University of Chicago course in "The Economic Order." Comments on (1) increase in accuracy on true-false test throughout the year; (2) changes in attitudes on controversial questions; (3) attitude scores that are less extreme at end of course; (4) lack of relation between attitude changes and Otis Intelligence Test results; (5) lack of relation between attitude changes and economic knowledge of student.

————. "Results from the Use of the Objective Tests and Questionnaires in a College Course on 'The Economic Order,'" *Journal of Business of the University of Chicago*, 1: 429–55 (1928); 2: 82–111 (1929).

KORNHAUSER, ARTHUR W., and SHARP, A. A. "Employee Attitudes: Suggestions from a Study in a Factory," *Personnel Journal*, 10: 393–404 (1932).

KULP, D. H., and DAVIDSON, H. H. "Can Neumann's 'Attitude Indicator' Be Used as a Test?" *Teachers College Record*, 22: 332–37 (1931).

Lapiere, R. T. "Race Prejudice: France and England," *Social Forces,* 7: 101–11 (1927).

Lasker, Bruno. *Race Attitudes in Children.* New York: Holt, 1929. 394 pp.
Finds fear the most vivid and lasting of conditioning influences. Concludes that perhaps promoters of peace would do better to build up resistance (criticism) against false racial suggestions than to try to combat the many everyday prejudicial situations.

Lasswell, Harold Dwight. "Measurement of Public Opinion," *American Political Science Review,* 25: 311–26 (May, 1931).

Lewerentz, Alfred S. "Attitude Differences of Social Groups," *Sociology and Social Research,* 16: 553–57 (1932).

Likert, Rensis. *A Technique for the Measurement of Attitudes* (Ph. D. thesis, Columbia University. Archives of Psychology, no. 140). New York, 1932. 55 pp.
Bibliography, pp. 54–55.

Lockhart, Earl Granger. *The Attitudes of Children toward Law* (Ph. D. thesis. University of Iowa Studies in Character, vol. 3, no. 1). Iowa City: University of Iowa, 1930. 61 pp.
Bibliography, p. 38.

Lundberg, George A. "The Measurement of Attitudes," in the author's *Social Research,* chap. 9. New York: Longmans, Green, 1929.
Textbook treatment of developments up to 1929. Has annotated bibliography on measurement of attitudes, social institutions, sources of social data, etc.

————. "The Newspaper and Public Opinion," *Social Forces,* 4: 709–15 (1926).
" . . . the relation between the policies of several newspapers and a generous sample of readers of each. He found poor correspondence between the avowed policy of the paper and the voice of the readers on specific candidates or referendum propositions." — G. B. Vetter, *Journal of Abnormal and Social Psychology,* vol. 25, p. 28.

————. "Sex Differences on Social Questions," *School and Society,* 23: 595–600 (1926).
" . . . Contrasted with men, the women college students were more conservative in regard to labor questions, changes in government, religion, and domestic and moral matters. They were more in favor of government ownership and more anti-war. They apparently were 'taken in' more by propaganda tales of the late war. Women strongly favored economic equality, but objected to 'Dutch treats' when with men. . . . Radical and conservative attitudes did not seem to be generalized or to carry over from one field of opinion to another." — G. B. Vetter, *Journal of Abnormal and Social Psychology,* vol. 25, p. 28.

McMILLEN, ARDEE WAYNE. *Measurement in Social Work* (Ph. D. thesis, University of Chicago. Social Service Monographs, no. 12). Chicago: University of Chicago, 1930. 154 pp.

MANRY, JAMES CAMPBELL. *World Citizenship: A Measurement of Certain Factors Determining Information and Judgment of International Affairs* (Ph. D. thesis. University of Iowa Studies in Character, vol. 1, no. 1). Iowa City: University of Iowa, 1927. 67 pp.

"The Measurement of Public Opinion," *American Political Science Review,* 19 : 123–26 (February, 1925).
Report of Round Tables on Political Statistics, National Conference on the Science of Politics.

MOEDE, WALTHER. *Experimentelle Massenpsychologie: Beiträge zur Experimentalpsychologie der Gruppe.* Leipzig: S. Hirzel, 1920. 239 pp.

MOORE, GWYN, and GARRISON, K. "Comparative Study of Social and Political Attitudes of College Students," *Journal of Abnormal and Social Psychology,* 27: 195–208 (1932).

MOORE, HENRY T. "Innate Factors in Radicalism and Conservatism," *Journal of Abnormal and Social Psychology,* 20: 234–44 (1925–26).

MURPHY, GARDNER, and MURPHY, LOIS BARCLAY. *Experimental Social Psychology.* New York: Harpers, 1931. 709 pp.
A standard treatise. Bibliography at ends of chapters; bibliographic note, p. 694.

NAFZIGER, RALPH O. "A Reader-Interest Survey of Madison, Wisconsin," *Journalism Quarterly,* 7: 128–141 (June, 1930).

NATIONAL LEAGUE OF WOMEN VOTERS. *Report of the Radio Committee of the National League of Women Voters for 1931 and 1932.* Washington, D. C., 1933. 31 pp.
An experimental study of the radio as an influence in changing public opinion, based on the reactions of groups of listeners during the electoral campaign of 1932.

NEUMANN, GEORGE BRADFORD. *A Study of the International Attitudes of High School Students* (Teachers College Contributions to Education, no. 239). New York: Columbia University, 1926. 120 pp.

PAGE, KIRBY. "Nineteen Thousand Clergymen on War and Peace," *The World Tomorrow,* 14: 138–49 (1931).

PENNINGROTH, PAUL WILLIAM. *A Study of Public Opinion in International Relations in Certain Communities* (Ph. D. thesis, Columbia University, 1932). Tampa, Florida, 1932. 111 pp.
Bibliography, pp. 109–10.

PORTER, ELIOT. "Student Opinion on War" (unpublished Ph. D. thesis, University of Chicago, 1926). 247 pp.
Bibliography, pp. 242–47.

REED, E. F. "Does the Individual Tend to be Consistently a Progressive or a Conservative?" *Social Forces*, 6: 49–52.

RICE, STUART ARTHUR. "Behavior Alternatives as Statistical Data in Studies by William F. Ogburn and Ernest W. Burgess," *Methods in Social Science*, pp. 586–608. Chicago: University of Chicago, 1931.

——. "Differential Changes of Political Preference under Campaign Stimulation," *Journal of Abnormal and Social Psychology*, 21: 297–303 (1926).

——. *Quantitative Methods in Politics.* New York: Knopf, 1928. 331 pp.

——. "Undergraduate Attitudes toward Marriage and Children," *Mental Hygiene*, 13: 788–93 (1929).

RICE, STUART ARTHUR, editor. *Statistics in Social Studies.* Philadelphia: University of Pennsylvania, 1930. 222 pp.
By twelve different authors, covering a wide variety of subjects.

RICE, STUART ARTHUR, and WEAVER, W. W. "The Verification of Social Measurements Involving Subjective Classifications: Measurement of Newspaper Content," *Social Forces*, 8: 16–28 (September, 1929).
Has bibliography.

RIDDLE, ETHEL MARIE. *Aggressive Behavior in a Small Social Group: Bluffing, Risking, and the Desire to Beat, Being Studied by the Use of a Poker Game as an Experimental Technique* (Ph. D. thesis, Columbia University. Archives of Psychology, no. 78). New York: Columbia University, 1925. 196 pp.

ROBINSON, V. P. "The Conception of God of College Students," *American Journal of Religious Psychology and Education*, 3: 247–57 (1908–09).

SCHNEERSOHN, F. "Experimentelle Massenpsychologie," *Ethos*, 1: 311–20 (1925–26).

SEYMOUR, J. S. "Rural Social Distance of Normal School Students," *Sociology and Social Research*, 14: 238–48 (1930).

SHIDELER, E. F. "The Social Distance Margin," *Sociology and Social Research*, 12: 243–352 (1928).

SONQUIST, DAVID EMMANUEL. *Techniques for Discovering the Interests of Young Men: The Discovery and Meaning of Interests in Pro-*

gram Building (Ph. D. thesis, University of Chicago, 1931). New York: Association Press, 1931. 177 pp.

Methods of discovering interests; written primarily for Y. M. C. A.'s. Bibliography, pp. 167–69.

STALNAKER, J. M., and EGGAN, F. "American Novelists Ranked: A Psychological Study," *English Journal*, 18: 295–307 (1929).

STURGES, H. A. "The Theory of Correlation Applied to Changing Attitudes," *American Journal of Sociology*, 33: 269–75 (1927).

SUMNER, WILLIAM A. "Reading Interests and Buying Habits of the Rural and Village Subscribers of a Daily Newspaper," *Journalism Quarterly*, 9: 182–89 (June, 1932).

SWABEY, M. C. "Publicity and Measurement," *International Journal of Ethics*, 41: 96–114 (October, 1930).

SYMONDS, P. M. "A Social Attitude Questionnaire," *Journal of Educational Psychology*, 16: 316–22 (1925).

"Symonds gave a social attitudes questionnaire to students of varying degrees of maturity: i. e., eighth-graders and college seniors. He concluded that the liberal-conservative attitudes are formed very early and remain fairly constant because the 8th graders were as liberal as the college seniors. Five judges made the decision of what constituted radical, liberal, progressive, conservative." — G. B. VETTER, *Journal of Abnormal and Social Psychology*, vol. 25, p. 29.

VAUGHAN, W. F. "An Experimental Study of Political Prejudice," *Journal of Abnormal and Social Psychology*, 25: 268–74 (1930).

VETTER, GEORGE B. "The Measurement of Social and Political Attitudes and the Related Personality Factors," *Journal of Abnormal and Social Psychology*, 25: 149–89 (1930).

————. "The Study of Social and Political Opinions," *Journal of Abnormal and Social Psychology*, 25: 26–27 (1930).

Contains a review of developments in the description of reaction patterns, and deals with such quantitative studies as were available at the time of writing.

WAPLES, DOUGLAS, and TYLER, RALPH W. *What People Want to Read About*. Chicago: Published for the American Library Association by the University of Chicago Press, 1931. 312 pp.

Analysis of statements of preference of more than a hundred groups, ranging from telephone operators to captains of industry.

WASHBURN, M., and others. "The Moore Test of Radicalism and Conservatism," *American Journal of Psychology*, 38: 449–52 (1927).

WATSON, GOODWIN BARBOUR. *The Measurement of Fair-Mindedness*

(Teachers College Contributions to Education, no. 176). New York: Columbia University, 1925. 97 pp.

―――. "Orient and Occident: An Opinion Study," *Religious Education*, 24: 322–28 (1929).

―――. *A Survey of Public Opinion on Some Religious and Economic Issues.* New York: Teachers College, Columbia University, 1927.

WATSON, GOODWIN BARBOUR, and GREEN, GERALDINE. "Scientific Studies and Personal Opinion on Sex Questions," *Journal of Abnormal and Social Psychology*, 27: 130–46 (1932).

WEINLAND, J. D. "An Objective Method for the Measurement of Attitudes," *Journal of Applied Psychology*, 14: 427–36 (1930).

WILCOX, W. F. "Attempt to Measure Public Opinion about Repealing the XVIII Amendment," *Journal of American Statistical Association*, 26: 243–61 (September, 1931).

WILKINSON, F. "Social Distance between Occupations," *Sociology and Social Research*, 13: 234–44 (1929).

WILLEY, MALCOLM MACDONALD, and RICE, STUART ARTHUR. "William J. Bryan as a Social Force," *Journal of Social Forces*, March, 1924. "Willey and Rice, seizing an opportunity to measure the power of the famous orator, Bryan, made up a list of questions on religious matters and gave them to a student body. The test was given after Bryan's speech, and the experimenters used the shift in opinions as recorded, to measure the efficacy of Bryan. . . . It is of interest here only as bringing out the fact that . . . questions or questionnaires are sensitive enough to bring out changes due presumably to the effects of a single exposure to oratory." — G. B. VETTER, *Journal of Abnormal and Social Psychology*, vol. 25, p. 30.

WILLOUGHBY, R. R. "A Sampling of Student Opinion," *Journal of Social Psychology*, 1: 164–69 (1930).

WILSON, W. R. "A Large-Scale Experiment in Student Ratings," *Psychological Bulletin*, 28: 248 (1931).

YOUNG, D. "Some Effects of a Course in Race Problems on the Race Prejudice of 450 Undergraduates of the University of Pennsylvania," *Journal of Abnormal and Social Psychology*, 22: 235–42 (1927).

YOUNG, P. V. "Occupational Attitudes and Values of Russian Lumber Workers," *Sociology and Social Research*, 12: 543–53 (1928).

ZELENY, L. D. "A Measure of Social Opinions of Students," *Journal of Applied Sociology*, 11: 56–64 (1926). Opinions of a class in sociology.

ZIMMERMAN, CARLE CLARK. *Farmers' Marketing Attitudes* (Ph.D. thesis, University of Minnesota, 1925). St. Paul, 1927. 54 pp.

ZIMMERMAN, CARLE CLARK, and ANDERSON, C. A. "Attitudes of Rural Preachers regarding Church Union and Science," *Sociology and Social Research,* 12:144–50 (1927).

ZIMMERMAN, CARLE CLARK, and BLACK, J. D. *The Marketing Attitudes of Minnesota Farmers* (University of Minnesota Agricultural Experiment Station Technical Bulletin no. 45). 1926.

C. MEASUREMENT OF THE EFFECTS OF COMMERCIAL ADVERTISING

ADAMS, H. F. "Adequacy of the Laboratory Test in Advertising," *Psychological Review,* 22:402–22 (September, 1915).

————. "The Relative Memory-Values of Duplication and Variation in Advertising," *Journal of Philosophical, Psychological, and Scientific Method,* 13:141–52 (1916).

ADAMS, H. F., and DANDISION, B. "Further Experiments on the Attention Value of Size and Repetition in Advertisements," *Journal of Applied Psychology,* 11:483–89 (December, 1927).

ADVERTISING FEDERATION OF AMERICA. *The Measurement of Advertising Effect.* New York, 1930.

ASHER, E. J. "Association Test as a Means of Determining the Relative Familiarity of Retail Stores," *Journal of Applied Psychology,* 12:437–46 (1928).
Bibliography.

AUDIT BUREAU OF CIRCULATIONS. *Scientific Space Selections.* Chicago, 1921. 167 pp.
A text on selection of advertising media.

BARKLEY, K. L. "Development of a New Method for Determining the Relative Efficiencies of Advertisements in Magazines," *Journal of Applied Psychology,* 15:390–410 (August, 1931); 16:74–90 (February, 1932).

BRANDT, EDITH ROBERTS. *The Memory Value of Advertisements with Special Reference to the Use of Color* (Ph.D. thesis, Columbia University, 1925. Archives of Psychology, no. 79). New York: Columbia University, 1925. 69 pp.

BURCHARD, T. C., and WARDEN, C. J. "Effect of the Size of the Advertising Section upon the Value of Individual Advertisements in It," *Journal of Applied Psychology,* 10:162–70 (June, 1926).

BURTT, H. E., and CROCKETT, T. S. "Technique for Psychological Study of Poster Board Advertising and Some Preliminary Results," *Journal of Applied Psychology,* 12: 43–55 (February, 1928).

BURTT, H. E., and DOBELL, M. E. "Curve of Forgetting for Advertising Material," *Journal of Applied Psychology,* 9: 5–21 (March, 1925).

CAPLES, JOHN. *Tested Advertising Methods.* New York and London: Harpers, 1932. 276 pp.

FRANKEN, RICHARD BENJAMIN. "Advertising Appeals Selected by the Method of Direct Impressions," *Journal of Applied Psychology,* 8: 232–44 (June, 1924).

———. *The Attention-Value of Newspaper Advertisements.* New York: Association of National Advertisers, 1925. 55 pp.
Bibliography, pp. 53–55.

FRANKEN, RICHARD BENJAMIN, and LARRABEE, CARROLL B. *Packages That Sell.* New York: Harpers, 1928. 302 pp.

GALLUP, GEORGE. *Factors of Reader Interest in 261 Advertisements.* New York: Liberty Publishing Corporation, 1932. 51 pp.

GUNDLACH, E. T. "Math. vs. Psychology in Advertising," *Advertising and Selling,* 3: 32 (August 13, 1924).

HANCOCK, G. B. "Commercial Advertisement and Social Pathology," *Social Forces,* 4: 812–19 (June, 1926).
Has bibliography.

HELLER, WALTER STERN, and BROWN, WARNER. "Memory and Association in the Case of Street-Car Advertising Cards," University of California Publications in Psychology, 2: 267–75. Berkeley, California: University of California, 1916.

HOLLINGSWORTH, H. L. "Judgments of Persuasiveness," *Psychological Review,* 18: 234–56 (July, 1911).

HOLMES, J. L. "Free Association Methods as a Measure of the Efficiency of Advertising," *Journal of Applied Psychology,* 9: 60–65 (March, 1925).

HOTCHKISS, GEORGE BURTON, and FRANKEN, RICHARD BENJAMIN. *The Attention Value of Advertisements in a Leading Periodical.* New York: New York University, Graduate School of Business Administration, Bureau of Business Research, 1920. 32 pp.
"An experiment in measuring the relative attention secured by the various advertisements printed in the *Saturday Evening Post* of November 8, 1919."

————. *The Leadership of Advertised Brands* (New York University, Graduate School of Business Administration, Bureau of Business Research, Studies). Garden City: Doubleday, Page, 1923. 256 pp.
A study of a hundred representative commodities showing the names and brands that are most familiar to the public, published for the Associated Advertising Clubs of the World.

————. *The Measurement of Advertising Effects: A Study of Representative Commodities, Showing Public Familiarity with Names and Brands, Sponsored by the International Advertising Association.* New York and London: Harpers, 1927. 248 pp.

————. *Newspaper Reading Habits of Business Executives and Professional Men in New York.* New York: New York University, Graduate School of Business Administration, Bureau of Business Research, 1922. 24 pp.

————. *Newspaper Reading Habits of College Students.* New York: Association of National Advertisers, Inc., 1920.

KARWOSKI, T. "Memory Value of Size," *Journal of Experimental Psychology,* 14: 539–54 (October, 1931).

KISS, J. A. "Fatigue Point: A Vital Feature of Sound Advertising Composition," *Inland Printer,* 83: 93–97 (September, 1929).

KITSON, H. D., and ALLEN, I. "Pictures of People in Magazine Advertising," *Journal of Applied Psychology,* 9: 367–70 (December, 1925).

KITSON, H. D., and CAMPBELL, J. J. "Minor Studies in the Psychology of Advertising: The Package as a Feature in Magazine Advertising," *Journal of Applied Psychology,* 8: 444–45 (December, 1924).

KITSON, H. D., and MORGAN, H. K. "Minor Studies in the Psychology of Advertising: Ratio between Size of Type in Headline and Size of Advertisement," *Journal of Applied Psychology,* 8: 446–49 (December, 1924).

LEVY, JACK MORRIS. "Experiments on Attention and Memory, with Special Reference to the Psychology of Advertising," University of California Publications in Psychology, 2: 157–97. Berkeley, California: University of California, 1916.

LUCAS, D. B., and BENSON, C. E. "Historical Trend of Negative Appeals in Advertising," *Journal of Applied Psychology,* 13: 346–56 (August, 1929).

————. "Recall Values of Positive and Negative Advertising Appeals," *Journal of Applied Psychology,* 14: 218–38 (June, 1930).

————. "Relative Values of Positive and Negative Advertising Appeals as Measured by Coupons Returned," *Journal of Applied Psychology*, 13:274–300 (June, 1929).

————. "Sales Results of Positive and Negative Advertisements," *Journal of Applied Psychology*, 14:363–70 (August, 1930).

MARCUS, F. "What Not to Do: A Scientific Analysis of 3,237 Pieces of Mail," *Mail Bag*, July, 1924, p. 97.

NEWHALL, S. M. "Reliability of Order of Merit Evaluations of Advertisements," *Journal of Applied Psychology*, 14:532–48 (December, 1930).

NEWHALL, S. M., and HEIM, M. H. "Memory Value of Absolute Size in Magazine Advertising," *Journal of Applied Psychology*, 13:62–75 (February, 1929).

NIXON, HOWARD KENNETH. *Attention and Interest in Advertising* (Ph.D. thesis, Columbia University, 1924. Archives of Psychology, no. 72). New York, 1924. 67 pp.

————. *An Investigation of Attention to Advertisements.* New York: Columbia University, 1926. 36 pp.

————. "Study of Perception of Advertisements," *Journal of Applied Psychology*, 11:135–42 (April, 1927).

————. "Two Studies of Attention to Advertisements," *Journal of Applied Psychoolgy*, 9:176–87 (June, 1925).

POFFENBERGER, A. T. "Psychological Tests in Advertising," *Journal of Experimental Psychology*, 73:312–20 (August, 1924).

ROLOFF, HANS PAUL. "Experimentelle Untersuchung der Werbewirkung von Plakatentwürfen," *Zeitschrift für angewandte Psychologie*, 28:1–44 (January, 1927).
Also published in Schriften zur Psychologie der Berufseignung und des Wirtschaftslebens, Heft 34. Leipzig: J. A. Barth, 1927. 44 pp.

SEASHORE, CARL EMIL, and GOULD, H. H. *How to Measure the Merit of an Advertisement* (University of Iowa Extension Bulletin no. 75). Iowa City: University of Iowa, 1921. 11 pp.

SODERGREN, PHILIP J. *Principles of Advertising Based on a Psychological Investigation of Iowa Newspapers* (University of Iowa Extension Bulletin no. 10. [N.S., no. 98]). Iowa City, Iowa: University of Iowa, 1915. 16 pp.
Bibliography, p. 16.

STARCH, DANIEL. "Testing the Effectiveness of Advertisements," *Harvard Business Review*, 1:464–74 (1923).

Strong, Edward K., Jr. "Effect of Size of Advertisements and the Frequency of Their Presentation," *Psychological Review*, 21: 136–52 (March, 1914).

————. "An Interesting Sex Difference," *Pedagogical Seminary*, 22: 521 (December, 1925).

————. "Psychological Methods as Applied to Advertising," *Journal of Educational Psychology*, 4: 393–404 (1913).

————. *The Relative Merit of Advertisements: A Psychological and Statistical Study* (Archives of Psychology, vol. 2, no. 17). New York: Science Press, 1911. 81 pp.

————. "Value of White Space in Advertising," *Journal of Applied Psychology*, 10: 107–16 (March, 1926).

Strong, E. K., Jr., and Laslett, H. R. "Further Study of Want vs. Commodity Advertisements," *Journal of Applied Psychology*, 11: 8–24 (February, 1927).

Strong, E. K., Jr., and Loveless, J. E. "Want and Solution Advertisements," *Journal of Applied Psychology*, 10: 346–66 (September, 1926).

Warden, C. J., and others. "Study of Certain Aspects of Advertising in the *Saturday Evening Post*," *Journal of Applied Psychology*, 10: 63–66 (March, 1926).

————. "Tendencies in the Use of Headlines in Magazine Advertising," *Journal of Applied Psychology*, 9: 225–29 (September, 1925).

Yerkes, Robert M. "The Class Experiment in Psychology with Advertisements as Materials," *Journal of Educational Psychology*, 3: 1–17 (1912).

D. MARKET ANALYSES

A few additional market analyses of marked sociological interest will be found in Part IV, Section F.

The federal government, many newspapers and chambers of commerce, some universities, and all the national advertising agencies engage extensively in market analysis, the investigation of the purchasing power, occupations, habits, desires, age, race, and cultural affiliations of selected populations. Campaigns are laid out months or even years in advance to bring the budgetary habits of buyers into conformity with the hopes of the advertiser's clients. It is worth noting that these studies are available to other pressure groups besides the purely commercial, as a basis for their programs for influencing public opinion.

The University of Illinois has published a market research bibliography (see below). Since this work and others are easily available, the titles quoted in the present bibliography do not pretend to completeness, but are inserted mainly to give some idea of the variety of such studies now under way.

1. BIBLIOGRAPHY

ASSOCIATION OF NATIONAL ADVERTISERS. *An Index to Distribution Research.* New York, 1929.

"A list of research studies conducted by various public and private organizations. It is expected that supplementary lists will be issued from time to time."

HAMLIN, INA M. *A Market Research Bibliography* (University of Illinois, Commerce and Administration College, Business Research Bureau, Bulletin no. 38, pp. 1–75). Urbana, Illinois: University of Illinois, 1931.

Contents: I. Market Analysis: Principles and Methods. II. Statistical Sources. III–VI. Reports of Specific Investigations: Marketing, Markets, Commodities, and Administration. VII. Some Sources of Additional Research Information.

SCHRAM, JENNIE L. *Outstanding Commercial Research and a List of Key Publications.* Chicago: Chicago Association of Commerce, n. d.

UNITED STATES DEPARTMENT OF COMMERCE, BUREAU OF FOREIGN AND DOMESTIC COMMERCE. *Market Research Agencies* (Domestic Commerce Series, no. 6). Washington, D. C.: Government Printing Office, annually, 1926 —.

"A list of publications on domestic market research by the federal government, state governments, colleges, publishers, advertising agencies, business services, chambers of commerce, individuals, business magazines, newspapers, and trade associations."

WILCOX, J. K. *A Checklist of Recent Industrial Surveys* (John Crerar Library Reference List no. 14, pp. 1–13). Chicago, 1931.

2. REFERENCES

AMERICAN ASSOCIATION OF ADVERTISING AGENCIES. *Market and Newspaper Statistics — 108 Cities.* New York, 1933. 255 pp., photolithographed.

"Selected information regarding markets and newspapers in cities having over 100,000 population."

AMERICAN ASSOCIATION OF FOREIGN LANGUAGE NEWSPAPERS, INC. *The Foreign Language Market in America.* New York, 1923.

A study of the racial and national groups in the United States, their geographical distribution, occupations, social and economic standing, the publications they support, with rates, circulations, and other data for the guidance of advertising agencies and advertisers.

BARTON, L. M., editor. *A Study of All American Markets*. Chicago: The 100,000 Group of American Cities, 1927. 606 pp.

Statistics on wholesale and retail distributors in 93 marketing areas.

EASTMAN, R. O., INC. *Zanesville and 36 Other American Communities: A Study of the Markets and of the Telephone as a Market Index*. New York: The Literary Digest, 1927. 188 pp.

"The results of personal interviews in 11,232 homes in Zanesville, Ohio, and 36 other cities of the U. S. The purpose of these visits, made under the direction of an independent research organization, was to present an analysis of the average American home."

LAZARSFELD, PAUL F. "The Psychological Aspect of Market Research," *Harvard Business Review,* October, 1934, pp. 54–71.

By a Viennese psychologist now engaged in market research in the United States.

PITKIN, WALTER BOUGHTON. *The Consumer, His Nature and Changing Habits*. New York: McGraw-Hill, 1932. 421 pp.

REILLY, WILLIAM J. "What Place Has the Advertising Agency in Market Research?" University of Texas, Business Administration School, Business Research Bureau, Research Monograph no. 3, pp. 1–31. Austin, Texas: University of Texas, 1929.

SWEENY, J. F. *A Study of the New York Times*. New York: The Times, 1923.

E. QUANTITATIVE NEWSPAPER, PERIODICAL, AND BOOK ANALYSIS : SPACE MEASUREMENT

BUSH, C. R. "A Critical Analysis of the Louisville *Courier-Journal*" (unpublished B. A. thesis, University of Wisconsin, 1925).

CHAFFEE, MARY. "A Comparison of Two City Journals Regarded as Social Stimuli" (unpublished master's essay, Columbia University, 1916).

COOK, K. E. "An Analysis of the Wisconsin *State Journal*" (unpublished B. A. thesis, University of Wisconsin, 1926).

CUMMINGS, ARTHUR R. "A Quantitative Analysis of a New York Newspaper and an Efficiency Test" (unpublished master's essay, Columbia University, 1914).

FOSTER, HARRY SCHUYLER, JR. "American News of Europe, 1914–1917" (unpublished Ph. D. thesis, University of Chicago, 1931). 355 pp.

———. "How America Became Belligerent: A Quantitative Study of War-News, 1914-17," *American Journal of Sociology,* 40: 464-76 (January, 1935).

FRANCE, GEORGIA P. "The Editorial Policies of Three New York Dailies" (unpublished master's essay, Columbia University, 1922).

GARTH, THOMAS R. "A Statistical Study of the Content of Newspapers," *School and Society,* 3: 140-44 (1918).

HART, HORNELL NORRIS. "Changing Opinions about Business Prosperity: A Consensus of Magazine Opinion in the U.S., 1929-32," *American Journal of Sociology,* 38: 665-88 (March, 1933).

———. "Changing Social Attitudes and Interests," *Recent Social Trends,* 1: 382-443. New York, 1933.

JANSKY, N. M. "An Analysis of the Wisconsin *State Journal*" (unpublished B.A. thesis, University of Wisconsin, 1926).

JOHNSON, GLENN. "News Variability in an American Journal" (unpublished master's thesis, Columbia University, 1916).

KINGSBURY, SUSAN M., HART, HORNELL, and associates. "Measuring the Ethics of American Newspapers," *Journalism Quarterly.* Series of articles: "Spectrum Analysis of Newspaper Sensationalism," 10: 93-108 (June, 1933); "News Interest Spectra of Important Papers," 10: 181-201 (September, 1933); "Newspaper Bias on Congressional Controversies," 10: 323-42 (December, 1933); "The Headline Index of Newspaper Bias," 11: 179-99 (June, 1934); "An Index of Pernicious Medical Advertising," 11: 276-300 (September, 1933); "Comparative Analysis of Newspaper Ethical Codes," 11: 361-81 (December, 1934).

MATHEWS, BYRON C. "A Study of a New York Daily," *Independent,* 68: 82-86 (January 13, 1910).

NEPRASH, JERRY ALVIN. "A Comparative Analysis of the Metropolitan Daily Press" (unpublished master's essay, Columbia University, 1926).

RICE, STUART ARTHUR, and WEAVER, W. W. "Verification of Social Measurements Involving Subjective Classifications: Measurement of Newspaper Content," *Social Forces,* 8: 16-28 (September, 1929). Has bibliography.

RIIS, ROGER W. "Are Newspapers Doing Their Duty?" *Independent,* 112: 117-18 (1924).

ROGERS, JAMES EDWARD. *The American Newspaper.* Chicago: University of Chicago, 1909. 213 pp.

SMITH, RUSSELL G. "Quantitative Problems in Press Analysis" (unpublished master's essay, Columbia University, 1914).

SPEED, J. G. "Do Newspapers Give the News?" *Forum,* 15:705–11.

STREET, ARTHUR T. "The Truth about Newspapers," *Chicago Sunday Tribune,* July 25, 1909.

TAUEBER, IRENE BARNES. "Material in Minnesota Weekly Newspapers," *Journalism Quarterly,* 9:281–89 (September, 1932).

TAYLOR, C. C. "The Country Newspaper as a Town-Country Agency," Proceedings of the Fourth National Country Life Conference, 1922, pp. 60–67.

TENNEY, ALVAN A. "The Scientific Analysis of the Press," *Independent,* 73:895–98.

WALKER, GAYLE COURTNEY. "A 'Yardstick' for the Measurement of Country Weekly Service," *Journalism Quarterly,* 7:293–302 (December, 1930).

WHITE, PAUL W. "Quarter Century Survey of Press Content Shows Demands for Facts," *Editor and Publisher,* vol. 57, no. 1 (May 31, 1924).

WILCOX, DELOS FRANKLIN. "The American Newspaper," *Annals of the American Academy of Political and Social Science,* 16:56–92 (1900).

WILLEY, MALCOLM MACDONALD. *The Country Newspaper* (Ph.D. thesis, Columbia University, 1926). Chapel Hill: University of North Carolina, 1926. London: Oxford University, 1926. 153 pp.
A study of the thirty-five country papers of Connecticut. Bibliography, pp. 129–33.

————. "The Influence of Cultural Change upon the American Newspaper," American Sociological Society Publications, 23:207–10 (1929).

WOODWARD, JULIAN LAURENCE. *Foreign News in American Morning Newspapers* (Ph.D. thesis, Columbia University). New York: Columbia University, 1930. 114 pp.
Bibliography, pp. 112–14.

F. POPULAR VOTE ANALYSIS

CATLIN, GEORGE E. G. "Harold F. Gosnell's Experiments in the Stimulation of Voting," *Methods in Social Science,* pp. 697–706. Chicago: University of Chicago, 1931.

FLORENCE, PHILIP SARGANT. *The Statistical Method in Economics and*

Political Science. New York: Harcourt, Brace, 1928. London: Kegan Paul, Trench, and Trubner, 1929. 521 pp.

GOSNELL, HAROLD FOOTE. *Getting out the Vote: An Experiment in the Stimulation of Voting.* Chicago: University of Chicago, 1927. 128 pp.
Studies effect of party organization and of racial, economic, and educational influences upon voting.

LUNDBERG, GEORGE A. "Demographic and Economic Basis of Political Radicalism and Conservatism," *American Journal of Sociology,* 32: 719–32 (1927).
Tax rolls and registration statistics in several voting districts in a middle western state yield the following conclusions: "(a) The radical is free from pressure of traditional social bonds produced by education, culture, or personality. (b) The radical is socially and economically insecure. (c) Radicals are much more numerous in new and undeveloped communities. (d) In general, ecological factors far outweigh in importance the factors of individual personality traits."

MCMACKIN, DENA LU VERNE. "The Correlation of Newspaper Circulation and Votes Cast on Selected Issues in Illinois" (unpublished M. A. thesis, University of Illinois, 1931).

MERRIAM, CHARLES EDWARD, and GOSNELL, HAROLD FOOTE. *Non-Voting: Causes and Methods of Control.* Chicago: University of Chicago, 1924. 287 pp.

NEPRASH, JERRY ALVIN. *The Brookhart Campaigns in Iowa, 1920–26: A Study in the Motivation of Political Attitudes* (Columbia University Studies in History, Economics, and Public Law, no. 366). New York: Columbia University, 1932. London: P. S. King, 1932. 128 pp.
Bibliography, pp. 124–26.

OGBURN, WILLIAM FIELDING, and TALBOT, NELL SNOW. "A Measurement of the Factors in the Presidential Elections of 1928," *Social Forces,* 8: 175–83 (December, 1929).

WOODDY, C. H., and STOUFFER, S. A. "Local Option and Public Opinion," *American Journal of Sociology,* 36: 175–205 (1930).
An examination of votes at over fourteen thousand local option elections on the liquor question in Massachusetts, Arkansas, and Michigan over a long period of years.

G. LEGISLATIVE VOTE ANALYSIS

BEYLE, HERMAN CAREY. *Identification and Analysis of Attribute-Cluster-Blocs: A Technique for Use in the Investigation of Behavior in Governance, Including Report on Identification and*

Analysis of Blocs in a Large Non-Partisan Legislative Body, the 1927 Session of the Minnesota State Senate. Chicago: University of Chicago, 1931. 249 pp.

HECOCK, D. S. "Social and Political Interests Revealed by Political and Geographic Cohesion in Congress" (unpublished M. A. thesis, Ohio State University, 1931).

RICE, STUART ARTHUR. *Quantitative Methods in Politics.* New York: Knopf, 1928. 331 pp.

H. STRAW BALLOTS

BEYLE, HERMAN CAREY. "The Editor Votes," *American Political Science Review,* 27:597–611 (August, 1933).
Straw ballots circulated among American editors, anent the "New Deal."

CARLSON, HAROLD SIGURD. *Information and Certainty in Political Opinion: A Study of University Students during a Campaign* (University of Iowa Studies, N. S., no. 209). Iowa City: University of Iowa, 1931. 48 pp.

ROBINSON, CLAUDE E. *Straw Votes: A Study of Political Prediction.* New York: Columbia University, 1932. 203 pp.

I. OBJECTIVE INTERVIEWING AND AUTOBIOGRAPHICAL TECHNIQUES

1. BIBLIOGRAPHY

BRADSHAW, FRANCIS F. "The Interview: A Bibliography," *Journal of Personnel Research,* 5:100–03 (1926).
"A selected bibliography prepared especially for the college personnel officer, but containing references of value to others using the interview."

MOORE, BRUCE V. *The Personal Interview: Annotated Bibliography.* New York: Personnel Research Federation, 1928. 22 pp.
Prepared by the Personnel Research Federation at the request of the Social Science Research Council.

2. REFERENCES

ARRINGTON, RUTH E. "Some Technical Aspects of Observer Reliability as Indicated in Studies of the 'Talkies,'" *American Journal of Sociology,* 38:409–18 (November, 1932).
An effort to effect "standardization of the observer as an instrument of measurement" of psycho-social data.

BINGHAM, WALTER VAN DYKE, and MOORE, BRUCE VICTOR. *How to*

Interview. Revised edition. New York and London: Harpers, 1934. 324 pp.

Practical rules for "objectifying" the interview. Contains bibliography.

BOGARDUS, E. S. "Methods of Interviewing," *Journal of Applied Sociology*, 9: 457–67 (1925).

Brief survey of the interview as used by physicians, lawyers, priests, journalists, detectives, social workers, and psychiatrists.

BOSE, PRABODH CHANDRA. *Introduction to Juristic Psychology*. Calcutta: Thacker, Spink, 1917. 423 pp.

The lawyer's manner of appraising psychological phenomena.

BOWERS, G. A. "Issues in Research Method," *Journal of Personnel Research*, 4: 155–61 (1925).

Finds the interview unreliable for fact-finding, but "an aid to discovery or verification through documentary and other sources."

BRANDENBURG, G. E. "Developing the Personal Interview," *Industrial Psychology*, 3: 229–35 (1927).

On interviewing in employment offices.

BROWN, MARION RALPH. *Legal Psychology*. Indianapolis: Bobbs-Merrill, 1926. 346 pp.

Chapter 4, on evidence, summarizes the studies on reliability of report. Bibliography, pp. 303–11.

BUELL, B. "Interviews, Interviewers, and Interviewing," *Family*, 6: 86–90 (1925).

For two years a committee of New York social workers originally organized by the American Association of Social Workers worked on analysis of the interview and its technique.

DOERMANN, HENRY JOHN. *Orientation of College Freshmen*. Baltimore: Williams and Wilkins, 1926. 162 pp.

Current practices in personal guidance and counseling. Bibliography, pp. 148–58.

ELIOT, THOMAS D. "Use of Psychoanalytic Classification in the Analysis of Social Behavior: Identification," *Journal of Abnormal Psychology*, 22: 67–81 (April, 1927).

Has bibliography.

FAMILY WELFARE ASSOCIATION OF AMERICA. *Interviews, Interviewers, and Interviewing in Social Case Work*. New York, 1931. 132 pp.

HERSEY, REX B. *Workers' Emotions in Shop and Home: A Study of Individual Workers from the Psychological and Physiological Standpoint*. Philadelphia: University of Pennsylvania, 1932. 441 pp.

Personal interviews were obtained over a three-year period and the material so collected was compared with production estimates, scores on psychological tests, and physiological changes.

LAIRD, DONALD ANDERSON. *The Psychology of Selecting Men.* New York: McGraw-Hill, 1925. 274 pp.

Chapters 6 and 8 discuss the use of the interview in employment processes.

LAPIERE, R. T. "Race Prejudice: France and England," *Social Forces,* 7: 102–11 (1928).

Interviews in England and France, casually introducing the question: "Would you let a good negro live at your house?"

LASSWELL, HAROLD DWIGHT. "Studies in the Objectification of the Psychoanalytic Interview."

In preparation at the University of Chicago. Analyzes relationship between verbal references and physiological changes.

————. "Study of the Ill as a Method of Research into Political Personalities," *American Political Science Review,* 23: 996–1001 (November, 1929).

See also chapter 11 in the author's *Psychopathology and Politics.*

LOOMIS, ALICE MARIE. *A Technique for Observing the Social Behavior of Nursery School Children* (Ph.D. thesis, Columbia University). New York: Columbia University, 1931. 100 pp.

"Carried on in the nursery schools of the Child Development Institute of Teachers College." Bibliography, p. 100.

LUNDBERG, GEORGE A. "The Interview and the Social Survey," in the author's *Social Research,* chap. 7. New York: Longmans, Green, 1929.

MAGSON, EGBERT HOCKEY. *How We Judge Intelligence* (*British Journal of Psychology,* Monograph Supplements, no. 9). Cambridge, England: Cambridge University, 1926. 115 pp.

A doctor of science thesis written under the guidance of Dr. C. Spearman at the University of London. Interview estimates of intelligence were found to be practically valueless. Bibliography, pp. 114–15.

MARR, HAMILTON CLELLAND. *Neuroses of the War.* London: H. Frowde; Hodder and Stoughton, 1919. 292+38 pp.

The methods of mental casetaking, partially discussed in the 38 end pages of this volume, may reveal effects of propaganda upon the unconscious mind.

MARSTON, M. "Studies in Testimony," *Journal of Criminal Law and Criminology,* 15: 5–31 (1924).

Compares various methods of eliciting testimony.

MAULSBY, WILLIAM SHIPMAN. *Getting the News*. New York: Harcourt, Brace, 1925. 310 pp.

Detailed study of techniques of interviewing in journalism.

MOORE, BRUCE VICTOR. "The Interview in Social Industrial Research," *Social Forces*, 7: 445-52 (1929).

MURPHY, GARDNER, and MURPHY, LOIS BARCLAY. *Experimental Social Psychology*. New York and London: Harpers, 1931. 709 pp.

Pages 575-79 review the literature of the "standardized" interview. Bibliography at end of chapter.

MYRICK, H. L. "Cross-Examination and Case-Work Interviewing," *Family*, 7: 121-24 (1926).

Points out that aid may be obtained by social workers from a study of books on evidence and cross-examination written for lawyers.

PECK, MARTIN W. *The Meaning of Psychoanalysis*. New York and London: Knopf, 1931. 270 pp.

Chapters 6 and 7 discuss the psychoanalytic interview.

RICHMOND, MARY ELLEN. *Social Diagnosis*. New York: Russell Sage Foundation, 1917. 511 pp.

Treatise on collecting evidence for social research and social case work. Bibliography, pp. 481-85.

ROBINSON, VIRGINIA POLLARD. *A Changing Psychology in Social Case Work* (Ph.D. thesis, University of Pennsylvania). Chapel Hill: University of North Carolina, 1930. 204 pp.

Bibliography, pp. 192-99.

TAFT, JESSIE. "Use of the Transfer within the Office Interview," Proceedings of National Conference of American Association of Social Workers, 1924. Also in *Family*, 5: 143-46 (1924).

TAYLOR, P. *A Treatise on the Law of Evidence*. London: Sweet and Maxwell, 1920. 2 vols.

On the nature and principles of evidence, the production of testimony, hearsay, witnesses, etc.

THOMAS, DOROTHY SWAINE, and associates. *Observational Studies of Social Behavior*. Series of volumes announced by Yale University Institute of Human Relations, 1933—.

———. *Some New Techniques for Studying Social Behavior*. New York: Columbia University, 1929. 203 pp.

Prepared by research workers at the Child Development Institute of Teachers College.

WHIPPLE, G. M. "The Obtaining of Information: Psychology of Observation and Report," *Psychological Bulletin,* 15: 217–48 (1918).
A manual for the Students Army Training Corps, to aid observers in reporting military facts objectively.

WHITE, WILLIAM ALANSON. *Outlines of Psychiatry.* Thirteenth edition. Washington, D. C.: Nervous and Mental Disease Publishing Company, 1932. 468 pp.
Emphasizes means of placing the patient at ease during the interview.

PART VII. PROPAGANDA AND CENSORSHIP IN MODERN SOCIETY

Selections from the vast literature that seeks to interpret the function of promotion in all its varied forms in contemporary civilization, together with titles that summarize social experience in striving to abolish or to regulate propaganda.

A. THE BROADER IMPLICATIONS OF PROPAGANDA IN MODERN SOCIETY

I. BIBLIOGRAPHY

DISBROW, MARY ETHEL. *Criticism of Newspaper Advertising in the United States Since 1915: A Selected Bibliography.* Madison: University of Wisconsin Library School, 1931. 61 pp., typewritten.

LIBRARY OF CONGRESS. *Advertising, with Special Reference to Its Social and Economic Effects: A Bibliographic List of Recent Writings* (Select List of References no. 1169). Washington, D.C., 1930. 13 pp. typewritten.

2. GENERAL EVALUATIONS OF PROPAGANDA

ANGELL, N. "What Advertising Might Become," *Spectator* (London), 138:935-37, 978-79, 1014-15 (May 28-June 11, 1927).

BELLOC, H. "On Advertisement," *Saturday Review,* 142:761-62 (December 18, 1926).

————. "True Advertising," *New Statesman,* 24:77-78 (October 25, 1924).

BROWN, H. C. "Advertising and Propaganda: A Study in the Ethics of Social Control," *International Journal of Ethics,* 40:39-55 (1929).

BROWNELL, WILMOT ATHERTON. "Publicity and Its Ethics," *North American Review,* 215:188-96 (February, 1922).

"Business," *Encyclopedia of the Social Sciences.* (By Dexter Merriam Keezer.)

CALKINS, EARNEST ELMO. *Business, the Civilizer.* Boston: Little, Brown, 1928. 309 pp.

CAMPBELL, J. M. "I Hold a Mirror Up to Advertising," *Advertising and Selling,* 13:18 (July 10, 1929).

CARR, WILLIAM G. "School Child and Propaganda: The Conundrum of the Educator," Proceedings of the National Conference of Social Work, 1931, pp. 597–605.

"Case for Industrial Publicity," New Statesman, 27: 351–52 (July 10, 1926).

CHAFEE, ZECHARIAH, JR. "The Conscription of Public Opinion," in Norris F. Hall, editor, The Next War. Cambridge, Massachusetts: Harvard Alumni Bulletin Press, 1925.

CHERINGTON, PAUL TERRY. The Consumer Looks at Advertising. New York and London: Harpers, 1928. 196 pp.

"Control, Social," Enyclopedia of the Social Sciences. (By Helen Everett.)

COOMBS, W. "Truth in Advertising," Nation, 122: 670 (June 16, 1926).

CRAWFORD, NELSON ANTRIM. Ethics of Journalism. New York: Knopf, 1924. 264 pp.
Bibliography at ends of chapters and pp. 241–59.

FLINT, LEON NELSON. The Conscience of the Newspaper. London and New York: Appleton, 1925. 470 pp.
Case book on newspaper ethics.

FLYNN, JOHN THOMAS. Graft in Business. New York: Vanguard, 1931. 318 pp.
On pressure activities and "ethics" of corporations.

FRUMUSAN, J. "Vulgarisation et publicité," Revue mondiale, série 9, 158: 410–14 (1924).

FULLER, R. "Honesty in Advertising," Nation, 125: 202–03 (August, 1927).

GALDSTON, IAGO. "Hazards of Commercial Health Advertisements," American Journal of Public Health, 21: 242–48 (March, 1931).

GARRETT, GEORGE PALMER. "Public Trials," American Law Review, 62: 1–12 (January–February, 1928).
"No one concerned with a criminal case which the newspapers have elected to make into a cause célèbre acts sanely. The public prosecutor becomes a public relations counsel and, before the trial, builds up a picture of the crime and of the guilt of the criminal in the minds of the general public by adroitly made statements. The defendant and his counsel seek to counteract the effect of this pre-trial with counter statements. The judge . . . tries the case from the point of view of the front page of the newspaper." This article analyzes examples of these practices.

GAZIN, HENRI. *De la publicité de la justice criminelle* (Université de Paris, Faculté de droit, Travaux de la Conférence de droit pénal, no. 10). Paris: L. Tenin, 1914. 57 pp.

GOODALL, G. W. *Advertising: A Study of a Modern Business Power,* with an introduction by Sidney Webb (London School of Economics Studies in Economics and Political Science, no. 41). London: Constable, 1914. 91 pp.
The rôle of the advertising man and his agency in England; who pays for his services and why, with reflections by Sidney Webb on how to bring him under " democratic control." Bibliography, pp. 90–91.

GOODE, KENNETH M., and POWELL, H. W. H. *What about Advertising?* New York and London: Harpers, 1927. 399 pp.
By successful advertisers.

GRISCOM, W. STUART. *The Press and Crime.*
Announced as a forthcoming volume in the Harvard Law School Survey of Crime in Boston, 1934.

HARRIS, FRANK. *The Presentation of Crime in Newspapers* (Ph. D. thesis, University of Minnesota). Hanover, New Hampshire: Sociological Press, 1933. 103 pp.
Proceeding from the belief that newspaper content reflects the interest of the reader, this study attempts to discover changing interest in crime by comparing the amount and type of crime news in Minneapolis newspapers with the volume and kinds of crime represented in court statistics.

HIGHAM, SIR CHARLES FREDERICK. *Advertising, Its Use and Abuse* (Home University Library). New York: Holt, 1925. London: Williams and Norgate, 1925. 256 pp.
Successful English advertising man.

――――. *Scientific Distribution.* London: Nisbet, 1916. 170 pp. New York: Knopf, 1918. 183 pp.

HODDER, F. H. " Propaganda as a Source of American History," *Mississippi Valley Historical Review,* 9: 3–18 (June, 1922).
Propaganda may become " history."

HULBERT, E. D. "Advertising Ethics and the General Welfare," *Survey,* 22: 425–26 (June 19, 1909).
Extent of " get-rich-quick " swindles.

KELLOGG, ARTHUR. " Minds Made by the Movies," *Survey,* 22: 245–50 (May, 1933).
115 films taken at random depicted 449 crimes. One person in three in the audiences was a child or an adolescent.

KITTLE, WILLIAM. "News Bureaus and Newspapers Advocating Corporation Interests," *Arena,* 41:440–45 (July, 1909).
Shock reactions of the muckraker.

LASSWELL, HAROLD DWIGHT. "The Function of the Propagandist," *International Journal of Ethics,* 38:258–63 (April, 1928).

LEWIS, WYNDHAM. "The Propagandist in Fiction," *Current History,* 40:567–72 (August, 1934).
English critic ruminates upon a growing tendency among readers and among other critics to view writers of fiction as propagandists, conscious or unconscious, in behalf of rival socio-political systems.

LÜDDECKE, T. "Der Einfluss der Reklame auf das Antlitz der Kultur," *Deutsche Rundschau,* 221:33–40 (October, 1929).
How advertising changes the visible social environment of our epoch.

LUMLEY, FREDERICK E. *The Propaganda Menace.* New York: Century, 1933. 454 pp.
Bibliography, pp. 433–45.

LYTTELTON, E. "Economic and Social Effects of Modern Advertising," *Hibbert Journal,* 23:510–15 (April, 1925).

MOGENS, V. "Politik, Propaganda, Presse, Publikum," *Deutsche Rundschau,* 213:171–78 (December, 1927).

NICHOLS, P. "Report of Special Committee on Advertising by Banks and Trust Companies, of the Massachusetts Bar Association," *American Law Review,* 60:264–73 (March, 1926).

POUND, R. "Public Opinion and Social Control," Proceedings of the National Conference for Social Work, 1930, pp. 607–23.

POWERS, JOHN O. "Advertising," *Annals of the American Academy of Political and Social Science,* November, 1903, pp. 469–74.

"Propaganda," *Economist,* 119:576–77 (September 29, 1934).
Should the democrat adopt the Catonian attitude and accept defeat on behalf of truth?

RUSSELL, BERTRAND. *Free Thought and Official Propaganda.* London: Watts, 1922. 48 pp.
Conway Memorial Lecture delivered at South Place Institute, March 24, 1922.

RUSSELL, GILBERT. *Nuntius: Advertising and Its Future* (Today and Tomorrow series). London: Kegan Paul, Trench, and Trubner, 1926. 96 pp.

STOCKING, COLLIS A. "Modern Advertising and Economic Theory," *American Economic Review,* 21:43–55 (March, 1931).
Reply by A. V. Abramson appears in the *American Economic Review,* 21:685–90 (December, 1931).

STRACHEY, J. ST. L. "Philosophy of Advertising," *Spectator* (London), 133:84 (July 19, 1924).

STRONG, ANNA LOUISE. "American Propaganda in Russia," *American Mercury*, 32:48–55 (May, 1934).
Should not Russia have withheld recognition of the United States, lest American propaganda advocate the overthrow of the Soviet form of government?

STRONG, E. K. "The Control of Propaganda as a Psychological Problem," *Scientific Monthly*, 14:234–52.

SUTHERLAND, E. H. "Public Opinion as a Cause of Crime," *Journal of Applied Sociology*, 9:51–56 (1924).

THOMSON, SIR BASIL. "Does International Propaganda Pay?" *Current Opinion*, 73:36–39 (July, 1922).

TINKHAM, JULIAN RUMSEY. *The Debunkment of Advertising and Prosperity, 1928–1930.* New York: Little and Ives, 1930. 131 pp.

TYLER, LYON GARDENER. *Propaganda in History.* Richmond: Richmond Press, 1920. 19 pp.
Much that passes for "history" was propaganda in its day.

VAUGHAN, FLOYD LAMAR. *Marketing and Advertising: An Economic Appraisal.* Princeton, New Jersey: Princeton University, 1928. 255 pp.
Bibliography, pp. 247–48.

WOLSELEY, R. E. "Propaganda and the Social Order," *Christian Century*, 51:151–53 (January 31, 1934).

3. INSTITUTIONAL READJUSTMENTS DUE TO PROPAGANDA

Propaganda both expresses and intensifies conflicting interests and sentiments in modern society. Efforts at reintegration have varied from "proportional representation" and "economic advisory councils," to "corporative" and "soviet" states. See also standard descriptions of the structure of government in the Soviet Union and in Italy.

ALGER, GEORGE W. "Unpunished Commercial Crime," *Atlantic Monthly*, 94:170–78 (August, 1904).

AMBROSINI, GASPARE. *Il Consiglio Nazionale delle Corporazioni* (Instituto Nazionale Fascista di Cultura, *Quaderni*, 2d Series, no. 9). Rome, 1930.

"American Credulity," *Outlook*, 96:759–60 (December 3, 1910).
Fraudulent promotion by mail: the Burr brothers and the Post Office Department.

AMERICAN MEDICAL ASSOCIATION. *New and Nonofficial Remedies.*

An attempt at social control by means of publicity. "Analyzes hundreds of drugs which have been found acceptable for specified uses. For the preparations not described and that do not have the sanction of the Council, a long list covering about 1,000 patent medicines is printed at the end of the volume. Here are found many well-known names. Each bears a specific reference to an article in the *Journal of the American Medical Association,* where it, or its method of exploitation, has been analyzed and found wanting."

APELT, DR. KURT. *Die wirtschaftlichen Interessenvertretungen in Deutschland, ihr Aufbau, ihr Wesen, und ihre Entwicklung.* Leipzig: G. A. Gloeckner, 1925. 104 pp.

Summarizes the history, activities, and organization of the principal contemporary economic groupings in Germany. Contains a brief bibliography.

BENN, E. "Advertising and the Standard of Living," *Electrician,* 103: 221–22 (August 23, 1929).

BENOÎT, FRANCIS DE. *La Représentation des intérêts professionnels.* Paris: Jouve, 1911. 164 pp.

Bibliography, pp. 159–62.

CASEY, RALPH D. "The Menace of Propaganda," *American Press,* 56: 2 (March, 1934).

Newspapers face readjustments owing to the spread of propaganda.

CLARK, JOHN MAURICE. *Social Control of Business.* Chicago: University of Chicago, 1926. 483 pp.

A standard treatise.

CLARK, JOHN MAURICE, and CLARK, F. E. "Appraisal of Certain Criticisms of Advertising," *American Economic Review,* March, 1925, Supplement, pp. 5–13 (vol. 15).

"Cleaning Up Health Advertising," *Journal of Social Hygiene,* 11: 291–93 (May, 1925).

COLE, GEORGE DOUGLAS HOWARD. *Social Theory.* London: Methuen, 1920. 219 pp.

Bibliography, pp. 210–13.

CRECRAFT, EARL WILLIS. *Government and Business: A Study in the Economic Aspects of Government and the Public Aspects of Business.* Yonkers-on-Hudson, New York, and Chicago: World Book Company, 1928. 508 pp.

Bibliography, pp. 485–500.

DENDIAS, MICHAEL. *La Problème de la chambre haute et la représenta-*

tion des intérêts à propos de l'organisation du Sénat grec. Paris: E. de Boccard, 1929. 463 pp.
Bibliography, pp. 13–69.

DIMOCK, MARSHALL EDWARD. *Congressional Investigating Committees* (Ph.D. thesis, Johns Hopkins University, 1928). Baltimore, Maryland: Johns Hopkins University, 1929. 182 pp.
Committee hearings offer opportunity for direct and open contact between pressure groups and legislatures. Bibliography, pp. 177–78.

GIANTURCO, MARIO. *La legislazione sindicale fascista e la riforma constituzionale.* Genoa, 1926.

GOSNELL, HAROLD FOOTE. "British Royal Commissions of Inquiry," *Political Science Quarterly,* 49:84–119 (March, 1934).

HAIDER, CARMEN. *Capital and Labor under Fascism* (Columbia University Studies in History, Economics, and Public Law, no. 318). New York: Columbia University, 1930. London: P. S. King, 1930. 296 pp.
The fact and the fiction of the corporative state. Bibliography, pp. 286–89.

HAUSCHILD, CLAUS DIETRICH HENRY. *Der vorläufige Reichswirtschaftsrat, 1920–1926.* Berlin: Mittler, 1926. 687 pp.
The most complete and authoritative account of the German Economic Council. Supplemented by a second volume published in 1931(?), it brings the story down to date. Contains an elaborate bibliography dealing with economic councils and the political representation of special interests. Bibliography, pp. 641–70.

HERRFAHRDT, HEINRICH. *Das Problem der berufständische Vertretung von der französischen Revolution bis zur Gegenwart.* Berlin, 1921.

HERRFAHRDT, HEINRICH, and MILLER, FRITZ. *Die Stellung der Berufsvereine im Staat.* Berlin, 1925.

HERRING, EDWARD PENDLETON. "The Czechoslovak Advisory Board for Economic Questions," *American Political Science Review,* 24:439–50 (1930).

———. "Legalized Lobbying in Europe," *Current History,* 31:947–52 (February, 1930).
Discusses bills in Congress to regulate the lobby through publicity.

———. "Special Interests and the Interstate Commerce Commission," *American Political Science Review,* 27:738–52, 899–918 (October and December, 1933).

HOUSE OF COMMONS, GREAT BRITAIN. "Discussion of the Representation of the People (no. 2) Bill" (official report, 1931), *Parliamentary Debates, House of Commons,* 249:1695–1811.

KEEZER, DEXTER MERRIAM, and MAY, STACY. *Public Control of Business: A Study of Anti-Trust Law Enforcement, Public Interest Regulation, and Government Participation in Business.* New York and London: Harpers, 1930. 267 pp.

KULEMANN, WILHELM. *Die Berufsvereine.* Jena: Fischer, 1908–13. 6 vols.
Volume 3 deals with German occupational organizations; the other volumes cover the various states of the world.

LAMBERT, PIERRE GEORGES. *La Représentation politique des intérêts professionnels.* Paris, 1929.

LASKI, HAROLD J., and others. *The Development of the Representative System in Our Times.* Geneva, 1928.

LAUTAUD, CAMILLE, and POUDENX, ANDRÉ. *La Représentation professionnelle: Les conseils économiques en Europe et en France.* Paris: Rivière, 1927. 285 pp.
Bibliography, pp. 267–73.

LINDNER, ELLI. *Review of the Economic Councils in the Different Countries of the World.* Geneva: Economic Committee of the League of Nations, 1933. 105 pp.

――――. *Die Wirtschaftsräte in Europa: Ein Beitrag zur Frage der Schaffung einer europäischen Wirtschaftsunion.* Berlin: Mittler, 1931. 55 pp.
Economic councils in Europe. Bibliography, p. 54.

LORWIN, LEWIS L. *Advisory Economic Councils.* Washington, D. C.: Brookings Institution, 1931. 84 pp.
Bibliography, pp. 83–84.

MANNZEN, KARL. *Sowjetunion und Völkerrecht: Die Fragen der Anerkennung der Schulden, der Auslandspropaganda und des Aussenhandelsmonopols.* Berlin: Stilke, 1932. 110 pp.
Bibliography, pp. 5–8.

MITWALLY, A. H. *La Démocratie et la représentation des intérêts en France.* Paris: A. Rousseau, 1931. 272 pp.
Bibliography, pp. 252–65.

MOYITCH, SAVA. *Le Parlement économique.* Paris, 1927.

"National Economic Councils," *Encyclopedia of the Social Sciences.* (By Emil Lederer.)

ODEGARD, PETER H. "Majorities, Minorities, and Legislation," *Annals of the American Academy of Political and Social Science,* 169: 29–46 (September, 1933).

POLLOCK, JAMES KERR, JR. "Regulation of Lobbying," *American Political Science Review,* 21:335–41 (May, 1927).

PRELOT, MARCEL. *La Représentation professionnelle dans l'Allemagne contemporaine.* Paris: Spe, 1924. 172 pp.
Origin and development of the Reichswirtschaftsrat (German National Economic Council). Bibliography, pp. 167–72.

"Proportional Representation," *Encyclopedia of the Social Sciences.* (By Harold F. Gosnell.)

REICHSARBEITSMINISTERIUM [Germany]. *Jahrbuch der Berufsverbände im Deutschen Reiche.* Sonderheft zum Reichsarbeitsblatt, 1930.
Publication of the German Ministry of Labor, containing an exhaustive list of all economic organizations in Germany, carefully classified, together with a large amount of information concerning them.

SCHAFFNER, MARGARET A. "Laws Concerning the Lobby in the United States," *Government,* 2:183–96 (December, 1907).

TATARIN-TARNHEYDEN, EDGAR. *Die Berufsstände: Ihre Stellung im Staatsrecht und die deutsche Wirtschaftsverfassung.* Berlin: Heymann, 1922. 260 pp.

——. *Berufsverbände und Wirtschaftsdemokratie.* Berlin, 1930.

UNITED STATES NATIONAL PLANNING BOARD. *Final Report, 1933–34.* Washington, D. C.: Government Printing Office, 1934. 119 pp.
Summary of activities of specialized planning agencies in the United States and abroad.

UNITED STATES SENATE, COMMITTEE ON MANUFACTURES. *Establishment of a National Economic Council* (hearings before a subcommittee of the Committee on Manufactures, 72d Congress, 1st Session, on S. 1625). Washington, D. C.: Government Printing Office, 1931. 2 vols.

WARNE, C. E. "Present-Day Advertising: Consumers' Viewpoint," *Annals of the American Academy of Political and Social Science,* 173:70–79 (May, 1934).

WEBB, SIDNEY, and WEBB, BEATRICE. *A Constitution for the Socialist Commonwealth of Great Britain.* London and New York: Longmans, Green, 1920. 364 pp.

——. *Methods of Social Study.* London, New York, and Toronto: Longmans, Green, 1932. 263 pp.
Chapter 8 describes "Royal Commissions and Committees of Enquiry as Sources for the Investigator."

B. THE BROADER IMPLICATIONS OF CENSORSHIP

Evaluations of the "moral worth" or social consequences of censorship efforts.

1. BIBLIOGRAPHY

SCHROEDER, THEODORE ALBERT. *Free Speech Bibliography, Including Every Discovered Attitude toward the Problem, Covering Every Method of Transmitting Ideas and Abridging Their Promulgation upon Every Subject Matter.* New York: H. W. Wilson, 1922. London: Grafton, 1922. 247 pp.

2. REFERENCES

AMERICAN SOCIOLOGICAL SOCIETY. *Freedom of Communication.* Chicago: Published by the University of Chicago, for the American Sociological Society, 1915. 202 pp.
Papers and proceedings of the ninth annual meeting of the American Sociological Society.

BEMAN, LAMAR TANEY, compiler. *Censorship of the Theater and Moving Pictures.* New York: H. W. Wilson, 1931. 385 pp.
A collection of arguments compiled to assist debaters. Useful as bibliography.

————. *Selected Articles on Censorship of Speech and the Press* (Wilson Handbooks, series 3, vol. 5). New York: H. W. Wilson, 1930. 507 pp.
Compiled to assist debaters. Bibliography, pp. 13–16.

BROYE, EUGÈNE. *La Censure politique et militaire en Suisse pendant la guerre.* Paris: Attinger, 1934. 200 pp.

BUTLER, N. C. "Law and Public Opinion," *American Law Review,* 49:374–88 (May, 1915).

CARR, F. "The English Law of Defamation," *Law Quarterly Review,* 18:255–73, 388–99 (1902).

CAUSTON, BERNARD, and YOUNG, C. GORDON. *Keeping It Dark, or the Censor's Handbook,* with a foreword by Rebecca West. London: Mandrake Press, 1930. 83 pp.

"Censorship," *Encyclopedia of the Social Sciences.* (By Harold D. Lasswell.)

"Censorship by Jury," *Law Notes,* 30:4 (April, 1926).

CHAFEE, ZECHARIAH, JR. *Freedom of Speech.* New York: Harcourt, Brace, and Howe, 1920. 431 pp.
Bibliography, pp. 377–86.

————. *The Inquiring Mind.* New York: Harcourt, Brace, 1928. 276 pp.
"A collection of essays on liberty and other constitutional problems including contemporaneous reviews of judicial decisions on free speech problems and industrial relations."

Constant de Rebècque, Henri Benjamin. *On the Liberty of the Press, or an Enquiry How Far the Government May Safely Allow the Publication of Political Pamphlets, Essays, and Periodical Works* (from *The Pamphleteer*, vol. 6, no. 11). London: The Pamphleteer, 1815. 31 pp.

" Copyright," *Encyclopedia of the Social Sciences.* (By Leon Whipple.)

"Dangers of Censorship," *Law Notes*, 30: 204 (February, 1927).

"Deportation and Expulsion of Aliens," *Encyclopedia of the Social Sciences.* (By J. M. Landis.)
Deportation may be used as a technique for control of public opinion. " The first English deportation statutes were temporary measures, which from 1793 to 1826 empowered high state officials to remove under severe penalty alien propagandists of the French Revolution."

Desjardins, Arthur. *De la liberté politique dans l'état moderne.* Paris, 1894.

Donogh, Walter Russell. *The History and Law of Sedition and Cognate Offenses, Penal and Preventive, with a Summary of Press Legislation in India and an Excerpt of Acts in Force Relating to the Press, the Stage, and Public Meetings.* Third edition. Calcutta: Thacker, Spink, 1917. London: W. Thacker, 1917. 285 pp.

Dreiser, Theodore. " The Meddlesome Decade: How Censorship Is Making Our Civilization Ridiculous," *Theatre Guild Magazine*, 6: 11–13, 61–62 (May, 1929).

Dufey, Enrique T. *La Defensa social: Medios preventivos y represivos* (thesis, National University of Buenos Aires). Buenos Aires: National University of Buenos Aires, 1913. 109 pp.
" Prevention and repression as means of social defense."

Ellis, H. " Obscenity and the Censor: Review of *To the Pure* by M. Ernst and W. Seagle," *Saturday Review* (London), 146: 642–43 (November 17, 1928).

Ernst, Morris Leopold, and Seagle, William. *To the Pure . . . : A Study of Obscenity and the Censor.* New York: Viking, 1928. 336 pp.
Bibliography, pp. 311–21.

Etzin, Franz. " Die Freiheit der öffentlichen Meinung unter Friedrich der Grossen," *Forschungen zur brandenbürgischen und preussichen Geschichte*, 33: 89 ff.

" Freedom of Speech and the Press," *Encyclopedia of the Social Sciences.* (By J. M. Landis.)

Garr, Max. *Parliament und Presse: Ein Beitrag zum Prinzip der*

parlamentarischen Öffentlichkeit (Wiener staatswissenschaftliche Studien, Band 8, Heft 2). Vienna: F. Deuticke, 1908. 75 pp.
Control of publicity by an official agency at the source.

GLEN, GARRARD. "Censorship at Common Law and under Modern Dispensation," *Pennsylvania Law Review,* December, 1933.

GRANT, SYDNEY SAUL, and ANGOFF, S. E. *Massachusetts and Censorship.* Boston: Boston University Law Review, 1930. 6 parts in 2 vols.

GREAT BRITAIN, WAR OFFICE. *Memorandum on the Censorship (Cd. 7679).* London: H. M. Stationery Office, 1915. 5 pp.
Official statement of policy on censorship of cables, posts, private and commercial communications, and press.

HAYS, ARTHUR GARFIELD. *Let Freedom Ring.* New York: Boni and Liveright, 1928. 341 pp.
"This book narrates some half dozen cases on freedom of education, speech and assemblage, press and residence, stage and opinion, with which the author happened to be connected. They all occurred between the years 1922 and 1927."

JACKSON, T. A. "Essays in Censorship," *Labour Monthly* (London), 11: 233–39 (April, 1929).

JOYNSON-HICKS, WILLIAM (VISCOUNT BRENTFORD OF NEWICK). *Do We Need a Censor?* (Criterion Miscellany, no. 6). London: Faber and Faber, 1929. 24 pp.

KALLEN, HORACE M. *Indecency and the Seven Arts, and Other Adventures of a Pragmatist in Aesthetics.* New York: Liveright, 1930. 246 pp.

KATZER, ERNST. *Das Problem der Lehrfreiheit und seine Lösung nach Kant.* Tübingen: Mohr, 1903. 53 pp.
Kant's solution of the problem of academic freedom.

KEATING, JOSEPH. "Civil Censorship, Theory and Practice," *Month* (London), 159: 239–49 (1932).

KRAUS, H. "Masse und Strafrecht," *Aschaffenburgs Monatsschrift für Kriminalpsychologie und Strafrechtsreform,* July, 1909.

KUHNERT, ERNST. *Staat, Kirche, und Buchhandel; Vortrag gehalten in der Vereinigung berliner Bibliothekare.* Berlin: Struppe und Winckler, 1930. 20 pp.
Bibliographic footnotes.

LAWRENCE, DAVID HERBERT. *Pornography and Obscenity* (Criterion Miscellany, no. 5). London: Faber and Faber, 1929. 32 pp.

"Libel and Slander," *Encyclopedia of the Social Sciences.* (By Theodore F. T. Plucknett.)

McCALLISTER, W. J. *The Growth of Freedom in Education: A Critical Interpretation of Some Historical Views.* London: Constable, 1931. 589 pp.
Bibliography, pp. 566–79.

MANNHEIM, H. "Pressrecht," *Enzyklopedie der Rechts- und Staatswissenschaft, Abteilung Rechtswissenschaft,* vol. 22(a). Berlin, 1927.
"Contains a good bibliography of continental literature." — J. M. LANDIS.

MAY, GEOFFREY. *Social Control of Sex Expression.* London: Allen and Unwin, 1930. 245 pp.
Bibliography, pp. 219–35.

MEYDENBAUER, H. "Der Staat als Zensor," *Preussische Jahrbücher,* 207: 94–96 (January, 1927).

MIGLIORE, B. "Il diritto di cronaca e le esigenze della morale," *Nuova antologia* (Rome), 251:235–44 (January 16, 1927).

MORRIS, H. B. "Censorship and Consequences," *Law Notes,* 32:99 (August, 1928).

MURRAY, G. "Obscenity in Literature," *Nation* (London), 44:876 (March 23, 1929).
Discussion, 44:908; 45: 11, 40, 72, 104–05, 156, 198–99, 235 (March 30– May 18, 1929).

NAUDEAU, L. "La Liberté de la presse et le fascisme," *L'Illustration,* 30:460–62 (October 30, 1926).

NEEP, EDWARD JOHN CECIL. *Seditious Offenses,* with an introductory note by Harold J. Laski (Fabian Tracts, no. 220). London: Fabian Society, 1926. 30 pp.

NOKES, GERALD DACRE. *A History of the Crime of Blasphemy.* London: Sweet and Maxwell, 1928. 178 pp.

PARK, ROBERT EZRA. *The Immigrant Press and Its Control.* New York and London: Harpers, 1922. 488 pp.

PATTERSON, JAMES. *The Liberty of the Press, Speech, and Public Worship, Being Commentaries on the Liberty of the Subject and the Laws of England.* London: Macmillan, 1880. 568 pp.

PERISCOPE (pseudonym). "Sedition and the Censor," *English Review,* 39:653–59 (November, 1924).

POLLARD, G. "The Role of the Censorship," *Labour Monthly* (London), 11:433–38 (July, 1929).

"The Pope and the Press," *Outlook* (London), 60:666–67 (November 19, 1927).

Discussion, 60:710, 746, 796, 824, 880–82 (November and December, 1927).

"Pornography and the Censorship," *New Statesman,* 34:219–20 (November 23, 1929).

PUTNAM, GEORGE HAVEN. *The Censorship of the Church of Rome and Its Influence upon the Production and Distribution of Literature: A Study of the History of the Prohibitory and Expurgatory Indexes, Together with Some Consideration of the Effects of Protestant Censorship and of Censorship by the State.* New York and London: Putnam, 1906–07. 2 vols.
Bibliography, pp. xvii–xxv.

RANDALL, R. G. "Youth and Censorship," *Nation* (London), 45:701–03 (August 31, 1929).

RIEGEL, O. W. *Mobilizing for Chaos: The Story of the New Propaganda.* New Haven: Yale University, 1934. 231 pp.
Bibliographic notes, pp. 215–22.

RIVARD. "De la liberté de la presse," Transactions of the Royal Society of Canada, 3d series, 1st section, 1923, vol. 17, pp. 33–104.
Has bibliography.

ROSENBERG, JAMES NAUMBERG. *Censorship in the United States: Address before Association of the Bar, New York City, March 15, 1928.* New York: Court Press, 1928. 28 pp.

SABATIÉ, L. *La Censure* (thesis, University of Paris). Paris: Pédone, 1908.

SAINTYVES, P. (pseudonym of E. NOURRY). *La Réforme intellectuelle du clergé et la liberté d'enseignement.* Paris: Nourry, 1904. 341 pp.

SCHROEDER, THEODORE ALBERT. *Constitutional Free Speech Defined and Defended in an Unfinished Argument in a Case of Blasphemy.* New York: The Free Speech League, 1919. 456 pp.

———. "Emotional Conflict, Liberty, and Authority," *Psyche and Eros,* vol. 2, no. 1 (January-February, 1921).

———. *"Obscene" Literature and Constitutional Law: A Forensic Defense of Freedom of the Press.* New York: "Privately printed for forensic uses," 1911. 439 pp.

SEAGLE, WILLIAM. *Cato, or the Future of Censorship* (Today and Tomorrow series). London: Kegan Paul, Trench, and Trubner, 1930. 96 pp.

STEPHEN, J. F. "Blasphemy and Blasphemous Libel," *Fortnightly Review*, N. S., 35: 289–318 (1884).

"Symposium of Criticism, Comment, and Opinion on the Subject of Censorship," *Laughing Horse* (Taos, New Mexico), no. 17, pp. 1–31 (1930).

UNITED STATES HOUSE OF REPRESENTATIVES, COMMITTEE ON THE JUDICIARY. *Sedition* (hearings, 66th Congress, 2d Session, February 4 and 6, 1920). Washington, D. C.: Government Printing Office, 1920. 288 pp.

————. *Sedition, Syndicalism, Sabotage, and Anarchy* (hearings, 66th Congress, 2d Session, December 11 and 16, 1919). Washington, D. C.: Government Printing Office, 1919. 64 pp.

VEEDER, V. V. "Freedom of Public Discussion," *Harvard Law Review*, 23: 413–40 (1909–10).

VILLARD, O. G. "What the Blue Menace Means," *Harper's Magazine*, 157: 529–40 (1928).

C. SPECIFIC INSTANCES OF CENSORSHIP

These titles illustrate the varied forms assumed by the problems of censorship.

"Angora on Trial," *Near East*, 27: 510 (May 14, 1925).

"Another Censored Message from India," *China Weekly Review*, 54: 128 (September 27, 1930).

APITZSCH, FRIEDRICH. "Die deutsche Tagespresse unter dem Einfluss des Sozialistengesetzes," in *Das Wesen der Zeitung*, vol. 1, pt. 3. Leipzig: Reinecke, 1928. 224 pp.

AUBARET. "La Censure en Irlande," *Journal des débats*, vol. 35, pt. 2, p. 841 (November 23, 1928).

"Australia and the *Labour Monthly*," *Labour Monthly* (London), 10: 215–16 (April, 1928).

BERGER, MARCEL, and ALLARD, PAUL. *Les Secrets de la censure pendant la guerre*. Paris: Édition des portiques, 1932. 382 pp.

BETTMAN, ALFRED, and HALE, SWINBURNE. *Do We Need More Sedition Laws?* New York: Civil Liberties Union, 1920. 22 pp.
Testimony before the House Committee on Rules.

BLOCH, A. R. "Liberty under the XIV Amendment (People v. Mintz, 290 Pac. 93)," *Journal of Criminal Law*, 21: 618–19 (February, 1931).

Booth, Philip. At the University of Chicago. Is preparing a dissertation on the post-war administrative and legislative history of criminal syndicalism in six states.

China's Attempt to Muzzle the Foreign Press: An Account of the Endeavors of Nanking to Suppress the Truth about Affairs in China. Shanghai: North China Daily News, 1929. 30 pp.

Civic Liberties Committee of Massachusetts. *The Censorship in Boston: Story as Told by Professor Zechariah Chafee.* Boston, 1929(?). 22 pp.

Communist Party of Great Britain. *The Communist Party on Trial: Harry Pollitt's Defense.* London, 1925. 31 pp.

———. *The Communist Party on Trial: The Defense of J. R. Campbell.* London, 1925. 31 pp.

———. *The Communist Party on Trial: Wm. Gallacher's Defense and Judge Rigby Swift's Summing Up.* London, 1925. 23 pp.

Crémieux, A. *La Censure en 1820 et 1821: Étude sur la presse politique et la résistance libérale* (thesis, University of Paris). Paris: Rieder, 1912.

De Voto, Bernard. "Literary Censorship in Cambridge," *Harvard Graduates' Magazine,* 39: 30–42 (September, 1930).

Dickinson, E. D. "Defamation of Foreign Governments," *American Journal of International Law,* 22: 840–44 (October, 1928).

Duranty, Walter. "Russian News and Soviet Censors," *Spectator* (London), 148: 207 (February 13, 1932).

Durham, M. E. "Very Free Press," *New Statesman and Nation,* 1: 352–53 (May 21, 1931).

Eaton, C. "Freedom of the Press in the Upper South," *Mississippi Valley Historical Review,* 18: 479–99 (March, 1932).
Has bibliography.

Engelbrecht, H. C. "Singeing the Beard of the Spanish Censor," *World Tomorrow,* 9: 222–23 (November, 1926).

"Fine Play Banned: Young Woodley," *New Statesman,* 30: 593–94 (February 18, 1928).

"Free State Censorship," *New Statesman,* 31: 632–33 (September 1, 1928).

"Freedom of the Press," *New Statesman,* 27: 4–5 (April 17, 1926).

"Freedom of the Press," *New Statesman,* 27: 116–17 (May 15, 1926).

GARRAUD, PIERRE, and LABORDE-LACOSTE, MARCEL. *La Répression de la propagande contre la natalité: La loi du 31 juillet 1920 réprimant la provocation à l'avortement et la propagande anti-conceptionnelle* (extrait des Annales de l'Université d'Aix, N.S., tôme 8). Aix-en-Provence: Imprimerie Nicollet, 1921. 88 pp.

GNAU, HERMANN. *Die Zensur unter Joseph II.* Strasbourg, 1911. 313 pp.
"Joseph II (1741–90) represents the purest type of enlightened despot . . . He . . . exercised a very tolerant censorship." — RUDOLPH STADELMANN, in *Encyclopedia of the Social Sciences.*

GRANT, S. S., and ANGOFF, S. E. "Recent Developments in Censorship," *Boston University Law Review,* 10: 488–509 (November, 1930).

GREEN, FREDERICK C. *Eighteenth Century France.* New York: Appleton, 1931. London: Dent, 1929. 221 pp.
Six essays, including one on censorship.

HALE, R. W. "Public Opinion as Contempt of Court," *American Law Review,* 58: 481–99 (1924).

"Has Shanghai a Free Press?" *China Weekly Review,* 41: 331 (August 27, 1927).

HAYES, A. G. *Trials by Prejudice.* New York: Covici, Friede, 1933. 369 pp.

HIGGINS, E. M. "Censorship in Australia: The Ban on Working Class Literature," *Labour Monthly* (London), 11: 57–58 (January, 1929).

HOBSON, J. A. "Liberty of Unlicensed Printing," *Nation* (London), 44: 831–32 (March 16, 1929).

Index librorum prohibitorum (Roman Catholic Church). Rome: Typis Polyglottis Vaticanis. Issued serially since 1551.

JOHNSON, THOMAS H. "Jonathan Edwards and the 'Young Folk's Bible,'" *New England Quarterly,* 5: 37–54 (1932).
On the advisability of censoring the Bible before giving it to children.

KUHL, ERNEST. "The Stationers' Company and Censorship (1599–1601)," *The Library* (London), 9: 388–94 (March, 1929).

LASKI, H. J. "Sedition: The Case of the *Daily Worker,*" *New Statesman and Nation,* 2: 743 (December 12, 1931).

LAUTERPACHT, H. "Revolutionary Activities by Private Persons against Foreign States," *American Journal of International Law,* 22: 105 ff. (1928).

―――. "Revolutionary Propaganda by Governments," Transactions of the Grotius Society, 13: 143–64 (1928).
By a prominent commentator on international law.

LIEBEN, S. H. "Beiträge zur Geschichte der Zensur hebräischer Drucke in Prag," Soncino-Blätter (Berlin), 3: 51–55 (1929).

MACPHERSON, HARRIET DOROTHEA. Censorship under Louis XIV, 1661–1715. New York: Institute of French Studies, 1929. 175 pp. Bibliography, pp. 169–75.

MANZI, A. "Il conte Giraud, il governo italico, e la censura: con documenti d'archivio e di cronache," Nuova antologia (Rome), 267: 359–80 (October 1, 1929).

MARTIN, G. "Venezuela Threatened with Civil War: Drastic Censorship Methods of the Government," China Weekly Review, 50: 346 (November 2, 1929).

MAXWELL, M. "Comment on Ansley v. Federal Radio Commission (46 F. (2d) 600), A Censorship Case," American Law Review, 2: 269–72 (April, 1931).

"Une Menace pour la littérature en Angleterre," Journal des débats, vol. 35, pt. 2, pp. 705–06 (November 2, 1928).

"Mr. D. H. Lawrence and Lord Brentford," Nation (London), 46: 508–09 (January 11, 1930).

MUSSEY, H. R. "The Christian Science Censor," Nation, 130: 147–49, 175–78 (1930).

"Nanking Abolishes Press Censorship," Pacific Affairs, 4: 64 (January, 1931).

"National Government's New Press Law," China Weekly Review, 55: 422–23 (February 21, 1931).

NELLES, WALTER. Espionage Act Cases, with Certain Others on Related Points. . . . New York: National Civil Liberties Bureau, 1918.

NELLES, WALTER, and KING, C. W. "Contempt by Publication in the United States," Columbia Law Review, 28: 401–31, 525–62 (1928).

Nostrums and Quackery. Chicago: American Medical Association, 1912–21.
Exposés of false claims by promoters of medicines, foods, and accessories.

ODGERS, W. B. A Digest of the Law of Libel and Slander. 6th edition, edited by R. Ritson. London, 1929.

"Opinion on Obscene Books," *Journal of Social Hygiene*, 17:354–58 (June 1, 1931).
Text of Judge Woolsey's opinion on Dr. Stopes's *Married Love*.

PALMER, FREDERICK. *With My Own Eyes: A Personal Story of the Battle Years*. Indianapolis: Bobbs-Merrill, 1933. 396 pp.
By the chief censor of news dispatches from the A. E. F.

POUND, R. "Equitable Relief against Defamation and Injuries to Personality," *Harvard Law Review*, 29:640–82 (1915–16).

PREUSS, LAWRENCE. "International Responsibility for Hostile Propaganda against Foreign States," *American Journal of International Law*, 28:649–68 (1934).

RIESCH, ERWIN. "Das Flugblatt im Luftkrieg," *Archiv für Luftrecht*, 3:65–75 (1933).

ROBERTSON, JOHN MACKINNON. *A History of Free Thought in the Nineteenth Century*. London: Watts, 1929. 2 vols.

RÖHR, JOHANN FRIEDRICH. *Wie Karl August, Grossherzog von Sachsen-Weimar, sich bei Verketzerungsversuchen gegen akademische Lehrer benahm. Aktenmässig dargestellt*. Hanover and Leipzig: Hahn, 1830. 48 pp.

RUSSELL, GEORGE WILLIAM. "Censorship in Ireland," *Nation* (London), 44:435–36 (December 22, 1928).

SALVEMINI, G. "Treatment of the Press in Fascist Italy," *New Statesman*, 28:412–13 (January 15, 1927).

SEAGLE, WILLIAM. *There Ought to be a Law: A Collection of Lunatic Legislation*. New York: Macaulay, 1933. 158 pp.

SELDES, GEORGE. *Can These Things Be?* New York: Brewer, Warren, and Putnam, 1931. 433 pp.
Sequel to *You Can't Print That!* Has a section on "the truth behind the censorship."

———. *The Truth behind the News, 1918–1928*. London, 1928. American edition: *You Can't Print That!* New York: Payson and Clarke, 1929. Garden City: Garden City Publishing Company, 1929. 465 pp.

SMITH, Y. B. "Liability of a Telegraph Company for Transmitting a Defamatory Message," *Columbia Law Review*, 20:30–50, 369–93 (1920).

"Still More Censorship — Case of H. L. Mencken," *Virginia Law Register*, N. S., 12:35–39 (May, 1926).

"They Snoop to Conquer," *Saturday Review* (London), 147:309–10 (March 9, 1929).

THOMPSON, C. D. "Is the Chautauqua a Free Platform?" *New Republic,* 41:86–88 (1924–25).

Treaties, Acts, and Regulations Relating to Missionary Freedom. London: International Missionary Council, 1923. 108 pp.

UNION OF SOUTH AFRICA. *Report of the Select Committee on the Prevention of Disorders Bill.* Capetown: Cape Times, Ltd., 1926. 15 pp.

VEEDER, V. V. "Absolute Immunity in Defamation," *Columbia Law Review,* 9:463–91, 600–16 (1909); 10:131–46 (1910).

———. "The History and Theory of the Law of Defamation," *Columbia Law Review,* 3:546–73 (1903); 4:33–56 (1904).

WARD, H. F. "Repression of Civil Liberties in the United States, 1918–1923," Publications of the American Sociological Society, 18:127–46 (1923).

WELSCHINGER, HENRI. *La Censure sous le premier empire; avec documents inédits.* Paris: Charavay, 1882. 400 pp.

WICKWAR, WILLIAM HARDY. *The Struggle for Freedom of the Press, 1819–1832.* London: Allen and Unwin, 1928. 325 pp.
Bibliography, pp. 316–22.

YEATS, WILLIAM BUTLER. "Irish Censorship," *Spectator* (London), 141:391–92 (September 29, 1928).
Discussion, 141:435–36, 488, 528 (October 6–20, 1928).

YUN, A. "American Revolt against Chinese Censorship," *China Weekly Review,* 57:421 (August 15, 1931).

ZÉVALÈS, ALEXANDRE BOURSON. *Les Procès littéraires au XIXe siècle.* Paris: Perrin, 1924. 278 pp.
On liberty of the press.

D. THE CENSORSHIP OF SPECIFIC CHANNELS OF COMMUNICATION

Specialized literature on this topic is rare, as it usually receives incidental treatment in works dealing with the channels of communication as such, or with censorship in general.

I. BOOKS

ADCOCK, A. ST. J. "Books That Have Been Banned," *Bookman* (London), 74:26–28 (April, 1928).

"Book Censorship in Ireland," *Saturday Review* (London), 146:262–63 (September 1, 1928).

BOWERMAN, GEORGE FRANKLIN. *Censorship and the Public Library, with Other Papers.* New York: H. W. Wilson, 1931. 298 pp.
Twenty essays, some reprinted from periodicals.

"La Censure des livres en Angleterre," *Journal des débats,* vol. 36, pt. 1, pp. 698–99 (May 3, 1929).

DARLING, LORD. "The Censorship of Books," *Nineteenth Century and After* (London), 105:433–50 (1929).

FARRER, JAMES ANSON. *Books Condemned to be Burnt.* London: E. Stock, 1892. New York: A. C. Armstrong, 1892. 206 pp.
Book fires in England.

GARÇON, M. "Les Livres contraires aux bonnes moeurs; avec une liste de livres condamnés en France," *Mercure de France,* 230:5–39 (August 15, 1931).

GILLETT, CHARLES RIPLEY. *Burned Books: Neglected Chapters in British History and Literature.* New York: Columbia University, 1932. 2 vols.
Bibliography, 2:667–702.

MORRIS, J. CONWAY. "Literary Censorship and the Law," *Quarterly Review,* 252:18–27 (1929).

PERRY, BLISS. *Pernicious Books.* Second edition. Boston: New England Watch and Ward Society, 1927. 15 pp.
Address delivered at the annual public meeting of the New England Watch and Ward Society at Old South Church, Boston, Massachusetts, April 22, 1923.

2. THE EDUCATIONAL SYSTEM

"Academic Freedom," *Encyclopedia of the Social Sciences.* (By Arthur O. Lovejoy.)

AMERICAN ASSOCIATION OF UNIVERSITY PROFESSORS. "Report of the Committee on Academic Freedom and Academic Tenure," *Bulletin of the American Association of University Professors,* vol. 1, pt. 1 (1915); vol. 2, no. 2, pt. 2 (April, 1916); vol. 2, no. 3, pt. 2 (May, 1916).

AMERICAN CIVIL LIBERTIES UNION, COMMITTEE ON ACADEMIC FREEDOM. *The Gag on Teaching: The Story of the New Restrictions by Law on Teaching in Schools, and by Public Opinion and Donors on Colleges; the Record Since the War. . . .* New York: American Civil Liberties Union, 1931. 31 pp.

BEALE, HOWARD KENNEDY. "Freedom of Teaching in the Schools" (Report of the Commission on the Social Studies, American Historical Association). Announced.

CATTELL, JAMES MCKEEN, and others. *University Control*. New York: Science Press, 1913. 484 pp.
"A series of 299 unsigned letters by leading men of science holding academic positions; and articles by Joseph Jastrow . . . etc."

HEIN, ADOLF. *Die Idee der politischen Universität*. Hamburg: Hanseatische Verlagsanstalt, 1933. 39 pp.

HOFFMANN, ERNST. *Die Freiheit der Forschung und der Lehre: Rede zur Reichsgründungsfeier am 17. Januar, 1931*. Heidelberg: Carl Winters, 1931. 22 pp.
Freedom of research and of teaching.

KAUFMANN, GEORG. *Die Lehrfreiheit an den deutschen Universitäten im neunzehnten Jahrhundert*. Leipzig: S. Hirzel, 1898. 48 pp.

"Legislation on Seditious and Blasphemous Teachings," *Law Times* (London), 163: 302 (1927).

LOWELL, ABBOTT LAWRENCE. "Academic Freedom," Reports of the President and Treasurer of Harvard College, 1916–17, pp. 17–21.

MÜLLER, MAX. *Die Lehr- und Lernfreiheit: Versuch einer systematisch-historischen Darstellung mit besonderer Berücksichtigung der französischen deutschen, und schweizerischen Verhältnisse*. Aarau: H. R. Sauerländer, 1911. 286 pp.

SCHMIDT, WALTER A. E. *Die Freiheit der Wissenschaft: Ein Beitrag zur Geschichte und Auslegung des Art. 142 der Reichsverfassung*. Berlin: Stilke, 1929. 149 pp.
Academic freedom under Article 142 of the German constitution. Bibliography, pp. 7–18.

SINCLAIR, UPTON BEALL. *The Goose-Step: A Study of American Education*. Second edition. Pasadena: The Author, 1923. 488 pp.

3. THE PRESS

"American Censorship in France," *Review of Reviews*, 57: 205–06 (February, 1918).

BLIVEN, BRUCE. "Little Liberty Left," *American Press*, 58: 17 (May, 1934).

BROWN, CONSTANTINE. "Censors Grip Most of World's Press," *Editor and Publisher*, 66: 15, 66 (April 21, 1934).

BROWNRIGG, ADMIRAL SIR DOUGLAS. *Indiscretions of the Naval Censor*. New York: Doubleday, Doran, 1920. 314 pp.
See in particular chapters 9, 10, and 14.

BRUNS, V., and HAENTZSCHEL, editors. *Die Pressgesetze des Erdballs*. Berlin, 1928–31. (Vols. 1–10 have appeared to date.)

BURLESON, ALBERT SIDNEY. "Postmaster General Explains to Editor Purpose and Operation of New Law," *Editor and Publisher*, 50: 5 (October 6, 1917).
Postmaster-General's policy in dealing with disloyal and seditious publications.

CALLWELL, SIR CHARLES EDWARD. "The Press Censorship," *Nineteenth Century*, 85: 1132–45 (June, 1919).

"Charles Evans Hughes Defines Functions of Newspaper Criticism in War Times," *Editor and Publisher* (May 4, 1918).

"Creel Announces New Censorship Rules for Guidance of Press Associations," *Editor and Publisher*, 50: 6 (August 4, 1917).

"Creel Formulates Press Censorship Rules," *Editor and Publisher* (June 2, 1917).
Regulations issued by the chairman of the Committee on Public Information.

DAVIS, RICHARD HARDING. "The War Correspondent," *Collier's*, 48: 21–22 (October 7, 1911).
Censorship in Russo-Japanese War.

DUNIWAY, CLYDE AUGUSTUS. *The Development of Freedom of the Press in Massachusetts* (expansion of Ph. D. thesis, Harvard University, 1897. Harvard Historical Series, vol. 12). New York and London: Longmans, Green, 1906. 202 pp.
Bibliography, pp. 175–86.

DURANTY, WALTER. "Russian News and Soviet Censors," *Spectator*, 148: 207–08 (February 13, 1932).
Soviet censorship is generally better and more reasonable than other European censorships.

ELTON, OLIVER. *C. E. Montague, a Memoir*. London: Chatto and Windus, 1929. 335 pp.
Chapter 6, "Press Censorship."

FAY, SIDNEY B. "German Press Today," *Current History*, 40: 100–02 (April, 1934).

FERGUSON, FRED S. "Honor-Bound Censorship Is Greatest Menace," *Editor and Publisher*, 56: 4 (November 24, 1923).
By a United Press correspondent who covered the Versailles Peace Conference.

"Frederick Palmer Explains 'Mysteries' of the American Censorship in France," *Editor and Publisher*, 50: 5–6, 27 (February 16, 1918).

GUSTI. *Die Grundbegriffe des Pressrechts* (Abhandlungen des Kriminalistichen Seminars an der Universität Berlin, N. S., Band 5, Heft 4). Berlin, 1909.

HALE, WILLIAM GREEN. *The Law of the Press*. St. Paul: West Publishing Company, 1923. 240 pp.

HARD, WILLIAM. "Mr. Burleson, Espionagent," *New Republic* (May 10, 1919).
Postmaster-General bars books and newspapers from the mails.

JÈZE, GASTON PAUL AMÉDÉE. *Le Régime juridique de la presse en Angleterre pendant la guerre*. Second edition. Paris: M. Giard et E. Brière, 1915. 185 pp.

JOHNSON, ALBIN E. "Three Hundred Million Citizens of Europe Living under Iron Rule of Censorship," *Editor and Publisher*, 67: 3–4, 38 (June 30, 1934).

MACDONALD, WILLIAM. "The Press and Censorship in England and France," *Nation*, 105: 287–89 (September 13, 1917).

MASON, GREGORY. "American War Correspondents at the Front," *Bookman*, 40: 63–67 (September, 1914).
Gives censorship regulations in force at outset of the Great War.

MONTAGUE, CHARLES EDWARD. *Disenchantment*. London: Chatto and Windus, 1928. 228 pp.
First-hand information about the military press censorship by the former *Manchester Guardian* leader writer who served as an assistant censor on the British front.

"Nazi Instructions to Press Cited," *Editor and Publisher*, 66: 37 (September 23, 1933).

NEUBERGER, RICHARD. "Germany under the Choke Bit," *New Republic*, 77: 13–15 (November 15, 1933).

PARDEY, HANS. *Das Recht der englischen Presse* (Hamburgische Universität, Seminar für öffentliches Recht, Abhandlungen und Mitteilungen, no. 20). 1928.

"Press Censorship in France," *Nation*, 108: 221 (November 8, 1919).

RANDALL, JAMES G. "Germany's Censorship and News Control," *North American Review*, 208: 51–62 (July, 1918).
Germany's press censorship during wartime.

———. "The Newspaper Problem in Its Bearing upon Military Secrecy during the Civil War," *American Historical Review*, 23: 303–23 (January, 1918).

RATHERT, HELMUT. *Die deutsche Kriegsberichterstattung und Presse als Kampfmittel im Weltkrieg.* Grossenhain: Plasnick, 1934. 52 pp.
Dissertation analyzing the use of the press for military purposes during the War.

RIPPLER, H. " Das Journalistengesetz," *Deutsche Rundschau,* 201: 253–57 (December, 1924).

SALMON, LUCY MAYNARD. *The Newspaper and Authority.* New York: Oxford University, 1923. 505 pp.
Chapters 2 to 6 inclusive.

SCHREINER, CAPTAIN GEORGE A. " Censorship Is Necessary, but Censors Muddle News of a Non-Military Nature," *Editor and Publisher* (June 23, 1917).

SHEARMAN, MONTAGUE, and RAYNOR, O. T. *The Press Laws of Foreign Countries.* London: Great Britain, Foreign Office, 1926.

SHEPHERD, WILLIAM G. " The Forty-two Centimeter Blue Pencil," *Everybody's,* 36: 470–82 (April, 1917).
How the censor works in wartime. Written by an American war correspondent.

SIEBERT, FREDRICK SEATON. *The Rights and Privileges of the Press.* London and New York: Appleton-Century, 1934. 429 pp.
Analysis and exposition of the contemporary status of the law in relation to the publication of news. Table of cases, pp. 401–18.

STONE, MAJOR DONALD L. " Press and Mail Censorship in War-Time," *Editor and Publisher,* 59: 5–6, 41 (August 14, 1926); 59: 7–8 (August 21, 1926).
On operations of American army censors in France during the World War.

SULLIVAN, MARK. " Creel-Censor," *Collier's,* 60: 13 (November 10, 1917).

" Suppression of Malicious, Scandalous, and Defamatory Newspapers and Periodicals by Injunction on Suit of the State Held to Violate the Constitutional Guarantee of Freedom of the Press," *Law and Labor,* 13: 153–58 (July, 1931).

THÉRY, J. " La Loi sur la liberté de la presse," *Mercure de France,* 212: 257–76 (June 1, 1929).

WANG, Y. P. " Legal Aspects of the Native Press in China," in *Rise of the Native Press in China,* pp. 35–44. New York: Columbia University, 1924.
Discusses at length the Press Law of 1914, and the censorship efforts of the Shanghai Municipal Council.

"What the French Are Not Allowed to Learn," *Independent,* 92: 499–500 (December 15, 1917).

WILDES, HARRY EMERSON. *Japan in Crisis.* New York: Macmillan, 1934. 300 pp.

WILLIAMS, WYTHE. "The Sins of the Censor," *Collier's,* 60: 6 (January 12, 1918).

"Wilson Names Creel as Censorship Chief," *Editor and Publisher,* 49: 18 (April 21, 1917).

WOOD, ERIC F. "The British Censorship," *Saturday Evening Post,* 189: 5–7, 101–02 (April 28, 1917); 189: 18–19, 105–06 (May 5, 1917). The British war censorship.

4. PROMOTERS

ALGER, ARTHUR N. *A Treatise on the Law in Relation to Promoters and the Promotion of Corporations.* Boston: Little, Brown, 1897. 302 pp.

BOND, FREDERIC D. "California Petroleum," *Moody's Magazine,* 15: 183–86 (March, 1913).
Stock market manipulation to attract attention. Testimony before the Pujo Committee.

CHASE, STUART, and SCHLINK, F. J. *Your Money's Worth: A Study in the Waste of the Consumer's Dollar.* New York: Macmillan, 1927, 1930. 285 pp.
Control of fraudulent promotion by counter-propaganda.

COWDRICK, SHEFFIELD. "Promoting Wildcat Mines," *World Today,* 13: 1231–34 (January, 1908).

DOUBMAN, JOHN RUSSELL. *Analysis of Display Advertising in Philadelphia Newspapers to Determine Its Express Truth or Falsity* (Ph.D. thesis, University of Pennsylvania, 1926). Philadelphia: University of Pennsylvania, 1926. 94 pp.

EHRIC, MANFRED W. *The Law of Promoters.* Albany: M. Bender, 1916. 645 pp.
A treatise on the law of promoters of private corporations, covering the rights and liabilities of promoters, and also the rights and liabilities of the corporation and the subscribers for and purchasers of its shares, the rights and liabilities of persons selling property to the corporation, and the rights and liabilities of all other persons as affected by the acts or omissions of the promoters.

FULLER, M. J. "Publicity as a Preventive of Abuses by the Retailer," *Annals of the American Academy of Political and Social Science,* 50: 83–85 (November, 1913).

HERRING, EDWARD PENDLETON. "Food, Drugs, and Poison," *Current History*, 40: 33–39 (April, 1934).
Discusses the history and current events of the perpetual propaganda battle over the pure food laws.

HEVENER, O. F. "Putting the Advertising Faker Out of Business," *Bankers Magazine*, 112: 844–45 (June, 1926).

HOUSTON, H. S. "The League for Truth in Trade," *Our World*, 5: 34–39 (July, 1924).

—————. *Winning the Fight for Honest Business*. New York: Associated Advertising Clubs, 1923.

ISAACS, NATHAN. "The Promoter: A Legislative Problem," *Harvard Law Review*, 38: 887–902 (1924–25).

LIBRARY OF CONGRESS. *List of References on Fraudulent Practices in the Promotion of Corporations and the Sale of Securities* (Select List of References no. 87). Washington, D. C., November 5, 1915. 9 pp. typewritten.
Relevant titles are included in the present bibliography.

MONIER, FERDINAND, CHESNEY, E., and ROUX, E. *Traité théorique et practique sur les fraudes et falsifications*. Second edition. Paris: Larose et Tenin, 1925–27. 2 vols.

ROUAST, ANDRÉ. *La Publicité frauduleuse et le droit pénal* (Université de Paris, Faculté de droit, Travaux de la Conférence du droit pénal, no. 4). Paris: Larose et Tenin, 1912. 25 pp.

SANTARO. "Frauds in Advertisements in Japan," *Trans-Pacific*, 11: 5 (October 4, 1924).

SIDENER, MERLE. "Patrolling the Avenues of Publicity," *World's Work*, 35: 638–42 (April, 1918).

WILEY, HARVEY WASHINGTON. *Harvey W. Wiley: An Autobiography*. Indianapolis: Bobbs-Merrill, 1930. 329 pp.
Describes informally and graphically the methods used to attract public attention to the dangers in foodstuffs when there is inadequate regulation and inspection.

—————. *History of a Crime against the Food Law*. Washington, D. C.: H. W. Wiley, 1929. 413 pp.
By the leading advocate of the pure food laws.

5. RADIO, TELEPHONE, TELEGRAPH, CABLE

A. BIBLIOGRAPHY

DETROIT PUBLIC LIBRARY, CIVICS DIVISION. *Radio Control: A List of References on the Subject, Resolved, That All Radio Broadcasting in the United States Should Be Conducted in Stations Owned and Controlled by the Federal Government.* Detroit, 1933. 11 pp., mimeographed.

LIBRARY OF CONGRESS. *Select List of References on the Regulation and Control of Radio Broadcasting in the United States and Foreign Countries.* Washington, D.C., 1933. 34 pp., mimeographed.

B. REFERENCES

BERMAN, M. K. "Regulation of Radio Broadcasting," *Boston University Law Review,* January, 1933.

"Cable Censorship Causes Stir Here," *Trans-Pacific* (Tokyo), 13:13 (January 16, 1926).

DAWSON, MITCHELL. "Censorship on the Air," *American Mercury,* 31: 257–68 (March, 1934).

GUIDER, J. W. "Liability for Defamation in Political Broadcasts," *Journal of Radio Law,* October, 1932.

"Indirect Censorship of Radio Programs," *Yale Law Journal,* 40: 967–73 (April, 1931).

KINGSLEY, R. "Bibliography of Radio Law," *Journal of Radio Law* (Northwestern University), 1:178–89 (April, 1931).

TREBLE, J. F. "Application of Sec. 237 of Federal Criminal Code to Censorship of Broadcasting by Federal Radio Commission," *Air Law Review,* 2:256–60 (April, 1931).

6. STAGE AND MOVIE THEATER

"Censorship of Films," *Law Times* (London), 170:519 (December 20, 1930).

"Censorship of the Stage," *Journal of Social Hygiene,* 17:181–85 (March, 1931).

CHASE, WILLIAM SHEAFE. *Catechism on Motion Pictures in Interstate Commerce: Shall This Interstate Business, Dangerous to Morals and to Politics, Be Nationally Controlled, a Trust Prevented, a Demoralized Business Be Reorganized, and an Attack upon Free Government Be Thwarted?* Third edition. Albany, New York: New York Civic League, 1922. 159 pp.
By the president of the New York Civic League.

ERNST, MORRIS LEOPOLD, and LORENTZ, PARE. *Censored: The Private Life of the Movie.* New York: Cape and Smith, 1930. 199 pp.

FEDERAL COUNCIL OF CHURCHES OF CHRIST IN AMERICA, DEPARTMENT OF RESEARCH AND EDUCATION. *The Public Relations of the Motion Picture Industry.* New York, 1931. 155 pp.
An investigation of the Motion Picture Producers and Distributors of America, Inc. (the "Hays organization").

GILDERSLEEVE, VIRGINIA CROCHERON. *Government Regulation of the Elizabethan Drama* (Columbia University Studies in English, 2d series, vol. 1, no. 1). New York: Columbia University, 1908. 259 pp. Bibliography, pp. 235–40.

GILLMORE, F. "Theatre Stands under the Shadow of a Padlock," *American Federationist,* 35: 316–20 (March, 1928).

HALLAYS-DABOT, VICTOR. *Histoire de la censure théâtrale en France.* Paris: E. Dentu, 1862. 340 pp.

NATIONAL COUNCIL OF PUBLIC MORALS FOR GREAT AND GREATER BRITAIN, CINEMA COMMISSION OF INQUIRY. *The Cinema: Its Present Position and Future Possibilities.* London: Williams and Norgate, 1917. 372 pp.

PARLIAMENT [Great Britain], JOINT SELECT COMMITTEE ON STAGE PLAYS (CENSORSHIP). *Report* (House of Lords, Reports and Papers, no. 214). London: H. M. Stationery Office, 1909–10. 2 pts., 413 pp.

PETZET, WOLFGANG. *Verbotene Filme.* Frankfort-on-the-Main: Sozietäts-Verlag, 1931. 160 pp.

RUTLAND, JAMES RICHARD, compiler. *State Censorship of Motion Pictures.* New York: H. W. Wilson, 1923. 177 pp.
Debate materials. Bibliography, pp. 16–28.

THOMPSON, ELBERT NEVIUS SEBRING. *The Controversy between the Puritans and the Stage* (Ph. D. thesis. Yale Studies in English, vol. 20). New York: Holt, 1903. 275 pp.
Bibliography, pp. 267–72.

UNITED STATES DEPARTMENT OF COMMERCE. *Australian Imports and Censorship of Films* (report no. 16, April 18, 1932). Washington, D. C.: Government Printing Office.

PREVIOUS BIBLIOGRAPHIES ON PROPAGANDA

AMERICAN HISTORICAL ASSOCIATION, COMMITTEE ON BIBLIOGRAPHY. *A Guide to Historical Literature*. New York: Macmillan, 1931. 1222 pp.

In this bibliography no section is devoted exclusively to propaganda, but the elaborate scheme of classification and the annotations (covering many books cited in the present bibliography) may be used to place propaganda studies in their proper historical perspective.

A Catalogue of Paris Peace Conference Delegation Propaganda in the Hoover War Library. Stanford University, California: Stanford University, 1926.

None of this material is included in Young and Lawrence's bibliography (*q. v.* below) except perhaps a few items by chance overlapping.

CHILDS, HARWOOD LAWRENCE. *A Reference Guide to the Study of Public Opinion*, with an introductory note by Edward L. Bernays. Princeton, New Jersey: Princeton University, 1934. 105 pp.

Prepared by a professor of government for the use of college students. Most of these titles are cited in the present bibliography.

Encyclopedia of the Social Sciences. New York: Macmillan, 1931–35.

Contains many articles of interest to students of propaganda. Bibliographies at ends of articles.

LANGER, WILLIAM L., and ARMSTRONG, HAMILTON. *Foreign Affairs Bibliography: A Selected and Annotated List of Books on International Affairs, 1919–1932*. New York and London: Published by Harpers for the Council on Foreign Relations, Inc., 1933. 551 pp.

Has a section on World War public opinion and propaganda.

LASSWELL, HAROLD DWIGHT. *Propaganda Technique in the World War*. London: Kegan Paul, Trench, and Trubner, 1927. New York: Knopf, 1927. 229 pp.

Bibliography, pp. 223–29. A good, though unannotated, bibliography. The footnotes are also suggestive.

LUTZ, RALPH HASWELL. "Studies of World War Propaganda, 1914–33: A Bibliographical Article," *Journal of Modern History*, 5: 496–516 (December, 1933).

These titles are included in the present bibliography.

MITCHELL, PETER C. *Report on the Propaganda Library [in the Intelligence Division of the War Office].* London: H. M. Stationery Office, 1917. 3 vols.

Appendix I, propaganda chiefly relating to nationalities; Appendix II, Germany and America.

PIERCE, BESSIE LOUISE. *Citizens' Organizations and the Civic Training of Youth.* New York: Scribners, 1933. 426 pp.

Lists many examples of propaganda as well as writings about it. Bibliography, pp. 353–408.

SALMON, LUCY MAYNARD. *The Newspaper and the Historian.* New York and London: Oxford, 1923. 566 pp.

Bibliography, pp. 493–516. Pages 381 ff. review the literature of caricature, cartoon, and illustration during the war.

Die Soviet Union, 1917–1932. Berlin: Ost-Europa Verlag, 1933. 186 pp.

Annotated bibliography of 1,900 books and articles on Russia published in German outside the Soviet Union since 1917. See Sections II, V, VI, and VIII.

UNITED STATES LIBRARY OF CONGRESS. *List of References on Publicity with Special Reference to Press Agents* (Select List of References no. 546). Washington, D. C., August 2, 1921. Typewritten.

Fifty-eight of these titles are included in the present bibliography.

—————. *Publicity and Public Opinion: A List of Books* (Select List of References no. 1172). Washington, D. C., May 15, 1930. Typewritten.

Relevant titles are included in the present bibliography.

YOUNG, KIMBALL, and LAWRENCE, RAYMOND D. *Bibliography on Censorship and Propaganda* (University of Oregon Journalism Series, vol. 1, no. 1). Eugene, Oregon, March, 1928. 133 pp.

This annotated work contains an introductory article by Kimball Young on "Censorship and Propaganda as Factors in Social Control" and a list of all manner of references from the early nineteenth century to 1927, in French, German, and English. The table of contents indicates the scope and organization:

PART I. CENSORSHIP

A. The General Features of Censorship
B. Political Censorship
C. War-Time Censorship
   1. World War Censorship (especially of the Allies)
   2. German World War Censorship
   3. Censorship in Other Wars
D. Censorship of Literature, Drama, etc.
   1. Censorship of Books
   2. Censorship of Stage Drama, Motion Pictures, Radio

Part II. Propaganda

A. The General Features of Propaganda
B. Political Propaganda
C. World War Propaganda
D. Propaganda of Economic Groups

Titles are taken from Cannon's bibliography *Journalism* (New York Public Library, 1924) and from *Reader's Guide* and *International Index* through May, 1927. The titles in the present bibliography include all the major works cited by Young and Lawrence; but no attempt has been made to reproduce their lists of lesser works, newspaper articles, and minor magazine articles.

INDEXES

AUTHOR INDEX

Coggeshall, Reginald, 286
Cohane, David B., 87
Cohen, B., 286
Cohen, Jacob M., 335
Cohen, Morris R., 123
Coker, Francis W., 252
Cole, A. H., 157
Cole, George D. H., 270, 378
Cole, Stewart G., 118
Cole, V. L., 286
Colegrove, K. W., 93
Coleman, Sydney H., 177
Collet, Octave, 191
Collins, A. S., 270
Collins, Kenneth, 131
Colm, Gerhart, 52
Comer, John P., 183
Commons, John R., 104, 107
Condliffe, John B., 93
Congdon, Charles T., 305
Connors, Francis J., 123
Consiglio, P., 220
Constant de Rebècque, Henri B., 383
Contreras, Francisco, 237
Conway, Martin, 52
Conwil-Evans, T. P., 125
Cook, A. B., 139, 151
Cook, Sir Edward T., 74
Cook, Elizabeth C., 286
Cook, J. G., 237
Cook, K. E., 364
Cook, R. C., 157
Cooke, Richard J., 118
Cooke, Sidney R., 157
Cooley, Charles H., 52
Coolidge, Calvin, 131
Coombs, W., 374
Cooper, Francis, 151
Cooper, Frederic T., 329
Cooper, Kent, 286
Corbett, E., 258
Corbin, John, 220
Cortissoz, Royal, 306
Cosmin, S., 287
Coste, Charles, 33
Coste, Pierre, 151
Cot, Pierre, 267
Coudenhove-Kalergi, Richard N., 165
Coultee, D. W., 139
Coulton, George G., 186
Counts, George S., 249, 312, 313
Couper, Walter J., 220
Coupland, R., 177
Couturat, Louis, 213
Cowan, Frances M., 126
Cowdrick, Sheffield, 398
Cowell, F. R., 68
Cowley, W. S., 270
Cozens, M. L., 258
Craig, G., Jr., 139
Crane, John O., 93

Cranfield, W. T., 306
Crawford, Nelson A., 109, 287, 374
Crawford, Sir William, 147
Crecraft, Earl W., 378
Creel, George, 74
Creelman, James, 306
Crémieux, A., 388
Crescott, D. A., 347
Creutzburg, A., 199
Critchfield and Company, 258
Crockett, T. S., 359
Croly, Herbert D., 89
Cronau, Rudolph, 33
Crook, Wilfrid H., 44
Crosman, Ralph L., 287
Crowell, Chester T., 287
Crowell Publishing Company, 259
Croy, Homer, 317
Crozier, Joseph, 74
Culpin, Ewart G., 177
Cummings, Arthur R., 364
Cunliffe, John W., 33
Cunow, Heinrich, 93
Curoe, Philip R. V., 105
Curry, Walter A., 324
Curti, Merle E., 186, 188, 267, 312
Curtius, Ernst R., 195, 225
Cushing, C. P., 139
Cutler, T. H., Jr., 349
Cynn, Hugh H. W., 168
Czarnowski, Stefan, 234

Dabney, Virginius, 225
Da Costa, Charles, 270
Dahl, J. O., 157
Dahl, Svend, 328
Dahlin, Ebba, 243
Dakin, Edwin F., 270
Daley, W. A., 207
Dameron, Kenneth, 157
Dana, H. W. L., 270
Dandision, B., 358
Daniélou, Charles, 74
Danilov, I. U., 74
Dannenberg, Willibald, 145
Dariac, A., 68
Dark, Sidney, 306
Darling, Lord, 393
Darras, M., 93
Darrow, Clarence S., 211
Dart, Rufus, 270
Darton, Frederick J. H., 328
Dascalakis, Ap., 287
Dasent, Arthur I., 306
Davenport, E. H., 157
Davenport, Frederick M., 53
Davenport, Walter, 89
David, Quentin J., 39
Davidson, H. H., 346, 352
Davidson, Jo, 328
Davidson, Philip G., 199

SUBJECT INDEX

Abolition, *see* Slavery and Abolition
Aborigines, protection of, 178
Academic freedom, 312, 384, 386, 393, 394
Action française, 196
Adams, Samuel, 271
Adult education, 122, 175, 259, 312, 316, 333, 334. *See also* Civic training; Educational systems; Workers' education
Advertisers, international, 343. *See also* Experts
Advertising, commercial, 31–43, 126–60, 258–63, 316–18, 321, 322, 325–26, 358–62, 373–77, 381; newspaper, 130, 132, 134, 135, 137, 144, 145, 146, 149, 152, 154, 225, 286, 301, 358–62, 373–77, 398, 399; social and economic effects of, 131, 136, 137, 145–48, 359, 365, 366, 373–81. *See also* Posters
Advertising agencies and firms, 133, 159, 363, 364, 375
Advertising effect, measurement of, *see* Advertising research
Advertising psychology, 131, 132, 358–62
Advertising research, 258–60, 262, 319–26, 358, 362–64, 375, 377. *See also* Advertising psychology; Propaganda, research
Agitation, 37, 41, 58; control of, 381–87
Agitators, psychology of, 269–76, 351, 354–56, 367
Agrarian groups, symbolism and propaganda of, 91, 107, 109–12, 157, 187, 198, 221, 224, 259, 270, 287, 313, 342, 358
Agrarian syndicalism, 109, 111
Agricultural bloc, *see* Agrarian groups
Agricultural education, 312, 313, 316, 333, 334. *See also* Agrarian groups
Agricultural groups, *see* Agrarian groups
Air mail contracts, propaganda concerning, 7, 159
Allied Patriotic Societies, 194
American Association for the Advancement of Atheism, 122
American Association of Advertising Agencies, 363
American Association of Foreign Language Newspapers, Inc., 363
American Association of Schools and Departments of Journalism, 192
American Association of Social Workers, 369

American Association of Teachers of Journalism, 292
American Association of University Professors, 156, 393
American Bar Association, 103
American Birth Control League, 209, 210
American Civil Liberties Union, Committee on Academic Freedom, 393
American Colonization Society, 214
American Construction Council, 174
American Defense Society, 194
American Farm Bureau Federation, 8, 11
American Federation of Labor, 104–05, 107, 108
American Historical Association, Commission on the Social Studies, 312; Committee on Bibliography, 402
American Jewish Committee, 124
American Legion, 194–97, 250
American Medical Association, 206, 378, 390
American Newspaper Publishers Association, 322
American Peace Society, 185, 188
American Political Science Association, Committee on Policy, 248
American Red Cross, 161
American Scenic and Historic Preservation Society, 175
American School Citizenship League, 185
American School Peace League, 185
American Steamship Owners' Association, 7
American Sunday School Union, 117
Americanism, history of the idea of, 243
Americanization, *see* Civic training
Anarchism and anarchists, 79, 197, 203, 255, 273
Anarcho-syndicalism, 187
Angell, Norman, 186
Animal protection movement, 175, 178, 181, 182
Anthony, Susan B., 113
Anti-Catholic movements, *see* Counterecclesiastical groups and individuals
Anti-clericalism, *see* Counter-ecclesiastical groups and individuals
Anti-Corn Law League, 183, 184
Anti-militarism, *see* Peace
Anti-radicalism, 194–97, 248–55. *See also* Civic training; Hyper-patriotism
Anti-rent agitation, 214
Anti-Saloon League of America, 211, 212

435